SONGBOOKS

Refiguring American Music
A series edited by RONALD RADANO, JOSH KUN,
AND NINA SUN EIDSHEIM

SONGBOOKS

★ *The Literature of* ★

AMERICAN POPULAR MUSIC

Eric Weisbard

Duke University Press   *Durham and London*   2021

Printed and bound by CPI Group (UK) Ltd, Croydon, CR0 4YY
Designed by Courtney Leigh Richardson
Typeset in Garamond Premier Pro by Westchester Publishing Services

Library of Congress Cataloging-in-Publication Data
Names: Weisbard, Eric, author.
Title: Songbooks : the literature of American popular music / Eric Weisbard.
Other titles: Refiguring American music.
Description: Durham : Duke University Press, 2021. | Series: Refiguring
American music | Includes bibliographical references and index.
Identifiers: LCCN 2020032092 (print) | LCCN 2020032093 (ebook) |
ISBN 9781478011941 (hardcover) | ISBN 9781478014089 (paperback) |
ISBN 9781478021391 (ebook)
Subjects: LCSH: Popular music—United States—History and criticism. |
Popular music—United States—Historiography.
Classification: LCC ML3477 .W457 2021 (print) | LCC ML3477 (ebook) |
DDC 782.421640973—dc23
LC record available at https://lccn.loc.gov/2020032092
LC ebook record available at https://lccn.loc.gov/2020032093

PRODUCED WITH A GRANT FROM

FIGURE FOUNDATION

PUBLICATION OF THE GLOBAL NATION

This book is dedicated to anybody who
ever wrote for the *Village Voice*
music section or presented at the
Pop Conference. My people!
Even if—especially if—we have argued.

CONTENTS

Introduction · 1

★ *Part I* ★

SETTING THE SCENE

First Writer, of Music and on Music:
William Billings, *The New-England Psalm-Singer*, 1770 · 20

Blackface Minstrelsy Extends Its Twisted Roots:
T. D. Rice, "Jim Crow," c.1832 · 22

Shape-Note Singing and Early Country:
B. F. White and E. J. King, *The Sacred Harp*, 1844 · 25

Music in Captivity: Solomon Northup,
Twelve Years a Slave, 1853 · 26

Champion of the White Male Vernacular:
Walt Whitman, *Leaves of Grass*, 1855 · 28

Notating Spirituals: William Francis Allen,
Charles Pickard Ware, and Lucy McKim Garrison, eds.,
Slave Songs of the United States, 1867 · 30

First Black Music Historian: James Trotter, *Music and Some Highly
Musical People: The Lives of Remarkable Musicians of the
Colored Race*, 1878 · 32

Child Ballads and Folklore: Francis James Child, *The English and Scottish
Popular Ballads*, 5 vols., 1882–1898 · 33

Women Not Inventing Ethnomusicology: Alice C. Fletcher,
A Study of Omaha Indian Music, 1893 · 35

First Hit Songwriter, from Pop to Folk and Back Again: Morrison
Foster, *Biography, Songs and Musical Compositions of
Stephen C. Foster*, 1896 · 39

Novelist of Urban Pop Longings: Theodore Dreiser,
Sister Carrie, 1900 · 42

Americana Emerges: Emma Bell Miles,
The Spirit of the Mountains, 1905 · 44

Documenting the Story: O. G. Sonneck, *Bibliography of Early
Secular American Music*, 1905 · 45

Tin Pan Alley's Sheet Music Biz: Charles K. Harris, *How to Write a
Popular Song*, 1906 · 47

First Family of Folk Collecting: John A. Lomax, *Cowboy Songs and
Other Frontier Ballads*, 1910 · 50

Proclaiming Black Modernity: James Weldon Johnson,
The Autobiography of an Ex-Colored Man, 1912 · 52

Songcatching in the Mountains: Olive Dame Campbell and
Cecil J. Sharp, *English Folk Songs from the Southern
Appalachians*, 1917 · 54

★ *Part II* ★

THE JAZZ AGE

Stories for the Slicks: F. Scott Fitzgerald,
Flappers and Philosophers, 1920 · 62

Remembering the First Black Star: Mabel Rowland, ed.,
Bert Williams, Son of Laughter, 1923 · 64

Magazine Criticism across Popular Genres: Gilbert Seldes,
The Seven Lively Arts, 1924 · 67

Harlem Renaissance: Alain Locke, ed., *The New Negro:
An Interpretation*, 1925 · 69

Tin Pan Alley's Standards Setter: Alexander Woollcott,
The Story of Irving Berlin, 1925 · 71

Broadway Musical as Supertext: Edna Ferber,
Show Boat, 1926 · 74

Father of the Blues in Print: W. C. Handy, ed., *Blues:
An Anthology*, 1926 · 76

Poet of the Blare and Racial Mountain: Langston Hughes,
The Weary Blues, 1926 · 78

Blessed Immortal, Forgotten Songwriter: Carrie Jacobs-Bond,
The Roads of Melody, 1927 · 80

Tune Detective and Expert Explainer: Sigmund Spaeth, *Read 'Em
and Weep: The Songs You Forgot to Remember*, 1927 · 82

Pop's First History Lesson: Isaac Goldberg, *Tin Pan Alley:
A Chronicle of the American Popular Music Racket*, 1930 · 84

Roots Intellectual: Constance Rourke, *American Humor:
A Study of the National Character*, 1931 · 85

Jook Ethnography, Inventing Black Music Studies: Zora Neale
Hurston, *Mules and Men*, 1935 · 87

What He Played Came First: Louis Armstrong,
Swing That Music, 1936 · 90

Jazz's Original Novel: Dorothy Baker,
Young Man with a Horn, 1938 · 94

Introducing Jazz Critics: Frederic Ramsey Jr. and
Charles Edward Smith, eds., *Jazzmen*, 1939 · 95

★ *Part III* ★

MIDCENTURY ICONS

Folk Embodiment: Woody Guthrie, *Bound for Glory*, 1943 · 104

A Hack Story Soldiers Took to War: David Ewen, *Men of
Popular Music*, 1944 · 106

From Immigrant Jew to Red Hot Mama: Sophie Tucker, *Some
of These Days*, 1945 · 108

White Negro Drug Dealer: Mezz Mezzrow and Bernard Wolfe,
Really the Blues, 1946 · 110

Composer of Tone Parallels: Barry Ulanov, *Duke Ellington*, 1946 · 111

Jazz's Precursor as Pop and Art: Rudi Blesh and Harriet Janis,
They All Played Ragtime: The True Story of an American Music, 1950 · 114

Field Recording in the Library of Congress: Alan Lomax, *Mister
Jelly Roll: The Fortunes of Jelly Roll Morton, New Orleans
Creole and "Inventor of Jazz,"* 1950 · 118

Dramatizing Blackness from a Distance: Ethel Waters with
Charles Samuels, *His Eye Is on the Sparrow*, 1951 · 120

Centering Vernacular Song: Gilbert Chase, *America's Music*, 1955 · 122

Writing about Records: Roland Gelatt, *The Fabulous Phonograph:
From Tin Foil to High Fidelity*, 1955 · 124

Collective Oral History to Document Scenes: Nat Shapiro and
Nat Hentoff, eds., *Hear Me Talkin' to Ya: The Story of Jazz as
Told by the Men Who Made It*, 1955 · 127

The Greatest Jazz Singer's Star Text: Billie Holiday with William Dufty,
Lady Sings the Blues, 1956 · 129

Beat Generation: Jack Kerouac, *On the Road*, 1957 · 133

Borderlands Folklore and Transnational Imaginaries:
Américo Paredes, *"With His Pistol in His Hands":
A Border Ballad and Its Hero*, 1958 · 136

New Yorker Critic of a Genre Becoming Middlebrow:
Whitney Balliett, *The Sound of Surprise: 46 Pieces on Jazz*, 1959 · 141

★ *Part IV* ★

VERNACULAR COUNTERCULTURE

Blues Revivalists: Samuel Charters, *The Country Blues*, 1959; Paul Oliver,
Blues Fell This Morning: The Meaning of the Blues, 1960 · 148

Britpop in Fiction: Colin MacInnes, *Absolute Beginners*, 1959 · 151

Form-Exploding Indeterminacy: John Cage, *Silence*, 1961 · 153

Science Fiction Writer Pens First Rock and Roll Novel: Harlan Ellison,
Rockabilly [Spider Kiss], 1961 · 155

Pro–Jazz Scene Sociology: Howard S. Becker, *Outsiders:
Studies in the Sociology of Deviance*, 1963 · 157

Reclaiming Black Music: LeRoi Jones (Amiri Baraka), *Blues People:
Negro Music in White America*, 1963 · 159

An Endless Lit, Limited Only in Scope: Michael Braun,
"Love Me Do!": The Beatles' Progress, 1964 · 162

Music as a Prose Master's Jagged Grain: Ralph Ellison,
Shadow and Act, 1964 · 167

How to Succeed in . . . : M. William Krasilovsky and Sidney Schemel,
This Business of Music, 1964 · 169

Schmaltz and Adversity: Sammy Davis Jr. and Jane and Burt Boyar,
Yes I Can, 1965 · 171

New Journalism and Electrified Syntax: Tom Wolfe, *Kandy-Kolored
Tangerine-Flake Streamline Baby*, 1965 · 173

Defining a Genre: Bill C. Malone, *Country Music,
U.S.A.: A Fifty-Year History*, 1968 · 175

Swing's Movers as an Alternate History of American Pop:
Marshall and Jean Stearns, *Jazz Dance: The Story of American
Vernacular Dance*, 1968 · 177

Rock and Roll's Greatest Hyper: Nik Cohn, *Awopbopaloobop
Alopbamboom*, 1969/1970 · 182

Ebony's Pioneering Critic of Black Pop as Black Power: Phyl Garland,
The Sound of Soul: The Story of Black Music, 1969 · 184

Entertainment Journalism and the Power of Knowing: Lillian Roxon,
Rock Encyclopedia, 1969 · 185

An Over-the-Top Genre's First Reliable History: Charlie Gillett,
The Sound of the City: The Rise of Rock and Roll, 1970 · 187

Rock Critic of the Trivially Awesome: Richard Meltzer,
The Aesthetics of Rock, 1970 · 188

Black Religious Fervor as the Core of Rock and Soul: Anthony Heilbut,
The Gospel Sound: Good News and Bad Times, 1971 · 190

Jazz Memoir of "Rotary Perception" Multiplicity: Charles Mingus,
Beneath the Underdog, 1971 · 193

Composing a Formal History: Eileen Southern,
The Music of Black Americans, 1971 · 194

Krazy Kat Fiction of Viral Vernaculars: Ishmael Reed,
Mumbo Jumbo, 1972 · 196

Derrière Garde Prose and Residual Pop Styles: Alec Wilder,
American Popular Song: The Great Innovators, 1900–1950, 1972 · 198

Charts as a New Literature: Joel Whitburn, *Top Pop Records,
1955–1972, 1973* · 201

Selling Platinum across Formats: Clive Davis with James Willwerth,
Clive: Inside the Record Business, 1975 · 203

Blues Relationships and Black Women's Deep Songs: Gayl Jones,
Corregidora, 1975 · 205

"Look at the World in a Rock 'n' Roll Sense . . . What Does
That Even Mean?": Greil Marcus, *Mystery Train:
Images of America in Rock 'n' Roll Music, 1975* · 207

Cultural Studies Brings Pop from the Hallway to the Classroom: Stuart
Hall and Tony Jefferson, eds., *Resistance through Rituals:
Youth Subcultures in Post-War Britain, 1976* · 211

A Life in Country for an Era of Feminism and Counterculture:
Loretta Lynn with George Vecsey, *Coal Miner's Daughter, 1976* · 214

Introducing Rock Critics: Jim Miller, ed., *The Rolling Stone
Illustrated History of Rock & Roll, 1976* · 216

Patriarchal Exegete of Black Vernacular as "Equipment for Living":
Albert Murray, *Stomping the Blues, 1976* · 219

Reading Pop Culture as Intellectual Obligation: Roland Barthes,
Image—Music—Text, 1977 · 221

Paging through Books to Make History: Dena Epstein, *Sinful
Tunes and Spirituals: Black Folk Music to the Civil War, 1977* · 223

Historians Begin to Study Popular Music: Lawrence Levine,
*Black Culture and Black Consciousness: Afro-American
Folk Thought from Slavery to Freedom, 1977* · 224

Musicking to Overturn Hierarchy: Christopher Small, *Music,
Society, Education, 1977* · 226

Drool Data and Stained Panties from a Critical Noise Boy: Nick Tosches,
Country: The Biggest Music in America, 1977 · 229

★ *Part V* ★

AFTER THE REVOLUTION

Punk Negates Rock: Julie Burchill and Tony Parsons, *The Boy Looked at
Johnny: The Obituary of Rock and Roll*, 1978 · 236

The Ghostwriter behind the Music Books: Ray Charles and David Ritz,
Brother Ray: Ray Charles' Own Story, 1978 · 240

Disco Negates Rock: Andrew Holleran,
Dancer from the Dance, 1978 · 242

Industry Schmoozer and Black Music Advocate Fills Public
Libraries with Okay Overviews: Arnold Shaw, *Honkers and Shouters:
The Golden Years of Rhythm and Blues*, 1978 · 245

Musicology's Greatest Tune Chronicler: Charles Hamm, *Yesterdays:
Popular Song in America*, 1979 · 247

Criticism's Greatest Album Chronicler: Robert Christgau,
Christgau's Record Guide: Rock Albums of the '70s, 1981 · 248

Rock's Frank Capra: Cameron Crowe, *Fast Times at Ridgemont High:
A True Story*, 1981 · 251

Culture Studies/Rock Critic Twofer!: Simon Frith, *Sound Effects:
Youth, Leisure, and the Politics of Rock'n'Roll*, 1981 · 252

A Magical Explainer of Impure Sounds: Robert Palmer,
Deep Blues, 1981 · 255

Feminist Rock Critic, Pop-Savvy Social Critic: Ellen Willis,
Beginning to See the Light: Pieces of a Decade, 1981 · 257

New Deal Swing Believer Revived: Otis Ferguson, *In the Spirit of Jazz:
The Otis Ferguson Reader*, 1982 · 259

Ethnomusicology and Pop, Forever Fraught: Bruno Nettl, *The Study of Ethnomusicology: Twenty-Nine Issues and Concepts*, 1983 · 260

Autodidact Deviance, Modeling the Rock Generation to Come: V. Vale and Andrea Juno, eds., *RE/Search #6/7: Industrial Culture Handbook*, 1983 · 263

The Rolling Stones of Rolling Stones Books: Stanley Booth, *The True Adventures of the Rolling Stones*, 1984 · 265

Finding the Blackface in Bluegrass: Robert Cantwell, *Bluegrass Breakdown: The Making of the Old Southern Sound*, 1984 · 267

Cyberpunk Novels and Cultural Studies Futurism: William Gibson, *Neuromancer*, 1984 · 269

Glossy Magazine Features Writer Gets History's Second Draft: Gerri Hirshey, *Nowhere to Run: The Story of Soul Music*, 1984 · 272

Theorizing Sound as Dress Rehearsal for the Future: Jacques Attali, *Noise: The Political Economy of Music*, 1977; Translation, 1985 · 274

Classic Rock, Mass Market Paperback Style: Stephen Davis, *Hammer of the Gods: The Led Zeppelin Saga*, 1985 · 275

Love and Rockets, Signature Comic of Punk Los Angeles as Borderland Imaginary: Los Bros Hernandez, *Music for Mechanics*, 1985 · 277

Plays about Black American Culture Surviving the Loss of Political Will: August Wilson, *Ma Rainey's Black Bottom*, 1985 · 280

Putting Pop in the Big Books of Music: H. Wiley Hitchcock and Stanley Sadie, eds., *The New Grove Dictionary of American Music*, 1986 · 282

Popular Music's Defining Singer and Swinger: Kitty Kelley, *His Way: The Unauthorized Biography of Frank Sinatra*, 1986 · 284

Anti-Epic Lyricizing of Black Music after Black Power: Nathaniel Mackey, *Bedouin Hornbook*, 1986 · 288

Lost Icon of Rock Criticism: Lester Bangs, *Psychotic Reactions and Carburetor Dung*, 1987 · 290

Veiled Glimpses of the Songwriter Who Invented Rock and Roll as Literature: Chuck Berry, *Chuck Berry: The Autobiography*, 1987 · 292

Making "Wild-Eyed Girls" a More Complex Narrative: Pamela Des Barres, *I'm with the Band: Confessions of a Groupie*, 1987 · 294

Reporting Black Music as Art Mixed with Business: Nelson George, *The Death of Rhythm & Blues*, 1988 · 295

Sessions with the Evil Genius of Jazz: Miles Davis with Quincy Troupe, *Miles: The Autobiography*, 1989 · 298

★ *Part VI* ★

NEW VOICES, NEW METHODS

Literature of New World Order Americanization: Jessica Hagedorn, *Dogeaters*, 1990 · 308

Ethnic Studies of Blended Musical Identities: George Lipsitz, *Time Passages: Collective Memory and American Popular Culture*, 1990 · 310

Ballad Novels for a Baby Boomer Appalachia: Sharyn McCrumb, *If Ever I Return, Pretty Peggy-O*, 1990 · 312

Pimply, Prole, and Putrid, but with a Surprisingly Diverse Genre Literature: Chuck Eddy, *Stairway to Hell: The 500 Best Heavy Metal Albums in the Universe*, 1991 · 314

How Musicology Met Cultural Studies: Susan McClary, *Feminine Endings: Music, Gender, and Sexuality*, 1991 · 318

Idol for Academic Analysis and a Changing Public Sphere: Madonna, *Sex*, 1992 · 320

Black Bohemian Cultural Nationalism: Greg Tate, *Flyboy in the Buttermilk: Essays on Contemporary America*, 1992 · 324

From Indie to Alternative Rock: Gina Arnold, *Route 666: On the Road to Nirvana*, 1993 · 326

Musicology on Popular Music—In Pragmatic Context: Richard Crawford, *The American Musical Landscape*, 1993 · 330

Listening, Queerly: Wayne Koestenbaum, *The Queen's Throat: Opera, Homosexuality and the Mystery of Desire*, 1993 · 332

Blackface as Stolen Vernacular: Eric Lott, *Love and Theft: Blackface Minstrelsy and the American Working Class*, 1993 · 334

Media Studies of Girls Listening to Top 40: Susan Douglas, *Where the Girls Are: Growing Up Female with the Mass Media*, 1994 · 338

Ironies of a Contested Identity: Peter Guralnick, *Last Train to Memphis: The Rise of Elvis Presley*, 1994 · 339

Two Generations of Leading Ethnomusicologists Debate the Popular: Charles Keil and Steven Feld, *Music Grooves: Essays and Dialogues*, 1994 · 344

Defining Hip-Hop as Flow, Layering, Rupture, and Postindustrial Resistance: Tricia Rose, *Black Noise: Rap Music and Black Culture in Contemporary America*, 1994 · 346

Regendering Music Writing, with the Deadly Art of Attitude: Evelyn McDonnell and Ann Powers, eds. *Rock She Wrote: Women Write about Rock, Pop, and Rap*, 1995 · 348

Soundscaping References, Immersing Trauma: David Toop, *Ocean of Sound: Aether Talk, Ambient Sound and Imaginary Worlds*, 1995 · 352

Sociologist Gives Country Studies a Soft-Shell Contrast to the Honky-Tonk: Richard Peterson, *Creating Country Music: Fabricating Authenticity*, 1997 · 354

All That Not-Quite Jazz: Gary Giddins, *Visions of Jazz: The First Century*, 1998 · 355

Jazz Studies Conquers the Academy: Robert G. O'Meally, ed., *The Jazz Cadence of American Culture*, 1998 · 357

★ *Part VII* ★

TOPICS IN PROGRESS

Paradigms of Club Culture, House and Techno to Rave and EDM: Simon Reynolds, *Energy Flash: A Journey through Rave Music and Dance Culture*, 1998 · 368

Performance Studies, Minoritarian Identity, and Academic Wildness: José Esteban Muñoz, *Disidentifications: Queers of Color and the Performance of Politics*, 1999 · 372

Left of Black: Networking a New Discourse: Mark Anthony Neal, *What the Music Said: Black Popular Music and Black Public Culture*, 1999 · 375

Aerobics as Genre, Managing Emotions: Tia DeNora, *Music in Everyday Life*, 2000 · 377

Confronting Globalization: Thomas Turino, *Nationalists, Cosmopolitans, and Popular Music in Zimbabwe*, 2000 · 378

Evocations of Cultural Migration Centered on Race, Rhythm, and Eventually Sexuality: Alejo Carpentier, *Music in Cuba*, 2001 (1946) · 382

Digging Up the Pre-Recordings Creation of a Black Pop Paradigm: Lynn Abbott and Doug Seroff, *Out of Sight: The Rise of African American Popular Music, 1889–1895*, 2002 · 386

When Faith in Popular Sound Wavers, He's Waiting: Theodor Adorno, *Essays on Music*, ed. Richard Leppert, 2002 · 388

Codifying a Precarious but Global Academic Field: David Hesmondhalgh and Keith Negus, eds., *Popular Music Studies*, 2002 · 391

Salsa and the Mixings of Global Culture: Lise Waxer, *City of Musical Memory: Salsa, Record Grooves, and Popular Culture in Cali, Colombia*, 2002 · 393

Musicals as Pop, Nationalism, and Changing Identity: Stacy Wolf, *A Problem Like Maria: Gender and Sexuality in the American Musical*, 2002 · 396

Musical Fiction and Criticism by the Greatest Used Bookstore
Clerk of All Time: Jonathan Lethem, *Fortress of Solitude*, 2003 · 399

Poetic Ontologies of Black Musical Style: Fred Moten, *In the Break:
The Aesthetics of the Black Radical Tradition*, 2003 · 401

Rescuing the Afromodern Vernacular: Guthrie Ramsey Jr., *Race Music:
Black Cultures from Bebop to Hip-Hop*, 2003 · 402

Sound Studies and the Songs Question: Jonathan Sterne, *The Audible
Past: Cultural Origins of Sound Reproduction*, 2003 · 404

Dylanologist Conventions: Bob Dylan, *Chronicles*:
Volume One, 2004 · 406

Two Editions of a Field Evolving Faster Than a Collection Could Contain:
Murray Forman and Mark Anthony Neal, eds., *That's the Joint!
The Hip-Hop Studies Reader*, 2004, 2012 · 410

Revisionist Bluesology and Tangled Intellectual History:
Elijah Wald, *Escaping the Delta: Robert Johnson and
the Invention of the Blues*, 2004 · 412

Trying to Tell the Story of a Dominant Genre: Jeff Chang, *Can't Stop,
Won't Stop: A History of the Hip-Hop Generation*, 2005 · 416

Refiguring American Music—And Its Institutionalization: Josh Kun,
Audiotopia: Music, Race, and America, 2005 · 420

Country Music Scholars Pioneer Gender and Industry Analysis:
Diane Pecknold, *The Selling Sound: The Rise of the
Country Music Industry*, 2007 · 423

Where Does Classical Music Fit In?: Alex Ross, *The Rest Is Noise:
Listening to the Twentieth Century*, 2007 · 426

Poptimism, 33⅓ Books, and the Struggles of Music Critics:
Carl Wilson, *Let's Talk about Love: A Journey to the
End of Taste*, 2007 · 429

Novelists Collegial with Indie Music: Jennifer Egan,
A Visit from the Goon Squad, 2010 · 432

YouTube, Streaming, and the Popular Music Performance Archive:
Will Friedwald, *A Biographical Guide to the Great Jazz and
Pop Singers*, 2010 · 437

Idiosyncratic Musician Memoirs—Performer as Writer in the Era
of the Artist as Brand: Jay-Z, *Decoded,* 2010 · 438

Acknowledgments · 443   Works Cited · 446   Index · 513

Introduction

Popular music, that oddity of capitalism and the democratic rabble, has long made writers bend taste, language, and professional standards—anything to ping-pong back the relentless flow of smashes and spins. The industry, Isaac Goldberg punned in the 1930s, as he wrote the first history, was a racket: noise in the service of a hustle. Would you call Irving Berlin, king of the Tin Pan Alley sheet music trade, a composer? He could only play in one key. Yet he wrote hits, so authors wrote explanations. Algonquin Round Table member Alexander Woollcott heard in slurry come-ons like "Everybody's Doin' It Now" the city's "alarum of the street cars," slang's "idiom of the sidewalks," and song plugging's relentless sales beat, "as much a part of the pace and rhythm of Berlin's music as that music, itself, is part of the pace and rhythm of America." Seventy years later, musicologist Charles Hamm detailed how Berlin songs gained middle-class legitimacy, himself legitimizing a topic that his discipline had led him to view as akin to pornography. Meanwhile, critic Jody Rosen pondered how the former Israel Baline wrote "White Christmas" and "Easter Parade," gleeful to quote novelist Philip Roth on what Berlin's assimilation did to goy holidays: "He de-Christs them both!"

Songbooks: The Literature of American Popular Music aims to capture all of that sequence and more. It's a critical guide to the authors, artists, and topics accruing a catalog as far back as William Billings's 1770 *New-England Psalm-Singer*.

The range of books makes an argument for intellectual history, comparable to pop's implications for music history. You'll find a blues novel by Gayl Jones and folk ballad mysteries by Sharyn McCrumb, memoirs by groupie Pamela Des Barres and industry figures Carrie Jacobs-Bond and Clive Davis, Top 40 charts books by Joel Whitburn and ragtime-era clippings collated by Lynn Abbott and Doug Seroff, glossy prose by Gilbert Seldes and Tom Wolfe. The provisional status of popular music authors, due to identity, funding, or creative obsession, shaped their output. Enduring stuff came from outsiders: women and/or writers of color, authors displaced by sexuality or partial education, deviants from orthodoxy. Efforts to fix music's meaning by discipline or genre have often meant less than a glimpse useful enough to pass around the way DJs would a breakbeat, comparable to the verse a songwriter distills from experience to suggest a world.

I define popular music primarily around songs, America as both place and influence, literature as something that captivates as much as it informs. My entries are short: suggestive rather than definitive. And they proceed in the order of publication date for the book that launched the career or discourse, putting foundational texts near others in a period and letting them all quest forward. In popular music, new forms required new interpretations: think Bob Dylan's Nobel Prize and the Is-he-literature? debate. Music writing's preemptive verbiage line-cut more traditional scholarship. Since the 1990s, academics have created a more formal literature: studies that extended other studies, shared keywords, university press book series. That's here, too. But professionalizing should not mean dismissing earlier writing. Hybridity and patched-together methods are not a weakness of popular music literature—they're its essence. Rereading expansively can be as revisionist as wholly new exploration.

Books on music have come in a few dominant forms: collections of songs that showed a subject existed; critical, autobiographical, and fictional salvos attuned to the timbres of pop culture; genre and disciplinary codifications meant to set boundaries; and cultural studies revisionism challenging such norms. To taxonomize:

Collected works made a case even as they made a sale, arguments about value and immensity. *Slave Songs of the United States* credited Black musical originality. Morrison Foster's 160-song collection sanctified his younger brother Stephen. John Lomax's *Cowboy Songs and Other Frontier Ballads* alchemized "Home on the Range" into a Library of Congress folk division. Whitburn's chart tallies valued commercial multiplicity.

As glossy magazines arrived, popular culture a staple, **arts criticism** supplied a tincture of modernity. Seldes of *Vanity Fair* tackled music within the "lively arts." Langston Hughes wrote for a trade publisher. The new journalism of Wolfe extended into rock and rap prose. A similar flair for language and encapsulation characterized the best **memoirs**, star turns of unexpected emphasis for Sophie Tucker, Charles Mingus, Chuck Berry, Bob Dylan, Jay-Z. Links between new sounds and shifts in the fabric were often first explored by **fiction writers**, from F. Scott Fitzgerald and lesser-known Dorothy Baker on the jazz age to Andrew Holleran's disco *Dancer from the Dance*. The desires of *Sister Carrie* met those of her later peers in *Rolling Stone* prodigy Cameron Crowe's novel *Fast Times at Ridgemont High*. Ethnicity got its thickest musical description in Jessica Hagedorn's *Dogeaters* and Los Bros Hernandez's comic series *Love and Rockets*.

Through **genre writing**, peer groups delineated estimable musical approaches. A jazz lingo solidified, as in the writers' collection *Jazzmen* or Nat Hentoff's multiartist synthesis *Hear Me Talkin' to Ya* creating collective oral history. Rudi Blesh decreed ragtime's worth. Samuel Charters and Paul Oliver foraged for blues. Charlie Gillett itemized rock and roll. Bill Malone put a honky-tonk center on country music. Rock and soul countercultures stressed a more transgressive populism. Amiri Baraka's *Blues People* voiced a funky perspective extended by Phyl Garland, Nelson George, and Greg Tate. Rock criticism came together in the *Rolling Stone Illustrated History*, Greil Marcus's *Mystery Train*, and collections from Richard Meltzer, Ellen Willis, Robert Christgau, Lester Bangs, and Robert Palmer.

Academic **disciplines** separated popular music, too, but by methods of analysis. The contributors to H. Wiley Hitchcock's *New Grove Dictionary of American Music* revamped musicology. Lawrence Levine brought folk laughter into American cultural history and archive digging into popular music writing. Bruno Nettl tracked the upstart field of ethnomusicology, raising comparative questions. Howard Becker and Richard Peterson fostered a sociology of culture, stressing institutions.

With Reagan and Thatcher in power and populist tastes no longer assumed progressive, **cultural studies** arrived, under Stuart Hall's leadership. Dissecting assumptions rather than, as earlier, deepening them, the approach was brought into rock criticism by Simon Frith, folklore by Robert Cantwell, jazz academia by Robert O'Meally's Columbia cohort, musicology by Susan McClary, ethnomusicology by Steven Feld, the African diaspora by Paul Gilroy, hip-hop by Tricia Rose, metal by Robert Walser, minstrelsy by Eric Lott, sound by Jonathan Sterne, Latinx scenes by Frances Aparicio, country by Diane Pecknold, Broadway musicals by Stacy Wolf. Similarly, fiction augmented the funky with the fantastic: the cyberpunk of William Gibson, future/past jumbles by Jennifer Egan. Post-boomer critics dug up once-deplored taste fringes: the poptimism of a Carl Wilson or Ann Powers, Alex Ross rooting classical in the popular sphere.

All of these approaches tended to overlap; another goal of this book is to put older work in conversation with those reworking it. William Billings was a young tanner when he self-published *The New-England Psalm-Singer*. In the 1955 *America's Music*, Gilbert Chase heralded Billings as "a natural genius, a true primitive." Richard Crawford, an early PhD in American music, recast that in 1993's *American Musical Landscape*, seeing a Billings who followed format rules. Those two scholars, getting U.S. popular sounds into music departments, left out the Billings who wrote sensationalist true-crime narratives akin to work by subsequent blackface minstrels like George Washington Dixon. Minstrels too had songbooks: a broadsheet of "Jim Crow" ran 150-plus verses. The dastardly versification obsessed the rock critic turned lore scholar W. T. Lhamon, who in staunch revisionism debuted the song's author-performer, T. D. Rice, on Harvard University Press more than a century after Rice's death. Lhamon also reprinted Constance Rourke's *American Humor*, 1930s speculation on minstrelsy as comic archetype.

Guthrie Ramsey Jr. worked at the junction of different traditions. His 2003 *Race Music* looked back to James Trotter's 1878 *Music and Some Highly Musical People*, the first take on Black music by a Black writer. Ramsey, pivotal in brewing up antidotes to essentializing non-Black perspectives, also celebrated white amateur Dena Epstein, a librarian who spent a quarter-century paging pre-1860s primary sources to create a compilation, the 1977 *Sinful Tunes and Spirituals*. His scholarship involved considering his own family narrative, from the South to Chicago: why the funk Gap Band's "Yearning for Your Love," heard at his dad's funeral, pushed against a music department urging him to concentrate on bebop pianist Bud Powell; why that raised issues of respectability you might take back to Alain Locke's 1925 *New Negro* anthology, or put him in a contemporary conversation with the post-soul public sphere interventions of Mark Anthony Neal, the critical freaky-deke of critic Greg Tate, the abstruse but telling ontologies of poet-critical theorist Fred Moten.

These tales have the same moral. Professionalism was always in question, same as primitivism. That was American music. That was American music writing. And it's all a very long story. Popular music involves not so much music and lyrics as music and the entire social and cultural field that supports and frames it. Writing that found a new way to chart an aspect of this universe, letting a part illuminate the whole, did the most for our understanding. To ramble, haphazardly and gleefully, through books that predate us, is to realize that while such matters as commerce versus creativity, novelty versus classics, Blackness versus "Blackness" constitute core dialectics, *popular* and *music* remain the most fundamental intersection. Each word subsumes a panoply of selves and note-taking practices.

THEMES AND VARIATIONS

Chronology rules the order of entries here, but a range of subjects recur. Nothing looms larger in American music than African American music—real, racially fantasized, and one-drop-rule conjoined, from blackface minstrelsy to spirituals, ragtime, jazz, blues, rock, soul, hip-hop, and EDM. Generalizing aggressively, I'd note through lines of discussion. First, a rhetoric that sought to humanize and institutionalize: Solomon Northup's memoir of slavery; Trotter's politic account as Reconstruction ended; James Weldon Johnson finding prose suitable to a songwriter-NAACP leader; Ralph Ellison, Albert Murray, Eileen Southern, O'Meally, and August Wilson ensconcing Jazz at Lincoln Center, blues on Broadway. Second, a countertrajectory that signified with strategic vulgarity: Zora Neale Hurston partying in her blues ethnography; Billie Holiday transcending propriety like a bad lyric; Baraka insisting on what Ishmael Reed later called *Mumbo Jumbo*. Even Sammy Davis Jr.'s new ethnicity fit this anti-anti-essentialist strand, theorized by Paul Gilroy and his adversary Fred Moten. And third, non-Blacks who analyzed Blackness as determinedly as others commodified it: origins from Natalie Curtis Burlin to Levine and Epstein, minstrelsy via Lott, blues from Samuel Charters to Elijah Wald. Jazz Blackness lured Mezz Mezzrow and Jack Kerouac; soul Blackness David Ritz and Peter Guralnick; hip-hop Blackness Jeff Chang and Jonathan Lethem; diaspora Blackness Steven Feld and Charles Keil.

To skim my table of contents is to notice women only sometimes credited elsewhere and never together. *Slave Songs of the United States*, the first collection of African American song, existed because coeditor Lucy McKim Garrison's parents were abolitionists and gender egalitarians. Olive Dame Campbell persuaded the English folk revivalist Cecil Sharp to extend her songcatching. Alice Fletcher, Natalie Curtis Burlin, and Frances Densmore, a trio whose field recordings were uncredited ethnomusicology, idealized antimodern outsider culture. That influenced *Show Boat* author Edna Ferber, who balanced ephemeral stage lights and eternal river. Emma Bell Miles's cultivation let her categorize "Some Real American Music" for *Harper's* in 1904, then publish *Spirit of the Mountains* in 1905. Her hard isolation was addressed in journals and stories, the first published only in 2014, the fiction in 2016. Carrie Jacobs-Bond, first rich woman songwriter, diminished posthumously, but her memoir, *The Roads of Melody*, now seems in a lineage with country songwriter Loretta Lynn's *Coal Miner's Daughter*. Baker wrote *Young Man with a Horn*, the first jazz novel; perhaps subsumed lesbianism gave her protagonists' "funny slant on things" a grounding, perhaps her awareness of race and class owed to fiction providing the critic's role jazz people would have denied her. Phyl Garland's *Soul* presented autoethnography as musicology before Ramsey; she'd pioneer cultural reporting at Columbia and still hasn't been fully anthologized.

Far more connections need drawing. One might link Lilian Roxon, writing herself into a male-dominated field with the *Rock Encyclopedia*, to Gina Arnold working through genre and gender with her alternative rock study *Route 666*; that common history was asserted in Evelyn McDonnell and Ann Powers's *Rock She Wrote*. Balance Garland's familial approach with Southern, her counterpart, who kept soul at a remove in *The Music of Black Americans* after years on the Black college margins but became Harvard's first Black woman full professor and original Afro-American Studies chair. Open the soul moment to the haunted blues of Gayl Jones, notice its absence in the acclaimed, brief rock criticism of Ellen Willis. The foundational figure for all of these placements and displacements would be Hurston, whose juke joint ethnography, *Mules and Men*, funded by university sources and an interventionist "Godmother," managed to both observe and observe herself observing in a manner we're still learning to appreciate. Hurston's influence lines led to Tricia Rose, the first hip-hop scholar, theorizing rupture and flow, to Lise Waxer's ethnography of salsa in the vinyl museum city of Cali, Columbia, to sociologist Tia DeNora's case studies of working women listening to songs to manage emotion.

The music business has been another perennial source of fascination and disgust, the pop perplex in a nutshell and a stand-in for shifting views of ethnicity, capitalism, aesthetics, and professionalism. Isaac Goldberg, finding "cosmopolitan culture" in what he contradictorily viewed as a "song factory," was not so different from Clive Davis calling his post-Monterey format juggling at Columbia Records "corporate nonconformity." Novelists and exposé journalists offered a more aggrieved barometer, including the lurid pulp original rock novel, Harlan Ellison's *Rockabilly*. A still different view came from how-to manuals, gushing in the early twentieth century, endlessly updated later as *This Business of Music*. In between decriers and celebrants, one found cultural studies–trained Keith Negus and former hip-hop bizzer Dan Charnas. Each captured outsider-insiders betting long and feeling queasy.

An ongoing approach here is to consider how literature collected around major figures, which Bert Williams turned out to be. He was considered liberal vaudeville in the wake of his 1922 death, viewed tragically circa the counterculture as plastic opposite of rock and soul, then regained iconicity for his masked identity as a figure of Black Atlantic double-consciousness. Like others, from Ellington and Holiday to Dylan and Madonna, the literature shaped around him changed as values and methods did. A similar pattern included books by artists themselves—more or less. Whether Jelly Roll Morton speaking over piano to Alan Lomax, all of David Ritz's ghostwriter projects, or classics of composite origin by Armstrong, Holiday, and Lynn, autobiographies raised enduring questions about voice and notation.

American popular music has connected to seemingly everything: race and ethnicity, gender and sexuality, class and capitalism, technology and modernity, theater and fashion, subculture and spectacle, Culture and culture. Similar questions came up even as the music changed. But it mattered if the askers changed, if topics were more canonical or conjunctural, if prose style in sentences shifted. Rereading the literature of American popular music entry by entry makes these issues acute. There isn't a subject in American popular music, from artist to genre, that hasn't dramatically altered its meaning over time. Confronting this through a display of examples (I can't pretend comprehensiveness) offers insights different from close-reading a particular work or era. JoAnne Mancini used "anthological modernism" to describe collections, like Harry Smith's *Anthology of American Folk Music*, LPs packaged to encompass the world in a document. There is something of that here. From Walt Whitman and his ever-expanding *Leaves of Grass*, how writers heard America singing has shaped what sort of book preserved the tale.

SENTIMENTAL AND VERNACULAR

But I have two more words to stress. Either "sentimental" or "vernacular" kept coming up as I read, so I started marking them down in entries as a heuristic device to see what connections might result. For sentimental, picture respectable women all feeling moved, emphasis on tears and the domestic sphere—the parlor. For vernacular, think regular guys talking shit, emphasis on laughter and the public sphere—the streets. We often simplistically narrate Victorian assumptions yielding to modern style, like one of those parlor women cutting her hair and going out dancing on the town. Embracing, in other words, the vernacular, which in American popular culture gets figured as the African American and immigrant, the urban and urbane, speckled with gay and working-class barroom touches, too.

Staying in overview mode, vernacular books started in the West with the Bible's translation into languages people spoke, a move connected to the enlightenment and modernity. Move that to the New World and you have, as vernacular, the "Yankee Doodle Dandy" style of U.S. politics and pop culture: Billings's "Chester" sung in the revolution, Rice jumping Jim Crow as founding fathers yielded to a Jacksonian democracy of scurrilous caricature. Much classic writing on American popular music bought into the equation of the vernacular and democratic, in opposition to a stuffy, European "genteel tradition": Chase's *America's Music*, Gillett's *Sound of the City*, Malone's *Country Music, U.S.A.*, Marcus's *Mystery Train*—it's especially clear in the first editions, before each author learned more and recalibrated.

Plenty connected vernacular, African American idioms, and technology. With recording, from different levels of audio production to movies and YouTube clips, what Barthes called "the grain of the voice" could be preserved, disseminated, and made essential to a specific vision of music. Michael Denning's *Noise Uprising* called the 1920s arrival of electrical recording a "vernacular music revolution," felt worldwide, which from New Orleans jazz to Egypt's Umm Kulthum allowed sounds to ripple out in a subaltern surge. Denning judged this a "decolonization of the ear," noting that the word vernacular came into parlance after the boom, used to describe commercial recordings as what Charles Seeger, musicologist and father of folk legend Pete, called "the musical vernacular of the 'common man.'" Vernacular, Denning wrote, was a term less fraught with nationalism than folk, more musically diverse than jazz, emphasized the spoken, and built up from *verna*, meaning a home-born slave.

Skip ahead a generation, turn up the sound, and think of LeRoi Jones, on his way to becoming Amiri Baraka, conjuring James Brown's grooves played in a bank, making that white institution "a place . . . where black people move in almost absolute openness and strength." Vernacular popular music went through an amplification process after World War II, the difference between trumpet and electric guitar, one microphone recording and magnetic tape edits, urban vaudeville and rock and roll. Charles Keil delineated this shift in *Music Grooves*, George Lipsitz found its political valence in *Rainbow at Midnight*, and Christgau wrote about Chuck Berry in the *Rolling Stone Illustrated History of Rock & Roll* as "heightened vernacular." Wolfe's pop art circus *Kandy-Kolored Tangerine-Flake Streamline Baby* was a partner to Baraka in the explosive release of this later vernacular literature, prose reaching to match what Palmer once called "The Church of the Sonic Guitar." Slangy, mass-produced sheet music already purveyed vernacular, but the twentieth century electrified it, as pop globalized, Americans below the median were targeted as consumers, and collective pride greeted Hank Williams, Elvis Presley, Soul Brother Number One. It was romantic, engaging writers across the wide spectrum this book surveys. Just as one revered funky Black music, not bland white pop or dead symphonic pomp, one wrote to uncover the kind of stories Jelly Roll Morton told.

But the rise of the vernacular, in music books and beyond, meant the purging of the sentimental. Try weeping to the "Murder Ballad" Morton chuckle-sang for Lomax. In books on American popular music, vernacular ideals rose as sentimental affiliations fell. Hughes and Hurston critiqued Harlem Renaissance respectability politics. Seldes, Woollcott, and Goldberg touted a sonic melting pot. Woody Guthrie built *Bound for Glory* around folksy address. Institutionalizers Marshall and Jean Stearns's *Jazz Dance* was subtitled *The Story of American Vernacular Dance*. Chase, urging musicology to embrace popular styles, thundered: "the American musical vernacular has been on the march through all these generations, and even our most academic composers are catching up with it, or being caught up by it." Levine stressed folk vernacular in *Black Culture and Black Consciousness*: African American secular song, he wrote, "cut through the sentimentality that marked most popular music."

This was a constrained definition of sentimentalism, which could also involve political identification with the downtrodden, bourgeois self-reflexivity over managing mood, and an aesthetic commitment to form-advancing uplift. Not to mention strong women. Sentimentality sponsored True Womanhood, melodramatic theater, and ballads of Home and Mother. It could also be a force for modernization, as when Fred Moten cited its connections to abolitionism in his evocation of a "Sentimental Avant-Garde" and wondered if the energies summoned to abolish slavery might one day be revived to abolish commodities. In the heavily commodified, Céline Dion singing "My Heart Will Go On" in *Titanic* sense explored by Carl Wilson, sentimentality still shaped romantic notions and popular art forms. Lauren Berlant's *The Female Complaint* called this "the unfinished business of sentimentality in American culture," connecting genealogies of the novel and theater pieces *Show Boat* and *Uncle Tom's Cabin* to challenge Lott's cultural studies view of minstrelsy. Berlant insisted that sentimentality's adaptability made it as forceful as blackface: Ferber's teary Americana united traumas of race, gender, class, and, implicitly, Jewish religion.

When McKim, a teenager still, went south during the Civil War and discovered spirituals, publishing "Roll, Jordan, Roll" as a prelude to *Slave Songs,* she wrote a friend a sentimental account. "Kneeling in that poor cabin with those who suffered scourgings at our hands . . . I vowed that if I ever forgot them, so might Heaven forget me!" One understands why Benjamin Filene called his roots music study *Romancing the Folk*. Yet describing Black singing for the magazine *Dwight's*, McKim became musicological: her sentimentality was adaptable to a professional discursive mode. Similarly, Fletcher, Curtis Burlin, and Densmore shuffled between sentimental and scientific, the way Ferber incorporated both sentimentalized climaxes (heroine Magnolia in white clutching the exposed as "passing" Julie in black) and the media savvy of her Algonquin peer Woollcott, mentioned in the novel.

Stephen Foster wrote blackface ditties, yet aspired to sentimental weepers and was valued for that in his day: friend Robert Nevin wrote in *The Atlantic* in 1867 that "his art taught us all to feel with the colored man the lowly joys and sorrows it celebrated." Berlin ragged "Swanee River" metaphorically in "Alexander's Ragtime Band," which Seldes called "utterly unsentimental" in his 1924 *Seven Lively Arts.* But we now value Berlin's utterly sentimental later songs, too: "White Christmas," again. Baker's jazz novel *Young Man with a Horn*, title from the *New Republic's* working-class jazz critic, Otis Ferguson, associated sentimental and commercial: "There is music that is turned out sweet in hotel ballrooms and there is music that comes right out of the genuine urge and doesn't come for money." To see limit in this critique recognizes the baggage that came with vernacular assumptions.

Just as early writing on popular music was never purely sentimental, the writing of the 1920s to 1970s was not purely vernacular: these were modes that writers relied on but supplemented. If sentimental writers used scientific and media idioms to toughen up, the best writers on vernacular used popularization to loosen up. David Ritz, turning from academia to ghost writing, worked this, as did young rock critic Cameron Crowe, celebrating the taste of older sisters. Cultural historians like Lewis Erenberg, communications scholars like Susan Douglas, fiction writers like Gibson all strategically interspersed sentimental and vernacular, the way Kiss suspended "Detroit Rock City" to get the lighters going with "Beth."

One final twist. If the sentimental was purged by the vernacular, much smart writing next purged the vernacular. Ellen Willis, among her critic peers, drew on feminist critique to question rock as a grassroots art form. The Birmingham Centre for Contemporary Cultural Studies writers considered belief in a counterhegemonic vernacular simplistic at a time of what Stuart Hall called "the great moving Right show." Simon Frith, joining Willis and Birmingham, knocked over rockism's house of cards, writing "It makes better sense to define pop as the sentimental song." DeNora analyzed *Music in Everyday Life* as professional women using sentiment as a tool. Jonathan Lethem urged that his fannish fiction and nonfiction be read for "impulses to beguile, cajole, evoke sensation, and even to manipulate." Wayne Koestenbaum used opera queens to revamp vernacular and sentimental altogether under the rubric of catharsis:

"the wish, condemned as effeminate, never to reassemble the socialized self, but, instead, to remain in tears forever, to stay where Puccini's *La Bohème* (1896) places us."

Ideas of sentimental and vernacular have pulled at each other over time, vernacular impulses purging the sentimental, then cultural studies and post-counterculture impulses purging the vernacular. That eternal reframing process has greatly affected lasting topics. Writing on African American music often at first turned on the sentimental: *Twelve Years a Slave*, for example. But every step toward Black Power added vernacular, through to 1970s Gayl Jones, who wrote: "The ballads were in the vernacular but they were oral. The 'people' made them, not 'writers.'" With Paul Gilroy's critique of hip-hop ghettocentricity as challenging to vernacular as Hughes or Baraka had been to sentimental uplift, a new wave valued Bert Williams's mask alongside Bessie Smith's realness. The film revival of *Twelve Years a Slave* readies us to reread James Trotter. And the revisionism of David Ritz, Farah Jasmine Griffin, and others position us to esteem the exaggerations in *Lady Sings the Blues* because, as Griffin put it, if you can't be free, be a mystery.

In particular, shifting views of sentimental and vernacular have turned on assumptions about gender and sexuality. When a Seldes or Chase attacked the sentimental, their figure of scorn was what Seldes called "the exact equivalent of a high-toned lady," Chase "the emulation of the elegant." The critique of the vernacular increased attention to such listeners and the music aimed at them. Feminists dissected rebellious masculine street identities as subcultural capital and celebrated bedroom fans. Eric Lott's revisioning of blackface minstrelsy abandoned the question of minstrelsy's truth as vernacular to present it as a contested terrain of sexualized cross-racial identification—the love that went with the theft.

The move from a jazz, rock, or hip-hop centered genre language of vernacular overcoming conservative constraints repositioned the music industry, too. Tin Pan Alley origins modernized via blackface minstrelsy, offering a slangy, theatrical mock-vernacular. It wasn't proper, but it sold. Then urbane taste flipped and what Karl Hagstrom Miller called the "folkloric paradigm" unquestioningly validated anti-genteel vernacular. Sentimentality became the doggie in the window: sweet sounds the most compromised. But rock and soul faltered in the wake of punk and disco, American populism elected Ronald Reagan, and the vernacular counterculture sparked in the Jazz Age, fused around midcentury icons of rebellion, found that the revolution was over. Cultural nationalist and not incidentally strong feminist Greg Tate complained: "Oh, the selling power of the Black Vernacular."

Noticing how sentimental and vernacular rhetoric thread through otherwise distinct music books can help us read and listen better. If a Céline Dion song is sentimental, and a Louis Armstrong scat is vernacular, Armstrong singing "What a Wonderful World" is a delicious hot toddy of a reminder not to assume purity in either category. (Speaking of Armstrong, whose entertainer side had to be reclaimed by critics such as Gary Giddins, let me note that while jazz factors heavily in this book, the goal is never to explain that genre as an art form set apart, always to view it as a category of popular music expression.) The vernacular is presumed to fight, thrill, and endure over time, recognized as art, while the sentimental fades, exposed as a kitschy fraud of well-meaning sanctimony. Figures like Armstrong or Elvis Presley have been thought to battle dual impulses, rebellious and conformist. This split was positioned as vernacular America against sentimental Europe, vernacular working class against sentimental middle class, vernacular Black—or Black *acting*—against sentimental white, and vernacular male against sentimental female.

That Whitman, Guthrie, Dylan, and Springsteen were overly gloried by this set of associations should not harden us to why popular music literature needed the vernacular to secure a position in American letters. To praise Armstrong's vivid, soloing genius over symphonic Paul Whiteman involved taste assertions useful in then esteeming blues. Chase needed the vernacular cudgel to turn American musicology upside down. But keeping the rhetorical nature of all this in mind illuminates why a jazz writer skeptical of vernacular claims might value Duke Ellington's *A Drum Is a Woman* television program, or why ideas surfaced in literary figures apart from at times stridently vernacular genre criticism.

The best approach would be to take more seriously what Ellington called tone parallels, the idea that music could evoke, however imperfectly, a Harlem airshaft. Or what Birmingham cultural studies writers called homologies, the way a leather jacket fit a rocker's subcultural outfit. In other words, the cultural epiphany produced by mixing music with something else. Books that managed to preserve, model, distill, flaunt, or critique some aspect of popular music, often at a cost to the writers, turned on these correspondences. They are at the core of this study, the works I have prioritized over others. Often, we interpret music by applying a framing model from far outside the world of songs to a specific performer or work. Here, in a method that brings me back to my days writing and editing "Riffs" for the *Village Voice*, I let a range of material bounce together, bring whatever I can hoist to the table interpretively, comment and quote freely. I won't pretend to the finer points of each Hurston, Adorno, or Moten essay, each wrinkle in ethnomusicology and sound studies. My hope is to help connect the literature of American popular music and let readers hear the tone parallels.

Just as we might now regret the purging of the sentimental by champions of the vernacular, we should be cautious about writing that looks to purge the vernacular. That's critics identified as poptimists critiquing the taste assumptions of rockists. That's populism getting seized by Rush Limbaugh or Donald Trump, so vernacular looks like another bastion of *herrenvolk* democracy. But it's also university professors raising an eyebrow at hyperbolic sentences that overstate claims. Academic writing has been freeing topically but more constrained linguistically. We should continue to read what Frith, drawing on fanzine Socrates Frank Kogan, called low theory. We should also continue to write it. Confused statements, incipient forms, displaced intellectuals: these are at the core of the sentimental and vernacular half-syntheses, the loopy work, of our songbooks.

As I revise this introduction, I'm reading recent and forthcoming books. Brent Edwards, from jazz studies, makes the literary essential to jazz in *Epistrophies*: more about the scatology of Armstrong's scat than you'd have expected, to consider why that free flow was part of a syntax, a way of dropping words that also dropped sounds—he has to photograph the great man's own documents when transcription won't do. Matt Brennan's *When Genres Collide* compares *Down Beat* and *Rolling Stone*, querying why jazz and rock criticism embraced such different perspectives; old battles now, as we retrace popular music's changing same. But he turns up another lost woman writer, Ruth Cage, who wrote about R&B for *Down Beat* in the 1950s, then stopped and became a theater publicist; somebody should collect her stuff. My wife, Ann Powers, has a book outlined on Joni Mitchell, in whom everything collided, so she is planning multiple chapters: Beats, Laurel Canyon, soul songwriters, love languages, tribute acts. There's Christgau's *Book Reports*, a reminder that many entries here started with him dipping into a writer who gave the big question, how pop music made us rethink culture, a new tale or tone. Fast-forward a few months more to the copyedits coming back and there are upcoming books by Maureen Mahon, Daphne Brooks, and Danyel Smith, among others, to eagerly await, sure, like Mahon's take on the likes of LaVern Baker as a rock and roller, to amplify the role of Black women in the literature as both authors and artists—the combo striking a power chord.

All these books feel akin to mine: perhaps the shared project is to find the literary glimmering in unexpected places. Deafened and jaded by neoliberal spectacles of sanctioned resistance, we have lost faith in popular music, or any popular culture, as idiomatic rebelliousness. But the far-flung chronicles that our songs have generated remain inspirational. Across eras and styles, wherever the story led, they constitute a great reckoning with the least ruly of cultural forms.

READER'S NOTE

Because this book surveys many other books across a large number of entries, the story it tells overlaps in many ways. You can read through or hopscotch. Here are some basic structural details.

If you see the name of an author or musician in this book in boldface, that means there is a separate entry elsewhere on that person. Go there for a fuller account of whatever is being referred to. The Works Cited list at the end should give full titles and publication details for all books and articles mentioned along the way.

Entries proceed chronologically from the publication date of the book that initiates the story being told in an entry. Within entries, however, the discussion often moves forward in time to survey how an author evolved, how views of a performer changed, or how opinions on a subject mutated.

Some entries focus on writers, some on musical figures, and some on key topics. The section breakdowns are purely chronological, but my titles for each suggest commonalities. And the titles for each entry in the table of contents can also help you figure out what to choose if you're pursuing a particular topic. Still, nothing is wholly contained. It can't be.

PART I

SETTING THE SCENE

FIGURE I.I
Title page, *Slave Songs of the
United States*, 1867. University
of Alabama Libraries Special
Collections.

———

FIGURE I.2
Cover, Emma Bell Miles, *The
Spirit of the Mountains*,
1905. University of Tennes-
see at Chattanooga Special
Collections.

SLAVE SONGS

OF THE

UNITED STATES.

New York:
A. SIMPSON & CO.,
1867.

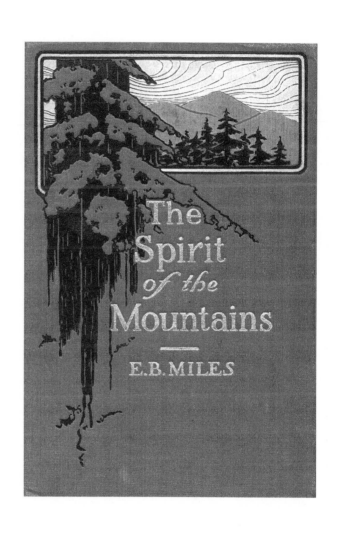

The
Spirit
of the
Mountains

—

E.B. MILES

FIGURE 1.3 Oscar George Theodore Sonneck, *A Bibliography of Early Secular American Music*, 1905; 1964 Da Capo reissue with preface by one of Sonneck's inheritors, Irving Lowens. Author's collection.

———

FIGURE 1.4 James Weldon Johnson, *The Autobiography of an Ex-Colored Man*, 1912, Library of America *Writings* edition, 2004. A novel that had to be published anonymously originally now belongs to the nation's most prestigious legacy imprint. Author's collection.

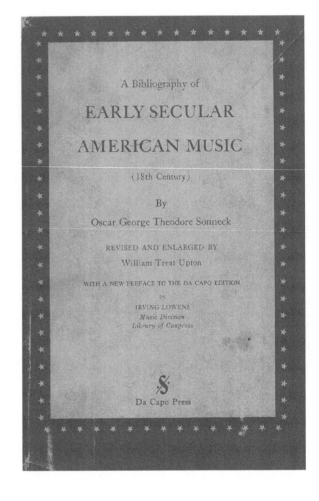

A Bibliography of

EARLY SECULAR

AMERICAN MUSIC

(18th Century)

By

Oscar George Theodore Sonneck

REVISED AND ENLARGED BY

William Treat Upton

WITH A NEW PREFACE TO THE DA CAPO EDITION

by

IRVING LOWENS
Music Division
Library of Congress

Da Capo Press

James Weldon
Johnson

Writings

The Autobiography of an Ex-Colored Man
Along This Way
Essays and Editorials
Selected Poems

FIRST WRITER, OF MUSIC AND ON MUSIC

William Billings, The New-England Psalm-Singer, *1770*

———

Here is a particularly American place to begin. Billings, 24 and a tanner by trade, published the first collection of tunes by a native, with a frontispiece by Paul Revere, no less, and a lyric for "Chester" that would soon be sung in the Revolution: "Let tyrants shake their iron Rod / And slav'ry clank her galling chains / We fear them not; we trust in God / New England's God forever reigns." As notable a writer about culture as a writer of culture, Billings's author notes emphasized his youth and musical inexperience, with a sarcastic air that still comes off: "I think it best for every *Composer* to be his own *Carver.*" The book sold few copies, but a sequel, *The Singing Master's Assistant,* proved a hit, including the parody "Jargon," written to be discordant and directed to be sung like "a hog who is extream hungry." Billings was not allowed to copyright his work, fell out of fashion, and died poor.

This archetypal figure wrote psalm tunes because in Puritan New England that was allowed, and because the elders had disliked the oral tradition of "lining out" enough to start singing schools in the 1720s. Meant to train congregants to respect the notated text, the schools became places to drink, dance, and make sexually merry. For composers like Billings, they also provided choirs trained enough to handle the polyphony of fuguing-tunes. An English inheritance, staid by London standards, psalmody became a form of rebellion and nationalism, though by 1800 the door was shut again, as churches returned to older sounds, music snobs looked to Europe, and rebels went to newly opened theaters.

Billings would be revived much later, musically in the Americana explorations of the 1930s and intellectually with **Gilbert Chase**'s 1955 *America's Music.*

FIGURE 1.5 Paul Revere frontispiece, William Billings, *The New-England Psalm-Singer,* 1770. American Antiquarian Society.

For Chase, looking to celebrate all in the U.S. archive that was not European classical, Billings, who "gloried in his musical independence," was the precursor to a later New England composer and outsider—Charles Ives. The musicologists who followed Chase included **H. Wiley Hitchcock** ("William Billings and the Yankee Tunesmiths" appeared, exotically, in *Stereo Review*) and psalmody PhD **Richard Crawford**, coauthor of a 1970s Billings biography, who analyzed his songbook tunes as a conscious mix in *The American Musical Landscape: The Business of Musicianship from Billings to Gershwin.* A four-volume scholarly edition of the tunebooks now sits on music library shelves near Brahms. Former Society for American Music president Michael Broyles gave a chapter to Billings in his 2004 *Mavericks,* which also covered Ives, Cage, Zappa, and Meredith Monk. The young carver of hides and psalms had come to represent American popular and art music inseparably linked.

Later authors reined in Chase's vernacular exuberance, stressing Billings more as a student of different rules, not opposition to all rules. Yet Broyles, looking at Billings's writings outside his psalmody, including magazine articles, found a parallel fascination with true crime narratives and lurid family dramas, suggesting a kinship to tabloid editor and early blackface minstrel George Washington Dixon. (Perhaps in both directions: the scholarly volumes were edited by Hans Nathan, also a noted minstrelsy historian.) From this perspective, one of Billings's last takes on music, a Q&A between "Master" and "Scholar" as part of *The Continental Harmony*, published by his friends as an act of charity in 1794, anticipated the minstrel interlocutor's dialogues with his end men: status anxiety never fully dispelled. "I was fool enough to commence author before I really understood either *tune, time,* or *concord*," Billings wrote, not the last American to discover that mastering music in maturity was the antithesis of gaining popularity in youth.

BLACKFACE MINSTRELSY
EXTENDS ITS TWISTED ROOTS

T. D. Rice, "Jim Crow," c.1832

Thomas Dartmouth Rice never wrote a book, which violates the rules of this book. Then again, violating rules is one of this book's themes—and Rice too fundamental to ignore. The national, then international craze for his "Jim Crow" song-and-dance theater routine established blackface minstrelsy as the first genre of American pop, gave a name to segregation after the Civil War, and made it impossible to mistake American vernacular for pure folk. Rice took a very basic banjo line, with room for an extended couplet, attached a chorus about a performer dancing, and created a musical skit you could extend forever—comment, then mocking, peripatetic signature. The earliest sheet music had a soon-iconic cover image of a putatively Black performer about to leap from verse to chorus: clothes shabby, hat tilted, feet raised, one hand on hip and the other enacting a tangled particular. Then a music page of verse, chorus and four more verses, a subsequent page of forty more verses, and a blank final page. Other printings offered as many as 150 or 160 verses. We might compare it to a *Hee Haw* comedy segment, banjo playing between punchlines, or unlikely chapters of R. Kelly's "Trapped in the Closet" series. Rice, a stage performer from New York, toured the country and then England in the era of Andrew Jackson.

FIGURE 1.6 Cover of E. Riley edition of "Jim Crow," picturing performer T. D. Rice as the character, circa 1831. Source: the Beinecke Rare Book and Manuscript Library, Yale University.

When we look at the sheet music variants, complexity emerges. The lyrics are in dialect: "I's jist from Tuckyhoe," voicing a character who chases women, fights indiscriminately, gets drunk, calls himself a "niggar," hits a "Sambo," and talks about animals like he is one. On the other hand, Tuckahoe is where Jefferson grew up and the character is a fiddler who compares himself to Paganini, cites a brutal Jackson victory in the War of 1812 to contextualize his orneriness and a 700-pound human spectacle alongside "a glass case of monkeys" in a Barnum-style street museum to contextualize his freakishness. Rice's text references racial topics: slave labor as more "honest" than white, the "white Negro" precursor "I'm so glad dat I'm a niggar, An don't you wish you was too, For den you'd gain popularity, By jumping Jim Crow." Most of all:

"Should dey get to fighting / Perhaps de blacks will rise / For deir wish for freedom / Is shining in deir eyes."

To linger on this song is to spiral into topsy-turvy, fun for Gilbert and Sullivan biopics, problematic for pop built on racial appropriation. All recent minstrelsy scholarship has unpacked "Jim Crow" as its first move: what **William Billings** offered musicologists, Rice offered 1990s rock and rollers having second thoughts. **Eric Lott**'s *Love and Theft* used the cultural studies framework of **Stuart Hall** and others to see in blackface a jittery white working-class response to the early capitalism of "wage slavery." Dale Cockrell's *Demons of Disorder* archived Rice's interracial social milieu and argued that middle- and upper-class audiences shifted minstrelsy's meaning in uniformly racist directions. Most devoted was W. T. Lhamon Jr., English professor and 1970s *New Republic* rock critic, then author of a 1950s study, *Deliberate Speed*, that rejected traditional cultural boundaries to put the gay sex antecedents of Little Richard's "Tutti Frutti" in conversation with Thomas Pynchon and Jackson Pollock. For Lhamon, Daddy Rice was an unrecognized antiracist rabble-rouser.

Lhamon, at heart a radical folklorist, saw "lore cycles" of raw and then cooked popular music as more central to American culture than any pop/folk divide. He first wrote about minstrelsy in *Raising Cain*, locating its heartbeat in the workers a step down from artisanal craftsmen, building the Erie Canal. Rice attracted his attention, and he followed with a second book, *Jump Jim Crow*, that started with a ninety-page overview of "Extravagant and Wheeling Stranger" Rice's life and work—how, for example, in New Orleans, his performances exchanged material with the Little Richard–like (he thought) Black entertainer Old Corn Meal. The bulk of the volume gave Rice the book he never published: editorially reconstructed composite texts of songs, plays, and street prose, all carrying the Jim Crow story deeper into race and class reversals, with Lhamon's notes the only guide. Not done, he shortened that dizzying collection into *Jim Crow, American*, part of the John Harvard Library series Harvard University Press devoted to canonical literary figures: Cooper, Twain, Hawthorne. Rice had become an American classic.

SHAPE-NOTE SINGING AND EARLY COUNTRY

B. F. White and E. J. King, The Sacred Harp, *1844*

———

Kiri Miller's ethnomusicology, *Traveling Home*, traced a group of shape-note singers, appearing on the Oscars the year *Cold Mountain* featured their rough harmonies, who brought to that stage Sacred Harp tunebooks. Not to sing from. To confuse viewers into investigating. Shape-note singing, one of the oldest and most enduring folk traditions, involved performing hymns "fasola" style, those notes and *mi* notated with particular shapes, printed in an oblong edition that allowed for categories of tenor, treble, bass, and maybe alto to sing out at the directive to take up, say, page 30. Only those who have "used" the contents have fully read such works. It's a likely dwindling population. But no study of American popular music literature would be complete without its most performed book.

One-sided lore from Joseph Summerlin James's *History of the Sacred Harp* (1904) claimed Benjamin Franklin White was cheated by William Walker, his South Carolina brother-in-law, who took all credit for the 1835 *Southern Harmony and Musical Companion*. That book sold a purported 600,000 copies and its 1854 expanded edition is still visited yearly in Benton, Kentucky. White moved to Georgia, started the Southern Musical Association, and with *The Sacred Harp* created a volume that supplanted rival Walker's. Both books drew on Isaac Watts hymns, **William Billings** fuguing syncopations, and reworking of New England singing-school styles from camp meetings of the Second Great Awakening. Yankee teachers had bred southern traditionalists, paradigms that then permeated gospel and country music styles.

An account of sacred harp as savvy on invented tradition as **Robert Cantwell's** *Bluegrass Breakdown* doesn't exist (Miller comes closest), but pieces can be assembled. Gavin James Campbell's "Old Can Be Used Instead of New" traced how the four-shape-note approach diverged from more modern seven-shape gospel singing after 1880; *The Sacred Harp* got five revisions to balance between old and new, with James's *Original Sacred Harp* (1911) winning the retro branding battle. Singing conventions, part of a broader antimodernity, kept strict rituals, and by the 1930s hundreds of these events epitomized white southern populism. George Pullen Jackson's *White Spirituals in the Southern Uplands*, a major influence on **Gilbert Chase's** *America's Music*, called the participants "country singers," to be contrasted with audience-centered urban pop. Jackson also, as in *White and Negro Spirituals*, obsessively asserted, with white-supremacist defensiveness, that Black voicings derived from white antecedents. A more literary account, northerner Carl Carmer's *Stars Fell on Alabama*, put singing conventions up against fiddler's conventions, moonshiners, blues juking, lynchings and Klan rallies, calling Bama "a strange country" and the shapenoters "outlandish gibberish."

Some forty years later, soon to be ex-academic Buell Cobb created the singers' favorite account of themselves, *The Sacred Harp: A Tradition and Its Music*, more tolerant racially than Jackson but still stressing a dubious "musical innocence." Cobb worked in partnership with Hugh McGraw's efforts to better scaffold the subculture; McGraw oversaw the now-dominant 1991 edition of the 1936, 1960, 1967, and 1970 Denson revisions of that 1911 James revision of *Sacred Harp*. *Cords around My Heart*, written after Cobb retired from business, went deeper on the belated acceptance by white groups of aging Black singers (a *Colored Sacred Harp* dated to 1934) just before their conventions died off. Cobb, able in the twenty-first century to recall figures who spanned the full twentieth, romanticized the Cullman, Alabama, courthouse singings that preceded him, admitting his community's whiteness but not stressing, as Carmer had, its signs: "Nigger, Don't Let the Sun Go Down on You in This Town!"

By the time Miller went to ninety conventions in fifteen states, between 1997 and 2006, shape-note singers had formed a diasporic network open to northern folkies yet still focused around the eternal book. She wrote, "The *Sacred Harp* is a teaching tool, propaganda vehicle, multivalent symbol, and transcendent canon in one." Critical distance precluded understanding, Miller found; one had to participate in a shape-note paradigm. Traditionalism, however compromised and constructed, was a core component of literary appreciation. At a New England convention, "Things proceeded more or less as I expected—until a leader on his way into the square took a starting pitch from a pitch pipe. With a visceral shock of indignation, I immediately shut my book and sat out his lesson. At that point I recognized myself as a Chicago singer."

MUSIC IN CAPTIVITY

Solomon Northup, Twelve Years a Slave, *1853*

———

"I was born in Tuckahoe," the great civil rights leader Frederick Douglass began his *Narrative of the Life* in 1845, and readers heard an echo. **T. D. Rice**'s "Jim Crow" had launched: "Come, listen all you galls and boys / I's jist from

Tuckyhoe / I'm goin to sing a little song / My name's Jim Crow." Douglass hated blackface minstrels, calling them "the filthy scum of white society, who have stolen from us a complexion denied to them by nature, in which to make money, and pander to the corrupt taste of their white fellow citizens." But he allowed for a different take in his *My Bondage and My Freedom*: "It would seem almost absurd to say it, considering the use that has been made of them, that we have allies in the Ethiopian songs; those songs that constitute our national music, and without which we have no national music. They are heart songs, and the finest feelings of human nature are expressed in them. 'Lucy Neal,' 'Old Kentucky Home,' and 'Uncle Ned,' can make the heart sad as well as merry, and can call forth a tear as well as a smile. They awaken the sympathies for the slave, in which antislavery principles take root, grow, and flourish."

The mixed message here will extend through many entries in this book. Music, acknowledged as a Black gift, yet under derogatory framing, occupied leading African American intellectuals far more than white thinkers. Within this literature, the sentimental/vernacular divide operated in complex ways. Sentimentality, to our assumptions a Victorian, middle-class, "white" orientation, radicalized abolitionist efforts to wake sympathy to Black suffering and humanity. Some 1850s minstrelsy took this path, with **Stephen Foster** songs like "Old Kentucky Home" weeping like *Uncle Tom's Cabin*. Vernacular Black expression was more easily reduced to a "happy darky" minstrel slander. Yet to deny it was to deny vital African American culture.

There was no way to unriddle the dichotomy, which forced what W. E. B. Du Bois would call double-consciousness and Paul Gilroy in *The Black Atlantic* a counterculture of modernity. Douglass's *Narrative* dwelled on the oppositions ("They would sometimes sing the most pathetic sentiment in the most rapturous tone"), distanced from his own slave past "within the circle" singing "those wild notes." The tears they caused him gave him "my first glimmering conception of the dehumanizing character of slavery," and why hearing joy in slave song was ghastly. Du Bois's chapter "Of the Sorrow Song" ended *The Souls of Black Folks* in 1903. He called spirituals "weird old songs in which the soul of the black slave spoke to men." They were "the music of an unhappy people," and as a message "naturally veiled and half articulate. Words and music have lost each other." This groping poignancy he contrasted with the "caricature" of minstrelsy and his own era's coon song.

A key twenty-first-century text for questioning "Black" music as it pained pleasure and pleasured pain was the film version of an 1853 strong seller, aimed at Douglass's admirers, about a northern tavern fiddler and odd-jobs entrepreneur captured into bondage. Solomon Northup felt "in the possession of abundance" in upstate New York: wife, kids, home, audience of young people. His memoir, cowritten with a white editor in ways we can't fully reconstruct, used sentimentality to evoke horror: "I seemed to stand on the brink of madness!" On the block alongside him, Eliza, children pulled from her, sought the grave: "the only resting place of the poor slave!"

While a fellow abductee was rescued by friends, Northup remained surrounded by rank strangers: "in all the crowd that thronged the wharf, there was no one who knew or cared for me." And this included the slaves he'd spend the years with, written about more as They than We. Steve McQueen's film added work songs and spirituals. Northup, excepting an almost anthropological section on the whoops and dances of Indian Creek, concentrated on the perversion of leisure and show business—captivity required a song. In the original slave pen, "we were again paraded and made to dance." On the plantation, Master Epps, who loved "dancing with his 'niggers,'" held a whip through the proceedings; there was to be no stopping. Vernacular Black culture—patting Juba, singing to a Christmas feast—appeared rarely in the book. It was so embedded in minstrelsy and mastery, as Lara Langer Cohen demonstrated in "Solomon Northup's Singing Book," that its accompanying sheet music made no sense paired with the verse printed below it. Words and music lost each other. Northup said he earned seventeen dollars once, playing a party—a slave millionaire. This too lingered in the literature: fast money for pop of no consequence, less important than the fish trap he invented to stave off wormy bacon.

CHAMPION OF THE WHITE MALE VERNACULAR

Walt Whitman, Leaves of Grass, *1855*

If blackface minstrelsy followed what **Eric Lott** called "love and theft," bad faith and tortured identification, the PR-poet of American democracy preached, as "I Sing the Body Electric" put it, "love and resistance." A teen in greater New York as blackface minstrelsy emerged, Whitman wrote: "I often saw Rice the original 'Jim Crow' at the Park Theatre filling up the gap in some short bill— and the wild chants were admirable—probably ahead of anything since." But "I never could, and never will admire the exemplifying of our national attributes with Ethiopian minstrelsy." He came closer to what he sought from American music in the Cheney Family, who took after the abolitionist Hutchinson Family Singers in their blended, earnest anthems. In "Art-Singing and Heart-Singing," published by Edgar Allan Poe's *Broadway Journal*, Whitman wrote: "the elegant simplicity of this style took us completely by surprise, and our gratification was inexpressible. This, said we in our heart, is the true method which must become popular in the United States—which must supplant the stale, second-hand, foreign method, with its flourishes, its ridiculous sentimentality, its antirepublican spirit, and its sycophantic influence, tainting the young taste of the republic." Whitman, champion of the rebellious white male vernacular over the imported, feminized sentimental, drew lines no less problematic than minstrelsy's, and equally enduring.

Leaves of Grass had multiple editions. The almost self-published original, with its manic preface and still untitled "Song of Myself," introduced "Walt Whitman, an American" as "one of the roughs, a kosmos,/ Disorderly fleshy and sensual . . . eating drinking and breeding, / No sentimentalist," the I of "I sing my barbaric yawp over the roofs of the world." David Reynolds, in *Walt Whitman's America*, viewed it as a summation of Jacksonian popular culture: "The street rowdies who swore, fought, and loved sensation novels and melodramas. The brash actors who introduced a stormy 'American' style to the stage. The slang-whanging orators who jousted with their audiences. The reformers who agitated constantly. The blackfaced minstrels who parodied polite culture in free-flowing, disjointed songs. The native humorists, whose quirky style had interested Whitman since the late forties. The spirit-rappers, free lovers, mesmerists, and trance poets who paraded their odd marvels." But the 426-page deathbed edition of 1891–92 added Civil War poems and robust sexuality grown patriarchal. A debut album by a scuffling bohemian had led to a career-spanning box set. **Langston Hughes**, rewriting "I Hear America Singing" as "I, Too" would go down Whitman's open (if closeted) road, joined later by **Woody Guthrie**, Allen Ginsberg, **Bob Dylan**, and Bruce Springsteen.

In conceiving his poetry as democratic song, "belched words" for an artisanal republic threatened by materialism, sectional divides, and parlor platitudes, Whitman gave popular music writing lasting mandates, traced partly in Bryan Garman's *Race of Singers*. The working-class hero inhabited his (very much his) subject in a showy performed representation. The vernacular arts promulgator cataloged slangy expressions of work and leisure. The child of Adam, "he that aches with amorous loves," assaulted norms of behavior for a middle-class audience. And the newspaperman, party flack, and lecturer to the Brooklyn Art Union in 1851, reading Baudelaire and Hegel in a borough surging from a population of five thousand to two hundred thousand, was not only a member of the first generation to grow up with American popular culture. He created the category, coined much later by critic **Robert Christgau**, of the semipopular artist.

NOTATING SPIRITUALS

William Francis Allen, Charles Pickard Ware, and

Lucy McKim Garrison, eds., Slave Songs of the United States, *1867*

––––––––

Bohemian blues scholar **Samuel Charters**'s final book, *Songs of Sorrow*, documented the radical networks that produced this first collection of African American song. Lucy McKim's parents were abolitionists (her father took John Brown's wife south to witness his execution) and gender egalitarians. Brought to Port Royal, South Carolina at age 19 to work with freed slaves, she had no hesitation using her piano and prose skills to author the inaugural intellectual treatment of spirituals for the eminent publication *Dwight's Journal of Music*. It was 1862 and the Civil War had already made a sheet music hit of "Go Down, Moses"; McKim added a version of "Roll, Jordan, Roll" to the ranks.

She wrote her best girlfriend a passionate Victorian account: "Kneeling in that poor cabin with those who suffered scourgings at our hands, & listening to that child-like old preacher calling down blessings on their new friends who had come 'so far, 'way from de beautiful Norf' to deliver them, instead of cursing every Anglo-Saxon, as he had cause & right to do—I vowed that if I ever forgot them, so might Heaven forget me!" But for *Dwight's*, she was musicological: "odd turns made in the throat; and that curious rhythmic effect produced by single voices chiming in at different irregular intervals . . . the leader, who, if he be a good one, is always an improvisator."

Five years later, she and new husband Wendell Garrison, first literary editor of *The Nation*, got a book out, aided by Emily Dickinson champion and Black troop commander Thomas Higginson, whose own spirituals article appeared in the *Atlantic* and his war memoir. Scholar William Allen, later mentor to frontier thesis proponent Frederic Turner, and his song-collector cousin, Charles Ware, did much of the commissioned work. Allen's introduction— best when it lifted from McKim, Higginson, and other collectors—too often equated Black with "barbarous." It solidified a white authenticity rhetoric for Black musicality as antidote to commercial pop. Denouncing minstrelsy, Allen romanticized the danced-out ring shout, which already had "connoisseurs." The book's 136 lyrics and piano melodies for solo singing (notation became a constant question) turned on white stirring at Black suffering. In his article, Higginson wrote, of the spiritual that went "I'll lie in de grave and stretch out my arms" (Du Bois would excerpt it, too): "Never, it seems to me, since man first lived and suffered, was his infinite longing for peace uttered more plaintively than in that line."

Slave Songs, for all its historic influence and reclamation during the Harlem Renaissance, was a commercial flop. Garrison and her husband had written in the *Nation*, "We shall be disappointed if many of the airs do not become popular." That did happen a few years later, as the Fisk University Jubilee Singers, a Nashville troupe raising funds for Black education, found fame singing to white congregations, their strongest support in former abolitionist strongholds. This, too, produced a book: J. B. T. Marsh's *The Story of the Jubilee Singers: With Their Songs* added an admiring sketch of the troupe to two earlier collections of their songs. The work would be updated in some thirty-five national and international editions by 1903, a sequence that librarian **Dena Epstein later** traced to honor fellow scholar **Eileen Southern**, supplemented definitively by Sandra Jean Graham's recent history, *Spirituals and the Birth of a Black Entertainment Industry*. In Marsh's book, performers were photographed and individually profiled, with an emphasis on choral singing in the transcriptions meant for at-home use. Whites were mesmerized. As Graham wrote, *Slave Songs* had "failed to convey the essence of spirituals, which was located in sound." Jubilee performance, as folk and commercial mix, spawned a new Black popular path.

These two books, a literary slow burner and non-literary hit, set into the record key tendencies: white esteem for Black culture as a disappearing space of authenticity; and literary discourse and idealistic staging framing musical styles of no small popular appeal as the antithesis of pop. (For these complexities, see Ronald Radano's *Lying Up a Nation* and especially Jon Cruz's *Culture on the Margins,* which developed an argument for the spiritual in white northern cultural analysis, finding "ethnosympathy" for Black song but not post-slavery Black political struggle.) Minstrelsy had an opposition, not just in live performance but in print, where *Slave Songs'* "Michael Row the Boat Ashore" or the Jubilee Singers' "Swing Low, Sweet Chariot" took on a wonder we now associate with **John Lomax**'s *Cowboy Songs'* "Home on the Range" or **Robert Johnson** at the crossroads.

FIRST BLACK MUSIC HISTORIAN

James Trotter, Music and Some Highly Musical People: The Lives
of Remarkable Musicians of the Colored Race, *1878*

––––––

Trotter, called "America's First Black Music Historian" by musicologist Robert Stevenson, fit that role into much else. Born a slave in 1842, manumitted by his birthfather/owner, and given the best education Ohio abolitionists provided, he was promoted to a Civil War lieutenancy, relocated to Boston's somewhat integrated elite, and published his one book before receiving the most plum patronage job Washington offered Blacks and dying from malaria at fifty. His son, sent to Harvard, tussled with Woodrow Wilson in the White House. The book was as strategic as its title, revealing the goal only in the subtitle left inside the covers. Trotter wanted to send a message of uplift at a far from uplifting moment: the abandonment of Reconstruction.

So, after four chapters of bland Victorian sentiments about the virtue of music, he cast around for success stories, exaggerating the popularity of the opera singer Black Patti; diminishing the questions raised by piano savant and otherwise inarticulate Blind Tom; and accepting a Blacks-in-blackface minstrel company as musicians of prowess with potential to be "diversified and elevated in character," while ignoring their comic leader, satchel-mouthed Billy Kersands. His greatest heroes sang spirituals and arias: the Fisk University Jubilee Singers, "perhaps the most picturesque achievement in all our history since the war"; the Luca family, touring with the Hutchinson family in 1859 to rally antislavery sentiments; Thomas Bowers, "the American Mario," who demanded theaters be integrated.

Current-day scholar **Guthrie Ramsey Jr.** has argued that "the collision between Trotter's racial politics and his Euro-based aesthetic perspectives formed an important and persistent tension in future work on black music." Another musicologist, Lawrence Schenbeck, focused on uplift, calling Trotter's work "advocacy wrapped in conciliation, which is to say representation." The need to find winners forced Trotter well beyond the era's composer-centered accounts. Justin Holland, who the Ramsey of *Race Music* might call an Afromodernist, fit the bill: he made his living creating arrangements of other people's works for guitar and authored an instructional book. *Some Highly Musical People's* perspective, what Schenbeck in *Racial Uplift and American Music* termed a "culture of dissemblance," poorly anticipated blues. But it aptly fit vaudeville's **Bert Williams** and George Walker, the Broadway hit *Shuffle Along*, Harry Belafonte, Jimi Hendrix, Beyoncé—a subsequent century of pragmatic spectacularists.

Consider the Hyer Sisters, still teens: "Our talented artists had now acquired throughout New England a fame so fair, that Mr. P. S. Gilmore felt warranted in inviting them to appear at the great Peace Jubilee concerts; and here, before an audience of fifty thousand people, and in the company of several of the great solo-vocalists of the world, surrounded by a chorus of twenty thousand voices and an orchestra of one thousand performers, these gifted girls occupied a proud position." Does it matter that the sisters were singing in Italian and German? Placing them in Trotter's sentimental spotlight created a lineage of its own.

CHILD BALLADS AND FOLKLORE

Francis James Child, The English and Scottish Popular Ballads,
5 vols., 1882–1898

———

With this massive compendium of 305 archaic songs in all their archived lyrical variants, soon central to the repertoire and lingo of every strumming singer from Carl Sandburg to Pete Seeger and Joan Baez, a Harvard English professor codified a genre and academic discipline at the same time. The Child collection, Bertrand Bronson wrote in 1959, "has been the indispensable anchorage of all serious study of its subject for more than half a century . . . it is so far in the lead that its rivals are not even in sight." And as literature the Child ballad itself was old testament poetry, whether altered like "Lord Randal" (see "A Hard Rain's A-Gonna Fall") and "Riddles Wisely Expounded" ("Scarborough Fair") or kept intact to tone up festival performances and other arty-folksy poesy.

But.

Because Child never actually finished his own personal statement on the words he had sifted and itemized, the closest we can get to one comes from an introduction his academic successor, George Lyman Kittredge, wrote for the single-volume Student's Cambridge Edition. "A ballad has no author," Kittredge wrote. Instead, and the subsequent italics were his: "*The popular ballads are really popular, that is they belong to the folk.*" Who were these folk? In Kittredge's word, "homogenous." As a definition of canonical art, this notion of the popular embraced diversity: no text but only texts, a poetry formed in the sung wash of time. In other regards, it was exclusionary, rejecting pop and American multiplicity.

No solution sufficed. Francis Gummere, like Kittredge a Child inheritor, was one of many to discourse on the individual versus communal origins of great songs: "the ballad wars," D. K. Wilgus called this in a history, with Hustvedt's *Ballad Books and Ballad Men* even chattier. **Olive Dame Campbell and Cecil Sharp**'s trips to Appalachia made Child's already transatlantic endeavors still more U.S. focused, finding tunes and living informants in the mountains, while **Alan and John Lomax** (John a Kittredge student) stockpiled field recordings in the same spirit. Bronson, a professor well located in Berkeley, added notated melody in *Traditional Tunes of the Child Ballads* and a fun essay collection, *The Ballad as Song*, that liberalized the ballad conceptually—"a fluid entity soluble in the mind." Come 1964, he chuckled at "the fact that academics were, in this country, responsible for the beginnings of what we now perceive as a mass phenomenon."

Then Dylan went electric. Against an amplified vernacular, the folk-popular shrank in stature. When an academic, Philip Bohlman, took up folk again, with *The Study of Folk Music in the Modern World* (1988), he was a **Bruno Nettl** student from the now-governing discipline of ethnomusicology, esteeming cultural studies notions of bricolage, **Robert Cantwell**'s antipurist bluegrass book, and anybody open to "mass-mediated traditions." Child et al. were conservatives, ruled by an "ethnocentric, racist evolutionary bias." Benjamin Filene's history *Romancing the Folk* further undercut ballad hunting, emphasizing a more inherently impure roots vision open to non-WASP presences. For Mark Slobin, giving folk music *A Very Short Introduction*, the story wasn't even roots, it was routes, as the ethno cliché went, like his book on klezmer incarnations; the ballad war stuff "seems like a pointless quarrel today."

"I want, if I can, to make a ballad-book that will last," Child had written early on, and perhaps there were chapters for future appreciation. Mary Ellen Brown's monograph centered on his correspondence with collaborators the world over, from Denmark's Nikolaj Grundtvig to William Macmath, a Scottish amateur working unpaid on the project for more than thirty years. Bohlman returned to folk in *Song Loves the Masses* via Johann Gottfried Herder, who'd first defined its *geist* in the 1770s while writing about one of Child's future ballads, "Edward." Herder sought to animate nationalism in Germany but also collected songs with a world music anthropologist's ecumenical zest and hopes the raw material would spark artistic adaptation. In Bohlman's conceptualization, Herder's translator's spirit, not any essence of fidelity, was his contribution to rethinking ethnomusicology. After all, even in the twenty-first century, that academic discipline, straitlaced as Child in some regards, struggled with how to register the "messthetics" a post-vernacular critic like **Simon Reynolds** archived so much more freely in work like *Rip It Up and Start Again*. And Reynolds wasn't as far ahead in time from *English and Scottish Popular Ballads* as that was from some of the dusty ballad manuscripts Child once had collated on a Cambridge desk.

Child, as multilingual as Herder if less intellectual, used correspondence to generate correspondences. A future scholar might well revisit each booked ballad for its afterlife. Sandburg gave 1920s "sinners" an *American Songbag,* with hell-bound ditties from Child, like "House Carpenter," called "Antiques." The Seegers scrutinized and popularized ballads as professors, composers, and performers. Folk-to-rock singers like Baez heard them as silver daggers of gendered rage. And experimentalists, from compositional Sam Amidon to the postpunk Amps for Christ, contemporaries of Reynolds, picked up on something in the tunes that Herder called "melodic manner," wavering on the modalities.

WOMEN NOT INVENTING ETHNOMUSICOLOGY

Alice C. Fletcher, A Study of Omaha Indian Music, *1893*

If writing on African American music moved from sentimental to vernacular, literature on native sounds—well-surveyed in Michael Pisani's *Imagining Native America in Music*—traveled from sentimental to scientific. It was a road built on Edison cylinder recordings and dry-as-dust write-ups by women confronting the sexist structure of academia. Fletcher, given a solid 1980s biography by Joan Mark, was born in 1838, four years before *Slave Songs* compiler **Lucy McKim Garrison**, and similarly educated in feminist circles. She lectured on prehistoric topics in the Association for the Advancement of Women and went west to study Native Americans in 1881, politicking land allotment while working with Omaha tribesman Francis La Flesche. Harvard's Peabody Museum of Archeology and Ethnology took a rich couple's money to make Fletcher a Fellow, though the university allowed no female faculty or grad students and favored Franz Boas. Frances Densmore, studied more recently by Joan Jensen and Michelle Wick Patterson, saw Fletcher at the Chicago World's Fair and worked the same field until her death at ninety in 1957, recording and transcribing over twenty-five hundred songs and stacking up books as condition of a quarter-century of demeaning annual nonstaff contracts from the Smithsonian's Bureau of American Ethnology (BAE). A third figure, Natalie Curtis Burlin, studied as well by Patterson, took an artier path: with patronage, she popularized Indian songs with her writing and also worked on African and African American music, loving "primitivism" in the name of antimodernism.

A much-noted photograph of Densmore recording an Indian chief in headdress, phonograph between them, showed L-R three uncertain figures: Victorian woman, mercurial device, repository of lore. As Erika Brady documented in *A Spiral Way*, fourteen thousand cylinder recordings were made from 1890–1935; Béla Bartók said, "The father of modern folk-song studies was Thomas Edison." Pisani captured the stakes: "Under the aegis of scientific accreditation, ethnologists went in search of, as critical anthropologists might describe it today, distilled concepts of pure authenticities that could first be catalogued and then disseminated." Cylinders were cultural vitrines rather than aesthetic rivals to commerce like the **John and Alan Lomax** discs produced in the 1930s. **Jonathan Sterne**, launching sound studies in *The Audible Past,* compared cylinder recording to embalming and canning, a cult of death and afterlife. New womanhood concerned Mark, who highlighted Fletcher's household with seven-years-older companion Jane Gay and seventeen-years-younger "son" La Flesche. Jensen and Patterson viewed Densmore's path, erased personal history included, as a "professional discourse of objectivity and expertise."

To turn to the original books is not a chance to exhale. *A Study of Omaha Indian Music* identified its author(s) as "Assistant in American Ethnology, Peabody Museum, and Holder of the Thaw Fellowship, also Aided by Francis La Flesche, and With a Report on the Structural Peculiarity of the Music by John Comfort Fillmore." La Flesche deserved recognition for translation and context, while Fillmore's scoring—harmonizing melodies not performed that way—was felt necessary to reach a nation of piano players. Notions of sentiment permeated: Fletcher's success studying Indians credited to "winning their love," natives ministering to her in illness as "the heart and inner life of the Indian," and Fillmore sure that "Omaha songs mean *feeling*." At thrilling core was the Wa-Wan Ceremony, men exchanging Pipes of Fellowship: music as rebuke to the white contemporary, severed from class distinction, if also from a future or "the sustained intellectual effort essential to the development of poetic art." While Fillmore's "careful scientific study" of Indian harmonics produced hot air, his alertness to Omaha rhythmic command, to melody "covered up and hidden by overpowering noise," hinted, as did Fletcher's acuity on syllables as sound signifiers, at *awopbopaloobop*s to come.

Lacking relish in the vernacular, *A Study of Omaha Indian Music* contributed a canned, embalmed Indianness to popular and art culture, as documented in Pisani and also in John Troutman's *Indian Blues*. The "sound of Indian" dum-dum-dum-dum permeated vaudeville in comic numbers like "Big Chief Killa-hun" alongside a vogue for manufactured, sweet "Indian Love Songs." Composer Arthur Farwell debuted work based on Fletcher's collection and started Wa-Wan Press in 1901 to put Indian motifs in American classical music. Fletcher, who regretted pushing Congress to give natives private land, never achieved the Boas role of scientist with peers. Reworking Omaha material for two popular press books, *Indian Story and Song* in 1900 and *Indian Games and Dances* in 1915, she studied Pawnee ritual expertly in the less-read *The Hako* (1904), then emphasized La Flesche's work. He was coauthor of their important ethnography *The Omaha Tribe* (1911), a six-hundred-page deepening, and she provided research for his four volume Osage study, published after her death.

Densmore had gotten a musical education at Oberlin Conservatory and added "Music of the American Indians" to her women's clubs lectures after that Columbian Exposition encounter with Fletcher. She told her BAE editor, "The finished work must be neither theoretical nor sentimental, it must stand the test of scientific scrutiny," received modest funding in 1907, and bought a phonograph. *Chippewa Music* stressed the objectivity of recording: scientism crushed most of the book into classification schemes, as the two hundred songs recorded were grouped to within a semitone of their life spirit. A second Chippewa volume built the sample base to 340 songs; 240 Sioux songs allowed comparative work on 600 by 1918. Hints of other material—thunderbird dreams and ceremonies of public humiliation, a doctor given tutelage by "a little green man"—were kept marginal. By 1957, her work in *BAE Bulletin* 165 on Pueblo Indians cited seventeen previous BAE publications and a database well past fifteen hundred songs. Densmore could write for a general audience, as in *American Indians and Their Music* (1926), a warm overview. But her enormous energy was given to what she called a "system of tabulated analyses." Without academic anchor, she was vulnerable: when Congress halted BAE funding to nonstaffers in 1934, she scuffled, bitter that American Indians had ceded popularity to African American jazz.

Densmore's literary force, dulled in scholarship, glimmered in liner notes to seven early 1950s LPs of cylinder recordings, released by the Library of Congress; here, she highlighted the stakes of her work, limited by technical restriction to lone rather than group voices, modest accompaniment rather than full shake and rattle. Charles Hoffman, admiring her for anticipating ethnomusicology, released an LP of her cylinders in 1965 on Folkways and edited a 1968 memorial book with many early writings. Densmore had a new audience: the counterculture and American Indian Movement's longing for roots. Brady, later to write on phonographs and ethnography—the Victorian obsession with indexing objects of sentiment and the modern need to understand contexts—helped lead the 1979 Federal Cylinder Project, which returned recordings to the tribes Densmore had often imperiously worked with. And an even more belated plot turn: fifty years after warnings by Densmore had been ignored, a new audio archivist at the Library of Congress, Judith Gray, writing in the Jensen and Patterson collection, concluded that the original cylinder transfers had been at the wrong speed, too slow; the vast work would need revisiting, re-repatriating. Pulled from dreams, pinned by science, the songs of the Chippewa et al. awaited another ghost dance. An acclaimed 2018 album by tenor Jeremy Dutcher, *Wolastoqiyik Lintuwakonawa*, made experimental song from cylinder recordings connected to his own indigenous community in Canada.

Natalie Curtis, later Curtis Burlin, was the artiest of this trio of scholars. Born to a connected New York family and trained as a pianist and composer, she was captivated by Wagner, mystic theosophy, and Dvořák's call for music with native and African American sources; some of her compositions were published by Wa-Wan Press. Family friend Theodore Roosevelt granted permission in 1903 to work with Hopis kept by the Bureau of Indian Affairs from exhibiting native culture, the young men forced to cut their hair. Writing for *Harper's*, she called herself the *Pahana*, Hopi for white or American; though "I had a white face I was somehow 'Indian' inside." Charlotte Osgood Mason, later "Godmother" to **Zora Neal Hurston** and **Langston Hughes**, began her philanthropy of primitivism with Curtis's project. The result was *The Indians' Book* (1907), an elegant Arts and Crafts product with graphics in the style of each tribe, handwritten song notations, and a Roosevelt letter of endorsement. Curtis pledged "direct utterance.... The Indians sang the songs directly to the recording pencil." But this naïveté, Patterson noted, supported a defense of Indian culture more strident than Fletcher's; the book ended in dialogue with Yuma tribeswoman Chiparopai. Two books of African American and African folk song material followed; an essay in *Musical Quarterly*, using the same antimodern rhetoric of "vitality" that Curtis Burlin took from Dvořák and applied to natives, became **Edna Ferber**'s musical underpinning to *Showboat*. Curtis Burlin was dead by then, victim of a Paris car accident.

When **Gilbert Chase** wrote *America's Music* in the 1950s, the work of these women was central to his Indian tribal music chapter, including the detail that patron Mary Hemenway had sponsored J. Walter Fewkes's first-ever phonographic recordings of Indians. By the revised 1987 edition, much of that had been cut out. Disciplined. Men like Alan Merriam and his *Ethnomusicology of the Flathead Indians* owned the new story.

FIRST HIT SONGWRITER, FROM POP TO FOLK AND BACK AGAIN

Morrison Foster, Biography, Songs and Musical Compositions
of Stephen C. Foster, *1896*

———

Stephen Foster's older brother published an airbrushed short account of him with a staggeringly persuasive 160-song appendage, initiating a century's worth of books exploring the murky and short life (1826–64) of a figure vexing to parse whose minstrel songs became folk songs became sentimental ballads and whose parodies of Black identity became romantic artistry became pop craftsmanship. The shifting narrative around the first successful U.S. songwriter revealed changing notions of sentimental and vernacular, art and identity.

Morrison took from Stephen's friend Robert Nevin's 1867 *Atlantic Monthly* article, "Stephen C. Foster and Minstrelsy," the idea that Foster's legacy was benign feeling: "the art in his hands teemed with a nobler significance. It dealt in its simplicity with universal sympathies and taught us all to feel with the colored man the lowly joys and sorrows it celebrated." In Morrison's history, their father built a "White Cottage" in Pittsburgh, "town of refinement." Oldest daughter Charlotte Susanna touched hearts with her singing before dying of cholera. Young Stephen's "thespian company" had him sing blackface tunes for tips with nice white lads similar to the harmony singing club for whom he first wrote. In his work, "The grotesque and clownish aspect of negro songs was softened, and ridicule began to merge into sympathy." Foster made poor choices in commerce, fell apart when his beloved mother died in 1855, and never recovered his muse or fortune. Known for plantation melodies, "His poetic fancy ran rather to sentimental songs."

During Foster's life, critics carped about his tunes, with John Sullivan Dwight in 1853 likening their ubiquity to "a morbid irritation of the skin." But early scholars insisted on his importance: a songwriter fit the model of a composer, a popular author fit a democratic nation, and in translating seemingly African American sources he reworked the nation's most distinctive folk material. Frédéric Ritter's 1883 *Music in America* claimed "people's song . . . is not to be found among the American people," but excepted "the colored race" and Foster, "undoubtedly the most naturally gifted and most successful," his work "very naïve and simple" if "a little too sentimental." Louis Elson's 1904 *History of American Music* removed the objection. Foster was "the folk-song genius of America" *because of* his skill at sentiment: "The charm of all his popular songs was their directness and pathos," not unlike "his favorite poet," Edgar Allan Poe. Walter Whittlesey and **Oscar Sonneck**'s 1915 *Catalogue of First Editions of Stephen C. Foster (1826–1864),* institutional documentation, switched back to idealize a folk wheat within sentimental chaff: "Many of Foster's songs, of course, belong to the mid-nineteenth century type of sentimental American parlour 'ballad,' not exactly distinguished by either beauty or skill, but some of his songs possess the beauty and power of imperishable folk-songs." Taking the emphasis a step further, the first biography of Foster after Morrison's, by Harold Milligan in 1920, called him *America's Folk-Song Composer.* Unhelpful on the life or work, Milligan did unsympathetically note "a movement of protest against the use of certain of Foster's songs in the public schools," with Boston withdrawing seven Foster songs after a Black pastor called them "an insult to the whole colored race."

As pop boomed, new Foster patrons sanctified his legacy. Leading figures of Tin Pan Alley claimed him to cast their Jewish immigrant ditties as all-Americana: Irving Berlin asked in the 1911 "Alexander's Ragtime Band," "do you want to hear 'Swanee River' played in ragtime?" Retired Indiana manufacturer Joseph Kirby Lilly created Foster Hall, with a private curator and its own bulletin for collector conversation. A thousand facsimile collections of Foster songs, in metal cabinets, were sent to public libraries, while Lilly's collection went to the University of Pittsburgh. Morrison's daughter, Evelyn Foster Morneweck, shared family material with the genteel scholar John Tasker Howard for *Stephen Foster: America's Troubadour* (1934), extensive bibliography supplied by Foster Hall staff, and grouped more documents as *Chronicles of Stephen Foster's Family* (1944). Howard gave readers Foster's own tallies of song royalties and vexed relationship with minstrel George Christy, his 1870s resurrection when Swedish singer Christine Nilsson kept "Old Folks" current in her tours. Morneweck allowed Foster's troubled marriage and alcoholism. But the interpretation was unchanged: Foster's music, Morneweck wrote, was "American folk songs at their finest." Howard, in a reverse appropriation not even the 1939 Hollywood biopic supported, suggested Foster might "be responsible for some of the so-called Negro folk songs," meaning spirituals. To Howard, Foster was the opposite of pop: "when he was himself, the market never soiled his work." He dismissed "Beautiful Dreamer" because "It smacks somewhat of the idiom of **Irving Berlin**."

The next wave of American musicology redefined Foster's musical contribution as, at its best, insurgent. In *America's Music,* **Gilbert Chase** positioned vernacular sound against middle-class propriety and Howard in particular, arguing that if respectable people in the 1850s hated Ethiopian melodies, "the lowest dregs of music," the "worst of it is that Stephen Foster often had to fight the same battle in his own mind." Foster, Chase concluded, ended up "succumbing to drink and the genteel tradition." Rogue musicologist William Austin, inspired by Chase, generated a book-length study in 1975, *"Susanna," "Jeannie," and "The Old Folks At Home,"* considering Foster's blackface, Anglo-American ballad, and pathos-drenched incarnations. Austin looked for correspondences: incorporations of Thomas Moore and other tearjerkers; abolitionist and gold rush-parodies of "Oh! Susanna" as extensions; how uses by Dvořák, Charles Ives, and Ray Charles fit new definitions of artistry. Austin assumed "no sharp division between the music business and the rest of music," considered folk validity less important, and embraced the "too" sentimental Foster songs others dismissed. If Foster the unifier of Americana had evolved into what Austin bashed as the "smug American power of 1950," this account chimed with countercultural skepticism. **Charles Hamm** finished the job in his 1979 songs history *Yesterdays,* mocking pre-Austin studies of Foster.

The stage was set for rock critic Ken Emerson to claim Foster for readers who might savor minstrel George Christy as "Dick Clark, if you will, to Dan Emmett's Alan Freed." In the 1997 trade press biography *Doo-dah! Stephen Foster and the Rise of American Popular Culture,* Foster left folk identity behind: the first performance of "Oh! Susanna" in 1847 was "a firm date for the birth of pop music as we still recognize it today." Emerson recognized the racism of its second verse (ignored by Austin and all previous commentators), casual about Black mutilation, but also how the steamboats and railroads referenced reflected Jacksonian America beyond Chase, Austin, and Hamm's expansive musicality. Emerson stressed gender: "The American mass audience, at least at the outset, was predominantly female." And he argued, as a rocker would, that in blackface "disingenuousness paradoxically encouraged honesty . . . Gleefully flouting the proprieties of sincerity and sentimentality, blackface delighted unabashedly in its irony and even its humbug. That's what made it 'pop' and P. T. Barnum one of its patron saints and purveyors.'"

If Emerson's study confirmed the vernacular ethos, a successor had appeared just earlier in **Eric Lott**'s study of blackface minstrelsy, *Love and Theft*. Here, vernacular and sentimental were framed in cultural studies language: "Historically there was a move away from the more 'folk'-derived music (black, British, and Irish) imitated in early minstrelsy toward a more discursive, 'bourgeois' (actually petit-bourgeois) song in the commercial era of the midcentury minstrel show, and from comic or novelty tunes to earnestly sentimental ones." Lott's sympathies were, like most modern commentators, geared to the vernacular, "plebeian theatergoers . . . on the sanctums of respectable song." Yet to Lott, Foster's songs created "conflicted energies": stomping polkas of western expansion, Black erasure in "My Old Kentucky Home." And he admitted that songs such as "Old Folks," exuding sentiment, "sometimes performed liberatory racial work." Robert Nevins and Morrison Foster might have been onto something all along.

NOVELIST OF URBAN POP LONGINGS

Theodore Dreiser, Sister Carrie, *1900*

Almost nothing about popular music entered this novel, great in coverage if not style, but still read for what it knew about cities, shopping, women, and desire. That's to say it revealed more than any previous book about the longings urban pop addressed. White, middle-class Carrie Meeber, from small-town Indiana, came to Chicago at eighteen, courted even on the train by Drouet, the "drummer," meaning salesman "in the slang of the day." She was transfixed by department stores, where a new sheet music industry, David Suisman explained in *Selling Sounds*, targeted women buyers. For Carrie, "delicately molded in sentiment," music "awoke longings for those things which she did not have." Her second suitor, dressy bar manager Hurstwood, fell for her aspect: "one who might be upon the verge of tears." An amateur production of the melodrama *Under the Gaslight* let her triumph in a part "of suffering and tears," like a Céline Dion power ballad.

She and Hurstwood absconded to New York, where "celebrities were numerous" and Mrs. Vance playing piano next door reminded Carrie "her life was becoming stale." She and her friend walked Broadway together, absorbing "the flavor of riches and show"—Dreiser evoked a hit about swells and their fine outfits. Carrie entered show business, the chorus line first, then the whole "showy world," from theater magazines to hotels that comped her once she'd made a name. Hurstwood's bleak suicide went unnoticed. Carrie told her final beau, Ames, that music "always makes me feel as if I wanted something" and considered his advice to move from comedy to drama and "make your powers endure."

Life gave Dreiser two entry points into Carrie's pop populism: a brother, Paul Dresser, who wrote sentimental hits, including one, "On the Banks of the Wabash," for which Dreiser fashioned the lyrics; and arts journalism at women's magazines. Dreiser discussed Dresser in the "My Brother Paul" chapter of *Twelve Men*, with essays such as "Birth and Growth of Popular Song" and "Whence the Song" now collected in *Art, Music, and Literature, 1897–1902*. Yet unlike magazine writer **Gilbert Seldes**, a generation later, Dreiser was hesitant about popular culture. His interviews with classical impresario Theodore Thomas and singer Lilian Nordica stressed hard training as investments in enduring success; Dresser's "all-too-brief" vogue came from "a little luck and some talent," much as Carrie's had. The key was empathy, not skill: a strain of music "would capture his fancy and presently he might be in tears." Paul dressed as flashy as Hurstwood, saw titles such as "Just Tell Them That You Saw Me" become urban memes, repeated by "staid business men wishing to appear 'up-to-date.'" To become a songwriter, Dreiser wrote, was to be "the cynosure of all eyes, the envy of all men." You associated with women of vaudeville, "rouged and powdered" with "no maidenly reserve" but hardly evil. There were hirelings to take down "the melody which the popular composer cannot play." Yet as Dresser's own sad ending demonstrated, low on funds and no longer trendy, first the pop moment and (its own dramatic paragraph) "Then the wane."

Dreiser's view of all this, drawn to commodities but fearing materialism, embracing high culture but versed in slicker categories, remained productively ambiguous. His one huge failing: Blacks were almost invisible in *Sister Carrie*. Black songwriter Gussie Davis was mocked in "Whence the Song" for taking flat fees instead of royalties—"He could have several thousand instead of a few hundred, but being shiftless, he does not care. Ready money is the thing with him." Dreiser could not register the racial passing that coincided with class and gender crossings in the pop and bohemian quadrants of New York and Chicago.

AMERICANA EMERGES

Emma Bell Miles, The Spirit of the Mountains, *1905*

———————

If **Walt Whitman** sang of the open road, Emma Bell Miles's ballads shared the closed one. Daughter of teachers who moved to the Tennessee mountains for her health, she was educated on Thoreau and a ten-year pile of *Harper's,* fell in love with a local man, resisted study elsewhere to marry him, and befriended the area's literary MacGowan sisters, who got her "Some Real American Music" into *Harper's* itself. This led to a book contract—and career stasis. Five kids, a husband who never earned, youngest dead for no doctor, living in tents, tuberculosis—Miles died in 1919, just shy of forty. This writer of all sorts, painter, and occasional guitarist kept journals for eight years, released in large part only in 2014. There, and in her poems, stories, newspaper columns, paintings, and one full book, her life on Walden's Ridge proved as remarkable as any at Walden Pond.

Folklorist David Whisnant, introducing the 1975 reissue of *Spirit,* wrote of Miles's "biculturism," neither romanticizing the folk nor condescending. Split between the city-bourgeois world she distrusted and Appalachians who distrusted her, she caught gender divides shaping cultural ones: "The woman belongs to the race, to the *old people.* He is a part of the *young nation.* His first songs are yodels." A poem (she scraped to fund a collection; a posthumous one, from 1930, first proved her endurance) contrasted "The Banjo and the Loom," domesticity and "Possum up a 'simmon-tree" minstrel scamp. Her story "The Dulcimore"—among those collected in 2016—sketched a mother exiled by love to mountains hardship, watching a daughter do the same for a blacksmith who'd made her the lap instrument. Without the distance of a **Cecil Sharp**, she recorded in *Spirit* the "Cuckoo" ballad crooned over weaving ("an inconstant lover is worse than a thief"); then in the journals, the ice cream particulars of a country dance and a Black guitarist appearing to tell the tale of Stagolee. Her attraction to Frank Miles became kin to her love of music: "The ring and jangles of the music is like the very throbs of hearts." Horror at where that love had led, abortions induced to stay another unsustainable child, took her writing from frolic to a gothic akin to Hank Williams's "Alone and Forsaken" or Dolly Parton's "Down from Dover." Late in the journals: "If he spends my last cent and makes me pregnant again—perhaps then I will be allowed, even by Edith, to die in peace . . . one young victim of a drunken husband's neglect during childbirth looked up and said enviously, 'My goodness, Mis' Miles, your husband sure must love you.' I might have answered that there is a love that kills." Friend Edith brought her guitar to the sanitarium, but it had been left in damp weather and couldn't be tuned.

"The music of the Southern mountaineer is not only peculiar, but like himself, peculiarly American," she'd written for *Harper's* and reprinted in *Spirit*, the journalist not yet moved several verses down in her own song. Should we dub Miles, reading Zola to her daughter in place of dinner, the first literary figure in what we now call Americana, roots but a measure apart from country? She was a **Zora Neale Hurston**, too, in her dialect(ical) fusing of scholar, artist, and subject—"we git more out o' life than anybody"—though she never brought to race the prescience she did to gender. She decried Dixon's *Birth of a Nation* but compared mulattoes to "a spoilt white man. It gives me a peculiar vague horror." That left her in place, resisting friends who said live in Chattanooga, take in more vaudeville. "They are all romance, these luxuries of the mountaineer," she told her journal one September; "music, whiskey, firelight, religion, and fighting; they are efforts to reach a finer, larger life,—part of the blue dream of the wild land."

DOCUMENTING THE STORY

O. G. Sonneck, Bibliography of Early Secular American Music, *1905*

———

In "The Bibliography of American Music," Oscar Sonneck wrote: "it is only with a keen sense of humiliation that I, as an American writer on the musical life of America, lead you for a moment into this 'darkest Africa.' What I mean is simply this: We do not even possess a bibliography of books and articles on the musical history of our country." The invocation of African primitivism was not incidental. Sonneck, desiring "scientific" methods, disparaged "silly African and Indian tendencies" in national sound and only allowed that "the songs and dances of the Negro should be collected, winnowed, and examined in light of their 'white' impact." He backhanded the pop listener as "the utilitarian cretin for whom the click of the cash register is the sweetest of all music, or whose musical taste does not rise far above so-called popular music and mushy parlor ballads."

Nonetheless, he was a giant: the librarian at the Library of Congress who created the M for music scores, ML for music literature division that college catalogs still use; founder and editor of the *Musical Quarterly*, which pioneered musicology; figurehead of the Sonneck Society, now Society for American Music. A visionary of "musical life" beyond scores alone, he insisted on the importance of primary source evidence and sifted archives, becoming what his inheritor, fellow Library of Congress maverick **Gilbert Chase**, called "a precursor to the socio-cultural approach to musical history." (A second, **Dena Epstein**, reversed Sonneck's neglect of Black culture with her own excavations.) This Sonneck studied "Yankee Doodle" and defended it, writing "a tune of such vitality must have some redeeming features," contextualized ballad-operas through the cities where they were performed, and concluded of minor psalmodist James Lyon: "Not the absolute but the relative merits of his music attract our attention."

The same might be said of Sonneck's music writing, all focused on America through 1800, detailed bibliographically, funny in the interstices, and concerned to clear ground for others. The preface to *Early Concert-Life in America (1731–1800)*, his most cited publication, dedicated itself "to turn a virgin-forest into a garden." Sonneck self-published two books that led to his LOC hiring: *A Bibliography of Early Secular American Music*—songs, songsters, and period writing—and a double monograph on Lyon and founding father of both nation and secular song James Hopkinson. At the library, he published a volume on American anthems from Francis Scott Key to "Yankee Doodle." His books on *Early Concert-Life* and *Early Opera in America* studied different city scenes and different companies, capturing when what we might now call "classical" was more like "yuppie"—the culture-with-airs of upward strivers. Or not even that: a *South Carolina Gazette* ad, in 1773, noted that alongside a bill of French horn and guitar songs, "Mr. Saunders will let any number of ladies or gentlemen think of as many cards as they please, and the same will be found in a roasted leg of mutton, hot from the fire, which will be placed on the table." Essays on "Benjamin Franklin's Musical Life" and the history of the history of American music filled two more volumes.

Sonneck, American born but German university reared, sought academic rigor but his legacy was as much that first bibliography: he was an amateur collecting citations the way others would records. His ur-text might have been Andrew Barton's *The Disappointment; or, The Force of Credulity*, a ballad opera, interspersing popular tunes including the first mention of "Yankee Doodle." The inaugural performance was canceled for mocking society Philadelphians but it still became, in 1767, the first published American libretto. It was finally staged in 1976. Sonneck noted it in *A Bibliography*, delved further in

Early Opera in America, still deeper for the "Early American Opera" chapter of *Miscellaneous Studies*. He pondered questions of authorship and edition, even esteeming the vulgarity of the text's humorous gentlemen: Hum, Parchment, Quadrant and Rattletrap. For a moment, abandoned back pages made some noise.

TIN PAN ALLEY'S SHEET MUSIC BIZ

Charles K. Harris, How to Write a Popular Song, *1906*

———

As Daniel Goldmark documented in "Making Songs Pay," from 1899 through the 1930s more than fifty songwriting books sold their ability to help Americans sell their ability—an ouroboros of manufactured competence. Will Rossiter's *How to Write a Song and Become Wealthy*, published alongside his *How to Take Care of Your Dog*, launched the category, urging a positive, however staged, outlook: "when you 'smile,' the world 'smiles' with you (at two for a quarter)." Featured in Rossiter was Charles K. Harris, author of the massive sheet music hit "After the Ball," which he bragged cost him only a five-dollar ad in the *New York Clipper* to promote: "If it contains merit you cannot keep it down." Herbert Taylor said of lyrics: "Strive to have them ungrammatical. Three correct stanzas in a song are sufficient to kill it at the outset." Gussie Davis said of bohemian display: "you must always wear your hair long enough to show people that you are the real article."

An inherent conflict existed between bourgeois self-control and songs that could burn through a city. When Harris, who admitted in his memoir that "even to this day I cannot distinguish one note from another," hauled in $52,000, a teller "asked whether I had robbed a bank or held up a train." His *How To*, with chapters on "Lyric Writing," "Music Setting/Melody," and "Presenting Manuscript to a Publisher," plus rhyming dictionary, suggested factory production. But popularization required savvy: "Get out and hustle." The songwriter catered to "the great American 'unmusical'" and commercialism dictated: "Always look to the selling qualities of a song," he preached. This might entail rougher material, like coon song, yet he cautioned against "slang and vulgarism." His heart belonged to a middlebrow: Adelina Patti, singing

FIGURE 1.7 Charles
Harris, *How to Write
a Popular Song*, 1906.
Page 59, illustrating
the book's style and
precepts. Collection of
Daniel Goldmark.

CHAPTER VII.
HINTS AND DON'TS.

Watch your competitors. Note their success or failure; analyze the cause and profit thereby.

Note public demand.

If you do not feel confident to write or compose a certain style of song, stick to the kind you are sure of, and gradually, adapt yourself to the others, if possible, before publicly presenting your work.

Avoid slang and vulgarism; they never succeed.

Avoid many-syllabled words and those containing hard consonants, wherever possible.

In writing lyrics be concise; get to your point quickly and when you arrive there make the point as strong as possible.

Simplicity in melody is one of the great secrets of success.

Let your melody musically convey the character and sentiment of the lyrics.

Don't try and write your music with a fine pointed pen. Use either a stub or a three-pointed music pen.

Don't use blotting paper on your written composition; let the ink dry.

Use a good black ink for writing. You can buy regular Music Ink at any good stationer's.

Try and acquire a good hand for writing music. If you find you cannot accomplish this or acquire the knack with any degree of satisfaction, let some one do this who is competent.

A poorly written manuscript is always handicapped when presented to a publisher, artist or manager.

59

"The Last Farewell" for women and children, democratizing taste such that "any high class performer in the world will gladly sing a popular ballad." Harris, a Midwesterner who never mentioned his Jewishness, a former banjo-playing minstrel who described one Bingo as "a little darky bootblack," resolved what should have been far deeper issues of identity with marketplace sentimentality. "Argument in favor of their merit is undoubtedly proven beyond question by their enormous sale; and many a sad and weary heart has been made glad by the strains of these 'popular' songs."

David Suisman's *Selling Sounds* emphasized the shift from Harris's middle-American persona to Lower East Side immigrant Irving Berlin, from the waltz "After the Ball" with its prim story to the boozier, slangier, and sexier "Alexander's Ragtime Band" and "Everybody's Doin' It Now." How-to publishers labored to secure a new reasonable position. Samuel Speck's *Songwriters' Guide* admitted: "Some of our best writers have placed a lot of trash on the market simply to feel the pulse of the public." One contributor, Harry F. Williams, ventured an early version of the Top 40 credo of programming for mother and daughter: "Remember you're writing for Maggie, the servant, and you're trying at the same time not to insult the intelligence of the master of the house." E. M. Wickes's *Writing the Popular Song* extolled professionalization, from increased payments (the original payola) to performers who introduced sheet music in vaudeville to savvy about taste publics: "The consensus of opinions holds that the popular song should be aimed at the younger generation, especially the heart of the sentimental woman still in her teens." More suggestive lyrics remained dubious: "real songwriters" did without them.

By 1927, when *Variety* music editor Abel Green published *Inside Stuff on How to Write Popular Songs*, Tin Pan Alley "slanguage" (Green's phrase) earned aplomb as one of the ASCAP pro's tools. (This included recognizing ASCAP: the American Society of Composers, Authors, and Publishers, a trade organization.) Home and mother still appealed as topics, but so too romantic drama for flappers and blues tropes as well, especially for recordings. Immigrants like Berlin and Gershwin, "ambitious boys" from "ghettos," were the new models. "The 'popular' song, before it became a Jewish industry, was really popular," allegedly capitalist Henry Ford charged, using criteria that others from theorist **Theodor Adorno** to historian Suisman would take up, minus the anti-Semitism. *Melody* editor Robert Bruce, read as a source by Adorno, responded to such belittlement in his 1935 *So You Want to Write a Song?* A hit, he noted, might sell organically, but also because a publisher spent on promotion: "The explanation of this differentiation may not be clear, but neither is the differentiation." With Bruce, a new word entered how-to guides: the "standard," earning "steady demand over a period of years so it never grows old." Then again, standard had two meanings. Bruce asked, rhetorically, "Must popular songs conform to certain standards and patterns?" He continued: "The answer to this question is a very definite 'Yes.'"

FIRST FAMILY OF FOLK COLLECTING

John A. Lomax, Cowboy Songs and Other Frontier Ballads, *1910*

———

"Frankly, the volume is meant to be popular," John Lomax explained in his brief commentary to the first important collection of American folk tunes rather than transplanted English and Scottish material. He was no purist. The verses were composites, acquired from multiple sources for appeal to singers and the imagination, not a taxonomy of linguistic dispersion. Lomax made stirring drama out of collecting songs of "that unique and romantic figure in modern civilization," the cowboy. They'd been gleaned, he said, in saloons, campfires, and during a bronco-busting.

Scholars have unpacked and debunked the work of Lomax and his son **Alan** ever since; myth-mongering was folklore's strategic essentialism. In his memoir, *Adventures of a Ballad Hunter*, John (1867–1947) called his family, "the upper crust of the 'po' white trash,' traditionally held in contempt by the aristocracy of the Old South and by their Negro slaves." His biographer, Nolan Portersfield, noted a father who farmed on the edge of arability in Texas but kept subscriptions to national newspapers; John started as a college student late and stayed one through age forty, getting administrative work at the University of Texas and a 1906–7 fellowship to Harvard. There, faculty in American literature attached to **Francis Child**'s folklore legacy embraced his casual seminar suggestion that he might do cowboy ballads. This was Teddy Roosevelt's America, described in Gail Bederman's *Manliness and Civilization* as a discourse of manhood under corporate threat to virility. Roosevelt became president through his western, strenuous persona, yet Black men like boxer Jack Johnson had to be tamed and colonized. The Victorian cry of "The Dying Cowboy" ("O bury me not on the lone prairie") began the ballads. Cruder works followed, with damnation at the core of "The Old Chisolm Trail." But it was a balance: "Home on the Range" uncovered alongside outlaw ballad "Jesse James"; "Whoopi Ti Yi Yo" among the "sharp, rhythmic yells" used to push "little dogies." This was the "Anglo-Saxon ballad spirit," Lomax suggested; each song the group product of men living in "practical equality." Like Natalie Curtis for *The Indians' Book*, Lomax secured an endorsement from Roosevelt, original handwriting reproduced. Like **Alice Fletcher**, he touted Harvard on the cover page. But unlike those Native Americanists, his white manly erudition proved enduring.

The rest is something of a composite ballad: the groaningly fat Lomax collections, credited to father and son, still found in libraries. His first book a modest success and influence, John spent the next two decades selling bonds, sent Alan to Choate, and then the Depression left him jobless at sixty-five. But even as "Home on the Range" became a pop song for Bing Crosby, a network of folk romantics sponsored his renewed efforts, from Chicago newspaperman Carl Sandburg to Modern Language Association professors. The Library of Congress fit father and son with a field recorder in 1933 for the song-collecting safari he had earlier hinted at. *American Ballads and Folk Songs* (1934) reveled in the bounty of what John said amounted to one hundred folk collections he had inspired, notably Sandburg's *American Songbag*. After an expanded *Cowboy Songs* and *Our Singing Country* (1941), adding musical transcriptions by Ruth Crawford Seeger, *Folk Song: U.S.A.* (1947) attempted a musical "canon." Alan and Seeger pushed for more scholarship—overly so by 1960's *The Folk Songs of North America*. The accompaniment, once meant for piano, switched to banjo and guitar, as folk revivalism pivoted around songs the Lomaxes had made into a songbook.

Then came the revisionists. Benjamin Filene's *Romancing the Folk* was particularly acidic on John Lomax's paternalistic relationship with Lead Belly and racist construction of a chain-gang persona for the songster's performances. Lomax had used his political savvy to coerce convicts to perform for him and conceptualized the best of Black music as a vernacular separated from commercial "jazz" or educated art. His own words damned him and at the time strained his relationship with Alan, a progressive who, as he took over, added references to figures like **Zora Neale Hurston** into the Lomax bibliographies.

Still, as the *St. Louis Post-Dispatch* once said: "Frederick Remington had put the cowboy into art as Professor Lomax now puts him into literature." Chicago newspaperman Lloyd Lewis wrote Lomax: "you could hit the sharp, often piercingly right note that gave the song character, made it descriptive, made it a picture of somebody, or some mood." Lomax was a performer and hustler canny to popular appeal. Paige McGinley's *Staging the Blues* considered this Lomax, "singing lecturer," as much a blues stager as Lead Belly. Porterfield's biography captured him at eighty, feted just before the heart attack that killed him. "He was the center of attention, pulling out stories and songs from the ages, practicing his old magic as tale-teller and raconteur. He launched into a bit of gentle bawdy, singing, 'Big Leg Rose,' laughing heartily through the end: 'The only thing I ever done wrong, stayed in Mississippi one day too long.' As he finished singing, he slumped suddenly to the floor, unconscious." Even this, with **Bob Dylan** perhaps taking notes, supplied the seed of a song.

PROCLAIMING BLACK MODERNITY

James Weldon Johnson, The Autobiography of an Ex-Colored Man, *1912*

In Johnson's actual autobiography, *Along This Way*, he learned a song referenced in **James Trotter**'s 1878 *Music and Some Highly Musical People*, found in his father's library, to stump his musician brother J. Rosamond. The Trotter link is telling: add a 1915 *New York Age* column, collected in Johnson's Library of America volume *Writings*, on Trotter's son being asked to leave the White House—Woodrow Wilson called his antiracism "insolence." Johnson was a cultural politician: a school principal and lawyer, a songwriter, novelist, poet, and arts chronicler, recipient of signature university posts, and a leader in the National Association for the Advancement of Colored People (NAACP). Trotter, no less connected, wrote ahead of the Jim Crow backlash. Johnson matured in its depths, answering with "Lift Every Voice and Sing." Like Trotter, he knew what "some highly musical people" must encompass.

When *Autobiography of an Ex-Colored Man* was written, for initially anonymous publication (he asserted authorship publicly in the 1920s), Johnson ran the American consulate in Venezuela, patronage for efforts in the Colored Republican Club. That opportunity owed to his lucrative songwriting with Rosamond and Bob Cole of hits like "Under the Bamboo Tree," reworking the spiritual "Nobody Knows de Trouble I See" into a slangy love call. Was this the "great"—a word he used often—contribution he and his parents, part of the Black elite in Jacksonville, Florida, or his friends at Atlanta University, had imagined? Or was elitism itself at fault?

Each of Johnson's books overlapped, pondering such questions from a different formal vantage. *Autobiography of an Ex-Colored Man* oscillated between hailing ragtime ("music that demanded physical response"; "whatever is *popular* is spoken of as not worth the while") and belittling it: a classically trained German pianist shamed the narrator by effortlessly copying his hardest moves. The unnamed protagonist, influencing **Ralph Ellison**'s *Invisible Man*, achieved a pragmatic cosmopolitanism, but the novel still ended, "I have sold my birthright." (A close friend, model for the novel, passed on occasion, marrying a Jewish woman.) Noelle Morrissette's study, *James Weldon Johnson's Modern Soundscapes*, suggested that Johnson, who rhapsodized the spiritual authors in a poem, "O Black and Unknown Bards," valued "linguistic heterogeneity, not perfect translation but the inflection of one culture upon another." Brent Hayes Edwards, writing in **Robert O'Meally**'s *The Jazz Cadence of American*

Culture and his own *Epistrophies*, saw Johnson's focus as "the transcription of African-American folk forms," updating the *Slave Songs* compilers. Johnson heard "swing" style rhythms in a Black preacher, developed his thoughts on the "jes' grew" nature, the "blare and jangle and the surge," of Black folk greatness in prefaces to *The Book of American Negro Poetry*, *The Book of Negro Spirituals*, *The Second Book of American Negro Spirituals*, and the sermon poems *God's Trombones*. **Ishmael Reed** took notes for *Mumbo Jumbo*.

A description of the Black nightclub Johnson and friends favored, used for fiction in *Autobiography*, was interpolated as history in *Black Manhattan*, an account Johnson centered on phases of Black entertainment there: minstrelsy, then ragtime revues, uptown nightclubs, and a return to Broadway. These triumphs underwrote Harlem, a city within a city whose residents were able to ward off white mob attacks and support a creative class. Switching to the first person in *Along This Way*, Johnson set himself apart, noting his agnosticism, his curveball pitching, his belated "knowledge of my own people as a 'race'" teaching in rural Georgia.

The insights of double-consciousness spoke to this coworker of W. E. B. DuBois, whose artistic voice—tone parallel to **Bert Williams**, **Jelly Roll Morton**, **Duke Ellington**—turned on the not-quite vernacular. Johnson wrote the lyrics for "Lift Every Voice," the Negro national anthem, in 1901, for a Lincoln birthday affair in Jacksonville, where he'd created the first Black high school and used every bourgeois skill to escape a mob who saw him with a light-skinned journalist. Imani Perry's *May We Forever Stand* tracked the anthem's role as NAACP song, southern Black school ritual, and epitome of a "black formalism" whose nature more accompanied the vernacular than challenged it—"Lift Every Voice" was sung at Wattstax, the "Black Woodstock," for example. If his anthem furthered Black association, that was one aspect of Black show business too. He declared himself "born to be a New Yorker" and found the theater hustle intoxicating and no less open to elevation, as when he, Rosamond, and Cole "decided to write a comic opera satirizing the new American imperialism." *Along the Way* cycled between moments when politics called, because "I had not yet made a real start on the work that I had long kept reassuring myself I should sometime do," and near admission that popular culture was real work: "It is, however, in his lighter music that the Negro has given America its best-known distinctive form of art." By 1933, in contrast to his *Ex-Colored* protagonist, this survivor of Jim Crow saw whites in Harlem, "doing their best to pass for colored"—his novel with an alternate ending.

SONGCATCHING IN THE MOUNTAINS

Olive Dame Campbell and Cecil J. Sharp, English Folk Songs from the Southern Appalachians: Comprising 122 Songs and Ballads, and 323 Tunes, *1917*

––––––

One **Child** ballad collected here, "Barbara Allen," was printed in ten variants, ascribed to different singers, dates, and places—the earliest, by Miss Ada B. Smith, transcribed on December 16, 1907, in Knott County, Kentucky. Sharp, leader of England's folk revival, noted in the introduction that his own collecting amounted to just nine weeks in 1916. Mrs. Campbell, as she was called, had set down the rest. For more, one might turn to *The Life and Work of John Charles Campbell*, a six-hundred-page typeset manuscript deposited in university libraries in 1968. This was Olive Dame Campbell's tribute to her husband, a foundation administrator for Highlanders who died in 1919, begun when her directorship of the John C. Campbell Folk School ended in 1944, and completed by peers after her death in 1954. In it, she recalled going with John in 1907 to Hindman Settlement School, uplift for Appalachians, where director Katherine Petit had a girl play banjo and sing. "I had been used to sing 'Barbara Allen' as a child," Campbell wrote, "but so far from that gentle tune was this—so strange, so remote, so thrilling. I was lost, almost from the first note."

Campbell called the songcatching that followed "one of the most illuminating and rewarding experiences of my life" and ultimately recruited Sharp to help. Her own perspective was captured in the 1915 article "Songs and Ballads of the Southern Mountains." This described mountain ballads as "elemental" more than once, echoed **Lucy McKim Garrison** on slave spirituals in wonder at the "custom of inserting slurring half notes and unexpected quavers," and made her experience like a "local color" magazine article of the 1870s or travel copy today: "one who has not heard the ballad sung at the mountain-hearth cannot fully appreciate how it seems to express the temper and isolation of its environment." With logging and mining, Campbell worried, the folklore of Appalachia was "a store that is rapidly being lost." She appealed to whiteness, terming the ballads "an unconscious record of the character, temper, and development of our race."

Ventriloquizing again, Campbell completed her husband's survey volume, *The Southern Highlander and His Homeland*, letting songs from the book with Sharp contrast with census statistics and other tables. In discussions of hookworm and diet, the mountain folk were figured as apathetic and inert. In their ballads and hymns, best when "sung in a little mountain church dimly lighted by smoking, flickering pine torches," they were cherished as quaint people "out of the currents of modern life, yet who live, perhaps, more closely to the heart of things."

In 1932, an expansive new *English Folk Songs* appeared, edited by Maud Karpeles, a fellow British revivalist who had accompanied Sharp on his fuller U.S. collecting work, later cowrote two editions of his hagiography, then declared in a 1967 final edition that it was her work all along—she had just needed a male beard. The Karpeles *English Folk Songs* minimized Campbell. It kept Sharp's original introduction, at times provocative—"That the illiterate may nevertheless reach a high level of culture will surprise those only who imagine that education and cultivation are convertible terms"—and at other times viewing Appalachians as picturesque, less obsequious than English peasants, and in "full enjoyment of their racial heritage." Nothing found records Campbell's response to her displacement, but letters setting the original partnership live in the manuscript book. Sharp stressed that his work "discusses the whole matter scientifically." Olive Dame Campbell conceded: "I know nothing of the scientific side of the matter," then gave him a tip: "The mountain people are sensitive, proud and shy, but will do things for you if they like you and feel that you like them."

Twisted roots indeed, which successive scholars labored to bonsai, always noting how antimodern biases affected "folk" definition, gradually noticing that sexism and racism did as well. Sharp's renown pushed folk revivalists out of the library and into the field, if with a dubious mandate; D. K. Wilgus's sharply observed *Anglo-American Folksong Scholarship Since 1898* offered Edmund Wilson's 1926 worry that "folk-lore has become a science—running to the same narrow specialization and the same unintelligible amassment of data as the other sciences." Henry Shapiro's *Appalachia On Our Mind* traced those local color writers to Sharp and John Campbell as the region shifted from "America's opposite" to a prized cliché of culture. David Whisnant's still influential *All That Is Native and Fine* brought women and whiteness more into the story, centering on settlement schools and Campbell as one of many northern, middle-class white women rerooted in the mountains. Looking at English folk revivalists, Dave Harker was gleefully antibourgeois in *Fakesong*, while Georgina Boyes's more cultural studies, feminist *Imagined Village* recounted Karpeles's own sexist treatment.

But work remained on what Olive Dame Campbell and the women in her networks accomplished. Her folk school, Whisnant found, modeled on Danish examples, helped focus a crafts industry that gave the cultural cliché a cash cow—Jane Becker took that story further in *Selling Tradition*. Ballad singer

Jean Ritchie similarly packaged the music: her memoir *Jean Ritchie's Singing Family of the Cumberlands* was almost a settlement school keepsake, praising the women for keeping "the old mountain songs" in regular life, as contrasted to the radio that made it all seem shameful next to "slick city music." Daniel Walkowitz's *City Folk* laid off debunking folk definitions to dwell on their popularization, to communities as far from the mountains as New Englander Campbell had been before she came South and got lost in a song.

PART II

THE JAZZ AGE

FIGURE 2.1
J. A. Rogers, "Jazz at
Home" essay on jazz as
"a marvel of paradox,"
Alain Locke, ed., *The New
Negro*, 1925. Illustration by
Aaron Douglas. Author's
collection.

———————

FIGURE 2.2
Cover of Isaac Goldberg,
*Tin Pan Alley: A Chronicle
of the American Popular
Music Racket*, 1930. Notice
the full publicity style now
in effect. Collection of
Ryan Raul Bañagale.

JAZZ AT HOME

J. A. ROGERS

JAZZ is a marvel of paradox: too fundamentally human, at
least as modern humanity goes, to be typically racial, too international to be characteristically national, too much abroad in the
world to have a special home. And yet jazz in spite of it all
is one part American and three parts American Negro, and
was originally the nobody's child of the levee and the city
slum. Transplanted exotic—a rather hardy one, we admit—
of the mundane world capitals, sport of the sophisticated, it is
really at home in its humble native soil wherever the modern
unsophisticated Negro feels happy and sings and dances to his
mood. It follows that jazz is more at home in Harlem than
in Paris, though from the look and sound of certain quarters
of Paris one would hardly think so. It is just the epidemic
contagiousness of jazz that makes it, like the measles, sweep
the block. But somebody had to have it first: that was the
Negro.

What after all is this taking new thing, that, condemned

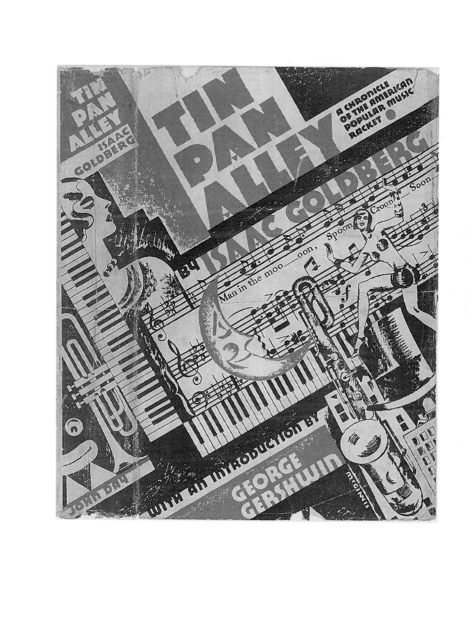

FIGURE 2.3 Zora Neale Hurston, *Mules and Men,* 1935 first edition, cover illustration by Harlem Renaissance staple Miguel Covarrubias, photographed copy. Special Collections and University Archives, Vanderbilt University.

FIGURE 2.4 Cover of
Frederic Ramsey Jr. and
Charles Edward Smith,
eds., *Jazzmen*, 1939. Harvest
Books/Harcourt Brace
reissue, 1977. Author's
collection.

STORIES FOR THE SLICKS

F. Scott Fitzgerald, Flappers and Philosophers, *1920*

———————

In "Bernice Bobs Her Hair," a story from his first collection, the Princeton-educated chronicler of smart-set misadventures declared with characteristic knowingness that "youth in this jazz-nourished generation is temperamentally restless, and the idea of fox-trotting more than one full fox trot with the same girl is distasteful." We might wonder about the idea of a generation nourished by a music only put on record in 1917: jazz, an *au courant* term, substituted for a perennial—ragtime. Music was mostly a backdrop, as were the musicians who played it. "The Offshore Pirate," a fantastic seduction, saw Ardita Farnam fall for the man playing white bandleader Curtis Carlyle, not his Six Black Buddies. African Americans only got a semiotic laminate, allowed symbolic entrance to modernity's passing strange, as in later novel *The Great Gatsby*: "As we crossed Blackwell's Island a limousine passed us, driven by a white chauffeur, in which sat three modish Negroes, two bucks and a girl. I laughed aloud as the yolks of their eyeballs rolled toward us in haughty rivalry. 'Anything can happen now that we've slid over this bridge,' I thought; 'anything at all. . . .'"

But what Fitzgerald missed about the Jazz Age as a Black music story he made up for on flappers as a white bourgeois one, presenting sequels to **Dreiser**'s *Sister Carrie*. Paula Fass named her history of American youth culture *The Damned and the Beautiful*, tweaking the title of his second novel: he illustrated her point about how peer cohorts defied norms in tandem. Ardita seduced "Curtis," too, with a forty-foot swan dive. Both were rebels, of a sort, and the goal was a companionate relationship, not separate spheres. "I know you don't like sentiment," Bernice said to her female rival in "the drama of the shifting, semicruel world of adolescence," who'd denounced "tiresome colorless marriages." Modernity removed social structure: Fitzgerald captured this in the metaphor of "hearing a phonograph record by a singer who had been dead a long time." That came in "Head and Shoulders," his anthology's third great story, in which a showgirl became known as a genius, her book *Sandra Pepys, Syncopated* promoted by Peter Bryce Wendill, "who happened at the time to be advocating the enrichment of the American language by the immediate adaptation of expressive vernacular words." Rights to the tale went to Metro Films for $2,500.

T. Austin Graham's work on Fitzgerald and pop songs—forget jazz, at least as a coherent entity apart from pop—has rescued this cash-in streak as literary innovation: "a new, musical mode of reading and writing," where songs coursed through characters' heads all the time, music was something one did things with rather than sifted into a canon, and an author positioned "between fandom and detachment on the subject of entertainment" used that space "to depict and engage with the complexities of his very busy cultural moment." To Graham, Fitzgerald was one the few to see that pop's "literary merits often lay in its very badness, that one's attitude towards it could not but be one of constant and often paradoxical readjustment."

Much like **Tom Wolfe** later, Fitzgerald refused to endorse the vernacular: he viewed pop culture as a romantic, materialist revisioning of the Victorian sentimental. His WASP focus imbibed racism and anti-Semitism, but he retained class contentiousness: elites "hipped on Freud and all that" were finding new means of breaking the noses of ordinary people. This is why adaptations of his work continue, like Baz Luhrmann's *Gatsby* film, a deco and hip-hop mélange. "I've got a streak of cheapness," said a character in *The Beautiful and Damned*. "I don't know where I get it but it's—oh, things like this and bright colors and gaudy vulgarity. I seem to belong here. These people could appreciate me and take me for granted, and these men would fall in love with me and admire me, whereas the clever men I meet would just analyze me and tell me I'm this because of this or that because of that."

REMEMBERING THE FIRST BLACK STAR

Mabel Rowland, ed., Bert Williams, Son of Laughter*, 1923*

————

In a letter to W. E. B. Du Bois asking for a contribution to this posthumous tribute book, Rowland described herself as the great comedian's publicist and confidential adviser for eighteen years. She'd later found an acting company and perform skits and monologues—one on Tin Pan Alley—that formed a second book, *Life with Laughter.* Not progressive enough to capitalize *Negro,* she did bring in Du Bois and Jessie Fauset, literary editor of NAACP house organ *The Crisis,* to testify alongside comedian W. C. Fields, legitimate theater maven David Belasco, and Williams's own father. The volume encapsulated a mystery that mostly waited for the twenty-first century: the vaudeville-topping Black man who brought his race to Broadway did so in blackface, his pokey character a required mask. His everyman role was "Nobody."

Williams came from the West Indies, then the West Coast; he'd partner with George Walker in comic routines that mixed coon song, cakewalk dancing, and increasing stage sophistication in revues such as *In Dahomey.* The company included Walker's spouse Aida Overton, a modernist force who danced Salome, poet Paul Laurence Dunbar ("We Wear the Mask"), and others who gathered at the Marshall Hotel in midtown, later seeding Harlem. They broke in 1897 and peaked in the early 1900s; then Walker died of syphilis, Aida shortly after. The company disbanded, with Williams taking lead roles in the otherwise white *Ziegfeld Follies* through the 1910s, dying at forty-six in 1922. As he passed, *Shuffle Along* had replaced Williams and Walker on Broadway, Bessie Smith's blues had replaced Williams's comic syncopations on Columbia Records, and though **Langston Hughes** skipped an exam at Columbia to attend the funeral, his Harlem Renaissance saw Williams as one era prior to the New Negro.

The way *Son of Laughter* told the tale, Williams sought a serious role with Belasco, then begged off. From childhood, he'd been "storing away dialects and little bits of mimicry." He played a Hawaiian in a troupe, then "studied the negro." His friend Alex Rogers, author of lyrics including "Nobody," said he chose "the line of least resistance"; unlike Walker, he "never strained the color line." *Theatrical Magazine,* Rowland noted, declared: "Nature has endowed him with a comic mask and he succeeds at obtaining with voice and gesture, ludicrous effects that are irresistible." His bromance with King Edward when the troupe ventured to London supplied other tales. Booker T. Washington proclaimed, "He has smiled his way into people's hearts. I have been obliged to *fight* my way." Rowland underlined Williams as reader, collecting a rare volume by Ogilby on Africa. "All Coons Look Alike to Me" originator Ernest Hogan wrote "The Phrenologist Coon" for him, a satire: "In ethnology I'se the thing." Yet by the *Follies* he was alone. Ziegfeld's staff didn't know how to shape material he could perform, Ring Lardner thought. Fields contributed a line that stuck: Williams was "the funniest man I ever saw and the saddest man I ever knew." Rowland denounced the "white problem of race prejudice" but quoted theater owner Shubert: "he is the whitest actor I've ever met in my life." To end the volume, Du Bois came through: Williams and his peers were "the smile that hovered above blood and tragedy; the light mask of happiness that hid breaking hearts and bitter souls."

Harlem intellectuals were inclined to be kind. Fauset shaped a fuller Williams criticism in her *New Negro* chapter "The Gift of Laughter." Like **Ellen Willis** later on **Bob Dylan**, this was an explorer's first cartography of an icon's extensive mask. She saw his West Indian identity as critical: "the ways of the American Negro were utterly alien to him." **James Weldon Johnson**'s *Black Manhattan*, a tale told by a fellow Marshall Hotel regular, drew a lineage from the 1890 *Creole Show* to Williams and Walker, "the strongest Negro theatrical combination that has yet been assembled." His oft-quoted remark about the "defection of Bert Williams to the white stage" came in a lineage of syphilis deaths undercutting the scene Williams supported, with Johnson concluding that a "real Negro theater" could only happen in Harlem, where "Negro performers played to audiences made up almost wholly of people of their own race."

The next book on Williams wouldn't emerge until 1970, when Ann Charters, connected to blues revivalists and Beats, wrote *Nobody*, the "story of a man neatly trapped by the prejudice and intolerance of his time." Charters made Williams's choices the result of "what looked to him like a hopeless situation," noting his standard remark at white society parties: "Is we all good niggers here?" An accompanying LP on Folkways, constrained to material "free from any overtone of racial stereotype," became the only full Williams album of the twentieth century. Eric Smith produced a dry, factually solid volume, *Bert Williams* (1992), that stressed theater over songs. **Gary Giddins**, looking for *Visions of Jazz*, made Williams and Al Jolson into originators, each tainted and vital, though his dichotomy was too neat: "While white minstrels spoke of the liberating influence of blackface, Williams expressed a loathing for its restraints."

For once, cultural studies canonized an artist: Paul Gilroy's work on the diasporic Black Atlantic taught scholars to appreciate a mask as a problematized conjuncture. Louis Chude-Sokei's insightful *The Last "Darky"* began with Lorca and Soyinka on masks and called Williams's legacy "as troubling then as it is productive now": his West Indian caricature of American Blackness revealed fault-lines in the "romantic nationalist notion that Blacks constituted a singular culture." Williams wasn't betrayer of vernacular so much as vernacular dualist, linked to calypso and Caribbean positionings. Daphne Brooks's take on Aida Walker in *Bodies in Dissent*, joined by writing on the dancer and the Williams and Walker company by David Krasner, Jayna Brown, and Karen Sotiropoulos, belonged to this new viewpoint. Camille Forbes's bland *Introducing Bert Williams*, from a dissertation supervised by Henry Louis Gates Jr., made Williams's signifying align with Black practice but also such American entertainment staples as the medicine show.

The Caribbean-to-Harlem author Eric Walrond, reviewing Rowland's volume in *Negro World*, predicted: "Some day one of our budding story writers ought to sit down and write a novel with a Negro protagonist with melancholia as the central idea. Bert Williams had it." Vastly later, St. Kitts–born Caryl Phillips wrote that diaspora novel, *Dancing in the Dark*, which played up Williams as a man who drank and slept alone; inflated George Walker's affair with white vaudeville star Eva Tanguay to a central plot point; and turned Williams and Walker accepting the taboo against portraying Black romance into a key framing. Phillips spoke of a desire to give Williams the interiority denied us in his archive.

For others, increasingly, that sense of the man came from his performances, a couple of silent films available on YouTube and the many audio discs he set down from 1901 until shortly before his death, collected by Archeophone on three discs released in the 2000s with extensive liner notes. Tim Brooks's *Lost Sounds: Blacks and the Birth of the Recording Industry* lingered over each release, finding triumph rather than compromise: "His recordings managed to convey his unique stage persona in a manner that appealed to both Black and white record buyers." A photo of Williams in the recording process, sans cork, made another kind of point. W. T. Lhamon's chapter on Williams in my collection *Listen Again* extended his work on minstrels like **T. D. Rice** and 1950s rockers to see "subaltern song" in the likes of "Borrow from Me" and find the creation of pop publics, the "excluded middle" that jazz denied, in the naysaying of "Nobody." Yuval Taylor and Jake Austen's *Darkest America* went still further: "To be categorical and plain, *Bert Williams treasured the minstrel tradition. But this fact is too horrifying for contemporary writers to face.*" Would blackface replace blues in our popular music historicizing? Would Williams replace **Robert Johnson**?

Fauset, in 1925, had already heard "compensating laughter," "emotional salvation," and an endowment for the portrayal of tragedy by later actors in Williams and his fallen players. She ended her essay for **Alain Locke**'s *New Negro* writing to ghosts: "I hope that Hogan realizes this and Cole and Walker, too, and that lastly Bert Williams the inimitable, will clap us on with those tragic black-gloved hands of his now that the gift of his laughter is no longer tainted with the salt of chagrin and tears."

MAGAZINE CRITICISM ACROSS POPULAR GENRES

Gilbert Seldes, The Seven Lively Arts, *1924*

———

One could argue for Carl Van Vechten, but most regard Gilbert Seldes as the first popular culture critic of note, able to parse form, recount history, and judge social shifts. An ecumenical music writer of the era, like **Sigmund Spaeth**, considered popular music alongside classical. Seldes put Irving Berlin and Al Jolson alongside Charlie Chaplin films, *Krazy Kat* comics, and *Ziegfeld Follies* variety theater. Attuned to talent, he recognized George Gershwin's revolutionary potential even before "Rhapsody in Blue." Intrigued by media forms, he noticed how movies resisted legitimate theater: "all of this is done *with the camera, through action* presented to the eye."

His personal connections were as powerful as his imaginative ones. A Harvard compatriot of e. e. cummings and John Dos Passos, then managing editor of the *Dial* (where "The Waste Land" first appeared), Seldes wrote *The Seven Lively Arts* at Edmund Wilson's behest for *Vanity Fair*; he finished it in Paris while mingling with Picasso, Joyce, and Gertrude Stein. Petitioning his book editor for abundant illustrations, cartoons, and photos, he urged—biographer Michael Kammen discovered—that his book appear "as removed from the genteel tradition as the subject matter." The modernist claim Seldes made, in resistance to gentility, was that only in categories counted secondary elsewhere could American culture be viewed as first rate. The title page illustration—busts of Aristophanes, slapstick director Mack Sennett, and Rabelais overhanging a Keystone comedy pantheon—set an arch tone for a survey that concluded with future Satanic Led Zeppelin influence Aleister Crowley gushing blasphemies over vaudeville vixen Eva Tanguay.

FIGURE 2.5
Ralph Barton
frontispiece,
"Custodians of
the Keystone,"
for Gilbert
Seldes, *The Seven
Lively Arts*, 1924.
Theme: high
and low culture,
brought ever
closer together.
University of
Alabama.

Seldes read slapstick as both "cinematographic" and "spectacle"; long before Richard Dyer considered Marilyn Monroe's star text or **Ellen Willis** savored Dylan's use of persona, he centered on "*Charlot*. The French name which is and is not Charlie will serve for that figure on the screen, the created image which is, and at the same time is more than, Charlie Chaplin, and is less." He contemplated gradations of artiness: "*The Kid* was undoubtedly a beginning in 'literature' for Charlie. I realize that in admitting this I am giving the whole case away, for in the opinion of certain critics the beginning of literature is the end of creative art. This attitude is not so familiar in America, but in France you hear the Charlot of *The Kid* spoken of as 'theatre,' as one who has ceased to be of the film entirely." Turning to dancer Irene Castle, he found something "unimpassioned, cool not cold, in her abandon," whereas "Jolson's vitality had the same quality as the impression I got from the New York skyline."

Seldes's nuanced best made his prejudices more saddening. If jazz, he saucily insisted, was "about the only native music worth listening to in America," it was not a Black triumph: "no negro band has yet come up to the level of the best white ones, and the leader of the best of all, by a little joke, is called Whiteman." (His one Black titan died young: ragtime's James Reese Europe.) To Seldes, "the negro is more intense than we are," but "we surpass him when we combine a more varied and more intelligent life with his instinctive qualities." In a 1957 second edition of *Seven Lively Arts*, he apologized for his earlier racial attitudes.

That still left the book's structuring gender opposition, lively men and sappy women. When Seldes wrote, "The lively arts which are continually jeopardized by the bogus," he meant the sentimental and bourgeois, "the exact equivalent of a high-toned lady." Casting popular culture's peaks as comic, unsentimental, spectacular, fun, and fantastic took Seldes far—but still left him short. Poet Conrad Aiken, Kammen found, picked up on the anxiety: "One suspects him, here, of over-simplification; and one suspects him also of having, towards his 'bogus' or 'pretentious' or faux bon art, what a psychiatrist would describe as an 'over-determined' feeling: for some reason, this vague nightmare excites him too much."

By the 1950s, bogus had become middlebrow and Seldes joined that hunt, recanting some claims in *The Public Arts* and calling for more "genuinely democratic entertainment." He didn't like crooners, nor the most avid female spectators: "women who listen to daytime serials suffer anxiety, frustration, a sense of futility." Perhaps that longer trajectory explains why Seldes now gets so little credit for a major feat: essentially inventing pop criticism.

HARLEM RENAISSANCE

Alain Locke, ed., The New Negro: An Interpretation, *1925*

———

Codifying the Harlem Renaissance, this collection put popular music at the center of Black Arts debates. Locke, the first African American Rhodes Scholar, esteemed cosmopolitanism and sought to elevate a folk culture created in slavery alongside Zionism, Irish independence, and other migrations "northward and city-ward." The book's Deco styling and high-contrast, heady author portraits were by German immigrant Winold Reiss; stereotype-courting nightlife paintings of jazz and blues came from Mexican artist Miguel Covarrubias. Strong emphasis fell on "Negro Youth," with emerging authors such as **Langston Hughes**, **Zora Neale Hurston**, and Jean Toomer made into peers of elders W. E. B. Du Bois and **James Weldon Johnson** or patrons Albert Barnes and Arthur Schomburg. Message: "Uncle Tom and Sambo have passed on."

A publication predating **Louis Armstrong**'s and **Duke Ellington**'s recognition could not have engaged jazz comprehensively, but Locke's take on jazziness differed from **F. Scott Fitzgerald**'s. For him, the spirituals cultivated by white collectors like **Lucy McKim Garrison**, popularized by Fisk Jubilee Singers, and declared central by Du Bois, were akin to the concert-hall music jazz later became. "Suppressed for generations," Locke wrote, "secretive, half-ashamed, until the courage of being natural brought them out." He admired how Toomer gave "a musical folk-tilt and a glamorous sensuous ecstasy to the style of the American prose modernist." But his preferred performers embraced formal music: Harry Burleigh, Roland Hayes.

Blues, already sold in bulk by Bessie Smith, turned up first in *New Negro* in Rudolph Fisher's noir short story, "City of Refuge"; the language likely inspired Duke Ellington's "Harlem Air Shaft." "An airshaft: cabbage and chitterlings cooking; liver and onions sizzling, sputtering; three player-pianos out-plunking each other; a man and woman calling each other vile things; a sick, neglected baby wailing; a phonograph broadcasting blues; dishes clacking; a girl crying heartbrokenly; waste noises, waste odors of a score of families, seeking issue through a common channel; pollution from bottom to top—a sewer of sounds and smells." For Ellington and Fisher, such a setting, rather than genre innovations, cultivated sound.

Black popular success had manifested in vaudeville, revues, and full musicals, from **Bert Williams** and George Walker's *In Dahomey* to Sissle and Blake's *Shuffle Along*. The anxiety was whether, as Locke's Howard University friend Montgomery Gregory wrote, "fundamentally they carry-on the old minstrel tradition." Jessie Fauset, literary editor for the NAACP's *Crisis*, recalled Bert Williams's "hopeless frustration" and felt encouraged by Paul Robeson's modernist work in Eugene O'Neill dramas.

Should jazz be heard in the context of spirituals and modernism or vaudeville and white-centered "buffoonery"? Given the "Jazz at Home" essay, freelancer J. A. Rogers, later to write *100 Amazing Facts About the Negro with Complete Proof*, chose optimism about commercialism, not unlike a **Gilbert Seldes**. Jazz for him was "a marvel of paradox," something that "ranks with the movies and the dollar" as "modern Americanism" and "joyous revolt from convention." He assembled a pantheon: James Reese Europe, **Ethel Waters**, Florence Mills, Eubie Blake, and dancer Bill Robinson, "inimitable artists, with an inventive, improvising skill." Still, he flinched, saying white orchestras like Whiteman's were "demonstrating the finer possibilities."

Next in Locke's volume, however, came a second dose of Hughes poetry, "Jazzonia," entirely sculpted from the "none too respectable cabaret" that Rogers feared. Generations later, Kevin Young would use this same verse—substituting jazziness as vernacular myth for Blackness as dialect ghetto, a hard distinction philosophically, but essential artistically—to start his anthology *Jazz Poems*. As with Fisher's airshaft, jazz was in the literature. Just not, yet, in the discourse.

TIN PAN ALLEY'S STANDARDS SETTER

Alexander Woollcott, The Story of Irving Berlin, *1925*

On his 1932 recording of "Say It Isn't So," originally popularized live on his radio show, Rudy Vallee introduced the song as Irving Berlin's first in a while. That the crooner, as artistically suspect as Berlin's plastic ditties and sob ballads, recognized his listeners would care reflected how Russian immigrant Israel Baline had become America's national icon of moon-June-spoon. Alive for more than a century (1888–1989), his career spanned Tin Pan Alley, Broadway musicals, Hollywood, and television—hundreds of songs performed for dozens of purposes. Jeffrey Magee noted, "we actually know quite a bit about Berlin's life. We are just beginning to come to grips with the vastness of his work."

Philip Furia, solid modern-day biographer for musical analysis and social history, found coverage of Berlin's songwriting magic and Lower East Side rags-to-riches tale as far back as 1910, a year before "Alexander's Ragtime Band" broke pop paradigms. "The Man Who Is Making the Country Hum" told the *New York World:* "You must be able to switch your lyre to something else. If not, a new writer will take your place." Some early stories, including Berlin essays on songwriting, were collected in Benjamin Sears's *Irving Berlin Reader*. Critic **Gilbert Seldes** recognized Berlin as a central figure of popular modernism in *The Seven Lively Arts*, saying of "Alexander's": "it was simple and passionate and utterly unsentimental and the whole country responded to its masterful cry, *Come on and hear!*"

But Berlin literature accelerated with *The Story of Irving Berlin*, the first biography of a living popular music figure, written by theater critic and Algonquin raconteur Alexander Woollcott, overwriting like an early **Tom Wolfe**. Woollcott heard in Berlin's Tin Pan Alley commerce less melting pot than banging pots:

> He transmuted into music the jumbled sounds of his life—the wash of the river against the blackened piers, the alarums of the street cars, the roar of the elevated, the frightening scream of the fire engines, the polyglot hubbub of the curbs and doorsteps on his own East Side, the brassy jangle of the hurdy-gurdies, the cries of the fruit vendors and push cart peddlers, the chants in the synagogues, the whines and squeals of Chinatown, the clink of glass and the crack of revolvers in saloons along the Bowery, above all the plaintive wail of his sorrowing tribe, the lamentation of a people harried and self-pitying since time out of mind.

Berlin, to him, meant "the idiom of the sidewalks," equating "loose-living, alcoholism, bobbed hair, distrust of government, and disrespect for old age." And his sales tallies were their own headline; $160,000 in copyrights for one year alone, million sellers in sheet music and on record. This was part of the noise Woollcott hit readers with: "the very selling method is as much a part of the pace and rhythm of Berlin's music as that music, itself, is part of the pace and rhythm of America in the third decade of the Twentieth Century."

There wouldn't be another Berlin biography for twenty-five years, when **David Ewen**'s middlebrow corpus gave him one of the four volumes by Ewen in Holt's Musical Biography Series. The others, tellingly, were on Gershwin, Strauss, and Haydn. Along with his rise in cultural hierarchy to author of standards, the mood Berlin evoked had gotten softer: "his capacity to discover the root need and sentiment of all our American lives," with "White Christmas. A full chapter documented "God Bless America" and other patriotic endeavors, but already it was hard to encompass the full work—Berlin's movie productions received scant paragraphs. In 1974, Michael Freedland, a BBC radio host, wrote a "show business story" about the author of now three thousand songs; his trick piano that transposed keys for his rudimentary playing skills, ensconced in the Smithsonian; and his long marriage to Ellin Mackay, who eloped against her Catholic father's wishes. *Irving Berlin and Ragtime America*, by Ian Whitcomb, a rocker turned pre-rock pop essayist, revived the noise by emphasizing the early work as "the gunpowder plot that banged us into what we are today." It was Woollcott in a new generation's idiom.

Posthumous work went deeper. Oldest child Mary Ellin Barrett's memoir presented her parents as social moderns, her mother raising three girls with Passover Seders and Catholicism alike. Along with Furia's book, acute and concise on changes in the work over time, and Laurence Bergreen's *As Thousands Cheer*, a detailed but mean-spirited take, Edward Jablonski's *Irving Berlin: American Troubadour* drew on telephone friendship with the reclusive elderly Berlin to detail life episodes. The *Reader* captured a no bizzer like show bizzer who retained some humor about that hustle but ultimately instantiated mainstream America's conflict over what commercial entertainment meant. Conductor Leopold Stokowski defended "God Bless America" for "dignity, simplicity and a wonderful sincerity"; a Black newspaper saluted Berlin for excising "darky," belatedly, from the sheet music for a song in the blackface-featuring film *Holiday Inn*; and *Times* critic Brooks Atkinson hedged on Berlin's last great triumph, the 1946 *Annie Get Your Gun,* calling it a "large, noisy, lavish, vulgar commercial musical show."

A definitive biography, drawing on boxes Berlin gave the Library of Congress, still awaits, but recent work has been more targeted. **Alec Wilder** set a model in his 1972 *American Popular Song: The Great Innovators*, in which—despite a permissions denial Bergreen gleefully recapitulated—his Berlin chapter broke down a craftsman centered on work, not art. Musicologist **Charles Hamm** used *Irving Berlin: Songs from the Melting Pot: The Formative Years* to chart a switch from working class, ethnic, vaudeville humor to *Watch Your Step* in 1914, a musical aimed at legitimate theater and a ballads-admiring middle-class public. Jeffrey Melnick's *A Right to Sing the Blues* put Berlin—rumored for decades to have "a little black boy" secretly writing his hits—at the center of debates over Jewish uses of Black forms. In a similar vein as Melnick, and the superb Berlin chapter in Gerald Mast's musicals overview *Can't Stop Singin'*, critic Jody Rosen's *White Christmas* took novelist Philip Roth's jibes about Berlin, the Jew who wrote "Easter Parade" and "White Christmas," in *Operation Shylock* ("what does Irving Berlin brilliantly do? He de-Christs them both!"), to read "good Jewish music" as assimilated Americana.

Berlin, who for years lagged Gershwin and other more complex songwriters in acclaim, gained from taste shifts that critiqued genre boundaries. In a *Visions of Jazz* chapter, **Gary Giddins** compared him to Louis Armstrong as a "progenitor of modern song—the agent of transition," amused that Berlin once said "You know, I never did find out what ragtime was." Todd Decker's *Music Makes Me: Fred Astaire and Jazz* used dancer/singer Astaire to build analyses of mainstream musical motion, from *Top Hat's* "Cheek to Cheek," which formally "routined itself," to "The Yam," written by Berlin after Astaire admired Black Lindy Hoppers. Jeffrey Magee's *Irving Berlin's American Musical Theater* revisited the stage work Hamm had highlighted, seeing in Berlin "genre profusion" rather than confusion—how he learned to think as much like a producer as an artist, "abandoning the last remnant of the operatic impulse." Magee's conclusion—that Berlin's output was "as riddled with contradictions as the country for which he saw his work as a 'mirror'"—might have damned him for decades. In the twenty-first century, it was a calling card.

BROADWAY MUSICAL AS SUPERTEXT

Edna Ferber, Show Boat, *1926*

———

Begin with the 1936 Hollywood film: Paul Robeson and torch singer Helen Morgan. Examine the script for the 1927 Broadway debut, belatedly published by the Library of America in 2014 (Laurence Maslon edited), to see how Oscar Hammerstein wed book to lyrics and forever changed the musical. Then turn to the now little-read Ferber and realize the amount this infinitely adaptable "supertext" (literary theorist Lauren Berlant's phrase; *Show Boat* has been no less a cottage industry for analysis) owes to its originating mainstream novel. Robeson's performance of Hammerstein and Kern's "Ol' Man River" gave a modernist, operatic lift to slave spirituals like "Go Down Moses," but Ferber's work made constant homage to spirituals as enduring folk statement and voguish source material. Figuring the Mississippi as "the great untamed," she put an 1870s riverboat in the same pantheon as an 1890s World's Fair hootchie-kootchie dance and 1920s Times Square. She thought about America as a spectacle, about Americans as modernizing peasants, about "Tuh-rue LOVE" as "The Simple Charm That Opens Every Woman's Heart." Her eternal themes of self-made women and assimilating outsiders, her instincts for cultural analysis beyond history or "demon statisticians," gave American music a sentimental apotheosis.

Ferber was not known for musical knowledge; Todd Decker's *Show Boat* study found her take on Black musicality plagiarized a Natalie Curtis Burlin *Musical Quarterly* essay. But the liftings established a lineage: Ferber back to

Curtis Burlin and back to **Alice Fletcher** and **Lucy McKim Garrison**. The key image, played out in novel, musical, and film alike, of Black dockworkers singing spirituals as they labored, harkened to 1860s feminist abolitionists. Spirituals surged first after the Civil War, then in the 1920s when *Slave Songs* was republished, as both an antidote to blackface minstrelsy and coon songs and as a source material for cultivated art. Ferber, who came at 1920s commodity culture with skepticism we associate with **F. Scott Fitzgerald**'s *The Great Gatsby*, romanticized Black primitivism as a power supply for white women navigating stormy modernity. What Curtis Burlin called a "current of musical inspiration" became popular culture itself in Ferber: "the warm electric current that flowed from those river audiences." The central character, Magnolia "I sing Negro songs with a banjo" Ravenal, wondered if Mississippi vitality lived in her daughter Kim, performing on the Great White Way a variant on what showboat cook's helper Jo and passing-for-white leading lady Julie had taught. Negro songs were the family business. Where musical and film ended on Magnolia reconciled with gambler husband Gay, Ferber closed back on the river boat, preserving a homey Americana.

Show Boat represented a literary take on American popular music; its success as a musical generated a secondary literature. Ferber was a media figure herself, reflected in the novel's mentions of writing partner George Kaufman and Algonquin crony Alexander Woollcott. Something of how critics addressed different adaptations can be gleaned from Miles Kreuger's documentary narrative of the musical's many forms. **David Ewen**'s Broadway histories positioned *Show Boat* as the start of a tradition of epics leading to *Oklahoma*! and eventually *West Side Story*. Richard Dyer's *Heavenly Bodies* and Shana Redmond's *Everything Man* gave special weight to Paul Robeson's burden, navigating a role that added to his culture hero status but required toting stereotype. Musicologists, such as Geoffrey Holden Block in *Enchanted Evenings* and **Richard Crawford** in *America's Musical Life*, used *Show Boat* to consider the Broadway musical's component forms, as it ranged from pseudo-blues to romantic balladry; Raymond Knapp's *The American Musical and the Formation of National Identity* brought racial themes forward. This was explored further by Decker, whose book was subtitled *Performing Race in an American Musical* and accompanied by a second study of "Ol' Man River" in multiple recordings. Where Kreuger reveled in *Show Boat*'s incendiary race language ("Imagine the shock"), Decker critiqued Ferber's stereotyping, valued Hammerstein's "popular music plot," and saw each iteration as reworked cultural hierarchy.

Literary scholars also weighed in, with Berlant (*The Female Complaint*) positioning sentimentality and Linda Williams (*Playing the Race Card*) melodrama as the root of Ferber's cross-platform legacy, emphasizing gender and sexuality more than the musicologists. For Berlant, looking back to *Uncle Tom's Cabin*, the musical's "gloss on the Confederate/pseudo-black vernacular minstrel/ text evokes a breathtakingly complex set of revisions and elisions"; liberalism lite. For Williams, who more charitably juxtaposed Ferber's Jewish assimilationism with *The Jazz Singer*, "It is that mainstream vernacular, and not just the 'pure' New Orleans-descended jazz, that permeates American popular culture." Views seemed likely to keep shifting, like stagings of *Show Boat*'s second act.

FATHER OF THE BLUES IN PRINT

W. C. Handy, ed., Blues: An Anthology, *1926*

———

Handy amassed and helped define a great cultural catalog. Born in Alabama in 1873, his modernity was Jim Crow law and Beale Street respite. He used secular music his pastor father despised for status as a bandleader catering to whites, a touring minstrel, and eventually a songwriter and publisher. At about thirty, he heard the blues in Mississippi. At about forty, in Memphis, he had a sheet music hit with a loose version of those blues—but sold the copyright prematurely. He wrote more hits and set up Pace-Handy, a sheet music publishing company in the New York of **Bert Williams** and George Gershwin, just held on as sheet music faltered, then partnered with lawyer and populist music critic Abbe Niles to secure his business and burnish his reputation. *Blues: An Anthology*, came with an expansive introduction and song notes by Niles in conversation with Handy and illustrations, as with **Alain Locke**'s *New Negro* and later **Zora Neale Hurston**'s *Mules and Men,* by Miguel Covarrubias. The volume helped turn Handy into a figure the Harlem Renaissance, publishing organization ASCAP, and *New Republic* alike could regard as his later memoir's title: *Father of the Blues.* And when *A Treasury of the Blues* updated the earlier anthology, in 1949, it included "Memphis Blues"—rights back, it was noted explicitly.

The playing of Charley Patton—who Handy biographer David Robertson said hoped to join Handy's Mississippi band but couldn't read music well enough—locally and eventually everywhere defined Delta blues as vernacular expression. Handy's compositions, inserting blue notes into ragtime, tango passages into twelve-bar verses, were compromised but versatile. **F. Scott Fitzgerald**, William Faulkner (who heard Handy play the state's college town, Oxford), and Flannery O'Connor incorporated his songs into their fiction; Florence Dore described the effect, particularly important to white southern modernism, in *Novel Sounds*. Gershwin, Whiteman, and the Castles connected Handy compositions to orchestras. To Niles, whose early essays deserve a book, Handy understood that "the essence of jazz is spontaneous deviation from the score," finding space in "the breaks" for soloing just as he found room within pop for "the mocking, ironic, or defiant discontent of the old folk-blues." Handy, he insisted, conscious of the Harlem Renaissance tendency to view popular music as raw material for classicizing, "has never professed to 'improve' the snatches of folk songs that appear here and there in his songs." Yet *Blues: An Anthology* was hardly folkloric. It featured **Langston Hughes**, called "likely to do for the blues verses what Handy will be shown to have done for the airs," and material from Gershwin's "Rhapsody in Blue" alongside the founding folk blues ballad "Joe Turner."

Father of the Blues, Handy's life story, presented a triumph: from the father who said music meant the devil and gutter and the Fisk-trained teacher who accepted Wagner but not spirituals to honored patriarch at an ASCAP festival alongside Kern, Garland, and **Carrie Jacobs-Bond**. Yet Handy rued racist restaurant service heading to that ASCAP event and complimented communists for their Scottsboro work. He valued himself as "a trouper" and saw worth in minstrel hokum without minimizing Orange, Texas, where whites routinely shot up train cars of Black entertainers. His tales of hearing blues, first a lone singer at a railroad junction, then a string trio showered with silver dollars, have been repeated ever since. But the material on the music business he went up and down in, that "sharp contest for financial advantage," said more about the blues spirit he personally embodied. His success carved out a mainstream space that proved essential for figures like emerging jazz great Louis Armstrong, whose album of Handy standards was presented to the writer before his death in 1958.

Handy learned young, he wrote in *Father of the Blues*, to "fight my way out, and yet be considered sufficiently 'submissive' by those who held the whip hand." That sardonic spirit, "an olive among the marshmallows" Nile wrote, became cosmopolitanism to join Cuban rhythm and Mississippi mud, create optional dialect about a St. Louis woman with her diamond rings, and persuade Boss Crump's chamber of commerce that "Memphis Blues" was good for business—hence Handy Park, where Bessie Smith joked that Black homeless could tell off white cops. At the time he heard those lines about the Southern crossing the dog, Handy was leading a Knights of Pythias band, a Black fraternal organization for secular advancement in segregated America. The pro songwriter and publisher it made him plundered freely, worked diverse networks in promotion, held court to brand self, form, race, and nation—and retained copyright.

POET OF THE BLARE AND RACIAL MOUNTAIN

Langston Hughes, The Weary Blues, *1926*

———

At twenty-four, with a first book of poetry out and a second on its way, the Harlem Renaissance's most enduring literary figure issued a manifesto, "The Negro Artist and the Racial Mountain," in the *Nation*. "Let the blare of Negro jazz bands and the bellowing voice of Bessie Smith singing blues penetrate the closed ears of the colored near-intellectuals until they listen and perhaps understand. Let Paul Robeson singing 'Water Boy,' and Rudolph Fisher writing about the streets of Harlem, and Jean Toomer holding the heart of Georgia in his hands, and Aaron Douglas drawing strange black fantasies cause the smug Negro middle class to turn from their white, respectable, ordinary books and papers to catch a glimmer of their own beauty." If the *Nation*, sixty years previously, had been white sponsors to **Lucy McKim Garrison** and company's collection of spirituals, Hughes substituted uptown blues as emblem of modern racial pride, with a perfect transitional gesture: a sentimental appeal for the vernacular.

He, too, relied on white sponsors: though Du Bois and Jessie Fauset's *Crisis* published his anthemic first poem, "The Negro Speaks of Rivers," *Weary Blues* came to trade publisher Knopf through his enduring friend Carl Van Vechten, *Vanity Fair* advocate of blues and author, the same year, of the infamously titled novel *Nigger Heaven*. "The Cat and the Saxophone (2 A.M.)" showed Hughes's hybrid assemblage, interspersing a recent hit, "Everybody Loves My Baby," with conversation at closing time, words splayed and jazzy, like e. e. cummings. Hughes's memoir, *The Big Sea*, revealed he heard **Ethel Waters** sing the tune the night he met both Van Vechten and **James Weldon Johnson** at an NAACP benefit on Lenox, where he "got in free, being a writer for the *Crisis*." Hughes needed the comp, in from Europe with a quarter in his pocket.

These bohemian, political, and fashionista credentials count because, as much as race or the shadowy sexuality pursued by Isaac Julien's documentary *Looking for Langston*, they framed his relationship to music—minimal by note-oriented or collector standards ("what I really know about Jazz would fill a thimble!"), but essential for a populist who identified with hustlers. For "The Weary Blues," he incorporated a blues he remembered hearing in Kansas City with his grandmother, once married to a member of John Brown's raiding party. But he put it in quotes—separated himself from the dialect language. Even Bessie Smith, whom he met awkwardly at Van Vechten parties and more comfortably with **Zora Neale Hurston** on tour in the South, appeared in his writing as force rather than peer. His fan move, arriving in New York in 1921, was attending *Shuffle Along*. That Black theater milieu was his dream, pursued in failed or half-successful Broadway ventures throughout his lifetime.

The Weary Blues and its successor volume, *Fine Clothes to the Jew*, were devastating for how tidy poems—"In a Harlem cabaret / Six long-headed jazzers play"—comported with each other ("sleek black boys in a cabaret"), stretching language—"Play, plAY, PLAY!"—in what Hughes called a "lazy sway." Stretching norms, too: "Hello, sailor boy . . . Let's go, sweetie!"; "Hit me again, / Says Clorinda"; "White girls' eyes / Call gay black boys / Black boys' lips / Grin jungle joys." Hughes noted his voyeurs: "White folks, laugh! White folks, pray!" He could be sentimental ("Beautiful, also are the souls of my people"), global ("Mexican Market Woman," "Danse Africaine"), find a jazz of sobs as much as gaiety, locating (as Shane Vogel has noted) an after-hours, queer, Black Harlem that almost dispelled "white mist."

As with many popular musicians, nothing matched his early stuff, and he struggled—like counterpart **Duke Ellington**—to move from brilliant miniature to longer forms. Recordings caught his **Walt Whitman** cadences and a quaver akin to Allen Ginsberg's. He exegeted the poems through memoirs and correspondence that informed Arnold Rampersad's massive biography and became published volumes. If he never learned jazz, jazz learned him. After he updated to Bird and Dizzy in "Montage of a Dream Deferred" ("Be-Bop boys / Implore Mecca / To achieve / six discs with Decca"), he recorded *The Weary Blues with Langston Hughes*, with music by **Charles Mingus,** and wrote a poem, "African Woman," for Randy Weston's *Uhuru, Afrika!* "Langston was the only black writer writing about us in those days," said Weston. "Jazz as Communication," presented at the Newport Jazz Festival in 1956, valued "Brill Building Blues" and "communicating for money," not to mention rock and roll, while the thorny dozens poem, "Ask Your Mama," took free jazz risks at book length and eventually received Carnegie Hall and Apollo Theater musical adaptations, featuring performers as diverse as opera singer Jessye Norman and hip-hop band the Roots. With late work such as *Negro Music Makers*, the entertainment overview *Black Magic*, and the children's books *First Book of Jazz* and *First Book of Rhythm*, Hughes also branded himself a cherished popularizer.

It's easy to see continuity from Hughes to Kevin Young, the poet, *New Yorker* editor, and Schomburg Center director. A forward by Young rightfully augmented Van Vechten in the 2015 Knopf edition of *Weary Blues*. Young wrote, "Hughes was in fact the first to write poetry in the blues form. He was the first to realize the blues are plural—to see in their complicated irony and earthy tone the potential to present a folk feeling both tragic and comic, one uniquely African American, which is to say, American. The blues made romance modern; modernism borrowed from the blues a new way of saying what it saw: Hughes made the blues his own, and ours too."

BLESSED IMMORTAL, FORGOTTEN SONGWRITER

Carrie Jacobs-Bond, The Roads of Melody*, 1927*

———

The "female **Stephen Foster**," first successful woman songwriter and indie icon for self-publishing, is overdue to reclaim her place in the history of American music—which diminished rapidly after her interment, at eighty-four in 1946, as Hollywood's Forest Lawn Cemetery's second Blessed Immortal. This entry is more predictive than grounded: there is little to draw on beyond Jacobs-Bond's own memoir. But that, for all its vagaries, merits a place: ancestor to **Loretta Lynn**'s *Coal Miner's Daughter* and the strategically emotional works by Dolly Parton et al. that followed.

Which is not to say it did not have precursors, notably two memoirs by nineteenth-century songwriters. George Root's *Story of a Musical Life* recalled performing and teaching in singing schools that dated back to **William Billings**, where being a musician "wasn't reputable, I knew." He was nervous enough about reputation to have published his first songs, inspired by Stephen Foster, under a pseudonym. But he came to embrace "people's song"—not as aesthetically preferable to Schubert, but as an inducement to "crave something higher," and as inspirational: Root's "Battle-Cry of Freedom," aka "Rally

'Round the Flag," was said by a former general to have made Union troops indomitable. The book's most cited passage, however, recalled Henry Russell—a star even before Foster—performing his own compositions, such as "Woodman! Spare that Tree!" These "were exceedingly pathetic, and always made people cry when he sang them. He looked so pitiful and so sympathetic—'he felt every word,' as his listeners would think and say—and yet, when he retired to his dressing room, he was said to have been much amused at the grief of his weeping constituents." Root rebuked Russell, saying good taste meant respecting the emotions you excited.

In turn, Russell's own memoir, when not bemoaning the "chaotic" sounds he heard at age eighty-three, made no bones of having helped a friend use music in "the birth of his sentimental nature." Nor had he qualms about speeding up "Vesper Hymn" to produce the minstrel "Buffalo Girls." And he caricatured both Blacks and provincial Americans, smiling decades later at "the innate drollery of the primitive people with whom I mixed." His self-justification turned on a perennial distinction: "the decay of honest sentiment, and the advance of drivel."

Jacobs-Bond might conceivably have read both books before bringing out her own debut, in 1901, with financial help from a popular American opera singer. *Seven Songs as Unpretentious as the Wild Rose* contained her enduring wedding song, "I Love You Truly"; her setting to music of the eventual standard "Just a Wearyin' for You"; and from her most private parlor, "Shadows," about the unexpected death of her second husband. Beyond songs, there were three poems, homey bromides that punctuated her live appearances: "You say I see the little things / Well yes, I guess I do. / For big things seldom come along / To folks like me, that's true. / And little things are all I have / To come and help me thru." Supporter Elbert Hubbard—an antimodernist whose William Morris–influenced Arts and Crafts group, the Roycroft Shop, inspired Jacobs-Bond's own Bond Shop—had his review in *The Philistine* reprinted: "gentle, spontaneous, and unaffected . . . child-songs."

Research by Phyllis Ruth Bruce and Max Morath helped understand Carrie Jacobs-Bond as both, in Morath's words, "the tough-minded business executive and the dreaming idealist." *Roads of Melody* began in 1895, Jacobs-Bond a widow with a son aged eleven, pursuing a career of necessity and suffering a Chicago poverty that counterbalanced the "fantastic fairy story" to follow. She wrote about hardship as a Republican: "That is the way with the world— if it finds some one really in need, those who have the money are willing to give." Harder to gauge were her attitudes on race: moved by a Blind Tom performance in her youth, she collaborated with Paul Laurence Dunbar on setting lyrics to music and said a servant of hers had been the model for Aunt Jemima. But networks of women were essential, from the bohemian who launched her in Chicago to that opera singer, Jesse Bartlett Davis, and others the text concealed—Governor Yates's wife, President Harding's wife. By the time of her memoir, a category had formed around her: Christopher Reynolds has amassed a database of over sixteen hundred Anglo-American female songwriters working from 1890 to 1930. With her earnings she moved to California. She embraced Hollywood, wrote her third big hit, "The End of a Perfect Day," about a sunset, and cemented a life built around her associations with socialites and celebrities.

One could dismiss Jacobs-Bond as easily as Evelyn Waugh's novel and the later film *The Loved One* did Forest Lawn: as a pile of sentimental claptrap. But a twenty-first-century vantage point notes her self-chosen hyphenated last name. Carrie Jacobs-Bond, like Foster and the nineteenth-century public, was molded by cataclysms, personal and economic: "Without warning the whole world seems to change for me." Like the great women country singers, she used traditionalism with calculation, to pursue art and business on her own terms, taking help where needed and feeling dazzled at all she affected. During World War I, "Perfect Day" served as "White Christmas" would in the next conflict. Jacobs-Bond wrote, "It was then that I felt glad to be a writer of home songs and songs that touch the heart, rather than a great musician, after all." Sentimentality wasn't her weakness: it was her gift and her PR campaign.

TUNE DETECTIVE AND EXPERT EXPLAINER

Sigmund Spaeth, Read 'Em and Weep: The Songs You
Forgot to Remember, *1927*

———

It's hard to be sure which of Spaeth's thirty-plus books to emphasize. America's leading middlebrow music scholar ranged from a Milton and music dissertation to *Barber Shop Ballads and How to Sing Them*, key in the barbershop quartet revival; an *Art of Enjoying Music* that colleges assigned for classical appreciation courses; and—a work for hire more than love, he confessed later—an overview *History of Popular Music in America*, clumped with songs and proceeding year by year. But he was a media figure too, education director of the American Piano Company turned "Tune Detective" of radio and later TV, with a newspaper column called "Music for Everybody" and a marquee sign for a Radio City Music Hall appearance. Spaeth thought people didn't play enough, sing enough; if they couldn't recognize the tune inside the symphony, he'd knock off a book (*Great Symphonies: How to Recognize and Remember Them*) of new lyrics as a mnemonic aid. His open ears closed when rock and roll arrived—"there are limits to human tolerance."

Read 'Em, ditties with basic piano melody and chatty notes, represented his aesthetic contribution if we turn it upside down and value only what he took lightly. "This is not in any sense a scholarly work," Spaeth declared at the onset. "Its chief object is that of entertainment." But that casualness produced tolerance in defining "the folk-song of a highly diversified but easily diverted nation," as when Spaeth wrote of "Only a 'ittle Dirly Dirl'": "Most people have a prejudice against baby-talk songs, but this one is so terrible that everyone is sure to like it." It was, no question, a minstrelsy-informed ecumenicalism: "Get up some dialect, Irish or Dutch," the book's invocation read; "Jokes done in black-face don't have to be much." Parodist Charlie Case, Spaeth wrote, killed himself: "Mixed blood was the chief reason." Spaeth delighted in the punch-line to "Casey Jones," where a mother tells her child not be devastated about a dead conductor father, "Cause you got another papa on the Salt Lake Line." Song note: "It seems there were two Irishmen!"

To Spaeth, the warps of the popular were as modernistic as atonal classical: "modernism and jazz amount to the same thing. Both may be most simply defined as the distortion of the conventional in music." Sometimes he was funnier about it: "in fact, jazz itself, as they once said of Wagner, is not so bad as it sounds. Be thankful at least that it is our folk-music and not our art-music." Until rock and roll, he was sanguine about lesser ditties: "Most of our smutty song texts can be more effectively spoofed than viewed with alarm." The jazz partisans who appeared in the 1930s, the "jitterbugs and hepcats," were no more worth validating than too-serious fans of serious music. He hated, in all forms, what he called the "contempt of the exclusive musical set for anything short of their own standards."

At core, Spaeth derived his sense of music from scores and sheet music; he wasn't sure which was "popular"—that crowd pleaser Beethoven?—and which was "classical"—**Stephen Foster** generations later? The divide, he thought, might have been "practically wiped out." His all-time favorite was George Gershwin, the composer and weaver of jazz, Tin Pan Alley, and symphonics. He never learned to recognize performers as artists: **Louis Armstrong** got two sentences in *History of Popular Music*; **Duke Ellington**'s compositional relationship to Billy Strayhorn, symphonies, and jazz purism received far more.

But he recognized from the start that musical sophistication had little to do with penning lasting tunes; that it was worth saluting **Irving Berlin** for "his unerring grasp of popular taste and his unique ability to satisfy it." After all, Spaeth's celebrity required he pull off the same trick.

POP'S FIRST HISTORY LESSON

Isaac Goldberg, Tin Pan Alley: A Chronicle of the American Popular Music Racket, *1930*

———

Goldberg was well situated to advocate noisy commercial pop as good culture: Harvard-educated scholar of languages; writer for H. L. Mencken's *American Mercury*; author of studies of musical theater's Gilbert and Sullivan, social theorist Havelock Ellis, drama critic George Jean Nathan, and the literature of Brazil; and soon to be George Gershwin's first and most lasting biographer, starting from three articles in *Ladies' Home Journal*. In 1899, he noted, author Rupert Hughes had declared: "To formulate ragtime is to commit synecdoche, to pretend that one tone is the whole gamut, and to pretend that chaos is orderly. The chief law is to be lawless." Goldberg embraced that lawlessness the way Alexander Woollcott recently had **Irving Berlin**. "While our academicians were debating about the qualities of a truly American music, the thing they scorned and unconsciously feared was rising from the musical slums of the nation, from the poundings of the Tin Bohemia." Commercialism was a good governor: "Seeking to capture, for profit, the ear and heart of the American public, these jongleurs were compelled to interpret that public—to speak for it, sing for it, recreate it in terms of its own lingo and tune." Pop was a melting pot of outsiders pandering their way to poetic cacophony. Song pluggers, paying vaudeville acts to sing, were part of the vernacular. Even "denatured products" could still have a true ring. *Tin Pan Alley* gave the products of the sheet music industry—everything from Stephen Foster's southern fantasies to the Hollywood musicals craze—their first synthesis.

Racket is not twenty-first-century reading, especially on race. Goldberg perceived an element of "social criticism" in Black songwriter Ernest Hogan's notorious "All Coons Look Alike to Me" and treated the long night of Sambo stereotype as "our catharsis." His own Jewish take on a very Jewish music business (developed further in *George Gershwin: A Study in American Music* and *The Story of the House of Witmark*, co-authored with the publisher Isidore Witmark) assumed that one oppressed people were akin to another and that what began as mimicry would lead to "understanding and sympathy." The idea was that the "unwittingly modernistic" impulse that lyrically turned dying babies into juicy babes, or "Puritan into Jazzer," would transcend additional prejudices. He revered W. C. Handy's ability to publish the blues without grasping **Louis Armstrong** or Charley Patton's ability to play blues. "What began as Afro-American folksong became transformed into cosmopolitan culture," he wrote.

But the clang of the sentences here still resonates. Goldberg, as he made clear in his Gershwin book, loved "good copy." (And immoderate sound: the opening of "Rhapsody in Blue," he wrote, "with its defiant cachinnation, was a perfect musical parallel to **Walt Whitman**'s 'barbaric yawp.'") This early history was nonetheless situated at the end of a long story. The publishers of 1890s ballyhoo, represented in how-to books by the likes of **Charles Harris**, were being acquired by film studios and radio networks on the cheap. Songwriters like Cole Porter were aiming at "smaller and better audiences." Provocations of minstrelsy, ragtime, and jazz had aged into repertoire. An era was ending, and Goldberg's wry sensibility captured its discount democracy. Music historian **Charles Hamm** has bemoaned, "Few writers were as free from stifling narratives as Goldberg, and his book gave impetus to no school of critical or historical writing on popular music." Perhaps we are ready to appreciate him better now.

ROOTS INTELLECTUAL

Constance Rourke, American Humor: A Study of the
National Character, *1931*

———

While other intellectuals debated whether the nation's young, greedy, democratic spirit allowed for great art, Constance Rourke documented potent Americana. "This book has no quarrel with the American character," she wrote in *American Humor*; "one might as well dispute with some established feature in the natural landscape." For Rourke, overlaps between Davy Crockett almanacs and Henry James's *The American*, Lincoln's mock oratory and the minstrel

"Negro," were obvious—each reworked tropes shared nationwide. Neither folk nor highbrow, this was popular culture. Her first book, *Trumpets of Jubilee*, defended Harriet Beecher Stowe's weepy style ("the unbroken force of that emotion produced depth") and its category: "popularity is a large gauge and a lively symbol . . . registering much that is essential and otherwise obscure in social history."

As documented in Joan Shelley Rubin's biography, Rourke, born in 1885, grew up in the Midwest with a powerful working mother who embraced Dewey's ideas of progressive education. Rourke was taught and employed by Vassar, published a vaudeville article in 1919 in *New Republic*, then became a professional writer. Harcourt, Brace published her books; *Trumpets* was serialized in *Woman's Home Companion*; *Davy Crockett* was optioned by Hollywood. Ecumenical, she divided time at home with her mother in Grand Rapids with culturally engaged visits to New York and London. Versatile, her subjects extended from Gold Rush trouper Lotta Crabtree to an interview book with modernist painter-photographer Charles Sheeler, who "may be said to have discovered, or uncovered, the industrial subject for American art," and such friends of his as William Carlos Williams. Before a fall killed her in 1941, she worked on a multivolume study, posthumously published in part as *The Roots of American Culture*. This challenged the way "'folk' is draped with quaintness and sentiment," viewing "arts as common utility." It gave historical shape to theatricality and symbolic Americas from Indians to early feminists, nationalist pageantry, and travelling companies; found early American music in the "populism" of **William Billings**; presented Shakers as a constructed folk community; urged folklorists to connect changes in form to changes in social fabric; and cited anthropology to defend non-European culture.

American Humor, short and pointed, focused on three persistent figures of fun: the Yankee, the backwoodsman, and the Negro minstrel. The trio, Rourke argued, had differing qualities—taciturn ingenuity, rhapsodic fantasy, politicized travesty—but also many overlaps, feeding into later creations such as urban Mose the Bowery b'hoy. **Walt Whitman**, singing himself and America, was formed from this nexus; so, too, Twain, the fictional Irish bartender Mr. Dooley, and comedian Will Rogers, among others. Rourke wrote nonspecialist sentences and disclaimed "abstract theory," but her research was thorough: it would be sixty years until **T. D. Rice**'s minstrel play "Bone Squash" reappeared in W. T. Lhamon's scholarship.

Long before David Reynolds argued for popular culture "beneath the American Renaissance," Rourke manifested its many influences. Rubin's biography noted her contribution to American Studies, which still regularly awards a Rourke prize. *American Humor* informed both notions of vernacular style developed further by John Kouwenhoven in works like *Made in America* and *The Beer Can by the Highway*, and the myth and symbol school extending from Henry Nash Smith and Leo Marx to **Greil Marcus**'s *Mystery Train*. Rubin also argued that Rourke's faith in tamed wildness, popularized folk, art versions of lore, and American hybridity reflected her own structured freedom: "Aware of the power of fantasy, Rourke turned to a means of dealing with it that was safe—writing." Rourke spoke to Lhamon and Marcus, who both wrote introductions to reissues of *American Humor*, with her sense of the best Americana as "a lawless element, full of surprises." She resonated too with **Albert Murray** and **Ralph Ellison**, who cited the book for defining American culture as racially and regionally blended.

We might question Rourke's belief that for Jews and Blacks, stereotypical humor would lead to respect: "A figure enters as comic; then gradually, when the full light of comedy has been cast upon him, human lineaments begin to appear and he is included in a larger realization." But this, too, was a literary move, the same one that let her write about a range of arts, in a manner that didn't sweat what turned out to be the small stuff—putatively modern taxonomies of expertise, in retrospect blinkered categorization and defeatist Eurocentrism. Rourke knew better, as an unpublished line Rubin cited made clear: "A new and abundant tradition exists in our literature if this can only be extricated from the mass of preconceptions, inferior work, and a widespread belief that our past accomplishment is minor."

JOOK ETHNOGRAPHY, INVENTING
BLACK MUSIC STUDIES

Zora Neale Hurston, Mules and Men*, 1935*

———

It began, half in jest, "I was glad when somebody told me, 'You may go and collect Negro folk-lore.'" Born by race and region to the job, Hurston explained, her perspective was altered by anthropology training; but then she was in a position to alter anthro, too, working with Blacks evasive of white fieldworkers. Other parts she did not explain. Biographer Valerie Boyd documented that the research was funded, beyond academia, by a white patron Hurston called

Godmother, who regulated what she could reveal. Publishers turned down all-folklore manuscripts, such as one discovered generations later—now in print as *Every Tongue Got to Confess*. But *Mules and Men,* inserting her as a protagonist, did get published, becoming the first ethnography of Black culture by an African American, the first key book on music by a woman of color, and a literary gem. If gleeful in the freedoms Hurston claimed as a strategy, *Mules* was cagey, too, in its enactment of what Hurston called "featherbed resistance." She performed a feat of literary magic: an appearing trick that took decades to complete.

The study of Black folk culture by a largely white cohort of scholars and collectors had already generated something of a thick literature, little used today for reasons of its scientism and assumptions about African Americans as a primitive, premodern people. Classical music critic Henry Krehbiel's 1914 *Afro-American Folksongs* supported composer Antonin Dvořák's controversial insistence on the originality of Black communal sounds, but via "scientific observation." Howard Odum, founder of University of North Carolina's sociology department, worked with former student Guy Johnson on the collections *The Negro and His Songs* and *Negro Workaday Songs* in the mid-1920s, characterized by Bruce Jackson as reading "like a Music of the Darkies with a bit of enlightened sociological body English." Jackson was prefacing a reissue of Newman White's *American Negro Folk Songs*, itself viewing racial progress as "ominous" for the music's purity, which depended on "an imitation frustrated by imperfect comprehension." Dorothy Scarborough's *On the Trail of Negro Folk-songs* was no better, a determined pastoral invention even as **W. C. Handy** purveyed blues songs on Tin Pan Alley.

Nor, necessarily, was the Harlem Renaissance's impact a decisive revision. **Alain Locke**, the instigator of New Negro reformulations of Blackness as art and style, saw folk and pop culture as ideally leading to weighty composers: "The real damage of the popular vogue rests in the corruption and misguidance of the few rare talents that might otherwise make heroic and lasting contributions," he wrote, as noted in Jeffrey Stewart's biography. **Langston Hughes**, Hurston's collaborator before their falling out, did value jazz and blues: Hurston wrote him, in a letter Stewart cited: "Negro folk-lore is <u>still</u> in the making, a new kind is crowding out the old." But Hughes, too, was removed from the culture's southern origins, more likely to rework blues lyrics for his own poetic purposes than to document that culture. To Stewart, "Locke's greatest failure of this period was his inability to acknowledge Zora Neale Hurston as the preeminent American scholar of the 1920s." Part of the issue was personal bearing: Locke "could not see past Hurston's crude, unsophisticated, and anti-bourgeois exterior to value her as a powerful anthropological thinker."

Hurston grew up in Eatonville, Florida, an all-Black municipality where her father was a preacher, mayor, and central figure in an oral culture of "woofing": men swapping stories on a general store porch, women bantering back, the same vernacular extending to songs, dance, and sermons. After lost years following her mother's death and father's remarriage, she arrived into the world of Black colleges, the Harlem Renaissance, and then the New Deal, but would return to Eatonville for material and authentication. That porch centered fieldwork in *Mules*; short stories for the Renaissance collections *The New Negro* and *Fire!*; a failed play, *Mule Bone*, written with Hughes; theatrical spectacle (*The Great Day*); essays for academic journals and Nancy Cunard's *Negro*; novels *Jonah's Gourd Vine* and *Their Eyes Were Watching God*; memoir *Dust Tracks on a Road*; musical field recordings; and pioneering documentary film. **James Weldon Johnson**, the Floridian elder she mocked as "passing for colored," was a cultural politician. Hurston, Trudier Harris wrote, was "performing personae": scholar, storyteller, and trickster icon of the folk.

In her day, Hurston delighted and concerned notables from Locke and anthropologist Franz Boas to Hughes, who called her "a perfect book of entertainment in herself." A celebrity of the 1920s, she amassed books in the 1930s, took criticism from Richard Wright and others for insufficient militancy, then faded before her death in 1960. She was revived with the Black Arts movement, which valued her vernacular emphasis, and proto-Black feminism: "there is no book more important to me than this one," Alice Walker wrote of *Their Eyes*. Hazel Carby critiqued the revival by 1990, seeing "tensions arising from Hurston's position as writer in relation to the folk as community that she produces in her writing." More recently, Roshanak Kheshti found new inspiration in Hurston's "sonic infidelity" and attentiveness to the lore in folklore: "those dreams, fictions, and fantasies that emerged postemancipation."

To read, as a popular music obsessive, *Mules and Men* and writing done in the same period by Hurston is to notice other prescience: what registered to Carby as a backward-looking valuing of rural "folk" anticipated how guitarists in country joints would, with R&B and rock and roll, claim the future. For Cunard, Hurston wrote: "Musically speaking, the Jook is the most important place in America. For in its smelly, shoddy confines has been born the secular music known as blues, and on blues has been founded jazz." Long before **Ralph Ellison** or **Albert Murray**, she defined blues as dancing, sex, theater, and race pride: no need for light skin if your singer "could hoist a Jook song from her belly."

What "Characteristics of Negro Expression" itemized, *Mules* located: blues as a living, evolving culture, from "Babe Brown, riding a running-board, guitar

in hand" to Polk County's Ella Wall and her "good boody." Refusing both dialect and smoothed-out transcription, Hurston pursued idiomatic exposition,
urging informants to see their testimony as fun "lying"; "Am'm gointer lie up
a nation," George Thomas said. The results ranged from testimony on how to
properly eat fish at a fish fry to Hurston's own testimony on how she avoided
being stabbed by a woman named Lucy with the help of another named Big
Sweet, the kind of confrontation Tera Hunter would inscribe historically much
later as the essence of black popular culture in Jim Crow America.

Hurston threw in New Orleans hoodoo for good measure at the book's end,
but it hardly mattered. She had caught the life surrounding the blues in words,
song, and imagery as none before her, adding more in 1939 Florida Works
Progress Administration writing found in her Library of America *Folklore*
collection—tales of "Negro Mythical Places" like Diddy-Wah-Diddy, the Sanctified Church as "barbaric thunder poem." As she wrote in *Their Eyes*, when
not treated as mules, her people were "lords of sounds and lesser things." Hurston was their herald—and not shy about it.

WHAT HE PLAYED CAME FIRST

Louis Armstrong, Swing That Music, *1936*

Miles Davis famously made the point that you couldn't play anything on a
horn that fellow trumpeter Louis Armstrong hadn't tried first, "even modern."
This applies equally to the literature of jazz—all of it can be seen as a reckoning
with the man. The genre's first great soloist became pop singing's most vernacular early stylist, then pop culture's most mainstream African American. He refashioned his New Orleans, in the worst years of Jim Crow, into an emblem of
Americana he toured the world with as "Ambassador Satch." The live dates and
recording sessions never ended, along with radio and TV appearances, typed
letters and memoirs, home recordings and art collages.

Books tracking him started with two 1927 releases, *Louis Armstrong's 125
Jazz Breaks for Cornet* and *Louis Armstrong's 50 Hot Choruses for Cornet*, modernist deviations from earlier sheet music collections. They honored a performer, not a composer, part of the work and not the whole, and were transcribed from recordings, without which Armstrong would have remained a

literary description like precursor Buddy Bolden. If breaks, choruses, and the cadenza launching "West End Blues" bolted Armstrong into jazz immortality, his place in American music writing was less instantly audible. *Swing That Music*, his first autobiography, was jazz's first, with an asterisk. Paul Whiteman's had appeared a decade earlier—yet Armstrong's redefinition called his jazz status into question. Not that the *Swing That Music* ghostwriter was much different in tone from Whiteman (or his ghostwriter), turning now-lost material Armstrong delivered into lessons in "the difference between trashy, popular jazz and fine swing music," plus references to Mark Twain and "Ol' Man River." Another mishit took place a decade later, as notebooks Armstrong sent French jazz critic Robert Goffin became Goffin's embellished-for-effect book version of what we'd now call a biopic, *Horn of Plenty*.

Far better was the second autobiography, *Satchmo: My Life in New Orleans*. Covering only his upbringing, it belongs on a shortlist with Benjamin Franklin's account and has similar qualities. Armstrong gave us not only the gritty stuff Goffin liked (bass drum street-parader and feared badman Black Benny was pivotal), but the traits he'd relied upon to transculturate his origins. Yes, his teen mother Mayann was a prostitute, like his first wife, but "she always held her head up." Armstrong was proud of his work ethic: "I was determined to play my horn against all odds and I had to sacrifice a whole lot of pleasure to do so." And equally proud of his play ethic: "I'll probably never be rich, but I will be a fat man." He articulated Black urban folk culture as an inheritance: "any learned musician can read music, but they can't all swing." And his pragmatic "I always kept in the good graces of the grocery man" explained his "I have always loved my white folks" finesse.

Only lightly edited from Armstrong's ellipses and apostrophe-strewn typing (he wrote in jags, as he sang and blew), *Satchmo* deleted material that took the story into Armstrong's arrival in Chicago. Also unpublished in his life was prose that celebrated his discovery—and lifelong use—of marijuana. This all appeared only in 1999, alongside the Goffin notebooks and other private writing, in Joshua Berrett's *Louis Armstrong Companion* and Thomas Brothers's fuller *Louis Armstrong, In His Own Words*. The Brothers volume, almost a third autobiography, gave an end-of-life look at a Jewish family who'd helped him as a boy, with unvarnished takes on Blacks ("We were lazy and *still* are"); whites in New Orleans ("Nigger Hunting Time. Any Nigger. . . . My, my, my, those were the days"); **Jelly Roll Morton** (for claiming he was "No Cullud at all. . . . He was a big Bragadossa. . . . still had to eat in the Kitchen, the same as we Blacks."); and his second wife, Lil Armstrong ("As an improviser—Hmm—terrible"). A 1955 letter to his manager, Joe Glaser, was equally pointed on sex, race, class, and their balance of power if Armstrong was to play on. Academics ruminated on this extended Armstrong literature, first glimpsed only in archives, from William Howland Kenney's "Jazz: A Bibliographical Essay" in the 1980s to Daniel Stein's recent *Music Is My Life: Louis Armstrong, Autobiography, and American Jazz*. Stein saw in the above work, a 1957 Decca LP set, *Satchmo: A Musical Autobiography*, and Armstrong's self-reflecting movie roles and collages/home recordings "a web of autobiographical significances" and "transmedial impulse."

But jazz critics were more integral, constructing a figure whose voice and genius, itemized, secured their voice. An Armstrong chapter and his New Orleans narrative grounded **Frederic Ramsey Jr. and Charles Edward Smith**'s *Jazzmen*, the 1939 critics' collection that first outlined a jazz tradition. Goffin's countryman, Hugues Pannassié, in *The Real Jazz*, repudiated an earlier book for not seeing "most white musicians were inferior to black musicians" and called Armstrong "the greatest of all jazz musicians," despite a recent "decline." **Nat Shapiro and Nat Hentoff**'s oral history of the genre, *Hear Me Talkin' to Ya*, as much counterpart to *Satchmo* as *Jazzmen* was to *Swing That Music*, was named for an Armstrong recording and featured him on 104 of its 410 pages, making his way from New Orleans to Mississippi riverboats, Chicago, and beyond though relegating him to revivalism in the bebop end pages.

A debate within jazz writing, which separated out pop dross, was what to do with Armstrong's singing and mugging. Gunther Schuller said in *Early Jazz* that "West End Blues" had "made quite clear that jazz could never again revert to being solely an entertainment or folk music" but saw later work as a clichéd "labyrinth of commercialism." James Lincoln Collier's biography made Armstrong the victim of an "inferiority complex" whose "unanalytic approach to his craft hampered the development of his music," leading him to choose entertainment over art. Responding to Collier, **Gary Giddins** framed his *Satchmo* around sections on "The Artist as Entertainer" and "The Entertainer as Artist," illuminating pop specifics to match hot solos, using the then unpublished writing to show Armstrong's analytic depth, and declaring: "A jazz aesthetics incapable of embracing Louis Armstrong whole is unworthy of him, and of the American style of music making that he, more than any other individual, engendered." **Will Friedwald**'s books, from *Jazz Singing* to "Stardust" covers in *Stardust Melodies*, itemized Armstrong's jazzing up of American vocals. Terry Teachout's 2009 *Pops* finished the job: a working critic as passionate about Armstrong the singer of "Hello Dolly" and TV personality, force in pop culture, as the trumpet player. Teachout was drawn to, and later developed a play around, what may yet become another Armstrong memoir: his 650 reel-to-reel tapes, often conversations.

Academic Armstrong scholarship, such as **Robert O'Meally**'s two edited collections of new jazz studies (*The Jazz Cadence of American Culture* and *Uptown Conversation*) considered Armstrong apart from aesthetic advocacy: against the other Pops, Whiteman, or in relationship to his Betty Boop cartoon. Krin Gabbard made Armstrong's star text central to his edited collections *Representing Jazz* and *Jazz Among the Discourses*; his study of jazz and film *Jammin' at the Margins*; and his overview of jazz and trumpet, *Hotter Than That*, whose chapter on Armstrong offered the best short introduction to issues his life raised for his art. But the landmark academic work, still in progress, became musicologist Brothers's multivolume biography. *Louis Armstrong's New Orleans* grounded the long-standing view of the performer as a Black vernacular representative in an impressive range of contexts: church, blues, street hustling, ragtime, masculinity. *Louis Armstrong: Master of Modernism* chronicled the masterpiece years, 1922–32, against Black Great Migration, white redefinitions of artistry, and modernity overall. Brothers's close readings of solos and songs accounted for distinct audiences, recordings unleashing art and movies containing it, and melodic styles from blues to solo and paraphrase.

Areas of Armstrong's arc remained underdocumented. Perhaps Brothers would get to Armstrong the television personality, vital for understanding his eternal visibility. Penny Von Eschen's *Satchmo Blows Up the World*, looking at State Department–funded tours by 1950s jazz musicians, hinted at Ambassador Satch's global appeal. An as-yet-unwritten great book on Armstrong would follow shifting Black perspectives: the figure **Ralph Ellison** made iconically central to *Invisible Man*; the **Albert Murray** vision of blues in *Stomping the Blues*; the inspiration to become a white Negro for **Mezz Mezzrow;** and the scorned patriarch of beboppers Gillespie and Davis. Armstrong wrote Goffin, "I was never born to be a Square about anything, no matter what it is." Ellison wrote Murray, in a letter reprinted in *Living with Music*, "Man and mask, sophistication and taste hiding behind clowning and crude manners—the American joke, man."

JAZZ'S ORIGINAL NOVEL

Dorothy Baker, Young Man with a Horn, *1938*

————————

Baker claimed as musical inspiration for this first jazz novel an already iconic white trumpeter; Bix Beiderbecke, dead at twenty-eight in 1931 from drinking—and, if you were in the tribe, the need to suffer too many commercial philistines. There would be a movie version: *Casablanca* director Michael Curtiz, leading lady Lauren Bacall, and piano presence Hoagy Carmichael saturating the screen around Kirk Douglas, stormy but brilliant, like when he'd play Van Gogh a few year later. Terribly romantic: **Gary Giddins**, in an afterword to the novel's reissue, categorized the jazz novel, "especially as produced by white writers," as "associated with a rote cycle of banalities centered on a doomed, misunderstood genius, white or black; a wise black mentor or worshipful white acolyte; competing women (nice and marriageable versus evil and sexy); and friends who try in vain to impede his tragic demise. The hero is usually fixated on hitting a fatal high note, consumes alcohol or drugs, and is given to shuffling alone in the rain."

Young Man with a Horn was that novel, in some ways. Rick Martin, trumpeter, taught by Black musicians, got recruited into a white band led by a Paul Whiteman stand-in during the mid-1920s. Right up front, the novel's narrator (one of those sometimes tough, sometimes winking ones in the vein of Nick Carraway in **F. Scott Fitzgerald**'s *Great Gatsby*) told readers: "It is the story of a number of things—of the gap between the man's musical ability and his ability to fit it to his own life; of the difference between the demands of expression and the demands of life here below; and finally of the difference between good and bad in a native American art form—jazz music. Because there's good in this music and there's bad. There is music that is turned out sweet in hotel ballrooms and there is music that comes right out of the genuine urge and doesn't come for money." Baker set her tale in the era of hot jazz before swing, an anticommercial ideology (as with grunge much later) yet to move from the margins, but the writing and publication took place during that credo's mainstreaming.

She also noticed how jazz functioned as a Trojan horse for an invasion of dissident modernity. The novel replicated, without much outright condemnation, the casual racism and incuriosity of most "stag and unfettered" white collegiate jazz bands, then gave its protagonist a vastly different imaginary—not middle-class Iowan like Bix, but part of the scene on Los Angeles's Central

Avenue that RJ Smith documented later in *The Great Black Way*. Baker was beyond collegiate herself: comparing Rick Martin to Thomas Mann's novelistic protagonist Tonio Kroger; making her female protagonist, Amy North, an aspiring psychiatrist who wrote "white-hot lyrics heavily inspired from Baudelaire," kept reproductions of female nudes by Gaugin, Cezanne, and Matisse in her bedroom because she was attracted to women, and offered impassioned defense of "feminism."

Ralph Berton's *Remembering Bix* usefully revisited 1920s memories with 1970s freedoms; he called Beiderbecke "the first 'cool' jazz man" and offered only scorn for Baker's novel, "a piece of sentimental popular fiction" and "masterpiece of point-missing." (There was scorn to go around in white jazz hipsterland: Jean Pierre Lion, in *Bix*, said Berton's book's "literary conceits overwhelm its historical value.") Yet, from the racial validation sought in his opening Armstrong epigram ("those pretty notes went all through me") to another early gambit ("Like Jesus, Van Gogh, and other gifted outcasts, Bix found the world uninhabitable, and left it, I think, without regrets, dying as he had lived—casually, without ceremony, and of course broke"), it was Berton who could seem corny in retrospect. Still, he captured the "elitist and absolute" early "jazz fraternity," plus, controversially, his brother Gene's sexual "fling" with Bix. Baker's lesbianism, inflecting decades of married life and four novels, Giddins reported, was only part of what she brought to the first jazz novel. Her critic-without-the-byline's sense of the music, of race and class factoring in its manifestations, mattered too. She and her protagonists idealized moments when they could "push out farther than usual," with furtive hope for the future.

INTRODUCING JAZZ CRITICS

Frederic Ramsey Jr. and Charles Edward Smith, eds., Jazzmen, 1939

———

On one page here, experimental musician William Russell—a peer of **John Cage**, volunteer aide to Mahalia Jackson, and later first curator of the jazz archive at Tulane—gave an overview of boogie-woogie piano playing. He veered to a comparison with Balinese gamelan just because, then brought up Romeo Nelson, who ten years prior to the book's publication made "Head Rag Hop," described by Russell as "a masterpiece" with "the spirit of 'Man, I'm gonna ruin this piano.'" He praised boogie-woogie as "the most non-commercial music in the world." He told readers that the record had been reissued by the Hot Record Society (release #8), and where Romeo lived when he recorded. And that when Meade Lux Lewis went searching for him, he found one Romeo Briggs instead. Because, "evidently there's a "Boogie Woogie pianist in almost every house on Chicago's South Side; Briggs's *Detroit Special* was very good."

That was this book: the first generation of jazz critics rather than jazz criticizers, born out of record collecting and forced to invent a new set of standards by which to evaluate popular music. The results were mixed. Too often, they vaunted jazz by setting it apart from the rest of pop, especially Tin Pan Alley, and their attitude toward Black musicians could condescend even when appreciative. (Details are in John Gennari's superb history of jazz criticism, *Blowin' Hot and Cool.*) All the writers were male, all but one white: E. Simms Campbell, a cartoonist for *Esquire*, got a dream interview with songwriter Clarence Williams. Their subject was the blues, and while it was not the version of blues we might recognize—no guitarists, little regional vernacular—here were Black men dialoguing about race, music, and America for a general readership in 1939.

Even while rooting in interviews, discographies, and newly constructed lineages, these writers created a popular music Storyville: jazz myth, like the faded photograph of unrecorded pioneer Buddy Bolden; the multiple invocations, surpassing mentions of **Duke Ellington** even, of Bolden's rediscovered but inconsequential follower Bunk Johnson; the flowery prose conjuring New Orleans rhythms travelling out of a shut-down bordello district to Chicago—where some whites at Austin High got interested—and ultimately New York, eater of jazz souls. The perspectives were not naïve: tourism was noted, with **Otis Ferguson** particularly savvy on mediation. But the authors shut out blurrier pop aspects to pursue an obsession: the spread of a specific way of hearing and playing music, epitomized in the hot jazz solos of Louis Armstrong and lost soul, also white record collector stand-in, Bix Beiderbecke. This artistry required no note reading or classical composition and did not need to be elevated symphonically: Roger Pryor Dodge raged, in a standards-setting overview of jazz criticism, against sacralizing Gershwin's "Rhapsody in Blue." Before it was hip to be cool, the authors of *Jazzmen* were hot.

As Gennari has pointed out, *Jazzmen* was an early opus in what became an extended period of definitional contest: jazz as pop (swing), jazz as art (bebop), and jazz as traditionalism (Dixieland). Jazz histories were legal briefs in the discourse. *Jazzmen* supported the trad camp, with **Rudi Blesh**'s *Shining Trumpets* following its lead in opinions that can now seem bizarre: "**Billie Holiday** is not a real blues singer but merely a smart entertainer"; "Swing, which is not jazz, is a type of European music with transplanted Negroid characteristics." Sidney Finkelstein's *Jazz: A People's Music* was in part a response, criticizing *Jazzmen* for romanticizing southern Black experience to embrace any grassroots variation: "creation of art is a social function . . . music should be made for people to use." Even the "fetish of 'originality,'" Finkelstein thought, was "a product of commercialism." Barry Ulanov's *History of Jazz in America* went still further, stating flatly: "The truth is that there is absolutely no dividing line between swing and jazz." A half-century in, Ulanov had faith that jazz "will out, but not necessarily before large audiences." Almost twenty years after *Jazzmen*, **Marshall Stearns**'s *Story of Jazz* proposed an ecumenical synthesis. Written in a tone of academic popularization rather than fanzine fervor, the book put hot in conversation with the newer cool, to synthesize a range of scholarship three decades in the making across multiple fields—an immense accomplishment. Jazz was ready to be institutionalized.

This was, of course, only a partial blessing, and the legacies of these books varied with changing tastes and use. A young **Nat Hentoff**, inspired by Charles Edward Smith's overviews in *Jazzmen*, written "like a tribal poet-singer," was not seduced to traditionalism. Romanticization produced in him an affinity for musicians' voices that made his jazz oral history, *Hear Me Talkin' to Ya*, a striking contrast to the scholars when excerpted within Stearns. Blesh, hep to **Robert Johnson**'s "Hell Hound on My Trail" in *Shining Trumpets*, reveled in rock and roll for the book's second edition: "The 'funky boys' are not playing it safe. They want to play hot with deep, unabashed feeling; they want to rock and wail." Stearns, by contrast—ecumenical on minstrelsy, blues, and R&B, eager to deploy James Baldwin's notion of Black masking—called those same new sounds "a tasteless version of the real thing." Jazz's white critics were all radical in some ways, challenged by pop in others. Gennari concluded, "each of these works deserves belated recognition for contributing to the study of the lives and cultural practices of American common people." Jazz writing fought to keep the commercial rains away but served best as a leaky umbrella.

PART III

MIDCENTURY ICONS

FIGURE 3.1 Cover of Woody Guthrie, *Bound for Glory*, 1943. Reprint of the first edition, New American Library, 1983. Author's collection.

———

FIGURE 3.2 Cover of Billie Holiday with William Dufty, *Lady Sings the Blues*, 1956. Lancer Books paperback reissue, released while Berry Gordy worked with Diana Ross on the movie version, 1972. Author's collection.

LANCER BOOKS 75-081 95¢

LADY SINGS THE BLUES

BY

BILLIE HOLIDAY

—WITH WILLIAM DUFTY—

"A hard, bitter and unsentimental book, written with brutal honesty and having much to say not only about Billie Holiday, the person but about what it means to be poor and black in America." Gerold Frank, *New York Herald Tribune*

Now being filmed as a major Cinema-Center release

FIGURE 3.3 Cover of Jack
Kerouac, *On the Road*, 1957.
Signet paperback edition, 1958.
Collection of Marissa Moss.

———

FIGURE 3.4 Cover of Américo
Paredes, *"With His Pistol in His
Hands": A Border Ballad*, 1958.
University of Texas Press 1982
edition, to mark the film *The
Ballad of Gregorio Cortez*.
Author's collection.

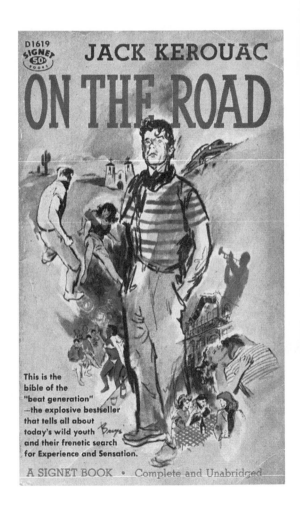

A BORDER BALLAD & ITS HERO by Américo Paredes

Now a Motion Picture, "The Ballad of Gregorio Cortez"

FOLK EMBODIMENT

Woody Guthrie, Bound for Glory, *1943*

In March, 1940, Guthrie blew into New York City from the hinterlands like Charlie Parker did with Kansas City bop. He convinced a Popular Front audience he was the Okie **Walt Whitman** at a *Grapes of Wrath*–themed benefit; recorded an oral history session in DC with **Alan Lomax**; befriended fellow songster and guitar busker Lead Belly; and found in twenty-year-old Pete Seeger his Dizzy Gillespie. He got a contract from major label Victor to make an "album" (still new in 1940) of *Dust Bowl Ballads*, which was done by July, and went back on the road in December, fed up. By 1942, the country was living like he did: dislocated, singing to raise spirits and amp war production. He put that, too, in the 1943 book contracted by E. P. Dutton. His 1944 included a burst of 160 songs for Moe Asch.

This hopped-up Guthrie—typing through the night at friends' apartments to keep the words storming out, conceiving the hootenanny with Seeger to match the bop academy of Parker and Gillespie at Minton's—evolved into the icon of folk, a style and scene destined to oppose Cold War America in a revival that included **Bob Dylan** and shaped rock. That was Guthrie phase two, during which he parented in Brooklyn with a Jewish Martha Graham dancer; slowed by McCarthy and Huntington's disease, he dwindled until dying in 1967. But there'd be a third phase, the archived Guthrie that wife Marjorie and daughter Nora fostered: thousands of lyrics, reams of prose, sex, whimsy and hybridity, exaggerations diseased or ahead of their time. Each phase sang to a notion of literature: folk embodiment, genre struggle, explosion of form.

For the vernacular first, we have *Dust Bowl Ballads* (Steinbeck wrote: "He sings the songs of a people and I suspect that he is, in a way, that people . . . there is nothing sweet about Woody"); the anthem "This Land Is Your Land"; and *Bound for Glory*, which began and ended in a boxcar, "men of all colors bouncing along." This train is bound for glory, this train! Guthrie swiped melodies from the Carter Family, attitude from singing brakeman Jimmie Rodgers, mediated folk wit from Will Rogers, humor in duress from silent films. But his rhetoric looked to Whitman: the cataloging of sorts, the mingling of bodies, the song of nation. His own family's boom and bust dominated the memoir, which marginalized his *Daily Worker* columns and popular culture efforts. Yet each anecdote told: days with the "boomtown rats" of lower Texas, "talking blues" for migrants at an apricot farm, "We Shall Not Be Moved" sung to defend Japanese immigrants. Add to this Guthrie the 1980 biography by Joe Klein, allowed by looser norms to detail harsher family drama, erotic graphomania, and communistic dreams—Woody making sure son Arlo knew the verse in "This Land" that mocked private property.

To know the artist who jumped big high walls—the boundary tester—read books mostly released later. Category reflections dominated the 1965 Robert Shelton collection *Born to Win*, including "Me and the Others"—Whitman, Sandburg, Will Rogers, even Pushkin—and "How to Make Up a Balladsong and Get Away with It." *Pastures of Plenty*, edited in 1990 by Dave Marsh and Harold Lowenthal, linked Guthrie's more pedantic writing (the introduction to Alan Lomax's *Hard Hitting Songs for Hard-Hit People*, for example) to rock. Michael Denning's *Cultural Front* put Guthrie in conversation with other *Grapes* versions and other national troubadours, theorizing the Popular Front's agitated vernacular. **Robert Cantwell**'s *When We Were Good* rooted folk revival norms in Guthrie's performance of identity and anti–show business group with Seeger, the Almanac Singers. Bryan Garman's *A Race of Singers* outlined why "Woody was never 'just plain old Woody'"; Peter La Chapelle's *Proud to Be an Okie* located the radio-host Guthrie from pre-Gotham 1930s California.

Then attention turned to Guthrie the sexual writer, the surrealist, the proto-postmodern pop savant. The album *Mermaid Avenue* and its sequels saw indie artists record Guthrie Archives lyrics unattached to sheet music—song concentrate. Edward Comentale, in *Sweet Air*, viewed Guthrie's ethos of dereliction, pushing beyond a folk audience into a talking blues form, as countercultural pop. Thomas Crow agreed, using art examples, in *The Long March of Pop*. Gustavus Stadler's *Woody Guthrie: An Intimate Life*, made his relationship with Marjorie, erotic writing, and work done as his illness worsened key elements in a full-on revamping. This Guthrie found support in two narrative books released posthumously, *Seeds of Man* and *House of Earth*, not as stirring as *Bound for Glory* but alive with erotic and sclerotic impulses—the glory troubadour telling more complicated stories. As acute interpreter Will Kaufman found while researching *Woody Guthrie, American Radical*, Guthrie wanted, ultimately, "to get my soul known again as the two, both, the sexual maniac, the saint, the sinner, the drinker, the thinker, the queer. The works."

A HACK STORY SOLDIERS TOOK TO WAR

David Ewen, Men of Popular Music, *1944*

————

Received wisdom can be tedious, even misleading: Sophie Tucker did not record a million-selling early version of "St. Louis Blues" for Victor—nor any, no matter how many accounts say so. Nobody was as prone to recapitulation as David Ewen, disgorging tomes on classical and popular music for fifty years. That George Gershwin story you liked the first time came back a dozen more, if you loaded a suitcase with wheels and took his corpus home. The Tucker error is in his 1957 *Panorama of American Music*, a book he condensed into a 1961 *History of Popular Music*, blew up a portion of for 1964's *Life and Death of Tin Pan Alley*—and don't skip *Great Men of American Popular Song*, *The Story of America's Musical Theatre*, or *Songs of America: A Cavalcade of Popular Songs*.

Then again, Ewen began writing at a moment when, for an Austrian Jew whose family had brought him to America, modernity was not necessarily a winning bet. *Hebrew Music*, in 1931, evoked **Walt Whitman** at the start: "I hear a nation singing . . . The nation is Israel, singing as it rebuilds Palestine." This study of Jewish composers ignored **Irving Berlin**, though Ewen did note: "Hebrew music is of the same haunting beauty as Negro Spirituals." A later book, the 1939 *Men and Women Who Make Music*, honored opera and spirituals singer Marian Anderson for her "triumph of genius" over "race prejudice," concluding: "*this*, after all, was America, and not Nazi Germany."

Men of Popular Music, repackaged in a pocket-sized Armed Services Edition for those serving overseas, captured—like "Boogie Woogie Bugle Boy"—a nation putting its modern culture up against the European canon. Ewen enthused: "the ragtime that was born in New Orleans, the blues that Handy crystallized in Memphis, the swing and the boogie-woogie evolved in Chicago—all

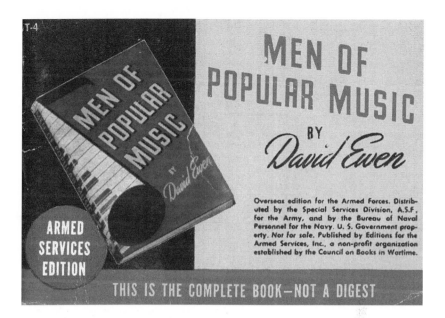

FIGURE 3.5 Cover of David Ewen, *Men of Popular Music*, 1944. This Armed Services Edition was produced to fit into soldiers' packs during the war. Author's collection.

this is so authentically American." His chapter subjects were Armstrong mentor King Oliver; Berlin; **W. C. Handy** and boogie-woogie pianist Meade Lux Lewis; **Duke Ellington;** Paul Whiteman and his arranger Ferde Grofé; Gershwin; Broadway's Jerome Kern, Rodgers and Hart, and Cole Porter; and swing's Benny Goodman and eccentric syncopator Raymond Scott. This emphasized composers more than a canon would now but recognized performers more than, say, **Sigmund Spaeth** had.

Still, if Ewen believed popular music "no longer a stepchild," he hedged: "when I use here such words as great or brilliant or important, the words are not to be read as meaning what they would mean if I used them in a discussion of serious music." He called ragtime "completely unschooled"; Berlin "had enough of ragtime's inherent abandon and animal spirits to give a new pulse and heartbeat to the effete popular music of the day." "St. Louis Blues" was hailed as a masterpiece. Ellington rated for his estimation by conductor Leopold Stokowski. Whiteman got defended from jazz snobs with an Ellington quote: "he gave composers a chance to write new, extended works." Gershwin reigned above all: technically flawed, but too vital to dismiss—concepts Ewen derived from Gershwin himself on jazz: "a very energetic kind of music;

noisy, boisterous, and even vulgar." The triumph of swing was the capper: "the emergence of a brilliant ensemble of white performers (that they were white was also a factor in making their music palatable to a larger audience)."

Thirty years later, having given much of his postwar writing to Broadway musical greats like Richard Rodgers (though still modernist enough to contextualize **John Cage** and Karlheinz Stockhausen in a book on *Composers of Tomorrow's Music*), Ewen resummarized. *All the Years of American Popular Music* was no pocket quickie but a tome that still overvalued "serious" music but registered a new received wisdom. Ragtime was now not unschooled but all Scott Joplin, esteeming his compositional ambitions. Country music deserved respect, like other tributaries unrecognized by ASCAP songwriters. Even as he cut Whiteman and Grofé way back and gave **Louis Armstrong** the space he deserved originally, Ewen kept a Gershwin detail he loved. In 1923, singer Eva Gauthier, in an Aeolian Hall recital that anticipated "Rhapsody in Blue" by a year, had Gershwin back her on piano for four of his songs, on a program that also covered Purcell, Bellini, Schoenberg, and Hindemith. "The jazz numbers stood up amazingly well," period critic Deems Taylor wrote, "not only as entertainment but as music." "I consider this one of the very most important events in American musical history," Carl Van Vechten hyped. Received wisdom shifted. It was, one surmised, the moment Ewen came in.

FROM IMMIGRANT JEW TO RED HOT MAMA

Sophie Tucker, Some of These Days: The Autobiography
of Sophie Tucker, *1945*

———

Circa chapter 9, Tucker—immigrant Russian Jew baby reared into "Last of the Red Hot Mamas" and cabaret royalty—got tossed from the *Ziegfeld Follies* for the vaudeville crime of upstaging the headliner. Mollie Elkins, veteran of the **Bert Williams** and George Walker company but now a stage maid, lifted her up, as Julie LaVerne did Nolie in *Show Boat*. Elkins paid her bills, gave her a yellow lace outfit to court uber-agent William Morris, then came on stage during that comeback performance, where Tucker—a former blackface coon shouter, meaning she sang assaultive songs for the double shock of transgressing race and gender—was introduced with the line, "I thought she was a colored girl at first." Supportive Elkins had no symbolic glove to take off: Tucker described her making the audience howl that night, "toddling as only colored people with their inborn sense of rhythm can." Tucker did help her own cause with range and novelty, "whistling a rhythm break" after a funny bit and a tearjerker. Next, Elkins found Tucker her first hit, Black songwriter Shelton Brooks's "Some of These Days." From that time, only monikers changed. Tucker: "I've lived through coon shouting, ragtime, jazz, swing, the hep-cat, jitterbug, and zoot suit eras."

In genre terms, Tucker's uneven race exchange was rewarded with the ultimate sanction: jazz's eternal indifference. In human terms, we might not be sure about this egotist, who left a young son behind in Hartford with her orthodox parents to pursue a singing career. And in censorship terms, we surely want more in the book of the humor one could read about in Lauren Sklaroff's Tucker biography: "Ernie, if you could learn to fuck we could fire the chauffeur!"—a punchline Bette Midler reused.

But the performer who started her memoir with her folks' twenty-five-cent restaurant as an ideal, then jerked away, like her hot vocal skids, remarking "There's no *oomph* to dishwashing"? That Tucker we need. So much mixed in this account: Yiddish bits, saying of the letter home when she didn't come back (spelling hadn't standardized yet) "I still like its *chutsba*." A running theme, personality. Modernism: she'd haunt the music publishers, like **Irving Berlin**; "Got something new, boys?" Tucker kept cool when customers shouted "give us the fat girl." And like show-biz memoirists back to P. T. Barnum she was full of tips: "make and keep friends"; "never fuss backstage"; "In show business clothes matter."

Recalling the club mogul who courted women and families as vaudeville customers, Tucker wrote: "Maybe Tony Pastor foresaw that this country was going feminist." She, too, foresaw that her legacy would be feminist: sex-positive anthems like "Life Begins at Forty," candor about "the bad effect on my husband of my making more money than he made." Her career, when the book was published, still had two decades to go: television loved her, as did England right through to the **Beatles**. Like peers Berlin, Fanny Brice, Eddie Cantor, and Al Jolson, Tucker's Jewish-American-vaudeville-jazz-populism amounted, as a performative identity, to ethnic Coca-Cola: drinkable any place or time. Ideal, no, but so much oomph.

WHITE NEGRO DRUG DEALER

Mezz Mezzrow and Bernard Wolfe, Really the Blues, *1946*

Most early guides to popular music asserted authority by proximity: a classical expert descended to familiar tunes, a magazine writer put jazz up against movies and comics. This memoir found expertise in what later subcultural scholars taught by **Stuart Hall** termed homologies: the preferences that connected loving a kind of music to loving a kind of person, drug, clothing, or slang. A clarinetist of limited gifts but an ace pot dealer, Mezzrow was Jewish by birth and African American by avocation, giving us the first book by what Norman Mailer a decade later would call "The White Negro." He presented his tale to Wolfe, former secretary to Leon Trotsky, future science fiction novelist and porn magazine contributor. To these men, hip music was a stall in the century's lifestyle market.

You can't read *Really the Blues* for firm history; the internet lets one notice that Blind Lemon Jefferson's "Black Snake Moan," which Mezzrow said he spent a day listening to in 1923 with the leader of the New Orleans Rhythm Kings, was recorded years later. A key early scene is set at a Black nightclub to illustrate the blues color line (Alberta Hunter performed), but two song lyrics Mezzrow offered as evidence were combined by country's blue yodeler, Jimmie Rodgers, into "Sidetrack Blues," complicating that assertion of racial difference. Gayle Wald, analyzing Mezzrow in her book on racial passing, *Crossing the Line,* saw his "voluntary Negro" role as a case study in "the commensurability between certain modes and gestures of transgression and the preservation (or even expansion) of gender and race hierarchies." His Boswell, Wolfe, thought he was full of it and wrote stiff essays in response on "Negrophilia," like "Ecstatic in Blackface," that influenced Frantz Fanon's *Black Skin, White Masks.*

But much like **Jelly Roll Morton**'s equally unreliable Library of Congress oral history recordings with **Alan Lomax**, *Really the Blues* proved prescient on repertoire and behavior. Mezzrow distinguished white or mixed-race jam sessions from all-Black cutting contests, smoking weed from addiction to heroin. He wrote about how the "hipster stays conscious of the fraud of language" and (anticipating **Albert Murray**) the blues as psychological ballast. He tracked **Louis Armstrong** on jukeboxes, not to mention his need for drummer Zutty Singleton. He considered Harlem jive in relationship to southern Black speech. The details mattered. They were Mezzrow's bounty, unlike his stale framing ideas: "the public hears only the bastard version and goes crazy about it, figuring it's the real thing."

Trad if viewed as a jazz fan of 1946, Mezzrow was modernistic if recast as a white rocker before the category existed. He raved about New Orleans pianist Tony Jackson's "bawdyhouse blues," which went "Keep a-knockin' but you can't come in." Since 1958, most have heard those lines as a Little Richard song, just as Mezzrow's love of Louis Armstrong's scatted "Eef, gaff, mmmff" in "Heebie Jeebies" became **Nik Cohn**'s love of "Awopbopaloobop." Mezzrow appreciated Original New Orleans Creole Jazz Band pianist Lil Hardin, mocked by most jazz critics for limited virtuosity, whose "steady four-four rhythm . . . helped rock the band." He gave us the first meaning of punk, the male recipient of another man, in telling of a prison riot sparked by Jim Crow southerners hating that a Black inmate received sexual favors from a white one, valuing what the memoir called "riot-in-music." Mezzrow, as an early jazz hipster, identified with antipop, sexist assumptions: "A guy who's really serious about his music likes to take it straight, without getting it all tangled up with sex." Mezzrow the "mellow" viper and riff rocker prophesied the Beats and white counterculturalists who came next.

COMPOSER OF TONE PARALLELS

Barry Ulanov, Duke Ellington, *1946*

———

This *Metronome* editor and future Columbia English professor's biography of jazz's greatest composer and bandleader—in what turned out to just be midcareer—encapsulated most written since on Sir Duke. Ulanov foregrounded the music's relationship to racism and New Negro resistance, linked Ellington's greatest achievements to work with a core of touring musicians, and supported the maestro's innovations in form, from emotionally multivalent recordings to extended suites presented at Carnegie Hall to the derision of classical and jazz critics. Equally, he raised an eyebrow at how manager Irving Mills and the white-oriented Cotton Club positioned Ellington as a genius beyond dance tunes. He captured the bandleader's key collaborator, Billy Strayhorn, in as close to an open "salon" banter with "roommate" Aaron Bridgers as the 1946 closet allowed. Ulanov heard then-recent "Black, Brown and Beige" as a "tone parallel to the history of the American Negro" and called the band American and democratic. He put on the table a question that would stay unresolved: whether "this gives his work greater sociological meaning than musical, which is the height of praise or the depth of scorn, depending on the aesthetic philosophy." Ulanov, a leading "modernist" jazz critic, supporting bebop over "moldy fig" Dixieland traditionalists, was well positioned; see his colleague Leonard Feather's *Inside Be-Bop* (aka *Inside Jazz*) for broader views of that period, or a chapter in Bernard Gendron's *Between Montmartre and the Mudd Club* for the kerfuffle.

By the time Ellington died in 1974, his cultural position was more residual and traditionalist, however much he'd resisted the category—or any. A trio of books appeared, via English journalist Stanley Dance. Dance's *World of Duke Ellington* brought sociology-of-culture specificity to his idol's combined callings: road life as sonic material, prospecting players, dance numbers defended as much as concert hall works, conversations with virtually every living one-time member of the band. *Music Is My Mistress*, compiled by Dance from hotel pads Ellington filled in spare moments, gave each musician a positive (if barbed) appraisal, while Ellington allowed his poetry ("Music" as a "topless chick" you "like to see shake it" but "never quite make it") and prose poems on subjects as critical as "Categories" to paint and splatter what jazz conservators had rendered "quite scholastic." Ellington recalled rolling a piano on wheels to back Sonny Greer's pop, jazz, dirty, torch, and Jewish songs in late night gigs and then spending the tips on hookers; he credited Mills, whose "roots were always in music publishing. . . . He could feel a song." And he mocked "the music people insisted on calling jazz," more interested in the hybridities of his satiric musical *Jump for Joy* or the Shakespeare-inspired *Such Sweet Thunder*. "The whole world is going oriental," he predicted, "and nobody will be able to retain his identity." Son Mercer Ellington, who best knew his dad acting as his road manager, talked more than Ellington was willing to about romantic partners, business frustrations, and racial challenges in the book he wrote with Dance, *Duke Ellington in Person: An Intimate Memoir*.

Ellington couldn't get away from the jazz era's estimation, evaluated by every leading critic and many others. Peter Gammond's *Duke Ellington: His Life and Music* was an early attempt to compile some of this, but Mark Tucker's *Duke Ellington Reader* was exemplary: more than one hundred pieces, from Abel Green's earliest show-biz reviews and Dave Peyton in the Black press. What emerged was how appraising the work meant appraising appraisal. R. D. Darrell invented Ellington criticism in *Phonograph Monthly Review* and the 1932 essay "Black Beauty": "Ellington has emancipated American popular music from text." Ellington sought greater emancipation: "I am trying to play the natural feelings of a people" and "what is being done by Countee Cullen and others in literature is overdue in our music." Ellington predated jazz, but jazz writers, Tucker showed, tried to steer his choices. They protested suave rather than growling trombonist Lawrence Brown and essentialized hot rhythms, where Ellington wrote in 1933 that he wanted "to describe emotions, moods, and activities which have a wide range" and composed "Mood Indigo" "specifically for microphone transmission." It boiled over as swing peaked, with John Hammond especially vicious on Ellington's "slick, un-negroid musicians." (Eric Porter's *What Is This Thing Called Jazz?* devoted an acute chapter to their battle.) Classical composers, whether positive (Aaron Copland), or quite negative (Paul Bowles on *Black, Brown and Beige*), also imposed. The figure illuminated in Ulanov and Dance's books could be glimpsed in a 1944 *New Yorker* profile, Strayhorn's essay on "The Ellington Effect" for *Down Beat*, a 1955 Senegalese novel excerpt Tucker had translated, and novelist Ralph Ellison summing up his hero's equipoise and wit.

The *Reader*'s archiving stood in for a far greater codification, as the Smithsonian added Ellington's papers. Tucker used them for *Duke Ellington: The Early Years*—acute on the music if dispassionate on extramusical questions. John Hasse, curator of American Music for the National Museum of American History, immersed to produce *Beyond Category: The Life and Genius of Duke Ellington*. It began with testimony from Wynton Marsalis, whose strictures of jazz repertoire honored Ellington's music but not his interest in, say, making a Technicolor *A Drum Is a Woman* spectacle for network TV. By contrast, Hasse drew upon social history by Lewis Erenberg and others, as well as Henry Louis Gates Jr.'s notion of signifying in Black aesthetics; he understood that "his success on the stage has escaped many writers on Ellington, because they have focused single-mindedly on his recordings." This was Ulanov with depth, full-career coverage, and latitude: Strayhorn's sexuality discussed openly, details on Cotton Club chorus girls and gangsters. Harvey Cohen's *Duke Ellington's America* made still more extensive use of the Smithsonian holdings, working with Hasse for an account rich in detail on Ellington's later years and business dealings, but awkward as writing on popular culture.

The next major biography, Terry Teachout's *Duke*, took up a different aspect of Ulanov's account: how Ellington's longtime band members felt betrayed over time, given less authority and cut off from some writing credits. (Brown told him: "I don't consider you a composer. You're a compiler.") To Teachout, admirably, "the politer black musical styles of the period were as 'authentic' as the dance-based working-class music that today's listeners esteem." He was an attentive listener and supple writer, contrasting the wah-wah of Bubber Miley and more speechlike yah-yah of Sam Nanton and developing a theory of Ellington's mosaic structure of composition and issues with pop melody. But in dismissing all of Ellington's political aspirations for music and most of the second half of his career, he became the latest white male writer lecturing Duke Ellington on what to play.

Hints of where writing on Duke Ellington might progress could be found. Brent Hayes Edwards, writing in the **Robert O'Meally** jazz studies collection *Uptown Conversation*, proposed that "the literary is less an *analogy* for Ellington's music than an inherent element in his conception of music itself and a key formal bridge or instigating spur in his compositional process." Ellington, for Edwards (who esteemed *Music Is My Mistress*), conceived his longer works as "parallels," to literature and life. Edwards approvingly cited Graham Lock, who in *Blutopia* had grouped Ellington with Sun Ra and Anthony Braxton to see Ellington's work as futurism and alternative history. Shane Vogel's *Scene of Harlem Cabaret* took up, briefly, the floor shows that spurred Ellington's sense of how to work. Lynn Spigel's *TV By Design* viewed the *Drum Is a Woman* broadcast as part of midcentury middlebrow modernism. Perhaps a new interpretation of Ellington, to finally move past Ulanov, would have to go not just beyond category but beyond music.

JAZZ'S PRECURSOR AS POP AND ART

Rudi Blesh and Harriet Janis, They All Played Ragtime:
The True Story of an American Music, *1950*

———

This collaboration between a traditionalist jazz critic and an art world author-patron turned on how, from Sedalia, Missouri, the opera-obsessed composer Scott Joplin created "classic ragtime," transcending racism and Tin Pan Alley pabulum. Four years later, veteran vaudeville performer Tom Fletcher published *100 Years of the Negro in Show Business*, reducing Joplin to one-hit-wonder status ("Maple Leaf Rag," 1899) and a single paragraph. His hero was Ernest Hogan, whose 1896 "All Coons Look Alike to Me" was a larger hit, popularizing both syncopated rhythms and the coon caricatures that took "Jim Crow" minstrelsy into the actual Jim Crow era. The divide—pinning the essence of a genre versus accepting its breadth—would dominate the literature of ragtime, shorthand for urbanity and new norms.

James Weldon Johnson's 1912 novel *The Autobiography of an Ex-Colored Man* and 1930 study *Black Manhattan* first and forever summoned Fletcher's subject: the ragtime, coon song era of Ike Hines's mixed-race ("black-and-tan") sporting saloon, the Black-run Marshall Hotel, **Bert Williams** and George Walker's revue *In Dahomey*, and James Reese Europe's musicians-for-hire Clef Club. This scene made its leading entertainers too big for their concessions to stereotype to fully dispel the credit given them for racial uplift. **Alan Lomax**'s 1938 oral history with **Jelly Roll Morton**—a master New Orleans musician breaking down ragtime and jazz variants as the ultimate cultural flaneur—informed Blesh and Janis, who put it out on their Circle record label in 1947 ahead of the book, *Mister Jelly Roll*. Ragtime, a dance beat, crossed to sheet music and the society cabaret of white fox-trotter Vernon Castle and his bobbed-hair wife Irene. The post-World War One era, indulging popular culture traditionalism for the first time, recalled it via a combo: *Shuffle Along*, the showy 1921 smash musical by Eubie Blake and Noble Sissle (Truman later campaigned on its "I'm Just Wild about Harry"), and a folk subculture of acute piano players stuck in bordellos.

They All Played Ragtime, which followed Blesh's trad jazz history *Shining Trumpets*, was dedicated to Joplin: "the genius whose spirit, though diluted, was filtered through thousands of cheap songs and vain imitations." It declared the "real story of ragtime is that of a song that came from the people and then got lost." The authors turned Joplin's white, Sedalia-based music publisher, John Stark, into a model for later evocations of Sam Phillips working with **Elvis Presley** at Sun Records: "prophet, champion, and zealot." Yet within the problematic framing, ragtime took on mythic resonance: itinerant performers working the 1893 Chicago World's Fair midway to popularize the sound; avid artists Joplin, James Scott, and white but "thoroughly Negroid" Joseph Lamb; honky-tonks like the Maple Leaf Club. Figures still around were interviewed: Tom Campbell in Missouri, "ragtime kid" acolyte Brun Campbell. Eubie Blake was especially vivid, recalling how Black musicians had to pretend they couldn't read notes. More bohemian than stuffy, the book anticipated blues revivalism, bracketing jazz and pop.

By contrast, *100 Years* welcomed anything musical that boosted business: "True, ragtime has been played in many different styles since it was first brought out, automobiles have also been made in many different styles since they were invented, and they are still automobiles. So whether you call it swing, jump, boogie woogie, syncopation, jazz, or what have you, it is still ragtime, and it is the rhythm that was discovered and introduced by Ernest Hogan in 'All Coons Look Alike To Me,' copyrighted and published by Witmark and Sons in New York City in 1896." Accenting entertainment removed authenticity— Fletcher grumbled at "great brains" denouncing Blacks in blackface—but not judgment: he raved about Aida Walker, "a Florence Mills and Josephine Baker rolled into one." Stride pianist Willie "the Lion" Smith took a similar view in his *Music on My Mind*: "I've played it all, barrel house, ragtime, blues, Dixieland, boogiewoogie, swing, bebop, bop—even the classics." He knew Joplin's widow for her boarding house, an after-hours joint; celebrated getting to play on Mamie Smith and Her Jazz Hounds' genre-dissolving "Crazy Blues." **Duke Ellington**, who dug his style, wrote the introduction.

Ragtimers, after *They All Played Ragtime*, became a tweedy subculture, cheery and innocuous. In 1971, Joplin received a two-volume academic edition, intro by Blesh ("Scott Joplin: Black-American Classicist") and sheet music alongside his finally performed opera *Treemonisha*. Eubie Blake, bigger as an octogenarian, got a coffee-table account (Kimball and Bolcom's *Reminiscing with Sissle and Blake*) and Al Rose biography. Collector-type David Jasen's accounts ranged from a useful survey of Black songwriters to an A–Z coauthored with Trebor Jay Tichenor, declawing ragtime as "a racially ambiguous commodity whose earliest composers had no common racial identity, nor the desire to promote their music under an ethnic banner." Terry Waldo's *This Is Ragtime* was a tranquil survey for folks who'd seen Newman and Redford in *The Sting*, while John Edward Hasse, soon a Smithsonian curator, edited essays for his *Ragtime*, including the backstory of *They All Played Ragtime*. Edward Berlin emerged as the musicologist of this bunch, his *Ragtime* and a Joplin biography (expanded greatly in 2016) correcting *They All Played Ragtime* factually, if cramped conceptually.

A novel, E. L. Doctorow's *Ragtime*, gave a fuller cultural story, with the Coalhouse Walker character a Clef Club member with Joplin dreams; strands connected New Womanhood and dance, immigration and labor, in a pastiche that made ragtime Manhattan something like a postmodern city. Others filled in the details. Lewis Erenberg's *Steppin' Out* brought social history to the cabaret, while Kathy Peiss's *Cheap Amusements* and Nan Enstad's *Ladies of Labor, Girls of Amusement* took up women dancing and consuming. Thomas Riis's *Just Before Jazz* surveyed the **Bert Williams** and George Walker theater milieu. Reid Badger's *A Life in Ragtime* gave a solid biography to James Reese Europe, first to stage Black music at Carnegie Hall in 1912 and musical director for the Castles—themselves profiled in Eve Golden's *Vernon and Irene Castle's Ragtime Revolution*. Tera Hunter's revelatory *To 'Joy My Freedom* found ragtime-era documentation in crime reports on Black Atlanta night-clubs. David Wondrich's *Stomp and Swerve* rooted for "hot" American music of all kinds—ragtime as agitating principle. Tim Brooks's *Lost Sounds* itemized Black recording artists prior to Mamie Smith's 1920 hit "Crazy Blues." Most comprehensively, **Lynn Abbott and Doug Seroff**'s *Out of Sight* compiled reporting on all African American popular music from 1889–95, as ragtime germinated; they proceeded forward with *Ragged but Right* and *The Original Blues*.

But ragtime, as **Ishmael Reed**'s 1972 novel *Mumbo Jumbo* had already insisted, wasn't necessarily meant to be put right: its "Jes Grew" qualities (a phrase taken from James Weldon Johnson) became the focal point of many a theory-drenched cultural studies project on subjectivities. Susan Glenn's *Female Spectacle* put Eva Tanguay, vaudeville shocker and George Walker mistress in *Mumbo*, on the cover to explore "the theatrical roots of modern feminism"; chorus girls received a fine reading. Karen Sotiropoulos's *Staging Race* focused on the "hyperconsciousness" of the likes of Williams and Walker musical director Will Cook, noting period Black critics such as Sylvester Russell. Daphne Brooks's *Bodies in Dissent* used spectacle as a centering device to work on *In Dahomey* and Aida Walker dancing Salome, while Jayna Brown's *Babylon Girls* took up Black chorus performers and the dancing body itself. In a different register, experimental graphic novelist Chris Ware published the *Ragtime Ephemeralist*, an occasional magazine aiming to "provide a dense sense of the whole era," Ware told a reporter; "the more I learn about it, the more fascinated and horrified I become." Those emotions informed *Jimmy Corrigan: The Smartest Kid on Earth* (2000), set in part at the 1893 World's Fair and themed around patriarchy and racism in the White City.

When David Gilbert resumed the study of ragtime proper in his *Product of Our Souls*, Scott Joplin once again became a footnote. If the core subject now was how "black and white Americans alike understood ragtime as a symbol of American urbanity and cosmopolitan U.S. modernity," then Kevin Mumford's work on *Interzones* of early sex districts mattered as much as sheet music tempo. Gilbert focused on Black Manhattan, concerned with the ways that uplift rhetoric precariously coexisted with the mobility of "ragtime identities." James Reese Europe, called "the Martin Luther King of music" in *Reminiscing*, called an enemy of Joplin in Berlin's biography, took center stage. Not for his compositions, but for being the best at "ragging uplift." Blesh and his inheritors hadn't quite grasped what Ernest Hogan never forgot—in Gilbert's words: "social dancing changed the color and sound of popular entertainment."

FIELD RECORDING IN THE LIBRARY OF CONGRESS

Alan Lomax, Mister Jelly Roll: The Fortunes of Jelly Roll Morton,
New Orleans Creole and "Inventor of Jazz," *1950*

———

"It took me four years of rewriting to render his prose on the page so that at times you can almost hear him talking," Alan Lomax remarked in the introduction to the second edition of the book he fashioned out of extended 1938 conversations with Jelly Roll Morton at the Library of Congress. "As far as I know, this was the first recorded biography to be made into a book." Lomax and his father **John Lomax** were renegade folk music collectors already, willing to create composite lyrics if it would attract a public readership. Their fieldwork quickly centered on tape-recording performances, because "what these people had to say and their way of saying it was as good as their songs." Morton, with his New Orleans history in ragtime, jazz, and swing—almost mass culture in 1938—had anything but a folk pedigree: "At that time, jazz was my worst enemy," Lomax said later. But at the recommendation of Alistair Cooke, a fellow traveler in discovering Americana, he met with Morton, then running a bar in Washington, DC. Lomax invited him to record, reminiscing and playing, and was so intoxicated by how Morton spoke that they kept going for months. As Lomax's biographer, John Szwed, wrote: "Despite the grand piano and the concert hall, it was still a field recording session in the Library of Congress."

In some ways, Alan Lomax could not have been more ready. He had seen how not to impose a narrative on a great storytelling songster with his father's treatment of Lead Belly; he had recently traveled to Haiti with **Zora Neale Hurston**, documenting Creole culture in ways he couldn't ultimately pull together. And he had mastered the New Deal cultural apparatus enough to move between cataloging folk material, producing it, and commenting upon it, though he was still in his early twenties. Morton's creole origins, his wanderings (the first story he recorded was cued to "Alabamy Bound"), his nonchalance recounting whorehouses, race riots, and social rhythms from classical gatherings to gay balls, made him a perfect subject for detailed scrutiny. And so did the Popular Front moment. As Michael Denning's *Cultural Front* illustrated, in examples from "Strange Fruit" to *Citizen Kane*, the mandate to make culture progressive created formal intensities, art remixes of the popular, whose implications often took generations to play out.

FIGURE 3.6 Illustration from Alan Lomax, *Mister Jelly Roll*, 1950. Nik Cohn later wrote that the book had steered him to an obsession with music, particularly the "racy line drawings. An octoroon showed off her cleavage in a doorway." Author's collection.

That was the case with this sometime book, sometime box set: released in a botched edition by ragtimers **Rudi Blesh and Harriet Janis** in 1947; affixed to the LP format with jazz correctives for Morton's overblown claims by Martin Williams in 1957; and published as a standalone book in 1950, as Lomax prepared to flee red-baiting America for England. The work was reissued in 1973 as the middlebrow Americana Lomax had turned to, alongside pseudo-academic cantometrics, to escape ideology; then again in the early 1990s, with Lomax protesting how the tap musical *Jelly's Last Jam* distorted Morton's life. As late as the 1990s, Rounder Records was asked to delete the dirtiest bordello material, to prevent political outrage over government-funded culture. A second avenue of inquisition challenged Lomax's valorization of Morton as the bard of the boudoir. The book's non-musical rival as oral history, Theodore

Rosengarten's *All God's Dangers: The Life of Nate Shaw*, looked at a sharecropper with a bourgeois streak and union affiliations; *Mister Jelly Roll* thrived on demimonde sacralization. Perhaps the transcript, provided as a PDF alongside the original recordings when it all finally came out—book attached—in 2005, might now suffice on its own, without Lomax's romantic reconfigurations.

The permanent wink in Morton's voice could never be fully captured in words. But his book-sized contribution remained a challenge for all synthesizers of American popular music. Will our conceptions of its multilayered meanings ever encompass his cosmopolitan ramble? Charles Hersch's *Subversive Sounds: Race and the Birth of Jazz in New Orleans* came the closest for Morton's home turf, determined to concretize "good-time people," Creole/African American cultural exchanges, and signifying across musical lines.

DRAMATIZING BLACKNESS FROM A DISTANCE

Ethel Waters with Charles Samuels, His Eye Is on the Sparrow, *1951*

———

At one point in this pioneering performer's autobiography, a fellow traveler checked out her act—comedian-singer **Bert Williams**: "friends had told him I was a girl-singer with his droll quality." Like Williams, Waters entertained by dramatizing Blackness from a distance, producing work whose immense popularity across race lines led to semantic confusion and disinterest as the twentieth century codified Black vernacular, then a renewed fascination as the twenty-first reconsidered. Donald Bogle's biography, *Heat Wave*, documented Waters from a rough Philadelphia upbringing to success with "St. Louis Blues" and a shimmy, first locally, then in front of Bessie Smith's crowd in Atlanta; then in Harlem; then on the white circuit, with hit records, Broadway and film roles, radio and TV. Bogle noted, too, the same-sex relationships *His Eye* only hinted at. James F. Wilson's *Bulldaggers, Pansies, and Chocolate Babies* and Shane Vogel's *Scene of Harlem Cabaret* brought cultural studies vantages, putting Waters alongside Florence Mills and the character Lulu Belle. Wilson called her starring revues a "continuously shifting parade of racial and sexual identities," with a song like "Hotentot Potentate" creating "a space for surreptitious community-building among gay men." Emily Bernard's *Carl Van Vechten and the Harlem Renaissance* took up Waters's long friendship with the white patron of interracial

New York society, another clue. Scholarship by John Szwed on *Lady Sings the Blues* made clear how Billie Holiday—who hated Waters personally—sought with her own, even more dramatic as-told-to account to equal this one's Book of the Month Club appeal. *His Eye* codified a genre, akin to noir, confessional cabaret, and the thematic LP.

"I never was a child." "I was always an outsider." "By the time I was seven I knew all about sex and life in the raw." It may have been untrue that Waters's mother conceived her after being raped at age twelve; Stephen Bourne's *Ethel Waters* showed otherwise. But the narrative turned on this sentimental framing, from Louise's withheld affections to their full conveyance at the close: "my heart filled up, and my eyes," seeing hands held out to "her unwanted one, whom she had borned so long ago in such great pain and sorrow and humiliation." That back-and-forth was trademark, from vernacular "life in the raw" and hatred of "dictys" feeling "superior to plebeian folks" to uplift via polish and pathos. "I never had that loud approach," she said; her key was "characterizations," even when pushing Fletcher Henderson to play "that chump-chump stuff that real jazz needs." With a diction never dicty, she savored whores, Harlem "drags," and the drug choices of West Indian Johnny.

One of Waters's many crossover moments, from "Stormy Weather" at the Cotton Club to a maid's role as Beulah on 1950s television, was "Supper Time"—an **Irving Berlin** number that preceded "Strange Fruit," about a woman who'd never serve dinner to her lynched husband, sung to that white circuit on Broadway. Waters explained that she sang recalling Macon, when the lynch mob dumped a boy they'd killed in the lobby of the theater she was due to play. She also hailed the producer who fought to keep the number in, taking a canny perspective: "it was the showman in Sam Harris that made him insist, over all opposition, that 'Supper Time,' a fantastic thing in a revue, stay in. It was the emotional impact on an audience that Mr. Harris reveled in. That was his real pay, as it has always been mine." Vogel cited an essay by Harlem Renaissance visionary Rudolph Fisher, "The Caucasian Storms Harlem," that captured some of this vernacular-sentimental mastery. In a raucous Edmond's Cellar, Waters would "stand there with a half-contemptuous nonchalance, and wait. All would become silent at once. Then she'd begin her song."

CENTERING VERNACULAR SONG

Gilbert Chase, America's Music: From the Pilgrims to the Present, *1955*

––––––––––

It was 1955. Elsewhere: Little Richard, Chuck Berry. But in Gilbert Chase's new book, *America's Music*, it was also 1721 and Cotton Mather was complaining about how "singing has degenerated into an odd noise, that has more of what we want a name for, than any Regular Singing in it." Chase challenged readers to revere those quavers and semiquavers. The "Regular Singing" that Mather liked meant proper pitch and time. In response, a repertory of Scottish tunes "provided a firm foundation for the improvisations and embellishments of the folk style." By the 1987 revision, Chase could refer to cultural anthropology, ethnomusicology, and the modern science of folklore for context. And he'd learned about a fun acronym from the period, ARSs, meaning antiregular singers. But in 1955, he gave a history to American noise.

Chase turned a Library of Congress Music Division job—where he took inspiration from the legacy of **Oscar Sonneck**—into media work, writing handbooks for the NBC radio program *Music of the New World*; he adjuncted at Columbia University, where folksy opera composer Douglas Moore commissioned a history. Chase consciously reversed John Tasker Howard's *Our American Music* in his study: "My own approach to America's music is not at all respectable—my bête noir is the genteel tradition, and I take my stand with that." He saluted **Constance Rourke** as inspiration, resurrected Arthur Farwell's *Music in America*, and underlined *vernacular*: "The American musical vernacular has been on the march through all these generations, and even our most academic composers are catching up with it, or being caught up by it."

In this new narrative, the greatest composers picked up on vernacular lineages: deviations in performance, especially African American, that created hybrids—what Chase called "syncretism," drawing on nascent ethnomusicology and anthropology from Richard Waterman and Melville Herskovits. History lagged, so he found Benjamin Franklin discoursing on ballads and demonstrating the sheer Americanicity of the popular: "if you had given it to some country girl in the heart of Massachusetts, who has never heard any other than psalm tunes or 'Chevy Chase,' the 'Children in the Woods,' the 'Spanish Lady,' and such old, simple ditties, but has naturally a good ear, she might more probably have made a pleasing popular tune for you than any of our masters here." Chase credited **Stephen Foster** with merging folk and pop and called blues intonation "an original and unique contribution of the Negro race to

America's music." Charles Ives capped the narrative—the resurrected author of popular-song-quoting symphonies, his second then only recently conducted in its entirety for the first time by Leonard Bernstein.

To champion vernacular origins and compositional refashioning, Chase constructed a problematic version of the substrata of popular work he deplored: "The genteel tradition is characterized by the cult of the fashionable, the worship of the conventional, the emulation of the elegant, the cultivation of the trite and artificial, the indulgence of sentimentality, and the predominance of superficiality. Its musical manifestations are found chiefly in a flood of vocal literature that presumably drew tears or sobs from its original listeners or filled them with chills and thrills in its more dramatic moments, but that in the cold light of the twentieth century seem to us more silly than pathetic, more ludicrous than impressive." Henry Russell, author of "Woodman, Spare That Tree," took a terrible beating; Broadway musicals held little appeal. Much of this was walked back in later editions, as a chapter that turned on a nineteenth-century fad that unleashed female sexuality, the dance move the Grecian Bend, concluded: "Moral: whatever Santayana may have said on the subject, never underestimate the social impact of the 'Genteel Tradition'!"

Chase also had trouble seeing African Americans as more than vernacular contributors. He was sympathetic to the "exuberant vitality" of blackface minstrelsy, feeling "Something genuine did come through." He reductively asserted, "All true Afro-American music is 'hot,' whether it be a spiritual, a work song, a blues, a banjo tune, a piano rag, or a jazz piece." Learning too much, perhaps, from jazz critics at the time, he declared "true minstrels of American music were not those of the stage, but those itinerant Negro singers and players." He contrasted "real jazz" with "slick commercial competition," and worried that **Duke Ellington**—arguably a good fit for his Ivesian model—"succeeded, at the price of turning jazz away from its traditional channels." Once again, Chase reversed himself in later editions, apologizing to Ellington and blaming **Rudi Blesh**'s *Shining Trumpets*, "surely one of the most bigoted books ever written about jazz."

The two subsequent editions of *America's Music*, a 1966 partial update and 1987 full revision, made for fascinating comparison to the original, not unlike the shift in Chase inheritor **Bill Malone**'s *Country Music, U.S.A.* By 1966, much of the rhetoric of fighting for the vernacular had gone away, replaced by joy in the experimentalism of the era: a new last chapter on the 1960s avant-garde. In 1987, an introduction by Chase's successor, **Richard Crawford**, contextualized his contribution and virtually every field of initial study had been fleshed out, from **Dena Epstein**'s work on pre–Civil War Black music and

J. H. Kwabena Nketia on Ghana to **Américo Paredes** on cultural pluralism and *corridos*. Opera in the United States now started with Joplin's *Treemonisha* and ended with Philip Glass's *Satyagraha*. A last chapter swept in all previously omitted: country, soul, folk, and rock. Chase was still Chase: the Residents, avant-gardists playing with the popular, received more attention than the **Beatles**. But America's music was more Chase than ever.

WRITING ABOUT RECORDS

Roland Gelatt, The Fabulous Phonograph: From Tin Foil

to High Fidelity, *1955*

––––––––

Since nearly every music writer—and many musicians—began with records, the subject appeared throughout the songbook literature. But there was a divide between studies of machinery and studies of how songs interacted with those machines. Records marked a split that two terms addressed: acousmatic, meaning sounds one heard but couldn't see; and schizophonia, meaning the displacement of a sound when reproduced. If pop, as music, was a kind of forceful modernization, dissolving the culturally solid into if not air then a sugary beverage, then recording studios were the alchemist's beaker, records the can that we sipped from, and mediated songs the carbonated bubbles. With downloads and streaming, the physical object dissolved too. Or did it?

The first book touching on the subject was by the earliest record producer, Frederick Gaisberg. *The Music Goes Round* recalled when Edison cylinders battled Berliner discs—ten people gathered grinning around a phonograph, listening through ear-tubes—and how the global pursuit of sounds became a cosmopolitan odyssey. "Another and totally strange world of music and people was opened up to me. I was like a drug addict now, ever longing hungrily for newer and stranger fields of travel." Electrical (or electronic) recording, replacing acoustic imprecision in the 1920s, was his technology Mecca; the recording of divas ("lost to posterity if I failed") his musical apex; and racism ("lazy like a carefree darky") his deep scratch in the shellac.

Gelatt's phonograph book, originating in the magazine for stereo obsessives, *Hi Fidelity*, added a third phase: magnetic, aka analog and editable tape recording, the stuff of 45 singles and LPs replacing 78s. *Fabulous* zipped through inventor litigation, nickel machines letting entertainment beat white-collar office dictation, an ultra-collectible Bettini cylinder, and the 1901 moment when, with Eldridge Johnson of Victor Records and its improved talking machine, records came of age. Caruso was the author's ideal—quality producing high sales. Notably, for takes on vinyl versus CDs to come, in this account something was lost when electric recording arrived—the organic nature of acoustic sound, and somehow, too, classical music's centrality. A 1977 update grudgingly accepted the **Beatles**.

As Gelatt added the rack jobber, getting product on store shelves, to his generative study, omnivores replaced snobs, record collections formidable as their book racks. Critics and academics met at the Brooklyn College conference "The Phonograph and Our Musical Life." A **John Cage** performance built on playing vinyl and cassettes fed into a Muzak exec's presentation. Jazz's Martin Williams talked performance on record with rock historian **Charlie Gillett** and blues scholar Bill Ferris. **Charles Hamm** hailed vernacular recording outdoing printed score. The proceedings were edited and published by **H. Wiley Hitchcock**. *The Recording Angel*, Evan Eisenberg's dazzling literary exploration, embraced this same eclecticism but saw clutter and rot, too. Collector fetishes gave him pause: "Records fracture. They are well suited to a society where everyone is off pursuing his own dream." Eisenberg wrote of his campy opera friend from Harvard, Tomas, buying records in Chile, theorized semiseriously how discs "shattered the public architecture of time" and compared heavy metal to a motorcycle accident. With *Repeated Takes*, critic-scholar Michael Chanan brought records fully into postmodernism, embracing Pierre Schaeffer's notion of the acousmatic to capture the recording's "continuous present." Examples ranged from Sartre on the **Sophie Tucker** song "Some of These Days" to Tom Dowd's engineering at Atlantic, the third world "cassette culture" just analyzed by ethnomusicologist Peter Manuel, and of course rap. Friedrich Kittler's *Gramophone, Film, Typewriter* served a trippy blend of lit, scientism, and froth: "*Funkspiel*, VHF tank radio, vocoders, Magnetophones, submarine location technologies, air war radio beams, etc., have released an abuse of army equipment that adapts ear and reaction speeds to World War $n+1$. Radio, the first abuse, leads from World War I to II, rock music, the next one, from II to III." Nick Hornby's record store novel, *High Fidelity*, belonged to this moment of records as pomo lit, taking Eisenberg's questions to heart: "The unhappiest people I know, romantically speaking, are the ones who like pop music the best."

Hornby was a recovering rockist, but others were less self-aware. Andre Millard's *America on Record* assumed that corporate "Empires of Sound" routinized what indie types created. In *Rhythm and Noise*, another ur–baby boomer, Theodore Gracyk, built an argument about "Louie," Big Star, and rock aesthetics as rooted in the record as centering text. How hip-hop related, or didn't, went unexamined. Travis Elborough's notes on the LP, *Vinyl Countdown*, memorialized a span from the first Alex Steinweiss album covers to the arrival of compact discs. Representing Generation X, Greg Milner's *Perfecting Sound Forever* gave undue space to Steve Albini complaining about CD audio, though many appreciated Milner's no-nonsense survey of recording phases and ability to stand apart from claims of digital utopianism.

More sober than Eisenberg or Chanan, an academic cohort took up the ecumenicalism of recordings. William Howland Kenney's *Recorded Music in American Life* brought cultural history specificity to such topics as the first recording artists (Coney Island types), Caruso and "good music" approaches, foreign language records, and the birth of race records and hillbilly categories. The putative topic, cultural memory, registered less than the range of people hearing their identities for the first time. Alexander Weheliye's *Phonographies: Grooves in Sonic Afro-Modernity* made the divide recordings generated exemplary of Afromodernism, using Derrida to help Du Bois speak to DJs and finding in **Ralph Ellison**'s *Invisible Man*, with his basement of Armstrong records, "the crevice made by the audiovisual disjunction engendered by the phonograph." Musicologist Mark Katz used *Capturing Sound* to assess "the phonograph effect" across violin vibrato, jazz, turntable battles, and the ethics of Fatboy Slim samples—there had not been a better overview written.

One lesson of this new literature was that music history reopened if recording culture was viewed as a *Soul Train* line for different cohorts to dance down. Albin Zak's *I Don't Sound Like Nobody* revisited the 1950s with the new prominence of the studio recording—not rock-and-roll nostalgia—as a focus, to generate an intriguing historiographical departure. Edward Comentale's *Sweet Air* saw recording as a modernist abstraction, performers from Charley Patton to Buddy Holly as vernacular modernists, and the deadness of studio space as akin to a painter's canvas. David Grubbs's *Records Ruin the Landscape* used **John Cage**'s aversion to records as a representation to rethink experimental music history. And Michael Denning's *Noise Uprising* looked globally at how 1920s electric recording made vernacular eruptions like tango the sonic roots of postcolonial rebellion.

And finally, a twist: vinyl rebounded, in the literature as much as at retail. Richard Osborne's *Vinyl: A History of the Analogue Record* noted that "digital technologies are not formats at all." Disagreeing, **Jonathan Sterne** published his sound study *MP3: The Meaning of a Format* that same year. But Osborne had a point. The nature of vinyl as material culture was proving pivotal. Amanda Petrusich profiled collectors as if they were performers in *Do Not Sell at Any Price*. Dominik Bartmanski and Ian Woodward's collaboration, also *Vinyl*, carried the story to Europe and linked it to a return to city centers. Paul Winters's *Vinyl Records* drew upon a mix of academic and critical sources to survey "fidelity," from Beatles reissues to retro-rocker Jack White's Third Man Records. Once again, records—technology humanized—demanded a double-sided cultural role.

COLLECTIVE ORAL HISTORY TO DOCUMENT SCENES

Nat Shapiro and Nat Hentoff, eds., Hear Me Talkin' to Ya:
The Story of Jazz as Told by the Men Who Made It, *1955*

———

The *men* who made it? This innovative book, which collated artist interviews into a collective rather than individual "oral history," did feature women. Primarily singers, such as **Billie Holiday** and Anita O'Day, pointing out jazz's gender-skewed focus on instrumental virtuosity rather than singing, composing, producing, or selling music. But also piano players like Lil Hardin and Mary Lou Williams, or scene figures—Fletcher Henderson's widow, Leora. So perhaps there was more to the title. Shapiro and Hentoff, white progressives working at *Down Beat*, consciously challenged jazz fans to think about race, but by eliding questions of gender. Music magazines, traditionally, were sold to advertisers as men's magazines. The behind-the-scenes oral history was a male fantasy of music, allowing the reader to put himself on the bandshell, not to mention backstage.

Hear Me Talkin' to Ya relied on its era's flourishing publications for source material: the continuing legacy of *Jazzmen*; *Down Beat* and *Esquire* coverage; memoirs by **Ethel Waters**, **Jelly Roll Morton**, Hoagy Carmichael, and **Louis Armstrong**; essays by **Duke Ellington**; oft-circulated letters of Bunk Johnson and Stan Getz. It did not challenge jazz's settled myths so much as augment them. Danny Barker, later to cowrite his own memoir, proved a great source on New Orleans, itemizing the picturesque treatment with a list of "Different Types of Joints." **Mezz Mezzrow** repeated the fable of Bessie Smith being turned away at a white hospital. An endless chapter on Bix Beiderbecke (twenty-four pages) found clarinetist Pee Wee Russell declaring "In a sense, Bix was killed by his friends." Carmichael elaborated: "Jazz was dying and the man who was its epitome was dying, too."

But as many magazine editors would learn, the advantage of the oral history was that it made palatable to readers arcana that would be cut from a critic's account. *Hear Me Talkin'* lingered impressively on the ups and downs of the Fletcher Henderson band and Count Basie band, on T-Bone Walker's perspective on twelve-bar blues and Jo Jones learning the art of "dropping bombs" on drums from Walter Page, with material on jamming bop at Minton's and Monroe's that Scott DeVeaux would later use in his social history. That most of these were Black voices was no small thing, though of course Shapiro and Hentoff chose which words to include—an important distinction, favoring stories of racism involving southern police, for example, over stories of the racism of white musicians and publishers.

Hear Me ended its narrative mocking Stan Kenton's art pretensions: "Ours is progressive jazz." Promoter Norman Granz muttered, "Stan read a few books or something." Yet Kenton's concern, "Jazz for a long time was mixed up with pop music," was shared by the editors: they often left out the pop side of jazz, whether Armstrong's crossover vocals or syndicated radio programs. The men's magazine format here created a template that future non-jazz oral histories could easily appropriate. Bunny Berigan might have been leading a big band, but what his trombonist, Ray Conniff, recounted to Shapiro and Hentoff set the tone for every pastiche of a tour diary to follow: "Oh, it was a mad ball. You should've seen those hotel rooms. Ribs, booze, and women all over the place."

Hentoff, a key critic, wrote that because of *Hear Me*, "I expect that my most long-lasting book will be the one that has no words of mine in it." Nevertheless, he served as a bridge figure, between moldy fig and modernist taste, apolitical and Black Power perspectives, and best-of lists and academic studies. For Hentoff, who wrote as much about the politics of race and liberty, jazz musicians were models of iconoclastic expression: in his wife Margot's words, "larger-than-life characters in a novel."

Growing up Jewish in the Irish Boston of Father Coughlin broadcasts and the Depression, Hentoff came to jazz as a teen through a club, the Savoy, that allowed Black performers and white regulars to mingle. *Down Beat* brought him to New York to edit, then fired him for hiring a Black receptionist. He scuffled, writing a non-music column for the *Village Voice* and freelancing in the biz, from liner notes to A&R and production, befriending **Charles Mingus**. There were three coedited books: *Hear Me Talking*, the equally artist-focused *Jazz Makers*, and *Jazz: New Perspectives*, which stressed academic approaches.

All of this went into *The Jazz Life*, which Hentoff called "not technical music criticism but rather an attempt at socio-economic description of the backgrounds of the music and its players." Less precise than Francis Newton (pseudonym of historian Eric Hobsbawm), whose *Jazz Scene* he cited, Hentoff knew more stories, including the central one: younger musicians reacting against what the Modern Jazz Quartet's John Lewis called an "attitude that Negroes were supposed to entertain people." Like sociologist **Howard Becker**, Hentoff saw in jazz mores constructions of deviance that had to be viewed in terms of constructions of normality: "The jazz musician, Negro and white, is generally on the defensive against the day people." He mocked Norman Mailer's view of jazz as orgasm and psychopathic outsiderism, citing James Baldwin and Thelonious Monk by contrast. Hentoff examined "the changes" that remade jazz as serious without always approving of them. He detailed codes of apprenticeship that built careers for new players; contrasted studio sessions by Armstrong (casual) and Davis (months in planning, then edited); and took the "perennially bland" Count Basie, puncher-back Mingus, and norm-shatterer Ornette Coleman for case studies.

A year later, **LeRoi Jones (Amiri Baraka)**'s *Blues People* made *The Jazz Life* seem timid, and Hentoff after that was more of an eminence: welcoming **Bob Dylan** to the Village, testifying for Lenny Bruce, writing shorter pieces that reworked the same musician stories in books such as *Jazz Is*. He had his avuncular place: the kid who cut classes at Boston Latin School for a burlesque parlor, Georgia Southern grinding to a Tricky Sam Nanton homage: "I look into the pit and there, playing that swivel-hipped solo, is my jazz-crazy neighbor, who winks at me."

THE GREATEST JAZZ SINGER'S STAR TEXT

Billie Holiday with William Dufty, Lady Sings the Blues, *1956*

Metabiographer John Szwed, in *Billie Holiday: The Musician and the Myth*, neatly checked off the revered singer's many followings: "jazz fans, feminists, classical musicians, black militants, beats, gays, nightclub sophisticates, political leftists, showbiz insiders, punks, pop stars, each with its own particular image of her." Holiday's musicianship made a bracingly original synthesis of

Louis Armstrong's vernacular expressiveness, the intimacy of microphones and electric recording, and the cultural radicalism of the Popular Front. Yet her imprisonment for heroin, abusive relationships with men, struggles to stay solvent, and death at forty-four left her a challenging icon to celebrate. "I ain't got no legit voice," she told musicians at a taped rehearsal offered as a bonus disc in *The Complete Verve Sessions*—cherished by some for offering her undiluted. Deathbed confidences form another recent portrayal: *Billie Holiday: The Last Interview and Other Conversations*. To critics like Szwed, comfortable with mirrors of mirrors, the multiplicity itself suggested a thesis. Black feminist scholar Farah Jasmine Griffin declared, in *If You Can't Be Free, Be a Mystery*, "there is no getting back to the genuine, 'real' or 'authentic' woman." New jazz studies leader **Robert O'Meally** suggested in *Lady Day* that we see her as a "modernist on fire."

Lady Sings the Blues, published in 1956 and read steadily since, was a strange classic: William Dufty knew her pretty well, but she didn't let him record her talking and much was edited for fear of libel suits. Szwed called it "autobiographical fiction," Griffin "the autobiography of the stage persona." The text seemed overly insistent on Holiday as a drug addict—*The Man with the Golden Arm* had been a best seller. Szwed looked at uncut drafts and found stories about Charles Laughton, Tallulah Bankhead, and others that would have positioned Holiday in a celebrity culture of sexual experimentation. He suggested that Dufty's own *New York Post* writing after Holiday's death be added to future editions, though the most recent instead offered longtime ghostwriter **David Ritz**'s tribute. To Ritz, the book, like Holiday, existed to "express emotion." Line after devastating line signified: touring with Artie Shaw as his first Black singer, Holiday was said to have said "the hills were full of white crackers." *Lady Sings the Blues* marked readers with language of bitches, dikes, and rats, calling a song like "I Cried for You" "my damn meat." Holiday or her persona entered over-the-top situations and reacted with bravado. Jazz and singing were rarely explored: "Give me a song I can feel."

Critical discourse, however, insisted on Holiday's artistry, working changes on her at least tripartite musical legacy: bounding sides for Columbia, star turns and statements in her middle passage, adult jazz and searing shards for Verve and the final LPs. This work was sampled in Leslie Gourse's *Billie Holiday Companion*: an excerpt from John Chilton's biography *Billie's Blues*, which favored the early recording years in kinship with her first advocate, John Hammond; her English champions Max Jones and Leonard Feather, who defined her for cosmopolitans; midcentury American scene stalwarts **Nat Hentoff**, Ralph Gleason, **Whitney Balliett**, John Wilson, and Dan Morganstern; and the subsequent generation's critics revising those views, with **Gary Giddins** acute on the final years as jazz maturity, **Will Friedwald** advocating the pop singing in the middle. There was more in books by each of these white men, who also—as Griffin sharply noted—dominated the BBC documentary by John Jeremy, *The Long Night of Lady Day*.

Alongside tabloid and jazz attention, Holiday enjoyed what critic Francis Davis, in another essay collected by Gourse, called "a sainted second existence in our national imagination . . . a recurring apparition in novels, poems, plays and literary memoirs." Those kept out of white male jazz discourse found recourse in literature. Holiday appeared in *New Yorker* fiction writer Alice Adams's *Listening to Billie* as a muse, stand-in for white women's struggles. She represented queerness, a distorted representation of the night, in Elizabeth Hardwick's fictionalized memoir *Sleepless Nights*; a diva figure stopping gay men's breathing in Frank O'Hara's poem "The Day Lady Died"; an aesthetic puzzle ("oxymoronic qualities") for composer Ned Rorem in his autobiography. Hardwick wrote: "One thing she was ashamed of—or confused by, rather—that she was not sentimental."

Above all, she was taken up by African Americans. She authenticated Malcolm X in his jazz hipster days according to that autobiography; she was the "Dark Lady of the Sonnets" for **Amiri Baraka**, mocking white critical myopia and embodying, as Griffin demonstrated, blues poetry in life but also form. She sang of the dark man of love and abuse, who haunted **Gayl Jones** in her poem "Deep Song" and novel *Corregidora*; she testified to a speculative character in Ntozake Shange's novel *Sassafrass, Cypress and Indigo*. And in an oft-quoted memoir scene, she told Maya Angelou's son that "Strange Fruit" was about "when they take a little nigger like you and snatch off his nuts and shove them down his goddam throat." Apart from books, we might include Diana Ross's role as Holiday in the Motown movie *Lady Sings the Blues*.

If literary treatments exploded the identity questions that tabloids had caricatured and jazz critics tamped down upon, academic studies of Holiday made the music wear her subjectivity and cultural position. In a key book, *Lady Day: The Many Faces of Billie Holiday*, and a documentary of the same name that reversed Jeremy's work by focusing on Black and female commentators, O'Meally drew heavily upon **Albert Murray**'s view of blues as balance, maturity, and the full range of human emotion, not pathological alienation. O'Meally called Holiday "able to invent for herself a shining identity as an artist," not a "pitiable black victim," doing this by "access to the nightworld, which she perceived as the only real alternative to the straight world represented by her mother and family." He embraced *Lady Sings the Blues* as "a dream book, a collection of

Holiday's wishes and lies." And if he viewed the results as jazz, "*To play with and against* is the jazz mode." This was jazz defined not as musical notes but African American expression—the double consciousness Du Bois wrote of in her singing, the blues life training Baraka wrote of in her life choices. Angela Davis concentrated on the politics of Holiday's reworking of white pop form in *Blues Legacies and Black Feminism*. Michael Denning's *Cultural Front* positioned "Strange Fruit" as the Popular Front's merging of swing jazz, left politics, and even tabloids like *PM*. Griffin's *If You Can't Be Free, Be a Mystery*, the culmination, drew on personal memoir and inheritors such as Mary J. Blige more than archival research, to create "an alternative fictional Holiday," interpreted "in a way that empowers us to realize our own potential." Here, the partiality of *Lady Sings the Blues* was contextualized: "Feminist literary critics have taught us women's writing is filled with gaps, silences, ellipses that we must learn to read."

That still left an even more challenging and amorphous Holiday text. "The older girls fuck the younger ones. Sneak 'em candy, talk nice to 'em, and when they catch 'em in bed, they fuck them." This was Mary "Pony" Kane, speaking to Linda Kuehl in a 1994 Donald Clarke biography of Holiday. In the early 1970s, Kuehl interviewed about 150 people, researching a bio she was unable to pull together. After Kuehl killed herself, the material was sold or donated to different writers. Figures like Pony, who knew Holiday at Baltimore's House of Good Shepherd for Colored Girls and Alice Dean's good-time joint, floated through the resulting literature; perhaps the recordings will too, someday—unexpurgated, a variant on the **Jelly Roll Morton** oral history described earlier.

Kuehl's research threatened the new academic synthesis. O'Meally drew modestly on the transcripts, blunting lines like the one I quoted. Biographer Clarke built *Wishing on the Moon* around long passages from Kuehl, making Holiday a masochist aware of her desires, who told pianist Carl Drinkard that she respected one husband because he "could beat her without leaving a mark." Griffin, unwilling to pay for Kuehl's work, condemned Clarke and Gourse's anthology for ending with testimony Kuehl had secured of another accompanist, Jimmy Rowles, tucking in a slatternly Holiday. She recommended, instead, the Kuehl-free Stuart Nicholson biography, *Billie Holiday*, which had excellent archival research on Holiday's emergence, but broke down trying to confront her star text.

We might hope for sexuality studies scholars to weigh in, or wish Kuehl's archive had been a subject of Szwed's recent book—so good on *Lady Sings the Blues* and the complexities of capturing Holiday's musicality, drawing on Gunther Schuller's excellent work in *Swing Jazz* on why transcription couldn't capture her vocals. (Nina Sun Eidsheim, trying to divorce any notion of racial essence from our experience of sound, made the overuse of Holiday's personal life and Black woman's iconicity a major case study in *The Race of Sound*.) Instead, there was *With Billie*, in which Julia Blackburn, the first author allowed tapes rather than transcripts, built a book from Kuehl interviews, one subject at a time. Rowles showed up again: "She had to have a cat that beat the shit out of her three times a week, to keep her happy." And a coda, set at a club in 1942 where Nat Cole played, Buck Clayton, too, and Holiday screamed "You motherfucker! Let 'em have it!" Lester Young sat with a whisky, saying "Isn't that nice! Isn't that nice!" Then he stood and blew the room away. Rowles: "It was really wild! Those that were there will remember!" Fragments and question marks continued to permeate Holiday's literary legacy.

BEAT GENERATION

Jack Kerouac, On the Road, *1957*

The counterculture's founding novel dangled glimpses of its author, called Sal Paradise, inventing a bohemian postwar America with Neal Cassady, called Dean Moriarty. Bop: "somewhere between its Charlie Parker Ornithology period and another period that began with **Miles Davis**." Scene: "rising from the underground, the sordid hipsters of America, a new beat generation." Whiteness: "Sighing like an old Negro cotton picker, I reclined on the bed and smoked . . . They thought I was a Mexican, of course; and in a way I am." Aesthetics: "I like it because it's ugly." Art appreciation: "Blow, man, blow." Therapeutic ideals: "We're trying to communicate with absolute honesty and absolute completeness everything on our minds." Jokes: that last bit continued, "We've had to take benzedrine." Goals: "we had never dared to play music as loud as we wanted." Purged homosexuality left on the typed scroll published fifty years later: "She says she loves his big cock—so does Carolyn—so do I."

Born in 1922, Kerouac wrote until he died in 1969; those he loved wrote, too; piles and piles accumulated, unsiftable as Guided by Voices records. Allen Ginsberg's "Howl" brought the style to poetry and later to rock lyrics. William Burroughs's *Naked Lunch* gave it a steeliness that presaged punk and industrial. Joyce Johnson's *Minor Characters* provided a feminist afterword. Her oldest surviving friend Hettie Jones's *How I Became* recalled marriage across color lines to LeRoi Jones, not yet **Amiri Baraka**, whose *Preface to a Twenty Volume Suicide Note* and *Blues People* stirred similar waters. Diane Di Prima wrote and defined *Revolutionary Letters*, even appearing on the Band's *Last Waltz* finale. Out of it all came what a Library of America collection, edited by Glenn O'Brien, later called *The Cool School*: **Bob Dylan**, for example, and novels by **Ishmael Reed**, Harvey Pekar comix, and the critical prose of **Lester Bangs, Richard Meltzer,** and **Greg Tate**. *On the Road* updated troubadour **Walt Whitman**'s songs of the open road as **Woody Guthrie** had (he and Kerouac don't seem to have met, but that scroll read like talking blues), in this case for the post-Depression consumer boom that shaped an interstate highway system.

Did Kerouac represent subterranean pop or libertarian flight, rebellion or a taste-shifting elite? The Guthrie, swing jazz, Popular Front left of Michael Denning's *Cultural Front* yielded after the war to abstract art, undanceable jazz, and hipsters, then rock and roll beatniks. Some saw inspired hybridity. W. T. Lhamon's *Deliberate Speed* considered *Visions of Cody* Kerouac's most realized statement: "consciousness exceeding its carrying capacity," akin to **Ralph Ellison**, Robert Frank, Chuck Berry, even Wittgenstein. This strand of beat, Lhamon wrote, was redeemed by the bop character's message in Thomas Pynchon's novel *V*: "keep cool, but care." Daniel Belgrad's *The Culture of Spontaneity* called the Kerouac of "Essentials of Spontaneous Prose" a revolt against "corporate liberalism," folding information, kicks, and shame into narrative: "the best writing is always the most painful personal . . . honest, ('ludicrous')," Kerouac wrote. Joel Dinerstein's *The Origins of Cool in Postwar America* based its perspective on Ginsberg's comment "Howl is all 'Lester Leaps In'"—Black jazz from Young's tenor to Parker's alto valorizing rebel resilience—and defended Kerouac, "something of a scapegoat in literary studies," for poems detonating like a bop soloist. But Barbara Ehrenreich's *Hearts of Men* saw Kerouac, the Mailer of "White Negro," the Salinger of Holden Caulfield, and the Hefner of jazz-revering *Playboy* as part of a broader male "flight from commitment." Grace Hale's *A Nation of Outsiders* framed the same continuum around the white middle class seizing the category of outsider. And Leerom Medovoi's *Rebels* theorized "identitarianism" as a sanctioned form of niche capitalism.

A unifying theory of beat literature could begin with Kerouac and Charlie Parker, one of his Buddha figures, called in the, uh, 239th chorus of "Mexico City Blues" a "great creator of forms / That ultimately find expression / In mores and what have you." Former rock critic John Leland's salutary and brief *Why Kerouac Matters* separated the Jack/Sal character in *Road* as a writer, a multiple, from the Neal/Dean id. "This ability to see things in two states at the same time—to see Dean as both myth and rat, or Hollywood as hollow and resonant—is a model for Sal's lessons in storytelling and time. It underlies Kerouac's quest to find Whitman's America in the post-Whitman landscape. Like the book's structure, it employs a jazz way of knowledge, completing a chorus by improvising on it from every angle, with each version contributing to the whole." If Lhamon and others emphasized an electrification of the folk, while Ehrenreich et al. made the issue social abdication, this perspective would see collegiate bohemians and jazz knowledge redefining Americana from frontier to bedroom.

Speculatively, what might a beat-bop American studies overview entail? It would include the still-tortured Charlie Parker literature, from white bohemian and record-store owner Ross Russell's novel (*The Sound*) and biography (*Bird Lives!*) to former *Village Voice* critic Stanley Crouch, a reconstructed antibohemian, laboring decades to profile Parker's upbringing in *Kansas City Lightning*. Gillespie's autobiography, *To Be, or Not . . . to Bop*, Robin Kelley on Thelonious Monk, or **Guthrie Ramsey Jr.** on Bud Powell could further represent the intellectual aspirations of bop musicians. The memoir of a Parker-revering, heroin-addicted white alto player of about the same age as Kerouac, Art Pepper's *Straight Life*, would be in this pantheon, filtered through professor Terry Castle's fellow-white-trash appreciation, "My Heroin Christmas." *On the Road*'s soundtrack, driven by favorites of New York DJ Symphony Sid, would reveal a surprisingly rock-and-roll take on jazz: the manic likes of "The Hunt" and "Gator Tail." But Kerouac's notes in the novel about "what it was to signify" and "world beat" would be cited as prescient, with the final section's scorn for an assimilated **Duke Ellington** proto-jazz studies. The "Reichian orgone accumulator" in the *On the Road* scroll and "vision of a great rucksack revolution" in *Dharma Bums* would link to **Ellen Willis** and **Tom Wolfe**'s counter-countercultures. Room would have to be found for all those references to the self-doubting Melville of *Pierre* and *Confidence Man*, the abundant chat in *Visions of Cody* about component pieces in "the living American melodic symphony that rings in my brain." It might be impossible.

Still, consider the reference points summoned within just a single, recent, minor book, Ann and **Samuel Charters**'s *Brother Souls*, about Kerouac's relationship to John Clellon Holmes. Holmes published the first Beat Generation article and novel (*Go*) in 1952, referencing the Kerouac, Ginsberg, Cassady circle from his own strained marriage. Then came a jazz fiction, *The Horn*, fitting characters modeled on Parker, **Billie Holiday,** and Monk to American Renaissance figures such as Poe, Dickinson, and Melville. The Charters's marriage, dating to a second reading of "Howl" (he divorced somebody else; she arrived as the date of Peter Orlovsky, soon Ginsberg's life partner), was part of this tale.

Ann became a tenured professor and Beat scholar, author of the first Kerouac biography, within a *Rolling Stone* book series, and editor of umpteen compilations. Her bibliography nestled with Sam's blues studies. In *Brother Souls*, they recalled get-togethers with the whole gang in Connecticut. Ginsberg had a fondness for Rabbit Brown, a singer on the 1950s Harry Smith–curated Folkways Anthology of early commercial recordings across the color line. Everybody seemed to have a take on Dostoevsky. Undergrounds, it turned out, needed roots, too.

BORDERLANDS FOLKLORE AND
TRANSNATIONAL IMAGINARIES

Américo Paredes, "With His Pistol in His Hands":
A Border Ballad and Its Hero, *1958*

––––––––––

In one of the great runs by a returning student, Paredes came back from overseas service in 1950 to get his bachelor's, master's, doctorate, teaching position, and even a university press book at University of Texas by 1958. Yet *"With His Pistol,"* the most successful folklore of its era, gained notice slowly. Paredes became respected in his field in the 1960s, an elder for the Chicano movement in the 1970s, and a revered ethnic studies precursor in the 1980s. Then 1990 saw the belated release of *George Washington Gomez*, a novel of the Lower Rio Grande border that this 1915-born child of the Mexican Revolution wrote before World War II. It, an even earlier poem, "The Mexico-Texan," short stories from his enlisted years in Asia, and tales of his border radio show on XERA and short marriage to singer Chelo Silva made him, by his death in 1999, a visionary of what Ramón Saldívar called "the transnational imaginary." This imaginary, turned into *narcocorridos* and other styles of Chicano and Tejano border music, would preoccupy generations of scholarship: migrations of people, music, and methods for telling the tale.

"I am the hand with the death grip / That murders and surprises; / My name is Higinio de Anda / And I have seen Paris." These were lines from a *corrido*, the outlaw-oriented story songs of Mexico and what Paredes termed "Greater Mexico"—over the border in land seized by the United States or beyond that in movements of modernity. The name for the ballad genre derived from the Spanish verb *correr*—to run, to flow like a river. Paredes set out not so much to capture that flow as swell it. He threatened his book's publication by defining Texas Rangers as *rinches*, "Americans armed and mounted and looking for Mexicans to kill." The Rangers offered slaughter or prosecution to border Mexicans like Gregorio Cortez, who in 1901 killed the sheriff who shot his brother, fled, and was only belatedly captured, hence his ballad. Paredes recounted the legend, with details to make "your neck-feathers rise." He dug up court records and pursued historical memory before the concept was codified to trace how Cortez was fit by Borderers into existing myth. He then cast the 1830s to 1930s as a "corrido century" of such figures as landowner Juan Cortina, shooting the Brownsville city marshal in 1859, fighting Confederates, but kept in Mexico City later by the U.S.-accommodating strongman Porfirio Díaz. The dedication hailed Paredes's dad, "who rode a raid or two with Catarino Garza" against Díaz. *"With His Pistol"* conveyed the transculturation of trauma, both Mexican and Greater Mexican, into sung revolutionary spirit. Paredes told Saldívar he'd centered on disparities between antimodern, patriarchal folk respectability and corrido culture's modern (we might say proto-gangsta rap) pleasures.

Subsequently, Don Américo became donnish: editing the *Journal of American Folklore* and directing the University of Texas Center for Intercultural Studies in Folklore and Oral History; translating and contextualizing *Folktales of Mexico*; editing *The Urban Experience and Folk Tradition* and *Toward New Perspectives in Folklore;* and writing *Folklore and Culture on the Texas-Mexican Border* plus a songbooks collection, *A Texas-Mexican Cancionero*. His advocacy of performed folklore, seeing the folk in "special groups" rather than peasants and primitives alone, sat well with the likes of hillbilly-loving folk scholar D. K. Wilgus or African American dozens (street banter) admirer Roger Abrahams. At times bland in print, Paredes intellectually advocated a folklore with teeth. His doctoral student of conjunto, Manuel Peña, liked another line, recalled in *Música Tejana*: "A purely Mexican-American folklore must be sought in the conflict of culture."

That conflict was vividly explored in the creative work Paredes's corrido book subsumed. "The Mexico-Texan," drafted as a high school senior in 1934, used dialect verse ("he no gotta no lan'") with the barbed urbanity of a **Langston Hughes** and a doubled doubleness of Borderer and teen, explored more fully in the posthumous *Cantos de Adolescencia: Songs of Youth (1932–1937)*. Later poetry, published as *Between Two Worlds*, saw in Chicano internationalism the "dream of my young and isolated years" and offered a rooted cosmopolitanism—"With my guitar / In a Tokyo bar." *The Shadow*, a second novel, written in the 1950s blur, ended with an echo of Paredes's favorite, "El corrido del hijo disobediente," the main protagonist riding into flames: "I am Antonio Cuitla, father of all you bad boys." As Saldívar wrote, "In Paredes's literary and journalistic writings, insight into a new configuration of national and ethnic identity was emerging that was neither fixed, immutable, and essential nor simply vague, dispersed, and undecidable."

The masterpiece of this early period, discovered late, was *George Washington Gomez*, reworked autobiography that problematized patriarchy, substituted a wavering assimilationist (Guálinto/George) for Cortez's populist resistance, and put working-class, urban *conjunto* into a crucial scene. Paredes offered "no vision of communal resistance," wrote another superb Paredes scholar, José Limón, "but only leisure-oriented entertainment that fostered unfocused male violence and unregulated female sexuality." The novelist's stand-in, his road not fully taken, knew what music represented: "Guálinto threw his head back and his nostrils widened to the challenge in the music. How sweet it must be to kill what you hate with all your being!"

Paredes's borderlands were augmented by scholars like Peña, whose *Where the Ox Does Not Plow* recalled his family of seasonal cotton pickers; participation in a rock-and-roll sock-hop group that threw in rancheras and corridos, too; musicianship to support César Chavez rallies and Chicano activism; and then transformation encountering Paredes: "With each sentence I read, the shame that had been my burden since I was in grade school was being swept away." With *The Texas-Mexican Conjunto*, then *The Mexican American Orquesta* and *Música Tejana*, Peña connected working-class politics to musical notions of *lo ranchero*, meaning "manliness, self-sufficiency, candor, simplicity, sincerity, and patriotism." Conjunto split on class lines from the snobbier (or *jaitón*) orquesta, though with the Chicano movement, middle-class students claimed vernacular style to ridicule assimilation. Using anthropology, cultural studies, and decades of musical exchange, Peña linked conjunto to blues and honky-tonk country trends. Los Tigres del Norte, the *norteño* group who seized working-class mexicanismo away from conjunto by the 1970s, were in the tradition, playing for newer migrants. Others, like eventual pop star Selena, struggled with a Tejano genre label that presumed regional and blue-collar limits.

Borderlands ballads, and the cultural personas they reworked, proved eternally current: hybridity ideals to postmodernism, resistant networks to neoliberalism critics, divisible into multiple musical and dance styles, borders definable around nation, regions, class, gender, and *Latinidad* itself. Stressing barrios more than borders, with Greater Mexico represented by Los Lobos as end product, Steven Loza surveyed Los Angeles's Mexican American music in *Barrio Rhythms*. As early as 1904, Charles Lummis recorded Mexican folksongs in L.A., publishing *Spanish Songs of Old California* in 1923. The 1930 corrido "El lavaplatos" (The Dishwasher) told a tale of Hollywood disillusionment. Zoot-suit riots during World War II involved a subculture that in L.A. was as much Mexican American as Black. Octavio Paz notably described these *pachuco* youth in *Labyrinth of Solitude*, though Paredes and others took issue with Paz's pessimistic conclusions of cultural sterility. Anthony Macías supplemented Loza, showing pan-Latin identity evolving in Los Angeles ballrooms with *Mexican American Mojo*. Chicano groups in the late 1960s and 1970s merged rock and soul to make movement statements.

Border questions took new forms in the 1990s, with the North American Free Trade Agreement (NAFTA) creating a neoliberal trade zone even as California's Proposition 187 spurred antimigrant policy. As Helena Simonett noted in *Banda: Mexican Life across Borders*, L.A. radio station KLAX topped ratings in 1992 with a "Mexican hillbilly music" given technobanda synth touches for a hats-and-boots crowd with hip-hop connections; now, Los Tigres and others specialized in narcocorridos, using an old form to tell stories of the drug trade. **Elijah Wald**'s *Narcocorridos* made the new subgenre serve a Mexican travelogue, interested in the "raw deal" of industry and media indifference to the biggest category of U.S. Latinx record sales and taking cocaine with musicians in his research. Mark Edberg's *El Narcotraficante* returned to borderlands issues, seeing the trafficker as social bandit and figure of unfettered mobility, mixed on whether to see such mediated pop as truly subaltern. Sydney Hutchinson's *From Quebradita to Duranguense* focused on "transnational dance," applying Peña's concepts of *lo ranchero* style to styles looking back to the zoot suiters, with ethnographies of scenes in Los Angeles and Tucson. Cathy Ragland's *Música Norteña* mapped norteña, "a genre that is not viewed as purely 'Mexican' by the mainstream Mexican music industry." The *mojado*, avoiding capture and attached to neither Mexico nor what Paredes called *afuera*, the places the border crossed, was both norteña's subject and a way of noticing identity complexities: "one must distinguish the Tejano from the Chicano and the Mexican-American from the Mexican national."

As both author and editor, Alejandro Madrid synthesized many of these perspectives, beginning with *Nor-Tec Rifa!* on the Nortec Collective's intersection of EDM and norteña, a middle-class and underground-identified "changing measure of the real under globalization." Tijuana, long a border site for U.S. vacationers seeking exotica, became "third-degree kitsch" in the bohemian Nortec group's repurposing; "local individuals are able to profit from the libidinal economy that places them as exotic or immoral others," Madrid wrote. A collection he coedited with Ignacio Corona, *Postnational Music Identities*, gave a section to U.S.-Mexico border topics, noting precursors: Gloria Anzaldúa figuring borderlands; Nestor Garcia Canclini on hybrid cultures; Homi Bhabha on third spaces and in-betweenness. A later collection, *Transnational Encounters: Music and Performance at the U.S.-Mexico Border*, was more extensive, proliferating styles and theoretical approaches; one section, drawing on **Josh Kun**'s keyword, explored "Trans-Border Cosmopolitan Audiotopias." Limón reflected on Tejano fanship as a collegiate separation from the *banda* of recent immigrants. Simonett looked at post-NAFTA Sinaloa, where cosmopolitan slogans created "victims of a cultural modernity." Madrid's chapter on Black Seminoles singing spirituals evidenced a Blackness that Mexican discourse erased—though the community, frustrated with researchers, stopped singing. Kun stockpiled Tijuanas, Herb Alpert's faux version into other "networked ecologies." Ramon Rivera-Servera's ethnography, "Dancing Reggaeton with Cowboy Boots," started with a gay couple in Phoenix, at a Mexican migrant dance club, grinding to a hit by Puerto Rico's Calle 13.

Diva studies troubled a different border imaginary, opening associations of ranchera country and manliness to feminist and pop practices. Folklorist María Herrera-Sobek's *The Mexican Corrido* itemized and critiqued archetypal roles played by women in the songs. Yolanda Broyles-González's *Lydia Mendoza's Life in Music*, an as-told-to memoir with added analysis, captured the signature figure of San Antonio's music scene, from "Mal Hombre" in the 1930s and onward for decades. Deborah Paredez's *Selenidad*, a product of cultural studies, looked at the mourning for Selena after her murder in 1995 as charged interstices: Selena's use of disco as a Spanglish, not fully crossover move more akin to Elvis than Madonna; the 1990s Latinx pop boom that left out most Tejano figures; a hands-on populace kept from retouching a monument built in Corpus Christi; queer repurposing as a Chicano notion, *rasquachismo*, akin to the *chusmeria* José Esteban Muñoz found in Cuban queerings. As a summation, Deborah Vargas's *Dissonant Divas* bookended Mendoza and Selena, considering overlooked figures in between them: "Rose of Texas" Rosita Fernandez, a San Antonio cultural ambassador literalized with a bridge named after her on the Riverwalk; Chelo Silva, symbol of all that her ex, Paredes, left out of his masculinist framings, as she used the supposedly *jaitón* bolero for populist ends and became an elder with teeth; Eva Garza and South-South borders between Texas and Cuba.

With borders proliferating, at least as songs in motion and cultural imaginaries for groundbreaking scholars, a rejoinder became inevitable: what about the actual people trying to cross, for whom a flow or corrido was much more labored and dangerous? Dolores Inés Casillas's *Sounds of Belonging* offered one kind of reworking, concentrating on the rising category of Spanish-language radio—itself dating to border stations in the 1920s and 1930s—to focus on listeners and DJs creating a Greater Mexico together, culminating in the massive public protest marches of 2006. Alex Chavez's *Sounds of Crossing* then went further, using ethnographies of yet another border style, *huapango arribeño*, to think about how sound claimed—rather than transcended—space. He contrasted transnational music movements, of the sort Madrid and his cohort quantified, with a racialized politics of illegality, especially questioning commercialized pop: "popular culture is less crucial to the issue than the vernacular and the everyday." The descriptions of a multihour *topada* performance, two ensembles facing each other with sound and *décima* poetry, could be lively: "Don't you go to sleep, bitch, they're about to play in A major." Verses he captured, "utopian glimpses of life beyond the language spaces of austerity," were wondrous: like missives from **Nathaniel Mackey** avatars. But his mandate kept the contemporary migrant in mind, as even Paredes had failed to do. Theory required he identify an "alternative biopolitics"; musicianship put him inside events that featured a starker language of performance: "I CROSS MOUNTAINS AS A WETBACK."

NEW YORKER CRITIC OF A GENRE
BECOMING MIDDLEBROW

Whitney Balliett, The Sound of Surprise: 46 Pieces on Jazz, *1959*

———

He was hired out of Phillips Exeter Academy and Cornell as a utility player by the *New Yorker,* which recognized its own in his clausal respirations. Appointing him jazz critic, his post for over four decades, was editor William Shawn, a fine Fats Waller–type pianist, he thought—worth quoting on Benny Goodman at Carnegie Hall in 1938. Balliett understood that the scandal cabaret of the Harlem Renaissance had by the latter 1950s become a middlebrow staple. Norman Granz, running Jazz at the Philharmonic and a record label with his "bullying eyebrows," oversaw a multimillion-dollar jazz business, but the results were too often "luxurious wastes," not unlike the Newport Jazz Festival's "bulging, General Motors proportions." Armstrong, subsidized by the State Department, had "made a spectacle of himself around the world." Stan Kenton's self-proclaimed "progressive jazz" was really "a self-conscious music that was caught—strident and humorless—somewhere between the pseudo-classical, jazz, and popular music." The coiner of the "sound of surprise" tag had read Bernard Rosenberg and David Manning White's *Mass Culture* takedown.

Balliett coolly valued how books by the likes of Marshall Stearns were supplanting the "hot, gassy prose" of earlier jazz writer-collectors, but revisiting *Sound* in his *Collected Works* confessed to some vapor of his own. Cecil Taylor, "brilliant, uncompromising" then, had "not become a revolutionary force." The sides of austerely avant Jimmy Giuffre "now seem pallid and a little cute." Where the critic excelled, however, was not just in what his own later critics, those he called "the musicology boys," viewed as imprecise metaphors and attention-grabbing description—"Thelonious Monk, who approaches a keyboard as if it had teeth and he were a dentist." Rather, Balliett's use of literary devices attuned him to extramusical impulses in others, pushing back against jazz's tendency, as it canonized itself, to disregard the popular and fetishize the recorded text. For example, he found Horace Silver's worthy hard bop guilty of "rigid monotony," but went all in on Charles Mingus for writerly lyricism and "unruly urgency," unlike contemporaries who "play as if at chess." And when he romanticized a player, it was more likely to be Big Sid Catlett, Armstrong's favorite drummer in the postwar All-Star years, than Ella Fitzgerald or Gunther Schuller, whose erudition he mistrusted. Ignoring the schism bebop represented, Balliett's jazz was an urbane folk of classical longevity.

As the years went by and jazz for a time reradicalized, Balliett waited, preferring James Brown at Newport to Coltrane in full squall. He didn't like to see race foregrounded, scorning **Albert Murray**'s *Stomping the Blues,* and sexuality escaped him, but he eagerly featured Blacks and women in his writing, esteeming **Jelly Roll Morton**'s voice alongside Dorothy Donegan's temperament. Not long after *Sound of Surprise*, Balliett put his *New Yorker* sentences to a second task, "portraits in jazz," collected in *American Musicians II* and the second *American Singers* edition. These pieces emphasized, with long quotations, the voices of performers and their familiars. They told more about the music than a review could, and most about the musician's path, from training to occasionally interrupted retirement. (Roy Eldridge kept a card from his wife, "How to Know You're Getting Older," as in "Your back goes out more than you do.") Songwriter, author, and oddball **Alec Wilder** (a Joseph Mitchell character if ever there was one) got an indelible portrait and frequent cameos. Balliett became part of jazz's pension plan; recognition's safety net. "It is silly to argue that art progresses," he once wrote. "The best thing that ever happened to jazz is the recording machine." He was happy to function as one.

PART IV

VERNACULAR COUNTERCULTURE

FIGURE 4.1 Cover
of LeRoi Jones (Amiri
Baraka), *Blues People*, 1963.
Harper Perennial reissue,
1999. Author's collection.

————

FIGURE 4.2 Cover of Tom
Wolfe, *The Kandy-Kolored
Tangerine-Flake Streamline
Baby*, 1965. Pocket Books,
1970 edition. Collection of
Robert Fink.

75¢

75135

the Kandy-Kolored Tangerine-Flake Streamline Baby by Tom Wolfe→

FIGURE 4.3 Cover of Bill C. Malone, *Country Music, U.S.A.*, 1968. In style, this first edition paid homage to the graphics in Harry Smith's anthology of commercial folk music for Folkways. Author's collection.

FIGURE 4.4 Cover of Greil Marcus, *Mystery Train*, 1975. Revised and expanded edition, Dutton, 1982. The book's discography section would outgrow its original contents over multiple editions. Author's collection.

NEW EDITION, REVISED AND EXPANDED

MYSTERY TRAIN

Images of America in Rock 'n' Roll Music

GREIL MARCUS

"PROBABLY THE BEST BOOK EVER WRITTEN
ABOUT ROCK" – *ROLLING STONE*

BLUES REVIVALISTS

Samuel Charters, The Country Blues, *1959; Paul Oliver,* Blues Fell This Morning: The Meaning of the Blues, *1960*

––––––––

With *Country Blues* and *Blues Fell This Morning,* the music of **Robert Johnson** and Mississippi John Hurt belatedly found white advocates with some of the clout of jazz cognoscenti—cultural forces who'd resurrect performers after decades, produce reissue albums, and provide the boomer generation a historical arc different from jazz's New Orleans cradle. The two authors were opposites and rivals. Neither claimed to speak for Black experience, as **LeRoi Jones (Amiri Baraka)**'s *Blues People* soon would. And neither was as savvy about contemporary sounds as **Charles Keil**'s mid-decade *Urban Blues.* But their long bodies of work were more ecumenical than most who followed, and the contrast was instructive—Charters a bohemian with literary aspirations, Oliver much more categorical and academic.

With *Country Blues,* Charters hoped to stir people to find bluesmen before they died and embody liberalism in a conservative decade: "If my books from this time seem romantic it's because I tried to make them romantic." His narrative started like a dry run for **Greil Marcus**, in "a poor, shabby room in the colored section of Houston," where "a thin, worn man sat holding a guitar." The man was Lightnin' Hopkins, about to sing "Ain't No More Cane on the Brazos," teaching **Bob Dylan** and the Band. Charters, unlike Marcus and other rock critics later, didn't just observe: he recorded the session and wrote liner notes for the Folkways LP that grew into his longer volume. Elsewhere, he recounted Fanny Kemble's plantation listening in the 1830s, Newman White's lyrics collecting in 1904 Auburn, **Bert Williams**'s business cronies and Mayo

Williams's A&R work with Paramount. He told folkies, pointedly: "The finest body of ethnic music collected in the South was that collected by the commercial recording directors in the South in the late 1920s." And though his intent was to follow Black listener taste, he made an exception for Johnson, noticing how whites goggled at his "sullen and brooding" persona even before the *King of the Delta Blues Singers* LP appeared. Charters was no purist: the "blues mafia" of collectors responded with *Really! The Country Blues*, an anthology designed to point out proper genre taste. He esteemed Big Bill Broonzy's popularizations, wrote about **Elvis Presley** with rare balance for the time, and urged white fogies to go to Black record stores and discover "a strong, vital current of the blues singing that has continued into many of the modern records."

Almost fifty years later, in his collection *Walking a Blues Road*, Charters recalled growing up in Sacramento, where a pal was Russ Solomon, soon to found the temple of omnivorous selection, Tower Records. Charters stocked Tower bins in the world's cultural imaginary: his no less revisionist book *Jazz* presented *A History of the New York Scene*, often spurned as a dilution, as instead a changing space of modernism and popularization. His wife Ann, a Columbia PhD and Beats scholar (thanked in *Country Blues* for having "taken time from her own research to discuss the manuscript"), took photos—highlighted much later in *Blues Faces*—that treated performers as charismatic artists, not social documents. *The Poetry of the Blues* saluted Ida Cox, who "insisted on the same freedom," sexually, as men; *The Bluesmen*, more Charley Patton and Delta focused, resisted romanticization enough to appreciate Johnson for his recording artistry. *The Legacy of the Blues*, subtitled *An Informal Study*, profiled twelve artists. *Sweet as the Showers of Rain* followed *Bluesmen*'s Mississippi and Texas story into the cities of Memphis and Atlanta, the prose still a touch too much: "Furry Lewis is a small, gentle man who spent most of his life sweeping the streets of Memphis."

Oliver, meanwhile, an architect in his paid life, found structures to overcome his obstacles. Yes, he was a Brit who'd never been to the United States, but *Blues Fell* mined U.K. record collectors to survey lyrical themes—migration away from sharecropping, Jim Crow, romantic battles. This was protoacademic scholarship, and Oliver easily affiliated university work in a 1990 second edition. His *Conversation with the Blues*, the result of a U.S. interview trip partially funded by the State Department, put quotes from musicians in separate short topical blocks, treating each as a specimen on a museum wall—the effusive Victoria Spivey resisted that, recounting her teen record "Black Snake." *Screening the Blues* turned thematics into sport, with more than a hundred pages of "Blue blues"—**Jelly Roll Morton** sexually unexpurgated alongside Lucille

Bogan. *The Story of the Blues* sought to give rockers an overview, though a generalizing Oliver overwrote worse than Charters had: "Blues is the wail of the forsaken." Oliver was better as a specialist, overseeing a series of blues paperbacks that included his own *Savannah Syncopators*, an argument for griots from Senegal, Gambia, Mali, and Niger affecting blues more than drummers from other regions of Africa.

Charters went to Africa for griots too, in *The Roots of the Blues*, ignoring Oliver's work. Their differences were basic. Charters wrote trying to find traces of an experience, traveler more than scholar. He'd put music into impressionistic creative fictions and memoirs such as *Jelly Roll Morton's Last Night at the Jungle Inn, Elvis Presley Calls His Mother after the Ed Sullivan Show*, and best, *The Day Is So Long and the Wages So Small*, on a summer in early days with Ann recording Joseph Spence—the couple a new generation telling more formally dressed white cruise boaters that "we had had an experience in the Bahamas that they had missed." Burned out by the sixties, they spent decades in Sweden—his book on that country's fiddlers is not available in English. Returning to New Orleans, site of his pre-blues jazz writing, after Hurricane Katrina, he embraced the repertoire tesseracted on Frenchman Street, setting off a final burst of books: *New Orleans: Playing a Jazz Chorus*, an avuncular ethnography; *A Trumpet Around the Corner*, updating the indexical earlier *Jazz: New Orleans* and thin on scholarship, if rich in Jelly Roll Morton stories. *A Language of Song* surveyed the African diaspora; at one point, Joseph Lamb, who'd known Scott Joplin, came bursting into the Charters' Brooklyn flat to tell his story, a 1959 anecdote published in 2009, connecting nineteenth to twenty-first century. That set the still-political Charters up to discuss a Joplin festival held in a whites-only neighborhood. *Songs of Sorrow* looked back to his and Ann's spiritual ancestor, **Lucy McKim Garrison**.

Oliver aligned himself with collectors and popular music studies academia. *Blues Off the Record* put his personal history into the narrative: farm work alongside American soldiers in 1942, a segregated few digging a trench: "'they're singing a *blues*,' Stan hissed at me." He hinted at a failed study of Texas blues with collector Mack McCormick: "The material we amassed reached Titanic proportions, and unfortunately the work met its own iceberg." (Alan Govenar compiled a version after both men's deaths, *The Blues Come to Texas*.) And he complained, well in advance of **Elijah Wald** and Marybeth Hamilton, that "we have imposed upon blues a rigidity of definition which the singers and musicians themselves didn't share," including the possibility that the blues had spread as much from city to country as the reverse. His corresponding study, *Songsters and Saints*, went looking for new narratives, making race records overall—religious, pop-secular, dancing, coon song, not just blues records—the focus of another thematic compendium. A couple of decades later, invited to give the **Alain Locke** lectures by Harvard, he produced one final parsing, *Barrelhouse Blues*, still seeking the origins of what he now called "proto-blues." His acknowledgments, characteristically, centered on Robert Dixon and John Godrich's *Blues and Gospel Records* (first published, at Oliver's suggestion, in 1964, up to some twenty thousand different items by its fourth edition in 1997, some just names on a ledger), and Austria's Johnny Parth, of Document Records, "whose self-directed mission was to make available on record all the items listed in the discography."

BRITPOP IN FICTION

Colin MacInnes, Absolute Beginners, *1959*

———

As George Melly, no slouch, put it in *Revolt into Style*, "The first adult to recognize the significance of pop and to make an attempt to formulate his conclusions was not only outside the pop world but well outside the teenage age-bracket, too. He was the novelist and critic, Colin MacInnes." These were both English writers, yet the echo back to America of Melly's next point was vital: "what MacInnes realized was that pop was not simply an empty pseudo-American sub-music but that it was also the banner of a new class."

MacInnes, born in 1914, swung many ways: a white jazz fan who referred to the "Negro period" of his (ambiguous) sex life in a letter reprinted in the collection *Absolute MacInnes*; an interpreter of teen pop Britain for Stuart Hall at *New Left Review*, while publishing a study of music-hall antiquities (*Sweet Saturday Night*) during peak hippiedom. His "London Trilogy" novels, particularly *City of Spades* and *Absolute Beginners*, captured in fiction what his *England, Half English* essayed in prose. A Britain of dark-skinned immigrants from Africa and the Caribbean, encountering hatred from subcultural Teddy Boys and respect of sorts from an emerging scene of teen idols like Tommy Steele; gay-friendly clubs for jazz traditionalists and Marxists; and anything that could be glimpsed from a Vespa. This was the birth of Britpop.

As an essayist (role model Orwell), MacInnes viewed "Young England, Half English" as a shared displacement, the teen idols "speaking American at the recording session and English in the pub round the corner afterwards." They were between countries, but also between classes (Tommy Steele was "every nice young girl's boy, every kid's favourite elder brother, every mother's cherished adolescent son"), between brows. In "Pop Songs and Teenagers," he saw youth as classless, amused, an "underground of joy," but also "raw material for crypto-fascisms of the worst kind." The trigger, if it all went off, would be racism: "A Short Guide for Jumbles," an essay he expressed regrets over later, answered the question of whether white and colored could be friends with a reluctant No.

His novels weren't the same as his treatises, MacInnes insisted, just responses to seeing a social theme move in on his life, "romantic in mood, and as rigorously analytic as I can be, by implication." *City of Spades* contrasted the stories of Montgomery Pew, discharged from the Colonial Department Welfare Office for becoming "too familiar," and Johnny Fortune, in from Lagos to meet his half-white half-brother in a late 1940s milieu of "ponces" (pimps), "smoking weed" (smoking weed), and American GIs who danced to Eckstine, Horne, and calypso at the Cosmopolitan dance hall. It ended badly. One Karl Marx Bo called Pew and his friend Theodora "full-time professional admirers of the coloured peoples, who like us as you like pet animals." Theodora echoed "Guide for Jumbles": "love, or even friendship, for those people is *impossible*."

Absolute Beginners, made into a 1980s Julian Temple film with David Bowie, added British pop idolatry, narrated by an unnamed protagonist from the "teenage epic": a photographer who lived in a house with mixed-race Modern Jazz Quartet fan Mr. Cool and lesbian ponce Big Jill; Ed the Ted threw a rock at him yelling "Go ome, Yank." His girl, Suze, had a fondness for Black men and an arranged marriage looming with an older white gay man. The prose anticipated **Tom Wolfe**'s new journalism at times: "'It's daddy who gets horsewhipped these days,' said the ex-Deb-of-last-year." Portraits of "culture-vultures" were astute, like Ron Todd, "a Marxist, and closely associated with the ballad-and-blues movement, which seeks to prove that all folk music is an art of protest." The Nottingham race riots provided a conclusion of sorts: "this was supposed to be the British isles," the narrator bemoaned.

MacInnes was hardly a pop music expert: Melly, **Nik Cohn**, and music managers such as Simon Napier-Bell, Andrew Loog Oldham, and Joe Boyd wrote better guidebooks. But his mix of pop, ponces, and pogroms outlined English subculture, detailed more by Hanif Kureishi's films (*My Beautiful Laundrette*, *Sammy and Rosie Get Laid*) and coedit with Jon Savage, *The Faber Book of Pop*.

MacInnes worried about "songs sung *by Englishmen in American*." Yet his ability to balance cynicism and hope, to understand that neither pop diversity nor white rage were going away, made him the first great expositor of a music he never named in *Absolute*: rock and roll.

FORM-EXPLODING INDETERMINACY

John Cage, Silence, *1961*

————

"Static between the stations. Rain. We want to capture and control these sounds, to use them not as sound effects but as musical instruments." Cage (1912–1982), the most influential American experimental music theorist, emitted variations on this theme all his life. If other composers chose between Schoenberg and Stravinsky, Cage razor-edited Marcel Duchamp ready-mades, *Finnegans Wake* word-splurge, Marshall McLuhan media massage. He and his partner, choreographer Merce Cunningham, put on dance productions with sets by painter Robert Rauschenberg: art as theater, downtown sensibility as boho sexual tolerance.

Cage's best-known piece, " 4'33"," put on the piano an empty score that made listening to one's surroundings compulsory. His book, *Silence*, referenced twenty years of stylizing a Zen, wild mushroom, and *I Ching*–adapted "chance operation" approach to prepared piano, off-beat percussion, magnetic tape collages, and other musique concrète. Within *Silence* were interstitial, interpolated, and underlined parts of *Indeterminacy*, a recording that irradiated ninety one-minute shaggy-dog stories, told in Cage's flat affect (akin to Andy Warhol), with David Tudor's piano jabs and portions of a noise piece. Released as a double album on Folkways, it ranked with **Jelly Roll Morton**'s oral history-over-piano Library of Congress recordings as form-exploding music literature. Nothing imbued the experimental like intersecting machine sounds and "I love this machine more than I do your Uncle Walter" schtick.

What did Cage have to do with popular music? As a work on Wesleyan University Press, *Silence* achieved unusual sales and dozens of translations. Cage, inclined in the book to separate "serious music" from jazz or folk, defined an omnivorous artistry for countless successors, from friends Yoko Ono and John Lennon to the *NoBrow* imbrication of pop and Lincoln Center described by John Seabrook. Cage shunned consumerism: he and peers like composer Morton Feldman were seen as kindred spirits by Frankfurt School theorist **Theodor Adorno**, who wrote, "As a joke they hurl culture into people's faces, a fate which both culture and people richly deserve." But cultivating experimental fellowship amped his brand: the first sentence of *Indeterminacy* mentioned sculptor Isamu Noguchi. Cage, profiled in *The New Yorker* by art-scene chronicler Calvin Tomkins (collected later in *The Bride and the Bachelors*), was treated as a brave pursuer of the "new and highly unpopular course," hissed by Philharmonic orchestras and kept at arm's length by universities. The profile wended its way, single column, through more than fifty pages of ads for portable Magnavox television sets and the like.

Meanwhile, in a story David Grubbs told in his revisionist account of Cage, *Records Ruin the Landscape*, Henry Flynt, a would-be experimentalist transformed by rock and roll and reading **Samuel Charters**'s *The Country Blues*, stewed. After playing Cage some of his music in Ono's loft in 1961, and telling him of his full musical palette, Flynt heard back: "'If that's what you're interested in, well, what are you doing here?'" Flynt noted, "And he was right, actually." He reflected, "I was listening to black music and I began to think that the best musicians were receiving the worst treatment." Cage's first prepared piano had come at the request of a Black dancer looking to perform an African-themed program. His emphasis on rhythm over harmony, on expanding notions of musical notation, anticipated hip-hop and EDM. His book *Notations* recruited hundreds of marvelously disparate examples of how to write down sound. Yet Cage refused to consider his "meeting" with Sun Ra a collaboration, highlighted no Black composers in *Notations*, and seems to have never invoked the vernacular as a force in art.

Cage would write one more *Silence*-like book, *A Year from Monday*, then concentrate on "mesostics," poems with a capitalized theme down the middle and even more destructured coherence: "sparrowsitA gROsbeak betrays itself by that peculiar squeakariEFFECT." His first major interpreter, Richard Kostelanetz, prioritized *John Cage, Writer* quite usefully. Kyle Gann's short book on "4′33″" gave the best account of Cage as a downtown musician. Kenneth Silverman's *Begin Again*, a full biography interested in sexuality questions, resembled an eternal cocktail party. The Grubbs book, by a musician from a generation that shared Flynt's natural tastes, offered the hint of a full-scale rethink still to come, as Cage's dismissal of recordings—even as he made great ones—informed a broader take on experimentalist assumptions.

As historian of gay America Jonathan Katz noted in the David Bernstein and Christopher Hatch–edited volume *Writings through John Cage's Music, Poetry, and Art*, Cage often seemed determined to closet any personal voice from his work. So let the composer have the last remark, a hint at how he was thinking, unconvinced by the era of countercultural vernacular, back and ultimately decades ahead, to wider realms of fantastic sentiment. "Noises, too had been discriminated against; and being American, having been trained to be sentimental, I fought for noises."

SCIENCE FICTION WRITER PENS FIRST
ROCK AND ROLL NOVEL

Harlan Ellison, Rockabilly *[Spider Kiss], 1961*

As rock and roll emerged into American consciousness in 1955, twenty-one-year-old Harlan Ellison fled Ohio State for New York, where he published one more issue of his science fiction fanzine, *Dimensions*, and sold his first story to a magazine. In 1956, the year **Elvis** broke, he cashed checks (small ones; rates were a penny or two per word) for one hundred such acts of pulp fiction. If *Rockabilly*—which Ellison had titled *Spider Kiss* (its name in all subsequent reprintings), the first American rock and roll novel, had nothing to do with music criticism, the author knew culture in other ways. Before there was Quentin, or Steven King, there was Harlan.

This pulp style was a delinquently juvenile genre culture, regardless of category. Science fiction, Ellison's bastion, had been an adjacent part of the Popular Front in the 1930s, with a group of boundary testers calling themselves the Futurians (see novelist Frederik Pohl's memoir, *The Way the Future Was*), not unlike the Hot Clubs of swing. The 1950s version made lurid comics and shock horror stories a funhouse mirror to the noise of electric guitar. When Private First Class Ellison, with Texan "Party Doll" singer Buddy Knox in his barracks, contributed a $64.50 story about a messed-up rock star to *Trapped* that he grew into a paperback, he knew what mattered topically. An overnight sensation from poor white southern origins. Show business people conflicted about the noise they sold, not unlike a certain pulp writer. Teen passion. A fall to go with the rise. Framed by commercial dread as much as the jazz novel, this rework feared success more than failure.

One part Jerry Lee Lewis the Killer, one part **Elvis Presley**—his Svengali was another Colonel, Freeport—Stag Preston in this novel fed the "animal murmuring of the audience, mostly teen-age girls with tight sweaters and mouths open-crammed by gum." Preston had real talent, but no self-control. "You're an animal," the woman who once mothered him said as he cast her aside. Ultimately, he ripped the clothing off a fan who fought to get away and fell to her death, killing his career as well. It was a narrative predictive of Ellen Sander's experience covering Led Zeppelin a decade later, published in her book *Trips*. Assaulted, dress ripped by band members, she concluded, "If you walk inside the cages of a zoo, you get to see the animals close-up, stroke the captive pelts and mingle with the energy behind the mystique. You also get to smell the shit first-hand." Ellison's stand-in as second protagonist, Shelly Morganstern, smelled a lot, becoming Stag's procurer, hating the "Jungle York" of "hipsters," meaning cool commercialized. "Substitute hipness for emotions, substitute sharp clothes and possessions for work that matters, that keeps a guy clean, substitute cigarettes for muscles." Preston, Ellison had Morganstern say, in an echo of horror flicks like *The Blob* and anticipation of 1990s Thomas Frank essays, was "a slime-thing I created with Freeport and the hip scene. He's a product, that's all."

Science fiction's literary mentality would continue to infuse rock. SF zines helped originate rock criticism. The two merged in **Bob Dylan** and Philip Dick scholar/**Jonathan Lethem** mentor Paul Williams's *Crawdaddy*, which published Ellison. Greg Shaw's SF-oriented *Entmoot* preceded his garage-rock *Bomp!* Ellison, past thirty, represented youth in a confrontation with Il Padrone captured in Gay Talese's immortal feature "**Frank Sinatra** Has a Cold." He edited *Dangerous Visions* and *Again, Dangerous Visions*, anthologies of "new wave" SF freed of pulp rules. Among science fiction authors, Samuel Delany, an occasional music writer, described in a memoir encountering Dylan while Delany performed at a Village folk night. J. G. Ballard's *Atrocity Exhibition* would be used for album titles by Joy Division and Danny Brown. And Michael Moorcock's Cornelius Quartet, beginning with *The Final Programme*, featured a psychedelic rock milieu; he'd work with a band of that type, Hawkwind. Ellison's view of the rock star as slime thing, false God, arty delinquency, influenced *The Man Who Fell to Earth*, a vehicle for David Bowie; *A Clockwork Orange's* psychosis-inducing use of classical music as antipop; George R. R. Martin's pre–*Game of Thrones* rock saga *The Armageddon Rag*; and other stagings of bottled apocalypse. We'll pick up with cyberpunk later on.

As for the rock novel, two of the most cherished of the first generation retained Ellison's mass cultural angst. Thomas Pynchon's *Crying of Lot 49*, a switch from his jazz-focused *V*, made its main protagonist's squeeze a Top 40 DJ, hopelessly compromised, while a local, goofy **Beatles**-type band was named the Paranoids. If Pynchon updated Elvis to Fab Four, Don DeLillo's *Great Jones Street* centered on a Bob Dylan figure, renamed Bucky Wunderlick, dropped out of culture-hero pursuits (Dylan's Basement Tapes as Wunderlick's Mountain Tapes) and trying to stay alive to the downtown scene—in the East Village, Great Jones is one off of (Positively) 4th Street. Pulpier rock treatments, like Anne Rice's *The Vampire Lestat*, persisted into the 1980s, but in other ways the tone became more affectionate and global. Roddy Doyle's *The Commitments* tracked friends in Dublin starting a soul band; Haruki Murakami's *Norwegian Wood* used the **Beatles** song to reflect on the late 1960s Japanese counterculture, becoming his nation's most popular novelist. But many popular music readers wound up with quirky favorites. **Greil Marcus**, for example, at the 2019 Pop Conference, highlighted David Helton's *King Jude*, about "a Texas guitar player named Jude who comes to New York and all but watches from a distance as stardom steals his soul." My own suggestion would be Anne Tyler's *A Slipping-Down Life*, which came at rockabilly again, yet from a perspective more attuned to women and southerners than Ellison's frustrated New Yorkism.

PRO-JAZZ SCENE SOCIOLOGY

Howard S. Becker, Outsiders: Studies in the Sociology of Deviance, *1963*

———

Two remarks established this sociologist's extradisciplinary bona fides. "I was for some years what is called a Saturday night musician, making myself available to whoever called and hired me to play for dances and parties in groups of varying sizes, playing everything from polkas through mambos, jazz, and imitations of Wayne King." And: "I found as many good ideas in fiction, drama, film, and photography as I did in what I was 'supposed' to be reading." *Outsiders*, a rebuke to mainstream judgment, opened with Faulkner: *"It's like it ain't so much what a fellow does, but it's the way the majority of folks is looking at him when he does it."* The 1982 *Art Worlds*, his second major book, used those weekend bandstand collaborators to explore culture as something people did together, not genius to unpack. Howie to all he met, a PhD at twenty-three still publishing in his late eighties, Becker made deviance a vernacular, social science a kind of **John Cage** chance operation, and the ordinary extraordinary in its implications.

Encouraged by University of Chicago mentor C. Everett Hughes, a sophisticate who loved to quote Robert Musil's unfinishable novel *Man Without Qualities* at stodgy peers, Becker published work on "dance musicians" and "marihuana users" as early as 1951 in major sociology journals. He set down how jazz values made players scorn their clients as squares and connected that to service occupations like nursing; put getting high alongside homosexuality as deviant only if society enforced that definition. Throughout *Outsiders*, the language was clear, categorical, blander than its implications: "Social rules define situations and the kinds of behavior appropriate to them, specifying some actions as 'right' and forbidding others as 'wrong.'" Becker looked to situations and interactions, leery of grand theories and set identities, avid for examples: a jazzman whose private theme song title was "If You Don't Like My Queer Ways You Can Kiss My Fucking Ass." The musician's deviance, Becker realized, fit career requirements. Subterranean values, a notion he shared with David Matza (*Delinquency and Drift*), Ned Polsky (*Hustlers, Beats and Others*), and Edgar Friedenberg (*Growing Up Absurd*), crossed many identity lines. Race, class, and gender were rarely highlighted, though the approach could fit Harold Finestone's "Cats, Kicks, and Color" on Black heroin users in Becker's 1964 collection *The Other Side: Perspectives in Deviance*, or Herbert Gans's work on taste subcultures in Becker's *Social Problems* anthology. *Sociological Work*, essays from his first twenty years, defined culture as "people doing things together" and scholarship as actively shaping values in "Whose Side Are We On?"

On the other side of the counterculture, Becker repositioned himself as a mixer of art and social science with the 1981 exhibition book *Exploring Society Photographically*, ranging from Bali to Venice Beach roller skaters. *Art Worlds*, by which he meant "the sociology of occupations applied to artistic work," illustrated categories more didactically developed in fellow sociologist **Richard Peterson**'s production of culture essay "Why 1955?"—modes of professional identity, legal constraints, etc.—with the flair of a grand lecturer. It moved from Harry Partch's constructed instruments, and what getting them played revealed about the conventions others accepted, to Ezra Pound's edits of *The Waste Land*. Far more academically sanctioned sociologist Pierre Bourdieu, emerging as his adversary, thundered about cultural capital and the field of production; Becker's "world" approach remained people trying things and finding what stuck.

This Becker, the emeritus Becker, worked the same vein for decades: *Writing for Social Scientists* joined *Tricks of the Trade*, an homage to Everett Hughes and the game playing tactics of Cage, and *Telling About Society*, overt about how writers such as Italo Calvino might inform sociology with their observation-studded fancies. And Becker returned to jazz, making it the focus of the multiauthor *Art from Start to Finish* and collaborating with fellow instrumentalist/sociologist Robert Faulkner on *"Do You Know . . . ?" The Jazz Repertoire in Action*, Saturday musicians writ large. This then spun off an e-book of the correspondence in writing that book, *Thinking Together*. Becker had long cited the likes of Calvin Trillin in the *New Yorker* as applied sociology; now that magazine profiled him as France's favorite kooky American scholar. Ordinary music as career in the conventions of deviance? Howie Becker owned the fake book.

RECLAIMING BLACK MUSIC

LeRoi Jones (Amiri Baraka), Blues People: Negro Music
in White America, *1963*

———

The body of literature this poet, playwright, essayist, agitator, and organizer amassed fused bohemian and vernacular like Joyce and "Howl," detonating the Black Arts movement and producing a lineage that shaped **Greg Tate, Fred Moten**, Kevin Young, and Afrocentric hip-hop. Along with **Tom Wolfe**, Jones, who changed his name to Baraka in 1965, after the murder of Malcolm X, exemplified the electric vernacular prose that would take much nonacademic music writing into the 1970s and beyond, especially rock and rap criticism. A generation past the Harlem Renaissance, Baraka put Black cultural definitions back up for grabs.

How he got there was a blast and a half. In his story "The Screamers," the Newark native to the birth of rhythm and blues recalled sax honkers—an urgent rather than refined sound. They played for the gang kids and a LeRoi Jones of "pitiful petty bourgeois origins," to quote his *Autobiography*, a book as obsessed with class as with race. Jones fantasized "the sweetest revolution, to hucklebuck into the fallen capital, and let the oppressors lindy hop out." At Howard University, before he dropped out, English professor and earlier "From Spirituals to Swing" cohost Sterling Brown showed him and A. B. Spellman, "classic submature campus hipsters," the music that preceded bebop, "with that 'tcch' sound such revelations are often armed with." Discharged from the air force for reading *Partisan Review*, Jones was hired as shipping clerk for a moldy-fig jazz store, befriending critics Martin Williams and **Nat Hentoff**. Then he put a devastating simple sentence atop the *Down Beat* essay "Jazz and the White Critic": "Most jazz critics have been white Americans, but most important jazz musicians have not been." This produced a book deal, offered by one of his many Beat friends, Joyce Glassman (later Johnson) at William Morrow.

Blues People flexed stylistically like a **Gilbert Seldes** or **Ralph Ellison** even as it disagreed with them, more in the tone of slick-magazine modernists than genre critics or social scientists. "A slave cannot be a man"; "The Negro could not ever become white and that was his strength"; "An idea of theater had come to the blues, and this movement toward performance turned some of the emotional climate of the Negro's life into artifact and entertainment." As John Gennari pointed out in his history of jazz criticism, *Blowin' Hot and Cool*, the authorial voice reworked mass-culture critics bemoaning the middle-brow, to which Jones assigned the Black middle class, cool jazz fans ("the tepid new popular music of the white middle-brow middle class")—but not, importantly, rock and roll such as the Coasters: "It is still raw enough to stand the dilution and in some cases, to even be made attractive by the very fact of its commercialization." In *Blues People*, vernacular expression was measured non-musicologically, as a continuum of Blackness formed outside the American mainstream: transplanted through slavery, imbued with leisure by emancipation, turned into a "classic blues" ironic satire by professionals, secured as art beyond middle-class sentimentalism by country folk, rendered cosmopolitan and boundary crossing in jazz, taken to the city by southern migration. The cycle was endless, a "continuous re-emergence of strong Negro influences to revitalize American popular music."

Though the subsequent *Black Music* collected liner notes and *Down Beat* columns like the white critic essay, Jones/Baraka titled another of that book's pivotal essays "The Changing Same (R&B and New Black Music)" because he saw the term jazz as a trap. Better to push hard boppers to try avant-garde Albert Ayler and Ayler fans to recognize that "the really nasty ideas" were in Motown hits and Bobby Bland. Above all, Jones/Baraka raised the question of James Brown, as challenging for Black Arts intellectuals as Fletcher Henderson for Harlem Renaissance ones, locating in Brown's "rhythm, instrumentation and sound" a place where Black people could "move in almost absolute openness and strength." Blues people had become, in this account, R&B people. The Baraka of later, thinner collections *The Music* and *Digging* would enthusiastically receive Bob Marley, Stevie Wonder, and Newark's Fugees, on the popular side, plus avant-garde regenerations by David Murray, Henry Threadgill, and the like. For a figure often described as didactic, Baraka manifested an expansive aesthetic.

But his writing always gave the vernacular shock treatments, made it a field of contestation and freedom taking. (For current academic treatments, see James Smethurst's *Brick City Vanguard* and Jean-Philippe Marcoux's edited collection *Some Other Blues*.) The early play *Dutchman*, with its Black male protagonist confronted and killed by a white woman in a ritual of ofay consumerism, mocked cosmopolitans: "If Bessie Smith had killed some white people she wouldn't have needed that music." "Changing Same" saw the prose become elliptical, beginning: "The blues impulse transferred . . . containing a race, and its expression. *Primal* (mixtures . . . transfers and imitations)." Sax honker Big Jay McNeely, "the first Dada coon of the age" in "The Screamers," playing to a crowd where all extremes were popular, was fed into the sixties woodchipper and came out the poem "Black Dada Nihilismus," read by Baraka over the New York Art Quartet, with lines like "rape the white girls. Rape their fathers." "Black Art," vocalized in jabs the group the Last Poets would soon trademark, words giving way to soundings of bomber planes, slick talk to profanity, was accompanied on record by Sonny Murray's drums, Ayler's sax, and Don Cherry's trumpet.

"Dagger poems," Baraka promised, continuing: "in the slimy bellies of the owner-jews." His anti-Semitism and anticommercialism constrained his take on music, denouncing a "Tin Pan Alley prison" of sentimental song by the likes of Jo Stafford, urging that "there be no love poems written until" the revolution, praising bebop as "anti-assimilationist," ungenerously greeting Prince for his androgynous presentation. A pivotal chapter in *Blues People* was called "Swing—From Verb to Noun," damning white commerce's reification of Black creativity. But if his interpretations were singularly unmeasured, Jones/Baraka revolutionized the discourse of American popular music. His friend Spellman, whose *Four Lives in the Bebop Business* offered the closest critical kinship, had asked, "What does anti-jazz mean and who are these ofays who've appointed themselves guardians of last year's blues?" Baraka, organizing an enclave in Newark that would breed a mayor, accepted a marginalization from slick publishing that left works like the 1974 experimental memoir "6 Persons" for later discovery. He devoted the remarkable introduction to his expanded *Autobiography* to his relationship with wife Amina as a love in struggle. And his poem "Return of the Native" encapsulated the culture of Black America in four words: "Harlem is vicious / modernism." Which, arguably, was everything anti-jazz meant.

AN ENDLESS LIT, LIMITED ONLY IN SCOPE

Michael Braun, "Love Me Do!": The Beatles' Progress, *1964*

———

For the 1995 reprint, Braun offered a summary of the Fab Four he could not have articulated in 1964, when he endeared himself to the band as more culturally aware than others in the media: "They were working-class urban lads who, had they been American, would have liked Frankie Laine, Frankie Valli or Frankie Avalon. Instead they listened to and talked about Muddy Waters, Little Richard and Buddy Holly. They were also interested in Fellini, Kerouac and marijuana. In fact they resonated to everything that we have come to call Pop Culture." Beatles books are limitless in number and pages, limited in scope, hardly changing after a cosmology was worked out, because as with Braun's subtitle they see in the Fab Four a pilgrim's *Progress.* This grand journey remade pop—a thing loved first and understood second. Instead of broader context, they offered exegesis, biblical books of John and—or versus—Paul. A "Beatle brain" appeared, knowing everything of them, little apart. Only the lives and songs mattered. Beatles could not be rethought, just compulsively anthologized.

One Braun competitor that first British Invasion year was Bill Adler's *Love Letters to the Beatles,* words by the girls screaming to "I Want to Hold Your Hand." Bea in Los Angeles: "Dear John, I am 4 feet 8. I weigh 92 lbs. I am all yours." Cookie: "I had an ankle sprained, my dress torn, a slightly scratched face, and a black eye. Isn't it WONDERFUL?" Alice in Pittsburgh: "I think a girl should wait until the man chases her. But I'm not going to wait forever." They were not to write their own books—save John's first wife's memoir and kids' lit—for fifty years, when Penelope Rowlands's, Candy Leonard's, and Nancy Hajeski's takes arrived. Gloria Steinem read Braun and reprinted Lennon's "women should be obscene and not heard" line in a sardonic 1964 *Cosmo* article; it's collected in a 2006 June Skinner Sawyer compendium of Beatles essays alongside Maureen Cleave, their first media friend, who'd imperil their 1966 tour with John's "bigger than Jesus" quote. So perhaps dissent simmered. But Braun got Beatle number one's "I get spasms of being intellectual" and "We don't want to learn to dance." He knew to marvel at Dizzy Gillespie requesting a George Harrison autograph and could explain Richard Avedon to the band. *Love Me Do!* captured Beatlemania—and also the boys' imperative to not become Cliff Richard, a pop artist scorned as female fans were. Lennon's own publication of poetry and drawings, *In His Own Write,* added luster. **Tom**

Wolfe, from a Murray the K article to an acid-era Beatles concert in San Francisco he attended with Ken Kesey, built new journalism around their new pop.

Where the first real book was John's, the second was Paul's. Hunter Davies turned an interview with McCartney quite different in tone ("The girls waiting outside. I don't despise them. I don't think fans are humiliating themselves") into the authorized 1968 biography *The Beatles*. Over forty years, Davies would add to the introduction and ending of the book. First, to comment about their pivotal manager, "One thing I regret was not being able to say that Brian Epstein was homosexual." An edition later, to preserve a McCartney call to vent about the canonization of his murdered songwriting partner. And eventually, to jibe at "the modern Beatles Brains. They know so much." But the main text stayed fixed. Davies became a primary text, canon, for typecasting John as anti-jazz rocker with a cruel streak, Paul as arty Londoner, Harrison as the one saying "I don't personally enjoy being a Beatle anymore," and all viewed more through drug use than song insights left "for the musicologists."

A note on those musicologists: early, London *Times* critic William Mann esteemed the Beatles for moves neither they nor their fans understood in such language. To Braun—who, like Sawyer, reprinted it—it was a sign they'd shifted from pop piffle to cultural establishment. Wilfrid Mellers, British specialist in American sounds (*Music in a New Found Land*, also published in 1964, was the U.K. counterpart to **Gilbert Chase**), compounded the problem with *Twilight of the Gods*, which analyzed the whole catalog but never moved from flatted sevenths to the imperatives of performance. A generation later, Allan Moore's short book on *Sgt. Pepper's*, for a series otherwise classical and "Rhapsody in Blue," added cultural studies awareness, genre lineages, and skepticism of great album claims, but better enumerated musicology's holes where Beatles pop was concerned than fixed them. Walter Everett's two-volume *The Beatles as Musicians* was a step back: "The blatant parallel fifths in Shannon's song are somewhat softened by Lennon's superficial consonant 6–5 suspensions." Tag teams within "popular musicology" gave Mozart-level attention to both *Revolver* (edited by Russell Reising) and again *Sgt. Pepper's* (edited by Olivier Julien), with Jacqueline Warwick useful on gendered listening experiences, Ger Tilleken itemizing those flatted sevenths once and for all, and Michael Hannan assessing "sound design."

If musicologists initially lacked a working language for this oeuvre, rock critics realized once the band broke up in 1970 how much they'd been provided one by all that wrestling with form and cultural status. (For the intellectual history, see Bernard Gendron's *Between Montmartre and the Mudd Club*.) *Lennon Remembers*, interviews by *Rolling Stone* founder Jann Wenner, was unprecedented

in American music lit for the artist's presumption of cultural power: "the Beatles deliberately didn't move like **Elvis**. That was our policy because we found
it stupid." Lennon touted wife Yoko Ono's ties to Ornette Coleman and **John
Cage**, but admitted "Whole Lotta Shakin' Goin' On" was as good as it got for
him. "Why do you think it means so much to people?" Wenner asked. "Rock &
roll? Because it's primitive enough and it has no bull shit." For **Greil Marcus**,
viewing the Beatles as "pop explosion" unifying a generation into the template
of a rock group in **Jim Miller**'s *Rolling Stone Illustrated History of Rock & Roll*,
Lennon's musical takes gave rock criticism an almost Platonic genealogy. British critics were less credulous: Roy Carr and Tony Tyler's *The Beatles* codified
that snarkier sensibility, evident earlier in George Melly's pop-theory *Revolt
into Style* and the anti-*Pepper's* stance of **Nik Cohn**'s *Awopbopaloobop*.

A different strand, Beatles memoirs, focused on scenery. Allan Williams's
The Man Who Gave the Beatles Away, by an early manager, put strippers,
speed, and show business into an account of Liverpool and Hamburg that first
mentioned Epstein's sexuality. In *The Longest Cocktail Party*, Richard DiLello
moved from U.S. high school senior when the Beatles played Ed Sullivan to
1967 London as "a fully fledged acid-drenched, pot-smoking American hippie
with a 14-inch Afro, a buckskin jacket, and a lust for adventure—and completely harmless." He became "house hippie" for the freewheeling Apple cor-
poration, founded by the group after Epstein was found dead in 1967. DiLello's
equally freewheeling 141 chapters (#27: "I'll ball you if you introduce me to
Paul McCartney"; two days later, "You bastard!") captured press events with
turkeys and other quirks. He'd eventually write Sean Penn movies like *Colors*,
rehearsing and then reprising **Cameron Crowe**'s life. No less flowery, if more
central, was Derek Taylor, Beatles "press officer" and ghostwriter of Epstein's
closeted *A Cellarful of Noise*, who released *As Time Goes By*. He knew the "pop
fringe is a strange piece of fabric" and clumped experiences from John with a
hooker on a U.S. Midwest radio tour to *Newlyweds* honcho Bob Eubanks, jazz
critic Ralph Gleason, and even Mae West as counterculture hangers-on. Taylor routinized Beatles books: helping George with terse memoir *I, Me, Mine*,
celebrating *Sgt. Pepper's* with *It Was Twenty Years Ago Today*, and prepping the
official *Anthology* at the time of his death.

As Taylor's oeuvre showed, rock criticism and hippie prose mulched into
Beatles books as standalone genre. Early, this was cute: Ron Schaumburg's
Growing Up with the Beatles recalled shouting at girls to shut up during a Kansas City *Hard Day's Night* screening, missing the concert there because "I had
to take my piano lesson," and becoming the "rotten hippie" of 1968, pictured
in Nehru jacket and peace chain. Nicholas Schaffner's *Beatles Forever*, still

treasured by Gen X fans as their gateway, mixed tiny type and large pictures, chattily smart on counterculture bits like drug use and on specific musical choices, noticing how the hippie albums "seemed entirely to shake off the black influences." Schaffner worked with Lennon's boyhood friend, Pete Shotton, on the sex-drenched retrospective *John Lennon: In My Life*. Geoffrey Stokes's *The Beatles* was more upscale, pricier binding for the photos by Avedon and other souvenirs, including a Leonard Bernstein intro touting "the Fuck-You coolness of these Four Horsemen of Our Apocalypse."

The tipping point was the best-selling biography that replaced Davies, Philip Norman's *Shout!* Another John book—claiming Lennon was "three-quarters of the Beatles" got him a Yoko session for the paperback and he later wrote a Lennon study, too—Norman's was the first full band bio, specific on which speed pills they took in Hamburg (Preludin), Epstein's rough-trade predicaments and business ineptitudes. There was also, strangely, information on what eight-year-old Mark Lewisohn was up to when *Sgt. Pepper's* came out; in the epilogue, Lewisohn, now twenty-two, was called the "Beatle Brain of Britain."

Who was this guy? An insatiable cataloger, apparently. The temptation, once the full Beatles saga concluded, with Lennon's murder in 1980 and the allowing of all sex, drugs, and money details, was to review it, over and over. This could be done genially, as in Tim Riley's survey of the records start to finish, *Tell Me Why*. Or touting info, as with Mark Hertsgaard's *New Yorker*–sparked, Abbey Road studio tapes–informed, critically feckless *A Day in the Life*. Or with a bit more of a manic edge: Ian MacDonald's *Revolution in the Head* became the judgy fan's favorite for his ability to specify, without reading like the musicologists, why a plunge from G major to unstable minor in "I Want to Hold Your Hand" earned Lennon's "that's it!" Answering the need for a book of Paul after *Shout!* was *Paul McCartney: Many Years from Now*, by bohemian friend Barry Miles. It included enough block quotes from the bassist, revealed to have helped on underground paper layouts (and bankrolls), to almost serve as official memoir.

But the heavyweight was Lewisohn, who called his 1986 *The Beatles Live!* "a reference work." The brain had given Norman research help on *Shout!*, producing, Lewisohn was thrilled to note, "the first-ever book to contain the true date Lennon met McCartney—6 July 1957." Drawing on a thousand-plus sources, the live book documented gigs from one on the back of a stationary coal lorry through to an undersold repeat engagement at Shea Stadium, one squib at a time. Its sequel, *Complete Beatles Recording Sessions*, earned an extensive McCartney interview—arty Paul really just liked one Stockhausen work, "The Song of the Young"; "I thought most of his other stuff was too fruity." Add *The Beatles*

Day by Day, The Complete Beatles Chronicle, and (with Piet Schreuders and Adam Smith) *The Beatles' London* (Derek Taylor foreword: "Like everything else bearing Mark Lewisohn's name it is relentlessly researched and as exact as human resources will permit"). Wait. The payoff was *Tune In,* a biography credited to "The world's only professional Beatles historian," either 960 pages or 1,728 in its "extended special edition," AND ENDING IN 1962. Sample: "A fledgling boyfriend-girlfriend situation developed with Sheila Prytherch, from number 8. 'Paul McCartney was my first kiss,' she says, 'and we held hands.'" Details stood out, like George Martin being given the Beatles to produce by a label head who couldn't fire him. No attempt was made at wider interpretation, just litany. Two more volumes were in the brain's offing.

Fans would only suggest more sources for the eternal exegesis, such as producer and engineer accounts. George Martin's began with 1979's *All You Need Is Ears,* on the Beatles but also how producers and A&R structured eclecticism; later came an edited how-to on *Making Music,* the *Sgt. Pepper's*–focused *With a Little Help from My Friends,* and a pricey *Playback* revisiting his full career. Geoff Emerick, who worked alongside Martin at Abbey Road, offered his insights in *Here, There and Everywhere*: now we knew what patchwork chicanery of vocal distortion it took to make John Lennon say good 'un. If solvent after choosing between the $375 and $674 versions of *Playback,* one might plunk another three digits for Brian Kehew's *Recording the Beatles*: an Amazon reviewer reported, "when I first opened the book I was greeted with a section on the changes made to the level meters on one of the mixing consoles. It detailed the changes in VU meter types and the technical details of each and the benefits of changing them out. I couldn't help the smile on my face."

Could the Blue Meanies be stopped from reifying all of Pepperland? A few authors tried to break loose. Devin McKinney's *Magic Circles,* Marcus-like in charged prose tone, drew on the earthier parts of Allan Williams, the romantic frenzy caught by Bill Adler, to view Beatle worship as indeed a mania, a compact between fans and band that was butchered as the sixties progressed. Jonathan Gould's *Can't Buy Me Love,* more straight ahead stylistically, put British Invasion of the U.S. Top 40 in conversation with Bond and *My Fair Lady,* or Weber on charisma overcoming patriarchy, *Sgt. Pepper's* in the context of modernist ballet *Parade.* Peter Doggett followed Apple's unwinding in *You Never Give Me Your Money.* Ian Inglis offered a balanced, hence not acerbic enough, academic summation in *The Beatles.* Sociologist Candy Leonard went looking for "the fan voice *and* the female voice," noting: "for the most part, Beatles scholarship is a conversation among male observers."

But Rob Sheffield's funny, fannish, and deeply historiographical *Dreaming the Beatles* came closest to revisionism, applying his lifelong critical obsession: boys becoming men by watching and learning from girls becoming women. Cherry-picking the literature to serve his tropes, he made "Paul Is a Concept by Which We Measure Our Pain" a perfect chapter; offered twenty-six genre- and time-spanning examples of Beatles covers in the loosest sense to get outside the catalog; contrasted different decades' governing notions of the Beatles; played *Revolver* off *Sgt. Pepper's* once and for all; and thought about Lennon in relation to depression. More by others was still needed: a fully feminist rereading; the Fab Four as homosociality in the context of emergent homosexuality; geographies of fandom and influence as sharp as Sara Cohen's work on Liverpool. Yet even fifty years ago today, it was hard to resist the music's Camelot spell and pull sword from stone.

MUSIC AS A PROSE MASTER'S JAGGED GRAIN

Ralph Ellison, Shadow and Act, *1964*

———

"When the first of these essays was published I regarded myself—in my most secret heart at least—a musician." The author of the great novel *Invisible Man* never did finish a sequel; *Juneteenth*, published posthumously, was a fragment. But his critical writing, especially on music, was nearly as vital, though it made him more grandmaster, less insurgent. Ellison, in 1943, speculated: "perhaps the zoot suit conceals profound political meaning." As late as 1977, he pondered ethnicity run amok: "a white youngster who, with a transistor radio screaming a Stevie Wonder tune glued to his ear, shouts epithets at black youngsters trying to swim at a public beach—and this in the name of the ethnic sanctity of what has been declared a neighborhood turf." Ellison never played music as well as heroes such as **Louis Armstrong**, **Duke Ellington**, or his southwest peers Charlie Christian and Jimmy Rushing. But he agreed with **Amiri Baraka**, otherwise an adversary, that African American music needed the "context of a total culture," supplying that in his fictional masterpiece and in the writing that illuminated it, collected in *Shadow and Act* and published during his moment of greatest influence.

Ellison pursued a particular Du Boisian double consciousness, seeing in Black and American identity, art and popular appeal, "Sound and the Mainstream," an enhanced wealth of perspective. Jazz musicians, like boxers or tap dancers, pushed against "accepted conventions of the hero handed down by cultural, religious and racist tradition." Novelists needed the same mix of lore and technique. He critiqued his first patron, Richard Wright, as "overcommitted to ideology" and not a good dancer, found a useful humanistic Americanism in Twain's Huck, and agreed with **Constance Rourke** that Black archetypes were central to U.S. identity. He validated Armstrong's mask: "When American life is most American it is apt to be most theatrical." Credited T. S. Eliot's "The Waste Land," including its interpolation of the **James Weldon Johnson** co-write "Under the Bamboo Tree," with sending him in quest of literature. And he had a still-powerful definition of the blues as early as 1945, developed with Tuskegee classmate **Albert Murray**: "The blues is an impulse to keep the painful details and episodes of a brutal experience alive in one's aching consciousness, to finger its jagged grain, and to transcend it, not by the consolation of philosophy but by squeezing from it a near-tragic, near-comic lyricism."

Invisible Man began with music, the unnamed protagonist imagining filling his wired lair with five recordings of Satchmo singing and playing "What Did I Do (To Be So Black and Blue)," a "beam of lyrical sound" that "made poetry out of being invisible," best heard on reefer so "the unheard sound came through." This was novel writing as sound studies and Afrofuturism, to use later terms, but then Ellison's work often registered as prophetic: Ras (anticipating Rastafarians), the "black nationalist"; the brotherhood (Communist Party) figure and hipster/zoot suiter Tod Clifton combining with the narrator, "chief spokesman of the Harlem district," into an antecedent of Malcolm X. Even, well before James Brown formed bands, a brother Maceo. Like **Zora Neale Hurston**, Ellison believed in "lying," that is, "the Afro-American folk term for an improvised story," as in a sharecropper's vernacular or church sermon. But his lore was as much a transition to electrification as Charlie Christian's guitar, shocking like the coins in the "Battle Royale" scene, amped by urban Harlem and modernist symbolism. Adam Bradley speculated in *Ralph Ellison in Progress* that Rinehart, the numbers runner and pimp in shades, summit of cool, might have centered the follow-up that Ellison never completed.

Ralph Waldo Ellison ended his novel not with a transparent eyeball, Emerson style, but a "disembodied voice" that his character suggested might speak to us on the lower frequencies. *Shadow and Act* pursued those matters explicitly. "Living with Music" took the "plunge into electronics" of *Invisible Man*'s hero as basis for a *High Fidelity* feature about Ellison's own sound-system tinkering and lessons in Harlem musical diversity—once more unto Ellington and Rudolph Fisher's airshafts. "The Golden Age, Time Past," for *Esquire*, cast bebop—whose antidance moves Ellison often mocked—in terms of the jam session at Minton's or Monroe's, "the jazzman's true academy." Key figures treated included Mahalia Jackson's fusion of "art with swing," of Bessie Smith and the gospel circuit; Charlie Parker's canonization by white beatniks interested in apolitical revolt; Charlie Christian enacting individual inside of group dynamics in ways the Brotherhood should have modeled. *Blues People* was denounced as sociology "enough to give even the blues the blues."

Ellison, by 1970, was an embattled figure, as an *Atlantic* feature reprinted in his *Collected Essays* reveals. But he'd emerge for our literature on the other side of that, fused into jazz studies by **Robert O'Meally**, whose edited *Living with Music: Ralph Ellison's Jazz Writings* included the novelist's great appreciation of Ellington's "aura of mockery" and letters to Murray, augmented in a massive *Selected Letters* compendium in 2019. "I wouldn't be a jazz critic for love or money," Ellison wrote his friend. But in his work, sound supplanted vision to make the color line a signifying riff.

HOW TO SUCCEED IN . . .

M. William Krasilovsky and Sidney Schemel,
This Business of Music, *1964*

———

Published under the auspices of the leading trade journal, *Billboard*, in ten editions and a half-million copies through 2007, this contracts-oriented "bible of the music industry" anticipated the production of culture perspective that **Richard Peterson** used in sociology and **Simon Frith** anchored to popular music studies—not to mention **Clive Davis**'s flip tone about how to sell rock, country, or soul in a culture war. It was also the story of Bill and Sid, two company men, dedicating the first edition to "our wives, Shirley and Phyllis, for their constant encouragement," taking the train in from the burbs to make legal boilerplate of any pop contingency. In a business of payola, cut-ins on publishing, and other shady dealings, these gents provided stability amid the overweening greed they viewed as perfectly healthy. Profiled by Kristin Hussey in the *New York Times* in 2007, as the industry structure finally gave way, Krasilovsky reported that he loved hearing "My Funny Valentine," since the estate of Lorenz Hart was a client: "I always know that there's a dollar sign behind it."

Record sales had soared from $48 million in 1940 to $200 million in 1946, $400 million in 1957, $658 million in 1963—a pace that, the authors bragged, "far outstripped the increase in the gross national product of the country as a whole." If earlier how-to books stressed that writing hit songs didn't require musical expertise, this era favored knowing the score: not quarter-notes but the contractual figures that upped bank deposits. "Are the Harry Fox Office fees of 3½ per cent (ordinarily 5 per cent for new publishers) being deducted in full by the publisher from mechanical receipts, or are they being limited to the 2½ per cent maximum provided in the AGAC contract?" A line in the introduction that survived many editions provided an ideology: "The industry still remains a highly viable one where fortunes can be rapidly built and lost." A good tune was not Krasilovsky and Schemel's expertise. They knew rack-jobbers and the supply line to customers in department stores, standard clauses and "mature artist" exceptions, independent producers and "hot masters," Judge Yankwich on fair use criteria, "Pepsi Cola Hits the Spot" launching jingles, and why "tax avoidance isn't tax evasion." The **Beatles** showed up in the technicalities of synch rights and performing rights involved in setting up a closed-circuit telecast to one hundred U.S. theaters.

Reading through the multiple editions of the series, one noted certain trends. Mature artists became "superstars," with power over repertoire and contracts that filtered into higher royalties and increased autonomy for newcomers, though some slipped back after the industry crashed between 1978 and 1984. Technology never stopped reshuffling the deck: the album disposition of the 1964 edition, the "cartridge television" presaging VCRs of the 1971 version, the discos of a 1977 printing, the CD by 1990, SoundScan tallies central as 1995 rolled off the presses. Government intervention mattered deeply, too: a new copyright framework in 1976 finally replaced the 1909 relic, feds forced MCA to divest its talent agency or put ASCAP and BMI under consent decrees. But the relationship of the United States to world markets became steadily more reciprocal, as Europe unified its trade and took a third of the gross alongside the North American third and Japanese 15 per cent. *This Business* appendices then shifted to the likes of the Berne Convention Implementation Act of 1988. Always, interpreting law took on epistemological qualities: "Standards of Originality," "Simulation of Artist Style," "Vicarious Liability." Economics strained as well: "It is difficult to conceive of anything more foreign to a conservative banker than the thousands of music publishers," they wrote, but a "satisfactory" accord had developed nonetheless. A second multiedition companion, *More about This Business of Music*, added chapters on structuring "serious music" (i.e., classical), jazz, church songs, printed scores, and touring networks. While the intro of each *This Business* stressed the huge number of amateur musicians, small number of professionals (the gap a reader might want to cross), the series said at least as much about the global army of service providers and risk managers required to stock music in all its popular dimensions. Radcliffe Joe's *This Business of Disco*, not technically in the series, used its structural approach to become the best book on that genre for many years.

And then came the internet, wrecking not just business models but standard operating procedures. As early as the eighth edition in 2000, with Schemel having passed away and new contributors adding language, the book anticipated media studies professor Henry Jenkins in proclaiming that "all media have converged." Industry figures confronted "a world of often confusing but always challenging acronyms" like MP3. Gone were "the old days when we could wonder at the beneficence of technology and its many gifts to the copyright industries." They cautioned, "The sky is not falling." Well. By 2007, the usual triumphal statistics about record sales had given way to hedging about iPod profits proving music's worth. Nobody knew how to calculate royalties anymore as all sought "a celestial cash register for the celestial jukebox." The end chapter pointedly warned, "Technology Is a Challenge, Not a Choice." The pros were replaced by amateurs, at least for a time, as the public became "producer, distributor, and promoter."

SCHMALTZ AND ADVERSITY

Sammy Davis Jr. and Jane and Burt Boyar, Yes I Can, *1965*

———

"I wanted to vomit." Sammy Davis Jr., still a teenager, experienced the full brunt of American racism in basic training during World War II. Nose broken, skin painted, made to dance for his tormentors, though a sympathetic drill sergeant turned him into an avid reader, loaning him *The Picture of Dorian Gray*. But Davis, appearing in vaudeville since age three, given a role in an **Ethel Waters** film at age seven, scuffling through the Depression, made it back on stage, teamed with a fellow, if white, soldier: the son of song-and-dance man George

Cohan. And when he performed, even the most brutal Texan "found something of me."

A six-hundred-page memoir, *Yes I Can* assumed "show people are different." It foregrounded its leading man's pathos, but found redemption in Mr. Entertainer connecting with audiences. The coauthors, Broadway columnists Burt and Jane Boyar, were friends who gave up their night jobs in the six-year process of getting Davis, born in 1925, to reflect on his first thirty-five years, then finished decades later with *Why Me?*—combined and edited, in *Sammy: An Autobiography*. Burt Boyar recalled: "I amused him by singing to him a la Al Jolson. I was a big Jolson fan, after seeing *The Jolson Story* six times, I knew all the songs and did a fair Jolson. When Sammy was down he'd say, 'Do that corny Jolson thing you do.' and I'd get down on one knee and sing 'Mammy' or 'California Here I Come' and believe me that would make anyone laugh and forget his troubles. You could say we exchanged humiliations."

Davis, like Judy Garland, grew up in a trunk, crossing the country with his father and "uncle" Will Mastin twenty-three times in the Will Mastin Trio by age fifteen. He would be buried between them, his first protectors. **Frank Sinatra**—whom he met when Blue Eyes sang with Tommy Dorsey—was his second, both a patron and artistic model, singing "free, unencumbered, as easy as if he were in a shower," and swinging through life in a related vision of freedom. But others helped: Mickey Rooney, Jerry Lewis, Milton Berle, Eddie Cantor—figures in the transition from blackface-era vaudeville to radio, Hollywood, and variety-show television. Davis, seizing postwar possibility, cut back what he saw as "shuffling," imitated whites as comically as he always had **Louis Armstrong**, made Civil Rights jokes. But he never modeled soul or delved into jazz; his blues were the Tin Pan Alley variety. At one point in *Yes I Can*, Harry Richman, the renamed Russian Jewish performer, declared "I'm turning 'Birth of the Blues' over to my young friend, Sammy Davis, Jr." Davis wrote: "I appreciated it for the gorgeous piece of show business schmaltz that it was."

Faced with racial adversity, Davis thought "I had to get bigger, that's all. I just had to get bigger." *Yes I Can* gave readers that story, as Vegas casinos let him perform and then reside, and as he helped Martin Luther King Jr. But its greatness as memoir was in showing Davis's unending shamings: racist imprecations on his homes in white neighborhoods, sidelining by the Kennedy campaign for his engagement to a white movie star (the mob contract, earlier, for dating a different white star was left for the later memoir), and abandonment by a Black audience who felt "you have removed yourself from Negro life." Davis, obsessed with his phoniness, hated listening to playbacks of his routines, knew his addiction to spending for catharsis meant not amassing wealth. He was who he was:

"primarily a nightclub performer" with roots in "the old vaudeville in which I'd been raised." Yet he also modeled the future: his "controversial" oddity left a marker for Elton John or Michael Jackson's; his car-wreck appearances in the tabloids put bodies in those pricey nightclub seats as "reality" show celebrity. The first memoir ended disingenuously, with Davis looking at his young daughter as a new path. The second noted that daughter's uncontroversial interracial, interfaith marriage as an achievement even his now-Republican entertainer friends, like Reagan, could take pride in. It ended in the place the Candyman with the replaced hip could never leave—onstage, talking to an audience.

NEW JOURNALISM AND ELECTRIFIED SYNTAX

Tom Wolfe, The Kandy-Kolored Tangerine-Flake Streamline Baby, *1965*

———

The flashiest reporter working the sixties beat, Wolfe told an interviewer that he regarded pop as "one of the great curses of my literary life. Pop is a word you cannot win with. There's no other meaning for it other than 'trivial.'" He was not averse to the term rock and roll, though he wrote about it as F. Scott Fitzgerald wrote about the jazz age: "now high styles come from low places." His "new journalism" defining articles related nothing about blues and **Elvis Presley**, but everything about how DJ Murray the K, producer Phil Spector, Warhol celebrity Jane Holzer, media guru Marshall McLuhan, hi-fi sex recluse Hugh Hefner, and silicone tits recipient Carole Doda had electrified syntax, rendered a "new sensibility—Baby baby baby where did our love go?—the new world, submerged so long, invisible, and now arising, slippy, shiny, electric—Super Scuba-man!—out of the vinyl deeps."

It helped that Wolfe was watching far more than participating, a Virginian turned on to popular culture studies by Marshall Fishwick at Washington and Lee University, languishing but learning through an American Studies PhD at Yale. Newspaper jobs led to a story on cars, California, and teenagers, which he wrote listening to Top 40 on WABC and set to that cadence of blather and beat, pages of "vignettes, odds and ends of scholarship, bits of memoir, short bursts of sociology, apostrophes, epithets, moans, cackles, anything that came into my head." *Kandy-Kolored* and its sequel, *The Pumphouse Gang*, were studies in "this incredible combination of form plus money." The post–World War II boom, a "happiness explosion," had given not only teens, but the southerners of NASCAR, the former proletarians and gangsters of Las Vegas, opportunity to "build monuments to their own styles." Hippies thought the counterculture transcended this commodified carnival. Wolfe, who'd used "psychedelic" as a description as early as 1965, knew better.

He took his seersucker on the bus with Ken Kesey's Merry Pranksters and wrote his first full book, *The Electric Kool-Aid Acid Test*, about a trip purging Black notions of cool in favor of a Grateful Dead and Stewart Brand strobing. Hefner, inclined to "split from *communitas* and start his own league," had anticipated this American segregation into "whole little societies" like the Sunset Strip rock scene. Wolfe was dazzled, but he was no convert. That became clear with *Radical Chic and Mau-Mauing the Flak Catchers*, which satirized a Leonard Bernstein party for the Black Panthers as status seeking by New Yorkers with enough apartment rooms. Soon, he'd call the 1970s a "Me Decade" of therapeutic hustlers like the EST trainer who said "Take your finger off the repress button!" The rock and roll of Jersey teens doing the Frug at the Peppermint Lounge took a new name: "Hundreds of young males may be seen dancing with one another to flashing lights and recorded music in a homoerotic frenzy, while prominent citizens, including politicians, lawyers, financiers, and upper-class matrons, as well as every sort of well-known figure in the arts, most of them heterosexual, look on, apparently greatly stimulated by the atmosphere. This is described in the native press as 'disco fever.'"

Profitable rock magazine *Rolling Stone* now supported his writing, both the astronaut story *The Right Stuff*, resurrecting Fishwick's studies of American heroes, and the serialized *Gatsby*/*Carrie* urban novel *Bonfire of the Vanities*, yuppies on Wall Street and the underclass in the Bronx. Wolfe would be seen as canny for his tabloid tale's anticipation of Bernard Goetz and Tawana Brawley. Or as racist and sexist, for again viewing the identity movements that emerged from the sixties, and the conservative backlash against them, as a zero-sum struggle over prestige. Wolfe knew the back pages of the new (the two references to Carl Van Vechten lurking in the pages of *Kandy* were telling), understood that an electrified vernacular would sooner or later short out. But even as he called for realism to revive and mocked modern art for antibourgeois posturing, his hole card was that he was a Victorian at heart, addicted to sensation, the precursor of modernism that offered a way to outlive it.

DEFINING A GENRE

Bill C. Malone, Country Music, U.S.A.: A Fifty-Year History, *1968*

———

There are instructive differences between the first edition of this book—more central to its genre's self-understanding than any other genre book—and its later revisions. The original account, a history dissertation published in a folklore series, was concerned to make two cases: First, that a scorned hillbilly music had become "a multi-million dollar industry and one of the most durable forms of American entertainment." And second, that it remained "as 'country' as rapid urbanization and commercial pressures will allow it to be." By the 1985 retake, Malone had less to prove: country's importance was evident. Its countryness remained a question.

Malone could craft a richly detailed history because networks of record collectors and folk scholars had created lineages for the early material: the fabled 1965 "Hillbilly Issue" of the *Journal of American Folklore* began with guest editor D. K. Wilgus's complaint, "We consider *commercial* and *folk* such antithetical concepts that anything other than domestic folk tradition seems to belong in a single non-folk category, when we are willing to consider it at all." Archie Green considered the term *hillbilly*, a pejorative-comical description that had stuck, dating back to the efforts of Ralph Peer, who wrote Green: "It is quite true . . . that I originated the terms 'Hillbilly' and 'Race' as applied to the record business." The only solid source Green could use was Linnell Gentry's 1961 *History and Encyclopedia of Country, Western, and Gospel Music,* a mix of reprinted older press accounts and short bios. In a roundup of sources elsewhere in the issue, Ed Kahn mentioned a novel, Borden Deal's *The Insolent Breed*; a biography by Jimmie Rodgers's widow Carrie; *Hubbin' It,* Ruth Knowles's long-lost biography of Western Swing bandleader Bob Wills; a 1952 Grand Ole Opry account by William McDaniel and Harold Seligman; and two recent *Billboard* "World of Country Music" special issues.

This was all changing, however. The folkies formed a John Edwards Memorial Foundation (JEMF) at UCLA, named for an Australian collector. The genre's trade organization, the Country Music Association (CMA)—in the process of creating a Country Music Hall of Fame—worked to sponsor an official history. Robert Shelton, best known for being the first to write about **Bob Dylan** in the *New York Times,* dedicated his 1966 *Country Music Story* to the JEMF and CMA. It started with an image from a 1930s medicine show and the lines, "Vaudeville never died. It moved to Nashville, Tennessee." Then Shelton qualified: "Here is a music that is unashamed of being sentimental and nostalgic, a music that places sincerity higher on its ladder of values than refinement." And he noted the "drift toward a modern, sleek sound" in response to **Elvis Presley**, spotting a debate—the terms came from jazz—"between traditionalists and modernists." He gave Hank Williams much less attention than Jimmie Rodgers—the pantheon had not been fully set beyond the earliest years of hillbilly. But he also pointed out the exclusion of Black contributions from country's evolving narrative, the "area that folk fans find the most difficult to accept."

Malone's history was itself touched by the folk revival: the first edition's cover graphics and take on early commercial recordings was shaped by the look and content of Harry Smith's box set, the *Anthology of American Folk Music*. Yet Malone, who'd grown up in Texas, wrote about southern music as a native, with more erudition than Shelton but also more identification. He was drawn to Uncle Dave Macon's showy, modernized folklore, to Jimmie Rodgers's "effortless informality," to the Blue Sky Boys "refusing to surrender to commercialism," to working-class southern white men storming the beaches of urbanization and electrification. His key contribution conceptually was to underline the term *honky-tonk* for the amplified music that emerged out of Texas oilfield bars, gave language to the style that Rodgers's blue yodels anticipated, Williams's lost soul anthems sanctified, and fans both inside and outside the Nashville mainstream could revere: a hardcore country, neither folk nor pop.

With Malone exemplifying how to write academically solid music history with trade organization resources, and with honky-tonk a hardcore ideal to reconcile folk, region, and commercialization, a country literature was free to flourish, and did for a generation. Paul Hemphill's *The Nashville Sound* was singular journalism as rock bent mainstream country at the turn of the 1970s. *Country Music* magazine emerged to publish *Rolling Stone* rock-critic types: Patrick Carr edited *The Illustrated History of Country Music* for it while Michael Bane published a book on *The Outlaws*, sanctioned rebels, and John Morthland's albums guide, *Best of Country Music,* represented a working canon. The Country Music Foundation (CMF), connected to the Country Hall, produced a coffee-table gift-shop offering with much stronger editorial than typical: Paul Kingsbury's *Country: The Music and the Musicians*. In it, the museum's head, Bill Ivey, offered a chapter on business practices—musician, producer, and label exec Chet Atkins jingling change: "'That,' says Chet, 'is the Nashville Sound.'" But the volume also had room for **Nick Tosches**, who'd published a "twisted" take on *Country* elsewhere, to cover honky-tonk as "The Bartender's Muse." In larger terms, this was a cohort ranging from bluegrass scholar (with CMF backing) Neil Rosenberg to roots biographer Nolan Porter and leading journalist

Chet Flippo, author of the first substantial Hank Williams account. There was even space for the anarchic likes of art critic Dave Hickey, whose "In Defense of the Telecaster Country Outlaws," for *Country Music* magazine helped define that hardcore insurgence in the first place; his later book, *Air Guitar*, is a classic of mixed-media arts criticism.

Still, hardcore country was an inherently sexist, reductive formulation and Malone was shrewd enough to realize that. By his 1985 revision, he became more attentive to the role played by women in creating country music. Personally, he never lost his fanship for a country style that became increasingly "alternative" to Nashville norms: the 2010 edition gave its account of more recent music to Jocelyn Neal because Malone felt he hadn't kept up; the 2018 account of the twenty-first century, by Tracey Laird, was more Americana focused. Malone did grow more appreciative of the role played by commercialism and its blurry stylings, writing a shrewd small book on the subject: *Singing Cowboys and Musical Mountaineers*. He confronted assumptions of country's political conservatism, more prevalent after the late 1960s, arguing for the music's working-class artists as populist and ideologically eclectic: for a fuller account see his *Don't Get above Your Raisin.'* His instinct, from the start, had been that change "did not kill country music, it merely transformed it," that "the 'folk' do not always act in the manner in which some people think they should." As a bibliography of writing that would top one hundred pages by the third edition followed in his wake, it became clear that Malone—an academic who loved journalistic writing more, a fan with a historian's bent for objectivity—had not only written the first great history of country. He'd set down a sustainable tradition, as surely as that other Bill M. in bluegrass.

SWING'S MOVERS AS AN ALTERNATE
HISTORY OF AMERICAN POP

Marshall and Jean Stearns, Jazz Dance: The Story of
American Vernacular Dance, *1968*

———

For generations, the dance clarified the song, gave music added social momentousness like the lyric. Blackface minstrelsy's "Jim Crow": arch and spin of the racialized body alongside chorus and rejoinder. Tap dancing and Lindy hops:

the jazz conquest of pop. *American Bandstand* or *Soul Train* dancers on TV by day; disco all night. But dance's imprint was frustrating to preserve. No sheet music, no LP, just a stage, film, or TV performance witnessed, and then ether until YouTube arrived. Social dancing? Even murkier. So writing substituted. Malcolm X, in *The Autobiography*, recalled Harlem's Savoy: "They'd jam-pack that ballroom, the black girls in way-out silk and satin dresses and shoes, their hair done in all kinds of styles, the men sharp in their zoot suits and crazy conks and everybody grinning and greased and gassed . . . My long-suppressed African instincts broke through and loose." In their needs, constraints, their corollaries, dance and pop presented as fraternal twins.

Marshall Stearns, the hot club organizer turned critic, professor, and Institute of Jazz Studies founder, worked for years with his wife, Jean, on a massive number of interviews that became *Jazz Dance*, finished just before his fatal heart attack in 1966 and culled for stories and participant viewpoints to this day. Tera Hunter, evoking working-class Black dancing in Atlanta in *To 'Joy My Freedom*, used a *Jazz Dance* tale by vaudeville's Coot Grant about Sue, who worked furnaces like a man in Birmingham. "When Sue arrived at my father's tonk, people would yell, 'Here Comes Sue! Do the Funky Butt, Baby! As soon as she got high and happy, that's what she'd do, pulling up her skirts and grinding her rear end like an alligator crawling up a bank." For the Stearnses, this defined "American vernacular dance," which they traced back to Africa in the manner of Melville Herskovits and compared directly to contemporary rock and roll: **Elvis Presley** "a relatively tame version of the ancient Snake Hips of the Negro folk, popularized in Harlem by dancer Earl Tucker during the twenties."

Not every detail proved accurate. But the discernment shown in calling such dancers "a kind of folk avant-garde," a phrase used by many thereafter, mattered and shaped the anecdotes into a show-business savvy and ecumenical, if apolitical, synthesis. The Stearnses esteemed tap as "one of the highest artistic achievements" and considered vaudeville the "reservoir of American vernacular dance," rather than its caricature. They worried that the tradition was fading, like swing bands, and noted without reproach star Hollywood dancer Gene Kelly's complaint that "the field is dominated by homosexuals." But they were also conscious of vaudeville's Cholly Atkins tutoring Motown acts and Latin dancing at New York's Palladium taking on some of the Savoy's old energy. By the time the book was republished in the 1990s, jazz dancing, like swing and tap, had thoroughly revived—if in a form as racially indeterminate as that early Joan Crawford Charleston they'd savored in the 1928 feature *Our Dancing Daughters*.

Historically, dance had always turned on who paired with whom—with African American identity's role in the exchange the most charged. Paul Cressey's 1932 *Taxi-Dance Hall*, reporting from a Juvenile Protection Association officer, found the ten-cents-a-dancers catering to Filipinos, Chinese, Mexicans, various Europeans—but not Blacks. Similarly, in *Cheap Amusements* historian Kathy Peiss found "Dance Madness" in the immigrant working class-women of early twentieth-century New York, including "tough dances" that simulated sex, but in racially segregated dance halls. Lewis Erenberg's cabaret study, *Steppin' Out*, resurrected the Latin "tango pirate," viewed as a potential threat to middle- and upper-class women.

Some of these divisions proved lasting. Joanna Bosse's recent *Becoming Beautiful*, an ethnomusicology of ballroom dancing in Illinois, found a schism of Standard and Latin in the instruction led by an Asian American owner and silence around Black dance legacies. Similarly, in *American Allegory*, "carnal sociologist" Black Hawk Hancock was fired as a dance instructor for talking too much about the Black origins of the Lindy. Brenda Dixon-Gottschild's 1996 *Digging the Africanist Presence in American Performance*, a pivotal intervention, sought to correct this skewed multiculturalism, invoking Carl Van Vechten's 1930 warning, in his novel *Parties*: "Nearly all the dancing now to be seen in our musical shows is of Negro origin. But both critics and public are so ignorant of this fact that the production of a new Negro revue is an excuse for the revival of the hoary old lament that it is pity the Negro can't create anything for himself, that he is obliged to imitate the white man's revues. This, in brief, has been the history of the Cakewalk, the Bunny Hug, the Turkey Trot, the Charleston, and the Black Bottom. It will probably be the history of the Lindy Hop." Constance Valis Hill's thorough social history, *Tap Dancing America*, stressed its entwined Black and Irish qualities

If Black vernacular underlay every step dance took, feeding largely uncredited into star turns, ballroom beautification, and other fantasies of gender and sexuality, where did that leave African Americans? Lynne Emery's *Black Dance*, by a white author citing Malcolm X's inspiration in the early 1970s, critiqued racist accounts (with words for the Stearnses on minstrelsy), reorienting to such Black writers as dancer-anthropologist Katherine Dunham, **Zora Neale Hurston**, **Langston Hughes**, and **Alain Locke**. Emery presented the blues and *Shuffle Along* Broadway movers as prelude to concert-world dance figures such as Pearl Primus and Alvin Ailey. Katrina Hazzard-Gordon's *Jookin'* connected Black dance to institutions: a "jook continuum" outside white scrutiny and the licensed "commercial urban complex." The first mattered more: "The African-American jook may very well be the most significant development in American popular dance and popular music history." Jacqui Malone's *Steppin' on the Blues* took a similar position with new jazz studies rhetoric: "**Albert Murray** calls the African American public dance a ritual of purification, affirmation, and celebration. It helps drive the blues away." Ingenious chapters connected vernacular to Black college marching bands and fraternities: "One attends a social event to hear the gutsy scream of James Brown and to witness his smooth dance moves; to see the precision stepping of Black sororities and fraternities and to hear their polyrhythms, chants, and songs of allusion; to listen to the halftime music of the FAMU Marching 100 and to watch the high-stepping drum majors and musicians strut their stuff."

Less central to popular music studies, the swing-Lindy-jitterbug-tap years through World War II were favored by dance writers. Norma Miller and Frankie Manning memoirs revisited Whitey's Lindy Hoppers, the most visible of the Savoy dancers. Manning was particularly acute on how Savoy drummer Chick Webb interacted with the Lindy elite—an epitome. Erenberg's *Swinging the Dream* looked for fan experiences, placing ads in two hundred papers to secure anecdotes that fed a great chapter on swing as youth culture and others on white swing leaders Benny Goodman and Glenn Miller. Joel Dinerstein's retitling, *Swinging the Machine*, saw an "aesthetics of acceleration" in a line from the architect Le Corbusier: "The Negroes of the USA have breathed into jazz the song, the rhythm and the sound of machines." The fusing of energy and control marked swing as it was writ large, from Busby Berkeley musical scenes to the Lindy as a machine aesthetics gone airborne; Dinerstein gave particular attention to "tap segregation" and other white appropriations. Manning's memoir fondly recalled the moment he danced with pin-up celeb Betty Grable as an enlisted man; Sherrie Tucker's *Dance Floor Democracy* stressed the imbalances of such moments, using cultural memories of the famed Hollywood Canteen to capture swing's intersection of dance, gender, race, pop culture, and nationalism. Christi Jay Wells's 2021 *Between Beats: The Jazz Tradition and Black Vernacular Dance* will likely be the subject's new benchmark.

A field developed around dance studies, collected in such volumes as Thomas DeFrantz's *Dancing Many Drums*, Julie Malnig's *Ballroom, Boogie, Shimmy Sham, Shake*, Guarino and Oliver's Stearns homage of sorts, *Jazz Dance*, and Anthony Shay and Barbara Sellers-Young's *Oxford Handbook of Dance and Ethnicity*. DeFrantz's anthology put the Stearnses in historical context, unearthed vaudeville's Whitman Sisters—including male impersonator Bert—itemized dance instruction songs, and looked at a radical work by Katherine Dunham suppressed in Cold War America. Malnig's surveyed women Apache dancing in 1910s New York; the "mambo body' in New York and Havana; teen dance fads from the Twist era; Jack Cole's modernist dance to Goodman's "Sing, Sing, Sing"; and the "insertion of social dance in the modern-dress musicals." Much to cover—a different set of roots and branches than pop. Joseph Schloss's *Foundation*, an ethnomusicology of B-boys and B-girls in New York, found dancers to be largely Latinx, drawing uprock moves from older Afro-Latin styles, the counterpart to hip-hop emerging musically from Latinized funk. *American Allegory*'s Hancock, irritated by the racial imaginary of swing, took solace in the contemporary Black counterpart: steppin'.

Powerful dance writing, past and present, hinted at possibilities beyond cultural studies. The writings of Roger Pryor Dodge, the dancer and jazz critic whose 1929–64 essays saw movement as the bodily counterpart to Bubber Miley's trumpet work, or Savoy dancers as a dance of "doing," were finally collected in the mid-1990s. Brilliant Latin American correspondent Alma Guillermoprieto described Brazilian *Samba*. Robert Farris Thompson distilled his pivotal theories of *African Art in Motion* into a single study, *Tango: The Art History of Love*, which covered "Tango in Hollywood" as much as the form's Black origins, milonga, "the conscience of tango" and risked a literary analogy: "Tango as dance, in the phrasing of Cormac McCarthy, contains within itself its own arrangement, history, and finale." Marta Savigliano's earlier *Tango and the Political Economy of Passion* was more theorized but no less audacious in its authorial presence. Love, passion: these combined more easily with the vernacular in dance writing, it seemed, than in music writing, where **Elijah Wald**'s case for dancing girls as the engine of pop history, *How the Beatles Destroyed Rock 'n' Roll*, remained an invitation rarely taken in hand. Ann Powers's *Good Booty*, picking up on dancers throughout the twentieth century and into the Britney-as-cyborg neoliberal moves of this one, was the most ingenious and comprehensive integration of dancing and pop music by far—even Deadhead moves got a tumble.

Megan Pugh's *America Dancing* came closest to a one-volume synthesis, a **Greil Marcus**–inspired but academically trained author favoring examples that subsumed multitudes and exploded meaning, aware that "we are forever recombining vernacular forms" and eager to vivify the process. Pugh's book spanned cakewalk to moonwalk: Bill "Bojangles" Robinson as dance's Bert Williams; Fred Astaire via Morris Dickstein's great reading in *Dancing in the Dark* as an icon in the vein of machine-beating folk hero John Henry; *Oklahoma!* choreographer Agnes de Mille inventing an Americana that obliterated Black dance stagings; Folkways recordings reconstituted for art dance by outlaw Paul Taylor; and one Michael Jackson. She leapt eras: "This is the 'wing' part of the nineteenth-century buck-and-wing, by way of the Charleston, carried forth by minstrel men to Macon, Georgia, where it was funkified by the Godfather of Soul, and mimicked by a little boy from the Midwest." So much history, it turned out, danced in search of the latest answer to Black Panther Stokely Carmichael's question: "How can black people inside of this country move?"

ROCK AND ROLL'S GREATEST HYPER

Nik Cohn, Awopbopaloobop Alopbamboom, *1969/1970*

———

"The way I like it, pop is all teenage property, and it mirrors everything that happens to teenagers in this time, in this American twentieth century. It is about clothes and cars and dancing; it's about parents and high school and being tied and breaking loose; it's about getting sex and getting rich and getting old; it's about America; it's about cities and noise. Get right down to it, it's all about Coca Cola." Cohn was in his early twenties when he wrote this, one of England's "Young Meteors," swinging through the sixties and among the first to express a **Tom Wolfe** sensibility from inside the baby-boom experience. There would be other versions of how Americanization produced British Invasion and eventually globalization: Reinhold Wagnleitner outlined *Coca-Colonization* from Austria, while German director Wim Wenders provided artistic vantage on Kinks and westerns in *Emotion Pictures*. Cohn's strengths were caught by the flap copy for a U.S. printing, *Rock from the Beginning.* (That and *Pop from the Beginning* in the United Kingdom were initial 1969 titles, the better title, a "Tutti Frutti" bleat, used from 1970 on.) "His words make music, capture the flash and speed, raucousness and vulgarity, guts and glory of rock." Already author of a rock novel, *I Am Still the Greatest Says Johnny Angelo*, Cohn would write text for *Rock Dreams*, paintings by Guy Peellaert of the music's mythological figures, then give *New York* magazine "Tribal Rites of the New Saturday Night," optioned into *Saturday Night Fever.* A prophet of fizz.

In *Lipstick Traces,* **Greil Marcus** noted Cohn's father, Norman, author of a classic study of revolutionary millenarians, but Nik countered with his own saga as time progressed. *Yes We Have No* roamed techno England in the 1990s to find Manolo Blahnik stilettos in the Newcastle night zones that had taught him about Kerouac and pot. *Triksta* updated to the bounce rap of 2000s New Orleans, where the "old white fuck" got enough seed money from a flailing former label head to make himself a player. But the book also circled back, revealing that he'd fallen for the city reading the **Alan Lomax** setting of his **Jelly Roll Morton** jazz oral history, *Mister Jelly Roll*, in 1959 at age 13. He'd loved, he recalled, the book's "racy line drawings. An octoroon showed off her cleavage in a doorway." But best were the pimps, the sports Morton described walking with a style "called shooting the agate." Johnny Angelo had the same agate moves down pat, cited explicitly, in the novel Cohn had built around his sociopathic rise and fall, a figure "satanic, messianic, kitsch and camp, and psychotic, and martyred, and just plain dirty," though mostly inflated from an interview with Texas pop sensation P. J. Proby. That, Cohn realized four decades later, was his central narrative: Male groups, gangs like Vincent's "Faces" in the Mod-type lingo he'd assigned to a Brooklyn disco set. And their leaders, his surrogates, from Morton to **Elvis** and beyond. The facts hardly mattered. "When in doubt, shoot the agate."

Awopbop had called modern pop a mix of Black beats and white sentiment, beginning with the deaf and off-key Johnnie Ray, who "generated more intensity than any performer I ever saw" before one too many arrests for male solicitation. Cohn valued the "highschool" pop of Paul Anka types, worried about the sophisticated notions that the later **Beatles** and especially **Bob Dylan** stood for. Proby—and his "attendant," Bongo Wolf—came up again: "The darkened room, the bourbon, the knickers, the fat Texan drawl—this was true heroism and it made me shake." Sure, there was better music, but "since when was pop anything to do with good music?" As the 1970s moved in, Cohn worried that rock was reducing his realm of myth, pop splitting up, "reduced to human beings." So he fought back. Even before he conjured Travolta one muddy Brooklyn night, he distilled his pop vision into the text of the Peelaert art gallery devoted to "images and obsessions." Proby appeared once more, surrounded by clouds of naked and crying girls, holding a mike and shimmying to the currents. "'I don't do,' said Proby. 'Maestro, I am.'"

EBONY'S PIONEERING CRITIC OF BLACK
POP AS BLACK POWER

Phyl Garland, The Sound of Soul: The Story of Black Music, *1969*

Family ties anchored the musical analysis of this *Ebony* writer's account of soul at the height of Black Power and Aretha crossover. Garland's mother would go on to be the first woman editor-in-chief of leading Black newspaper the *Pittsburgh Courier* and could perform a mean version of **Ethel Waters**'s "Down Home Blues." Her father, a photographer, was also a trombonist and capable of resurrecting his father's ragtime favorites on piano, with stories of watching Ella Fitzgerald win amateur night at the Apollo. Garland received some classical music training and grew up with a jukebox in the living room, "a soulful thing in itself," with records like "After Hours" by Avery Parrish with Erskine Hawkins's band, a lot of Dinah Washington, Nat Cole fighting it out with Muddy Waters. Not all of this was soul music, as 1969 defined that. But it belonged to the same family: "the rhythm and the feeling were always there, in the lilt of a popular ballad, in the unbridled stretching out of a big brass ensemble and in the buoyancy of a blues shout." Garland's reporting uncovered other family stories. Nina Simone, asked about her classical instruction, told her "I was colored long before that!" and explained how she'd sung gospel, jazz, and blues with her mom. Helen Dowdy defined Strawberry Woman in *Porgy and Bess* only after her mother taught her not to sing the part conservatory fashion. B. B. King, by contrast, had blues estrangement from family: house surrendered to ex-wife, no desire to live with dad, owning a building with white tenants who had no desire to live with him.

It would take **Guthrie Ramsey Jr.**, in *Race Music,* to theorize such familialism as musicology; Garland declared herself an amateur. Her ties were to culture reporting, which she'd go on to teach at Columbia. Her music writing, deserving of anthology, continued in *Ebony* through 1978, with a column in *Stereo Review* through 1992 and text for a Michael Jackson photo book. Her *Ebony*-refined tone, celebrating Black achievement, rubbed some radicals wrong: Nikki Giovanni wrote in *Gemini* that "Garland is saying, if we just had a few more white people singing the blues, all would be right with the world." But open-mindedness led to an interesting expansiveness: the assertion that there was no generation gap in Black culture, unlike rock culture; the use of **Amiri Baraka**'s *Blues People* to set the beginning of blues in 1619. Drawing on James Baldwin, she defined soul as "to be present in all that one does, from the effort of loving to the breaking of bread."

Sound of Soul was shrewder on racial appropriation than Giovanni recognized, when compared to the more conventional, if more voluminous overview offered in Arnold Shaw's *World of Soul.* The profile of Aretha Franklin ranged from a portrait of her at home in Detroit to her lineage across gospel and R&B: "No answer could be more soulful than that," the last line, became both a musicological and intensely domestic summary. Garland focused on the cultural politics of shades of dark skin, Cole's issues obtaining ad sponsorship, Hendrix's white following, and the radio division between soul stations and Top 40. **Eileen Southern**'s *Music of Black Americans*, a radically different synthesis appearing soon after, esteemed William Grant Still, Dean of Afro-American Composers; Garland threw snark at his out-of-print catalog and called the orchestrated spirituals of Burleigh and Dett a poor substitute for earthy gospel. She found the collegian in Booker T., staged a conversation between country/ urbane soul figures Albert King and Al Jackson Jr., and used Billy Taylor and Les McCann to pinpoint soul's jazz roots. Her centrist instincts, writing for *Ebony* readers, were structurally revisionist.

ENTERTAINMENT JOURNALISM AND THE
POWER OF KNOWING

Lillian Roxon, Rock Encyclopedia, *1969*

———

"He is great," Roxon wrote in her entry on Fred Neil, "and everyone inside rock knows it." Roxon, born Liliana Ropschitz in Italy in 1932 to a family of Polish Jews who made it to Australia just before the war started in Europe, might not have been presumed "inside rock": too old, foreign, female. As Lisa Rhodes documented in *Electric Ladyland,* her study of women in the early rock era, writers and editors at *Rolling Stone* and elsewhere "systematically belittled or ignored" women. Rhodes saw two key exceptions among women rock writers: **Ellen Willis**, a great critic, and Roxon, an entertainment journalist who turned the *Encyclopedia*'s vogue into a *Tonight Show* appearance and columns in *Mademoiselle* and the *New York Daily News* before dying of asthma-related symptoms in 1973. Both were revived, Willis as the ultimate embodiment of *Rock She Wrote,* Roxon as *Mother of Rock* in a Robert Milliken biography that captured her centrality to the New York music media world of the early 1970s, and a documentary film, where the likes of Iggy Pop, Danny Fields, and Helen Reddy remembered her asking a snarky question at a Brian Epstein press conference, holding court at Max's Kansas City, making the scene.

Roxon typed herself into rock, finding a knowing tone—that of media and industry insiders, capable of quickly identifying why something worked or didn't, noting an outré detail—that was not specifically feminist but used by many women: Gloria Stavers at *16 Magazine*, for example, or pop-rock columnist Lisa Robinson; even Roxon's feminist provocateur Australian rival Germaine Greer and perhaps friend Linda Eastman, soon McCartney, who took her book's author photo. The six-hundred-page tome didn't read like one: dashed off in seven months, it started with Acid Rock and romped through Zombies. Eric Andersen was "Gangling and innocent and perhaps just a little too beautiful." Eric Burdon's voice: "when America knew the English meant business." Frankie Avalon's star rose, fell ("the sort of adult-controlled love scene the Beatles saved us from"), and lingered: "lately there has been a sentimental swing back to that era." No record collector, Roxon rarely singled out classics for attention, but she could place a Baez or Who, told the history of rock through the Beatles, and located subculture: Hamburg Fab Four as "rough-trade rocker" types, then "Dylany"; Blood, Sweat and Tears as "Bar Mitzvah Soul." The Blues Magoos had the "best coif-genius" in New York, namely "scowling Christopher Pluck at Vidal Sassoon."

While she was quite happy to acknowledge "bowdlerization" of Black music, Roxon wrote from a white rock perspective: her James Brown entry led with his performing for "white New York," her entry on Leonard Cohen (alert to his importance quite early) ran much longer than her one on Sam Cooke, and she bought into stereotypes of Motown as "a sort of watering down of soul for the white pop market." Nor was she much better on women as performers, players, and fans. The **Beatles**, her Lesley Gore entry argued, "put a finish to shrill female nastiness" and her groupies entry, a cataloging of types, threw out: "The most clever groupies get jobs in the industry and often persuade themselves they aren't groupies at all."

But Roxon's voice would linger, recurring in *Entertainment Weekly* pieces by writers who likely never read her, in the conversation at industry lunches on somebody's card. The key was to make it feel that you were there, had always been there, watching Hendrix freak out the moms and kids opening for the Monkees; watching the Monkees get evaluated up into "underground pets" by actual bands taken by their sincerity; relating how a collage of Beatles tunes by Harry Nilsson charmed their press agent Derek Taylor, who turned it over to John Lennon, who talked of nothing else in a May 1968 visit to the United States. It was understanding why the Velvet Underground mattered more than their record sales, and relating to experimentalist **John Cage** ("you hear Cage you realize that rock isn't all that bold and daring") but discotheques and campy Mrs. Elva Miller, too. This wasn't rock as revolution so much as pop looming way too large for an entertainment reporter not to track the biggest story of her life.

AN OVER-THE-TOP GENRE'S FIRST RELIABLE HISTORY

Charlie Gillett, The Sound of the City: The Rise of Rock and Roll, *1970*

———

There were no books on rock and roll that mattered when Gillett set out to expand his Columbia Teachers' College master's thesis of 1966, with help from fellow British music collectors; there would be several by 1970. **Nik Cohn** captured the excitement of Anglo-American teens with *Pop from the Beginning*. **Lilian Roxon**'s *Rock Encyclopedia* paraded New York scene attitude. Paul Williams and **Richard Meltzer** undertook the first American rock-critic books. Carl Belz's *The Story of Rock* pursued a rock as folk-art notion that raised questions **Simon Frith** would answer better years later. Anthologies, including two *Age of Rock* collections by Jonathan Eisen and **Greil Marcus**'s *Rock and Roll Will Stand*, had scattershot success. But Gillett's history endured.

A thesis structured his methodology: rock and roll, at best, was an independent record label creation that embraced diversity, in particular African American and southern styles that the majors rejected. This let him survey label rosters and make the music industry a mobile presence in his account, built poring over *Billboard* microfilm. Second, as with **Paul Oliver** earlier in U.K. blues writing, he had great access to records. It might not matter whether the following sentence was accurate: "Ted Taylor, with one of the more distinctive voices of his time, was even more obviously influenced by the high intense style of Roy Brown than were B. B. King, Bland, and Parker, but Taylor too had a touch of their gospel flavor." But having that range put him beyond his peers.

As with **Bill Malone**'s *Country Music, U.S.A.,* a certain aesthetic editorializing—"softening rock 'n' roll into something that did not sound too aggravating inside suburban living rooms"—was more prominent in Gillett's first edition than his 1980s revision. He thought the best of the music had been weakened in the *American Bandstand* era and found **Elvis Presley** on RCA "more theatrical and self-conscious" than Elvis on Sun. Rock after 1967 was harder for him to enjoy: he'd edit out his initial gripe that Aretha Franklin songs "sounded much the same as one another," but struggle even in the later edition to see the Black Power in James Brown's having "turned all his attention to the function of funk for dancers, reducing the verbal content of his records to repeated phrases and exhortations." For a book called *Sound of the City*, urbanism remained strangely underexamined.

Yet most of what Gillett esteemed in 1970 remained vital in 1983 and through to today. (He'd write a second book, about Atlantic Records, work on new wave records with Ian Dury and Lene Lovich, then DJ for the BBC, a key advocate for African music.) His basic outline gave a solid four-stage periodization: rock and roll, its R&B underpinnings, how Black music went on after rock and roll, and the "transatlantic echoes" of British and counterculture rock. That joined with an aptitude for quick summary of artistic qualities: he wrote of Smokey Robinson, "The sadness was an aura, never a pool he wallowed in as did so many others," while the **Beatles** "provided in meat and bone and a sharp glance across a room the spirit" Angry Young Man British theater and film had lacked.

Gillett knew his sounds and the cultural revision they represented. He cared about Black music as lineage and living force. He was a rock and roller, not a hippie. One of the lines cut after the first edition represented a savvy early critique of rockism. "But while the contrived bubblegum sound was recorded by independent companies, rock was almost entirely under the control of majors, confirming the impression that, despite the vaunted political implications of the music, this was a formulated product, whose audience was often more, rather than less, gullible than the bubblegum and soul audiences they sometimes belittled."

ROCK CRITIC OF THE TRIVIALLY AWESOME

Richard Meltzer, The Aesthetics of Rock, *1970*

———

Gilbert Chase, pioneer for belatedly bringing U.S. popular music to musicology, commissioned wooliest early American rock critic, Richard Meltzer, for an issue of *Arts in Society*, and got "Recent Reinstantiations of Flea-Flop in the Mustard Tusk Scene." Not exactly Charles Ives. But Meltzer—who mentioned Bartók and Schoenberg up top, then evoked "non-non-navigational" rockers, deploying his "grocery list" approach—doesn't seem that different, in retrospect, from avant-garde figures emerging in the latter 1960s. It was merely Meltzer's task to derive mandalas from the Trashmen's "Surfin' Bird," whose repeated lyrics he transcribed, with descriptive note at one point in the text: "prolonged sound of vomiting." To this Yale philosophy dropout, Blue Öyster Cult crony, and pioneer of psychedelic jitter-prose, rock was "a particular blend of the earth-shattering and the forgettably trivial . . . trivially awesome."

Meltzer was easy to wrongly dismiss: an actual philosophy professor, Theodore Gracyk, later pointedly subtitled his book *Rhythm and Noise, An Aesthetic of Rock*, making fewer claims as he detailed why the recordings focus of pop-rock differed from scores or live performance. Others, like Albin Zak, then picked up on Gracyk's claims. Meltzer became a crank who thirty years later, in "Vinyl Reckoning" (collected, like "Recent Reinstantiations," in 2000's *A Whore Just Like the Rest*), attacked **Robert Christgau** and **Greil Marcus** for stealing his thunder—and cooties. We might never wholly grasp his "unknown tongues" approach, accounting for the germinal no matter how inane the origins. *The Aesthetics of Rock* just went on. "Here is where rock 'n' roll enters. All music is overstatement of a sort, any music after **Cage** and company is overstated overstatement, and rock 'n' roll is overstated overstatement taken as subtlety (as well as itself)." No chapter breaks or breaths. As Meltzer liked to write, so what?

The leaps in prose worked a bit like how he'd described Hendrix, who asked him if he'd written it stoned: "a paisley, metaphorically wondrous and elusive enough to be even more all-encompassing without the 'of relevance' attached." He and his fellow "noise boys," **Nick Tosches** and **Lester Bangs**, were the punk riposte to Christgau, Marcus, and **Ellen Willis**'s little magazine discursiveness. Even more than Bangs, Meltzer loved subcategories (enchanting later askew critics such as **Chuck Eddy** and Frank Kogan); his footnotes cavorted. Meltzer's grocery-list, epistemological toe-jam *Aesthetics* held up over time as a precursor of not just punk but blog rock and indie everything. Grumping, he rightly predicted, when the mopey singer-songwriter was still a teenager, "Pretty soon it's gonna be *all* Jackson Browne all over the place."

Meltzer lived to become the purest example—though comix artist Harvey Pekar was more famous—of the intellectual underclass status awaiting a certain kind of half-abandoned privilege. *Gulcher*, his second book, pulled away from pop even as it gave first sightings of Mapplethorpe and Smith. *A Whore Just Like the Rest* documented, over 128 pieces, the one-draft Beat writing style he kept through 1974 and innumerable record company junkets, his contempt for women from Yoko to Blondie, and for Bowie, too. Still, he grew, embracing Los Angeles punk as a DJ and singer; working out takes on Lawrence Welk,

Bud Powell, and Throbbing Gristle; finally considering race and appropriation after the Rodney King uprisings; making a kind of post-everything poetry of the memory of a Jaki Byard album he played after his girlfriend's abortion. Many of his peers stood for rock and roll over rock pretense. Meltzer, insisting "I want to terminate the academy" as it all but made him into a version of a card catalog marked for the dumpster, stood for rock pretense as rock and roll.

BLACK RELIGIOUS FERVOR AS THE CORE
OF ROCK AND SOUL

Anthony Heilbut, The Gospel Sound: Good News and Bad Times, *1971*

———————

Dedicated to "all the gospel singers who didn't sell out" in its first edition, this trade book genre study had its postscript updated for decades, as the central assertion—Black religious fervor was the stylistic core of rock and soul—became accepted, but the performers interviewed and befriended passed on. Marion Williams, for example, died within a year of receiving a MacArthur fellowship and honors at the Kennedy Center, where Little Richard told her, "Honey, *you* made me a star because you gave me my high note." That anecdote pointed out another evolving theme, Heilbut's increasing ability to note publicly what his first edition made history even lightly registering: the central role of gays and lesbians in gospel's "theatrical" presentation style. Much later, in *The Fan Who Knew Too Much*, he took this further, calling gospel "the blues of gay men and lesbians" and remembering how, as a white atheist child of Holocaust escapees, performers like Alex Bradford "presiding over proud and open gay people" helped him explore his own sexuality.

Heilbut loved gospel as a vernacular unicorn. The music was intensely physical, but with a gender fluidity of "male sopranos and female basses" that "recognized the importance and creative capacity of women." Its initial disreputability in the Black community won more crossover respect than propriety. Williams marveled, "They used to talk about us like dogs, call us crazy and Holy Rollers, and now those white children are carrying on worse than we ever did." The style wasn't that old, professionalized in the 1930s, with a "gospel highway" circuit of venues in the golden era of 1945–60. Everything, at best, balanced: showmanship without stylization, founding songwriter Thomas Dorsey's mix of "low-down gospel and a more sentimental middle-class music," vaunted singer Mahalia Jackson importing the blues. Getting figure after figure interviewed just in time—like Jackson or her more secular rival, Sister Rosetta Tharpe—Heilbut sketched a world of song publishers, radio DJs, Holiness churches, and pass-the-hat "free-will programs," some stars but many greats, like Willie Mae Ford Smith, never to rise up; for them, "gospel pays like unskilled labor." Though, as Sam Cooke proved, singers were "as worldly as any in show business," gospel in this telling was popular culture minus what Heilbut's taste deemed overkill. To read the book in conversation with the chapters in *The Fan* exploring the sexuality of figures like Bradford ("Am I Wrong?") or James Cleveland, then taking up Aretha Franklin and the male soprano whoop, offered a rarity: the same author both essentializing a genre and later queering it.

Much that followed *Gospel Sound* took up one or the other pursuit. Codification, first: the gospel quartet received scholarly scrutiny in Kip Lornell's Memphis-focused *Happy in the Service of the Lord*, with much detail added by **Lynn Abbott and Doug Seroff**'s 1870s Fisk Jubilee to late twentieth-century Bessemer, Alabama, chronicle, *To Do This, You Must Know How*. Michael Harris's *The Rise of Gospel Blues* took Dorsey from dirt-farming boyhood amid "the plaintive twang of his uncle's blues guitar" to Decatur Street Atlanta's pleasure spots and a religiosity he learned to popularize musically, giving gospel a blues voice with the personal message of "Take My Hand, Precious Lord." Horace Clarence Boyer, a former singer himself, recounted *The Golden Age of Gospel* with charismatic brevity. Jerma Jackson's *Singing in My Soul*, academic social history, drew on fellow scholars Tera Hunter and Evelyn Higginbotham to show how "sanctified communities" developed, with much on Tharpe and "entrepreneurial black capitalism." Robert Darden, a former *Billboard* gospel music editor, encapsulated highlights from spirituals through Moby samples in *People Get Ready!* Jerry Zolten's *Great God A'Mighty* studied the Dixie Hummingbirds, exiting South Carolina in the 1930s, employed by Paul Simon on "Loves Me Like a Rock" in the 1970s: decades on the gospel highway as "gentlemen of song." Robert Marovich's 2015 *City Called Heaven*, about Chicago as gospel central, came thick with details, like soul progenitor Clyde McPhatter's cousin working with Bradford—but no sexuality.

By this point, the omission was noticeable. Beyond Heilbut's second tour of gospel, others arrived to relay a more erotically inclusive and stylistically fractured account. Gayle Wald's *Shout, Sister, Shout!* celebrated Tharpe as the greatest unknown rocker ever, from her "Rock Me" rewrite of Dorsey to how she coinvented electric guitar style. If gospel stood outside pop in many treatments, Wald made secular connections a through line of the larger history, using

Tharpe's involvement in everything from John Hammond's 1930s "From Spirituals to Swing" concert to Ellis Haizlip—host of the PBS show *Soul* (subject of Wald's subsequent book)—staging "Soul at the Center" in the 1970s. That name nodded to Lincoln Center, but also soul as central to everything and gospel central within that. The treatment of Tharpe's connection to more-than-singing partner Marie Knight made clear that ambiguous sexuality was now as presumed a part of gospel as melisma. So too pop machinations: concert bookers, looking for hype material to fill a stadium for Tharpe, told her to stage a marriage. "Rosetta, find a husband. We'll promote the wedding."

Gospel, queered, turned out to equate to pop, cubed. When Mark Burford, with Bourdieu categories in mind, surveyed *Mahalia Jackson and the Gospel Field*, he captured a different concert than Wald: five thousand attending Golden Gate in Harlem in 1948, to synch with New York's Apollo Records— led by Bess Berman, a rare female label head—promoting the great smash "Move on Up a Little Higher." Gospel here was a highly mediated celebrity form, for all its community connections, that didn't repudiate respectability politics in the name of vernacular so much as rework them in "a determined rebranding of 'whoop-it-up' singing as 'good music.'" Ann Powers's *Good Booty* saw gospel as the key to rock and soul's body pop, using the unrecorded lyrics of "Tutti Frutti" in her title as license to explore all the sacred/secular, gay/straight accelerations of form and function.

Ashon Crawley's *Blackpentecostal Breath*, using the hybrid academic/poetic language of **Fred Moten** and **Nathaniel Mackey**, positioned itself "in the nexus of performance theory, queer theory, sound studies, literary theory, theological studies, and continental philosophy." James Baldwin's gospel-reared queer-of-color critique—represented in such work as *The Fire Next Time*, about Pentecostal worship producing a "rocking church," and his novel, *Just Above My Ahead*, also about the church as training ground and the presence of gay singers within it—factored into this study of the music as a way to "live into the flesh as a critique of the violence of modernity." (For more on Baldwin and Black music, see Ed Pavlić's *Who Can Afford to Improvise?* Appearing just as this book went through copyedits, Alisha Lola Jones's *Flaming? The Peculiar Theopolitics of Fire and Desire in Black Male Gospel Performance* seemed likely to become a major text on queerness in gospel, focused on the choir-director stereotype in particular as it unpacked gender dynamics.) The Hammond B3 defined "black-queer sociality." Crawley detailed how feeling the spirit in choir had led to an encounter with another boy in the church bathroom. The gospel breath, "black pneuma," created "the capacity for the plural movement." To put it another way: "Nothing's got to be real for Kant, he's no Patti LaBelle."

JAZZ MEMOIR OF "ROTARY PERCEPTION" MULTIPLICITY

Charles Mingus, Beneath the Underdog, *1971*

———

At one point in Billy Bones's pimp monologue, *Beneath the Underdog* flashed readers its claim as the next chapter in authorially blurry musical autobiography, in the spirit of **Billie Holiday**'s *Lady Sings the Blues* or **Jelly Roll Morton**'s performed oral history. "Mingus, here's how to save yourself from depending on what rich punks think and critics say about jazz, true jazz, your work. By my reckoning a good jazz musician has got to turn to pimpdom in order to be free and keep his soul straight. Jelly Roll Morton had seven girls I know of and that's the way he bought the time to write and study and incidentally got diamonds in his teeth and probably his asshole." Krin Gabbard's excellent *Better Git It in Your Soul* offered an account of what made the way Mingus told his life story so distinctive—personally written (rare for popular music) in 1963, then halved and reshuffled, with his attentive permission, in 1971, starting with a line, "In other words, I am three," that emphasized the disjunctions to come.

Morton, too, was participant-observer in jazz as Black struggle, funkybutt sexuality, and performed composition, but Mingus upped the art-house quotient, giving recordings such titles as "All the Things You Could Be by Now If Sigmund Freud's Wife Was Your Mother." Early in the book, like an episode in a David Mitchell novel, the narrator became Mingus: "I climbed up on the white table where Baby was laid out and materialized myself into the big hole over his left eye." Immigrant Simon Rodia's outsider-art Watts towers also featured, as did "Nature Boy" singer and mystic Eden Ahbez and avant-garde poet Kenneth Patchen. Mingus at times allowed musicology: "Swing went in one direction, it was linear, and everything had to be played with an obvious pulse, and that's very restrictive. But I use the term 'rotary perception.' If you get a mental picture of the beat existing within a circle you're more free to improvise."

This artist of complicated racial origins, who rued, early in life, "There really was no skin color exactly like his," made Black voices in conversation dominate his story. Trumpeter Fats Navarro and Bones talked resistance to white power in different registers. Jazz musicians on the bandstand discussed whether to take money from dubious women and dubious bandleaders. A paradigm shift or two later, **Jay-Z**'s autobiography would make clear why just being a great rapper wasn't enough—you needed to be a hustler/entrepreneur. Mingus, like Morton before him, put this element of Black music's changing same down in

a form that fit his bohemian, proto–Black Power moment, but which also illustrated the "extended form" compositions on his albums. In the memoir, that
became getting high in the Hollywood Hills on a mix of pot and hash prepared
by a Filipino houseboy for the wealthy white woman who turned out to be a
madam. Or how the Nigerian porter who recognized Mingus at the airport and
nodded to soul internationalism merged into Mingus snorting coke with a pimp
"cousin," whose number-one lady taught Mingus's woman vaginal muscle tricks.

It might have been illuminating to learn more of Mingus's work in a jazz co-op,
or starting his own record label, Debut, with Max Roach. But *Beneath the Underdog* was never less than clear about its terms: jazz as verb rather than noun, performance and conversation to showcase the bravura of Black male multiplicity.

COMPOSING A FORMAL HISTORY

Eileen Southern, The Music of Black Americans, *1971*

———

The prose in this attempt at a summation was studiously bland: "The fusion of
blues and ragtime with brass-band and syncopated dance music resulted in the
music called jazz, a music that developed its own characteristics." When Southern did find some dramatic verve, as in the account of the Nashville Students
(neither from Nashville, nor students, she joked) offering the first formal concert of syncopated music in 1905, her facts were shaky: they had been billed
that time as the Memphis Students, the second edition clarified. Yet her loyal-
ties were clear, to musicians striving to orchestrate Black music through a racism that stretched from music schools to coon-song Tin Pan Alley. "Whatever
opinion critics of the future may have regarding the intrinsic value of the music
of the black pioneers just discussed, these men remain historically important as
the first composers to truly assimilate the characteristic idioms of Negro folk-
song into a body of composed music."

Southern, daughter of a professor and trained as a concert pianist, wrote a
master's thesis, "The Use of Negro Folksong in Symphonic Form," for University of Chicago in 1941, taught for a decade in Black colleges, then another decade in public schools while getting a PhD, unfunded, from NYU—she studied
with a Renaissance scholar and wrote a dissertation on the fifteenth-century
German Buxheim Organ Book. *The Music of Black Americans*—which she

attributed to colleagues in CUNY music departments scoffing at Black music beyond jazz—had wide recognition on Norton, accompanied by a *Readings in Black American Music* edited volume. Southern, turned down for graduate study by Harvard, became its first Black female tenured full professor and chair of Afro-American Studies from 1975 to 1979. With her husband of sixty years, Joseph Southern, handling business details, she launched *Black Perspectives in Music* in 1973, the field's first musicological journal.

Samuel Floyd became inspired by her example, directing an Institute for Research in Black American Music at Fisk, founding *Black Music Research Journal*, and moving both to Columbia College, where he became a dean and edited a bibliography of *Black Music in the United States* with Marsha Reisser. Floyd's important study, *The Power of Black Music*, integrated Henry Louis Gates Jr. on signifyin(g) and Sterling Stuckey on the ring shout with the more evidentiary lineage that Southern and others had traced, the whole operating through a theorizing of Call/Response. This was followed by his editing *The International Dictionary of Black Composers*. Posthumously, his *Transformation of Black Music* appeared, extending Floyd's overview to encompass a diasporic perspective on Black rhythm but also African American composers—and a fascinating chapter, inspired in part by Stuckey, on Melville's observations of Black culture and the relationship of *Moby Dick* and "Benito Cereno" to a nascent blues mood. One chapter in *Transformation*, on Afro-modernism in jazz and R&B, was contributed by **Guthrie Ramsey Jr.**, subsequent editor of *Black Music Research Journal*. Each of these figures saw their work in a lineage, African American scholarship compiling and theorizing Black American music in a tradition dating back to **James Trotter**.

Floyd called the essay he wrote in his and Josephine Wright's Festschrift for her, "Eileen Jackson Southern: Quiet Revolutionary," stressing her ability to work "squarely within the musicological tradition, cherishing its modes of inquiry and its scholarly products, with no desire to undermine or reject the accepted tenets and practices of the profession. What is revolutionary about Southern is her desire to correct all traditional wrong-headed Establishment assumptions about black music, and to accomplish this using Establishment tools." He noted **Richard Crawford**'s parsing of two traditions of Black music research, one more scholarly (Trotter, **Locke**, Maud Cuney-Hare), the other more literary (Du Bois, **Baraka, Murray**). Floyd claimed the second edition of *Music* subtly merged the two.

A comparison of all three editions through 1997 shows change—less despair about Scott Joplin, as his opera and reputation revived, more stuff on travelling companies and theatrical presentation, or the institutionalization of jazz at Lincoln Center, rap making the final version. But Southern remained, at core, an admirer of William Grant Still, "Dean of Afro-American Composers," inclined to rank Ellington's more formal Sacred Concerts above his other achievements. Her 1982 *Biographical Dictionary of Afro-American and African Musicians* had informative information on pre-1920 critic Sylvester Russell and no entry at all on George Clinton. For the person who wrote the Afro-American Music entry in the 1986 *New Grove Dictionary of American Music*, representing the whole category, this was problematic. Gates, brought in to lead African American Studies at Harvard in 1991 in part on the basis of work highlighting Black vernacular devices, represented an opposite perspective: Clinton, not Russell, appeared in Gates's 2008 *African American National Biography*.

Yet Southern should not be dismissed. She rescued nineteenth-century Philadelphia bandleader Frank Johnson, the Ellington of his day, from obscurity, and used Olly Wilson, both composer and admirer of Clinton, a key figure in theorizing Black sound, to end the second edition of her *Readings*. Her Renaissance perspective easily spanned the centuries her subject represented. She admired Trotter and Ernest Hogan for different accomplishments, dismissive of, but not repelled by, wrinkles in the popular. And she upheld a still-enduring tradition, however in eclipse to the vernacular. For her contribution, look to a line by blues-compiler **W. C. Handy**, from a 1940 *Etude* essay in her reader: "I am proud of being the first to collect their elements in orderly documentation."

KRAZY KAT FICTION OF VIRAL VERNACULARS

Ishmael Reed, Mumbo Jumbo, *1972*

Jes Grew, the idea of diasporic African American culture virally spreading across genres and continents, was a phrase that Ishmael Reed took from pioneering critic **James Weldon Johnson** and gave to many others—George Clinton, for example, once had Reed come on stage at a P-Funk concert and present a Sir Nose (i.e., devoid of funk) award to the whites who ran his record labels. Add to the mix Cecil Brown, Reed's intellectual sounding board in turn-of-the-1970s Berkeley, and Richard Pryor as he readied his comedic transformation. Reed, as writer, editor, publisher, performer, and provocateur, augmented a bohemians-of-color network that would eventually encompass **Greg Tate**, Frank Chin, **Jessica Hagedorn**, Walter Moseley, Colson Whitehead, and many others. He loved a gumbo and hated a monoculture, even a Black one. *Mumbo Jumbo*, his third novel, eclipsed the rest of his oeuvre—a countercultural freeze-frame.

It was set in the 1920s, sort of, when "We got reports from down here that people were doing 'stupid sensual things,' were in a state of 'uncontrollable frenzy,' were wriggling like fish, doing something called the 'Eagle Rock' and the 'Sassy Bump'; were cutting a mean 'Mooche,' and 'lusting after relevance.' We decoded this coon mumbo jumbo. We knew that something was Jes Growing just like the 1890s flair-up." Reed summoned **Louis Armstrong** on second lines as spiritual possession and **Zora Neale Hurston** before her revival, with a dedication to "George Herriman, Afro-American, who created Krazy Kat." His narrative offered a thriller, sort of, with PaPa LaBas of the Mumbo Jumbo Kathedral putting his voudon up against a raft of Garveyites, occultists, evil "Atonists," a Malcolm X stand-in, Knights Templar, and a Carl Van Vechten stand-in, too, with time for a parenthetical slam at Albert Goldman and cites of J. A. Rogers in *The New Negro* and Paracelsus, "who startled the academicians by lecturing in the vernacular." "What's that sound?" a character asked another. "It's a loa that Jes Grew here in America among our people. We call it blues."

Born in Tennessee in 1938, Reed had a working-class upbringing plus some college in Buffalo, then five years in New York City that included cofounding the *East Village Other*. His voice was in place by the time he settled for good in the Bay Area: outlaw scholar of Neo-HooDoo and Warren Harding, prose counterpart of Thomas Pynchon in the paranoid Nixon moment but no less of Harlem Renaissance satirist George Schuyler (*Black No More*) in the not-paranoid tradition of African American *ahem*. After *Mumbo Jumbo*, a relatively focused work with its Jes Grew through line, his novels were less noticed in public discourse than his essays contesting feminism. But to read through Bruce Dick and Amritjit Singh Reed's collected *Conversations with Ishmael Reed* is to marvel at his anticipatory sense. Decades before the musical, Reed noticed Alexander Hamilton: "He was black, and Aaron Burr shot him because they were so jealous of him because he was so tricky and groovy with the women." (His *Haunting of Lin Manuel-Miranda,* a critique of *Hamilton,* was staged in 2019.) If Brent Hayes Edwards made jazz's literary qualities a centerpiece, Reed earlier observed: "I think some of the most inventive writing that I've seen is the titles and lyrics of bebop songs, or songs that Fats Waller composed."

An advance taste of *Mumbo Jumbo* appeared in the John Williams and Charles Harris anthology *Amistad* as "Cab Calloway Stands in for the Moon" or "D Hexorcism of Noxon D Awful," described on the title page as "another one of those mean incoherent frequently nonsensical hallucinogenic diatribes by Ishmael Reed." Harding here was Nixon, or Noxon, with his wife Minnie D Moocher, their offspring a thing in the closet with five o'clock shadow and the USA possibly a stage set discarded by Ziegfeld. The satire was buckshot: "This *Marioprocaccino* started off as a one-liner and then it grew larger and larger until now its taken over 20 tables in Toots Shor and has threatened to call up reinforcements." Others in the two volume Black Studies survey included Addison Gayle, whose aesthetic theories Reed dismissed; a vast interview (shepherded, *still*, by Van Vechten) of radical-to-pulp novelist Chester Himes, whom he admired; Mal Watkins on James Brown lyrics as art ("he is not singing *about* black life, he *is* black life"); and similarly recent fiction by Toni Morrison and **Gayl Jones**, rivals in prominence. Morrison, portrayed pushing Reed's patriarchal buttons in his article "Shrovetide in New Orleans," became the Nobelist, while Reed battled unsuccessfully for tenure and Jones abandoned hers and then writing altogether. But Reed endured, somehow, a Schuyler fan for a reason: jazzed by interstices.

DERRIÈRE GARDE PROSE AND RESIDUAL POP STYLES

Alec Wilder, American Popular Song: The Great
Innovators, 1900–1950, *1972*

———

Irving Berlin said hell no to "all that analysis crap," perhaps irked over Wilder's opinions about the repetitive qualities of "Always." But almost everybody else approved what had to be the most copyright permissions of any book in this book: hundreds of musical and lyrical examples. A songwriter and composer himself, born rich, living eccentrically at the Algonquin Hotel, a treasured friend and a mean drunk, Wilder had his *Octets* produced by one **Frank Sinatra**, who also recorded his "I'll Be Around" for the *In the Wee Small Hours* LP that prototyped the concept album. In the office of his publisher, Howard Richmond, with James Maher as his Boswell, Wilder set up with a piano and all the Tin Pan Alley sheet music on earth, then ruminated, examining songs "as attentively as if they were Schubert lieder," a *Times* rave declared. Maher, a jazz scholar, called the approach a "tweedy huff of Edwardian urbanity."

Much turned on the details this method favored. Dylan Hicks, not incidentally a songwriter, told me: "in a brief and appropriately equivocal analysis of

John Klenner's 'Just Friends,' he writes that for him it's the lyricism of measure thirteen that distinguishes the song more than the unexpected chromatic notes in bars three and seven (the chromaticism that probably helped lead Charlie Parker and others to make the tune a jazz standard), and though I don't necessarily side with Wilder there, I always like the opportunity to argue or agree with (and learn from) him on the songwriters' specific melodic and harmonic choices. I like, too, that he's not overreverent about the material." Indeed: summing up George Gershwin, Wilder said, "I jump from enthusiasm to critical reservation like the lines of a fever chart."

But to judge the songs of vaudeville, Broadway, and Hollywood solely as words and scoring was to leave out everything secured by performance, staging, technology, media, life. At times, Wilder gave in, recalling the time he first came across Hoagy Carmichael, singing and playing on a Paul Whiteman recording of "Washboard Blues." There could have been so much more: Wilder's circle included not only Sinatra but the cult cabaret icon Mabel Mercer, pianist Marian McPartland, Columbia Records A&R chief Mitch Miller. Jazz evoker **Whitney Balliett** profiled him in the *New Yorker* and built a book around the results, *Alec Wilder and His Friends*. That work, with its examples of the epistolary Wilder, may have led to *Letters I Never Mailed*: a memoir in the form of harangues. "To Marian: Do you know that you inadvertently depressed the hell out of me by conning me to do that television show? For Christ's sake! When I looked at the playback of that videotape I damn near threw up and fainted, in that order." Wilder also revamped his book into a series of allegedly somewhat more personal radio programs for NPR.

The Wilder of the 1970s represented what he and Balliett called the "derrière garde," a now residual pop style that needed recuperation as standalone art. A strong advocate was Gunther Schuller, who worked with editor Nancy Zeltsman on the 1991 *Alec Wilder: An Introduction* and published Wilder compositions on Margun Music. But Schuller was best known for two books— *Early Jazz* and *The Swing Era*—built on an equally obsessive gleaning: "the assumption that virtually every record made . . . has been listened to, analyzed, and if necessary discussed."

Arguing with Wilder and his fellow monomaniacs produced its own rich literature. Gerald Mast, a hugely productive film scholar connecting theory with the specifics of screwball comedy before an early death from AIDS, wrote one book on musicals, *Can't Help Singin',* that supplied everything Wilder (WASP, sexually ambiguous even to his biographer Desmond Stone) avoided: musicals as the work of gays needing to appeal to goys. Anticipating theater studies to come (Lauren Berlant was a thanked colleague), he was no less eager to challenge *American Popular Song*'s judgements: "Always," for example, was worthy as in fact "precisely repetitive." And it mattered that Berlin's biggest hit was "a singing Christmas card," or that *Show Boat* was far better than Wilder believed, when you accounted for its treatment of race and show biz. Mast saw in Disney animation innovation Wilder wouldn't, "the independent play of music and images," Snow White as a "female impersonator." He traced the field through *Fiddler on the Roof* and *La Cage aux Folles*, out works of Jewish and gay identity, contrasting the latter with its Stephen Sondheim Tony Awards rival, *Sunday in the Park with George*: "the modernist metaphoric conception without tunes which left nobody laughing; the old-fashioned show with laughs, tunes, and legs. Of course, many of its legs were no longer female legs, but male legs pretending."

Wilfrid Sheed, novelist and essayist coming of age in the 1940s, had planned a book with Wilder, and decades after Wilder's death in 1980 supplied it anyway with *The House That George Built*. Sheed wasn't savvy with sheet music, recordings, or pop culture factoids. His was the bull-session approach—anything goes. Unlike Wilder, he wasn't "allergic to Gershwin." And his heart was in "sophistication for the masses," blendings across race and class (though white guys were still the central protagonists) that happened "naturally and spontaneously," given that jazz was also pop. Sure, later "the fussbudget Alec Wilder would be enthralled by Arlen's pure musicianship," but really "the rough-and-ready give-and-take of the bandstand had been his finishing school, and the Cotton Club was the name on his diploma." Richard Rodgers supposedly said "I can pee melody." Harry Warren couldn't get over how famous he wasn't. And Johnny Mercer defined the songwriting breed ("All roads lead through John," Wilder told him) with his mix of "sadism and sentimentality." That was the ticket: messy men who, when they didn't play music, still played at something—Gershwin's tennis partners ranged from Hoagy Carmichael to Arnold Schoenberg.

There would be other interesting distillations of the Great American Songbook, through to critic **Will Friedwald**. Laurence Maslon's *Broadway to Main Street*, focused on cast albums and popularization, an ingenious genealogy with room for early A&R types like Tin Pan Alley publisher Max Dreyfus; landmarks nobody else commemorated, like Eddie Cantor hosting NBC radio's *Chase and Sanborn Hour* in 1931; *My Fair Lady* going on sale the same day **Elvis** first appeared on nationwide TV; and show tunes as "Adult Contemporaneity." Writers pulling up a bar stool to a piano kept reinterpreting the essence of pre-rock standards, much as jazz musicians reworked the actual numbers. Wilder told Balliett, "improvisation is a lightning mystery. In fact, it's *the* creative mystery of our age," more or less negating his book. What a load of bull!

CHARTS AS A NEW LITERATURE

Joel Whitburn, Top Pop Records, 1955–1972, *1973*

———

Nashville's public library interlibrary loan office emailed to say that *Record Research (1955–1969)*, the almost mythic first survey of *Billboard* charts hits fashioned by a Midwestern 45s collector, resided only in noncirculating copies in eighteen institutions. So let's work from the second edition. In 1973, the year of *American Graffiti* and its Top 40 nostalgia, the renamed *Top Pop Records* turned into the juggernaut it has remained: an approach to compiling popular music success as flexible as a jukebox or radio format. Over time, Whitburn published books on Top R&B Records, Top LPs, Top Country, Top Easy Listening, and Top Pop before the arrival of rock and roll. They were pricey but the only spot for a rundown on when a song appeared in the charts, how long it remained there, and how many other hits the performer had.

Whitburn courted controversy with *Pop Memories*, a fascinating, inevitably flawed, attempt to reconstruct chart history from almost the earliest days of recording, 1890–1954. His claims in 1973 to offer "a factual history of the United States' most popular recorded music" were overblown, given the corruptible nature of chart tallying. Nonetheless, because *Billboard* emphasized hit-record listings as rock and roll became a national youth craze, charts told the story of this pop-rock-Top 40 era. Tin Pan Alley had the novelty sheet music hit and standard, sung by a range of performers. Jazz, notably, had the amateur-compiled discography, centered on musicianship in the studio. As the "Discography" entry in the Charles Garrett–edited second edition of the *Grove Dictionary of American Music* documented, this began in 1930s European collector circles with Charles Delaunay's *Hot Discography* and picked up speed with *Jazzmen* coeditor **Charles Edward Smith** et al.'s *Jazz Record Book*, but became totemic with Brian Rust's ever-expanding survey of 78 RPM works, *Jazz Records A–Z*; additional Danish and Belgian efforts led to Canadian Tom Lord's thirty-four volume *Jazz Discography*, online after 2004.

Pop/rock, instead, was about a unique record featuring one performer, concoctions ratified by airplay. This process, almost always involving accidents as much as genius, held its own fascination: a corollary series to Whitburn's work was Fred Bronson's *Billboard Book of Number One Hits*, which through multiple editions (and variants like Christopher Feldman's poignant *Billboard Book of No. Two Singles*) gave an anecdotal page to each chart smash. It might have seemed, when Whitburn started offering his summations, that hits had been

FIGURE 4.5 Sample page 183 from Joel Whitburn, *Top Pop Records 1955–1972*, 1973, showing Whitburn's methodology: release date, peak chart position, and weeks on chart for hit performer recordings. Author's collection.

Date	Pos.	Wks.	ARTIST — RECORDING	Label
			PATTY & THE EMBLEMS	
6/20/64	37	11	MIXED-UP, SHOOK-UP, GIRL..........	Herald 590
			PAUL, BILLY	
11/4/72	1	16	** ME AND MRS. JONES.................	Philadelphia International 3521
			PAUL, LES, & MARY FORD	
11/2/55	38	9	AMUKIRIKI..........................	Capitol 3248
11/2/55	96	2	MAGIC MELODY	Capitol 3248
1/18/56	91	2	TEXAS LADY.........................	Capitol 3301
2/1/56	49	12	MORITAT (THEME FROM THREE PENNY OPERA) (LES PAUL ONLY).....	Capitol 3329
2/8/56	91	1	NUEVO LAREDO.......................	Capitol 3329
1/2/57	35	14	CINCO ROBLES.......................	Capitol 3612
8/24/58	32	10	PUT A RING ON MY FINGER...........	Columbia 41222
4/30/61	37	10	JURA...............................	Columbia 41994
			PAUL & PAULA	
12/29/62	1	15	** HEY PAULA.......................	Philips 40084
3/16/63	6	10	* YOUNG LOVERS.....................	Philips 40096
6/1/63	27	8	FIRST QUARREL......................	Philips 40114
8/24/63	77	5	SOMETHING OLD, SOMETHING NEW	Philips 40130
10/5/63	60	4	FIRST DAY BACK AT SCHOOL.........	Philips 40142
			PAULETTE SISTERS	
11/9/55	92	2	YOU WIN AGAIN	Capitol 3186
			PAVONE, RITA	
6/6/64	26	9	REMEMBER ME.......................	RCA Victor 47-8365
			PAYCHECK, JOHNNY	
12/18/71	91	2	SHE'S ALL I GOT...................	Epic 10783
			PAYNE, FREDA	
4/25/70	3	20	* BAND OF GOLD	Invictus 9075
9/12/70	24	12	DEEPER & DEEPER...................	Invictus 9080
2/13/71	44	8	CHERISH WHAT IS DEAR TO YOU (WHILE IT'S NEAR TO YOU)........	Invictus 9085
6/5/71	12	13	BRING THE BOYS HOME..............	Invictus 9092
10/2/71	52	8	YOU BROUGHT THE JOY..............	Invictus 9100
1/8/72	100	2	THE ROAD WE DIDN'T TAKE	Invictus 9109
			PEACHES & HERB	
12/31/66	21	12	LET'S FALL IN LOVE................	Date 1523
3/25/67	8	12	* CLOSE YOUR EYES.................	Date 1549
6/24/67	20	8	FOR YOUR LOVE	Date 1563
9/30/67	13	9	LOVE IS STRANGE...................	Date 1574
12/16/67	31	8	TWO LITTLE KIDS...................	Date 1586
2/24/68	55	5	THE TEN COMMANDMENTS OF LOVE...	Date 1592
5/18/68	46	8	UNITED............................	Date 1603
11/9/68	75	4	LET'S MAKE A PROMISE	Date 1623
3/1/69	49	7	WHEN HE TOUCHES ME	Date 1637
8/16/69	74	4	LET ME BE THE ONE................	Date 1649
6/26/71	100	2	THE SOUND OF SILENCE.............	Columbia 45386
			PEANUT BUTTER CONSPIRACY	
3/11/67	93	3	IT'S A HAPPENING THING...........	Columbia 43985
			PEARLETTES	
3/10/62	96	2	DUCHESS OF EARL..................	Vee-Jay 435
			PEDICIN, MIKE	
3/7/56	79	1	LARGE LARGE HOUSE...............	RCA Victor 47-6369
2/1/58	71	2	SHAKE A HAND.....................	Cameo 125
			PEDRICK, BOBBY, JR.	
11/16/58	74	4	WHITE BUCKS & SADDLE SHOES.......	Big Top 3004

replaced by rock, soul, and country identity statements. But by 1973, as Elton John sang "Crocodile Rock" and Top 40 rebounded on radio, it was again clear that charts pop would continue chronicling the rival mainstreams of American music.

Even *Top Pop Records 1955–1972*—a slim volume compared to the gargantuan revised and expanded seventh edition of *Billboard Book of Top 40 Hits* for 1955–2000 (pre-website)—contained 2,735 artists and 11,041 records, according to the introduction. Pop was voluminous, welcoming; to make it onto a weekly rundown of one hundred records like the *Billboard* Hot 100 was far less arduous than competing for an Academy Award or an election. With categories added, as in the related books, a performer who failed at pop could register in country, adult pop, Black-oriented listings. Each hit, Whitburn stressed, was big enough to function as a repository of memory, evoking an era. His guides trained readers to approach the geography of popular music through markers vertical (how high did it chart) and horizontal (for how long), to measure careers by one-hit wonders or names filling much of a page. You could dip in from Abaco Dream ("Life and Death in G & A," A&M Records, six weeks, peaked at 74) to—just before Zombies and ZZ Top—Pat Zill ("Pick Me Up on Your Way Down," Indigo, one week, peaked at 91). Alphabetized song titles associated "Lonely Boy" with "Lonely Bull," "Lonely Chair," Crowd, Days, Drifter, Guitar, Island, Life, Man, One, Saturday Night, Soldier, Street, Sumer, Surfer, Teardrops, Teenager, Weekends, and Winds. Was it all the same, then? Pictures of those Whitburn reckoned the Top 100 artists of the Hot 100, 1955–72, suggested otherwise: **Elvis**, **Beatles**, Boone, Ricky Nelson, and Connie Francis, yes, but then Fats Domino, Ray Charles, Supremes, James Brown, and Brenda Lee, through to Bobby Bland at 100.

The Whitburn books were not literature in any traditional sense, but they turned up in every used bookstore's music section, were cited in every book on music prior to the internet supplanting them, and even then held an almost mystical place in pop-rock lore. To get a song, another song, a concert's worth of songs, onto the charts was to visit the promised land. Joel Whitburn, out in Wisconsin, kept the ledger sheet of who had passed through the gates, how high they'd ascended, and how long they had been permitted to remain.

SELLING PLATINUM ACROSS FORMATS

Clive Davis with James Willwerth, Clive:
Inside the Record Business, *1975*

———

As head of Columbia Records in the golden years of the rock boom, Davis was understandably busy. Still, he told us in this memoir, he'd halt the phone calls, mail, and networking whenever sales figures came in. "I could never *stop* reading them, impractical and time-consuming as it was." They were his favorite form of literature. On Wednesdays at 11:00 A.M., at the record division offices at the "Black Rock" midtown building of the full CBS network, Davis would host a weekly meeting: about twenty-five execs from A&R and marketing at the table, another fifty backbenching, to go over those figures, decide how to bump up a Top 40 track or a classical album. When artists or managers considered signing to Columbia, they'd sometimes be invited to these meetings, which would then be staged to highlight hits rather than near-misses. They were his favorite form of theater.

Davis was not the most likable mogul: after eight years of rising to the helm at Columbia and then steering it to record profits, he was summarily fired, allegedly over $93,000 in unauthorized expenses, by rumor over worries about payola for record promotion, especially in the Black music division he'd championed. His style clashed with the blue-blood William Paley legacy of the "Tiffany Network," so he was replaced briefly by his predecessor, show-tunes cast albums and soundtracks champion Goddard Lieberson. But ultimately the job went to Walter Yetnikoff, a promotions maniac with even fewer graces. The Davis style, it turned out, was needed to ship platinum and stock an artist roster across commercial categories. *Clive*, the book Davis wrote to justify his Columbia tenure, is the best book on that style. (Forty years later, he'd write a second, less impressive memoir. For a better sequel, try Yetnikoff's *Howling at the Moon*.) It's less judgy than Steve Chapple and Reebee Garofalo's New Left academic study *Rock 'n' Roll Is Here to Pay*; more balanced, though less fun, than Fredric Dannen's mob-obsessed *Hit Men*; not as rock specific as the touring-band journalism of Geoffrey Stokes's *Starmaking Machinery* and Bob Greene's Alice Cooper–centered *Billion Dollar Baby*.

Where aging hippies feared rock's mass popularization, Davis, born in 1932, viewed the counterculture affectionately from a distance and made an ideal of mainstreaming. Growing up in Brooklyn, he'd favored baseball—a game of statistics. Promoted out of the legal department at Columbia in 1965 to oversee its struggling record sales, he applied the same numbers mentality to renewing the contracts of Andy Williams, an MOR star with a television show, no cultural cachet, and the most solo album sales in the country; Barbra Streisand, a diva with reliable fans and album numbers; and **Bob Dylan**, a culture hero whose dismal sales tallies were "the best-kept secret in the record business." *Clive* turned on such itemizations, meant to illustrate that there was not a single formula for commercial success but ingredients that had to be spiced properly. Rock had to become more like MOR, MOR more like rock, country and R&B like both, because for Davis the most salutary word was *contemporary*: "Barriers were breaking down, and diffuse forms of popular music were sweeping everything before them."

In one fraught moment, Grand Ole Opry legend Minnie Pearl confronted Davis about why his country label head, Bob Johnston, was failing the test of "Nashville politics." Davis schooled himself in what that meant ("I had to let them know—regularly—that I fully appreciated their music"), brought in producer Billy Sherrill to be his emissary, and moved on, just as he insisted on Black promo men when R&B radio programmers rejected white ones. A generation later, in *Music Genres and Corporate Culture*, sociologist **Keith Negus** would treat this capitalist multilingualism as the essence of the post-1960s music business. Davis partied strategically with Janis Joplin and **Miles Davis**, moved operations as needed to a bungalow at the Beverly Hills Hilton, and tried to persuade both his bosses and the snoots at *Rolling Stone* that it was viable to "combine business acumen and creativity." He was hardly perfect in his predictions: "Ten Years After, Neil Diamond and Pink Floyd. These three deals will stand the test of time." But two out of three ain't bad, to cite Meat Loaf, who he passed on, too. The last artist mentioned in this book, finished in 1974? "Billy Joel began to stake his claim."

BLUES RELATIONSHIPS AND BLACK WOMEN'S
DEEP SONGS

Gayl Jones, Corregidora, *1975*

Gayl Jones's poem "Deep Song," named for a **Billie Holiday** recording and citing another ("Crazy He Calls Me"), pinpointed the increasingly fixed, almost burdensome tradition she was aligning herself with, as an African American woman from Kentucky in her early twenties in the Black Power era. "The blues is calling my name . . . Sometimes he is a good dark man / Sometimes he is a bad dark man." There was a countermelody in the verse, free as the 1970s: "He sits with his knees apart. / His fly is broken. . . . I tell him he'd better / do something about his fly."

Her own story would remain mysterious: a creative-writing student at Brown, where a mentor, Michael Harper, referred her to then–Random House editor Toni Morrison, she burst to prominence with *Corregidora*, a novel about a blues singer struggling with the legacy of slavery and her own family, men and sexual desire. The story made generation, birth and the passage of years, a metaphor for Black diasporic modernity. The good dark man/bad dark man here was Mutt, who pushed Ursa down stairs and left her barren; a generation later, she returned to him. A generation after *Corregidora*, Jones gained new public attention: she'd married an unstable man, Robert Higgins, and given up a tenured position with University of Michigan to flee the United States with him so he could avoid responding to a felony charge. Both came back to care for her dying mother in the late 1990s, then Higgins stabbed himself to death when police tried to apprehend him. There has been little information on her life in Kentucky since, but in the spring of 2020, volumes of a newly published novel, *Palmares*, set in Brazil's slavery era, appeared on Amazon, with talk of its full publication by Beacon Press in the fall of 2021.

In an interview with Harper, Jones talked about loving writers like Marquez, Fuentes, Joyce, and back to Chaucer: "writers who I feel can hear . . . Chaucer had to hear because he was writing in the 'vernacular' at a time when 'writers' wrote in Latin. The ballads were in the vernacular but they were oral. The 'people' made them, not 'writers.' Of course, black writers—it goes without saying why we've always had to hear." Jones told Harper she revered *Their Eyes Were Watching God* but questioned if **Zora Neale Hurston** had fully subsumed her anthropological education in letting the vernacular speak her novel. To heal that division, she sought "connection with the oral storytelling and black music continuum." She talked of finding forms "that can bring in everything," of her gender sketches as "blues relationships. . . . Blues acknowledges all different kinds of feelings at once." And she returned to Holiday: "Why sing something the same way twice? I'm thinking about Billie Holiday here, of course. That's the tradition. I like to change a tune."

For white fellow Kentuckian Elizabeth Hardwick—who helped Jones get her college scholarship—writing in *Sleepless Nights*, Holiday remained other: "her singing created a large, swelling anxiety. . . . To speak as part of the white audience of 'knowing' this baroque and puzzling phantom is an immoderation." Jones gave us the other literary path: connection. Emily Lordi, in *Black Resonance: Iconic Women Singers and African American Literature*, sought to "recover the sounds that make writers want to align themselves with musicians in the first place and the literary effects that could make such an effort worthwhile." Lordi, white as well, saw Jones and Holiday as "timbral virtuosos," unfixed in their artistry rather than imprisoned by their biographies or by a static notion of the blues, jazz, or any other folk/art/race constellation. "In this reading, black literature is not authenticated by a stable image of black music but instead serves to make music newly, productively, strange."

Corregidora affirmed such a reading, from the astonishing opening pages of the confrontation between Ursa and Mutt (reminiscent of the following year's start to *Coal Miner's Daughter*, though in that exchange **Loretta Lynn** landed the spousal blows) to the oral sex ending it. The language was as blunt as **Jelly Roll Morton** Library of Congress recordings or Lucille Bogan's 1935 "Shave 'Em Dry," but with soul-era politics addressing racism, colonialism, and sexism without indirection. On the Brazilian slave owner, Corregidora: "My grandma was his daughter, but he was fucking her too." A friend and adversary: "I heard Mama talking bout women like that. Mess up their minds and then fuck up their pussy." The quintessentially vernacular Mutt: "You not such a hard woman. You try to sing hard, but you're not hard." Another friend/adversary: "Like Ma [Rainey], for instance, after all the alcohol and men, the strain made it better, because you could tell what she'd been through."

A larger exploration of the questions raised by Jones's iconic novel and troubled history might look to her mentors and counterparts. Morrison explored *Jazz* in one novel, *Whiteness and the Literary Imagination*. Activist intellectual Angela Davis noted that a Morrison character "might well have been a blues woman had she only found her voice." Davis, studying *Blues Legacies and Black Feminism* through the work of Holiday, Bessie Smith, and Ma Rainey, wrote in the cultural studies era, citing **Stuart Hall** on Blackness and intersectional analyses of race and gender. She noted the lag between her subjects and Black women like Jones, Toni Cade Bambara, Sherley Ann Williams, Mary Helen Washington, and Alice Walker, thinking about them through fiction. (One might add poet Nikki Giovanni, playwright Ntozake Shange.) Jones would never summarize all this. But she might have epitomized it in her great novel, where the language, italicized, at times was allowed to explode. Ursa, in her mind, the repetitions songful, aimed the following at her blues-fearing mother, explaining why singing was her (re)generation: "*let me give witness the only way I can. I'll make a fetus out of grounds of coffee to rub inside my eyes. When it's time to give witness, I'll make a fetus out of grounds of coffee. I'll stain their hands.*"

"LOOK AT THE WORLD IN A ROCK 'N' ROLL SENSE . . . WHAT DOES THAT EVEN MEAN?"

Greil Marcus, Mystery Train: Images of America
in Rock 'n' Roll Music, *1975*

———

The critic who wrote *the* book on his subject was, unsurprisingly, relentlessly quotable—this was maybe 80th percentile: "Rock 'n' roll is a combination of good ideas dried up by fads, terrible junk, hideous failings in taste and judgment, gullibility and manipulation, moments of unbelievable clarity and invention, pleasure, fun, vulgarity, excess, novelty and utter enervation, all summed up nowhere so well as on Top 40 radio, that ultimate rock 'n' roll version of America." But the language revealed the method. To invoke a fellow critic, the "**Ellen Willis** test" was to judge sexism by how a singer's words resonated when you imagined a woman performing them. The undeclared Greil Marcus test was to take each cultural item, noble or sordid, as it came, and see if the dough leavened, see if the candle kept, unfathomably, burning.

Those everlasting flames he collected. Not like most collectors, genre definers. His was a critic's compendium: songs, film scenes, ad hypes, all sorts of performances that affected him entered in the register and given fitting prose. Once in, they stayed. You (he often used the second person) might read *The History of Rock 'n' Roll in Ten Songs* and realize that Neil Young line on rock and roll being older, in spirit, than country and blues had appeared before in Marcus's writing, in an *Artforum* column collected in *Ranters & Crowd Pleasers*, aka *In the Fascist Bathroom*. Raves and equally enthused slams became entries in his decades-spanning Top Ten columns, compiled as *Real Life Rock*, or the ending of *Stranded*, an edited volume of desert island LP essays capped by his fifty-page list of records to explain rock and roll to a Martian. (As obdurate about his dislikes, he had to be forced to include Stevie Wonder.) When **Elvis Presley** died, Marcus loved Col. Parker's response: "Hell, I'll keep right on managing him." Marcus did the same with the discourse. He kept "Presliad," the ending of *Mystery Train*, named for an Elvis recording, in the present tense, but applied what followed to a Notes and Discographies section that ballooned over six editions to outgrow the original book itself. Presley compiling required a subsequent *Dead Elvis* study, then *Double Trouble* on Elvis b/w Bill Clinton.

Mystery Train was written as Marcus turned thirty, a Northern Californian free-speecher who'd dropped out of Berkeley grad studies for the new *Rolling Stone*, then contributed to *Creem*, which published "Rock-a-Hula Clarified" in 1971. This key essay provided the scene of Little Richard on *Dick Cavett* that kicked the book off four years later, based more on fractured memory than actual text, he admitted decades afterward on his Ask Greil web page, after YouTube brought the *Cavett* installment into availability. But where in *Creem* he'd worried about pop's deeper meaning, about Grand Funk Railroad and rock fragmentation as the sixties ended, Marcus made *Mystery Train*'s subject America and let Elvis contain the fragments. A reclaimed ancestor, Delta bluesman **Robert Johnson**, lost between his young death in 1938 and a 1961 compilation (Marcus: "There has not been a better album in the history of the recording industry"), paired with a permanently obscure one, early white rocker Harmonica Frank. The inheritors, too, hit limits: the Band constrained by stage fright and Canadian/cracker remove, Randy Newman by small popularity, Sly Stone by the consequences of his LP *There's a Riot Going On* as a Herman Melville-sized NO. Elvis headlined as YES, cornpone and lifeless spans not severable from "the nerve to cross the borders he had been raised to respect." The Greil Marcus test left the book a lasting story of rock and roll because his NO was for the later form rock as baby-boomer reification, official *Rolling Stone* history. Marcus, semisanctioned, voiced the loyal opposition.

Mystery Train emendations in subsequent editions deserve notice. The first explored how Newman responded to brief "Short People" fame, then returned to the margins. The second, an asterisk, confessed that it had been naïve in the Sly chapter to romanticize Black Panthers Eldridge Cleaver and Huey Newton as figures in the pop-lore lineage of Staggerlee, the mythic bad man of song. But the majority of revisions took place in Notes and Discographies. This reflected the passage between the first edition, when **Joel Whitburn**'s chart summaries were still young and Marcus had no scholarly frame (by "Allan Lomax" in 1910, he meant not just **Alan Lomax** [changed in second edition] but actually his father **John** [fourth]), and the growth of a cottage industry reissuing recordings in ever-expanded sets, accompanied by a literature of fanship, fiction, biography, and memoir. Staggerlee met the Clash in the 1982 volume, where *Elvis: What Happened* was deemed "worth reading" and **Lester Bangs**'s obit sealed the end of a subsection. The third edition recognized Staggerlee was now a rapper, "But that is another chapter in another book." The fourth, in 1997, proclaimed itself the first updated for the CD era, scorning Johnson and Band boxes.

In 2008, after the longest gap, the fifth edition ramped up the Notes when Marcus felt under siege—**Elijah Wald** and others calling Johnson a myth he'd helped create. This, Marcus rejoined, was to "extinguish any spark of transcendence." Undyingly productive Newman aside, the *Mystery* cast had now seen its own flame fade—Marcus wrote up the deaths of Band members, each failed Sly Stone comeback. The real question was whether the light had gone out on rock and roll itself, particularly the unruly apostrophe version he cultivated. Younger critic Rob Sheffield, Marcus noted, had written that for Newman—who prospered on soundtrack high fructose corn syrup—to write a good song for a movie like *Babe* was worse, in a rock and roll sense, than to write a bad one. Newman, asked by Marcus about this, responded: "If you want to look at the world in a rock 'n' roll sense—I don't know what you'd make of it. What does that even mean?"

One can read Marcus's vast bibliography as an effort to answer that question and expand the *Mystery* notes. He was a charismatic editor, a force behind the illustrated *Rolling Stone* histories that **Jim Miller** edited; Anthony DeCurtis's later version he called "a lump." *Stranded* was a rock critic free-for-all in the best sense: shaggy-dog essays on beloved albums. *Psychotic Reactions*, the first Lester Bangs collection, stressed the idea that the best writer in America had been an unsung rock scribe. *The Rose & the Briar*, edited with Sean Wilentz, searched for the crevices in folk balladry. Most strikingly, Marcus worked with Werner Sollors to compile *A New Literary History of America*, magic moments–themed anti-academicism ranging across arts and letters. His own second major book, *Lipstick Traces* (more in the entry on punk books), explored rock and roll after punk and alongside the Reagan-Thatcher regimes, an Anglo-European focus with space for women's voices *Mystery Train* had never allowed. Negation, the Sly Stone NO, prevailed as Marcus sought exile.

Bob Dylan and Folkways *Anthology* compiler Harry Smith were marginal presences in *Mystery Train*. It was several editions before Marcus acknowledged that his Epilogue's song summaries were nods to Smith's. Dylan's live and recorded work with the Band was still almost all unreleased in 1975, when Marcus imagined the King singing "I Threw It All Away" and laughing. *Invisible Republic*, which looked at the *Basement Tapes* of 1967 through Smith's folk-revival collection of pre-Depression commercial vernacular, summoned an Old, Weird America—Dock Boggs, not Sam Phillips, as secret hero. Dylan books stacked up: a full-length on "Like a Rolling Stone," then the collection *Bob Dylan by Greil Marcus*, arcing Dylan's late work as a return to Smithtown.

Marcus, like Dylan, was a rare boomer icon still looked to for new work. Sometimes his essays highlighted indie icons Sleater-Kinney, the Mekons, and Pere Ubu; sometimes he took books to consider Van Morrison, the Doors, or the film *Manchurian Candidate*, but always he worked from the particulars of a performance to the correspondences that let him fully absorb it. Too much credence to history, he reiterated in his *Ten Songs* book and a *Three Songs* one as well, killed off the individual actor making that history, the agency involved. A president of the United States now sang Robert Johnson songs like he'd heard them all his life. What more could you ask? Well, a reissue of that demo version of "Without You," finally revealed to be by Johnny Bragg in the sixth edition, that had been what Presley aspired to in his first full Sun Session and Marion Keisker had held on to, and he'd heard it once, sounded like a . . .

CULTURAL STUDIES BRINGS POP FROM THE HALLWAY TO THE CLASSROOM

Stuart Hall and Tony Jefferson, eds., Resistance through Rituals:
Youth Subcultures in Post-War Britain, *1976*

————

The text looked mimeographed. Chapters, often coauthored, could read as if
put together by committee. Yet articles originally designed for a double issue of
the Working Papers of the Centre for Contemporary Cultural Studies (CCCS)
at the University of Birmingham in England, then shoved into a book, proved
decisive in reorienting academic takes on pop. If Phil Cohen's notion of subcultures offering "magical" solutions to real problems had inspired this free-form
collection of U.K. leftists, they, in turn, as cultural studies, magically inspired
everybody else. Popular music studies beanstalked out of these pages.

At Birmingham, the "culturalist" Marxist orientation of Raymond Williams
and E. P. Thompson confronted postwar consumer culture, first under the
leadership of Richard Hoggart (whose *Uses of Literacy* explored English worker
behavior), then Stuart Hall, a Black Jamaican who cofounded *New Left Review*
and cowrote *The Popular Arts,* an early popular culture study, warm to African
American blues and jazz, cold to commercialized rock and pop. At the CCCS,
Hall moved from aesthetic evaluation to a "conjunctural analysis" that drew
on antifascist theorist Antonio Gramsci and others to view popular culture as
a stage—style and ideology in strut against the problematics of a particular moment. To quote, as countless would, a separate essay, "Notes on Deconstructing
'The Popular'": "Popular culture is one of the sites where the struggle for and
against a culture of the powerful is engaged: it is also the stake to be won or
lost in that struggle. It is the arena of consent and resistance. It is partly where
hegemony arises and where it is secured. It is not a sphere where socialism, a
socialist culture—already fully formed—might be simply 'expressed.' But it is
one of the places where socialism might be constituted. That is why 'popular
culture' matters. Otherwise, to tell you the truth, I don't give a damn about it."

The CCCS authors took up the British youth subcultures that had made a
splashy media impact since the 1950s: Teddy Boys, Mods, rockers, skinheads,
glam Bowie. Rejecting traditional Marxist notions of false consciousness, but
also populist celebration, *Resistance through Rituals* explored the "double articulation" that linked stylish youth from factory families to working-class culture and the mediated mainstream. This involved a process they swiped from
anthropologist Claude Lévi-Strauss, *bricolage*, refashioning the two larger cultures by repurposing objects, spaces, and sounds. Music worked through ho-

mology: the preferred tunes of a motorbike boy had to match the rest of his cultural ensemble. That might all seem dry, but it offered a path for future work as sturdy as Ramones barre chords: the culture around music mattered and did not have to be romanticized or rated like albums. Every realm of popular and underground sound was restored to a blank slate.

Dick Hebdige, whose chapters in *Resistance* focused on Mods and Rastas, was first to popularize the approach with *Subculture: The Meaning of Style*, which incorporated punk and registered in its pocket edition's flashy cover as poppy new wave. Hall and cohort emphasized class against a media assumption that youth was all that mattered. Hebdige valued bohemian and gay subversion: his first reference was to Jean Genet (Bowie's "Jean Genie") and a confiscated tube of Vaseline. *Resistance* argued that "spectacular features" of subcultures were a hype to deconstruct. Hebdige hailed them for this: they "signaled in a spectacular fashion the breakdown of consensus in the post-war period." Like punk, Hebdige flaunted subculture as noise, more chaos and art school "cut up" than dole kid representation. He also made the central assertion that U.K. subcultures had always had a shadow history, built around disparate views of immigrant Black Britain. Hebdige would extend his insights, from motor scooters to Pop Art, in the essay collection *Hiding in the Light*, but add a cautionary note: with punky subversion now a consumer staple, he no longer believed in youth negation as a strategy. Later, he was the subject of Chris Kraus's obsessed takedown *I Love Dick*: for a limited time and a limited number, the cultural studies author became, like the critic earlier, a kind of cult stud.

Angela McRobbie contributed "Girls and Subcultures," written with Jenny Garber, to *Resistance*, critiquing the inherent sexism in valorizing street cultures, an easier preserve for boys, over girl cultures of fandom or family. Extending this was her "Settling Accounts with Subculture: A Feminist Critique," lambasting Hebdige's *Subculture* and *Resistance* coauthor Paul Willis's *Learning to Labour*, an extended homological ethnography. Her edited collection, *Zoot Suits and Second-Hand Dresses*, connected music and fashion, finding that cultural studies had ignored subcultural entrepreneurs. *Feminism and Youth Culture* brought together her essays, often focused on women's magazines. The second edition's introduction, in 2000, questioned her 1970s sense of estrangement from working-class Birmingham women but easy familiarity with arty types like the members of the Au Pairs. McRobbie always probed at cultural studies from within. Other work included *Postmodernism and Popular Culture*, aestheticized everyday life *In the Culture Society*, and *The Aftermath of Feminism*, which questioned "vernacular features of resistance and opposition" as empowerment language became *Sex and the City*. Each twist influenced American media studies figures such as **Susan Douglas**.

If *Resistance* writers demonstrated music's homologies with other cultural touchstones, then Iain Chambers, author in that collection of a rudimentary sketch of rock and roll's racial underpinnings, took this farthest in two postmodern studies, *Urban Rhythms* and *Popular Culture: The Metropolitan Experience*. Both used quotations actively, so Walter Benjamin in the abstract and producer Glyn Johns in the specific suggested how "you envelop the commodity with desire." Chambers, even more than McRobbie—who moved along edges from postpunk bands to drum 'n' bass in her writing—reclaimed pop as such and its "widely assumed banality," tagging the displacement of Black music by countercultural rock chauvinists. For Chambers, pop was "the contemporary urban vernacular . . . an affirmation of your right to inhabit the present."

With the exception of guest-CCCS participant **Simon Frith**, writing on youth culture with Paul Corrigan, none of the *Resistance* writers played a continuing part in popular music writing; Hebdige's reggae book *Cut 'n' Mix* was thin on details and overreaching conceptually. But the Birmingham influence quickly altered the literature that framed popular music analysis. Paul Gilroy, in *The Black Atlantic*, wrote from an avowedly African diaspora perspective, reversing the white view of immigrants in much Birmingham writing. His notion of a Black diaspora and Blackness as a "counterculture of modernity" reshaped the African American vernacular centrality of many studies, though later work seemed surprisingly dismissive of post-soul culture. **Eric Lott** applied cultural studies methods to minstrelsy in *Love & Theft*, another deviation from vernacular primacy: theatrical instability, rather than blues balance, as an origin story for pop. Michael Denning's conjunctural analysis of *The Cultural Front* reshaped notions of 1930s popular arts: again, work by figures such as Paul Robeson, suspect aesthetically from a blues or jazz perspective, was reclaimed using cultural studies notions of social formation affecting artistic form. Frith's *Sound Effects* combined cultural studies with rock criticism. In *Black Noise*, **Tricia Rose** invented academic writing on hip-hop by transposing CCCS framings. Sarah Thornton added "subcultural capital," via Bourdieu for *Club Cultures*. Lawrence Grossberg theorized American rock, and the community it generated, in cultural studies terms as a set of "affective alliances," an early example of what academics would soon embrace as affect theory. This is a very partial list.

Most influential, however, was Stuart Hall, just coeditor of *Resistance*, one of four credited authors of its key theoretical introduction, seemingly allergic to writing books on his own. Yet as CCCS director until 1979, an essayist for journals and newspapers, and the British media figure in the age of Thatcher captured in John Akomfrah's documentary *The Stuart Hall Project*, he was a dazzling voice for radical analysis. Hall might be compared to **John Cage**: he went into a very structured discourse (Marxism, not musicology) and questioned every rule, imparting a collaborative spirit and recontextualizing the world. Cultural studies writers with Hall in them often came off as ungainly: really, conjunctural analysis? But that kept them, at best, from becoming blandly academic or apolitically postmodern. And the method was critical for seeing why the vernacular music revolution—as Denning later called it in his *Noise Uprising*—turning working-class culture, via youth culture, into counterculture, was never as secure as it appeared. When the tide turned, in what Hall called "the great moving right show," cultural studies was there, disillusioned but not disarmed, mapping away.

A LIFE IN COUNTRY FOR AN ERA OF FEMINISM AND COUNTERCULTURE

Loretta Lynn with George Vecsey, Coal Miner's Daughter, *1976*

————

There were three versions of the title words, each reflecting a different cultural form and social moment. The 1969 song, written fully by Lynn, focused on family and working-class pride: kin to Merle Haggard's pride in being an Okie, both responses to James Brown's "Say It Loud—I'm Black and I'm Proud." The verses, trimmed in production but still longer than most soul, pop, or rock, worked up to that "proud to be a" moment, building a case; the music at that point, having stayed modal and repetitive as folk, modulated into pop-rock superstardom effects, announcing not only Lynn's move from hominess, but country's. The 1980 film, only loosely based on Lynn's work, stressed feminism without the name, highlighting Lynn's relationship with fellow singer Patsy Cline, whose legacy the movie revived.

In between was the memoir, where as so often with musical autobiographies, authorship proved more complicated. Lynn, whose lack of formal education was part of her artistic persona, worked with a cowriter, a *New York Times* staffer but fellow Kentuckian, the preface stressed. Once again, popular music literature turned on inherent questions about the nature of all three terms. If the song aimed at country partisans and the movie at a woman-defined mainstream, the book sought countercultural readership alongside Fan Fair attendees, with Lynn constantly positioning herself as both a mother and a supporter of abortion rights, antiwelfare yet anti-Vietnam. The central character, besides Lynn, was her older husband Doo, who "whipped me in line a little" but stood aside as she ascended. The resulting balance, where Doo raised the kids but also raised hell, could be hair raising: "Like one time Doo got mad at a dog that was barking too much. So right in front of me, he just hit it once with a club and killed it. I just went to bed and stared at the ceiling for twenty-four hours." If that was not a Loretta Lynn song, it was a Lucinda Williams song.

Coal Miner's Daughter was tersely composed. Seven evocative pages on Cline, another four on Lynn's songwriting, just hints of her—then under litigation—relationship to the Wilburn Brothers, television singers who hired Lynn as their "girl singer" and brought her to wider attention. But two simply made points anchored the memoir. Lynn wrote, "See, the men are supposed to be the head of the household in the country. But the women lots of times find it easier to get along with office work and stores." In other words, women as white- or pink-collar workers, service-sector employees, disrupted male country's preferred blue-collar men, motherly women narrative. Similarly, "I've got to be honest and say I don't like playing clubs because of the hard work and the way a few guys carry on." That endorsed state fairs, theaters, and media over honky-tonks. The longest chapter, "On the Road," started with a blueprint of Lynn's tour bus and itemized it as both home and office. PS: her band called her "Mom."

Pamela Fox, exploring women's country memoirs in *Natural Acts: Gender, Race, and Rusticity in Country Music*, demonstrated how Lynn's book, only the second memoir by a country artist (after Johnny Cash), and first by a woman, created a category for the likes of Dolly, Reba, and others, "establishing their own cachet as authentic country artists, exploiting *and* rewriting the music's gendered cultural scripts." As "working female celebrities," Fox continued, "these figures forfeit not only their traditional pasts but also their present maternal identities." This got at the stakes underlying the apparently chatty *Coal Miner's Daughter*, which Fox called "an unflinching and essentially unapologetic look at reluctant—as well as absent—mothering."

Lynn, in working into book form the persona she'd evolved within show business for a style that turned on theatrical presentations of sincerity and authenticity—the Holler *and* the mansion—was not only giving women a model. She was doing the same for country, as it moved from genre to format, from the Ryman auditorium Opry that left her awestruck long after she'd conquered it to the suburban Opry that was "just another arena." Country wasn't quite mainstream yet in 1976: "television's not ready for us yet to be ourselves," Lynn complained, even as she singled out Dolly Parton, who'd advance the process a bit more in subsequent years as her closest peer since Cline. "We're good friends because we talk the same hillbilly language." Lynn told readers, "In Nashville, we've got this saying, 'closet country,' meaning you've got to enjoy it in secret." Lynn's words opened that closet.

INTRODUCING ROCK CRITICS

Jim Miller, ed., The Rolling Stone Illustrated
History of Rock & Roll, *1976*

An oversized book resembling the physical magazine during that hallowed time, *The Rolling Stone Illustrated History of Rock & Roll* began its first edition with large photos of an obscure white rocker (Ersel Hickey), police holding back white girl Beatlemaniacs, and a golden-oldies revived Black vocal group (the Five Satins). This was a fan projection, not star-oriented. Editor Miller's introduction itemized essentials: "social statements (again), drug anthems, personal confessions, the evocation of an heroic American past, and this kaleidoscope of folk music past and future, amplified through the medium of rock, epitomized for me the music's magic, the reason I have listened to it since the first time I heard **Elvis Presley** on the radio, the reason why rock has defined more than one generation's sensibility, style of life, and fantasies." Then he caught himself. "As for the question: is this for real, for fun, or for money— well, it was for all three, and that's rock and roll."

The note, connecting commerce, art, and popular expression in a way jazz critics would mostly have resisted, distinguished this first generation of rock critics, all white, almost all men, mid-twenties to mid-thirties in these mid-1970s, a little past reckless mythologizing but still a counterculture. **Greil Marcus** on girl groups: "That the crassest conditions the recording industry has been able to contrive led to emotionally rich music is a good chapter in someone's thesis on Art and Capitalism, but it happened." **Lester Bangs** on the British Invasion bands: "The reason they seem quaint is that they were, by and large, junk: perfect expressions of the pop aesthetic of a disposable culture. Which is all right. In the fatuity of their enthusiasm lay their very charm."

Robert Christgau on the Rolling Stones: "It is sometimes argued that such modulations of sensibility belie the group's artistic integrity; in fact, however, the Stones' willingness to 'exploit' and 'compromise' their own bohemian proclivities meant only that they assumed a pop aesthetic."

It fell to Ellen Willis to note that the ideas that had launched rock criticism, launched the magazine, were unsustainable.

> The hippie rock stars of the late Sixties merged two versions of that hardy American myth, the free individual. . . . The combination was inherently unstable—Whitman's open road is not, finally, the Hollywood freeway. . . . For a fragile historical moment rock transcended those contradictions; in its aftermath our pop heroes found themselves grappling, like the rest of us, with what are probably enduring changes in the white American consciousness—changes that have to do with something very like an awareness of tragedy. It is in this context that Janis Joplin developed as an artist, a celebrity, a rebel, a woman, and it is in this context that she died.

Willis perhaps resisted a notion of pop or rock as a reasonable path to white male liberation because she wrote as a woman left marginal by the discourse. We'll never know how Black critics such as Vernon Gibbs or Margo Jefferson would have spoken in these pages, where Robert Palmer discussed rock and roll's origins through "the influence of black music on white"; Peter Guralnick philosophized on soul ending with Martin Luther King Jr.'s murder and nobody mentioned funk; Russell Gersten dismissed Aretha Franklin's pre-Atlantic work as "not particularly black"; and Dave Marsh said of Eric Clapton's blues playing: "He had finally felt the music as deeply as anyone, matched Robert Johnson blow for blow, sorrow for sorrow."

(Marsh, selling the bulk of his books as Bruce Springsteen's hagiographer, radical politically and yet hostile to punk or any kind of arty gender bending, blasting figures like Neil Young for works now generally revered in *The Rolling Stone Record Guide* he coedited, was proof of how complicated the question of rock critic values could be. In *The Heart of Rock & Soul: The 1001 Greatest Singles Ever Made*, published in 1989, he gave a single entry to Elton John's "Bitch Is Back" as "the only time he ever convinced me"—one more than to David Bowie. That book blended Top 40 songs and outliers, the best stuff finding the right tag—"I Want to Know What Love Is" as "the Sistine Chapel of cock rock"—or getting a good story; the "Louie Louie" entry led to his second-best book. It touted obscurities YouTube now summons, like the Schoolboys, "Please Say You Want Me." Call it the only time he ever fully convinced *me*. Miller was a problematic critic, too, his history of rock and roll, *Flowers in the Dustbin*, premised on the notion that the music's period of artistic impact ended with punk. To be fair, there were even worse baby-boomer rock critics kept out of the *Stone* anthology: Bruce Pollock called his overview *Hipper Than Our Kids*.)

For all one might carp, this was a truly great book. Palmer, not only a rare southern voice but a rare musician's presence, was adept on rock and roll's "rawer" origins, if light on the pop side, and gave James Brown his first detailed musical account. The discographies alone, working from Joel Whitburn's research, with two full pages on Motown hits, solidified a still vague story, as did essays on New Orleans, Chicago, and many other key cities. There was poetry of sorts, Barry Hansen (aka syndicated radio's Dr. Demento) capturing Clyde McPhatter in 1952, Joe McEwen the Impressions in 1958, Nik Cohn an adrift Phil Spector in 1969. Christgau was definitive on Chuck Berry's artistry; Marcus proposed the concept of the Pop Explosion, uniting a generation, to explain the Beatles; Bangs wrote about heavy metal as a disuniting, teens resisting critics. Classically trained John Rockwell was profound on rock as art in an age of pop anti-art: "The point here is that art rock is hardly to be equated with complexity, no matter what British working class bands enamored of studio fanciness may think . . . much of the artistic energy in Manhattan has been taken up by performance art, and part of that art has manifested itself as rock and roll." Each entry spoke to the last.

The second edition, just four years later in 1980, featured an incredible cover display (Pere Ubu's David Thomas next to Jim Morrison, among scores of juxtapositions) that emphasized a new intent: to place somewhat less popular music into the story, reflecting punk rock and its stress on underground traditions. Miller's new intro shrugged off Presley's passing ("So while the King is dead, the show goes on") but stressed the Sex Pistols: "The institution of rock has faced a revolt. The consequences have yet to run their course." Best in show was Tom Smucker's overview of disco, epitomizing the post-hippie sensibility: "by the late Seventies we were awash with so many fools, hacks and clods working the hustle of significance that 'significance' itself had become a problem. Punk attacked the impasse with a revolt from below—an honorable rock idea. Disco solved it with an equally honorable pop idea—reducing everything to its surfaces." Miller, oddly in retrospect, put his ultimate faith in another white male savior, Elvis Costello: "Going beyond the troubled mythology of Bruce Springsteen and the pure nihilism of the Sex Pistols, he has taken aim at the heart of our current great depression." The third edition in 1992, edited by Anthony DeCurtis and others, featured mostly blander new writers—Chuck

Eddy on newer metal the exception. *Trouble Girls*, editor Barbara O'Dair's collection of writing on women musicians, was a far worthier sequel. But the *Illustrated History*'s first two versions remained the most coherent encapsulation of why early rock critics thought they could have it all—then were forced to change their mind.

PATRIARCHAL EXEGETE OF BLACK VERNACULAR AS "EQUIPMENT FOR LIVING"

Albert Murray, Stomping the Blues, *1976*

———

Simply publishing books was an elongated process for Murray, born in 1916 and debuting with *The Omni-Americans* in 1970. Two years younger than friend and fellow Tuskegeean **Ralph Ellison**, he retired from a twenty-year military career before a second adult lifetime writing and discoursing full-time from his apartment in Harlem—Romare Bearden once borrowed the view. He lived to ninety-seven, with a legacy that included a Library of America nonfiction anthology of six volumes plus; four music-filled novels with alter-ego "Scooter"; correspondence book with Ellison; an as-told-to memoir with Count Basie; posthumous books of interviews with drummer Jo Jones (*Riff-tides*) and others (*Murray Talks Music*); consulting at Jazz at Lincoln Center; onscreen Yoda in Ken Burns's *Jazz*. As jazz giants passed, Murray became their patriarchal exegete.

The Harlem Renaissance was long over, soul's Black Arts movement under siege, when Murray published *Omni-Americans*, responding to the "social science fiction" of such studies as the Moynihan Report attacking the Black family and "negritude promoters" like Eldridge Cleaver. He declared American culture mulatto and African American culture, "the blues idiom," a modernist triumph: "idiomatic equipment for living." Fonder of classic American Studies treatises by **Constance Rourke** and John Kouhenhoven than of Black Power statements by James Baldwin, Murray above all idolized **Duke Ellington**, for his ability to swing the blues and transform its folk elements into a stylized statement of experience transformed. In *South to a Very Old Place*, which like *The Hero and the Blues* mixed blues as music with blues as literature, he called himself "a writer whose nonfiction represents an effort to play literary vamps and intellectual riffs equivalent to the musical ones."

Stomping the Blues, Murray's most developed exploration of popular music, talked about blues as a "counterstatement" that responded to adversity with good-times and renewed feeling, not pathos and alienation. Given that he was writing well into the era of Led Zeppelin, Stevie Wonder, and **Robert Johnson** revivalism, there was counterstatement aplenty in his insistence on seeing blues as, at best, a jazz reworking of honky-tonk and juke joint material, a signifying too on pop and even classical, rather than as rural expression electrified for arenas. Murray was happy to hail Hemingway as a blues writer. Rock and soul, by contrast, he saw as "charged with sentimentality rather than earthiness."

Yet because the celebration of rock, soul, and the down-home blues they owed to became dominant, Murray's take on the stuff that moved from vaudeville circuits to elements of swing jazz sets functioned as a critical corrective, setting the stage for Robert Johnson revisionism and anti-rockism. He resisted seeing blues as self-expression or social reporting: "It is not so much what blues musicians bring out of themselves on the spur of the moment as what they do with existing conventions." He valued Charlie Parker for his Kansas City groove and complained about blues writers who wanted the music to leave the dance hall for the concert hall. Folk authenticity, he japed, was as pious as classical music snobbery. "The stylizations of Leadbelly, Blind Lemon Jefferson, Tampa Red, Leroy Carr, Lonnie Johnson, Muddy Waters, and Lightnin' Hopkins are not less artificial than those of, say, Floyd Smith, Charlie Christian, Otis Spann, and George Benson, only less sophisticated." For Murray, the choice was between a modernist vernacular and "the same old essentially sentimental assumptions that make for pastoral literature."

He was more doctrinaire than Ellison, who apologized, in a letter in *Trading Twelves*, for loving R&B pioneer Smiley Lewis's "Blue Monday"— "Call that primitivism if you want to." But Murray let loose, too: he wrote back saluting how "that goddamn Ray ass Charles absorbs everything and uses everything. Absorbs it and assimilates it with all that sanctified, stew meat smelling, mattress stirring, fucked up guilt, touchy violence, jailhouse dodging, second hand American dream shit, and sometimes it comes out like a sermon by one of them spellbinding stemwinders in your work-in-progress, and other times he's extending Basie's stuff better than Basie himself." Then he got the gig coauthoring Basie's autobiography and let the bandleader's studied blandness promote his credos nonetheless: "we had our own thing, and we could always play some more blues and call it something, and we did our thing on the old standards and the current pops." His talks with Basie's more irascible drummer, Jo Jones, located blues in show business versatility: "I was in the carnival shows and circuses, then I was a singer, a dancer, a dramatic artist, then I went through the trumpet, the saxophone, the piano, and now I'm the drums." For Murray, in *Blue Devils of Nada*, Ellington "fulfilled the ancestral aesthetic imperative to process folk melodies." Seven decades later, the omni-American from Tuskegee was still defining Harlem's renaissance.

READING POP CULTURE AS INTELLECTUAL OBLIGATION

Roland Barthes, Image—Music—Text, *1977*

———

His own interest in reproducible art forms ran more to photography, but this superstar French decoder gave popular music studies a notion, "the grain of the voice," used ever since. *Image—Music—Text*, a kind of best-of for English readers, came out as punk was emerging. Barthes spoke to that subculture's toying with significance. Queer theorists like D. A. Miller returned to him posthumously (he died in 1980, hit by a van), bringing him "out" of his "neuter" persona. He represented mid-twentieth-century intellectuals, of the sort studied by Daniel Horowitz in *Consuming Pleasures*, engaging popular culture in an increasingly agile fashion. To itemize those Horowitz covered and suggest the range of thinkers by this point used to "read" pop culture, you had Lawrence Alloway and Richard Hamilton on Pop Art; Reyner Banham on Los Angeles and Michael Venturi on Las Vegas as pop cities; Walter Benjamin revived as a prophet of reproducible forms; Umberto Eco for semiotics and best-selling potboilers; Herbert Gans on taste publics and ethnicity; Jürgen Habermas on the public sphere; Richard Hoggart and **Stuart Hall** building British cultural studies; C. L. R. James on cricket and Afro-Caribbean identity; Dwight Macdonald on middle-brows; Marshall McLuhan on media; David Riesman on other-directed conformity; Susan Sontag on camp; and Raymond Williams on culture itself. Within this large array, Barthes played a key role in thinking through the turn from embracing vernacular to reclaiming sentimentality. Above all, his sensibility emanated: demystification at its most encompassing, negation of negation if needed, but in a spirit of play.

The 1957 *Mythologies*, based on magazine columns, appeared truncated in English in 1972, in full in 2012, and ranged from wrestling ("a spectacle of excess") to a Billy Graham revival in Paris and the mythos of steak-frites, probing at cultural formations that rendered middle-class behavior as universal and timeless.

"The Bourgeois Art of Song" hugely anticipated *American Idol* hatewatching as it denounced virtuosos who favored melodramatic displays of technique, such as Gérard Souzay, to salute prosodic, less "respiratory" styles. Barthes the culture critic would become increasingly academic, embracing structuralism. His libidinal writerliness still came through: a structuring of narrative, driest part of *Image—Music—Text*, at least X-rayed the Bond novel and film *Goldfinger*. *S/Z*, a long study of a Balzac short story, turned on a castrato living as a woman.

Though his terms would change repeatedly, Barthes sought angles on meaning that eluded the consensus views he called doxa. *Image—Music—Text* found him taking up photographs as "message without a code," then showing they were socialized nonetheless, concluding "the more technology develops the diffusion of information (and notably of images) the more it provides the means of masking the constructed meaning under the appearance of the given meaning." Barthes's own mythologies approach needed sharpening after ad agencies used the same insights: "a mythological doxa has been created." He postulated the filmic as "that in the film which cannot be described, the representation that cannot be represented," just as his prose sought to "write in the novelistic without ever writing novels." This spirit informed his famous "Death of the Author," asserting readings over locatable voice, the even better "From Work to Text," proposing a joyful interdisciplinarity in the teeth of patriarchal canon, and "Writers, Intellectuals, Teachers," offering the Marx Brothers film *A Night at the Opera* as "allegorical of many a textual problem."

As the book's two essays on the topic revealed, musically Barthes never quite found his Harpo—he was more suspicious of phonograph than photograph, revered Schumann as a student of classical piano and voice, and never mentioned a specific popular musician. "Musica Practica" complained, in **Theodor Adorno** Frankfurt School cadence: "passive receptive music, sound music, is become *the* music (that of concert, festival, record, radio): playing has ceased to exist; musical activity is no longer manual, muscular, kneadingly physical, but merely liquid, effusive, 'lubricating.'" Still, "The Grain of the Voice" offered an aesthetic defense applicable to a **Bob Dylan** or **Billie Holiday**, song as a form of writing rather than flashy prowess. Here, doxa was pheno-song (language from Julia Kristeva), freedom was geno-song, "a signifying play." Denouncing the baritone of Dietrich Fischer-Dieskau as "expressive, dramatic, *sentimentally clear*," Barthes warned of an ebbing vernacular, using the older sense of non-Latin national idioms: the French were "abandoning their language . . . as a space of pleasure, of thrill, a site where language works for *nothing*, that is in perversion." He concluded, "The 'grain' is the body in the voice as it sings, the hand as it writes, the limb as it performs." And he noted that he intended his categories to apply to popular music as well.

After the death of his beloved mother, Barthes found his emotions rerouted. *Mourning Diary* included the lines "In taking these notes, I'm trusting myself to the *banality* that is in me" and "listening to Souzay* sing: 'My heart is full of a terrible sadness,' I burst into tears. *whom I used to make fun of." The memoir of writer as text, *Roland Barthes,* ended: "One writes with one's desire, and I am not through desiring." Miller and others would note the category-churning author's block on what desires he could identify. But boy could he write.

PAGING THROUGH BOOKS TO MAKE HISTORY

Dena Epstein, Sinful Tunes and Spirituals: Black Folk
Music to the Civil War, *1977*

———

Epstein is one of the few authors in this book with a YouTube documentary. It proved impossible not to romanticize how an Illinois librarian in 1953 decided to read through "slave narratives, travel accounts, memoirs, letters, novels, church histories, and polemics on slavery"—everything apart from newspapers—for pre-1867 references to African American music, then two dozen years later published the results in a book that scholars have been drawing upon ever since. Why do we get to marvel at a sentence from a New Orleans visitor in 1819, that "on Sabbath evening the African slaves meet on the green, by the swamp and rock the city with their Congo dances"? Because Epstein found it in a pseudonymously published 1824 collection, paging through yet another old tome—"when I least expected it, a significant document would be uncovered," she wrote in her preface.

As a **Lawrence Levine** review noted, Epstein's archive cinched the argument that Black American music had African origins. An instrument like that continent's banjo could be traced to 1621 references, including sketches, and forward to its use in blackface minstrelsy. "Wherever the Africans were taken," Epstein wrote, "the music went with them, merging to a degree with the white man's culture, but never losing its distinctive qualities. How it was modified by its new surroundings and how it modified the music of the whites is a fascinating aspect of music in the Americas." Unlike Levine's history, *Black Culture and Black Consciousness*, her scope of inquiry included the West Indies before 1800, since in those earlier plantations, acculturation accelerated ahead of the colonies that formed the United States.

Epstein did not pretend to be an ethnomusicologist, but brought important skepticism to scholars who'd let preconceptions skew evidence: "A heated, confused, and prejudice-ridden controversy over the origins of the Negro spiritual has been carried out for years by professors of English literature, musicologists, and theologians, none with adequate backgrounds in American history or African music and culture." *Sinful Tunes and Spirituals* explored the world **Solomon Northup** knew, in which the spirituals grew up. It documented how Black fiddlers, playing jigs in Virginia in the 1790s, represented the first Black-to-white cultural crossover there; how the signifying improvisations of "singing the master" evolved in work songs, commenting in code; how the revivalist camp meetings witnessed by observers such as a favorite source, Swedish feminist Fredrika Bremer, overlapped not only Black and white but sacred and secular, leader and chorus, melody and rhythm. Concentrating on another feminist, **Lucy McKim Garrison**, Epstein gave the first detailed history of *Slave Songs of the United States*, treating its "amateur" compilers with as much respect as her disdain for the so-called experts.

Epstein's unerring sense of what to trust in the archival record provided access to the materials needed to shape new analysis. Along with **Gilbert Chase**, she may have been **Oscar Sonneck**'s greatest successor. By the 2003 reissue, she happily noted the emergence of two new journals of Black scholarship on Black music, *Black Perspective in Music* and *Black Music Research Journal*, as well as a Black banjo revival. If African cultural contributions, and the need to recognize and document them, were Epstein's passion, then her book proved a second point: the history of American popular music owed its archival backbone to the efforts of independent scholars.

HISTORIANS BEGIN TO STUDY POPULAR MUSIC

Lawrence Levine, Black Culture and Black Consciousness:
Afro-American Folk Thought from Slavery to Freedom, *1977*

———

American history had never seen a major figure center a book on music before, though Levine counted American Studies pioneer John William Ward as a predecessor, Harlem Renaissance scholar Nathan Huggins as a peer, and was part of a UC Berkeley history department more open to popular culture than any other: Robert Toll's minstrelsy dissertation, *Blacking Up*, beat Levine into publication. History was changing and Levine wrote from a middle position—part of the non-WASP contingent Carl Bridenbaugh decried in a 1962 American Historical Association presidential address, but tackling, as a white Jew with immigrant roots, akin to almost academic **Nat Hentoff**, a subject that Black scholars were rapidly making their own.

Levine responded with staunch disciplinarity, drawing upon folklore, ethnomusicology, and anthropology—along with many nonacademic writers—but positioning himself as a historian engaged in the study of folk consciousness, not debates about musical origins, African survivals, or aesthetic innovation. His view of culture, "not a fixed condition but a process: the product of interaction between the past and present," downgraded such exactitude. Rather, he stressed transformation, the ways in which African Americans between the 1840s and 1940s refashioned the world that confronted them into "an improvisational communal consciousness." The viewpoint resembled what **Stuart Hall**'s Birmingham cultural studies already theorized as the bricolage habits of subculture, and anticipated aspects of what theorists such as **Nathaniel Mackey** and **Fred Moten** would underline in Black studies, but Levine was no theorist. He amassed evidence, making an assertion to start a paragraph and then supporting it with multiple examples from archives equally tolerant in definition: contemporary (Nina Simone, Dick Gregory) alongside plantation; no censoring for language, dialect or obscene.

Levine's landmark had fewer examples of slave musical culture than **Dena Epstein** did, but enough to dispel ideas associated with historian Stanley Elkins, that the peculiar institution had left its victims "atomized and psychically defenseless." Music, Levine wrote, gave participants "change, transcendence, ultimate justice, and personal worth." Secular song, subject of a one-hundred-page blues chapter, "cut through the sentimentality that marked most popular music" and "reinforced deeply inculcated dreams and ideals in a world which daily disproved them." That note about sentimentality was telling, as Levine wrote at the moment of vernacular triumph, challenging, too, some Black middle-class views: "Negro children were hardly socialized to the vernacular of their own group before they learned of its disadvantages and low status in the larger culture." Levine uncritically cited work, such as **John and Alan Lomax** on Lead Belly, that subsequent scholars problematized because it fit his expansive definition of folk expression. Music connected to humor and storytelling; urban culture cross-fertilized rural.

Levine went on to a second influential book, *Highbrow/Lowbrow*, that argued a "sacralization of culture" in the late nineteenth century had removed Shakespeare, opera, and related styles from a "rich shared public culture" into temples of aestheticism. Unfinished fuller study of 1930s Depression culture produced essays, collected in *The Unpredictable Past*, on movies and music as "the folklore of industrial society." Though he endorsed Janice Radway's *Reading the Romance* and saw parallels between blues and soap operas, a full reckoning with sentimentality as much as vernacular, or cultural studies critiques of folk identity, eluded him. But his legacy offered a way of studying popular culture, particularly music, within American history. Lewis Erenberg's cabaret book, *Steppin' Out*, and jazz sequel, *Swingin' the Dream*, might be cited here, through to such later archives-rooted efforts as Penny Von Eschen's *Satchmo Blows Up the World*; Karl Hagstrom Miller's *Segregating Sound*; Robin D. G. Kelley's biography of Thelonious Monk and related studies of Black cultural radicalism; Diane Pecknold's *The Selling Sound*; Charles Hughes's *Country Soul*, and David Suisman's *Selling Sounds*. Music could now be slotted by historians in studies like Tera Hunter's *To 'Joy My Freedom*, capturing Black female domestic workers in Atlanta on the dance floors of Decatur Street in one fantastic chapter. Inspired by Levine's digging and line-drawing, historians refused notions of mass cultural passivity, stacking up voices rather than faltering over categories.

MUSICKING TO OVERTURN HIERARCHY

Christopher Small, Music, Society, Education, *1977*

———

In the late 1990s, retired to Spain, Small argued himself into devaluing the music he loved most: "Who am I that I should go on wanting to play and hear the works of this repertory?" For three books, he had ramped up a contrast between western classical music—taught as the great product of great composers but in his critique vainglorious bourgeois industrial capitalism—and vernacular African American music, a ritual performance connecting audiences to art rather than an object held separate. Small's influential term for music as action was musicking. If classical flexed temporally, with a top-down canon, musicking triumphed spatially in bottom-up global reach: "Here, surely, is the central music culture of the west in our time, which despite its commercialism and the starmaking inflicted upon it remains a music of participation rather than spectacle, in which all are invited to join, and through which even the most downtrodden members of industrial societies can come to define themselves rather than have definition thrust upon them." **Amiri Baraka** critiqued the shift in jazz from verb to noun: Small wanted to restore a sense of music as activity, not possession or even artwork.

Small's background had taken him from a New Zealand undergraduate music degree to a 1961 U.K. scholarship that never gelled, mixed experiences with the avant-garde, and low-level university teaching in music programs. His debut book, written (Small said in an autobiographical piece published by Robert Walser in *The Christopher Small Reader* after his death) "off the top of my head from my lectures and classes," came out of a meeting with a small London publisher to do something else entirely. Walser, along with **Susan McClary** in academia and **Robert Christgau** in criticism a fierce champion, called him "the perfect example of an undisciplined scholar," meaning neither a musicologist nor ethnomusicologist, but in this book's terms placing him in the lineage of many such figures. *Music, Society, Education*—a success from the start with the support of Wilfrid Mellers, a kindred spirit—was republished in Walser and Susan McClary's Wesleyan series, Music/Culture, as the transformation in attitudes he'd helped further solidified, especially in the United States. The book rejected as a "bewitchment" the western notion of tonal harmony, connecting it to scientism, desire to command nature, and capitalist work discipline severing leisure from life. Looking for alternatives, Small found the musicology of **Gilbert Chase** and the American story of **William Billings**, picked up on blues from rogue academic **Charles Keil**, saw education through counterculturalist Paul Goodman. Musically, he seemed most comfortable with avant-garde tests of tonality: **John Cage**, Harry Partch, Steve Reich, LaMonte Young, the rock of the Velvet Underground, the Grateful Dead's opus "Dark Star," and the Isle of Wight Festival in 1970, where the Who, well past bleary midnight, resembled for him a nonteleological gamelan.

Small, in the 1970s, was thinking in parallel to vernacular champions he had not yet read: **Albert Murray**, Robert Farris Thompson, **Dena Epstein, Lawrence Levine, Bill Malone,** John Storm Roberts, **Charlie Gillett,** Paul Willis, **Simon Frith.** That new evidentiary base emboldened *Music of the Common Tongue*, glossing African American music history as "one brilliant tradition" that "fulfilled in me not only an emotional but also an intellectual and a social need." It moved from slave diaspora to Bob Marley and hip-hop, defining musicking as blues writ large, "the *only* consistent thread . . . through the whole of modern popular music." Suspicious enough of commercialization to credit Debord's notion of spectacle, of recordings if they deviated from the live performance he idealized, Small insisted that the rock narrative "had the effect of writing black musicians out of their central role" and valued DJ scratching as proof of "black genius for humanizing the mechanical." Yet the book rarely showcased Small creatively interpreting specific examples of the music he was putatively touting—he didn't relate to recordings in that fashion, describing in Walser's *Reader* an ambivalent response to what was probably a Tina Turner concert.

Musicking returned to a space Small found vexing but familiar: the symphony hall, "where middle-class white people can feel safe together." Drawing confusingly on anthropologist Gregory Bateson's theories of ecology and mind, Small refamiliarized as popular culture the embedding of classical performances. Staged by conductors symbolically enacting power over professionally distanced orchestra players, using scores from Mozart to Mahler to enact a ritual drama of relationships with gender as much as class implications, perhaps they were musicking after all. Small knew norms could change. Born in 1927, in 2006 he married his longtime partner Neville Braithwaite, a Black West Indian with dance expertise; McClary's afterword in the *Reader* focused on Braithwaite as the key to Small's work on diasporic African vernacular. Intellectually, he became no less free to consider how Tchaikovsky's gay sensibility worked against classical music's "vision of order." Confronting Thatcherism and the many blows to what he'd loved about the 1960s, he wondered if all he had steeped in, and still musicked playing with Catalan choirs or piano at home, needed abandoning. A pivotal chapter held up a nonliterate flute player for contrast, understanding the dangers of romanticization but unwilling to discard sentimentality. He had gone as far in his spiritual/intellectual travels as he was able to go, so he mostly stopped, pondering in one late essay, collected by Walser, a Republican party gathering that featured a bluegrass band covering—perhaps for the shock value—Pete Seeger's "If I Had a Hammer." His friend Charles Keil, he told interviewer Christgau, was prone to thunder about what was and wasn't valid musically. Small didn't draw lines so dramatically. "Creative Reunderstandings," after all, had been his lifework.

DROOL DATA AND STAINED PANTIES FROM
A CRITICAL NOISE BOY

Nick Tosches, Country: The Biggest Music in America, *1977*

———

In the chapter "Orpheus, Gypsies, and Redneck Rock 'n' Roll," Tosches more or less invented what **Greil Marcus**—formally, an intellectual peer—would call secret history, tracing the folk song "Black Jack David" back to Orpheus, with stops for early modern diarist Samuel Pepys and TV gameshow host Wink Martindale. But his motivation was a Sun Records B-side to the faux-primitive (many would say racist) "Ubangi Stomp." That song epitomized "the tough, churlish strain of country music" called rockabilly. And rockabilly was "the glorious florescence of white rock-and-roll." Tosches could accelerate his prose in other ways, as when he noted "some added drool-data" about Orpheus and boys. That wording linked him to **Richard Meltzer** and **Lester Bangs** in the punky "noise boys" brigade of rock critics. But he brought a folklorist's passion to such assertions as "the purest mountain airs . . . were once the pop junk of urban Britain."

In *The Nick Tosches Reader,* he explained turning sixteen in 1965 around his dad's bar in Newark. As the music shifted with "Satisfaction" and **Bob Dylan**'s "From a Buick 6," his sense of writing flipped after Hubert Selby's white working-class *Last Exit to Brooklyn,* whose biblical epigrams suggested to him that the dark topics rock and Beat literature explored were eternal and unresolvable. By 1970, he was calling Black Sabbath "bubblegum Satanism" in *Rolling Stone*; a few years later, he profiled a different stage shocker, Screamin' Jay Hawkins, for *Creem,* in the dress rehearsal for what ultimately became *Unsung Heroes of Rock 'n' Roll.*

Country, his first book, was less about Nashville pop than the subtitle affixed to the 1990s reissue of the lightly revised 1985 edition: *The Twisted Roots of Rock 'n' Roll.* All his preoccupations were on display: Jerry Lee Lewis as "last American wildman," blackface minstrel Emmett Miller as blurry forerunner (his version of Marcus's Harmonica Frank and later Dock Boggs), even a mention of Dean Martin as **Elvis Presley**'s unlikely idol. Tosches threw the N word around freely, a white rock usage common then (fellow New Jersey punk Patti Smith defended the practice in an interview Tosches put in the reader) but jarring now. The premise, as in a chapter called "Stained Panties and Coarse Metaphors," was that country was a music of miscegenation and had never not been a rough sport—even Roy Acuff worked blue, and a drunk western swing bandleader, Spade Cooley, made his daughter watch as he murdered her mother. Twisted roots never got less apologetic treatment. As Tosches wrote in *Unsung Heroes*, on the "lurid excess" of Wynonie Harris and his counterparts—included an invented Jesse Presley—"Nothing can better bring together a black man and a white, a young man and an old, a country man and a city man, than a dollar placed between them. Rock 'n' roll flourished because it sold."

Topically, Tosches's path was now set: his next set of books included a full biography of Lewis, *Hellfire*, that interspersed the Killer with first cousin Jimmy Swaggart and said of "Whole Lotta Shaking": "It bloodied virgins and stirred new housewives to recall things they never spoke of." Women always seemed malleable clay for the maniacs Tosches revered, including Lewis's teen wife Myra, also his cousin. The writing pushed unblinking description and outré mentalité over moral judgement, trying to match in language what Tosches heard in the recorded vernacular. His prose became men's magazine writing, manliness at the edge of civilization generations after Tarzan stories, with Tosches akin to a Gay Talese or Frank Deford. He put music aside to write about a mobster and Vatican financier in *Power on Earth*, tried a crime novel, wrote a Hall and Oates biography—to pay a tax bill, he fiercely disclaimed—and porn stuff he didn't hide, for *Penthouse* and others. The great study *Dino: Living High in the Dirty Business of Dreams* followed Dean Martin from Steubenville to Jerry Lewis, **Frank Sinatra**, and stasis, a fierce equation of entertainment ("dreamland") and crime ("shadowland"). Martin had been chosen for his underlying quality of *Menefreghismo*, not giving a fuck.

Soon, novels took over alongside $50,000 *Vanity Fair* assignments; a killed 1990s *New Yorker* piece on country singer George Jones as cipher, in the *Reader*, deserves noting. But *Where Dead Voices Gather* offered a pro bono return to Miller, yodeling before Jimmie Rodgers seized the crown, doomed to a career of blackface anonymity apart from his glorious "Lovesick Blues" and "I Ain't Got Nobody." Academics, insulted roundly by Tosches, would benefit to weigh his unqualified assertions, as Louis Chude-Sokei did in his **Bert Williams** study, *The Last "Darky."* Tosches argued that minstrelsy's racism had to be placed against "every other manner of ethnic fraud" rooting popular culture, wop song alongside coon songs; that the appreciative pro-blues flatulence of a Carl Van Vechten set the stage for those 1960s white folkies known perfectly as New Christy Minstrels; that **Robert Johnson** and his Delta fraternity were "far from primitive." It was all, for Tosches, "a perfect representative of the schizophrenic heart of what this country, with a straight face, calls its culture."

PART V

AFTER THE REVOLUTION

FIGURE 5.1 Cover of Robert Christgau, *Christgau's Record Guide*, 1981. Dog-eared copy from author's collection.

———

FIGURE 5.2 Cover of Simon Frith, *Sound Effects*, 1981. Pantheon trade paperback, showing Frith's ability to write for both a scholarly and general audience, 1983. Author's collection.

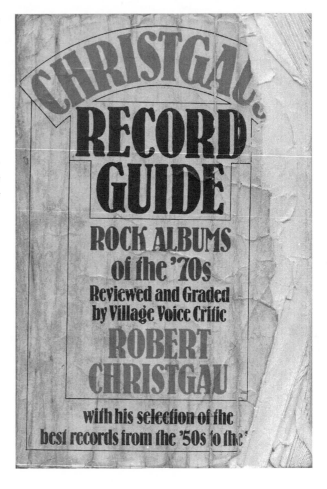

CHRISTGAU'S
RECORD
GUIDE

ROCK ALBUMS
of the '70s
Reviewed and Graded
by Village Voice Critic

ROBERT
CHRISTGAU

with his selection of the
best records from the '50s to the '

SOUND EFFECTS

Youth, Leisure, and the
Politics of Rock 'n' Roll

by Simon Frith

"The one book [for] anybody eager to attain an
understanding of how rock and roll works."
The Village Voice

FIGURE 5.3 Cover of
August Wilson, *Ma Rainey's
Black Bottom*, 1985. The
Plume paperback edition
repurposes the cover image
from the Broadway *Playbill*.
Nashville Public Library
copy.

_____

FIGURE 5.4 Cover of
Pamela Des Barres, *I'm With
the Band*, 1987, mass-market
paperback edition. Author's
collection.

I'M WITH THE BAND

CONFESSIONS OF A GROUPIE

PAMELA DES BARRES

Includes Candid Photos!

JOVE · 0-515-09712-8 · ($5.25 CANADA) · $3.95 US

PUNK NEGATES ROCK

Julie Burchill and Tony Parsons, The Boy Looked at Johnny:
The Obituary of Rock and Roll, *1978*

———

"**Bob Dylan** broke his neck—close, but no cigar," it began. This scabrous obit would not prove to rank with the most-read books on punk: Dick Hebdige's *Subculture*, **Greil Marcus**'s *Lipstick Traces*, Jon Savage's *England's Dreaming*, Legs McNeil and Gillian McCain's *Please Kill Me*. Its feminist impulses, from the title's origin in a Patti Smith lyric to the line two dedication to Joan Jett and Poly Styrene, have to be qualified. Julie Burchill's politics would prove more Thatcherite than progressive and even here, the publishers dissociated themselves from the line 4 dedication to the Israeli Likud Party's Menachem Begin.

But *Boy*'s skimpy, self-contradicting, but ever-so-collectible qualities (Pete Townshend blurb: "Gross callousness"), the book version of a 45 single rather than a full LP, reboot this *Songbooks* story. In the late 1970s, as right-wing governments took power in the United States and United Kingdom, a subcultural backlash against rock was joined by a mass cultural backlash against pop: the Disco Sucks movement. Vernacular countercultures from rock and soul to country and gospel had been energized by an electrification of sound, by newly affluent niche audiences, by the sense that something collective was being spoken, loudly, for the first time. Now that revolution was done: punk stuck a fork in it. The Year Zero attitude, registering here even more than in Caroline Coon's inaugural punk book, *1988*, repudiated previous pop-rock alliances, the book version of the Clash singing "no **Elvis**, **Beatles** or the Rolling Stones in 1977" and "I'm So Bored with the U.S.A." Punk wanted to destroy.

Destroy what, though? From some perspectives, Dylan *was* a punk, his sneer ineradicable, copied by the garage bands collected as early "punk" in Patti Smith guitarist Lenny Kaye's *Nuggets* (see Steve Waksman's *This Ain't the Summer of Love* and Clinton Heylin's *From the Velvets to the Voidoids*). New York City fans of those sounds and the arty Velvet Underground started a fanzine, *Punk*—later anthologized by editor John Holmstrom. Add the 1-2-3-4 rush of the glue-sniffing Ramones, headliners at downtown's CBGB, and it wasn't clear who was a go-Rimbaud flaneur and who liked three chords and a cheeseburger. Poor-selling albums like Television's *Marquee Moon* got outsized appreciation from *Village Voice* rock critics, **Robert Christgau** formulating the concept of the "semi-popular" around them. The punk ethos glimmered in Robert Duncan's *The Noise* chapter on the Dictators, then got full treatment in *Please Kill Me*, an oral history by former *Punk* editor Legs McNeil and Gillian McCain's—scene tales like Dee Dee Ramone's failed gay street hustling and doomed lover Connie Gripp. Patti Smith, Richard Hell, and David Byrne memoirs showed how their dissidence had been considered and formal, akin to Sam Shepard plays or Robert Wilson operas. Will Hermes made that cross-cultural renaissance central to his tale of New York City's civic punking, *Love Goes to Buildings on Fire*. Kembrew McLeod viewed *The Downtown Pop Underground* as a decades-long Andy Warhol screen test.

British punk showily spit in people's faces. Sex-shop impresario Malcolm McLaren, his partner, designer Vivienne Westwood, culture-jamming artist Jamie Reid (given a portfolio in *Up They Rise*), and the band they put together, Sex Pistols—led by John Lydon as Johnny Rotten—created "Anarchy in the U.K." and the banned-yet-charting "God Save the Queen" to fire a global subculture. Fred and Judy Vermorel, McLaren cronies and pop theorists who'd go on to put out small gems of books on *Starlust* and Kate Bush, captured the frenzy with *The Sex Pistols: The Inside Story*, released just as the band broke up. A publicist recalled: "suddenly in October, the whole thing exploded and a complete scene came out of almost nowhere. And there were bands like the Vibrators, the Damned, the Clash, they were all formed within a matter of weeks of each other. And suddenly it was 50 punk bands playing in London." A diary by McLaren office manager Sophie Richmond hinted at a backstory. January 11, 1977: "I keep thinking of that quote—situationist, I think, 'The majority of men & women live lives of quiet desperation'—my life, the Sex Pistols, the Heartbreakers maybe especially, lead lives of loud desperation. We shout it, display the wounds, shove them in people's faces." More on Situationism, a left agitprop resistance to consumer spectacle embraced by McLaren and Reid, emerged in the 1981 edition. The key was *detournement*, "which is turning the establishment's codes, forms and values (ie the hit parade) against itself." McLaren, the Vermorels thought, "didn't always take Situationist ideas as seriously as Jamie. But they *worked* so he carried them on."

If Burchill and Parsons were guillotining rock, the Vermorels insisted "We will never understand the Sex Pistols if we think of them as a rock and roll band," echoing Clash manager Bernie Rhodes: "one can't talk about the Pistols as a rock'n'roll band. One's got to talk about them as a media phenomenon." The punk provocation as subcultural media baiting sparked academic cultural studies, with Dick Hebdige's *Subculture*, slim and visually snarling as *Boy*, a surprise hit in literary circles—he took the ideas of **Stuart Hall**'s *Resistance through Rituals*, connecting Teddy Boys now to safety pin and mohawk gobbers in a postwar arc. **Simon Frith** joined punk and cultural studies to rock criticism in works like *Sound Effects* and *Art into Pop*; Dave Laing gave punk early popular music studies treatment in *One Chord Wonders*. Punk became postmodern—music for footnotes, read by art-school kids who started more bands.

Thornier punk engagement came from rock critics drawn to a palpable revolt within the genre discourse they held in protective custody. If Coon, Burchill, and the Nick Kent of *The Dark Stuff* represented a British press taxed with weekly accounting, Americans took essayistic liberties. **Ellen Willis** wrote about the Sex Pistols' "Bodies," arguing its humanity-hating extremity tested her radical feminism. **Lester Bangs** replaced dissolute mentor Lou Reed with the earnest Clash and took idealist aim at the scene's racism in "The White Noise Supremacists." The second *Rolling Stone Illustrated History* edition viewed punk as rock and roll's capstone. Dissenters like Dave Marsh (*Fortunate Son* preserved his queasiness) were now reactionaries. A new canon appeared in Ira Robbins's punk- and new-wave-focused *Trouser Press Record Guide*: artists like the rock-crit resembling Elvis Costello.

Two critics, the English Jon Savage and American Greil Marcus, wrote punk's classic studies, Marcus as Sex Pistols–type intransigent, Savage as Clash-type interpreter. *Lipstick Traces* presented a "secret history" that heard in Johnny Rotten singing "I am an antichrist" Middle Ages heresy, French revolution across centuries, and art movements like dada. How punks, before and later, "hurled themselves at social facts" was Marcus's story, set pieces collected like singles and played for the reader, not assembled as narrative history. In flight from Reagan and the pop explosion, Michael Jackson, that followed his beloved Elvis and Beatles, Marcus sought art to negate dark ages. As charismatic on a Slits or Mekons obscurity as on Guy Debord's theories of *derive*, Marcus prose—like punk, the way he framed it—"came to life as demands on the symbolic milieu of pop music—demands that produced a voice it had never used."

Savage in *England's Dreaming* was eternal observer, aware of McLaren's first encapsulation of the Pistols vibe in the unfinished film *Oxford Street*, or how punk played out in Cleveland, but also bigger stories the genre reflected. He'd later write a history of the teenager, coedit the best anthology of British pop writing, dive into pop-rock summit year 1966, and craft sharp essays on sexuality in music. In *England's Dreaming*, Vivienne Westwood and fashion gained centrality: "She is the first Sex Pistol," Savage wrote of a Westwood shop employee, Jordan. Compared to Marcus, he worked from a tolerant definition of punk, from Throbbing Gristle to Kraftwerk as "hidden soundtrack of 1977," from the role of record shops to subcultural theory. If *Lipstick Traces* sought the indelible, *England's Dreaming* stuck with Joe Strummer through *Cut the Crap*.

Most of the books beyond the classics were warty documents meant to establish, as commercial results hadn't, the legacy of different scenes. Los Angeles had a multiracial, boho punk that devolved into largely white hardcore, then pop-punk: start with club manager Brendan Mullen and Marc Spitz's *We Got the Neutron Bomb*, portions of Michael Azerrad's *Our Band Could Be Your Life*, then performers: Alice Bag's *Violence Girl* and John Doe of X's *Under the Big Black Sun* and *More Fun in the New World*. Washington, DC had straightedge and Dischord, the punk politics Mark Andersen and Mark Jenkins documented in *Dance of Days*. Stephen Blush's *American Hardcore* surveyed the scene that replaced punk in the U.S. overview and whirled into its topic, both in book and DVD versions; *Mutations: The Many Strange Faces of Hardcore Punk*, by Sam McPheeters, offered a performer's look back. David Widgery's *Beating Time* and George McKay's *Senseless Acts of Beauty* caught politicized punk communities in England; Stewart Home's *Cranked Up Really High* honored punk Savage and Marcus disdained, like oi! **Simon Reynolds**'s *Rip It Up and Start Again* interviewed players in the next U.K. wave, postpunk. And the 33⅓ series of album studies revealed the primacy given punk work, with looks at Joy Division, Ramones, Costello, Throbbing Gristle, Smith, Pogues, Wire, Television, Talking Heads, Gang of Four, Hell, Devo, Dead Kennedys, Blondie, Modern Lovers, Young Marble Giants, Raincoats, and Fugazi.

Women had become marginal to much punk codification—changing that back again fed subsequent writing. Vivienne Westwood got more acclaim than McLaren in exhibit catalogs like Andrew Bolton and the Metropolitan Museum of Art's *Punk: Chaos to Couture*. Angela McRobbie's cultural studies works outnumbered Hebdige's. Jayne (formerly Wayne) County's *Man Enough to Be a Woman* storified CB's in contrast to the aggro sexism of *Please Kill Me*. Deborah Curtis's *Touching from a Distance* recalled Joy Division's suicidal lead singer from his less arty widow's perspective. And two performer memoirs drew raves: Alice Bag's *Violence Girl* for L.A. and Viv Albertine's *Clothes, Clothes, Clothes, Music, Music, Music, Boys, Boys, Boys* for England. Vivien Goldman, a sometime performer and more prominent journalist on the scene, summed up the whole of this legacy with her *Revenge of the She-Punks*. Jenn Pelly's *Raincoats* book saw a younger feminist generation reframing these questions.

Destroy what? The question lingered, explored academically by Neil Nehring (*Flowers in the Dustbin*, theorizing what Marcus postulated), Ryan Moore (*Sells Like Teen Spirit*, punk as "the beginning of a long wave of neoliberal capitalism"), and Waksman's *This Ain't the Summer of Love* (metal blurrers like Motörhead). Roger Sabin's *Punk Rock: So What?* collected a thoughtful mix of British critics and academics; Stephen Duncombe and Maxwell Tremblay mixed old and new writing in *White Riot* to further the race questions Bangs had raised. John Lydon's memoirs, *Rotten* and *Anger Is an Energy*, made clear why the Sex Pistols *were* a rock band, with a great lead singer working through his issues. Punk epistemology lingered in books of all kinds: a moment mixed with other moments, for artists retracing their paths (Marc Almond's *Tainted Life*, Lavinia Greenlaw's *The Importance of Music to Girls*) or critics realizing how much they'd been affected (Frank Kogan's *Real Punks Don't Wear Black*, Luc Sante's *Kill All Your Darlings*). Punk hadn't ended rock, let alone rock and roll. It was no hip-hop or even metal in larger impact. But it bequeathed to music literature a mandatory intellectual revisionism.

THE GHOSTWRITER BEHIND THE MUSIC BOOKS

Ray Charles and David Ritz, Brother Ray: Ray Charles' Own Story, *1978*

Ritz, music's most prolific "as told to," "with," or "and" autobiographer—especially notable for his devotion to telling Black performers' stories that might have been lost otherwise—gave his own life a memoir, *The God Groove*. Early, he saw jazz singers Jimmy Scott and **Billie Holiday**, then adored her memoir *Lady Sings the Blues*. At SUNY Buffalo, where he befriended a fellow student, blues author and eventual ethnomusicologist **Charles Keil,** his mentor was his dad's friend, literary scholar and maverick popular culture defender Leslie Fiedler. Then he had a stint in advertising, music and marketing to remain a favorite mix. Ritz was a lifelong married guy with sexual history with men, a Jew baptized Christian, a renouncer of drugs and booze with misgivings about the twelve steps, an academic who realized that giving up his voice to embrace the role of ghostwriter was his true calling.

Brother Ray, his first collaboration, was followed by *Divided Soul*, turned biography after Marvin Gaye was murdered by his father. That story might not have appeared otherwise: Ritz and Gaye had tussled over authorship of "Sexual Healing," born during time together. Ritz noted several songs on his author's pages, alongside novels that came to include collaborations with rapper T. I. *Respect*, a biography of Aretha Franklin, joining Charles and Gaye as the final artist in his trinity, followed a 1998 as-told-to he'd never liked, yet was as much in the voice of his many prior book subjects as his own. Rather than abdicate authorship, Ritz deployed a cut-up approach, recognizing the permeability of the borders between spoken voice and musical voice, between history and literature. Cagey about letting categories such as race, gender, and class supplant family history and unique psychology, Ritz favored artists and narratives along the lines of what Willie Nelson told him in their 2015 pairing: "My integrity is what it's always been: a flexible thing, just like my music. It can bend this way and that."

The Charles biography set the template. Vernacular: "I'm a country boy. And, man, I mean the real *backwoods*." But also, pivotally, sentimentality: "When I sing, I often cry. Crying is feeling and feeling is being human. Oh yes, I cry." Language only available because the right interview subject had final approval: "A school for the blind ain't the easiest place to jack off." Unexpected family dynamics: Charles's relationships with two very different mother figures. And a strong thesis: the performer's great passion was for levels of control not expected of him, from blindness overcome to drug use he insisted never hurt him to the musical authority held from the first Atlantic sessions to his country album of 1962, even the buildings he purchased to create an office complex: "Now everything surrounding me was mine." To capture the voice, Ritz wrote later, meant altering words, condensing, getting at a deeper meaning. Construction.

"You'd have to call me a drug addict and a sex freak. Didn't you write the same thing about Ray Charles?" Gaye's comment to Ritz wasn't fair. In his case, the theme was the connect between tortured, sexually insecure performer— "Marvin never recovered from being an abused and battered child"—and work that made that torment indelible. Ritz came to the singer's attention as a passionate defender of his divorce-settlement album *Here, My Dear*. *Divided Soul* presented a collapse as total as *Brother Ray*'s consolidation, yet felt part of the same invented world, like a Western or gangster flick made of the soul singer's journey. *Rage to Survive*, with Etta James, less thematized rage than naturalness ("Her vernacular was all-the-way black"), mother issues ("Miss Hip"), grudging accommodation ("It's just that I'm choosy about whose ass I'm gonna kiss"), and productive relationships with gays and wrong, violent men. *Blues All around Me*, written with B. B. King, mocked **Robert Johnson** blues acolytes and pledged allegiance to R&B urbanity: "I've never been a purist" said the "conglomerate" with fifteen children, seventeen guitars named Lucille, and collections of books, records, and porn tapes. Jimmy Scott, unwilling to even control his own book, let Ritz steer a 2002 study of a lost singer whose Kallmann syndrome made him androgynous, epitomizing "the jazz life" for rediscovery by a post-punk rock world. Ritz worked for hire: pianist Lang Lang from Cultural Revolution China to Carnegie Hall, coke-addled record exec Walter Yetnikoff laughing over "Fuck the Bunny" fights with Warner's and "Old School Horny." But his preferred figures shared his music and sense of scene, like Atlantic Records' Jerry Wexler on Jewish "bagel babies" at NYC Latin clubs, Mitch Miller as "first modern A&R director," and how Stax's funkiness "knocked my dick in the dirt."

Decades of assemblage coalesced in the Franklin study. Old friends—Etta James, more indelible than in her own book, gushing over how the pre-Queen "pissed all over" "Skylark" and why "gentleman pimps," sometimes aka producers, were justifiable risks; Wexler a chatterbox throughout—met new ones: booker Ruth Bowen, Aretha's siblings. This was the motherlode, from father C. L.'s abusive affair with gospel singer Clara Ward to how his favorite child took *Sparkle* from out lesbian sister Carolyn. Franklin was both an indomitable, adaptable life success and a traumatized abyss—perfect Ritziana.

DISCO NEGATES ROCK

Andrew Holleran, Dancer from the Dance, *1978*

———

Dancing Madness, edited by Abe Peck for Rolling Stone Press, of all places, was the first disco book in 1976, and surprisingly sharp: short essay by founding disco critic Vince Aletti; Latin music scholar John Storm Roberts talking salsa with Willie Colon; a Frank Robertson vignette of an interracial couple straddling each other on the floor to the Isley Brothers' "Fight the Power." As with much disco writing, confronting a span of backdrops that ranged from fisting on poppers at black-leather parties to suburban bar mitzvahs, the literary glinted through a catalog not subjectable to judicious reckoning. Remember, **Nik Cohn** making up a story about a Brooklyn club, based on his memories of Mod-era England, gave us the article optioned to become *Saturday Night Fever*. So it figured that a writer, Eric Garber, taking the pseudonym Andrew Holleran (in some editions, Honey Soundsystem) as he ventured between Manhattan and outer Long Island like a latter-day **F. Scott Fitzgerald**, would encapsulate disco's decade of Saturday nights well before strong scholarship arrived.

The novel opened with letters exchanged between friends in crumbling New York City ("Flamingo had a White Party last night—two muscle numbers came in DIAPERS") and rehab in the South, where the narrator promised "A gay novel, darling. About all of us," including, especially, "the failures." Admitting failure was critical. Holleran, drawing on his experiences at clubs like the Loft and 10th Floor, wrote a much-cited passage about that revolutionary subculture:

> They lived only to bathe in the music, and each other's desire, in a strange democracy whose only ticket of admission was physical beauty—and not even that sometimes. All else was strictly classless: The boy passed out on the sofa from an overdose of Tuinols was a Puerto Rican who washed dishes in the employees' cafeteria at CBS, but the doctor bending over him had treated presidents. It was a democracy such as the world—with its rewards and its penalties, its competition and snobbery—never permits, but which flourished in this little room on the twelfth floor of a factory building . . . because its central principle was the most anarchic of all: erotic love.

But he also used the phrase "guilty pleasure" and noted the racism of his queeny protagonist Sutherland, the conformity of the anti-queen clone look forming ("They *all* wear plaid shirts, and they all have moustaches"), and the sterility of some of the "roller-skating music they're turning out now that discos are big business." Well before AIDS, "an odd sensation of death" hovered. If Sutherland, "who turned frosty at the slightest sign of complaint, self-pity, or sentimentality," had with his friends brought gay vernacular into a counterpublic sphere, Holleran's other protagonist, Malone, dreamed of picket fences. His narrator concluded that gay people "come, piss and shit together, but they cry alone!"

The Disco Reader that is hugely needed would pair trade magazine and *Rolling Stone/Village Voice* writing by Aletti (compiled in his *Disco Files*) and remixer and *Billboard* columnist Tom Moulton with such key period essays as Richard Dyer's "In Defence of Disco," explaining the dualities of gay materialism to the British left; Andrew Kopkind's "The Dialectic of Disco" doing the same for the U.S. left; and Tom Smucker's "Disco" chapter in the *Rolling Stone Illustrated History of Rock & Roll* adding aesthetics and early poptimism. **Nelson George**'s *Death of Rhythm & Blues* would be excerpted sparingly for his fear of disco stealing soul from Black music, a parallel to the scorn of *Punk* magazine. And Walter Hughes's "In the Empire of the Beat" would show how disco benefited from queer academic brilliance on par with **Wayne Koestenbaum** on opera or D. A. Miller on musical theater. Hughes wrote: "disco is 'mindless,' 'repetitive,' 'synthetic,' 'technological' and 'commercial,' just as the men who dance to it with each other are 'unnatural,' 'trivial,' 'decadent,' 'artificial,' and 'indistinguishable' 'clones.'"

Three ambitious twenty-first-century books began to give disco's club history, pop scope, and identity issues something like comprehensive treatment. Tim Lawrence's *Love Saves the Day*, built on extensive oral histories, took the New York DJ and club story from David Mancuso's countercultural rather than polyester Loft parties, with a membership list and immaculate sound system, to DJ record pools, Studio 54, and Larry Levan's Paradise Garage. Lawrence juxtaposed the inclusive Loft and Paradise sensibility, mixing race, gender, and class audiences, with an A-list of white gays at places like Flamingo, prepping a neoliberal night shift. His efforts reconstructed the "downtown party network" that anchored disco long after records were burned in Chicago in 1979—including in Chicago, where Frankie Knuckles took what he'd learned from Mancuso and Levan to start house music.

If Lawrence synopsized oral history, Peter Shapiro's overview, *Turn the Beat Around*, made disco's multiplicity its mission statement, everything from Nazi Swing Kids and theorists Deleuze and Guattari on "desiring machines" to a seventeen-page set piece on "smiling faces" tropes in R&B. Shapiro, a writer for adventurous music magazine *The Wire*, belonged to a cohort that valued secret history in electronic music far more than in rock: Mancuso protégé Nicky Siano's work with varispeed turntables interested him as much as the work of drummer Earl Young on Salsoul Records. Still, like Lawrence, he romanticized disco, calling it "the last gasp for integration in America."

Alice Echols asked tougher questions, bringing a history of work that included a study of radical feminism, a Janis Joplin biography, and the important exploration of racial polarization in popular music that provided the title essay of her *Shaky Ground* collection. *Hot Stuff* turned on an inherently academic perspective, how disco "broadened the contours of blackness, femininity, and male homosexuality," but Echols incorporated critics like Aletti; if Lawrence was disco's best oral historian and Shapiro its best detailer, she was its best literature reader. Chapters explored Barry White's soul moves as "refusing black macho"; treated underground gay disco as more akin than opposed to later mainstreams; and provided the first substantive exploration of women and disco. Investing Holleran and Lawrence's insights on white gay racism, Echols also questioned gay macho, wondered at the revisionist halo draped on Sylvester (subject of a good biography by sociologist Joshua Gamson), looked at Nik Cohn's fabrications as a transnational disco story, and advocated work on suburban disco experience.

Disco, once a plastic fantastic popped balloon, then a lost underground history, was by the early 2000s performed by groundskeepers at baseball stadiums where the records were once blown up; studied by musicologists like Mitchell Morris and Charles Kronengold; connected to subsequent dance culture and hip-hop by critics Will Hermes and **Simon Reynolds** and to immigrant experience by Karen Tongson. It was almost the white-picket-fence story Malone had dreamed of. "Go out dancing tonight my dear," *Dancer* ended, "and go home with someone, and if the love doesn't last beyond the morning, then know I love you."

INDUSTRY SCHMOOZER AND BLACK MUSIC ADVOCATE FILLS PUBLIC LIBRARIES WITH OKAY OVERVIEWS

Arnold Shaw, Honkers and Shouters: The Golden Years of Rhythm and Blues, *1978*

This music publishing vet was born the same year as Benny Goodman and Gene Krupa, the latter the subject of his first book(let), a 1945 fan bio. He added a Tin Pan Alley novel, *The Money Song*, and full studies of Harry Belafonte and Frank Sinatra before turning to overviews. *The Rock Revolution*, to critic **Robert Christgau**, read like an old man using press clippings to pretend to keep up; musicologist **Gilbert Chase** scorned its many subcategories: "The exegesis of Rock Culture has become weighty indeed!" His final books, on the jazz 1920s and 1930s, are thin on what preceded him. He's the third key hack in my overview, alongside **Sigmund Spaeth** and **David Ewen**.

But Shaw rack-jobbed the music of the 1940s to 1960s, especially the Black music, with an industry type's energy and liberal eclecticism. His Belafonte book, dedicated to his parents for teaching him "to be gentle, kind, and color-blind," had a running "Stereo" section that juxtaposed the star's experiences with racism with those of many others, positioning Belafonte's radical beliefs as a response to American cruelty. Show-biz cruelty, though, came off as natural order entertainment ethics; Shaw enjoyed his cat-and-mouse games with Belafonte in a publishing negotiation and was equally malleable on genre categories. *The World of Soul* celebrated "black nationalism in Pop," connecting blues to R&B and soul around "black musical originators and white polishers and popularizers." Shaw built on *Billboard* pieces to cover a sweep, if with dubious assertions: Lead Belly as "a con man," James Brown "primitive," Curtis Mayfield's Impressions white-oriented "Oreo Singers." *The Street That Never Slept*, later retitled *52nd Street,* was the best in this batch, as Shaw's experience and interviews detailed the clubs that brought jazz downtown: Onyx popularizing "The Music Goes Around and Around" to launch Decca Records; Coleman Hawkins's "Body and Soul" reflecting late nights at Kelly's Stable; the Milt Gabler–fostered progressive hot fanship at Ryan's.

Shaw hunted popular music lore with the gusto that had led him to secure a 50 percent share in "Sh'Boom" from Atlantic. *The Rockin' 50s* claimed his passing **Elvis** Sun singles at Col. Parker's behest to DJ Bill Randle ignited a major-label bidding war, celebrated the pop cash-in efforts of a Dot Records in Tennessee, and defended white covers against **Gillett**'s outrage as profit for indie labels who still made money from the publishing. *Honkers and Shouters*, more than five hundred pages of R&B stories, proved a testament. Adding interviewed voices to the *Sound of the City* approach, it was less reliable than either that book or John Broven's much later *Record Makers and Breakers*, but Shaw caught Louis Jordan and T-Bone Walker just before they died (the tapes are now at UNLV, where he taught), and his notion of R&B worked with his label exec blasé: "artlessness, a product of fumbling amateurs, introduced an experimental freshness." Shaw proclaimed: "R&B was rejected, ridiculed, and renounced by the avant-garde as well as the 'moldy figs,' by scholars as well as social snobs, by white liberals as well as white Southern racists." Phyl Garland understood her familial connection to Avery Parrish's "After Hours"; Shaw knew Parrish was bashed in the head with a stool during a gig, near-paralyzed, then finished off later when he fell down stairs.

Shaw, whose trade books filled popular music shelves in 1980s libraries, an entry point for many growing up then, was more sketcher than scholar. Though he'd next attempt a more formal *Black Popular Music in America*, its good bibliographies rarely integrated into the text beyond the spirituals section and a correction of the Bessie Smith myth he'd propagated in *World of Soul*. Instead, the one-time general manager of Edward B. Marks Music Company extended the legacy of Edward B. Marks, music writer—industry schmoozer as filter of pop in flux.

MUSICOLOGY'S GREATEST TUNE CHRONICLER

Charles Hamm, Yesterdays: Popular Song in America, *1979*

In his career-summing anthology, audaciously titled *Putting Popular Music in Its Place*, music historian Charles Hamm recalled arriving at Princeton in 1957 as a grad student and being directed to a single library room, which had all the books, articles, scores, and other materials a PhD aspirant needed to master. To study material outside this room, Hamm wrote, felt like indulging in pornography. That included popular music, "the work of non-academics, chiefly journalists and dilettantes." Hamm responded by creating an alternative structure, no less sturdy, not a canon but a two-hundred-year unbroken lineage of popular song. The music Americans actually listened to revamped European and African sources to fit New World themes: nostalgia and separation, slangy modernity. The song, which could skim opera and ragtime with equal dispassion, was the perfect vehicle; commercial viability the only true measure; the sheet music ditties and recordings that resulted simple but ingenious. Hamm listened, researched, and illustrated.

Yesterdays was the result: American song from the onset of nation and copyright. Early British imports favored pleasure-garden songs with rustic settings and the occasional reference to orgasm. Critics already battled over pop minimalism and an early favorite songwriter was named Hook—the key to any tune or recording. War, slavery, and immigration marked American topical preferences, with the plaintive airs of Thomas Moore ("Tis the Last Rose of Summer") heard as wilder than Italian melodies. A "tune family," Hamm argued, ran from Moore to Stephen Foster, the first working professional American songwriter. But there were "Scotch snaps" to consider, rhythmically, and translated operas like Rossini's *Cinderella*, stage works like the 1843 *The Bohemian Girl*. We were who we became; Hamm had the details. He documented the non–African

American nature of blackface minstrel music, though here his **Alec Wilder**–like score-focus underplayed performance qualities that connected blackface to rock and roll, which he saw as more of a rupture than later historians. He unearthed the protest songs of the abolition- and temperance-supporting Hutchinson Family, documented the New York sensibility of Tin Pan Alley, and argued that even jazz bent to the pop song, not the reverse. Hamm was more concerned that we study unhip but very pop bands like the Casa Loma Orchestra.

One book couldn't contain Hamm's legacy: his account in *Putting Popular Music* of narratives that reduced the huge sweep of music to different authenticities was as vital a start for poptimism as **Simon Frith.** He also, in that book, offered remarkable scholarship on South African *mbaqanga*, the unmeasured-by-charts effects of pop repertoire on network TV, and George Gershwin as a mass-mediated composer. *Music in the New World*, though a textbook less virtuosic than *Yesterdays*, went deeper on African American musicianship and blackface paradoxes. And there was a late study of early **Irving Berlin**, who exemplified the possibilities of a raggy beat, three chords, and anything but the truth. "A song is a song is a song," Hamm wrote, and none have so demonstrated the breadth and rootedness of that sentiment.

CRITICISM'S GREATEST ALBUM CHRONICLER

Robert Christgau, Christgau's Record Guide:
Rock Albums of the '70s, *1981*

———

Reviewing an album by Pink Floyd casualty Syd Barrett for his Consumer Guide of capsule-length, letter-graded evaluations, Christgau wrote, characteristically: "While my superego insists I grade it a notch lower, I know damn well it gives me more pleasure than *The Dark Side of the Moon*." That calibration, between the demands of personal listening and populist listening, between an idea or judgement call produced by a single example and a lifetime thinking about pop in general, between a casual tone and critical rigor, was Christgau at his best. The bohemian *Village Voice* sheltered his approach from 1969 through the late 2000s, and his mock title, the "Dean of American Rock Critics," reflected his importance there as writer, editor, and "poobah" of the Pazz & Jop Critics'

Poll. The *Voice* music section, especially as he defined it from the 1970s into the 1990s, was at the core of nearly all important U.S. music criticism, mixing in-the-moment commentary, freeform writing style, and a sense of criticism as community. The *Voice* was never quite as diverse as it seemed, except next to any of its competitors. The weekly's music section took the *Rolling Stone Illustrated History* approach two beats farther in topics covered, identities expressed, and reader-service gleefully ignored.

This anthology showed Christgau's criticism at its most influential—there were 1980s and 1990s books, too, and a fifty-year run of the capsules lives at RobertChristgau.com. With mainstream music, he had many blind spots: one could create an A–Z, from Abba, Black Sabbath, and Carpenters to Isaac Hayes, Queen, and ZZ Top. He more than made up for it with the obscurities he championed as "semipopular": that other A–Z might go Air, Big Star, and Leonard Cohen through Pere Ubu, Wild Tchoupitoulas, and Tom Zé, with strong support for reggae and African pop. He found similar off-center values in certain work by the biggest acts: notably, the Rolling Stones' *Exile on Main Street*. Applying 1950s and early 1960s ideals of integrated rock and roll and Pop Art–worthy Top 40 to late 1960s rock and its too-precious countercultural ambitions, he solved the politically chastened but subculturally burgeoning 1970s of Al Green and Joni Mitchell, disco and punk. The wink went to Hobbes when Christgau called his preferred music "nasty, brutish, and short." But rooting his taste was the most expansive application imaginable of "the heightened vernacular" of "my man **Chuck Berry**." Berry, with his attention to sharp, tight wording within an unconstrained beat, his emphasis on fun you could take to the bank, not to mention his African American revolutionizing of jump blues into a conversation on pop modernity others could share and extend, obviously fed into the Stones and then the New York Dolls. But the idea of listening for that conversation, noticing how one dynamic spliced into another, riffing on riffing, might include what **Miles Davis** heard in Jimi Hendrix, what Kate and Ana McGarrigle and Loudon Wainwright heard in a dissolving marriage, what Brian Eno revealed about "middle-class feminism, a rock and roll subject if ever there was one."

Positioning himself as a new journalist—a nonmusic piece, included in a **Tom Wolfe** collection, helped his early career, which started alongside his then-partner, **Ellen Willis**—Christgau reported on his listening and reading, roaming through unfathomable quantities of sounds and sentences. Much more ecumenical in taste than his great friend **Greil Marcus**, he was always, on some level, trying to let the thing in front of him stand in for the full constellation—the rock and roll *and* story that he would chase through categories of taste, politics, and deportment. He secured his legacy by mocking Jackson Browne while chomping through twenty-three albums by James Brown; as an editor, he championed the two most influential Black critics of the era, **Nelson George** and **Greg Tate**. He delved into the country catalogs of Merle Haggard, Willie Nelson, and Dolly Parton as an appreciative outsider. But he was not driven to open himself up to hard rock, which he depreciated without considering class, or salsa and other Latin pop, which he ignored. The flourishing of New York punk, bohemian to the core, was his vision proliferated: Blondie, Television, Patti Smith, Talking Heads, Richard Hell, Ramones, eventually Sonic Youth. He mistrusted Los Angeles and England and skipped the rest of Europe almost altogether. His notion of vernacular righteousness made peace more easily with Peter Stampfel experiments than Laura Nyro's art rhythms or other ways of bending gender and sexuality. And calibrations—How many Bonnie Koloc albums did he review?—kept him from the unified "theory of pop" his later memoir, *Going into the City*, told us he sought.

Still, the ideas were all there, just chopped into record reviews and the essays on artists and authors that came to fill multiple books, not to mention the week-by-week unveiling of his larger influence in each *Village Voice* issue, one with a "lead riff" and several more to accompany that one. Perhaps a column on jazz by **Gary Giddins**; his fellow residents of 193 2nd Avenue Vince Aletti on soul and Tom Smucker on the intersection of music and politics in the post-Left imaginary; perhaps a **Simon Frith** "Britbeat"; or some great writing by a figure the rest of the world wouldn't discover for decades, like Dave Hickey on country. Or maybe one of the new kids he encouraged even after he'd stopped being the music editor, like **Ann Powers,** Rob Sheffield—or me. In his early essay "Rock Lyrics Are Poetry (Maybe)," wrongly left out of his first collection, *Any Old Way You Choose It* (title from, what else, a Chuck Berry verse), he stressed that you had to hear the voice of the singer inside the production for the whole effect to come off. Christgau made it the job of the *Voice* to look for voices, then edit them to make their realized, idiosyncratic diction as important as any assertions. His consumer guides were a labor that precluded writing full-on books. But nobody's book of pages, written and edited, included more songs. What gave him the fortitude to keep going as rock and roll's revolution imploded? His sense that case by case, the story of those caught up in it, working and living away, was inexhaustible, even when it made you gag just a little. As in this reaction to Peter Gabriel: "Remember the immortal words of Chuck Berry: beware of middlebrows bearing electric guitars."

ROCK'S FRANK CAPRA

Cameron Crowe, Fast Times at Ridgemont High: A True Story, *1981*

At a minimum, we might credit this story (truth irrelevant) and subsequent film with Crowe's career as the writer-director of suburban white rock teen dramas, a category that dated to the earlier *American Graffiti,* then flourished in this moment with *Valley Girl,* John Hughes's oeuvre, *Fast Times* director Amy Heckerling's *Clueless,* Richard Linklater's *Dazed & Confused,* and beyond. Crowe also helped shape the sensitive rock-critic books of Nick Hornby, Rob Sheffield, and Chuck Klosterman. And, of course, we thank him for Fountains of Wayne's only real hit, "Stacy's Mom." Hired stunningly young by *Rolling Stone* for his awe at hanging with Poco, Crowe was never a great critic. A book by his idol, **Lester Bangs**, popped up in the grunge Seattle film *Singles,* then Bangs became a character in Crowe's filmic memoir, *Almost Famous.* But ultimately, he was an older sister's boy, intrigued by rock's connection to young women's liberation from strict parents, the endless California summer where the boys dug Zeppelin and the girls quoted "Landslide" in their yearbooks. In that iconic scene in his movie *Say Anything,* middle-class stand-in John Cusack held up the boom box wearing a Clash shirt, but he played Peter Gabriel's "In Your Eyes" because that's what his sweetie preferred.

Crowe, born in 1957, represented the younger seventies generation that packed arenas, appeared apolitical, and frightened their sixties elders. Collected on his website, The Uncool, Crowe's music writing replicated his feature subjects' mythologizing more than challenging it, hanging beyond dawn with David Bowie in 1976 as Mr. Stardust pronounced: "I've still not read an autobiography by a rock person that had the same degree of presumptuousness and arrogance that a rock & roll record used to have." Peter Frampton, another regular subject, became a lifelong friend: "Through the peaks and valleys and peaks of his career, he's always been the same guy," Crowe wrote later. He put Crosby, Stills, Nash and Young in a 1977 Top 10 for *Stone*'s tenth anniversary, writing "If punk is any indication of the alternative, I'll stick with the Sixties wimps." Instead, Crowe left music journalism to write *Fast Times,* turned book into script into directing, and wound up in Seattle when Pearl Jam were forming. They appeared in *Singles*; two decades later, he made *Pearl Jam Twenty* to capture another rock cohort, "the inspired children of pro basketball and Cheap Trick and Led Zeppelin and Black Flag and Kiss."

"The original title of Fast Times was Stairway to Heaven," Crowe recalled. "I was still writing about rock, but from a different perspective." The cast of the film—young Sean Penn as surfer Spicoli, most notably—can overshadow the shrewdness of Crowe's book, which began on a note to his bosses at *Stone* about that "enormous whale," "The Kids." Ridgemont's high schoolers equally seemed to view their part in the post-counterculture as a required Speech course. Stacy Hamilton, losing her virginity to a vet (not Vietnam, animal doctor—this was a fully middle-class, hetero narrative, with only one Black character, footballer Charles Jefferson), got back home, called the local FM rock station, and requested "Stairway," as "the supreme lullaby for her rite of passage." There had always already, somehow, been sex, drugs, and rock and roll. "One of the most common phrases heard in high school was now: 'I went through my *drug* phase in junior high.'" Crowe faltered when he tried to bring **Tom Wolfe** prose to his young charges: comparing the Mist-Blue Newport II tux at a prom to a 1956 Cadillac. But he could relate to Randy Eddo, the school ticket scalper, celebrating Ritchie Blackmore's birthday each April with twelve hours on the stereo, from Screaming Lord Sutch sidework to Deep Purple. Friday at Ridgemont one week was "Punk or Disco Day." Every graduating class got an overnight at Disneyland. Spicoli gave a class speech at the end of spring semester: "Everything was going great in the sixties. . . . Then everything went off-balance . . . who knows what will happen in the future?" In Crowe's influential opinion, more of the same.

CULTURE STUDIES/ROCK CRITIC TWOFER!

Simon Frith, Sound Effects: Youth, Leisure, and the
Politics of Rock'n'Roll, *1981*

———

For intellectually minded rock readers in the 1980s, he was everything: critic enough to turn up in **Greil Marcus**'s *Stranded* and hold down a *Village Voice* column; academic enough to turn up, too, in **Stuart Hall**'s *Resistance through Rituals*, trace a lineage for how writing on pop had evolved in the collection *On Record*, showcase new directions with essays recruited for *Facing the Music*, explore postmodern criticism in *Music for Pleasure*, and do much of this scholarship via a trade publisher, Pantheon. *Sound Effects* became the model for how to write books within a new field, popular music studies. It would be followed by a later monograph, *Performing Rites*, and essays collected in *Taking Popular Music Seriously*. Frith was interdisciplinary, teaching in sociology, English, media studies, and music departments. But he was also antidisciplinary. Saluting "low theory," he made Frank Kogan fanzines central to his critique of Bourdieu. He used pop advocacy to deconstruct countercultural rock assumptions. And he reclaimed the sentimental for a silly-love-songs karaoke with the vernacular.

A non-musician baby boomer raised on singles in England (his brother avant-garde fixture Fred Frith), Frith got his doctorate in sociology, including a stint at Berkeley as the 1960s ended, which linked him to **Howard Becker** and paralleled him to **Richard Peterson** academically, to the *Rolling Stone* world journalistically. *Sound Effects* began as the more traditionally academic *Sociology of Rock*, featuring a 1972 survey of young British listeners; most manifested pop/rock divisions of class and gender, yet some elided both and age gave them a shared T. Rex consciousness. Partnering with Angela McRobbie from Birmingham cultural studies, Frith explored cock rock and teenybop cultures in "Rock and Sexuality" (complicating his views in a new wave "Afterthoughts")—he always took *Top of the Pops* over dude bluster. "The Magic That Can Set You Free: The Ideology of Folk and the Myth of the Rock Community" pioneered anti-rockism, picking apart boomer male certainties. Frith was a Marxist finding his way through punk and Thatcher. Yet he remained inspired by his local record store's product: "Rock interested me academically as a discourse in which the contradictions at issue for all music-making in a capitalist society were constantly, self-consciously addressed." And he esteemed the clerks: pop was "first theorized by practitioners rather than academics."

Sound Effects touted its author as leading "a double life," going rogue on academia and offering a British take on "How American music was generalized." In its view of rock as "a mass-consumed music that carries a critique of its own means of production," the book became instant canon. Frith was also among the first to lay out how white rockers trivialized, as pop, their Black inspirations. He viewed the music industry in more complicated terms than most New Left figures, treating its creative commerce dilemmas as structuring contradictions rather than simply major labels plundering indies, or merchandisers stealing from artists. If a great corrective to hippie bullshit, punk pogo, and rock authenticity overall, the book's account of a "struggle for fun" lacked a clear delineation of rock's larger contexts: postindustrial and postmodern shifts to an information-based capitalism; the dueling surge in R&B, country, and adult pop; pre-rock popular styles.

Frith's subsequent work pursued such issues but retained the core vision of pop as the greatest contradiction of all. He wrote about technology disrupting the organic and corporate, with music video a particular focus and subject of another edited collection, bringing prescient attention to a shift within industry economics from recorded product to "rights exploitation" (still another collection, on copyright). *Art into Pop*, written with Howard Horne, used British art-school rockers to explore the sequence from 1950s Pop Art to Thatcherite graphic designers—imagists of the "dialectic of authenticity and artifice that pop entails." *Music for Pleasure* declared "the rock era is over" and stressed suburbia, middlebrow prewar hero Gracie Fields "smiling through," and New Pop, if also fondness for strains of post-punk. Writing "Toward an Aesthetic of Popular Music" in 1987, Frith pushed—in an upending characteristic of his prose—to pursue not what music revealed about people but how it constructed them, "an experience that transcends the mundane, that takes us 'out of ourselves.'"

This became the core of *Performing Rites*, which stressed the values assigned to "low art" by performers but also fans performing identity as they listened; film-music cues that turned on associations of sound and emotions or particular places and times; voices heard as personally expressive, not just musically; recordings putting listeners inside the music, too. Frith drew from Jonathan Swift and Adam Smith alike, and also a deranged Metallica fan, probing music as an imagined real. Rhythm, and its exaggerated association with African American sexuality, was part of the survey, though Frith was often too eager to challenge group identity claims to take insight from Black writers. Still, if **Lawrence Levine**—like others attached to vernacular—saw a blues lyric as inherently more realistic than a love song, Frith wondered why a sappy expression could not be true to life as well: "it makes better sense to define pop as the sentimental song," he wrote later in a "Pop Music" definition for the *Cambridge Companion to Pop and Rock*. Starting as a dissenter from rock orthodoxy, he positioned himself better than any of his peers to explore its antecedents, successors, and parallel lines.

A MAGICAL EXPLAINER OF IMPURE SOUNDS

Robert Palmer, Deep Blues, *1981*

––––––––––

The short bio in *Deep Blues* came off as the best résumé in music writing. Palmer grew up in Arkansas, playing in "blues, rock, soul, and jazz bands," and organizing blues festivals. He then went to New York, where he became chief pop-music critic of the *Times* and wrote for *Rolling Stone* and *Penthouse* but also the *Journal of American Folklore* and *Ethnomusicology*. But *Blues & Chaos*, compiled by Anthony DeCurtis a decade after Palmer died needing a liver and lacking health insurance, put his struggles with drug addiction on record: "I'm from the William Burroughs school of junkies," he had told rocker Robbie Robertson. Nobody explored the deceptive depth of American vernacular music—the links between Muddy Waters microtones, Black Sabbath thud, Jajoukan mysticism, and La Monte Young art drone—with the ease of Palmer, whose exposition made peers of general interest readers, scholars, and musicians. But this tour guide was a rock and roller from the Lou Reed school of Dionysians.

When Palmer wrote about James Brown for *Rolling Stone* in the early 1970s (see *The James Brown Reader* and *Rolling Stone Illustrated History*) and again for *Rock & Roll: An Unruly History*, companion to a PBS miniseries, he vaulted over other rock critics for his southern sensibility, valuing of rhythm over song, and ability to write about musicianship accessibly. The closest he had to an equal in that regard among early critics, and it wasn't close, was Jon Landau, whose writing would be collected in *It's Too Late to Stop Now* before Landau devoted himself to managing Bruce Springsteen. If Brown represented an extreme, taking out melody to lock on groove, Palmer had the background in academic and avant-garde classical and jazz to see Brown's kinfolk. **H. Wiley Hitchcock**, who hosted Palmer at the Institute for Studies in American Music—leading to Palmer's short 1979 monograph, *A Tale of Two Cities: Memphis Rock and New Orleans Roll* (other short books focused on Leiber and Stoller, Jerry Lee Lewis, and the Stones)—was a classical guy reaching to pop and an art fringe. Palmer worked that in reverse, charming an Eric Clapton, Terry Riley, or Sam Phillips into a great interview; alert to Bo Diddley devices musicologists missed, how Diddley "cut off his phrases as percussively as he chokes his guitar." In 1975, in *Down Beat*, Palmer lectured: "we need a set of procedures which will allow us to evaluate Charles Ives *and* James Brown." He created them.

Palmer, "the first white kid to start showing up at all the black shows" in Arkansas, saw in *Deep Blues* "an epic as noble and as essentially American as any in our history" and produced new versions for Fat Possum Records after he left the *Times*. Waters was at the book's center, moving from Charley Patton and Robert Johnson's plantation Mississippi to Chess Records Chicago and Rolling Stones revival. Reporter and critic at once, Palmer centered a "preference for impure sounds," the use of electricity to amplify rawness and physicality, a crossroads meeting of trickster mojo, personalized lore, and "wide open" sin towns. He asked at book's end: "How much history can be transmitted by pressure on a guitar string?" Marybeth Hamilton, in her revisionist account of blues mythologizers, wondered about Palmer's role in this; at one point he asserted functional illiteracy as vital to Waters, Bobby Bland, or Joe Turner's singing. Palmer, salivating over an "I'm Gonna Murder My Baby" not even Phillips dared to release, was captured by, as much as capturing, the ethos pushing white rock from Black blues.

John Lennon called Palmer on his shit, singing "Pardon me if I'm sentimental" at the Dakota after the critic called "Starting Over" sappy in the paper of record. Palmer would always be less comfortable with "treacle," with women as performers if they weren't noisy (his fraught marriages and parenting were chronicled in a daughter's family documentary, *The Hand of Fatima*), than with proclaiming Ray Charles "as enduring as anything in the history of American vernacular music." *Rock & Roll: An Unruly History* became his mission statement, committed to the music as antipop, "dangerous to racists, demagogues, and the self-appointed moral guardians," squashed by major labels. Still, Palmer knew rock was "semi-sanctioned rebellion within the music business," esteeming thugs like Teddy Reig who stole bucks from Chuck Berry but also made "The Hucklebuck" by stealing a riff from Charlie Parker. His ethnomusicology of rock origins, always cutting edge, here positioned Cuba as "Mississippi Delta of the Americas." He gave drugs more than their due, putting psychedelia within larger debates over "sound organized by consciousness." A "Church of the Sonic Guitar" chapter sustained resonances from Charlie Christian to Sonic Youth. He even found room for Cleveland punk and Lee Perry dub, as he had found room in a *Times* piece *Blues & Chaos* collected for the Swans and Nick Cave. Rock, he wrote in that column, was "abrasive by birthright."

FEMINIST ROCK CRITIC, POP-SAVVY CULTURE CRITIC

Ellen Willis, Beginning to See the Light: Pieces of a Decade, *1981*

———

Nobody generalized better about rock and roll's impossible relationship to collective and individual freedom than Willis. **Bob Dylan**: "exploited his image as a vehicle for artistic statement." Woodstock: "What cultural revolutionaries do not seem to grasp is that, far from being a grass-roots art form that has been taken over by businessmen, rock itself comes from the commercial exploitation of blues. It is bourgeois at its core, a mass-produced commodity, dependent on advanced technology and therefore on the money controlled by those in power." The lead singer of Big Brother: "It was seeing Janis Joplin that made me resolve, once and for all, not to get my hair straightened." The Velvet Underground: "the first important rock-and-roll artists who had no real chance of attracting a mass audience." Punk: "the paradox: music that boldly and aggressively laid out what the singer wanted, loved, hated—as good rock-and-roll did—challenged me to do the same, and so, even when the content was antiwoman, antisexual, in a sense antihuman, the form encouraged my struggle for liberation."

Willis's first book was named after a Velvets song, a pun in the subtitle—pieces are unromantic writer speak for articles, but also this *New Yorker, Village Voice,* and *Rolling Stone* essayist knew her communications from halcyon late 1960s to backlash late 1970s were shards as much as synthesis. Freedom was the topic, divided into rock and roll primarily in the opening section ("Out of the Vinyl Deeps" a phrase taken from **Tom Wolfe**), feminist politics in the second. What complicated its pursuit was Willis's vantage: woman, Jew, lower-middle-class child of a policeman, elite college educated, white, leftist, and pop-conscious bohemian. Her sentences highlighted the tensions, bringing critical distance to a "personal is political" moment. Music mattered less to her than feminism. After her death from lung cancer in 2006, her daughter Nona Willis Aronowitz edited a collection, again *Out of the Vinyl Deeps,* entirely of her rock criticism—primarily *New Yorker* columns from 1968 to 1975. And with that, she took her place in the first generation's first rank, alongside peers **Robert Christgau** and **Greil Marcus**.

The full run of music criticism is patchy in some ways. Willis was at least as attuned as her former romantic partner to what Christgau called the semipopular, validating the Velvet Underground, Gram Parsons, Modern Lovers, and New York Dolls, but she resisted the polish even of Black performers as brilliant as Stevie Wonder and B. B. King. Looking for women rockers, she questioned Joni Mitchell and Patti Smith out of her canon, most esteeming the never-recorded Ms. Clawdy. If "stuck in the sixties" is a questionable pejorative, Willis does read as stodgy in her dismissals of Bowie ("I felt just the slightest bit conned") and roots rock: "a pleasant dead end."

But *Out of the Vinyl Deeps* captured key disconnects within rock and roll: Willis confessed she "felt no emotional identification" with the 1950s stars—too prole, too hillbilly, too Black, whereas "who among us has soul so pure that he never liked Pat Boone?" So when, during the Nixon seventies, rock audiences fragmented beyond shared Dylan and Stones love, Willis was alert to "My Grand Funk Problem—And Ours." Having always understood the elitism within rock as it separated from rock and roll, she was as likely to feel sympathy for Black Sabbath as question the "virility cult" of New York punk. And understanding the sexism within the counterculture, she could both dissect "Wild World" with what became known as the Ellen Willis test—take a song written by a man about a woman and reverse the sexes, see if it becomes repulsive—and spot rockism instantly: "A group that is thought of as a teenybopper band won't be accepted by most serious rock fans no matter how good it is."

The achievement of *Beginning to See the Light* was to apply insights about the rock counterculture to political debates from abortion and rape to the new right. The politics of consumerism and the politics of sex both turned on a rebel urge that capitalism encouraged and mitigated; art might express a response, but not organize one. Willis's takes on Dylan as Whitman and ad man, on the Who's pop savvy and **Elvis**'s detachment, connected to *Deep Throat* and feminist battles over pornography and to Wolfe's spry conservatism and Herbert Marcuse's dissection of hierarchy. A piece about a brother turned Orthodox in Israel—twenty-two thousand words for *Rolling Stone*—ended the book, positioning rock as her religion and Dylan's "Like a Rolling Stone" as the Judaism of no direction home. If Willis no longer reviewed records, she still explored the bigger questions those records led you to.

NEW DEAL SWING BELIEVER REVIVED

Otis Ferguson, In the Spirit of Jazz: The Otis Ferguson Reader, *1982*

———

"I claim him as the first rock critic," **Robert Christgau** wrote on encountering this collection, and though he was probably right, we don't have to take that as a compliment. Ferguson was the **Lester Bangs** of his day, working-class born, dead too young (World War II service, not cough syrup), bringing flair to obsessive record listening—the impulse to wait for two bars by Bix Beiderbecke, and not even all of those, just the "pure jazz figure" section. He made listening its own kind of cutting contest, fanship a form of engagement no less than getting the music from lived experience. In jazz, between the 1920s and 1930s, that could not be an innocent transposition. Whites, in Ferguson's schema, lived jazz as male fraternalism without need of Black peers or women, exactly the model that big parts of rock culture would extend.

Mostly, Ferguson was known for his film criticism—collected in a separate volume—which took a pro-studio "genius of the system" position to cite the book that Thomas Schatz was researching at about the time of Ferguson's revival. The collective effort of men to make a product together that had some spirit to it and not a lot of pretension was Ferguson's sweet spot; he had to grapple with his reservations about Orson Welles's willfully maverick, yet great, *Citizen Kane*. In the New Deal and Popular Front era, swing bands were near equivalents to studio flicks, as David Stowe later demonstrated in *Swing Changes*. Ferguson, a jazz fan of long standing, was an assistant editor of the *New Republic*—he'd served in the Navy to earn the money to finish high school in New England, got a college scholarship, then the *New Republic* connection by winning their writing contest. He wrote, "I remember probably better than anything the time we were tied up in Shanghai with a ship that had come out later, and somebody on it had a record of 'Black and Tan Fantasy'—played, as I did not learn at the time because the hand-winding portable Victor belonged to the range-finder division, which is a division extremely particular in instances of who comes messing up its part of the ship, by **Duke Ellington**. That was a world heard through a porthole, and not to be forgotten." His first column came in 1936, just as Benny Goodman's swing popularized the band sounds of Ellington and Fletcher Henderson; his death in 1943 meant all his music writing came in the brevity of white jazz popular culture overlapping national mass culture.

Ferguson's Bix Beiderbecke essay, "Young Man with a Horn," gave **Dorothy Baker** the title of her novel, loosely based on Beiderbecke; he returned the favor by calling her "intuitive expression" better than any jazz monograph. The *Reader* contains more than one essay of his on slang, "good among sailors; it lives and is never still." That was Ferguson's obsession: the vernacular in motion. Unschooled Beiderbecke notes, sailor speak. For his music columns he went out on the road with the Goodman band as their "all-around stooge" (roadie before that term circulated) and observed recording sessions. For a hot jazz publication, he mocked John Hammond's trust-fund radicalism: "Every place he goes he presently spies the taint of commercialism in art of the sordid hand of capitalism clutching workers. He burns. He speaks out. And then he *is* out." But he respected Hammond's driving, burning rubber from New York to middle America to catch a band playing. Ferguson was one of the authors in **Frederic Ramsey Jr. and Charles Smith**'s *Jazzmen*, but John Gennari's summation of jazz criticism had little to say about him because his contemporaneous influence was minimal. Rather, his prose set a tone for the heightened vernacular to come, as when he caught a taste of a **Robert Johnson** record ("Kind Hearted Women Blues") and mocked Lead Belly by comparison. Symphonic jazz, whether Paul Whiteman or later **Duke Ellington**, wasn't to his taste. He wanted to be at the Savoy when "the dancers forget dancing and flock," to let **Louis Armstrong**'s "Shine" move him to "sadness, pride, and consciousness of other people outside myself," to live, like his beloved, bludgeoned Bix, in "the servants' entrance to art."

ETHNOMUSICOLOGY AND POP, FOREVER FRAUGHT

Bruno Nettl, The Study of Ethnomusicology: Twenty-Nine
Issues and Concepts, *1983*

———

In keeping with the writing of the grand old man of ethnomusicology, note that I first drafted this entry the morning after seeing Seu Jorge re-create live his Portuguese remakes of David Bowie songs, used in the movie *The Life Aquatic with Steve Zissou.* "Where are the investigations of urban American concert life, of the country-and-western scene, of modern music in the cities of Asia and Africa?" Nettl asked in this personable survey of "problem areas" for the field. "In all cases, the urban, mixed, popular genres, Westernized and sounding familiar, definitely come last." He would update and augment the book

(*Thirty-One Issues*), then again (*Thirty-Three Discussions*) as he turned 85 in 2015, but retained the conceit of imagining himself at a cocktail party, pushed to account for what his "oddball" associates *did*, tongue-tied and calling for a second scotch. It was his preferred fieldwork site.

Ethnomusicology, the 1950s rebranding of comparative musicology in a strategic alliance with anthropology, had long embraced the study of non-Western music, folk music, even—as Nettl's first book, published in 1956, was unfortunately called—*Music in Primitive Culture*. In 1964, Alan Merriam's *The Anthropology of Music*, dedicated to his mentor Melville Herskovits, became a classic in the field, critiquing Nettl's early definition of it as "the science that deals with the music of peoples outside of western civilization" to seek a more expansive theoretical framework. Nodding approvingly at **Alan Lomax, Gilbert Chase, Alice Fletcher,** and **Paul Oliver,** among others, the final citation was to **Nat Hentoff's** *Jazz Life*, as Merriam happily observed: "Of particular contemporary interest is the recent appearance of 'soul' music, an almost ideal situation for a case study of a contra-acculturative movement." It was not an opening Merriam pursued. A decade later, John Blacking—a fan of Webern who studied South Africa's Venda tribe—proclaimed, at the start of a series of lectures published as *How Musical Is Man?*, his conviction: "I can now see no useful distinction between the terms 'folk' and 'art' music, except as commercial labels." A mention of the early **Beatles** and a citation, at a friend's suggestion, of **Amiri Baraka's** *Blues People* notwithstanding, Blacking still missed a category: pop and its commercial mediation as an aspect of culture to study.

Nettl's own 1964 work, an ethnomusicology textbook that chewed out Frances Densmore for poor research methods, betrayed no awareness of the contestations within the field that awaited; but he was actually well suited for them. His parents, music intellectuals from Prague, dodged Nazis to land in public university Bloomington, Indiana. The mother he described in *Becoming an Ethnomusicologist* was a model of tender critical distance who struggled with health and career, taking her life the day after his wedding. His advisor George Herzog entered a sanitarium with manic depression. Nettl relied on library work for many years after his Harvard University Press debut, finally scoring his own Midwestern university perch. At the University of Illinois, he related in a different memoir, *Encounters in Ethnomusicology*, he joined a poker game with pivotal popular music studies musicologist **Charles Hamm.** The two set up a plenary at a joint AMS-SEM gathering in 1971, with Albert Goldman, **Charles Keil,** and bossa nova scholar Gerard Béhague, irritating more established scholars.

This personal and professional history animated *The Study of Ethnomusicology*, written as postcolonialism and postmodernism challenged all notions of white dude ethnography, then revisited on the other side of theory and the world music pop explosion. Nettl's emeritus persona in the books affably admitted to no big answers but defended comparative study, even a sneaky fondness for **Alan Lomax**'s Cantometrics. He practiced cosmopolitan paragraphs, returning regularly to his research on India's Carnatic classical music, Persian *radif*, and Native American Blackfoot song, not to mention the academic culture of the school of music, subject of his *Heartland Excursions*. Equally, he favored his bookshelves—scholars others might consider antiquated were put into a conversation with **Steven Feld** or Thomas Turino. What exactly was music, transcription, the boundaries of folk and art? Was music to be studied *in* culture or *as* culture? How should one approach fieldwork, authenticity, issues of Westernization as homogenization? In short essays—class sessions—Nettl considered. The 2005 and 2015 versions registered the field after Peter Manuel's 1988 *Popular Musics of the Non-Western World*, Ellen Koskoff's sustained gender studies, or Philip Bohlman's work on race and the folk in modernity. But the broad outlines of the 1983 egalitarian vision remained.

Popular music was never one of Nettl's areas of scholarly strength. He knew a bit about Iranian variants, strongly advocated for Virginia Danielson's book on Egyptian singer Umm Kulthum, and appreciated the extent to which those arriving in ethnomusicology after 1970 tended to have such sounds in their past. He edited an early collection of essays on urban music cultures and pushed for more work connecting music to dance. Echoes in his casual evidencing of **Simon Frith**, his friend Hamm, and other central figures suggested deeper commonalities that might have been pursued further. Ethnomusicology, as its limited presence in this book suggests, remained underwhelming in how it addressed pop's relationship to cultures in transition. But Nettl stood for more than his area of academia delivered. He still found relevant, he wrote, the notion of syncretism: cultures that joined up because their central qualities were compatible. That notion marked his scholarly instincts, as a force within a field as much as a writer or editor. The global musicking, past and present, that compelled Nettl—the need for studies of how individuals, and not just great musicians, formed their sense of music within differing cultural paradigms—this was as much a vision for where popular music scholarship might go as it was for ethnomusicology, his chosen nation, his invented tradition.

AUTODIDACT DEVIANCE, MODELING THE ROCK GENERATION TO COME

V. Vale and Andrea Juno, eds., RE/Search #6/7:
Industrial Culture Handbook, *1983*

———

The aesthetic favored "all things gross, atrocious, horrific, demented, and un-just," as "examined with black-humor eyes." The preferred method was Q&A segments with musicians, artists, and other provocateurs, followed by a Refer-ences page covering fave readings, viewings, listening. Formally, each volume was a large bound book, equivalent—for the zines that had nurtured punk through to its aftermath—of the graphic novels that collected comics. And the themes were often notable. This one was followed by *Incredibly Strange Films, Pranks!, Modern Primitives, Angry Women,* and *Incredibly Strange Music.* It took Andrea Juno to keep the autodidact deviance from sliding into clichéd male gonzo; once she departed, her name was expunged from reprints. But she had left a legacy worth reclaiming: this step beyond punk widened the new popular music category, alternative.

Vale Hamanaka, an employee of City Lights, the fabled Bay Area beat book-shop, started punk zine *Search & Destroy;* but *RE/Search*—probably created in conjunction with Juno, about whom no personal information seems to be cur-rently available—was more eclectic. A dark-side-of-the-force version of hippie bible *Whole Earth Catalog*, its indexing of the William Burroughs bohemian interzones had a similar effect, described in Fred Turner's *From Counterculture to Cyberculture*: mapping institutionalized legacies, building networks, nam-ing trends. *Issue #4/5*, first to go from zine shape to bound volume, combined Burroughs and his partner in the text cut-up, Brion Gysin, with avid younger admirer Genesis P-Orridge, whose Throbbing Gristle defined a new genre named after its self-run label, Industrial Records. Each got multiple interviews, packaged to emphasize arcana: survivalist flights by Burroughs; Gysin draw-ings as "cabalistic grid" to protopsychedelic Dreamachine; P-Orridge seen in "his little bunker, cluttered as it is with model skulls, videos, books, cassettes, decorated with stark posters and tasteful displays of meatrack pornography, furnished with low level couches of camouflaged foam."

RE/Search, at this juncture, more comfortably photographed Throbbing Gristle at Spahn Ranch to raise questions about Charles Manson than it ex-plored, say, homosexuality; "all that gay stuff was lost on me," said P-Orridge, who'd later pursue a Pandrogeny Project that included body modification with partner Lady Jaye. The *Industrial Culture Handbook* featured a white cast will-

FIGURE 5.5 Cover of V. Vale and Andrea Juno, eds., *RE/Search #6/7: Industrial Culture Handbook*, 1983. Note the severe aesthetic of this fanzine bulked into formidable book. Author's collection.

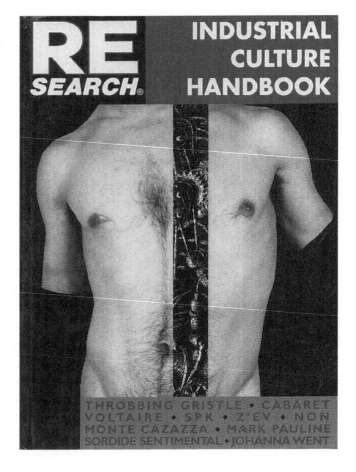

RE SEARCH®

INDUSTRIAL CULTURE HANDBOOK

THROBBING GRISTLE ◆ CABARET VOLTAIRE ◆ SPK ◆ Z'EV ◆ NON MONTE CAZAZZA ◆ MARK PAULINE SORDIDE SENTIMENTAL ◆ JOHANNA WENT

ing, like Boyd Rice of NON, to flirt with Hitler and say, like Stephen Mallinder of Cabaret Voltaire, "Instead of emulating ethnic primitivism we're modern primitives." The one woman, performance artist Joanna Went, was the only person not given a References list of avidities.

Yet those avidities could be dazzling. Survival Research Lab's Mark Pauline made fighting animalistic robots, built Went a blood-spurt device for a Statue of Liberty getup, and shone in *Pranks!* with his tale of defacing a Telly Savalas billboard. Rice, at work on the *Incredibly Strange Films* project, saluted trashy directors with Quentin Tarantino acuity and anticipated the RE/Search music books to come, calling Annette Funicello's "Jo Jo the Dog-Faced Boy" wilder than Captain Beefheart. As S. Alexander Reed has written, the RE/Search volumes were aggressively literary, demanding to know what scenesters read and pursuing a cross-category arts vision, whole from the start, that no other publication could match.

When alternative rock peaked, *RE/Search* became an elder itself, giving the Lollapalooza throngs the history of their modified skins and tattoos with *Modern Primitives*—from Fakir Musafar, born in 1930 and named for a Ripley's cartoon, who hooked and stretched everything, back to P-Orridge and wife Paula, pictured naked to feature all penile and labial insertions. Juno did sole interviews with figures like lesbian piercer Raelyn Gallina and SM mistress Sheree Rose. But her breakout was *Angry Women*, making an icon of Diamanda Galás, an extreme vocalist whose *Plague Mass* for AIDS victims and arrest in an ACT-UP die-in asserted the identity connections that earlier issues had refused in clinging to outsider artists as deviancy enough. "My brother *despised* cheap sentiment," said Galás, no fan of gentle sex and pictured holding a gun, as Burroughs once had been. This was the only *RE/Search* to interview Black artists, such as academic renegade bell hooks and poet Sapphire, alongside NEA-cheated playwright Holly Hughes and abortion-art activists Kerr and Malley. Sequel *Angry Women in Rock*, published by the short-lived Juno Books, featured riotous rockers like Tribe 8's Lynn Breedlove, exultant and free, and an unforgettable portrait of Jarboe of the Swans—abused within the noise model favored by bandleader Michael Gira.

In between came the *Incredibly Strange Music* volumes (1993–94), industrial's negation of punk negation, alternatives to alternative rock, with their loving attention to Martin Denny exotica or Moog-synth quartets. This anthological survey had a point it only half made: the stereophonic 1950–80 records as counterpart to the downhome pre-Depression recordings Harry Smith collected for his Folkways *Anthology*. The books would become a YouTube fantasy to listen with. Yet collector Gil Ray, urging us to try the Hi-Los—"they're trying to sound 'black,' but they don't at all. They just don't sound real"—revealed the limits of the form. *RE/Search* could summon every alt space save the African American counterculture of modernity.

THE ROLLING STONES OF ROLLING STONES BOOKS

Stanley Booth, The True Adventures of the Rolling Stones, *1984*

Booth could wait. His account of the world's greatest rock and roll band—reported on tour in late 1969 through Altamont, but interspersed with chapters set earlier, so founder Brian Jones's death all but coincided with concert attendee Meredith Hunter's—was a decade and a half coming out, following breakdowns. It had a title he hated, *Dance with the Devil*, and no publicity, save for his good friend and band guitarist Keith Richards's ultimate blurb: "the only one I can read and say, 'Yeah, that's how it was.'" Booth would revisit Richards at age forty-five, still bruised in the shoulders from drug injections, in his collection, *Rhythm* Oil, then author a full biography of the man he liked to call "the world's only blue gum white man." Richards wrote his own memoir, which started with the kind of southern scene Booth liked and added some details on blues chording. Robert Greenfield covered the 1972 tour that left Booth a dissipated one hundred pounds and the *Exile on Main Street* recordings. Rich Cohen skipped from time on the road with the much older band back to the start. But if all Rolling Stones music after a certain point was the same music, all tours the same tour, these were the same book. In the end, correct title appended, Booth's account was quintessential.

The idea was that all of this rock stuff had happened before. And it was perfect for a writer from the same remote part of Georgia as his friend, country-rock inventor Gram Parsons, coming of age in the Memphis where Furry Lewis, the great 1920s bluesman and his first profile subject, still strapped on an artificial leg each morning and went to work sweeping streets. Epigraphs invoked Buddy Bolden, gone insane blowing jazz, and the psychoanalytic theories of Freud, Jung, Norman Brown. The prose modeled hard-boiled Chandler: "Then she looked at me again and something happened in her green eyes." "She" was Shirley Watts, married to drummer Charlie, reading Priestley's *Prince of Pleasure* on the Regency era while Booth waited to talk to Stones assistant Jo Bergman; his ally because she loved Henry James and used that to speak "an even more esoteric language, Celebrity Code." Booth told singer Mick Jagger: "I am hip, I am fucking cognizant." That cognizance went beyond anything Michael Braun had offered the Beatles five years earlier, just as Stones music went farther. Everything was gulped down—mescaline, trips to Morocco, Kansas City Six recordings. Even the arena audiences started to smell like weed.

The second big idea, reinforced by the book's inordinate birthing: this moment was doomed. **Kerouac** passed away as Booth began his reporting. Parsons would be gone by 1973, body burned in the Mojave. Some of what ended, Booth thought inherently ridiculous: his fellow critic, Ralph Gleason, demanding the Stones play a free concert; writers and lovers **Robert Christgau** and **Ellen Willis**, referred to only as *Esquire* and *New Yorker*, turning up for "a joint interview with Jagger where we'll try to patch things up between us." Every time the Stones performed "I'm Free," Booth groaned about it, sure no mass version of freedom was real. Even Jagger, the groupies joked, was no Mick Jagger. But the real death was mythological. After Altamont, the band's transgressions seemed ludicrous; they played up their camp qualities. To Booth, "They may have been naïve, but they were much more interesting than the sensible people who came along later." You could quibble, but he'd earned his opinion, going down with the good ship Vernacular.

Yet a key piece remained unresolved. This was a book, a band, that peaked in Muscle Shoals, Alabama, where a Black-music-loving group of non-Blacks, the Stones plus Booth, area renegade Jim Dickinson on tack piano, and Atlantic Records head Ahmet Ertegun (piously discoursing: "Black music is the most popular music of all time—and has been since it got started good, about 1921") recorded "Brown Sugar," originally titled "Black Pussy." Unlike **Elijah Wald**'s *How the Beatles Destroyed Rock and Roll*, where this era was seen as cutting white music off from Black sources and girls dancing, here the process was sketchy appropriation, sifted in Jack Hamilton's *Just Around Midnight*. Booth just waited, observed: his own strong relationships with Black musicians, notably the mentally ill Memphis piano player Phineas Newborn, profiled in *Rhythm Oil*; Mick Jagger in 1969 laughing that *he* didn't want to be Black; Richards's four-year-old, during the Xpensive Winos era, telling Booth "I want to be a black girl." In the sixties-ending tour, Ike and Tina Turner opened for the Stones, with Jagger studying Tina's moves and partnering with an Ikette. At Altamont, the Black fan, Hunter, was stabbed to death by a white Hell's Angel. Jones's replacement on guitar, Mick Taylor, suggested they debut "Brown Sugar." Booth, writing all those years later, called it "a song of sadism, savagery, race hate/love, a song of redemption, a song that accepted the fear of night, blackness, chaos, the unknown . . ." In the absence of a conclusion, the list went on.

FINDING THE BLACKFACE IN BLUEGRASS

Robert Cantwell, Bluegrass Breakdown: The Making of the
Old Southern Sound, *1984*

———

Folklore almost dissolved in Cantwell's antidisciplinary, antigenre accounting. Commissioned to write about the Folklife Festival held on the Mall in

Washington, his chapters horrified his Smithsonian patrons, becoming his first book, the arcane *Ethnomimesis*. But with *Bluegrass Breakdown* and *When We Were Good* he brilliantly represented how the popular was remade by its past, generating avowedly literary but also theory-savvy renderings of a bluegrass pioneer inventing tradition; a baby boomer singing "We Shall Overcome" with powerful naïveté. Writing his subjects into a compelling blur, he made a kind of peace with pop commerce, or at least with folkies who ventured there. Blackface minstrelsy and that equally fake patrician Pete Seeger were lore, too.

Bluegrass Breakdown took up Bill Monroe and his legacy decades down the road, his Grand Ole Opry prominence having become, in **Alan Lomax**'s phrase, a "folk music in overdrive" created with Flatt and Scruggs for country fans at first, then hippie-infused revivalists who created a national tapestry of festivals. Cantwell's methodological range was as impressive as his subject: vivid scene reporting on a 1977 concert, the informed musical details of a kid raised on Pete Seeger's *How to Play the 5-String Banjo*. There was full literacy in folk music history from **Cecil Sharp** forward, centered by the influence of scholars such as Archie Green and Norm Cohen, and the critical understanding that "Hillbilly music has never been anything but entrepreneurial and commercial, prospering in the one commodity which in America is ever in short supply—the past." In one lineage, bluegrass was like a revivalist camp meeting. Just as much, it was the legacy of men like the Irish minstrel Dan Emmett, copying Blacks to sing of Dixie. **Eric Lott** had not yet connected cultural studies to blackface, but *Bluegrass Breakdown* anticipated "love and theft" in every sentence about the "high, lonesome sound" as "ritual, icon, and image," as "a form of 'sentimental' romance." "Bluegrass music is a representation," Cantwell wrote; "by imitating that representation, back-porch players make it real." Lore fossilized by commerce and power could spark anew: "The jazz disc of the twenties, in a word, was fiction, formed like coal from the transmutation of living matter to release its energy again in another world." If this was overwriting, a séance, the hallucination held.

The other books were more of the same. Like his peers W. T. Lhamon and **Greil Marcus**, Cantwell's vision could find similar outcomes in endless and disparate sources, though his validated the "festive" space of the communal arts over pop publics and secret histories. *Ethnomimesis* took up the "impulse to contextualize" culture as modernity in nine chapters: English enclosure acts and gardened landscape, World's Fairs, couscous-eating yuppie cosmopolitans. Guy Debord met Shakespeare: "Tom O'Bedlam was mad; now his madness, in the society of the spectacle, is our own cultural condition." A later collection of essays, *If Beale Street Could Talk*, put ethnomimesis in conversation with habitus, postmodernism with glocalism; against the mediated life's hyperreal encroachment, he wrote, he felt like a nineteenth-century abolitionist. *When We Were Good*, Cantwell's second pivotal work, claimed to be about the folk revival from the Kingston Trio in 1958 to the Beatles in 1964, peaking with those who all sang "Blowin' in the Wind" at Newport. It went well beyond that, anticipating Michael Denning in its take on the earlier folksong movement of **Woody Guthrie** and Seeger inside the Popular Front. Anticipating Marcus too, Cantwell wrote about Harry Smith's 1952 Folkways *Anthology*, not as old, weird America but as another example of folk's representatives shifting: from collected songs to collected records, from political messaging to a riverbed for what would become counterculture. The uber-indie Seeger, who could never have been a Marcus hero, was one of Cantwell's, like Alan Lomax and Joan Baez. Support for folk life came in many shapes: nobles and patrons, patriots and reds. He was more than happy to share the category.

CYBERPUNK NOVELS AND CULTURAL
STUDIES FUTURISM

William Gibson, Neuromancer, *1984*

———

Cyberpunk emerged as one part this celebrated novel and Gibson's prior short stories collected in *Burning Chrome*, one part the *Mirrorshades* collection that Bruce Sterling edited as a science-fiction manifesto. Gibson was Parker–**Kerouac**–**Marcus**–Sex Pistols: the language of the break. Sterling was Gillespie-Ginsberg-**Christgau**-Clash: the break's explanation. Cyberpunk fiction belonged in that dichotomy chain because it synthesized, digitized, the rock and roll connection to science fiction that Harlan Ellison had explored, to where the results fused into movies like *The Matrix*, albums like *OK Computer*, SF-adjacent novels like *Cloud Atlas*. Nobody redeployed Sterling's phrase "chipsters," but Gibson's terms cyberspace and sprawl entered vernacular. He used punk guitarist Robert Quine's name for Bobby Quine, hacker protagonist of "Burning Chrome," whose phrase "the street finds its own uses for things" itself reused the Birmingham subcultural studies led by **Stuart Hall**. Sterling, amid fiction of corporations (*zaibatsus*) akin to underworld gangs, mech and bio upgrades, conceived "Dori Bangs," where rock critic **Lester Bangs** and underground comix artist Dori Seda avoided dying young and dissolute, met, and had a modest afterlife. Cyberpunk's move to link computers and transgressive music insisted on homology, recasting futurism as rainy-day postmodern. Once again, a literary imaginary drew immensely from music, then influenced it just as much.

Gibson, who relocated to Canada to avoid Vietnam and managed a head shop, came to punk as "an age-designated noncombatant" (Steely Dan's mordant noir was closer to home), using it to rekindle his connection to science fiction and the Beats. Stories like "Johnny Mnemonic," "The Gernsback Continuum," and "Burning Chrome," and then the taut *Neuromancer* typed-out console cowboys hacking in parallel to posthuman AIs; lethally upgraded female mercenaries; dub reggae and voodoo loa Afrofuturists; the *gomi* detritus of earlier American modernities collected by Japanese. All shared one information-economy imperative: "have to find that Edge." Gibson came off as a popular culture evoker in the vein of a **Gilbert Seldes** or **Tom Wolfe**, slick in tone: "Really bad media can exorcise your semiotic ghosts." In *Neuromancer*, "Fads swept the youth of the Sprawl at the speed of light; entire subcultures could rise overnight, thrive for a dozen weeks, and then vanish utterly." Two sequel novels, tedious as *Matrix* sequels, were followed eventually by *Pattern Recognition*, a response to 9/11 set in the present. Its central protagonist, a woman named Cayce (instead of, as in *Neuromancer*, a man named Case), was a "cool hunter" and "dowser in the world of global marketing," yet now reduced to tears, implicated in a sentimental manner unlike previous Gibson characters. A short-term future had become no future.

Sterling was not as gifted at fiction or encapsulated modernity, but displayed immense network forum instincts—to use the language of Fred Turner's study of cyberculture—for defining core issues and socializing answers. *Cheap Truth*, a zine, preceded the *Mirrorshades* collection, followed by hacker-relevant manifestoes, e-books, and TED talks. The prescient short story "We See Things Differently"—published first in an issue of *Semiotext(e)*—found Sayyid Qutb, from the Arabic Caliphate, visiting Miami to take out Tom Boston, "Don't Tread on Me" nativist rocker for angry antiglobalists. "The media pop star, the politician. Was there any difference anymore? Not in America; it was all a question of seizing eyes, of seizing attention." If Gibson took on edgy cool, Sterling was a genre partisan, loving and lumping them as "slipstream." Imagining Bangs considering Seda, he wrote, anxious about cultural hierarchy Gibson would never cop to: "To make 'comic books' into *Art*—what a hopeless fucking effort, worse than rock and roll and you don't even get heavy bread for it." Notably, neither Sterling with *Zeitgeist* nor Gibson with *Idoru* proved successful focusing more directly on musical topics.

For that, two writers featured in *Mirrorshades* had better results. Pat Cadigan, an exception to the straight-white-maleness that limited cyberpunk, had "Rock On," about the boundaries of cybernetic and human identity lining off a mediated pop star from an audience member. If Gibson was punk negationism and Sterling the venture-capital-seeking indieness of South by Southwest conventions, then Cadigan defaulted to MTV new wave. In her novel *Synners*, implanted sockets allowed a transcendental experiential stream gushed out by a designated few reality stars, leaping out of their bodies: "*You and Gina and the rest of them, you synthesize the sound and the pictures into what they want to see and hear. You're the real synthesizers.*" **Dylan**'s "I Want You" sounded through the book, a boomer misgiving that insisted no amount of cybershimmy could remove the human need to flounder through personal relationships.

Even more of a fogey in new clothes, Lewis Shiner gave up cyberpunk for music novels of different kinds. *Slam*, set in a Galveston heterotopia of fringe publications like *The Abolition of Work*, put a pushing-forty hippie with rock band roots in a squatter subculture of hardcore punk Suicidal Tendencies fans and skaters. *Glimpses* used a fantastic premise: that a similar protagonist, stuck in the sixties as CD reissues took over, could mentally conjure unfinished songs and albums by the Doors, Beach Boys, and **Beatles**, working through his father's authoritarian streak and the erotic fading of his marriage. (A 2019 novel, *Outside the Gates of Eden*, revisited the sixties tropes once more.) Cyberpunk projected a near future. Shiner gave his hero the ability to astral project into the cherished recent past, taking up the fiction of *Star Trek* slash novels and other fanshipping: "That's me biting the celery on 'Vegetables,' a part played by Paul McCartney in another version of history, the one that ends up with *Smiley Smile*." *Say Goodbye* attempted a California rock novel, falling into the same problem that later sank **Jonathan Lethem**'s *You Don't Love Me Yet*: a hyperreal production culture, from Fleetwood Mac to Jenny Lewis, is not easily recast by realist or surrealist fiction. The repetition of intent was far from coincidental: Lethem, like Rick Moody, **Jennifer Egan**, Dana Spiotta, and many others, had joined cyberpunk's literary inheritors, venturing in the slipstream, between the viaducts of dreams.

GLOSSY MAGAZINE FEATURES WRITER GETS
HISTORY'S SECOND DRAFT

Gerri Hirshey, Nowhere to Run: The Story of Soul Music, *1984*

———

There was much to distrust about this best-selling baby boomer essentializing of romantic failure and betrayed 1960s ideals. It assumed a white perspective—key interview figures like Atlantic's Jerry Wexler and Stax guitarist Steve Cropper interpreted not only the music but its racial meanings. Hirshey blithely called Ray Charles music "undeniably black" and southern soul "rawboned and simple"; she declared, "James Brown has never had a number one hit on the pop charts—he is *that* black." Motown's "artistic confines" meant "style would all but supplant soul" and Cropper told her, "to me, Motown was white music." Well in, Reverend Al Sharpton discussed Brown as his surrogate father, the first time in the book that a Black person who wasn't a performer had talked about a Black performer. African American communal expression was left almost entirely off the table.

Hirshey's reportorial triumph was turning her glossy magazine feature–writer's gifts into interviews with many key soul artists, typically years after their peak, sharing anecdotes they wouldn't have earlier: Solomon Burke on performing behind a sheet to a KKK audience; Diana Ross expressing more tolerance of her female-impersonating fans than Hirshey had ("this is not the crossover Berry Gordy had in mind"); Aretha Franklin's notes on turning demos into finished songs; James Brown's scarred knees and evolving hairstyles; Jerry Wexler on ad-libs as the core of southern soul studio work; Sam (Moore) on his tormented relationship to drugs and Dave (Prater). Even Michael Jackson sat for a session that included his boa constrictor, caught in the midst of his *Thriller* heyday. This 1980s reckoning with soul, equivalent to the Woodstock survivors dancing to Motown in that *Big Chill* scene from the same moment, gave its readers a mythology to reckon with, however problematic.

Introducing the belated follow-up *We Gotta Get Out of This Place*, on "Women in Rock," Hirshey compared her time on the road reporting on musicians to women from Ma Rainey and Janis Joplin on tour. A bass player told her, "Honey, your line of work ain't natural." Screamin' Jay Hawkins echoed: "Your mama know what kind of work you do?" Thinking about her many features for *Rolling Stone*, she concluded: "I am a confirmed process junkie," a departure from her early assumption that she'd be an academic furthering her interest in **Roland Barthes** and the like: hers were just "finger-poppin' ethnographies."

Gender, from her twenty-first-century perspective, mattered less to her than expertise: "my peers are flexible professionals who have learned to go deep Zen when trapped for two hours in a hotel room with a half-dozen chain-smoking French journalists ('C'est dope!') while a hip-hop diva gets her nails lacquered to match her newest car." Her Obi Wan, wheelchair-bound Doc Pomus, was a bard to **Elvis, Dylan**, Lennon, Lou Reed.

Let's quickly recognize some of Hirshey's peers, the fellow second-draft authors whose biographies and scene studies are often more than half the contents of the music section of that pine-shelf bookstore near you.

Barney Hoskyns: the most comprehensive British narrative chronicler of boomer sounds, from California rock and all sorts of singer-songwriter epiphanies to glam, arena rock, and soul accounts, not to mention founder of the great writing clips site www.Rocksbackpages.com

Holly George-Warren: an editor, for Rolling Stone Press, of many a coffee table summation, of Beats, the 1970s, and the like. But on her own a skilled biographer, first of people who would have never otherwise gotten one (Gene Autry, Alex Chilton), most recently applauded for her take on Janis Joplin. Side passion: western wear.

Robert Hilburn: longtime *Los Angeles Times* rock critic and profiler to further his canonizing imperative. But after retiring from the daily beat, he wrote books about two of his favorite subjects, Johnny Cash and Paul Simon, as well as a memoir of his years in the trenches.

David Browne: That moment when Art sang Paul's "Bridge" over the top? Browne could fete it like few others: the most eager commemorator left of seemingly tapped baby boom high-water moments, from his useful book on *1970* to studies of Crosby, Stills, Nash, and Young; Jeff and Tim Buckley; and the Grateful Dead.

Greg Kot and Jim DeRogatis: cohosts of the Chicago radio show *Sound Opinions*, these Indie City fellows did things with their subjects that they couldn't with their ideas or sentences. Kot, after cementing his dad-rock daily newspaper critic credentials with a Wilco biography, rooted for the record industry's demise in *Ripped* and provided much needed attention to the Staple Singers. DeRogatis, deathly on psychedelia and Flaming Lips, gave Lester Bangs's life a narrative and heroically pursued *The Case against R. Kelly*.

Timothy White: participated in the transformation of Bob Marley into a rock star equivalent with a posthumous biography; became yet another *Rolling Stone* elongated features writer, with several collections and work on such boomer faves as the Beach Boys and James Taylor; editorialized like none before or since as *Billboard* editor, toastmaster-general style.

Hirshey would never explicitly confront her exoticizing of Black subjects and reliance on white cronies. Fortunately, **Nelson George, Greg Tate**, Joan Morgan, *Vibe* magazine, **Tricia Rose, Mark Anthony Neal, Guthrie Ramsey Jr.**, and many others would soon create pathways apart from white filtering, extending the 1960s legacy of **Phyl Garland**. But the intellectual position of Hirshey herself, thinking at thirty thousand feet "with solid interview tapes safe in the carryon," extending in turn the legacy of **Lilian Roxon** in her *Rock Encyclopedia* and celebrity journalist days, was worth valuing. Features, she insisted, turned "on moments." Almost all rockers could remember what they first wore on stage. Style and substance were inseparable. And though "we are a nation of inveterate rock critics, I have never tried to be one in print."

THEORIZING SOUND AS DRESS REHEARSAL
FOR THE FUTURE

Jacques Attali, Noise: The Political Economy of Music, *1977;*

Translation, 1985

———

This world-class omnivore, with a stint as economics consultant for Mitterrand's socialist party on his resume, able to juggle jongleurs, Bach, and Tangerine Dream, took an italics-filled stab at defining the totality of music's relationship to noise—very French. Brute noise, he wrote, was akin to murder, needing music to channel its disruption, evolving through different categories of organization: communal *ritual*, individual *representation* (meaning performance), stockpiled *recording*—en route to, he hoped, a liberatory ethos of *composition* on new instruments. Shrewdly, he set his prediction down as punk waved bloody flags and hip-hop used records as instruments of composition; by the time it was translated, it looked prophetic. Attali could come off supercilious in his assertions, an **Adorno**: the Woodstock Years reducing music subsequent to the late 1960s rock he admired to Muzak and minimalism; and, again, so French in his distanced invocations of "style forged in the furnace of black American music." Still, it made for quite a trip and he was tribe popular music in his call for "the only worthwhile researchers: undisciplined ones."

Many picked up on Attali's notion that music anticipated structural changes, sometimes by centuries, providing a "credible metaphor of the real" in the shifts from, say, court performance to bourgeois orchestra and the **Stones'** "Satisfaction." His reading included early American sociology of culture essays, leading to unromantic thoughts on music as anti-noise, a tool for silencing people. Equally vivid were his contrasts between formations—why the festival culture of ritualistic music gave no freedom to composers; how representation opposed that, as money-paying publics allowed performing stars and hit writers to function as new gentry of a liminal sort in an emerging capitalism. Squint a bit, and his take in this part on the artist as rentier explained Neil Young. Recordings were where he got stodgy, viewing them primarily as the replacement of collectivity with passivity. But even there, his stress on musical repetition as critical, producing consumer markets, held up well to subsequent scholarship. Attali returned more than once to druggy mystic Carlos Castaneda in this post-sixties theory book: singular high-low shamanism.

CLASSIC ROCK, MASS MARKET PAPERBACK STYLE

Stephen Davis, Hammer of the Gods: The Led Zeppelin Saga, *1985*

———

Much like Zeppelin, *Hammer* achieved disturbing popularity, selling millions of copies of its tales of groupies fucked by men wielding sharks in hotel rooms, whipped, or kept locked up at age fourteen; hotel rooms reduced to rubble; and a drummer given the nickname the Beast. Davis collected anecdotes like guitarist Jimmy Page would the artifacts of occultist Aleister Crowley. But he did have a strong thesis, stressed academically in Steve Waksman's *This Ain't the Summer of Love*: that unlike the **Rolling Stones**, who had Pop Art glamor Andy Warhol could admire and every music critic in their pockets, the biggest arena rock band of the 1970s was an embarrassment, the scorned secret of the little brothers and sisters of the counterculture. By the mid-1980s, mocked rock had become classic rock. Earlier revels in rock crudery like Jerry Hopkins and Danny Sugerman's Jim Morrison biography, *No One Here Gets out Alive,* set the tone. Mötley Crüe's later group memoir with sleaze student Neil Strauss, *The Dirt*, followed this model, too, reigniting the Sunset Strip.

Hammer was a noise story: about the moment it became clear that Iron Butterfly's "In-A-Gadda-Da-Vida" mattered as much to young people as Woodstock, about heavy-metal thunder and all that born-to-be-wildness. Rock, from this perspective, was not some **Bob Dylan**–generated art twist on rock and roll, though it shared with the singer-songwriter and punk stories a white removal from African American origins. This was more functional: you played electric blues guitar and fantasized **Robert Johnson** selling his soul to the devil, read *Lord of the Rings* and fantasized operatic battles. And if you were lucky, and arrived just as Madison Square Garden–worthy sound systems, high school–aged stoner and easy sex fans, and FM rock radio were locking into place, that fantasy—"Dazed and Confused" jamming, "Moby Dick" drum solos, the "Stairway to Heaven" itself—could be sustaining. It let you record in mansions, forego singles, demand 90 percent of the gate, use a three-hundred-pound manager (Peter Grant) as your battering ram.

"It was OK because Peter Grant was the street," Zep publicist and would-be mogul Danny Goldberg reminded readers. "Peter Grant could deliver rock and roll that was guaranteed to make money." In retrospect, the dollar amounts seem quaint: millions more than billions, the band accepting tax exile from the United Kingdom before those codes were rewritten to favor the rich. For more outraged views of what it led to, see Fred Goodman's *Mansion on the Hill*. For further analysis of Led Zeppelin, there would be **Pamela Des Barres** on the groupies, Ellen Sander on being treated like one, Waksman on the arenas, Chuck Klosterman on the fans, Erik Davis on the occult, and Susan Fast on the music. But this unauthorized biography held up for highlighting the group's ability to conjure a streak of hard-to-parse populism. Led Zeppelin toured the United States, again and again, every region, seven hundred thousand tickets snapped up in one 1975 day. Who were these fans? As Davis's best seller told it: "A despised segment of the rock audience—young, mostly male, mostly working class, cannon-fodder youth who identified with Led Zeppelin in a mytho-poetic fashion beyond the music itself. Led Zeppelin was a mystery cult with several million initiates. In the high school parking lots of every suburban American town in the 1970s, Led Zeppelin *ruled*." That's not "the street" as hip-hop would claim it. It wasn't clear how suburban equaled working class, either. And the role of women was deleted altogether. Readers were left with legends, of a band that hammered like gods and the Americans who worshipped them.

LOVE AND ROCKETS, SIGNATURE COMIC OF PUNK LOS ANGELES AS BORDERLAND IMAGINARY

Los Bros Hernandez, Music for Mechanics, *1985*

———

A bit over a hundred pages into the second massive collection of Jaime Hernandez's *Locas* stories, a character asked the main protagonists, Maggie and Hopey: "So, when did you decide punk was over for you? When it was time for a change?" This particular comic strip, anthologized in 2009, had been drawn in 1999. The friends and the *Love and Rockets* books they appeared in dated to the early 1980s. And the punk allegiance was all 1970s. "Never. It's something that stays with you forever," Maggie Chascarrillo replied. "It's like in everything you do. Like, I dunno, when you drink coffee in the morning." More than the words testified. Each panel offered details of expression, posture, and style that made the man asking not punk, his friends lingeringly so even as bodies and hair filled in. Lining characters, Jaime and his brother Gilbert drew out countless subcultural meanings.

The Bros had grown up in California, U.S.-raised with Texan and Mexican family heritages but fixated on rock, *Creem*-style glam, and the early L.A. punk that crossed race, gender, and sexuality, putting groups like Los Plugz alongside early Go-Gos before white-guy hardcore took over. That initial story went missing: it took decades to get Michelle Habell-Pallán's chapter "'¿Soy Punkera, Y Que?': Sexuality, Translocality, and Punk in Los Angeles and Beyond," in a book called, a la Jaime's, *Loca Motion*. Then came *Violence Girl: East L.A. Rage to Hollywood Stage, a Chicana Punk Story*, where Alicia Armendariz explained how she became Alice Bag. The Hernandez version, peripheral musically, achieved quicker renown as a literary echo. Fantagraphics, a Seattle underground comix label, built its list on *Love and Rockets*, assembled in graphic novels beginning with *Music for Mechanics*.

The connection between popular music and comics or cartoons has been too long-standing for extended summary here. *Krazy Kat* comics were appreciated alongside jazz by the likes of **Gilbert Seldes** for their equally skewed modernist lines; Louis Armstrong was reduced to a cartoon character more than once in movie shorts and Warner Bros. cartoons became a place for musical parodies ranging from radio hits to classical standards. But the same hippie impulses that launched Big Brother and the Grateful Dead in Haight-Ashbury encouraged Gilbert Shelton's *Fabulous Furry Freak Brothers* and the sexually leering

FIGURE 5.6 A portion of page 116 in Jaime Hernandez, *Locas II: Maggie, Hopey and Ray*. Fantagraphics Books, 2009. Originally from *Penny Century* #5 (1999), also Fantagraphics, a *Love and Rockets* spin-off comic from after the first run ended in 1996, featuring work exclusively by Jaime. Author's collection.

but visually stunning work of R. Crumb—more Scott Joplin than Janis in his personal tastes (though he drew Big Brother's *Cheap Thrills* album cover), as a series of trading-card drawings honoring old-time musicians and then the documentary *Crumb* made clear. Crumb's lifelong friend Harvey Pekar, who wrote text for a series of comix (the underground term) called *American Splendor*, becoming a *David Letterman* regular and the subject of a biopic, also looked backward. He was a jazz critic and hospital grunt who identified vernacular music's arc with the deindustrialization of places like his home, Cleveland. Pekar, the Hernandez brothers, and such later figures as the grunge era's Pete

Bagge (*Hate*) and Julie Doucet (*Dirty Plotte*), or Chris Ware's ragtime imaginaries, made comix a place for indie types to go worldmaking, to a subcultural music pulse.

Love and Rockets' borderland imaginary encompassed ethnicity, sustainable indie bohemianism, and dextrous genre bends. Punk rule breaking, especially impulsive sexuality, levitated immutable trauma. Gilbert joked that Jaime was Jekyll to his Hyde. The Maggie and Hopey stories began with a science-fiction streak and kept a female wrestling subthread, but became an extended family saga, rooted in the Latinx neighborhood Hoppers 13. Friends and sometime lovers, Hopey battled with anger in her bands and boho circles, Maggie with depression in more working-class, trad affiliations, all lovingly detailed as they aged into "has-been punks." Gilbert theorized culture more overtly: a strip in *Music for Mechanics* traced invented band Twitch City, 1977 becoming 1984, music returned "back to the good ol' indulgent/sexist/reactionary crap it's always made the most money at . . . But for a minute there, for a blink . . ." A later extended narrative, titled "Love and Rockets" as a wink to the real English band who'd borrowed the strip's title, wove rock, rap, the film biz, immigrant flower vendors, and other markers into a sonic mural of Los Angeles just pre–Rodney King. But most of Gilbert's work was set in the invented Latin American town of Palomar, liminal space of the rural becoming pop modern, where a Russ Meyer movie–proportioned heroine, Luba, gave baths, ran a theater, enforced laws with a hammer, and hit the nearest city to dance her head off. Bad things, personal and omnipolitical, scarred bodies. Palomar and Luba's clan pushed on.

More could be mentioned. Maggie and Hopey were first seen in a library, singing "Thirty-five dollars and a six pack to my name. Sixpack!" Credit to Black Flag at the bottom of the page. A Hoppers 13 punk reunion occupied Jaime's *Love and Rockets* portions in 2017–18. There was a flashback to glam and punk (but with an iPad present) in Gilbert's one-off book *Bumperhead*. An accordion teacher in magically real Palomar pushed *One Hundred Years of Solitude* on his indifferent wife, but in the other direction, Junot Díaz testified that he wrote his novel *The Brief Wondrous Life of Oscar Wao* to finish the work Los Bros started. "I don't read Spanish," Gilbert said to Enrique García in an interview published in a *Routledge Companion to Latina/o Popular Culture*. "But I made up my own story in my head."

PLAYS ABOUT BLACK AMERICAN CULTURE SURVIVING
THE LOSS OF POLITICAL WILL

August Wilson, Ma Rainey's Black Bottom, *1985*

———

In 2000, eight works into his ten-play, ten-decade twentieth-century cycle, August Wilson wrote his own encapsulation for the *New York Times*:

> The culture of black America, forged in the cotton fields of the South and tested by the hard pavements of the industrial North, has been the ladder by which we have climbed into the New World. The field of manners and rituals of social intercourse—the music, speech, rhythms, eating habits, religious beliefs, gestures, notions of common sense, attitudes toward sex, concepts of beauty and justice, and the responses to pleasure and pain—have enabled us to survive the loss of our political will and the disruption of our history. The culture's moral codes and sanction of conduct offer clear instructions as to the value of community, and make clear that the preservation and promotion, the propagation and rehearsal of the value of one's ancestors is the surest way to a full and productive life. The cycle of plays I have been writing since 1979 is my attempt to represent that culture in dramatic art.

A more elliptical way in: Ma Rainey, a Wilson character, was based on the singer from the world of Black tent-show companies that **Lynn Abbott and Doug Seroff** finally documented. She deferred recording, deferred signing the release forms, made the white record men wonder how long must they hesitate ("Hesitating Blues" a **W. C. Handy** copyright, but Handy took it from folk sources and Wilson sampled it in *The Piano Lesson*), because "They don't care nothing about me. All they want is my voice." Wilson himself, asked to let outside producers take his play to Broadway, refused to surrender control; later, he'd refuse to film *Fences* with a white director. Pittsburgh-born, in 1945, to an aspirational Black mom and a soon-absent white dad, loving a working-class Black stepfather who died, dropping out of school at fifteen but reading relentlessly in the library, he heard—his preface to *Three Plays* told us—Bessie Smith in 1965, while living in a rooming house; a 78 of "Nobody in Town Can Bake a Sweet Jellyroll Like Mine." That was the spark, plus 1960s Black cultural nationalism, the painting of Romare Bearden (blues in extra-musical form), and Borges's surreal fiction. Near forty, he trusted *Ma Rainey* to Lloyd Richards, who had directed *A Raisin in the Sun* on Broadway in 1959; Wilson's became the first Black play there since. He kept on until *Radio Golf* and his death in 2005.

Wilson baked his jelly roll from the freedoms of the sixties, the plunder of the twenties, and the backlash of the eighties. *Ma Rainey* was the only cycle play not set in Pittsburgh's Hill district, as if blues were the only way to carry forth the local. "White folks don't understand the blues. They hear it come out, but they don't know how it got there," a character said, challenging the Rainey character with a song lifted from Charley Patton before stabbing the only book-reading musician. (Wilson's preface called blues the "cultural response of a nonliterate people.") The play ended with a trumpet, "blowing pain and warning." A later play, *Seven Guitars*, updated the action to 1948, giving character Floyd Barton the Jimmy Rogers song "That's All Right" to record for a flat fee and still no royalties in the electric blues era. But the past wasn't letting go: the character who killed Barton, this time with a machete, relentlessly sang "I Thought I Heard Buddy Bolden Say." Wilson insisted, "I am not a historian"; he wanted for art "the contents of my mother's life . . . the song that escaped from her sometimes parched lips." Only some songs fit: Jim Jackson's "Old Dog Blue," from Harry Smith's *Anthology*, in *Fences*; a proto-blues Handy's *Anthology* made much of lending its title to *Joe Turner's Come and Gone*; **Alan Lomax** recording from Parchman penitentiary in *Piano Lesson*; Dinah Washington's "Red Sails in the Sunset" for fading memory in *King Hedley II*; **Irving Berlin**'s "Blue Skies" for Buppie deracination in *Radio Golf*.

Wilson was no purist. Compared to **Ralph Ellison** and **Albert Murray**'s canonization of **Duke Ellington**, a Henry Louis Gates Jr. signifying in academia, or a Stanley Crouch hitting neotraditional notes as a critic to further Wynton Marsalis, he was part of the W. C. Handy and **Zora Neale Hurston** continuum—the world's longest-running Black literary craps game. Struggle and song were his theater. It came down to stuff we might accuse a white chronicler of mythicizing. But this wasn't a sentimental in need of vernacular so much as the next step. Wilson started from the vernacular and then, through an artistic process steeped in Black Power, framed an updated myth to cope with the disappointments of its very partial triumph.

PUTTING POP IN THE BIG BOOKS OF MUSIC

H. Wiley Hitchcock and Stanley Sadie, eds., The New Grove Dictionary
of American Music, *1986*

From 1969 to 2000, Hitchcock's *Music in the United States: A Historical Introduction* (nicknamed MinUS by its author) kept tabs, across four revised, slim editions, of the unfolding literature its author administered. Hitchcock, a music PhD who had studied in Paris with legendary composer mentor Nadia Boulanger, initially noted "we know less about our own music than about that of western Europe" and pledged to cover "pop songs as well as art songs." His most influential formulation, declaring a nineteenth-century U.S. musical schism between "cultivated" and "vernacular" modes, drew on John Kouwenhoven's *Made in America* and anticipated **Lawrence Levine**'s *Highbrow/Lowbrow*—interdisciplinary American Studies. But he remained Boulanger's pupil, giving a full chapter only to Charles Ives: the composer who reworked the popular from the art margins. Through the final edition, edgy composers tied to the popular took priority; guitar symphonies by Glenn Branca (in a Kyle Gann–authored chapter) got more space than Hendrix.

But Hitchcock's greatest gift to popular music came from his administrative prowess. He used his perch within the CUNY system to launch the Institute for Studies in American Music, whose publications and programs allowed scholars like **Richard Crawford** and Carol Oja, critics like **Robert Palmer**, debuts for key framing work. Then he took the lead as coeditor of the decidedly plus-sized 1986 *New Grove Dictionary of American Music*: nine hundred contributors, over five thousand topics.

These four volumes were as much a consolidation of vernacular American music studies as the *Rolling Stone* author tomes of the time. **Charles Hamm** wrote the long entry on popular music. Rock and classical critic John Rockwell assigned pop-rock entries to peers such as **Greil Marcus**, Dave Marsh, Jon Pareles, and Ken Tucker. **Paul Oliver** spoke to blues, Gunther Schuller to jazz, **Bill Malone** to country, **Arnold Shaw** and Henry Pleasants to pop, Gerald Bordman to musical theater, Edward Berlin to ragtime, Crawford to psalmody. Judith Tick addressed the role of women, **Eileen Southern** the African American tradition, **Bruno Nettl** ethnomusicology. Once again, Hitchcock skewed the coverage: ample for classical and experimental music, good-sized for jazz, spare for pop genres, so La Monte Young got more words than Neil Young. The rock critics were asked to accept stiff prose edits (**Robert Christgau** withdrew from the project), which made it fun to see them try to elide the restrictions: Marcus called Creedence Clearwater Revival "as far-seeing an account of the limitations and opportunities of the American way of life as the rock idiom has produced."

One could find the limit of the enterprise in the minstrelsy entry, which positioned blackface in relationship to the genteel tradition but never attempted the intersectional reading of power dynamics that **Robert Cantwell** had already tried with bluegrass and **Eric Lott** would soon turn into his book *Love and Theft*. Cultural studies approaches—interpretations of **John Cage**'s sexuality in relationship to his music, notions of popular genres as constructed forms to unpack—were not part of this encyclopedia. Instead, Amerigrove, as the volumes came to be called, marked a summation of other sorts: the end of the three decades of exploration ushered in by *America's Music* (**Gilbert Chase** contributed one symbolic entry, on populist composer and pioneering music historian Arthur Farwell), canonically focused and narrative genre studies, identity politics, and rock and roll. Here, if in odd proportions, the full range of subject matter could be summoned for well-versed writers to parse. Never had so much vernacular knowledge been put down in one place, piece by piece. American music had truly become a field.

Without attempting a sustained contrast, it's worth noting Charles Hiroshi Garrett's eight-volume *Grove Dictionary of American Music,* which supplanted Hitchcock and Sadie in 2013. The preface stressed how thoroughly the coverage of country music had expanded as part of the now nine thousand entries by fifteen hundred contributors—a notable choice to make a representative example. But if the entries were more populist, what about the scholarship? Here, the steering figures were all academics: Frances Aparicio on Latinx music to Sherrie Tucker on jazz in advisory roles, a Loren Kajikawa on hip-hop, or Jacqueline Warwick on post-1945 pop, among many section editors. The legacy of critics and non-university types was pushed into the background of many an entry's bibliography. In this iteration at least, quite useful to be sure, custody of American music had been given over to university music departments.

POPULAR MUSIC'S DEFINING SINGER AND SWINGER

Kitty Kelley, His Way: The Unauthorized
Biography of Frank Sinatra, *1986*

———

"He is the great missed opportunity of American letters," neo-snob Terry Teachout complained in a 1995 *Times* review. "No musician seems ever to have interviewed him at length; no first-rate book has been written about his life. Instead of a novel, we got a trashy tell-all biography." Teachout was celebrating three then-new books. **Will Friedwald**'s *Sinatra! The Song Is You* distilled the "saloon singer" who set a standard for standards. Steven Petkov and Leonard Mustazza's *Frank Sinatra Reader* spanned forty years of press criticism, including Gay Talese's legendary write-around (profile without interview), "**Frank Sinatra** Has a Cold." And daughter Nancy's coffee-table book *Frank Sinatra: An American Legend*? There, Lauren Bacall called her fellow celeb "a complete shit" and the kids shaded his final wife. Maybe that tell-all was worthy after all—of the swinger, Reagan Democrat, and longing baritone who made American pop a star text.

The earliest book on Sinatra, by *New Yorker* writer and army vet E. J. Kahn Jr., captured that intersection in its title, *The Voice: The Story of an American Phenomenon.* Kahn heard the fellows asking, "What's he got that I haven't got?" Not only did the skinny 4-F sing "slow, dreamy love songs" to "the satisfaction of several million adolescent girls," but Walter Winchell claimed that his 1944 income of almost $1.5 million was the largest in the world. It had to be a hype: publicist George Evans was Kahn's preferred source, planting gossip-column items that the "lower middle-class" fans in "Teenage America" read religiously and used to form "a party line, like Communists." One fan, writing far down the road, Martha Weinman Lear (reprinted in the *Reader*), provided gender and musical insights Kahn could not: her peers would "practice swooning"; the vocal trigger a "skimming slur" that the Voice "would do coming off the end of a note." Another grown-up fan, tabloid columnist Pete Hamill, deepened the class reading: Sinatra spoke to the individualistic needs of Americans "transformed by the Depression and the war into unwilling members of groups" as "the first star to step out of the tightly controlled ensembles of the white swing bands to work on his own."

Still, for decades the bulk of Sinatra writing came in gossip columns. Richard Gehman's *Sinatra and His Rat Pack* dwelled on the Sinatra who'd always had, as Kahn put it, a "retinue." Talese's profile compensated for the rejected interview with scenes that showed Sinatra as "Il Padrone," demanding respect in his Italian American circles but musically from studio players who made his records classic

FIGURE 5.7 Cover of E. J. Kahn Jr., *The Voice: The Story of An American Phenomenon*, 1946, the first book on Sinatra. Author's collection.

and financially in his corporate clout. His sexuality was interpreted as rejection of nuclear domesticity, his outbursts as authenticating passion or a generation gap. Adept summarizer **Arnold Shaw** added musical detail to this arc in *Sinatra: Twentieth Century Romantic*: "No pop singer before him sought or achieved so complete an identification, both personal and emotional, with his material. Through him, involvement and intensity became the touchstones of popular singing, as they always were of folk and blues singing." One of Sinatra's loyal, then exiled, columnists, Earl Wilson, offered a ripped-from-the-clippings summation with the toothless 1976 *Sinatra: An Unauthorized Biography*. Sample: "Oh, he has been known to hit a woman, too—with provocation." Wilson did deflate the intensity Shaw celebrated: "He prospers, yes, prospers—even commercially—on brawls, lawsuits and headlines. The conflicts make him a bigger box-office attraction than all the happy singers."

His Way was more serious conflict: Kitty Kelley upended the Sinatra narrative. His feared mother Dolly, readers learned, performed abortions. (This, still waiting for a feminist reading, became an indelible part of the story: first wife Nancy's abortion as their marriage foundered; second wife Ava Gardner's two abortions; the girlfriends valet George Jacobs recalled taking for the procedure; daughter Tina's account of waking from one, to her father's dismay.) Hoboken clout helped Dolly fund and advocate for his early career, but her power also threatened him. Ava was his Dolly surrogate, the movie star breadwinner who bragged about his cock size and by dumping him—Nelson Riddle was said to have said—"taught him to sing a torch song." Comedian Shecky Greene: "He couldn't control her or dominate her." So, in Kelley's account, he settled for dominating all other women, with violence ranging from pushing one through a window to beating up young third wife Mia Farrow for working on *Rosemary's Baby*. If Swoonatra becoming Chairman of the Board was remasculinization, Kelley ripped off the toupee.

The obvious rejoinder was musical, but few had particularized Sinatra's work: he wasn't jazz enough, let alone rock. Henry Pleasants, mostly a classical critic, did the first heavy lift in his fascinating *The Great American Popular Singers*, which proclaimed Sinatra best in a lineage from Jolson to Streisand and analyzed how his bel canto approach and use of pitch variance worked the microphone to its fullest potential, creating a "sense of a personal relationship between singer and listener." Friedwald's Sinatra book, instantly definitive on much of the aesthetics, contrasted arranger Riddle with others like Gordon Jenkins; acknowledged his most sustained musical marriage, to pianist Bill Miller; considered Artie Shaw questions of art and ownership; and viewed the evolving music album as central—balancing multiple tracks, Sinatra switched attitude as others did keys. Its flaw was the author's anti-rock exaggeration: "The first major teen idol was also the last one not to pander to his audience." Charles Granata added to this musical underpinning with *Sessions with Sinatra*, focused on studio recording.

James Kaplan's two-volume biography, *The Voice* and *The Chairman*, combined Friedwald's work-by-work passion with much Kelley, though a less vengeful and more men's magazine variant, akin to **Nick Tosches** on Dean Martin. Kaplan was able to draw on the far greater number of memoirs by fellow stars now available—Gardner, Bacall, etc. He recognized in the Rat Pack at the Sands a "vision of unrepentant American masculinity that continues to reverberate"; the sex was less judged than tallied, like burgers sold at McDonald's. Kaplan cashed the register on Lana Turner's "love with the idea of being a movie star," then Ava Gardner's wanderlust ("Castro, Miles . . . She could keep up with Frank and his gangsters any day of the week"). The violence, too, got an accounts balanced, so that if Farrow's bruises were questioned, it was more workaday horrific that Sinatra had his pal Jilly break a baker's ankle when the buns weren't ready. Normal biographical transitions became disorienting, as the baker bit moved into an appreciation of the third *Man and His Music* program, with Ella Fitzgerald and Antônio Carlos Jobim: "Televised popular music simply didn't get any better."

While Kaplan's books stretched fifteen hundred pages to cover one life and its work, academics grappled to frame context. Keir Keightley never made a book of his 1996 dissertation on the singer as 1950s high fidelity, adult pop, and masculinity from suburbs to bachelor pads, but articles proliferated (see the Works Cited). Michael Denning's *Cultural Front* considered leftist working-class popular culture in the Depression and World War II era, explaining Sinatra the FDR advocate who championed civil rights in the film short and song "The House I Live In," words by the author of "Strange Fruit." Allison McCracken's *Real Men Don't Croon* positioned the crooner role that Sinatra transformed. Joel Dinerstein's *The Origins of Cool in Postwar America* gave a chapter to Sinatra's version supplanting Humphrey Bogart's noir. Karen McNally's *When Frankie Went to Hollywood*, focused on masculinity and "Sinatra's star identity," considered the postwar working class's anxious relationship to white-collar prosperity. One section explored the slinger of terms like "spook" on civil rights—for more, see **Sammy Davis**'s *Yes I Can* and *Mr. S*, George Jacobs's cutting houseman's memoir from the bedroom one wall-tap away.

In his novel *The Godfather*, Mario Puzo earned Sinatra's ire by imagining him as Johnny Fontane, indebted to the mob for his contract release and rebound film role. But other myths lingered, like the idea that Frank Jr. had staged his own kidnapping "for the attention of his father," Rona Jaffe said in Tina's memoir, which recalled a rich California suburb where Walt Disney gave train rides around his house on Saturdays and the Crosby boys fled over to escape Bing. Dad was divorced but sometimes spent the night. If he wasn't Fontane, was Sinatra the godfather? Something dark out of a James Ellroy novel? Kelley had the last laugh. "Frank destroys money," said his friend until he wasn't, baseball icon Joe DiMaggio, in *His Way*. And money always came back: $200 million at the end, claimed one of the books—John Lahr, another *New Yorker* author drawn in. "'Scuse me, while I disappear," the Voice sang, retiring in 1971, a year after he'd endorsed Reagan for governor. *Ol' Blue Eyes Is Back*, he announced in 1973. "He's one of *them* now," critic Ralph Gleason declared in a 1974 slam reprinted in the *Reader*. Kelley moved on to write about Nancy Reagan. Sure, she wasn't a music critic. But as the vernacular in general became the god that failed, her *Way* stood as the book Sinatra had coming to him.

ANTI-EPIC LYRICIZING OF BLACK MUSIC
AFTER BLACK POWER

Nathaniel Mackey, Bedouin Hornbook, *1986*

———

This punning (Hornbooks would be a great title for a collected look at the jazz literature) launched *From a Broken Bottle Traces of Perfume Still Emanate*, a currently five-book fiction of letters sent between 1978 and 1984 from an experimental musician, N., to his "Angel of Dust." Mackey's author photo worked that same margin: activist gaze, knit cap that even in black and white suggested red, gold, and green. But he was a literature professor at UC Santa Cruz, then Duke, releasing poetry books and journal criticism, editing the Black Arts site for writerly woodshedding *Hambone*, hosting a jazz and world music college radio show—everything but blowing. *Bedouin* appeared in a book series overseen by *Callaloo*, a postmovement journal where Mackey edited special issues and received his own. There, they called him Nate, reframing that *Emanate*. Reframing: it was constant here. *Bedouin* started with N. dreaming of playing "pipe" to a "crowd" (both quotes his) that wanted "Naima" but got an Archie Shepp version of "Cousin Mary" from *Four for Trane*. Particularly, reframing to endure a loss: "Perhaps Wilson Harris is right," the next paragraph began. "There are musics which haunt us like a phantom limb."

The fugitive style but counterpublic gains of jazz and Black Power provided funding lines for this steadily accruing amalgamation, diasporic Black anthological modernism that joined vernacular to avant-garde. The totality mattered as much, as time went on, as the particulars. Mackey used the social and even titling processes of free jazz, funk, Afrobeat, and beyond as a holistic vision of "discrepant" literature ranging from U.S. poets Robert Duncan and William Carlos Williams to Guyanese novelist Harris or Barbadian poet Kamau Brathwaite. N.'s band, Mystic Horn Society, later Molimo m'Atet, was a collective whose tribulations, mythic and all too human, produced strange compositions that went "into our book," meaning repertoire but also every link of jazz to the literary. N. became other avatars who appeared in "after-the-fact lecture/libretto" sections of the novels. Earlier, the N. letters appeared in "Song of the Andoumboulou," a serial work that would go on to number more than one hundred poems, including a CD with musical accompaniment. Mackey's essay "Othering: From Noun to Verb," in his criticism collection *Discrepant Engagement*, took up *Blues People*'s "Swing—From Verb to Noun" chapter with an aim in line with **Amiri Baraka**'s: to dispel white reification. His method was different, assemblages of reference and provisional practice to "accent fissure, fracture, incongruity, the rickety, imperfect fit between word and world." Yet the impact revealed itself as he moved from citer to cited, the inspiration for **Fred Moten**'s Black aesthetics exploration *In the Break* and such scholars as Brent Hayes Edwards, Anthony Reed, Nadia Ellis, and Ashon Crawley.

That same early *Bedouin* passage made a point to say: "The last thing I remember is coming to the realization that what I was playing already existed on a record." N. and his author arrived in popular music literature as the vernacular revolution crested. Moten would explore "the sentimental avant-garde" using Mackey, who had used **Steven Feld**'s ethnomusicology (and "participatory discrepancies" via **Charles Keil**) for his "Sound and Sentiment, Sound and Symbol." Orpheus and the orphic linked to orphan and abandonment. Song recuperated that imprecisely, across margins of race, gender, and sexuality, flamenco *duende* and Malian Dogon lore. Mackey wrote, in his later collection *Paracritical Hinge*, of "Palimpsestic Swagger." One learned that a letter in *Bedouin* was inspired by an artist he first saw in the San Francisco home/wonderland of poet Robert Duncan, an ally of the Beats, and his male partner the visual artist Jess. "Social estrangement is gnostic estrangement," Mackey concluded, "and the step from Satchmo's 'height of trumpet' to Sun Ra's 'intergalactic music' is neither a long nor an illogical one." Amid postmodern pastiche, Rock Hall canons, and neotrad jazz, Mackey focused on music and language: "Words are treated as though, rather than sticking, as Jack Spicer puts it, to the real, they were continually slipping from it." That went beyond vernacular. Like **Charles Mingus** explaining jazz, it was a multiple, with room for the bladelike syncopation in a Burning Spear cut, the dedication to blackface performer **T. D. Rice** in John Berryman's *Dream Songs*.

To Mackey, citing Ives, music was an "art of speaking extravagantly." In a gripping scene in *Bedouin*, N. attended the Crossroads Choir, whose crowd chanted "My house of cards had no foundation." An avatar named—for at least a time—Jarred Bottle, Gap Band funkifying his Kafka, announced, or tried to, "that the creaking word, the rickety, crackpot word, was at the root of all music, its motivating base." Two volumes later, balloons with not-so-explanatory captions started mystically appearing during Molimo m'Atet solos. Two volumes after that, the group offered a press release: "Legibility, we know, is an inflated claim."

LOST ICON OF ROCK CRITICISM

Lester Bangs, Psychotic Reactions and Carburetor Dung, *1987*

───────

During his short (1948–82) lifetime, rock critic Lester Bangs was unable to sell any U.S. publisher on a collection; the closest near-miss was a German translation. **Greil Marcus**—who had no such trouble in the same years, because his criticism illuminated as much as it embodied rock and roll wildness—noted at the onset of the posthumous anthology he edited: "Perhaps what this book demands from a reader is a willingness to accept that the best writer in America could write almost nothing but record reviews."

Psychotic Reactions took its title from a song by the sort of garage band Bangs made his name defending: "goony fuzztone clatter . . . pure folklore." (*Carburetor Dung* he made up, which mattered too.) He positioned clatter against "those Class albums that you just don't get any kicks out of." The superstar singer-songwriters of the 1970s, Bangs insisted, were—to quote the Stooges, one of the underground outliers he championed instead—"No Fun." It was "drowning in the kitchvats of Elton John and James Taylor, that I finally came to realize that grossness was the truest criterion for rock 'n' roll, the cruder the clang and grind the more fun."

Bangs took this attitude in 1971 to *Creem*, the Detroit publication that billed itself as "America's only rock 'n' roll magazine" in opposition to the rock, increasingly polished *Rolling Stone*. His championing of "the Party" as spirit and aesthetic in elongated first-draft essays connected with readers too young for 1960s folk-rock art—the new arena crowds. He could find groupies for southern rockers Wet Willie, use Black Sabbath to explore heavy metal before it was called that. Most notoriously, in repeated articles, he exchanged barbs with former Velvet Underground leader Lou Reed, an equally adamant rock and roll autodidact.

Then he gave Detroit up for New York as punk evolved from garage rock and Velvets into the *Punk* magazine scene of Patti Smith, the Ramones, and his new home's commune, CBGB. Bangs freelanced for the *Village Voice*, started a band, and reconsidered his principles. He'd been skeptical of righteousness profiling Bob Marley; now he embraced it profiling the Clash. He'd tossed off the N word in prose like he was Lenny Bruce and rock and roll required offensiveness; now he wrote the antiracist intervention "The White Noise Supremacists." (It's less evident that he ever confronted the guy-on-the-make sexism implicit in his aggro persona, though a passage in his book on Blondie came close: "I think that if most guys in America could somehow get their fave-rave poster girl in bed and have total license to do whatever they wanted with this legendary body for one afternoon, at least 75% of the guys in the country would elect to beat her up.") He tried to stop drinking. He died. Robert Duncan, his successor at *Creem*, sort of wrote Bangs's book instead: *The Noise: Notes from a Rock 'n' Roll Era*.

Marcus stressed the litterateur whose "love for apparent trash and contempt for all pretensions" predicted punk. Bangs's arena rock and free jazz sensibilities waited years for a second volume, John Morthland's more topically varied *Mainlines, Blood Feasts, and Bad Taste*. Unpublished writing there exhumed Bangs's trauma, in 1968, witnessing a Hell's Angels gang rape; telling a professor that now "artists of all stripes everywhere would feel blissfully free to cut themselves loose from their heritage, or not even learn that heritage." Jim DeRogatis's biography *Let it Blurt*, uninterested in Bangs's intellectual ambitions, presented him as one of the "Noise Boys," alongside **Richard Meltzer** and **Nick Tosches**: the Bangs portrayed in the movie *Almost Famous*; the Bangs akin to punk oral history *Please Kill Me*. Steve Waksman's *This Ain't the Summer of Love* started the task of connecting Bangs to rock studies; less punk, more Grand Funk Railroad. A new crop of transgressive academics, **José Esteban Muñoz**, Jack Halberstam, and Tavia Nyong'o, succeeded Bangs's crew as Noise Boys, at least hypothetically, as will be explored later on.

When and if the field gets there, Bangs will still have material ready for reconsideration. His typewriter solo runs always left spare rooms for self-doubt: "We got a groovy, beautifully insular hip community, maybe a nation, budding here, and our art is a celebration of ourselves as liberated individuals and masses of such—the People, dig?" He got the aesthetically indifferent (but to a strength not a fault) Dick Clark to say: "in this generation of young people who all wanta be individualistic, the line is 'Look, I wanna be different, just like everybody else!,' we are really coming into a carbon-copy generation." And he wrote, more to himself, about a line in **Peter Guralnick**: "Surely this is Sam Phillips buying his own myth, if not his own hype." It wasn't the glory of rock that made Bangs so much as a sense that he was a little late to it, a little square for it. He sipped on syrup and horrible noise.

VEILED GLIMPSES OF THE SONGWRITER WHO
INVENTED ROCK AND ROLL AS LITERATURE

Chuck Berry, Chuck Berry: The Autobiography, *1987*

––––––––

"Hey, you all know Chuck just as good as I do; I've just known him longer," said Johnnie Johnson, whose boogie-woogie piano anchored the songwriter who invented rock and roll as literature, to the musicians and film people gathered in St. Louis in 1986 for the sixtieth birthday tribute *Hail! Hail! Rock 'n' Roll.* Berry's great admirer, Rolling Stones guitarist Keith Richards, offered exasperated, impressed concurrence: "the more you find out about him, the less you know." The best biographer, Bruce Pegg, brought in Henry Louis Gates Jr.'s Black literary theory to center "Berry's own fascination with signifying itself." So it should be no surprise that Berry's memoir, out not long after the documentary, was no less playful about its revelations. A dedication pledged, with his characteristic wink and glide out of the frame, to cover "WHAT IS TRUE / PRAISED OR TABOO / HERE / ARE A FEW / THINGS THAT I DO / EXPOSED TO YOU / FOR YOUR REVIEW." As a Berry song put it, "Goes to show you never can tell."

In that late 1980s moment of Rock and Roll Hall of Fame inductions, compact-disc reissues, and white baby-boomer synopses of African American "influence," Berry—who stressed that he had used no ghost[white]writer—was as determined as his pursed-lip admirer, **Bob Dylan** in *Chronicles,* to not be pigeonholed. (*X-Ray,* the "unauthorized" and unreliable autobiography of Kinks front man Ray Davies, belongs in this subcategory, too.) The chapter on his recordings was no more important to him than recollections of a near-dalliance with a French journalist or his first visit to New Orleans, where strip clubs were closed to Blacks, so he watched with field glasses from doorways across the street and waited for the doors to open. The man who'd left his first prison stint "free, black, twenty-one, single, and unbelievably horny" worked African American changes on white archetypes as a matter of course. He'd taken the band from Johnnie Johnson with moves that made mixed St. Louis crowds ask "Who is that black hillbilly at the Cosmo?" Now, he made rock and roll liberation a Black swing generation high school kid's coming-of-age. Time ran in both directions for him: his final album, *Chuck,* released posthumously, rewrote the 1873 ditty "Silver Threads Among the Gold" as "Darlin.'"

In his book, Berry traced his origins to a plantation where the woman who ran it had a child with a man who slaved for it. He stressed his family's solidity:

college-educated mother who named a son for Paul Laurence Dunbar, father who labored for Drozda Realty nearly thirty years, sister who studied voice at conservatories. Berry found it all subservient. "Dad had a way of showing he was 'in his place' and not a trouble-maker." He heard Tommy Dorsey on a jukebox and bought drape pants, sang Jay McShann blues and Sinatra ballads for his first love, a lesbian. "Fetishes, latent in my anticipation," were explored when he married Themetta at twenty-two. Electric guitar and a reel-to-reel tape recorder unleashed his voyeuristic muse: "I was completely fascinated by its reproduction qualities." Still feeling like an amateur, he took two songs to Chess Records in Chicago, signed a contract knowing "I was being railroaded," and became a hit with "transistor-radio teenagers" though "married nigh six years, a veteran at paying bills."

Subsequent writers picked out larger meanings Berry hinted at. **Robert Palmer**'s "Church of the Sonic Guitar" outlined a lineage of Black electric guitar players that fed those dancing riffs. Steve Waksman's *Instruments of Desire* considered how Berry's lighter tone let a crossover figure deflect issues of Black masculinity. Albin Zaks's *I Don't Sound Like Nobody* focused on his "songs as records" use of aural language alongside wordplay. W. T. Lhamon's *Deliberate Speed* was typically shrewd about Berry's racialized masks and artifice.

Still awaiting elaboration, the issues remaining loaded, was Berry's sense of rock and roll freedom—"caressable, cold cash," sex across race and age lines, stints in prison or court every fifteen years, musical one-nighters with pickup bands. Berry stayed in St. Louis, stayed married, and for close to four decades stayed away from releasing new music. But did he, in other regards, refuse to stay "in his place"? No Black writer made him a subject of study, though the scenes of him with Little Richard and Bo Diddley in *Hail! Hail!*, available in full on the DVD reissue, cried out for a revisiting of this era. (For Little Richard, the sexually technicolor *Life and Times*, told to Charles White, should be read in tandem with Berry.) Berry Park, the 1957–74 interracial leisure spot and recording studio that Berry, dismissive of his other work, had such hopes for, might be seen as a precursor to Prince's Paisley Park. Much of what Berry wished for racist Missouri and American freedom remained closeted, sedimented. The book concluded with more mock verse. "Some days are like hours of music / Some songs are like stories you tell / Some views that came down from the hippies / are now classics, like rock is as well."

MAKING "WILD-EYED GIRLS" A MORE
COMPLEX NARRATIVE

Pamela Des Barres, I'm with the Band: Confessions of a Groupie, *1987*

———

"Something came over me in the presence of rock idols, something vile and despicable, something wondrous and holy." Later, Lisa Rhodes's *Electric Lady-land* soberly surveyed the mid-1960s to mid-1970s, documenting the sexism of a supposedly revolutionary moment: *Rolling Stone* condescending to women as musicians and fans. From that period emerged the figure of the groupie, whether Cynthia Plastercaster's concept-art provocation—fellate a musician, cast a sculpture of his member—or the arena rocker's angel of the tour circuit, Penny Lane, portrayed later in **Cameron Crowe**'s film *Almost Famous. Stone* used the groupie to brand itself, taking out a $7,000 ad in the *New York Times* for a special issue that later became a standalone book edited by Jann Wenner. But its coverage reduced a varied scene to a confining stereotype.

Des Barres, whom Rhodes had trouble assessing, broke that stereotype or gave it an all-time romanticization—it wasn't fully clear. Raised in Southern California at the perfect boomer moment, she had better-than-typical taste: friendly with cult-rocker Captain Beefheart, she transitioned from **Beatles** fan to Flying Burrito Brothers champion with effortless sophistication. Frank Zappa, a more mainstream undergrounder, encouraged Des Barres and other scenesters to become the band the G.T.O.s—Girls Together Outrageously. The groupies as group: that special issue drank it up. Before drugs and Zappa's recoil undercut them, the G.T.O.s embodied rock as female norm shattering, just like Beatlemania, or Joan Jett's first band the Runaways, formed on the Sunset Strip to be packaged as jailbait. Des Barres would notch Jimmy Page, Mick Jagger, Keith Moon, Waylon Jennings, and actor Don Johnson before settling with Michael Des Barres, and voicing with this best-seller what that brief G.T.O.'s heyday had only hinted at.

She wrote, "sitting up on Jimmy's amp, I almost felt like one of the group; I could see what they saw, and feel what they felt pouring from the frenzied fanatics. The wild-eyed girls looked up at me and wondered which member of the group I was sleeping with, and I felt so proud." She also confessed to worrying, at the time, about her "lack of accomplishments." In the 1980s, when so much sixties music lore was being reified, Des Barres's book made sure that "wild-eyed girls" would become a bigger, more complex part of the narrative than in the first accounts. But she begged questions with her optimism, particularly about young teen sex: if Page dated her at nineteen, he moved on to a fourteen-year-old, Lori Maddox, as Don Johnson did to fourteen-year-old Melanie Griffith.

As **Ann Powers**'s *Good Booty* argued in a particularly acute chapter, groupies were essential to the remaking of rock culture as a system, a standardized process, which has something to do with why there was such little outrage. Books on the topic, usually by women with musical leanings of their own, included five others by Des Barres; Jenny Fabian and Johnny Byrne's British account *Groupie*, fictionalized but through a sheer fabric; Patricia Kennealy-Morrison, herself a central figure in early rock writing, remembering her witch husband Jim in *Strange Days*; Bebe Buell's *Rebel Heart*; Cherry Vanilla's more industry aware *Lick Me*; and Catherine James's *Dandelion: Memoir of a Free Spirit*. Karinne Steffan's *Confessions of a Video Vixen* took this endlessly popular narrative into the hip-hop era, with Roxana Shirazi's *The Last Living Slut* explaining how its protagonist left Tehran for heavy metal. Another category to at least nod at, named by Victoria Balfour's book, was *Rock Wives*, a set including Cynthia Lennon's *A Twist of Lennon*, Pattie Boyd's *Wonderful Tonight*, and Angie Bowie's *Backstage Passes*.

Still, Des Barres's first account remained the boutique version of this eventually oft-told tale. Her authorial presence, not quite judging but never oblivious, imbued the prose. Page, for example, "was always in the mirror, primping on his splendid image, and putting perfect waves in his long black hair with a little crimping machine. He used Pantene products, and whenever I smelled them, for years afterward, I remembered being buried in his hair."

REPORTING BLACK MUSIC AS ART MIXED WITH BUSINESS

Nelson George, The Death of Rhythm & Blues, *1988*

———

Consider how the most accomplished Black music journalist of the soul into hip-hop era referenced the prior swing jazz years in two mentions of Jimmie Lunceford. Dave Clark, in George's genealogy the inventor of records promotion, began working with Lunceford and other Decca artists; fifty years later, as the overview in *Death of Rhythm & Blues* concluded, he was at Malaco in Jackson, Mississippi, still plugging. The other mention, in *Elevating the Game*—George's take on Black men and basketball—was through the Harlem Rens, short for Renaissance, a team whose exhibitions were followed by dances, some led by Lunceford. This was George's writerly signature, an ability to easily address the big history of African American music through facility with both Black business practices and Black aesthetic practices.

George, close in age to Michael Jackson, Prince, and Def Jam head Russell Simmons, described himself in *Buppies, B-Boys, Baps & Bohos: Notes on Post-Soul Black Culture* as a "working-class boy reared in Brooklyn projects by a single mother." But he also read Andrew Sarris on film and **Robert Christgau** on music in the *Village Voice*, interned at the *Amsterdam News* in 1978, and then earned the Black music editor staff position at *Record World* and *Billboard* while doing *Voice* essays. (A sampling of his early writing was collected in *The Nelson George Mixtape*.) Money from a quickie book on Michael Jackson helped fund Spike Lee's *She's Gotta Have It*. George worked on his own movies, *Strictly Business* and *CB4*, with the likes of Chris Rock, and wrote *Blackface*, a combination memoir, timeline, and analysis of African Americans and film. Such synergy, he argued, defined the story of what he called "post-soul culture": less idealistic than materialistic, but shrewder about leveraging profit.

His books explored what the death of soul but afterlife of record men and Rens suggested about the era of Reagan *and* Simmons. (Like the Run-D.M.C. rap, George went to St. John's University; he covered Def Jam's launch and cowrote the autobiography of Simmons, subsequently accused of rape by several women and moving to Indonesia to escape prosecution.) *Where Did Our Love Go?* used Motown family capitalism to argue for the "Production Line" as organizing metaphor, fascinated both by how Barney Ales forced money out of distributors and Smokey Robinson lyrics turned on paradoxes of love. Yet the book ended on a down beat: Motown sold, *Thriller* recorded for a bigger label with no connection to Black achievement.

Death of Rhythm & Blues manifested that loss: Black music was triumphant but the community that fostered it "a sad shell of itself," Aretha turned into Whitney, "not as gutsy or spirited." George celebrated Booker T. Washington over Du Bois and "race records" entrepreneurship over integration, with heroes like Al Benson selling products on the radio to Black Chicago, Ruth Bowen organizing Queen Booking with the help of Dinah Washington, and above all James Brown—for his touring schedule acumen as much as growing "There Was a Time" from live vamps. (Along with Alan Leeds, George edited *The James Brown Reader*, highlighting many forgotten Black critics.) But the corporate 1970s—with Harvard Business report pushing Columbia and other majors to start Black music divisions that required white crossover, mom-and-pop stores shut out of marketing, and radio an "urban" beige—led to 1980s communal suffering amid superstardom. George recognized Jackson and Prince as the "decade's finest music historians," but found "disquieting androgyny" in their work; better "homegirl" Anita Baker. If the conclusions deserved challenge, the book offered the best overview of Black pop since its model, **Amiri Baraka's** *Blues People*.

The question George skirted was hip-hop: resisted by a fading soul formation of radio and records people, yet supplying their replacements. *Buppies, B-boys, Baps & Bohos*, collecting his *Voice* writing, critiqued "ghettocentricity" in a manner akin to Paul Gilroy's cultural studies judgements, though George—unlike his *Voice* colleague **Greg Tate**—ignored that and all other academic writing. Columns ranged from rapper Scarface to playwright **August Wilson**, "my favorite living writer." *Hip Hop America* resisted hip-hop studies conclusions: the genre "survives even the crassest commercialism," George concluded. He analyzed its cross-racial appeal as fundamental, not problematic, and recalled Spellman women who read Ntozake Shange but partied to 2 Live Crew. The Simmons of Def Comedy Jam mattered as much as the hip-hop Simmons, George argued. Blacks needed to transform "the permanent business," so a Puffy Combs was admirable: "Never in the history of postwar black pop has a single man done so much so well."

Subsequently, the staggeringly prolific George revisited the post-soul era, with a memoir (*City Kid*), timeline of the 1980s (*Post-Soul Nation*), and revisionist take on *Soul Train* (*The Hippest Trip in America*). His efforts in film and television ranged from VH1 *Hip-Hop Honors* to funk documentaries and a hip-hop drama with Baz Luhrmann for Netflix. He also co-produced and featured in a documentary, *The Black Godfather*, on Clarence Avant, who—from the tutelage of Louis Armstrong manager Joe Glaser—became an industry advisor to *Soul Train* and Terry Jam and Jimmy Lewis, got home-run king Hank Aaron sponsorship deals: a perfect Nelson George subject of inquiry. There were novels like *The Plot Against Hip-Hop*, coding references from his criticism into action sequences. And his inheritors, like former music critic Cheo Coker, turned showrunner of *Luke Cage* for Netflix, did the same. George had become a godfather too, Fort Greene scholar-schmoozer.

SESSIONS WITH THE EVIL GENIUS OF JAZZ

Miles Davis with Quincy Troupe, Miles: The Autobiography, *1989*

————

In *Miles Beyond,* the first book on the electric music of jazz's coolest trumpeter—where **Louis Armstrong** was hottest—Paul Tingen recalled guitarist John McLaughlin asking pianist Herbie Hancock: "was that any good what we did? I mean, what did we do?" Hancock replied, "John, welcome to a Miles Davis session." Just past forty when he pivoted in the late 1960s to studio edits and wah-wah trumpet over funk grooves and rock amplification, Davis was already a patriarch: the Parker and Gillespie–trained conceptualist who'd chilled bebop with *Birth of the Cool* in the late 1940s; boxed out hard bop with "Walkin'"; defined jazz romanticism with his muted trumpet and postwar Black rebellion with his refusal to Tom; and made the genre's quintessential album, the modal and serene *Kind of Blue,* with saxophonist John Coltrane. He then innovated with a second great band keyed off new sax ally Wayne Shorter, Hancock, and teen drummer Tony Williams. If he now kept James Brown, Jimi Hendrix, Sly Stone, and Karlheinz Stockhausen in his ears, no one bet against him, even if few understood what he and producer Teo Macero were up to as *In a Silent Way* became *Bitches Brew* and *On the Corner.*

The literature that grew up around Davis was equally provisional. That reflected his troubling of musical definitions jazz insisted upon, the race ripples of his culture hero persona—in critic **Greg Tate**'s formulation, "Miles Davis *is* the black aesthetic." As much, though, it had to do with his brutal treatment of people, especially women; Tate concluded, "Miles may have swung like a champion but on that score he went out like a roach." Jazz's most socially progressive and least musically restrictive white critics, notably **Nat Hentoff** and Ralph Gleason, were tolerated to interview him. Black writers had a special perch: Marc Crawford's 1961 "Evil Genius of Jazz" *Ebony* profile; Alex Haley debuting the *Playboy* extended interview, in 1962 with a Davis Q&A anticipating Haley's later Malcolm X memoir and *Roots*; Quincy Troupe's hiring for the blockbuster memoir Davis agreed to publicize. These works were controversial. Haley was accused of plagiarizing Crawford, Troupe of borrowing from previous biographers. Still, unless Davis's taped voice on the Troupe archive should ever supersede it, *Miles: The Autobiography* will orient accounts of this—his chosen term of praise—motherfucker.

Troupe, a poet, recalled in *Miles and Me* how he'd first encountered Davis in 1956, cursing out a white fan who wanted to shake hands: "I had never seen a white man treated like that by a black man." He felt less sanguine when Davis cursed him, too, years later, but ultimately "bought into his legend," writing: "Miles Davis was first and foremost all about sound, and so am I." *The Autobiography* started there, Davis engulfed in sound, hearing "Diz and Bird" as a 1944 teen already playing jump blues trumpet in St. Louis groups (he was an exact contemporary of **Chuck Berry**), resolving to master bebop. It continued with a family vignette: visiting Arkansas relatives where music seemed to come out of the trees, a "blues, church, back-road funk kind of thing." Those were his dueling impulses, as this account told it, rather than the Juilliard training footed by his dental surgeon father. *Kind of Blue* was Arkansas. *Bitches Brew* showed bop conviction that jazz not "become a museum thing locked under glass." Davis offered precise appraisals of what he'd heard in every stage of the music he'd reshaped—and he could reshape everything: "Plastic was coming in and plastic has a different sound." But he was no less pointed in characterizing women as a brew of bitches he could pimp, hit, or—as with wife Frances Taylor—cut off from careers.

Jack Chambers, whose two-volume *Milestones* stood for a time as authoritative, charged in a later reissue that the *Autobiography* represented "Freaky Deaky, his burnt-out alter ego," with factual information plagiarized from biographers including himself, Ian Carr, and Eric Nisenson. For Chambers, what Davis wouldn't recall about his old recordings was pivotal: the track-by-track history from "Now's the Time," with its brief solo in Davis's future tone, to the "monotony" of *On the Corner*. Chambers left room for divergent opinions (**Whitney Balliett** on "Now's," Eugene Chadbourne on electric Miles as "pure sound and sensation") but distrusted Davis's Arkansas streak: "the unsophisticated funk of a bar band" was typical of his evaluations. Carr, a trumpeter, had sympathy for the electric era but scant thesis beyond an ungrounded assertion of Davis's bisexuality. An updated edition of Nisenson's biography offered a fascinating preface on how he'd almost become Troupe: allowed into Davis's late 1970s seclusion as a gopher, then purged. The book read like a trial run for *Miles*, if less aggressively dark. The best biography to emerge was John Szwed's *So What*, less for new research than the author's firm sense of jazz's broader contexts: how Davis's beating by New York police in 1959, for example, entered Frank O'Hara's "Personal Poem."

Volumes collecting Davis writing also debated between cherry-picking from his oeuvre and engaging what it blew at American culture. Bill Kirchner sniffed, to start *A Miles Davis Reader*, "Warning: this is a book about Miles Davis, the musician." Still, from a 1950 interview by a rare woman jazz critic, Pat Harris ("likes to play what he believes is noncommercial bop"), to France's

André Hodeir assessing the "cool tendency" and a Q&A-based Columbia Records life study by George Avakian in 1957 ("People ask me if I respond to the audience"), the content showed the frames shaping "Davis, the musician." Davis, the icon, could not be kept out. An excerpt of W. T. Lhamon's *Deliberate Speed* connected Pynchon's muted horn symbol in *The Crying of Lot 49* and **Jack Kerouac**'s *Visions of Cody* appreciation of Davis's "structure of iron on which tremendous phrases can be strung and hung and long pauses goofed, kicked along, whaled, touched with hidden and active meanings." Nor could one expunge Davis, the race man, who, drummer Steve McCall told **Amiri Baraka**, "transcended the slave mentality." To survey such texts showed that "electric Miles" was merely one mile in a long stretch of grooved pavement. In a *Jazz Life* excerpt included in Gary Carner's less musically restrictive *Miles Davis Companion*, Nat Hentoff tried to teach Francis Newton (legendary historian Eric Hobsbawm), to value Davis's "direct aggressiveness." Forget electric Miles—Hentoff captured Davis dealing with a racist electrician.

Posthumous writing on Davis drew upon critics for whom jazz no more defined taste than rock or hip-hop, instructed by cultural studies to see canonizing as a project to interpret more than perform. Gerald Early's collection *Miles Davis and American Culture* found the editor arguing the autobiography's summoning of Davis's voice mattered beyond its flaws. His approach saw Davis "being able to 'sell,' as an image, the iconoclastic," offering a genealogy of the "bad boy" via boxing and sporting life, and introducing a Q&A with Quincy Jones as a parallel for Davis's genre crossing ("Miles was a serious dramatist, you know"). Essays by such scholars as John Gennari on critics, Ingrid Monson on Davis's politics, Eric Porter on the response to Davis's "Electric Turn," and Farah Jasmine Griffin on Davis's relationship to women performers and aural vulnerability showed how jazz studies had made the unruly margins of Davis's jazz world presence its centerpiece. This was also the first book to include his defining *Playboy* interview—a proper home away from the jazz police.

Greg Tate had made the issues awaiting Miles Davis criticism clear in 1980s *Downbeat* articles reprinted in his *Flyboy* collection: "the music Miles made between 1969 and now demands revisionist history, and no writer in my reading has made sense out of its revolutionary aesthetics or adequately appreciated its visionary beauty. Nor have many, if any, of Miles's critics shown enough background in black pop to place his electric music within the cultural context which spawned it. Moreover, when it comes to his last mid-'70s band, I don't think many of my, uh, esteemed colleagues could make heads or tails of *Agharta* or dig it in reference to Funkadelic and a punk revolution that was just around the corner." Much work with such a synthesis in mind has appeared since, from

Tingen's pioneering overview of the "languages" of music and Davis as a blues player who moved into jazz, then back, rather than a bebop defector, with bassist Michael Henderson "the pivot around which Miles's bands revolved." Phil Freeman's *Running the Voodoo Down* connected Davis to *On the Corner* fan **Lester Bangs**—Tate's punk point. Ralph Gleason, the jazz-rock pioneer critic long a champion of Davis's assault on "old forms," received belated appreciation for his observation, in *Celebrating the Duke*, "There is more sound here than stereo can handle on record," and comparison of a Davis "rhythm orchestra" to an equally loud, less modulated, Who concert.

But as Krin Gabbard acerbically noted in his study of the trumpet, *Hotter Than That*, which contained a savvy if anti-electric Davis chapter, it would not be *Bitches Brew* that remained Davis's crossover: that status reverted to *Kind of Blue*, which became a cottage industry for books. Ashley Kahn's *Kind of Blue* took up its making from a studio and music industry perspective; Richard Williams's *The Blue Moment* gave a cultural reading of its links to adventurous pop and art music, from Davis to minimalism and Velvet Underground, or "So What" influencing "Cold Sweat." Griffin and Salim Washington's *Clawing at the Limits of Cool*, title taken from a poem by Baraka (for whom Davis was the lifelong cultural hero), made the Davis-Coltrane partnership a study in the last two jazz geniuses to register fully, urban hipster and down-home believer.

Davis revisited his work with Coltrane and arranger Gil Evans before his death, pushed by Quincy Jones, but it is hard to imagine him approving of his legacy reverting back to classic jazz. The 1980s era, in which his postmodern persona collided with MTV culture and he appeared on *Miami Vice* and courted hip-hop, remains a final frontier of Davis scholarship. No vantage on Davis was fully satisfactory; no assessment unbiased; no placement within jazz, Black expressive culture, or American iconoclasm extricable from the contradictions his artistry molded and exaggerated. He rebuked easy categorizing—a critical theorist in the form of a bandleader, producing the most sustained answer to **Theodor Adorno**'s disparagement of jazz as a form of mass culture standardization.

PART VI

NEW VOICES, NEW METHODS

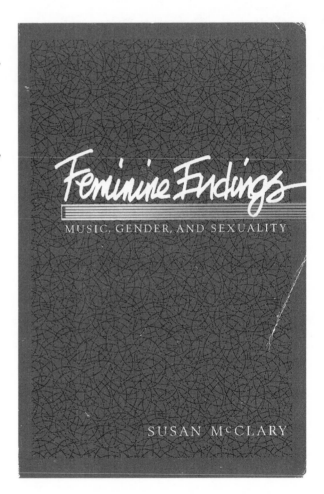

FIGURE 6.1 Cover of Susan McClary, *Feminine Endings: Music, Gender, and Sexuality*, 1991. Author's collection.

_____

FIGURE 6.2 Cover of Greg Tate, *Flyboy in the Buttermilk: Essays on Contemporary America*, 1992. Author's collection.

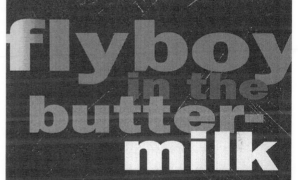

flyboy in the butter- milk

essays on contemporary america

an eye—opening look at race, politics, literature, and music

greg tate

foreword by henry louis gates, jr.

FIGURE 6.3 Cover of Eric Lott, *Love and Theft: Blackface Minstrelsy and the American Working Class,* 1993. Author's collection.

FIGURE 6.4 Cover of Charles Keil and Steven Feld, *Music Grooves: Essays and Dialogues,* 1994. Author's collection.

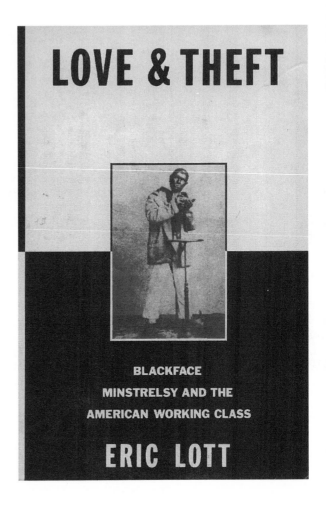

LOVE & THEFT

BLACKFACE
MINSTRELSY AND THE
AMERICAN WORKING CLASS

ERIC LOTT

LITERATURE OF NEW WORLD ORDER AMERICANIZATION

Jessica Hagedorn, Dogeaters, *1990*

———

If the United States, as colony to empire, had a "special relationship" with the United Kingdom that extended to music, perhaps such was true with the Philippines as empire to colony. Pop had always telegraphed ditties into the world: by the 1990s and afterward, the British invasion gave way to globalization, and transnationalism became a leading issue for American studies and sounds. Filipinos and Filipino Americans sang cover songs on cruise ships, fronted latter editions of the anthemic pop-rock Journey, and created hip-hop DJ crews like Invisibl Skratch Piklz—not to mention Bruno Mars, **Elvis** impersonator turned James Brown–evoking hitmaker. Back in the literature of music, Jessica Hagedorn proved an originary force. Arriving as a teen in the early 1960s Bay Area, she connected to the bohemia of magpie Kenneth Rexroth, the race-centered version around **Ishmael Reed**, and literary "satin sisters" Ntozake Shange and Thulani Davis. She embraced 1970s downtown New York City as it coalesced, fronting the band Gangster Choir and issuing a 1975 collection of poems, plays, essays, and stories: *Dangerous Music*, expanded later into *Danger and Beauty.*

Hagedorn drew upon the baby boom's pantheon of rebellion: one poem equated film's Sal Mineo, James Dean, and Marlon Brando with music's Little Richard, Fats Domino, and the Motown hit "Dancing in the Street." But her position on it was far more self-reflexive: "When I was ten / It was Etta James / I didn't know what she looked like, / If she was male or female," the early poem "Autobiography Part Two: Rock and Roll" offered. And critically, her take on popular culture equated Hollywood melodramas and cultural imperialism. Hagedorn quoted an adage attributed to an older author, Nick Joaquin, "The Philippines spent three hundred years trapped in a convent, and fifty years in Hollywood," adding: "there we were, seduced and abandoned in a confusion of identities, then granted our independence." Her dialectics were subtle: "pulp songs stupefy some, / awaken others. / revolution's sentimental, after all." Examples multiplied: Elvis Presley songwriter Otis Blackwell into Otis Redding—"otis uno / otis dos / otis tres, / fontella bass. / we're international citizens, / you understand." Yes, and global cosmopolitans of a scrappy kind, a dysfunctional family where "gossip is integral to conversation" and "we giggle at the dinner table / aunts and whores / brothers and homosexuals." As Arjun Appadurai would argue in *Modernity at Large*, global flows of information and capital were sweeping through cultures; global flows of people were far stickier. Christine Bacareza Balance's *Tropical Renditions*, drawing on Martin Joseph Ponce's *Beyond the Nation*, gave Hagedorn's muse its fuller translocal centering: neither depoliticized postmodern nor authentic postcolonial, but multi-everything.

Dogeaters appeared in 1990, in time for fantasies of New World Order and theories of spectacle and simulacra to dazzle left and right. Corazon Aquino, widow of murdered opposition leader Benigno, replaced the Marcoses in power, but the generals were hardly dislodged. Rock, meanwhile, calcified into its own dynastic corruption. The likes of Laurie Anderson—whose 1984 album title, *Mister Heartbreak*, Hagedorn borrowed for a chapter and protagonist in the novel—made genre-crossing art out of the contradictions, becoming acclaimed but hardly secure financially. Combining haunted legacies of colonialism with jolts of music and new sexual freedom, Hagedorn modeled a template as powerful as cyberpunk, influencing the likes of Junot Diaz and Zadie Smith. One character (as in a song by Duran Duran) was Rio, who watched Sirk films with a boyish gaze in 1956, danced the Madison to imported records in 1960, left for the United States not long after, and had a dying grandfather named **Whitman**: Spanish-American War, AIDS, and *Leaves of Grass* colliding. Another character named himself Joey Sands after Vegas, spun James Brown in a gay disco where Fassbinder picked him up, and had a GI father, Black as vernacular, he'd not met: "Joey Taboo: my head of tight, kinky curls, my pretty hazel eyes, my sleek brown skin." Finally, there was the general, vibing Dinah Washington with actress/lover Lolita on a Japanese sound system until she played Grace Jones and he kicked it to pieces; the general who told Daisy Avila, before his men raped her, that her father "was a sentimental man, with sentimental taste in music and movies," unlike his Eartha Kitt/Benny Goodman modernism.

Daisy would meet a transformed Joey, "disgusted by his own sentimentality," in the rebel camps.

Later Hagedorn productions drew out the sonic implications of her vision: a theatrical *Dogeaters*, the rock novel *Gangster of Love* with its imagined Hendrix conversations and Bay Area–to–NYC memoir details, the musical *Most Wanted*. Yet *Dogeaters*, queer and colonial, Downtown and canon, remained a masterpiece of popular culture *Disidentifications*—that ambiguous response to unequal representation detailed by **Jose Esteban Muñoz**. Hagedorn, Balance demonstrated, was Muñoz before Muñoz. The dream was vernacular lightning: "The sleep had lasted for centuries, but one day the thunderbolt struck, and in striking, infused life." The experience, captured in Hagedorn's prescient literature, was strategic anti-anti-sentimentalism, in the sense of Paul Gilroy's diasporic cultural studies concepts of anti-anti-essentialism—or what fellow rocker Warren Zevon, cleaning up from the counterculture howls of his past, called sentimental hygiene. "I remember the same doggish look about [US soldier] Neil," Sands told readers at one point, hating the affective power dynamics that made director Rainer stroke him, too, "how it always made me angry, how my anger always fueled the American's desire."

ETHNIC STUDIES OF BLENDED MUSICAL IDENTITIES

George Lipsitz, Time Passages: Collective Memory and
American Popular Culture, *1990*

————

Sixties girl group singer Ronnie Spector's autobiography, recalling a Hank Williams song she performed at a home recital, produced an ur–George Lipsitz moment: "So when the African-American, Native American, and Euro-American Ronnie Bennett sang 'Jambalaya' for her Puerto Rican, African-American, Native American, and Euro-American family, she was imitating a version of a Cajun song written and recorded by an Anglo-American singer who thought of himself as a Native American trained by African Americans, and who played in a band with a Mexican American and a Native American!" Lipsitz, first in *Time Passages*, then *Dangerous Crossroads*, and later *Footsteps in the Dark*, brought to popular music a passion for blended identities, for working-class people whose actions suggested a cultural imaginary outside conventional expectations. From a universe of potential musicians, he bonded most closely—writing two books about him—with Johnny Otis, born Ioannis Alexandres Veliotesa to Greek immigrants, who "passed" for Black and produced "Hound Dog," authored by two Jewish guys, for Big Mama Thornton.

Time Passages, the collection of essays that brought Lipsitz to prominence, was written as postmodernism and cultural studies started to systematically reshape academic work. Lipsitz, trained as a historian, struggled with that field's disciplinary myopia and moved toward American and ethnic studies, allying at University of Minnesota with musicology revampers **Susan McClary** and Robert Walser. "My own inquiries have often left me between fields," he wrote, "struggling to remain in the profession and keep my voice alive." **Lawrence Levine**, with whom he shared countercultural values and a passion for recognizing the folkloric worth of art created within commercial culture as much as outside it, fought to open up history for popular culture; Lipsitz saw popular culture as a way to take part in history: "For me, too, popular culture has been a way of expressing indirectly values and beliefs about which I had no direct means of expression." Joining Fredric Jameson, Pierre Bourdieu, and **Stuart Hall** to the social histories of Kathy Peiss and John Kasson, among others, evolving a language of "sedimented" lore and culture that resisted narrative "closure," Lipsitz hunkered down in the age of Reagan, assembling a living archive of counterexamples.

While *Time Passages* covered a range of topics, including ethnic television at the turn of the 1950s and Toni Morrison novels, its music chapters showed Lipsitz's retooling of American academic approaches. Critiquing **Simon Frith**'s pop sympathies, Lipsitz favored "rougher, wilder, blacker, and more working class music," using theory to cast such styles as "dialogic" in the Mikhail Bakhtin sense, or as creating an oppositional "bloc" in the Antonio Gramsci sense. His positioning of examples, rooted in research or interviews with the likes of St. Louis, then Rod Stewart guitarist Billy Peek, made the at times ponderous categorizing more persuasive. And two chapters in particular, on East L.A. music from "Pachuco Boogie" to Los Lobos and Mardi Gras Indians in New Orleans, provided spectacular examples of multifaceted music cultures establishing long lineages. This was not quite "secret history" in the vein of **Greil Marcus**'s *Lipstick Traces* at about this same time—more communal, yet equally likely to pressure standard narratives.

Lipsitz returned to music in *Dangerous Crossroads*, describing transnational sounds: the Haitian band Boukman Eksperyans, the "diasporic intimacy" of hip-hop's Zulu Nation, the Rasta encodings lurking within a Musical Youth crossover hit, Algerian rai and Québécois nationalism. *Footsteps in the Dark* took as its theme "hidden histories," including containerization in global trade, urban renewal as a force deindustrializing Black U.S. neighborhoods. Attuned to the stories of musicians, Lipsitz increasingly amplified a generation of ethnic studies popular culture scholars he'd exchanged inspiration with: Deborah Pacini Hernandez on bachata, Helena Simonett on banda, Deborah Wong on Asian American music making, Juan Flores on Puerto Rican Boricua pop. He'd helped to create, within a strand of academia, the kinds of networks, emplacements, and shared imaginaries that he'd spent so long documenting in music itself.

BALLAD NOVELS FOR A BABY BOOMER APPALACHIA

Sharyn McCrumb, If Ever I Return, Pretty Peggy-O, *1990*

For *The Rose & the Briar*, essays on American ballads edited by **Greil Marcus** and Sean Wilentz, McCrumb put her "ballad novels" in perspective with a story about six characters spending centuries acting out the fantasies of people singing. Folk became Victorian, modern, countercultural, and karaoke, and one time a weasel actually popped, but "Pretty Peggy-O" never went away, "long as the feelings were genuine." McCrumb was postmodern enough to have offered "Thanks from a Bricoleur" in the dedication of her first ballad novel, named after that same song. But she was also a fatalistic chronicler, with family roots in mountain folk culture to the 1790s, aware that for all her hippie cohort thought they were revolutionizing, "There's always a new dead girl to sing about. Always a dead girl."

So that was what she sang, putting music alongside the hurts that nursed and rehearsed it, a spiritual heir to **Emma Miles**'s *Spirit of the Mountains* when the century started. Vietnam veterans were a major element of *If Ever I Return*, their trauma placed against marriages lost to domestic violence, young men fantasizing survivalism, and a new left folk singer unromantic about the material she metamorphized. With *The Hangman's Beautiful Daughter*, psychic mountains lady Nora Bonesteel joined down-to-earth sheriff Spencer Arrowood as a series regular, and the values in play became clearer—an impoverished young mother's sacrifice representing permanent imbalances of power; corporate pollution affecting rivers; an Arrowood trip to a farewell Judds concert for contemporaneity; the past as open to endless reworkings as the folksong "In the Pines." *She Walks These Hills* saw McCrumb stretching her coverage, crosscutting an escaped convict unable to recall his life after 1968; the equally doomed tale of an eighteenth-century escapee from Cherokee abduction; a university researcher and a Yankee on community radio both confronting their liminality to folklore (Victor Turner dutifully cited); and more poor, young women with dead babies enduring absolute centrality to that tradition. "It wasn't the kind of thing anybody would write in the history books, but the people in these mountains always knew. The women did, anyhow."

Many would argue for Lee Smith's *The Devil's Dream* as the greatest novel of mountain ballads and country music, chronicling five generations of a Virginia family, from hollers to Opryland, the "dulcimer-and-calico story," **Robert Cantwell** wrote in a review for *Appalachian Journal*. If McCrumb never quite peaked as high, her decision to put her fiction in series form spoke to another way of trying to capture popular music's flow: not a solitary reckoning but a cultivation over time, the performativity of genre tropes matching how popular music settled one's life. Other fictional series with no shortage of music might be noted here: Walter Mosley's Easy Rawlins novels, always alert to Black music in Los Angeles, and Ace Atkins's Nick Travers mysteries, starting with *Crossroad Blues*. Stephen King, who sometimes played music in the proudly bad Rock Bottom Remainders, tucked rock and roll into his horror books whenever possible: the haunted 1958 Plymouth Fury in *Christine* playing death songs, radio tunes trying to warn Jack Torrance about the hotel in *The Shining*.

In McCrumb's fifth novel of this kind, *The Ballad of Frankie Silver*, among the series' best, a character told Sheriff Arrowood to play "Green, Green Grass of Home" at his execution. "That's a real tearjerker." Then McCrumb, fictionalizing the nineteenth-century Silver, who axed her husband to death (McCrumb thought) because he abused her and was threatening their baby, brought tears to a reader's eyes nonetheless: a scene where wealthier women in the Tennessee town gave Silver a fine white dress she'd craved, to die in. Many more ballad novels later, it was clear that there need be no end to these stories. The form of the mass-market paperback mystery novel guaranteed it, which made it the perfect position for McCrumb to keep exploring the intersection of the folk ballad and modern life. She walked the hills, went to the library, played Bascom Lamar Lunsford—a sublime songcatcher.

PIMPLY, PROLE, AND PUTRID, BUT WITH A SURPRISINGLY DIVERSE GENRE LITERATURE

Chuck Eddy, Stairway to Hell: The 500 Best Heavy
Metal Albums in the Universe, *1991*

———

Consigned and proud to serve hell, heavy metal generated an impressive literature. A memoir of piss-licking contests with Ozzy Osborne by Mötley Crüe; also young Crüe fanship in North Dakota by Chuck Klosterman, who called *Shout at the Devil* his *Sgt. Pepper's.* A Chuck Eddy album guide to the genre's true spirit that ranked Teena Marie over Iron Maiden. And marginal European academic Keith Kahn-Harris, deciding "reflexive anti-reflexivity" was just the term for "Detroit Rock City" spilling into Norwegian black metal. If books trailed documentaries for metal (*Spinal Tap, Decline of Western Civilization II, Heavy Metal Parking Lot, Some Kind of Monster*), these were still *awesome.*

Lester Bangs, youngest first-generation rock critic, was friendliest to metal, writing a *Rolling Stone Illustrated History* entry on its bratty succulence. Robert Duncan's *The Noise* gave the claims a lineage: 1973 as the proliferation of the sixties across America, not just *Roe v. Wade* and Watergate but the leather-and-whips act of Alice Cooper. Duncan's definition of metal would be perennially quoted: "pimply, prole, putrid, unchic, unsophisticated, antiintellectual (but impossibly pretentious), dismal, abysmal, terrible, horrible, and stupid music . . . made by slack-jawed, alpaca-haired, bulbous-inseamed imbeciles"—but hey, a money machine, "the music on which the music biz of the seventies founded its far-flung success." Linking punk to metal as the same sponsored (and no less real for it) hype, Duncan met up with Ross the Boss from the Dictators at the Garden watching Black Sabbath. "D'ya *hear* that?!? *That's* rock 'n' roll!"

A trio of books arrived in 1991, reflecting metal's resurgence in the MTV 1980s. Deena Weinstein's *Heavy Metal*, written in sociology academese, hid a part-time rock critic who knew "metal instruments must gleam, like polished metal," had fun proving Rush fans had no idea what *2112* was about, delineated "lite" metal from thrash versions, and called the genre's faithful "proud pariahs." Donna Gaines's *Teenage Wasteland*, both sociology dissertation and *Village Voice* cover story, looked at high school metal burnouts as "suburbia's dead end kids." After the suicides of four AC/DC–loving New Jersey teens from the "upper poor" white world, she went to the mall in search of "the children of ZOSO" and, after bonding over bands, was shown their razor scars. Rock in this corner of the world was also "The Rock," in Jersey a special-needs student campus. Gaines documented gender, black metal, and thrash's ties to hardcore punk. No book better anticipated the topical shift from sex to death about to make Metallica the biggest rock band of the second generation.

Neither Chuck was all that fond of Metallica, yet as critics they solidified the metal wing of rock writing, identifying with the music's distance from collegiate, coastal cool. Eddy's *Stairway to Hell*, the third 1991 metal publication, built around five hundred album picks, viewed the category as a less musical, more epistemological essence chasing: scourge of "left-wing 'political correctness' no less than right-wing 'moral propriety.'" He idealized 1970–73, "the Years of Sludge," valued Grand Funk Railroad and others deep in the purple, and agreed with critic Frank Kogan that the spirit had dissipated with genericism: "*heavy metal* has nothing to do with heavy metal." So he roamed, looking for populist punch or a stray echo in everything from the Godz, "Gotta Keep Running," to proto-grunge compilations. Eddy infuriated metalheads: by the second edition, including 1990s albums, he was telling such fans to check out Martin Popoff's metal guides instead. But for rock critics, his kaleidoscopic lists, continued in the putatively Def Leppard–inspired *Accidental Evolution of Rock'n'Roll* and article anthologies, used metal's genre liminality—was it rock or its own beast?—to question settled taste. Klosterman arrived at the start of a new century as the first voice of the 1980s youth raised on MTV metal. *Fargo Rock City* took up mall cassettes of Mötley, Axl Rose as "redneck intellectual," the stoned discussions of heavy versus hard you might have with Van Halen fans—and the endlessly fraught question that divided an Eddy from a Popoff: whether it was more rock or less when girls liked Lep and not Zep. He was too well adjusted to really get extreme metal or even "Fade to Black," but he was funny, and those inside and outside the genre loved reading him. A string of similar books followed, with lesser impact but rare popularity for critical writing, inspiring weaker versions of Klosterman like starchy Steven Hyden and even a pop-cult tone that authors including Bill Simmons and Shea Serrano used on such websites as *Grantland* and *The Ringer*.

Grunge earnestness had made flashy metal seem adorable. Neil Strauss, another *Voice* writer fascinated by metal, secured a Mötley Crüe oral history, *The Dirt*. The "big pile of blow" that David Lee Roth brought to their squalid Sunset Strip pad, the "reckless, aggravated testosterone" on display, was a given; but why would Tommy Lee possibly say this? "If there's one genetic trait that automatically disqualifies a man from being able to rock, it's curly hair." Later: "She was so worried her dad, who was the dean of the UCLA School of Engineering, would disapprove if he saw all my tattoos. I covered myself with towels." She being starlet Heather Locklear. With **Robert Johnson** references to rival **Greil Marcus**'s *Mystery Train*, *The Dirt* was rock myth of the zombie variety—like Bruce Campbell playing **Presley** in *Bubba Ho-Tep*. Pick your poison: "somebody's got to help her find her teeth"; "He pulled the tubes out of his nose, tore the IV out of his arms, and told everyone to fuck off. He walked out with only a pair of leather pants on"; "Like *Theatre of Pain*, *Girls, Girls, Girls* could have been a phenomenal record, but we were too caught up in our own personal bullshit to put any effort into it." Perhaps the oral history was metal's best book form: Jon Wiederhorn and Katherine Turman's *Louder Than Hell*, with sections on the Sabbath to Kiss origins, the New Wave of British Heavy Metal codification, Sunset Strip glam, thrash and industrial edges, nü-metal response to grunge plus death metal/black metal fueling millennial cores, became the best one-volume introduction to the genre. Slipknot's Robb Flynn, on page 666: "I passed out in my bunk in the new Depends. Woke up pruned and shriveled and urined. And happy."

Academics did have a few questions. Weinstein became a tribe elder, joined from musicology by Robert Walser, whose *Running with the Devil* modeled new forms of popular music study and insisted—as Gaines had more journalistically—on deindustrialization fueling a need to symbolically beat postmodernity. Power chords and power politics got an acutely written defense. Susan Fast's *In the Houses of the Holy*, on Zeppelin, legitimized rock studies, joined by Glenn Pillsbury's *Damage Incorporated*, on Metallica's sonic and public identity. But Keith Kahn-Harris's *Extreme Metal* did the most to codify "metal studies," treating the wilder and more European sounds that had dominated the underground since the 1990s. Taking up subculture, Kahn-Harris delineated "mundane" and "transgressive" forms of belonging. He viewed the power moves as less redemptive than Walser did. And in his formulation, "reflexive anti-reflexivity," he captured well the jokes that made metal bulletproof to scorn and consciousness raising, the insistence "on the illusion that the world is simple and obvious" that held modernity at bay and made "transgressive community" possible. Metal studies had a strong internationalist wing, too, with the Jeremy Wallach et al. collection *Metal Rules the Globe* and Andy Brown et al.'s *Global Metal and Culture*.

But what about the Chucks? Academics buried those not their own. Steve Waksman, interested in bringing hard rock into conversation with music in general, provided a key exception as a reader and thinker. *Instruments of Desire*, a study of electric guitar, took up in its Zeppelin chapter a range of writers to explore the technophallic instrument as power supply ripe for plunder away from normativity. (Later, Amber Clifford-Napoleon's *Queerness in Metal Music*, with its focus on a "queerscape" of fans and performers from Judas Priest's Rob

Halford to Joan Jett, all in leather, made clearer how some of this worked; the Florian Heesch and Niall Scott collection, *Heavy Metal, Gender and Sexuality* brought still more voices to the discussion.) Waksman's *This Ain't the Summer of Love*, rooted historically in the same *Creem* issues Eddy read, saw rock after 1970 as "metal and punk in dialogue"—lots of room for Grand Funk Railroad arena shows, Alice Cooper as akin to Iggy Pop, Metal Blade Records in relationship to hardcore's SST or indie's Sub Pop. Duncan's favorites the Dictators came up again, so that Waksman could look more closely at how singer Dick Manitoba had baited Wayne (soon to be Jayne) County into a physical confrontation at CBGB. Prioritizing layered history over sociology and musicology, Waksman spoke to the fuller literature.

In a different self-selection (genre, not academic discipline rules), the metal world published its own books, with Popoff's ever-expanding array of collector guides and album explications leading the way and Def Leppard given no quarter. Didrik Søderlind and Michael Moynihan's controversial *Lords of Chaos* was partial to the homophobically murderous and racist Scandinavian black metal world; more itemization came in Daniel Ekeroth's *Swedish Death Metal* and Peter Beste's *True Norwegian Death Metal*. Albert Mudrian, editor of the metal magazine *Decibel*, released *Choosing Death*, on death metal and grindcore extremities, while editing the album oral histories collection *Precious Metal*. (For more along those lines, Erik Davis's book on Aleister Crowley, magus, and the fourth Zeppelin album, in the 33⅓ series, supplied gleeful overkill.) Ian Christe gave the metal community a "complete headbanging history" to call its own with *The Sound of the Beast*, filled with freakographies and other mappings of the spirit—metal orthodoxy settled over every full-page PowerPoint summary. A two-volume Metallica biography, by Paul Brannigan and Ian Winwood, became the leading account of the now "old gods."

Two authors pointed out directions still to be fully taken. Laina Dawes's *What Are You Doing Here?* confronted her fanship as a Black female outsider ("The 'Only One' Syndrome") but ultimately found a scene of sorts in fellow outsiders, which raised issues of the lines between critic and academic, mundane and transgressive participant. Much more critical memoir of this sort needed writing. And John Darnielle blazed across the field like a star not willing to stay distant: his role as indie rock Mountain Goats singer gave way to accounts of his love for metal, with a fictionalized tale of an institutionalized kid that served as the 33⅓ take on Black Sabbath's *Masters of Reality*. Both, in a way, brought the story of metal back to where it had begun: dead-end kids, confronted with a deluge of albums and identities, claiming a voice with a really loud listicle.

HOW MUSICOLOGY MET CULTURAL STUDIES

Susan McClary, Feminine Endings: Music, Gender, and Sexuality, *1991*

A specialist in Renaissance and Baroque, McClary joined the University of Minnesota in punk rock 1977, determined to connect music to lived context, with a feminist interest in calling out norms like a composer's greatness outweighing his surroundings. The approach seemed outrageous to her field's "quasi-mathematical formal analysis," she recalled in "The Life and Times of a Renegade Musicologist." Rejected drafts "circulated samizdat-style, in paler and paler photocopies." But elsewhere in academia she was an up-to-date, cultural studies–informed postmodernist. *Feminine Endings*, with its "Live to Tell" case study, thrilled academic Madonna obsessives. By 1995, she had received a MacArthur, steered UCLA's music department as a new model, and oversaw a "Music/Culture" series on Wesleyan University Press with fellow former U of M'ers **George Lipsitz** and her spouse, Robert Walser. (Not only Prince and the Replacements broke out of the Twin Cities.) This book has detailed outsiders, often women. Here were new insiders.

What came with that shift? At least twice, she wrote variations of the same theme: "I had absorbed classical music as my vernacular"; "If I can be said to have a vernacular, Western classical would have to be it." By contrast, "I had to cast off my life-long prejudice against popular music." McClary wrote with a rock critic's sense of stakes, just about other topics: "The Blasphemy of Talking Politics During Bach Year." She narrated musical choices like others might **Elvis** strapping on an electric: "With a single stroke, the descent of *ab* to *g* in m. 84 announces unceremoniously what we should have known all along—that this whole A*b* excursion was a fantasy." And the awareness of how choices of tonality, like everything else presumed "absolute music," might be constructed—by sexuality, for example, in a controversial Schubert talk that made the *New York Times*—fed her popular music writing. "An emergent group often announces its arrival first and most intensely in the ways its music constitutes the body," she wrote, and detailed Tawny Kitaen videos for Whitesnake. McClary titled her essays collection *Reading Music* to make two points: those in classical needed context; those in pop needed notation—"The study of popular music should also include the study of popular music." Partnering with Walser for a "Musicology Wrestles with Rock" essay, she urged that both those in her department and outside it learn new methods to answer the question "Yeah, but do we kick butt?"

Walser made metal, in McClary's words "today's answer to baroque spectacle," the focus of his book-length study *Running with the Devil*; the guitar "tapping" of Eddie Van Halen accrued a lineage with Bach. As influenced by Lipsitz on popular culture as McClary on music, Walser theorized that deindustrialization accounted for the displays of frustrated power in 1980s favorites like Judas Priest. McClary linked gender to canonical mystification, revisiting in *Conventional Wisdom*'s "Talking Blues" the erasure of women from "a pure lineage of blues" before **Elijah Wald** started his **Robert Johnson** revisionism; Walser knew that rock critics hated metal as much as Tipper Gore did. Poorly slotted sounds were his meat, and articles on **Miles Davis** ballads, Public Enemy blare, and Earth, Wind & Fire groove deserved their own collection.

As institution builders (they'd eventually donate millions to fund graduate student research), McClary and Walser's influence created a paradigm shift: music departments increasingly sought popular music specialists, academic book series flourished. To cite just a few examples, Jacqueline Warwick's *Girl Groups, Girl Culture* expanded **Susan Douglas**'s "Why the Shirelles Mattered," with not just notes but singing, dancing, and grooming getting case-study close observation. David Ake's *Jazz Cultures* considered fault lines of jazz identity: Creole New Orleans, Ornette Coleman's resistance to cutting-contest masculinity; conservatory wariness of Coltrane beyond "Giant Steps." Charles Garrett, already overseeing the second *Grove Dictionary of American Music* edition, which codified the new cohort, wrote *Struggling to Define a Nation*: Charles Ives and ragtime; **Jelly Roll Morton**'s "Spanish tinge"; Armstrong and the great migration via "Gully Low Blues"; an opiated "Chinatown, My Chinatown." Mitchell Morris was the Walser of soft music with *The Persistence of Sentiment*: Barry White *and* Barry Manilow. Robert Fink's *Repeating Ourselves*, pointedly subtitled *American Minimal Music as Cultural Practice*, made Philip Glass's peers speak to Giorgio Moroder disco and to ad campaigns. He noted that "when I began this work in earnest, Susan McClary was not only a powerful musicological example—she was the *only* musicological example of the scholar I sought someday to be."

Two issues qualified this couple's massive intervention. First, what happened to George Lipsitz? While McClary and Walser made musicology a place for contextual work that included popular music topics, they were less interested in interdisciplinary or nonacademic collaborations: "absolute music" was gone, but not music department insularity. On a related note, where were the Black scholars in this field, launched in part out of a concern with gender? If new jazz studies, or conversations between the likes of **Guthrie Ramsey Jr., Mark Anthony Neal**, and **Greg Tate**, regularly showcased African American across category, critical musicology did not, either in the bylines or, to a lesser extent, the citations.

David Brackett's work, while hardly a full corrective, made for a useful contrast. *Interpreting Popular Music*, obscure on first release, was reissued with Walser's passionate support. It fit the model: a musicologist comfortable ranging from Bing Crosby and **Billie Holiday** versions of "I'll Be Seeing You" to Hank Williams and authenticity, James Brown and Blackness, Elvis Costello and the shifting of modernism away from classical. But Brackett drew more widely on work from multiple sources: Ramsey for R&B repetition; Paul Gilroy for anti-anti-essentialism on questions of race and music generally; trade publications and reviewers to capture thought within the field itself. Those concerns framed how he collected *The Pop, Rock, and Soul Reader* and then his later book *Categorizing Sound*, which looked at genre discussions: immigrant Americans as the first pop leapers, blues as messy theater in the 1920s, the positioning of R&B charts in *Billboard* in the 1960s. Brackett lacked McClary and Walser's authorial punch. But rather than insist that musicology find a single new model, he tended to assume that different portions of popular music required different methods. Musicology could expand and, with the right playlist lined up, take up the ultimate pop challenge: crossover.

IDOL FOR ACADEMIC ANALYSIS AND A CHANGING PUBLIC SPHERE

Madonna, Sex, *1992*

"We were wearing matching Christian Dior demi-cup bras and that made me feel even closer to her." To call the words supplied by Madonna (downtown scene fixture Glenn O'Brien edited) for her explicit photo book *Sex* the best thing written about her would not be relevant. Given her rise alongside the music video's doubling of the pop single's address, the celebrity complex's hyperinflation of star text, and the culture-wars battle over the legacy of sixties social movements, as government swung right and yuppies gained as much as Reaganites from increasing economic divides, nobody had standing to judge. Better to notice how much an overview could sponge up. By this measure, *Sex* was a Bounty, the quicker-picker-upper of paper towels. Gender, race, money, power, style, *demimonde*: everything that seeped out of pop music idolatry got an absorbent sheet.

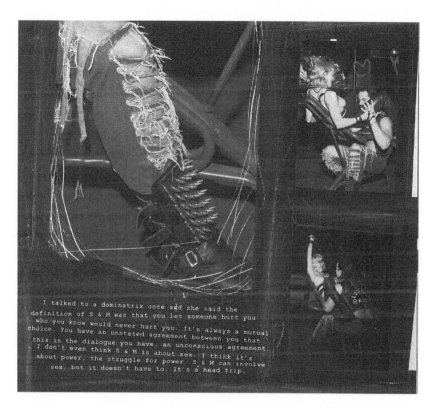

I talked to a dominatrix once and she said the definition of S & M was that you let someone hurt you who you know would never hurt you. It's always a mutual choice. You have an unstated agreement between you that this is the dialogue you have, an unconscious agreement. I don't even think S & M is about sex. I think it's about power, the struggle for power. S & M can involve sex, but it doesn't have to. It's a head trip.

FIGURE 6.5: Portion of a page from Madonna, *Sex, 1992*. The text, presumably by the singer, pictured in ways no previous major star ever had been, equated sexuality and power—a synthesis irresistible to academics, whose endless commentary revealed a major shift in the source of popular music writing. Author's collection.

The Queen of Pop emerged in a 1980s trinity. The best anthology of general writing, Adam Sexton's *Desperately Seeking Madonna*, included *New York Times* columnist Russell Baker, who made like that old coot Andy Rooney on *60 Minutes*: "It seems scarcely a year ago that the hottest of all possible stars was Michael Jackson, but while still digesting that fact I was astonished to discover that tremendous heat was suddenly being exuded by Prince, a male rock star whose wardrobe includes an ankle-length blanket of purple sequins." Yet only Madonna books proliferated in the 1990s, the bulk coming from a new group of cultural studies academics, mostly women. (For Jackson, the most impressive eventual book would be critic Margo Jefferson's *On Michael Jackson*, putting him in a showy lineage back to P. T. Barnum, and updated to engage questions about his predatory sexuality, with Steve Knopper's biography the least histrionic. Prince generated an even sketchier literature: Michaelangelo

Matos wrote superbly about the album *Sign 'O' the Times* for the 33⅓ series and recently released the full history of this pop moment, *Can't Slow Down: How 1984 Became Pop's Blockbuster Year*; one might also consult the articles compiled in the essential journalism database, Rock's Backpages.) It wasn't hard to mock when, for example, Cathy Schwichtenberg, editor of *The Madonna Connection*, wrote "I read Madonna's figuration against the backdrop of Baudrillardian theory where simulation is the pivotal term for a post-modern feminism that"—and so on. Heavily footnoted articles were the preferred form, with appreciation for the rest of popular music in short supply.

Rock critics—collected by Sexton, a former one ("I'm not a Madonna fan")—had the first crack at a mainstreamer of punk and disco they were inclined to distrust, complaining about "the degradation that Madonna heaps upon herself" and "rancidly Reaganite convictions" in places like the *Village Voice*. Critic Dave Marsh, sympathetic to a singles-oriented artist from Detroit, rode in, noting that "Nobody ever called Mick Jagger a strumpet." Joyce Millman, a rare woman's voice in the critical community at that time, proclaimed: "Madonna is the girl group of the eighties." Mary Harron, not yet a director, rerouted the pop/rock dichotomies for *Facing the Music*, edited by **Simon Frith**: "Madonna, with her unabashed artificiality and calculation is actually presenting a more genuine image of herself and her position than Springsteen, and finds her image easier to control." On the other side of "Like a Prayer" and Madonna's redefinition as oppositional, not Boy Toy, **Robert Christgau**'s "Madonnathinking" contrasted her overanalyzed, overstuffed videos with her underanalyzed, sleek pop songs. And years after Sexton's book, Mim Udovitch, in Barbara O'Dair's critical anthology *Trouble Girls*, epitomized how, in the vein of **Lillian Roxon**, to smartly identify pop cultural stakes: "my point is that one of the many ways Madonna has embodied and prefigured the decade-plus she has dominated from the start was by having a career that was virtually born in backlash (before backlash was in!), and that the force of the backlash, from whatever political or critical stance it has proceeded, has always had a direct correlation to how explicit sexuality has been a part of the text."

Cult studiers worked more from cracks between categories, letting ambiguity claim its own accrued stature. **Susan McClary**, in the *Feminine Endings* chapter Sexton included, used the lack of harmonic resolution in an oscillating "Live to Tell" as feminist commentary. Andrew Goodwin, in his book on music videos, *Dancing in the Distraction Factory*, made "Material Girl" the centerpiece of an exemplary study of how star text, video persona, and pop song intersected in a work whose "bourgeois feminism" shouldn't automatically be read as subversive. Lisa Frank and Paul Smith's collection *Madonnarama*, assembled in response to *Sex*, found academics and kindred spirits using an unlikely sort of book to refashion university "research": their contributions included handwritten letters and poems, transcribed dialogues, and John Champagne wondering if his own porn writing would affect his tenure prospects. The links between Douglas Crimp and Michael Warner's queer theory and Susie Bright, Carol Queen, and Pat Califia's sex-positive feminism made banter about *Sex*'s "dicklessness" or Madonna's exhibitionism cohere. On the border of academia and public intellectual writing, bell hooks remained Madonna's most persuasive detractor, calling her a plantation mistress in an essay Sexton reprinted and a purveyor of hedonism, rather than resistance, in *Madonnarama*. Carol Benson's *Madonna Companion*, a few years later, saw more backlash: articles like "Playing the Shock Market" and Daniel Harris's *Nation* critique of academic Madonna studies: "reverse cooptation involves the appropriation of a mainstream artist by a marginal group." Still, Pamela Robertson, in an excerpt from her book on feminist camp, provided a confident tracing of what made Madonna a Mae West for yuppies. Santiago Fouz-Hernández and Freya Jarman-Ivens's 2004 anthology, *Madonna's Drowned Worlds*, treated the performer less as postmodern marvel and more as "somewhat threatening presence" and "putative danger." By that time, music degrees dominated the author bios, Corinna Herr noting of "Justify My Love": "in the same way that the spectators were turned into voyeurs in 'Open Your Heart,' here the listeners are turned into voyeurs acoustically."

The majority of Madonna biographies were skippable, lacking new context, information, or perspective, but two general interest books broke ground after the phenomenon dissipated. Lucy O'Brien's *Madonna: Like an Icon*, stressed—in the vein of McClary and Christgau—musicality and artistic agency. In it, the performer who "used to go to shows by the Slits" (Ari Up claimed Madonna took her early fashion ideas from Viv Albertine), was explored through sources like the drummer on "Like a Virgin" explaining why it mattered that the beats there, at the singer's direction, were "big, fat and wide," one of any number of studio scenes pinpointing the icon as auteur. O'Brien brought the mix of music critic and academic chops seen in her women's music overview *She Bop*: Madonna's sound as "what cultural theorist **Theodor Adorno** would have called 'standardization' and rapper Vanilla Ice 'friendly-ass corny shit.'" And in the guise of a checklist, Matthew Rettenmund's *Encyclopedia Madonnica*, updated in 2015, provided a knowing fan's ontological distinctions at a micro level worthy of **Richard Meltzer**.

Finally, there were the fan accounts. The **Beatles**, early on, generated books of letters, and Fred and Judy Vermorel's *Starlust* collected fantasies. But with *I Dream of Madonna*, the new generation's academic slant let a folklore PhD, Kay Turner, collect women's imagining. "Fearlessness" was a keyword for Madonna in wannabe psyches; in dreams, either "she recognizes me" or the opposite. The star's response was regal: "I'd rather be on their minds than off." Grown-up bobby-soxer Martha Weinman Lear gave the *Frank Sinatra Reader* a key perspective; Laura Barcella's 2012 *Madonna and Me* asked dozens of women writers to trace their relationship to the icon over the years, often from grade school. Barcella recalled her look: "messy hair, the mesh tank top, the jelly bracelets, the crucifixes." For Courtney Martin, arising circa "Vogue," she "taught me to be brazen, unapologetic, and multidimensional." Stacey May Fowles connected because "I was probably about six years old when I first displayed an interest in domination and submission." Tamara Lynch needed *Sex* for the interracial Big Daddy Kane photos. Christine Bachman, raised by queer parents, enacted at seven a Madonna-Michael Jackson marriage with neighbor Lucy. Soniah Kamal, a Pakistani in Saudi Arabia, heard Madonna via an international school friend, calling her "the Mouse." Another fan—fifty as she wrote—who'd taken up boxing and ran for training, encountered Madonna at the Central Park reservoir and took satisfaction in exchanging a nod.

Were these magic moments musical? The MTV epiphany, with its megastars and postmodern politics, rerouted musical analysis: away from critics and toward cultural studies academia; away from rock and soul vernaculars and toward a multiplicity of musical add-ons that corresponded to new social and cultural identities. (John Champagne compared *Sex* to vacation slides: "Like all such images, they are chiefly of interest only to the sentimental traveler.") Madonna, mopping it up, wasn't exactly a progressive force. But her avidity and persistence, the challenge of reading her as much as listening, marked the break.

BLACK BOHEMIAN CULTURAL NATIONALISM

Greg Tate, Flyboy in the Buttermilk:
Essays on Contemporary America, *1992*

———

"I decided that what black culture needs is a popular poststructuralism," Greg Tate wrote in the pivotal "Cult-Nats Meet Freaky-Deke," and that is what he gave us, one "I mean" stray thought and coolness catalog at a time: "We talking a black **Barthes**ian variation on *Jet*"; "signifying like Muhammad Ali that Black and bad were once again synonymous: say it loud I'm funky and I'm proud. A generation before the Brown Bomber and bebop also proclaimed 'up you mighty race.' So goes the axis." On and on, inimitable, though the space he opened up in the 1980s, writing for the *Village Voice*, inspired everyone from **Mark Anthony Neal** to Colson Whitehead and film's Arthur Jafa, while it extended the rock critic lineage of a **Richard Meltzer** or **Lester Bangs**, the cultural studies mappings of a Dick Hebdige or Paul Gilroy. Tate was misleadingly identified with hip-hop: Henry Louis Gates Jr., in the introduction to this first collection of his work, called him "a leading intellectual exponent of the hiphop generation" and some marketer splashed "are you ready for the hiphop generation?" in big text on the back cover. Yet the photo there of Tate in full-on boho jazz regalia, taken by his Black Rock Coalition co-founder, guitarist Vernon Reid, said more than the words: Tate, second-generation Black cultural nationalist (hence Cult-Nats)—or umpteenth if you made his journey from DC to Harlem an Ellingtonian variation—was the ancient to the future of the funk.

When Tate, writing about the Chocolate City's hardcore and Rasta punks the Bad Brains in the *Voice* in 1982, invoked his "black radical-professional parentage," called himself a Black Bohemian Nationalist, and cited *Subculture: The Meaning of Style*, he was as much the subject as his subject. New Journalism had always allowed for that first person style, and in the Reagan era ("sheer savagery," Tate wrote) there was much for that persona to unpack: the crossover success and neotraditionalism of Wynton Marsalis, Prince, Michael Jackson, and Eddie Murphy; the avant-garde or theory moves of Ramm-El-Zee, Houston Baker, and **Nathaniel Mackey**; the problematic metropolitan New York culture heroes of the time—Public Enemy, Jean-Michel Basquiat, venerable **Amiri Baraka**. Equally unfazed by music, film, art, fiction, and theory, the Tate gallery of essays collected in *Fly Boy* suggested an updated **Langston Hughes**. The vernacular revolution was over, with mixed consequences. You could talk King Sunny Adé's Nigerian juju with Robert Farris Thompson in Yale; balance an appraisal of **Miles Davis**'s *Agharta* with feminist outrage at him as a roach to women; locate dub in **William Gibson**'s cyberpunk; cringe at Lee Atwater's electric blues inaugural for George Bush; and esteem Public Enemy's noise and agitprop—but not "whack retarded philosophy."

The dilemma for Tate, moving forward after his dazzling first decade, resembled what British cultural studies faced: immense sensibility, no institutional support for projects that took years to complete. His book on Jimi Hendrix was spotty and the one on James Brown never came out. His band Burnt

Sugar, with Tate on guitar and a shifting cast of Afronauts, made an arty New York variant on P-Funk and Sun Ra, stoner skronking that explored revered catalogs. His edited collection, *Everything but the Burden*, on white liftings of Black culture, provided a tag that lasted and ended with an essay by Jafa, whose *Love Is the Message, the Message Is Death*, a short film of edited clips, exactly captured that burden. Arguably, Tate's genius emanated through his circle as much as his writing. *Flyboy 2*, published in 2016, was more magisterial than mercurial, leaning toward artist interviews, obituaries, and keynote summations over reckonings with new sounds and styles. It did showcase his feminist explorations, a break with Black Arts movement antecedents. And it gave him a chance to preserve two key pieces on hip-hop: a 1993 poem ("Hiphop is digital chips on African lips") for *Vibe*, the 1990s Black-oriented music magazine where he was viewed in the elder role he'd accorded Baraka, and a 2004 assessment for the *Voice* of its fusion of African American ingenuity and global hypercapitalism. "Oh, the selling power of the Black Vernacular," Tate marveled, then threw in a **Ralph Ellison** comparison.

FROM INDIE TO ALTERNATIVE ROCK

Gina Arnold, Route 666: On the Road to Nirvana*, 1993*

———

Maybe—to play with the Brian Eno formulation about the Velvet Underground's seeding of new bands—there weren't many Replacements and Hüsker Dü fans gobsmacked as Nirvana and Pearl Jam sold millions during the 1991–92 school year, but each one wrote a book about it. Or maybe, as poet and Harvard professor Stephanie (then Stephen) Burt wrote in my first Pop Conference anthology, *This Is Pop*, indie-ish rock marked a shift: from rockers as pagan gods to rockers as grad students, poets, performance artists. (Add locavores, techies, realtors, *Portlandia* reenactors.) Those who nurtured college rock worried about the mass market. But class, gender, and sexuality were no less intractable concerns, producing a literature of quirky memoirs and double agents.

For Arnold, a Bay Area music columnist, "Nirvana's being on the radio means my own values are winning: I'm no longer in the opposition." St. Martin's Press modeled *Route 666's* design on Douglas Coupland's demographic manifesto, the novel *Generation X*, which offered coinages like McJobs, Decade Blending, and Musical Hairsplitting; a character, recalling his time in advertising, said "I'd wear bow ties and listen to alternative rock and slum in the arty part of town." Arnold had the K Records fanship to bond with Kurt Cobain over, the college radio background to contemplate the Lollapalooza festival. Her subject became how "a network started to form" in the fourteen years between the Sex Pistols' *Never Mind the Bollocks* and the chart-topping *Nevermind*, then the aftermath. Lurking was gender: "white girls from the suburbs get no respect," she wrote. Indie had fewer groupies in spandex, but "was always just as misogynistic." Female friends, from industry pathbreakers to fans, were ballast against the sneers of *Forced Exposure*'s Byron Coley or SST Records manager Joe Carducci's *Rock and the Pop Narcotic*, a well-written manifesto about rock as expressive guitar crunch only, not sociology, that defined out nearly all women. Arnold only partly noted riot grrrl challenging grunge, returning much later to the topic in her 33⅓ series monograph on *Exile in Guyville*. In between, *Kiss This* confronted the alt era of Green Day, Epitaph Records, and snowboarding. Arnold left journalism for a PhD; her study of rock festivals and power became a university press volume. The issues she had raised would linger.

To some indie/alt performers, largely male, the divide was one of class: the difference between the college DJ, *Voice* critic, or label rep type and artists with much more unsettled upbringings. Kurt Cobain's voice defined *Come as You Are*, released by Michael Azerrad months before the singer's death; audio from the interviews later became the documentary *About a Boy*. Alienated from rednecks and jocks in his logging town of Aberdeen, Washington, but also unlike the Sub Pop people in Seattle, sheltering under a bridge, this Cobain was a mythic construction—the working-class punk hero. Later biographies were corrective. Charles Cross's *Heavier Than Heaven* used the author's Northwest affiliations and access to Cobain's journals, themselves published soon after, to show his lifelong desire for rock stardom, only in this context a revelation. Azerrad extended his conversations with indie performers in *Our Band Could Be Your Life*, with chapters from Black Flag to Fugazi: men telling band-of-brothers war stories. These, too, became outsider lore—how did the Butthole Surfers do it?—as indie culture further gentrified. Azerrad would work with ex-Hüsker Bob Mould on a book, *See a Little Light*, that revealed Mould to have studied **Howard Becker** and connected indie and gay semiotics: "You learn the different signifiers." Bob Mehr's *Trouble Boys* got lost with the Replacements, Mould's great rivals: satisfying work on the class-liminal rocker.

The *Spin Alternative Record Guide* I edited with Craig Marks in 1995 stood as a New York media account, defining alternative rock against boomer variants. Entries ranged from Abba to Zorn, to expand beyond guitar bands. One found future novelists (Colson Whitehead on alt-rap, James Hannaham japing anticanonical); classical critic **Alex Ross** loving New Zealand indie; future Mötley Crüe biographer Neil Strauss detailing musique concrète. Michael Eric Dyson recruited for Public Enemy and Ice Cube. Will Hermes recounted Brazilian *tropicália*, foreshadowing the merge of salsa with punk, hip-hop, and minimalism in his 1970s New York City study, *Love Goes to Buildings on Fire.* **Ann Powers** wrote on central women performers such as PJ Harvey but also Nick Drake, "a perfect music for arty girls and boys just cracking their first volume of Keats's collected letters." Many beloved entries were by Rob Sheffield, a new waver who only laughed affectionately: "Robert Smith's artistic ambitions are so complex that it's easy to overlook the key to his undeniable greatness: he's ugly and his mother dresses him funny." Sheffield would become *Rolling Stone*'s most prolific Gen X critic. *Love Is a Mix Tape* mourned the loss of wife Renée Crist, also in the *Guide*, who died of an embolism in 1997; the University of Virginia couple listened to Pavement and compilations with names like *Ciccone Island Baby* together, charmed when grunge appeared at the mall. "Why not? We were easily amused."

Many other new writers entered public view connecting indie-alt to bigger subjects. For *Radio On*, Sarah Vowell spent 1995 listening to the radio and mourning Kurt Cobain. Vowell was heartland indie: a fan of Arnold's book and favorite band Fastbacks, of Ira Glass's war, with his show *This American Life*, on traditional NPR, droll on Billy Corgan's complaints about competing with "imitation Nirvanas," agape at her relatives in Muskogee. Thomas Frank's *The Conquest of Cool*, building on his work for lefty zine *The Baffler*, positioned itself—like rocker, record engineer, and scene bully Steve Albini—against all mainstreaming. Powers's *Weird Like Us*, by contrast, on her drug use, feminist cohort, and even our wedding, treated selling out as part of upper-bohemian mores. Vowell's ally Dave Eggers's *A Heartbreaking Work of Staggering Genius* made another Bay Area–Chicago–Brooklyn loop, the moving story of how his parents died and he cared for his young brother, but also of absurdist friends with "carefully messy Westerberg hair" starting *Might Magazine*, auditioning for MTV's *Real World San Francisco* ("I am a Kirk Cameron–Kurt Cobain figure, roguishly quirky, dandified but down to earth, kooky but comprehensible; denizen of the growing penumbra between alternative and mainstream culture; angsty prophet of the already bygone apocalypse, yet upbeat, stylish and sexy!") and appearing for eight seconds in episode two. Chuck Klosterman left an upbringing as remote as Vowell's for star *Spin* status as a young fogey with *Fargo Rock*

City, a take on alt and metal by a 1980s Crüe fan far more sincere than Strauss, able to explain perfectly why Axl Rose was done a disservice by the Cobain disdain that Arnold, for example, endorsed.

Academics, themselves often college radio or indie band vets, put the indie-alt-indie parabola into cultural studies lingo. In *Site and Sound*, Holly Kruse explored networks much like Arnold's, such as the Bay Area record label Alias, but with popular music studies grounding in the definition of local scenes. Richard Lloyd's *Neo-Bohemia* was a sociology capturing postindustrial Chicago in the Wicker Park, Liz Phair moment from creative industry types to bartender economies. **Josh Kun**'s *Audiotopia* had a chapter, "Rock's Reconquista" on *rock en español* in a moment of Café Tacuba making the college radio charts. Anthropologist Wendy Fonarow's *Empire of Dirt*, centered on British indie, captured how participation was ritualized from industry figures to hipsters. Joshua Clover's *1989*, subtitled *Bob Dylan Didn't Have This to Sing About* after a Jesus Jones lyric, merged rock critic, literary academic, and radical perspectives to synch post-boomer sounds from hip-hop and Top 40 to grunge's "inward turn." Steve Waksman's *This Ain't the Summer of Love*, like Klosterman, connected metal and alt, tracing that back to punk—SST Records met Metal Blade. Ryan Moore's *Sells Like Teen Spirit* covered similar terrain as soft-power neoliberalism: "Young, Gifted, and Slack" ventured from Richard Linklater and Sub Pop to Stone Temple Pilots and WTO protests.

Fiction writers and musicians sought to personify the 1990s crossroads. Denis Johnson's taut story collection *Jesus' Son*, named for a line in the Velvet Underground song "Heroin," achieved similar allure; Sonic Youth would take lines from Johnson's prose. Darcey Steinke's *Suicide Blonde*, named in turn for an INXS song, set itself in the urban slack Arnold, Vowell, and Eggers knew, but with a tougher appraisal; *Spin* sent her to interview Cobain. In underground comics, anchored by Seattle indie Fantagraphics, Peter Bagge's *Hate* made his Seattle based, after Hoboken and Minneapolis stints, alter-ego Buddy Bradley a stoned, underemployed, record-collecting type, dating women no less aggro and parsing the *Motorbooty*, Lisa Suckdog, Walt Kelley culturescape. Rick Moody, a novelist who listed the Feelies as a "primary source" for his Gen X *Garden State* and wrote about music regularly for *The Believer* (a publication Eggers helped create) described the death of cool, opening for Magnetic Fields, and his antipathy to drum machines in *On Celestial Music*. Marc Spitz, a novelist and playwright living on *Spin* assignments, described a later variant of alt-media well in *Poseur*: "We were the 'Lit Fucks.'" As Spitz wryly noted, "Years, later, in a *New Yorker* piece someone would refer to Pavement as 'Frat rock for the Bennington/Sarah Lawrence set,' and it's basically true."

Closer to the game, Jacob Slichter and his Harvard friend Dan Wilson started Semisonic, hit with "Closing Time," and couldn't repeat: "we were positioned as 'smart guys,' a potential selling point and incalculable liability." Slichter's *So You Wanna Be a Rock & Roll Star* broke down radio subformats and rocker prestige categories; he preferred funk, honestly, though Wilson was a pop lifer who would later cowrite for Adele. Jen Trynin's *Everything I'm Cracked Up to Be* cared even less about indie and alt, especially when mansplained, and traced its Boston singer-songwriter's participation in a bidding war: "This is when David Geffen tells me how much I remind him of Linda Ronstadt." In *Hunger Makes Me a Modern Girl*, much bigger Northwest rock star Carrie Brownstein—daughter of a closeted lawyer in Redmond, arrived at Evergreen circa Bikini Kill—noted that, faced with similar signing options, her band Sleater-Kinney "chose Kill Rock Stars. We stayed close to home." Brownstein, like Bob Mould, or Kim Gordon, formerly of Sonic Youth, in her memoir *Girl in a Band*, embraced the interlinkages of indie, calling herself a music nerd as she rendered gawky the riot grrrl exchanges Sara Marcus historically outlined in *Girls to the Front*. Of course, should she write a sequel, Brownstein would need to recount how Portland became *Portlandia* and *Hunger* was momentarily picked up for development by Hulu.

MUSICOLOGY ON POPULAR MUSIC—IN
PRAGMATIC CONTEXT

Richard Crawford, The American Musical Landscape, *1993*

———

Given an updated preface in 2000—and a helpful subtitle, *The Business of Musicianship from Billings to Gershwin*—musicologist Richard Crawford's case studies of how context and use solidified the texts his discipline abstractly unpacked became a meditation on the longer book they prepped him for: *America's Musical Life*. That title nodded at **Gilbert Chase**'s *America's Music*. In both his volumes, Crawford revamped predecessors **Oscar Sonneck** and Chase by placing performance over composition. Emphasizing business and select examples, Crawford's first stab posed enduring questions that his trade-press history only partially answered.

Crawford endorsed Sonneck's insistence that "bibliography is the backbone of history" but added historiography, interpretive structure for "the strain of randomness that, over nearly a century and a half of serious study, has run through histories of American music." He started constructing one: George Hood's primary source grounded *History of Music in New England* back in the 1840s; an even more obscure William Lines Hubbard edited 1908 *History of American Music*, one volume in a larger encyclopedia set, but good on popular genres; **H. Wiley Hitchcock**'s cultivated/vernacular distinction, which he liked for emphasizing attitudes over actual musical properties; through to **Charles Hamm**'s *Music in a New World* and its "acceptance of the musical market" over folk and art margins.

Business, Crawford declared, was actually "the very turf upon which American musical life has been constituted," not its antithesis. And he supplied examples no jazz, rock, or hip-hop critic could have: Lowell Mason, purveyor of secular music for schooling and uplift (making a fortune in the process); **William Billings**, learning to write psalms for the functional needs of a varied songbook: "Amherst owed its circulation chiefly to its metrical structure: It is cast in the pattern 6.6.6.6.4.4.4.4., the so-called hallelujah meter ... Amherst was chosen by many compilers because it best filled the hallelujah meter pigeon hole." He positioned the popular as "accessibility" against late nineteenth century classical music as "authenticity," then showed jazz and rock bringing authenticity into pop as well. He cited and illuminated songwriter George Frederick Root's populism: "Good taste requires that the singer should treat respectfully the emotion he excites."

Crawford added method and reach by reading more widely than other musicologists: jazz critics from 1920s dancer Roger Pryor Dodge to 1950s canonizer Martin Williams; mythmaking rock critics like **Greil Marcus** and popular music studies myth dispellers like **Simon Frith**, whose antiorthodoxies Crawford often paralleled; theorists like **Jacques Attali** on noise; American historians like the **Lawrence Levine** of *Highbrow/Lowbrow*. Some of his twentieth-century music analysis still felt secondhand: the great detail about the rising in pitch and volume of a Bigard clarinet behind the third chorus Nanton trombone solo in an Ellington recording came from Gunther Schuller. Focusing on performance, Crawford struggled with performativity: how recordings or mass media not only challenged notation but scripted identity. But when he experimented, for instance applying Sonneck on bibliography to the cross-genre recordings and film uses of Gershwin's "I Got Rhythm" in a striking chapter, he both conceptualized American music's historiographical tradition and extended the field's reach.

America's Musical Life suffered from Crawford's limits. Strong on the early years, it put Native American and Spanish language back in the narrative overall, showed why for the "pair of Georgia plain folk" who put Sacred Harp singing into book form, "formula was part of their power." Yet this was still a composer-slanted narrative: if performing mattered most, the Louis from Louisiana to get a chapter should have been Armstrong, not Gottschalk. Motown received a paragraph and Crawford failed to give James Brown's funk the musicological appreciation his younger colleague David Brackett had supplied. Crawford had nothing durable to replace the triad he relied upon, "transcendence of the classical, accessibility of the popular, and the continuity of the traditional," after it broke down when electrical recording in 1925 captured vernacular performance. He confessed he found rock and roll singing "rather grating."

Still, as *America's Musical Life* concluded, there were signs of the Crawford in *The American Musical Landscape*: grappling with how Black collective authorship connected jazz and hip-hop, considering performativity through PJ Harvey on the cover of a *Rolling Stone* book of women writers on women performers. He was less suited to summing up than nodding at patterns and looking ahead.

LISTENING, QUEERLY

Wayne Koestenbaum, The Queen's Throat: Opera,
Homosexuality and the Mystery of Desire, *1993*

———

Opera, **Lawrence Levine** showed us in *Highbrow/Lowbrow*, was very much American popular music in the nineteenth century: repertoire for theatrical revamping, like Shakespeare. Recordings historians William Kenney and David Suisman demonstrated that opera, too, was American pop in the twentieth century, if you applied Motown Records founder Berry Gordy's definition: "'Pop' means popular and . . . I never gave a damn what else it was called." Enrico Caruso discs were megasellers and opera's fitting of words to music, lightened as operetta, became Broadway song style that aspired to standards. But opera wasn't populist—Victor sold Caruso on a different color-coded catalog line than its vaudeville, just as race records were a color line removed from country.

Koestenbaum left this taste history to the margins, where queer opera obsession, centered on the diva's performance of gender ambiguity, resided. He wrote in the moment of Queer Nation and Silence = Death posters, as a thirty-three-year-old who remembered asking at eighteen, "Am I in love with Julie Andrews, or do I think I *am* Julie Andrews?" When he declared, "I devoted my twenty-first winter to Mozart's *Don Giovanni* (1787) and to the search for a boyfriend" or connected imitating opera singers to liberating his throat for fellatio, those private moments made larger claims. No closet now for the lonely opera queen's collected fantasies. Opera was popular music again: this listening narrative reinscribed it in the public sphere.

The canopy of queerness, strong as grunge in 1993 and no less fond of Abba, let an aesthetic emerge with relevance for popular music theory. Koestenbaum showed that fans loved the opera diva as much for her mistakes as her triumphs. Records gave them disembodied voices to fantasize through: "sonic drag." They craved "backstage knowledge," pursuing "diva speak" in memoirs of impugnable legitimacy. A chapter on Maria Callas saw in her work a reverse camp effect: she made opera seem more serious and believable. If popular music turned as much on camp theatrics of identification as on hip subcultures and vernacular authenticity, *The Queen's Throat* offered a manual in the form of a scrapbook of asides. Koestenbaum wrote: "This conviction that having a voice means having an identity is a cultural myth."

Overtly, he rhapsodized fragments of identity—nonnormative ambiguity emerging in personal and public crisis, opera as "an art of interruption, rupture, and bodily danger." But this approach required opera's solid position as a genre in the arts pantheon. As he showed, one could link terminologically the naming of bel canto singing and homosexuality to the 1860s and modernizing, discriminatory taxonomies. Still, that was also, Levine argued, when the pressure to sacralize cultural categories intensified. It was less clear why Koestenbaum, who admitted to loving Streisand as a kid but set such pop performers aside elsewhere in his book and apparently his life, only making movie references, could mention the film *Diva* but not the diva Grace Jones. Race, class, and cultural capital went to the periphery of a book by a Yale English professor who cited queer theorist Eve Sedgwick and gender musicologist **Susan McClary**.

Koestenbaum "listened, queerly" and in detail, prose, and erudition, his work was exemplary, worth partnering with D. A. Miller's equally artful *Place for Us* from a few years later, on gay men and musicals, from home listening to cast albums to piano bars and *Gypsy*. The quality of the writing alone helped solidify the category of literary nonfiction. One last taste of *Queen's Throat*: "Not camp, not bathos, not sentimentality: dignify queer emotion by saying *catharsis*, even if opera induces the wish, condemned as effeminate, never to reassemble the socialized self, but, instead, to remain in tears forever, to stay where Puccini's *La Bohème* (1896) places us." But those seeking to reckon with popular music had to approach this book from a differently queer angle. As noted more than once, the opera queen did not always want to mingle or even give a nod of shared recognition.

BLACKFACE AS STOLEN VERNACULAR

Eric Lott, Love and Theft: Blackface Minstrelsy and the American Working Class, *1993*

———

T. D. Rice's illegitimate offspring, blackface minstrelsy, generated tie-in books for a century: songsters for outfits such as Virginia Minstrels; overviews in the vein of Charles Day's *Fun in Black*; profiles of minstrels like George Christy and Dan Emmett; how-to-stage-a-show encyclopedias from sheet music publishers; Ike Simond's *Old Slack's Reminiscence* on African American troupes after the Civil War. Edward LeRoy Rice's 1911 *Monarchs of Minstrelsy*, by a second-generation performer who debuted in the wench role of outraged spouse, offered a yearbook of suggestive capsule biographies and photographs. Harold Weston, "a colored man, was one of the world's greatest banjoists"; Julia Gould, "the first woman to achieve prominence in minstrelsy"; Leon, "the dean of minstrel female impersonators." A photo near the end of a quite young, devilish Al Jolson noted how quickly he'd risen: "In the vernacular of the Rialto, Mr. Jolson was a 'riot.'" Dailey Paskman and **Sigmund Spaeth**'s coffee-table book, *Gentlemen, Be Seated!* tied the antiquarian bow.

Tambo and Bone inaugurated a second century of writing, serious this time; Carl Wittke was a history professor, later known for his immigrant account *We Who Built America*, though also an amateur minstrel as a student. His account accepted the racist myth that "plantation owners in America kept their Negroes happy and productive" by forcing them to sing and dance, calling the Black in minstrelsy "a somewhat different individual" from real life. But he detailed a saga, back to the eighteenth century and through to Al G. Field Minstrels closing in 1928, the end of an era—or not: "The future of minstrelsy seems to lie in the lap of Hollywood." At core, Wittke believed, Americans loved to see lowbrow defeat high.

While others, notably **Constance Rourke**, took up minstrelsy as Americana, the next major study came in 1962 from Hans Nathan, a German musicologist who'd fled Nazis to also work on **William Billings** and Israeli folk song. *Dan Emmett and the Rise of Early Negro Minstrelsy*, written in the spirit of **Gilbert Chase**, saw the form as anti-genteel, "an indigenous, sinewy popular art." Mining sheet music, Nathan found nuggets of folk expression, especially Emmett: his first big quartet, Virginia Minstrels in 1843, getting onstage in the Bowery like punk rockers, their "horrible noise (for they attempted no tune)" producing the eventual roots standard "Old Dan Tucker." Emmett's "Dixie" fortified both sides during the war. Lincoln declared after Lee's surrender: "I had heard that our adversaries over the way had attempted to appropriate it. I insisted yesterday that we had fairly captured it."

On the other side of the 1960s, minstrelsy's Sambo racism was a given. Yet in Robert Toll's 1974 *Blacking Up*, history in the Berkeley vein of **Lawrence Levine**, blackface became "a major vehicle through which Northern whites conceptualized and coped with many of their problems." With industrial capitalism and Jacksonian democracy, a "substitute for their folk culture" evolved: touring actors like Rice and George Washington Dixon, then bands like the Christy Minstrels, then bigger troupes staging shows. Sentimental songs prevailed during the war years. New rivals like variety and vaudeville arrived postwar, as Black performers claimed "Black" roles and white shows turned to extravaganzas.

All of these books were adjuncts to the tenured likes of **Isaac Goldberg**'s *Tin Pan Alley*, Chase's *America's Music*, and Levine's *Black Culture and Black Consciousness*, but Eric Lott's *Love and Theft* took an endowed chair center stage, called nothing less than—his highest compliment—a "pop explosion" by **Greil Marcus** in the foreword to its reissue. Lott brought **Stuart Hall**'s *Resistance through Rituals*–type cultural studies analysis to minstrelsy, reshaping American Studies as Marcus had with *Mystery Train*—maps of hegemonic instability replaced the hunt for white whales. His framework, appropriation as unwieldy desire, was catchy enough for **Bob Dylan** to call an album *"Love and Theft."* To the proud lowbrow, the anti-genteel folk artist, the Jacksonian democrat, Lott added identity-crossing bohemians. "'Lucy Long' was sung by a white negro as a male female danced," the *New York Tribune* had reported in 1853. Lott shot a full magazine of cultural theory at this: "America witnessed a simultaneous *hybridization* and *proliferation* of vernaculars." But he was talking

Mick Jagger, Norman Mailer, and Ronald Reagan too: the "seeming counterfeit" and "happy ambiguities" of minstrelsy were the origins of rock and roll and also its co-optation; the twisted roots of American music challenged any cross-racial class struggle.

Other white male rock and rollers followed Lott, mesmerized by blackface fissures of identity. *Demons of Disorder*, by historical musicologist Dale Cockrell, fixated on George Washington Dixon, whose minstrel hits preceded "Jim Crow." Dixon's character Zip Coon, an urban dandy of the North tripping on his faux sophistication, rivaled Rice's plantation antihero. His other obsession, publishing tabloids, resembled minstrelsy as un-"larned" pop culture. Cockrell, a geographer of the working-class New York streets that figures like Rice knew well, saw minstrelsy as charivari, ritual of carnivalesque misrule in the public sphere, like callithumpian bands banging on pots to make the night hideous. Factories threatened social cohesion; minstrelsy answered back. If Lott parsed side-splitting fun, Cockrell heard buckshot noise. His vintage quote came from the 1838 *Boston Post*: "The poor can but share / A crack'd fiddle in the air, / Which offends all sound morality." Later, his book *Everybody's Doin' It* extended the New York perspective to cover the city's bordello-sanctioned music scene from 1840 to 1917.

In the equally influential *Raising Cain*, W. T. Lhamon Jr.—later to bring Rice's songs and plays back into print—applied the term "mudsill mutuality" to the workers in such places as the Erie Canal, part of a "broad interracial refusal of middle-class channeling." He saw blackface's multiple stages as a lore cycle, "an arc of insouciant gestures rising toward containment and control." Lhamon's knack for the specific set piece made him a Lott rewritten by Marcus: secret histories ranging from the minstrel whistle fed to Jolson as Jack Robin in *The Jazz Singer*, Ida Cox performing as Topsy in *Uncle Tom's Cabin* revues before her blues days, Rice's *Bone Squash Diavolo* play, and even MC Hammer. In a more extreme version, anti-academic critic **Nick Tosches** used twentieth-century blackface yodeler Emmett Miller in *Where Dead Voices Gather* to effuse about "mixed and mongrel bloodlines," the "lies, pretenses, and falsehoods that define us." Tosches piled up mirrors to infinitize all claims of originality.

One weakness of rocker-scholar minstrelsy books was that they disdained the category's sentimental tendencies: Stephen Foster's "Old Folks at Home" and many other middle-class parlor numbers. William Mahar's dryly written *Behind the Burnt Cork Mask* was an early rebuke to Lott, finding in playbills and other primary sources a show-business eclecticism that made Italian opera derivations "as much a part of the whole burnt cork routine as any borrowed plantation dance." Lauren Berlant's chapter on *Show Boat* in *The Female*

Complaint defined a view of woman's adaptation in contrast to *Love and Theft*. Brian Roberts's *Blackface Nation* contrasted "Old Dan Tucker" with the abolitionist rewrite made popular by the Hutchinson Family Singers, "Get off the Track!" This bourgeois, female-friendlier sphere, too, Roberts argued, was American pop; a contrast to an insistence on a subservient "Blackness," enforced by riot in the 1834 Five Points New York glorified by Lott, Cockrell, and Lhamon. Michael Rogin's *Blackface, White Noise* made no pretense of distilling redemptive strands as it conceptualized Jews replacing Irish as immigrants using the cork to recode themselves as white.

The limits of the blackface corrective had become clearer. American music had to be understood as enduringly interracial, a complex blend. Musicologist Christopher Smith's *Creolization of American Culture* used William Sidney Mount paintings to evoke performances pre-recordings, along with scholarship reaching back to Nathan and including Robert Carlin's work, in *Birth of the Banjo*, on early star player Joel Walker Sweeney. Smith concluded that music was being "ragged" in performance long before ragtime, whites and Blacks learning from each other to deploy the "participatory discrepancies" **Charles Keil** attributed to groove music everywhere, from the urban North to the "riverine frontiers" of the South. Even minstrel dialect, Smith thought, was "a much more sincere attempt to render early nineteenth century, African American-inflected, working-class speech as it sounded."

But genealogies of the warped vernacular, in a sense the impetus of these books right back to Jolson in *Monarchs*, had little to say to Katrina Thompson's stress in *Ring Shout Wheel About* on how slaves performing for whites anchored American entertainment right back to the ships from Africa. The whip and rape were used to propagandize happy darkies, with only private frolics away from white engagement a possible exception. Her chapter on blackface was bluntly titled "Same Script, Different Actors." Minstrelsy, she wrote, was not "a display of black culture but instead was mimicry of the façade of slavery that pervaded the United States." Thompson's critique rubbed some cork from the very white pantheon of minstrel writing. (Exception: Wesley Brown's novel of Jim Crow, *Darktown Strutters*.) And Lott noted—highlighted in a Karl Hagstrom Miller review of minstrel books—that his love and theft meme had been taken up more than his interest in examining class and capitalism. Much still needed to be thought through. As the so-called *Jazz Singer* put it, you ain't heard nothin' yet.

MEDIA STUDIES OF GIRLS LISTENING TO TOP 40

Susan Douglas, Where the Girls Are: Growing Up
with the Mass Media, *1994*

————

She taught media studies but published trade books; mixed historiographical revisionism and personal memoir; and with two 1990s works, *Where the Girls Are* and *Listening In*, brought feminist incisiveness to topics like girl groups and Top 40 radio. "I am a woman of the baby boom," this study began, "which means my history is filled with embarrassment, littered with images I'd just as soon forget." But the effect was quite the opposite. After Douglas wrote "Why the Shirelles Matter," that they did wasn't even a question anymore. If men, as critics and academics, tended to prioritize the margins, her studies debated the center of pop culture, interested in works whose ambiguities and compromises spoke to the "warring selves" inside many a listener, especially girls.

Style mattered: a confident and direct address, making personal-political judgements about culture without belaboring ontology. Douglas's solid first book, *Inventing American Broadcasting*, a translated dissertation, explored radio's origins in cultural notions of the "inventor-hero," like Marconi, and amateur operators—tinkering men and boys—reinventing corporate orders. *Where the Girls Are* had an immediately different tone. There had been precursors, such as **Lillian Roxon** eluding the standard categories of *Rolling Stone* rock criticism with her *Rock Encyclopedia*. Barbara Ehrenreich's *Hearts of Men* and (as coauthor) *Re-Making Love* came even closer, picking apart the male rebellions of a *Playboy* or Kerouac in the first, singling out girls losing it for the **Beatles** as an origin point of feminism in the second. Douglas recognized herself in this; she'd read *Glamour* alongside *Ms*. She suspected that, at least in some eras, rather than "coopting rebellion, the media actually helped promote it." Hence the Shirelles: first Black women to top the charts, singing a song about whether to have sex, written by a young white couple. The soft, respectable strings in the arrangement were as powerful a signal as the lyric, contradicting the idea that the years between **Elvis** and British Invasion were fallow, but also representing a "euphoria of commercialism." Shows from much later, like *Charlie's Angels* and *Dynasty*, made her checklist, too; they "spoke volumes about our inner contradictions."

Listening In took up radio again, but for its effect on music, vernacular speech, and how the combination let men access socially feminized parts of themselves— or resist that. An early chapter, "Tuning into Jazz," explored the crooning and jazzy dance pop that Alison McCracken later devoted an important book to, *Real Men Don't Sing*. Other sections covered broadcast journalism, sports on radio, and radio research. Douglas's boomer narrative returned her to transistors and DJs like Wolfman Jack. As was often the case in her writing, Black culture gained focus mostly through white appreciation: "Black hipster slang signaled membership in a special, outcast community that seemed to laugh at and be above those clueless, cookie-cutter, tightassed white folks." But in connecting chapters on AM hit radio, FM underground resistance, and how shock jocks like Howard Stern represented a freedom lost on corporatized AOR, Douglas offered a music history entirely structured around broadcast media rather than the usual tour of genres. She ended on a down note, seeing a post-deregulation radio formation of chains and rigid programming: "I, and millions like me, don't have a radio station to listen to anymore."

Others would take the academic intersection of media studies and popular music farther: look to the work of Mary Celeste Kearney, including *Girls Make Media* and *Gender and Rock*, or Michele Hilmes's various radio projects, such as *Only Connect* and a compiled *Radio Reader*. Jacqueline Warwick's *Girl Groups, Girl Culture* supplied a fuller story for the Shirelles. Douglas, meanwhile, influenced by the later work of Angela McRobbie of Birmingham cultural studies, who focused on *The Aftermath of Feminism*, contemplated *The Rise of Enlightened Sexism*. Radio now meant Clear Channel promoting "The Breast Christmas Ever" and reality TV was "ground zero of enlightened sexism" that embraced gender dichotomies with "bratty tone and ironic distance." Not quite able to think through the class implications of what a Joshua Gamson (with help from **Ellen Willis**), in *Freaks Talk Back*, called "democratization through exploitation," Douglas stuck to first principles, gave thanks for *Buffy the Vampire Slayer*, and dreamed she could put a stake through a culture that had shifted from "Will You Love Me Tomorrow" to *Toddlers and Tiaras*.

IRONIES OF A CONTESTED IDENTITY

Peter Guralnick, Last Train to Memphis: The Rise of Elvis Presley, *1994*

———

In a *Rolling Stone Illustrated History of Rock & Roll* entry, Guralnick recalled the rare boomers still fixated on the King by the hippie 1960s: "Every fact which is presented in this essay was a mystery then, the subject for painstaking detective work, an intricately assembled collage which has since been exploded by knowledge. Most of all we labored happily in the wilderness, self-mocking but earnest, possessors of a secret knowledge shared only by fellow fans: Elvis Presley was to be taken seriously." Even Guralnick felt the white embodiment of rocking out to Black-identified sounds peaked with his indie Memphis recordings, calling later RCA hits "fundamentally silly records, a charge which could never be leveled at the Sun sides." Two historiographical thoughts present from this, useful in a pilgrimage to the mound of E-books. To take Elvis seriously required serious effort that deserves serious respect. But what that meant varied constantly, right down to the definition of serious.

A pre-rock critics' take on rock and roll, informed by jazz, swing, and popular culture legacies, has died in our memory. (Matt Brennan's recent *When Genres Collide* offered a corrective.) One Robert Johnson—not the bluesman but a *Memphis Press-Scimitar* columnist and nephew of Presley's ninth-grade homeroom teacher—inaugurated the literature in 1956 with *Elvis Presley Speaks!* A magazine with photos, its local details approximated those still accepted: sharecropper Tupelo to public-housing Memphis; fluke success in between country and R&B at Sun, helped by Marion Keisker and Sam Phillips at the label plus DJ Dewey Phillips; management given over to "shrewd businessman" Col. Tom Parker, major RCA signing and big media appearances on TV; embrace of cars, threads, girls, and buddies like Red West. To Johnson, once a swing kid, rock and roll was teens dancing again. James Gregory's fuzzier *Elvis Presley Story*, by a *Movieland Magazine* editor, continued into movies and military, with Dick Clark reassuring readers Presley would stay popular post-service. **Rudi Blesh**, recalled as an anticommercial Dixieland moldy fig, reveled in those who "want to rock and wail" in the second edition of *Shining Trumpets*. Institute of Jazz Studies founder Marshall Stearns, though, called the new sounds "a tasteless version of the real thing" in his *Story of Jazz*. **Samuel Charters**, popularizer of country blues, later wrote a novel called *Elvis Presley Calls His Mother after the Ed Sullivan Show*, shrewd on media in those days, women fans, and southern parents—a book of unresolved dreams and urges.

Fannish early rock critics shaped the next writing wave, with Elvis resurging via a TV special, Memphis soul studio recordings, and live coronations. To *Awopbopaloobop*'s **Nik Cohn** in England, later to write a pulpy detective novel featuring the singer's stillborn twin, *King Death*, "Elvis is where pop begins and ends," the "major teen breakthrough." "He was flash—he had four Cadillacs." And "Always, he came back to sex . . . those axis hips." **Stanley Booth** scored an *Esquire* feature, unearthing Dewey Phillips for "the lead of a lifetime," but it only saw print in his later book *Rhythm Oil*: "Talkin' about eatin' pussy, me and Sam Phillips used to make old Elvis sick with the stuff." Booth's focus was Graceland, his Elvis a southern Brando good young boy. Jerry Hopkins got the first full biography. The "I don't sing like nobody but me, I reckon," Presley in Johnson's magazine, talking to Keisker during their first meeting at Sun, now became the more iconic "I don't sound like nobody." Keisker too, famously, here recalled Sam Phillips proclaiming "If I could find a white man who had the Negro sound. . . ." Engineer-producer Bones Howe told Hopkins that Elvis "honestly dug the [black-identified] music. And so others began to show respect" and shattered the "total embargo on sex in pop." Critic **Greil Marcus** made an incandescent "Presliad" conclude *Mystery Train*. Breaking southern white working-class barriers that Hank Williams couldn't, his films inadvertent French surrealism, this King throwing it all away was an American studies symbol of contradictions. Marcus footnoted a dream he'd had about a Vegas ad appearing on Elvis's penis.

When Presley died at forty-two in 1977, one more rock critic take became hallowed: **Lester Bangs**'s obit, mourning the love his generation once shared for him: "we will never again agree on anything as we agreed on Elvis." The key to the literature that mushroomed afterwards turned out to be cracking apart that "we." First—and purchased by millions—was the newly out, seemingly predictive, *Elvis: What Happened?* Former "Memphis Mafia" entourage figures Red West, Sonny West, and Dave Hebler dished on the pill-popping "walking drugstore," touchy-to-borderline-homicidal deity who believed "he is a law unto himself"; whose sexscapades, before and after former young teen bed partner, then wife, Priscilla had her affair and blew away, were more trick-mirror voyeurism than smut, akin to his buying binges. Still, the tone was respectful, imploring their southern friend to redeem himself.

Not so Albert Goldman's *Elvis*, also informed by a Mafia figure—Lamar Fike collected royalties—but acidic on a redneck whose origins deserved no more respect than his home: "Though it cost a lot of money to fill up Graceland with the things that appealed to Elvis Presley, nothing in the house is worth a dime." Presley in his final girth was a "grotesque object," shitting the bed. The "Negro" in Keisker's Phillips quote, an outraged Marcus pointed out, shifted to the N-word in Goldman's telling, without either Sun figure's testimony. Goldman—a Lenny Bruce biographer and part of the pre-boomer pop culture intelligentsia who later undercut John Lennon with equal disdain—was savvy enough to call Presley's early music: "the put-on and the take-off, the characteristic fusion of enthusiasm and mockery that was almost universal in the pop culture of the fifties" and evoke *Mad*, Sid Caesar, Terry Southern, and Leiber and Stoller for comparison. But another line Marcus cited (dueling penile signifiers?), Goldman mocking Presley's "ugly hillbilly pecker," set the tone.

Elvis books of every kind spammed out along other velvet knockoffs in the 1980s and 1990s, a story unto themselves. Novelist Don DeLillo had trenchant comments on "Elvis Studies" in *White Noise* that cultural studies scholar Gil Rodman concretized in *Elvis after Elvis*: fault lines of race, cock, region, culture. Marcus policed the discussion, through *Dead Elvis* and the Bill Clinton, aka "Bubba," aka "Elvis"-aligned *Double Trouble*. He contested Guralnick's Sun-slanted taste, arguing that "there is no greater aesthetic thrill than to see minority culture aggressively and triumphantly transform itself into mass culture." There were more insider accounts, notably longtime road manager Joe Esposito's *Good Rocking Tonight* and original guitarist Scotty Moore's *That's Alright, Elvis*.

But the most vital revisioning came out of Linda Ray Pratt's "Elvis, or the Ironies of a Southern Identity," in the university press collection *Elvis: Images and Fancies*, which argued his original southern fans had never abandoned him, associating his shame with some of their own. For these millions, the sharecropper's son who revered his mother, enjoyed the American dream, and didn't at core change eclipsed those early rocking Sun sides. It was, Pratt noted, a "sentimental myth," but she agreed with W. J. Cash that southerners were "the most sentimental people in history." In a second telling point, Pratt wondered—in 1979—why women hadn't written more on Elvis; she could only find a Julie Hecht short story.

From this gender-region nexus a literature quietly blossomed, summed up neatly in Bobbie Ann Mason's brief portrait: "Elvis was great, so familiar—and he was ours!" Elaine Dundy's *Elvis and Gladys* became the go-to source on Tupelo and the family. American studies professor Karal Ann Marling's *Graceland*, starting with a firm rebuke to Goldman's dismissal of the objects there, offered a deep exploration of taste and class prejudice, especially good at links: Las Vegas and weddings, Elvis and Gene Autry films, the 1970s jumpsuit as "strange, special, quasi-liturgical garment." If Priscilla's blander memoir, *Elvis and Me*, dominated sales, June Juanico's *Elvis in the Twilight of Memory*, by a Biloxi girlfriend, picked up the summer of 1956 story right where the photos of Alfred Westheimer had left it. "Elvis was behind the wheel of a big pink Cadillac; his mother and father were next to him in the front seat." Vernon Chadwick's collection, *In Search of Elvis*, brought writing by Southern outsider artists and explored fan shrine Graceland Too. Erika Doss's *Elvis Culture* detailed fanship and visual depictions. Michael Bertrand's *Race, Rock and Elvis* provided a coroner's report on the invented quote that destroyed Presley's Black fan base, "The only thing Negroes can do for me is shine my shoes and buy my records," tracing it to the white-owned *Sepia*, and he documented young southerners across race lines battling to integrate concerts. Yet, tellingly, he also noted Sun performer Rufus Thomas on why Sam Phillips never mixed races on record: he believed "blacks and whites couldn't do it together." Alanna Nash was shrewd in her Elvis books: resurrecting Fike in snorting banter with two other Mafiosos for the first, drawing out details on Col. Parker for the second, and making delicious, psychosexual hash (playing off Peter Whitmer's hokum, in *The Inner Elvis*, about Elvis as "twinless twin") in *Baby, Let's Play House: Elvis and The Women Who Loved Him*. There, fan-clubber Kay Wheeler taught him "Rock & Bop" dance moves and Russ Meyer movie vixen Tura Satana taught him much more.

Meanwhile, Guralnick cemented his quasi-definitive take. A Bostonian running summer camps to fund his books, the ultimate roots-rock fan pursued interviews with leading soul and country performers, writing profiles with grace and a restraint quite the opposite of, say, **Nick Tosches**. His *Feel Like Going Home: Portraits* had chapters on the Sun sound and Charlie Rich, a great artist unable to fully realize his potential—first in what became a Guralnick litany of them. The piece earned him the friendship of the Phillips family, including the belated Sam interview that became the capper of his next collection, *Lost Highway*. "I never wanted to be a critic," Guralnick recalled there, preferring "passionate naiveté." But as with the parallel soul writing of Gerri Hirshey in *Nowhere to Run*, his biases, seemingly unimpeachable—who could be against staying true to yourself, or racial integration?—flattened pop stories fueled by inequity. *Sweet Soul Music*, ending this early trilogy with another Memphis indie, Stax, had more rich tales than ever but a continuing naïveté and dismissal of Black Power–era choices; Charles Hughes's *Country Soul* later gave a firm corrective.

Dubious beliefs can produce great art and *Last Train to Memphis* fit the bill: giving rock-critic sanction to the revisionist regional view, Guralnick vowed "to keep the story within 'real' time" and joined numerous interviews to Elaine Dundes's Tupelo contacts, the world of *Elvis Speaks!* and those Hopkins tapes. Ending with Elvis in the army kept the tragic part at bay. And the author made a concession he wouldn't have earlier: Elvis wasn't, in self-conception or even at his best, a blues singer. Guralnick's restraint was blatant in places: he held back Col. Parker's illegal immigrant status and made-up identity (long before revealed by Goldman) until *Careless Love*, the second volume, published after Parker's death. But the ultimate Elvis book had been written. The tragic sequel was less successful, with the author's disinterest in questions of gender, race, and capitalism meeting a slop he couldn't enjoy playing around in. Guralnick ended his bio-odyssey back with the Sun 78s, "that sense of aspiration." There was a service book: with the leading specialist on recordings, Ernst Jorgensen, he published *Elvis Day by Day*. But the real finale was a stellar, singular *Sam Phillips* biography, researched in friendship, about the figure whose aspirations more resembled what Guralnick heard in Elvis than Elvis did. If Pratt uncovered the sentimental myth of Elvis, Guralnick remastered his vernacular.

Little new Elvis canon followed—the king was gone and so, to play off an old George Jones song, was much of what used to be "you."(Mark Duffet's *Elvis: Roots, Image, Comeback, Phenomenon* gave a current overview from a thematic, academic perspective.) What propped up a "we" for so long—Marcus tending the fires so punk winds couldn't blow them out, Guralnick synthesizing a plausible origins myth—needed to yield still further. Not necessarily to the future: there was plenty to draw upon in early writers who saw Presley as the next popular culture chapter, not at core a brand-new one; in the death projected onto him long before his stardom was harvested; in the tackiness, shame, and sentiment that stamped region, gender, race. We still very much need to hear from Black authors on Elvis. Elvis books can only gain from an animating theme of failure, which is not the same as scorn. A deader Elvis belongs to popular music as we now hear it.

TWO GENERATIONS OF LEADING
ETHNOMUSICOLOGISTS DEBATE THE POPULAR

Charles Keil and Steven Feld, Music Grooves:
Essays and Dialogues, *1994*

———

Music Grooves was the *My Dinner with Andre* of popular music books. (Look it up!) Keil, author of *Urban Blues* in 1966—a paradigm shifter owing to its preference for new, loud, city sounds over the acoustic turns jazz collectors valorized—had become a kind of Old Testament culture radical. He wrote books on Nigerian *Tiv Song* and on the polka scene around him at SUNY Buffalo; with *My Music*, he supplied a pioneering reception study of the idiosyncrasies, eluding genre categories, found when oral history focused on how people listened and played. He was also a born collaborator: *Polka Happiness* with wife Angeliki and photographer Dick Blau, reprised in 2002 with *Bright Balkan Morning*, on Greek Roma musicians; *My Music* as a Music in Daily Life project that gave co-credit to two graduate students, Susan Crafts and future listening scholar Daniel Cavicchi. Keil had been the rare white man writing for *Muhammad Speaks,* dedicated *Urban Blues* to Malcolm X, then became disillusioned when Nigeria massacred the Ibos at Biafra. His 1965 essay "Motion and Feeling Through Music," included in *Music Grooves*, challenged Leonard Meyer and musicology more generally, seeing in jazz performance unnotatable qualities of "engendered feeling," like a drummer's personal tap. For Keil, communal participation was key, reification suspect, whether score, recording, or ledger sheet.

Feld, though younger, was no less accomplished: one *Music Grooves* footnote explained that the conversation that day took place after he received a MacArthur fellowship. A Coltrane fan and jazz player, he had studied ethnomusicology with Alan Merriam, felt the approach didn't capture songs very well, then worked both outside academia as a sound engineer and outside music departments as a communications scholar while pursuing fieldwork with the Kaluli of tropical New Guinea. *Sound and Sentiment*, canonical in ethnomusicology (and to authors outside it, such as **Nathaniel Mackey**), was written in New Testament cultural studies theory speak: "By analyzing the form and performance of weeping, poetics, and song in relation to their origin myth and the bird world they metaphorize, Kaluli sound expressions are revealed as embodiments of deeply felt sentiments." Yet his focus was maverick. A story of a boy who became a bird could underpin a whole musical system, the soundscape of animals and forest "layered" (his favorite approbation) with song, dance, and tears. As concerned to document Kaluli music as interpret it, he collaborated with locals in a process of "dialogic editing"; the thirtieth anniversary edition of the book called this "anthropology in sound." With Mickey Hart of the Grateful Dead, he put together a popular *Voices of the Rain Forest* CD for Rykodisc.

Music Grooves was a multilayer cake: original writing by each man, dialogues that framed the essays in advance and afterward, capacious endnotes to each dialogue, and, near the middle, an exchange of letters about Aretha Franklin. The first half took up issues of musical participation, the second issues of musical mediation. Keil played the curmudgeon, so identifying with R. Crumb and some of his antimodern musical tastes that a Crumb cartoon strip was included. He railed at cultural studies ("SNIVELIZATION REIFIES!"), including Feld's version ("Why do you feel that you have to live uptown, in a world of

high theory?), even as he tossed off his own great jargon: "participatory discrepancies" for the very human groove qualities that made a Bo Diddley beat
something more than shave and a haircut. Feld, a thorny read to be sure on
"Communications, Music, and Speech About Music" unwound: his Franklin
letter to Keil asked, "Does 'Sock it to me' mean fuck me or fuck off?" Picking
apart the power dynamics of Paul Simon's *Graceland*, he then went deeper on
world beat as a transition from schizophonia (the cutting of off sounds from
sources) to schismogenesis (differentiation achieved through interaction), using
his work with Hart as an example. They were two radicals, two white men anx-
iously indebted to Black music, two scholars and improvisers. *Music Grooves*
let them be retrospective, challenge methods, and reinforce expertise—crucial,
since ethnomusicology remained fairly closed to work on Western and non-
"folk" topics.

Feld contributed an audio soundscape to *Bright Balkan Morning* and in
2012 published *Jazz Cosmopolitanism in Accra*, about his time in Ghana with a
fellow Coltrane fetishist who was also a conceptual artist; elder of African jazz
Guy Warren (or Ghanaba); and a fleet of custom car honkers who worked fu-
nerals, not unlike brass bands in New Orleans. The book, naturally, linked to a
raft of DVDs and CDs that let those portrayed step to the front. For Feld—who
wrote that notions of bricolage should apply to the researcher as much as the
subject—ideas of vernacular or discrepant cosmopolitanism, of diasporic intimacy and intervocality, summoned the overlays of routes and detours he called
home. Like Keil, he was concerned not to reify. So he told stories; walked the
duration of borderlines; listened in stereo.

DEFINING HIP-HOP AS FLOW, LAYERING, RUPTURE, AND POSTINDUSTRIAL RESISTANCE

Tricia Rose, Black Noise: Rap Music and Black Culture
in Contemporary America, *1994*

———

"I owe mad thanks to the hip hop community," Tricia Rose wrote atypically
at the start of this, acknowledging a slight divide between a cultural studies
academic and the rappers, industry folks, and critics who had helped her study.

That divide vanished with *Black Noise*, which set the stage for innumerable Blackademic takes on hip-hop to follow, far more than rock produced a generation earlier. It was a good moment for such a study: the last possible that one could frame a work around the overtly political rappers Public Enemy and not the neoliberal rebels of G-Funk like Dr. Dre and Snoop, or Puff Daddy at Bad Boy and Jay-Z at Roc Nation; around eclecticism and not gangsta rap codification.

Belief in the strident and new Black music genre's political efficacy grounded this book. Yes, Public Enemy rapped "Bring the Noise," rap was "confusing and noisy" and raised the question "Is this really music anyway." But Rose, utilizing James Scott's language in *Domination and the Arts of Resistance*, found "hidden oppositional transcripts" inside those booming systems. She applied Dick Hebdige's notions of punk subculture to hip-hop's style "nobody can deal with." Rappers and rap producers offered a bricolage: anti-music only in the sense that they appropriated technology and conventional musicality to rework longstanding Black traditions of groove and cutting into that groove—James Snead's "On Repetition in Black Culture" factored critically here. The approach looked backward to **Amiri Baraka** and sideways to **George Lipsitz** more than ahead to ideas of Afrofuturism—there was no theorizing of a post-soul split. Rose had much to say about political messages in lyrics and videos and a sharp point about Black women's dialogic, rather than antagonistic, relationship to Black male rappers. But she lacked performance theory, a notion of identity as performative, or just writerly comfort with evoking how the delivery of a text theatrically affected the message.

The most lasting legacy of *Black Noise*, picked up on by **Mark Anthony Neal**, Jeff Chang, Imani Perry, Eithne Quinn, and many others, was in changing the framing of rap and hip-hop from postmodern to postindustrial. (Rose's own return to the subject with *The Hip Hop Wars*, in 2008, was much more schematic in its exasperation with the genre's mainstream compromises.) That might seem the kind of thing only academics would care about. But viewing sampling and other tactics as formal shuffling kept the focus on aesthetics—the rap of Blondie, Fab Five Freddy, and New York City downtown types. Seeing hip-hop through Robert Moses's cutting up the Bronx, or post-Fordism changing industrial economies into information economies, upped the stakes. Rose was a terrifically syncretic scholar, brilliantly applying a suggestion from cinematographer Arthur Jafa—that this postindustrial reclamation be viewed as operating through notions of flow (as a rapper might), layering (as a DJ might), and rupture (as Reagan-Bush policies might, or belligerent responses back at them). Rose wasn't, fully, a hip-hop expert, but nobody did more to map the conjuncture that brought the noise. She concluded, "hip hop style *is* black urban renewal."

REGENDERING MUSIC WRITING, WITH THE DEADLY ART OF ATTITUDE

Evelyn McDonnell and Ann Powers, eds., Rock She Wrote:
Women Write about Rock, Pop, and Rap, *1995*

Writing about popular music had been overwhelmingly male, overwhelmingly about men, but to only notice this missed deeper points. The enthusiasm that had driven such prose and such adulation was itself gendered, like **Walt Whitman**'s verse, or **Louis Armstrong**'s trumpet, or **Jack Kerouac**'s road, or **Amiri Baraka**'s nationalism, or a **Greil Marcus** set piece. You could write more about women. You could publish more writing by women. But did writing itself, as it reflected and amplified popular music, have to change? Was critique the first step? Or to create alternative styles no less compelling?

When Ann Powers and Evelyn McDonnell put together *Rock She Wrote*, they were *Village Voice* stalwarts in the tradition of **Ellen Willis**, hitting their stride as PJ Harvey, Liz Phair, Courtney Love, and riot grrrl remade rock. Read now, the collection seems underresearched: pre-internet xeroxes left even figures with books, like **Phyl Garland**, unmentioned. Academics were largely slighted: **Susan McClary**'s the only article with footnotes; **Tricia Rose** there, but with a *Voice* reprint. Yet the collection was utterly inspirational because the then contemporary alt-weekly talent pool was magnificent: with crafty, attitudinal sentences, these women brought vital criticism to rock and rap readerships that actively debated the politics of their genres. Donna Gaines on her Johnny Thunders, yes, Lou Reed not so much investiture, paralleled a ditty by Mary Gaitskill on Axl Rose and Joan Morgan working through Ice Cube—a power trio on the advantages of troubling rather than seemingly more sympathetic men. Gretchen Phillips moshed at the Michigan Womyn's Music Festival; Mim Udovitch found a funny pal named k. d. lang for a *Rolling Stone* feature. Sue Cummings opposed rockism with rave coverage, while Powers modeled language as surging and surgical as Harvey, greatest rocker of the day. Barbara O'Dair's collection *Trouble Girls*, a *Rolling Stone*–sponsored look at

"Women in Rock," featured similar strong authors, including McDonnell and Powers, and more targeted, if less idiosyncratic writing, with Harvey on the cover.

A reading list in back of *Trouble Girls* noted other key books as of that point. Lucy O'Brien's *She Bop* and Gillian Gaar's *She's a Rebel* were the best straightforward histories of women through the pop-rock years; Mary Bufwack and Robert Oermann's *Finding Her Voice* offered the same for country. More maverick accounts included **Andrea Juno**'s *Angry Women in Rock*, McClary's *Feminine Endings*, and a **Madonna** anthology edited by Cathy Schwichtenberg. Placed under "Books on Music Genres, Movements, and History," rather than "Women-Themed Books" was **Simon Reynolds** and Joy Press's *The Sex Revolts*. It focused on gender, not women, turning the pop, rock, rap, and avant-garde pantheon into a referendum: the sexism of the Stones or Clash but also, via cultural theory, male abjection in Nirvana or the rhizomatic Can. Patti Smith to Kim Gordon was read as "female machisma"; Kate Bush slotted with "chicks on broomsticks." Harvey received more attention than Madonna or Janet Jackson. And a key point was made: "the Dionysian rebel tradition in rock is played out."

Academic popular music gender studies arrived with Sheila Whiteley's anthology, *Sexing the Groove*, which made its orientation felt with the first article: Will Straw's pointedly titled "Sizing Up Record Collections." Emerging scholars like Norma Coates nodded at *Rock She Wrote*, but absorbed Judith Butler on performativity to make the issue how rock reinforced norms. Here, too, there was huge fascination with riot grrrl: answer to the calcified male moves of Springsteen and Jagger, though Stan Hawkins found comfort in Pet Shop Boys. Such work became a solid part of media studies: Mary Celeste Kearney's *Gender and Rock*, a generation later, gave a textbook survey to intervening books by Mavis Bayton, Whiteley, Marion Leonard, and Freya Jarman. But such authors struggled to engage the ideas or prose punch of Willis and the *Rock She Wrote Voice* contingent. Counterparts in other areas brought gender studies to jazz (Sherrie Tucker's edited volume *Big Ears*), country (Kristine McCusker and **Diane Pecknold**'s *A Boy Named Sue*), and Latinx pop (Frances Aparicio's *Listening to Salsa*). Meanwhile, a different kind of academic emerged, highlighted in Whiteley's later collection, *Queering the Popular Pitch*. Authors such as Judith, later Jack, Halberstam, writing about female masculinity and queer temporality, or Karen Tongson, with the *Voice*-style headline "Tickle Me Emo," aimed for language and presence as provocative as their subject matter. They were academic rockers, as Halberstam's *Gaga Feminism* and Tongson's *Why Karen Carpenter Matters* fully demonstrated.

When Joan Morgan, a *Voice* writer featured in *Rock She Wrote*, gave hip-hop feminism its launch with the 1999 *When Chickenheads Come Home to Roost*, she coined a phrase for this approach: "*we practice the deadly art of attitude.*" It wasn't just posturing. If Morgan was to question how women in the genre that outshone rock had been downgraded from flygirls to bitches and hoes, she had to leave no doubt of her power. Then she could put down a sentence like the much-quoted "I needed a feminism brave enough to fuck with the grays" and inspire a generation of academics and critics. A good example of her impact was *The Crunk Feminist Collection*, in which Brittney Cooper and her tenure-tracked counterparts got ratchet to fuck the patriarchy. Aisha Durham pondered her relationship to Nicki Minaj here, as a Karen Durbin once had her relationship to Mick Jagger. Rachel Raimist called out **Nelson George** and hailed Ava DuVernay's *My Mic Sounds Nice* documentary for BET. Soon, Raimist would film an episode for a series DuVernay ran: media practice overwhelming media studies, not unlike George's moves from critic to creator or critic dream hampton's move to direct the acclaimed and effective *Surviving R. Kelly*. Morgan published *She Begat This*, a look at *The Miseducation of Lauryn Hill*, the album that appeared the same year as *Chickenheads*. Holding her own prose back, Morgan built the book around conversations with different Black women: a fashion editor, a neoliberalism scholar, a DJ, the always provocative hampton. Once again, Morgan critiqued gender and experimented with form in response.

In their own work subsequent to *Rock She Wrote*, Powers and McDonnell were no less prolific and formally daring. McDonnell, after quick books on Björk and *Rent*, became a journalism professor (calling herself a "free press rock-n-roller" on the university website), published a biography of 1970s women rockers the Runaways, and then edited another compendium. *Women Who Rock* changed the phrase to something more active than *In Rock*. In some ways, McDonnell's approach was old-fashioned: women writing on women. But she had illustrations rather than photos accompany the articles and urged contributors to not be encyclopedic. The goal was to locate the power of each artist—and write back. Academic contributors included Gayle Wald, author of a biography that resurrected proto-rocker Sister Rosetta Tharpe; Daphne Brooks, due as this book comes out to publish the first in a trio of books on Black women and popular music, *Liner Notes for the Revolution*; and Shana Redmond, a powerful scholar of Black anthems and Paul Robeson. Critics were represented by punk era veteran Vivien Goldman, whose own solid history, *Revenge of the She-Punks*, appeared soon after, and younger critics such as indie supporters Jenn and Liz Pelly and country/Americana–focused Jewly Hight.

To imagine what a fuller roster of authors might have looked like had budget and time allowed reveals the extent to which music scribing had now become a *Rock She Wrote* world. Front of the line was Jessica Hopper, whose emo, Hole, Lana Del Rey, and R. Kelly immersion, *The First Collection of Criticism by a Living Female Rock Critic*, was **Lester Bangs**ian in its gleeful abrasiveness but avowedly feminist and aimed in part at readers such as those devoted to the online girls magazine *Rookie*. Both Hopper and McDonnell coedited books series for the University of Texas Press, neither explicitly women- or gender-focused but with plenty of room for that, so McDonnell's Music Matters series included Tongson's Karen Carpenter and Gaines's Ramones books, while Hopper's American Music series published Sasha Geffen's *Glitter Up the Dark: How Pop Music Broke the Binary*, Holly Gleason's edited *Woman Walk the Line* country collection, and Hannah Ewen's *Fangirls*.

But there were many one could mention: the features approach to roots writing modeled by Amanda Petrusich in the *New Yorker* and books like *Do Not Sell at Any Price*; McDonnell-Powers contemporary dating to *SF Weekly* Danyel Smith's work, from editing *Vibe* and *Billboard* to novels, essays bordering on prose poems that need collecting, and the 2021 book *Shine Bright: A Personal History of Black Women in Pop*; southern hip-hop rabble-rouser Regina Bradley's forthcoming *Chronicling Stankonia*; neoliberalism slayer Robin James in *The Sonic Episteme* on Rihanna and how to musically detonate bombs; Emily Lordi ad-libbing *The Meaning of Soul*. Would Zandria Robinson, moving from sociology academese to trauma-confronting literary nonfiction in her essays for places like the *Oxford American*, be next with a great book? *Rolling Stone* cover story go-to writer Brittany Spanos? *New York Times* contributor Lindsay Zoladz?

Still, and conflicts of interest be damned, it's just true, only one author was attempting to bring the full sweep of the work that had been published since *Rock She Wrote* into her own essays and books: my wife, Ann Powers. She held down critic's roles at the *New York Times*, *Los Angeles Times*, and then NPR, where she oversaw the multiplatform series "Turning the Tables" to challenge popular music canons. *Tori Amos: Piece by Piece* was an extended conversation with the art-pop singer-songwriter, on spirituality as much as harpsichord. But *Good Booty* was the key statement, a successor to *Sex Revolts* in its ranging engagement with sexuality and pop but reaching back to pre–Civil War New Orleans and making race a no less central concern. Nobody had attempted to synthesize this range of subject matter and scholarship. Powers was pulling off the intersectional analysis of what her subtitle promised—*Love and Sex, Black and White, Body and Soul*—by retaining the music critic's freedom to move from micro to macro as the story demanded, to trust in sentences as much as sources. From the jazz shimmy to gospel's role in bodying music to the sexual pull of Jim Morrison, groupie dynamics, cyborg Britney, and Beyoncé tweets, this was the most holistic reckoning to date. And it honored the *Rock She Wrote* impetus not only to foreground women but to do so in a way that made assertive writing central, gender as charged a subject as race, and the resulting conclusions a full-on rethinking.

SOUNDSCAPING REFERENCES, IMMERSING TRAUMA

David Toop, Ocean of Sound: Aether Talk, Ambient Sound and Imaginary Worlds, *1995*

———

Ruminating and revisionist, Toop challenged fellow sonic explorer Robert Palmer for calling Ornette Coleman's first free jazz recordings meandering and lacking a bluesy "basis in vernacular rhythms." Toop shot back: "passion existed before blues and besides, music not *going anywhere* is one of the most fertile developments of the twentieth century." This was not just a squabble between two enormous La Monte Young fans; it marked a divide. Palmer, champion of unruly rock and roll anchored in African American origins and electric eruptions, hailed the vernacular; Toop's unpacking of ambient sound revived a Euro-Asian sentimental.

An Englishman who passed through art school and the Flying Lizards, Toop mainly saw himself, his memoir *Flutter Echo* revealed, as a grassroots experimental musician dating back to the late 1960s, with ties to groups such as the London Musicians' Collective and the ambitious small magazine *Collusion*. Toop then wrote the first significant study of hip-hop, *Rap Attack*, which sprinkled subcultural studies on New York interviews (Spoonie Gee, working as a rehab supervisor), and a record hound's erudition: Latin connections, cross-dressing anthem "Another Man," jivers like Slim Gaillard, electro experimentalist Bill Laswell. This postmodern vantage stressed adaptation: "the mythological tricksters and heroes are replaced by electronic-age superheroes recruited from kung fu, karate, science fiction and blaxploitation movies, rerun television series, video games, comic books and advertising." Toop had less interest in rappers as new rockers, or African American enterprise: subsequent editions of *Rap Attack* dutifully nodded at N.W.A's breakthrough but heartily claimed fringier figures like DJ Shadow.

Ocean of Sound was several steps more ambitious, the product of his musical experiments turning in a computer sounds direction, his becoming a decently paid music journalist for *The Face*, giving him access to sources, and his marriage dissolving shortly before his ex-wife committed suicide, leaving him sole parent of a young girl. Of necessity, Toop's book all but conjured its own aural universe, juxtaposing times and places: Debussy hearing Javanese music at the 1889 Paris Exposition, Lafcadio Hearn's reinvention in Japan, Black science fiction impulses routed from Sun Ra to acid house, gurus **John Cage** and Brian Eno. *Ocean* celebrated shamanism and eroded genre: solid melted into aether. James Clifford's anti-authentic anthropology lent authority, but each new kindred spirit added to the lofty summations. "Ecology, anthropology, physics, semiotics, land art and conceptual art levered music into an area where sound and listening could take precedence over the intention of the composer." Toop's tastes remained predictive: the mavericks—Merzbow, Arthur Russell—that he complained of Tower Records in lower Manhattan neglecting became central to the hipster boutique Other Music across the street. A boomer-era rocker now found more edge in **Nick Tosches** on Dean Martin, in suburban withdrawal, than punk transgression: "Floating, amorphous, oceanic crooning (or crooning with attitude) seems to mirror the feeling of non-specific dread that many people now feel when they think about life, the world, the future; yet it expresses a feeling of bliss." Written in short, loosely connected sections, *Ocean of Sound* preferred electronic "bedroom bores" to **Lomax**-style folk explorers, but still ended with Kate Bush's Tennyson and Celtic moves, Victorian as much as hypermodern.

Toop's subsequent books *Exotica, Haunted Weather*, and *Sinister Resonance* were produced in conjunction with related soundtracks he'd compile and original recordings, too, as well as live collaborations with the likes of Sonic Youth's Thurston Moore. He continued sounding the oceans of material available from this open perspective; Les Baxter–style lounge music perspectives reordering genre ideals, like **Ellington**'s McLuhanesque orientalism, became a retake on jazz. Digital technology made sound studies and conceptual art as cutting edge as subcultural songs and rhythms once had been. A haunted listening house of spectral noises was presented with Toop's bluff mysticism: "But do we read Poe for sense, for logic or probability, or for the thickened, uncanny atmospheres of which he was a master?" His books sought the sublimity of improvisation, subject of his 2016 study, *Into the Maelstrom*—guitar gnostic Derek Bailey another pivotal guru—via snatches of other writing, invocation of cool recordings or conversations, art world travelogues.

But the goal was never Palmer's miscegenated rebellion. Toop's immersions gave him the capacity, rather, to absorb trauma in the manner of his totem Joseph Conrad: "I let my spirit float supine over that chaos." His taste and personal testing readied him for 9/11. A portion of *Haunted Weather* recalled that composer Stephen Vitiello had been artist in residence at the World Trade Center in 1999, positioning contact mics against the anechoic windows. Audiences after 2001 were moved; the Whitney Biennial transferred now unrecreatable recordings into a 5.1 surround. Soundmarks, Toop called this: a way of registering even absence.

SOCIOLOGIST GIVES COUNTRY STUDIES A SOFT-SHELL CONTRAST TO THE HONKY-TONK

Richard Peterson, Creating Country Music:
Fabricating Authenticity, *1997*

––––––––

Sociology's "production of culture" school dated to the early 1970s, highlighting the institutional factors that made it viable for styles to flourish. Changes in law, technology, managerial style, industry structure, and the like put Bing Crosby atop popular culture in one era, working an almost bureaucratic combination of syndicated network radio, Hollywood movie musicals, and Broadway standards, administered through major record labels and studios. **Elvis Presley**'s gyrations reflected a new moment, more entrepreneurial and arriviste, of independent record labels like Sun, localized Top 40 radio, 45 RPM records, and an R&B/country repertoire. That was Peterson in his article "Why 1955?" A childhood Dixieland jazz and bebop fan who stayed active long enough to study the alt-country scene, he had a knack for identifying underlying trends; another of his short studies, written with Roger Kern, was the much-cited "Changing Highbrow Taste: From Snob to Omnivore."

Mainstream country, mixing an industry format and stylistic genre, roots and show boots, was Peterson's perfect subject, helped by proximity as a professor at Vanderbilt in Nashville. *Creating Country* developed an evocative Peterson phrase: "the dialectic of hard-core and soft-shell," oscillations between honky-tonk rawness and "Achy Breaky Heart" crossover. Spanning the first hit "old-time" record by Fiddlin' John Carson in 1923 and the posthumous deification of Hank Williams in 1953, it emphasized how popularizing a scorned regional culture turned on pragmatic use of tradition and authenticity. The look at Carson considered the new Atlanta radio station that played him; the "value-neutral commercialism" of the furniture dealer there who pushed New York's Okeh to record him; and why that strip-mining approach only worked for a time, replaced by A&R pioneer Ralph Peer's move to share copyright and turn tradition into a "renewable resource," or Fred Rose's reinvention of Nashville as a regional Tin Pan Alley. Other threads surveyed the cowboy look merging with hillbilly sound, "hot records" production making honky-tonk jukebox hits boom out, Roy Acuff engineering a paradigm shift at the Grand Ole Opry, and Hank Williams as patron saint of a far from saintly industry.

Applying a value-neutral approach to commercialism, Peterson balanced **Bill Malone**'s genre partisanship and pointed out innumerable paths for future study. A footnote about the need for a study of the Country Music Association in a late chapter gave **Diane Pecknold** a topic for her *Selling Sound*; Jennifer Lena, a collaborator, developed genre theories of music in *Banding Together*; Karl Hagstrom Miller avidly applied the stuff on how race and repertoire was categorized in *Segregating Sound*. If Miller would prove more alert to the confines of that process, Peterson enjoyed how some commercial figures, like the Vagabonds, eluded them—not by being purists, but by being even less pure. He had a soft side for the soft shell.

ALL THAT NOT-QUITE JAZZ

Gary Giddins, Visions of Jazz: The First Century, *1998*

———

The longtime *Village Voice* columnist knew his core subject as far back as his 1977 obituary for category-confusing vocalist **Ethel Waters**, "mother of modern popular singing," which kicked off his first collection, *Riding on a Blue Note*, subtitled *Jazz and American Pop*. *Riding*'s second essay, on Bing Crosby, put "the genuine insouciance of the man" in the lineage of blackface minstrelsy. That appreciation led to *A Pocketful of Dreams*, first of a two-volume and growing biography that captured the *Kraft Music Hall* radio show world around the crooner while detailing how he reworked **Louis Armstrong** or inhabited a *Road* film. For Giddins, who zigged Satchmo as a kid when the world zagged **Beatles**, "modern" was a continuum. Charlie Parker's bop "Koko," Arthur Blythe and the 1970s loft scene, and Jason Moran's new-century "You've Got to Be Modernistic" all belonged. Giddins used obituaries, reissues, Ken Burns's PBS *Jazz* show, and university textbooks to parse, periodize, and celebrate the immensity.

While his first book looked at the Dominoes, Otis Blackwell demos for **Elvis Presley**, Bobby Bland, and Professor Longhair, Giddins's qualms at "stifling pop orthodoxies" and "illiterate musician's music" were deeply ingrained, like his hatred of jazz-rock fusions. He'd jab, "could anyone have imagined in 1970 that **Miles Davis** would someday be satisfied with his playing on *Agharta*?" and make a joke of the time Cecil Taylor disappointed him by asking to hear James Brown. But his ability to spot the prose and pop inside jazz more than compensated: artists from **Irving Berlin** to European avant-gardist Willem Breuker, treatments from a bar mitzvah–laden feature on Red Rodney to an oeuvre sift of James P. Johnson. Notably, his Art Pepper account, "The Whiteness of the Wail," engaged race more creatively than any take on jazz and Black power. The white Giddins credited **Albert Murray** as a mentor, alongside jazz's two leading white cartographers, *Jazz Tradition* author and Smithsonian compiler Martin Williams, and liner notes ace and Institute of Jazz Studies head Dan Morganstern. He cited the modernist Americana critics **Gilbert Seldes, Constance Rourke**, John Koeuenhoven, and Dwight MacDonald, or sentence seer **Whitney Balliett** far more than **Amiri Baraka** and his inheritors.

Rhythm-a-ning focused on jazz's "neoclassical" centering without overpraising Wynton Marsalis: "I don't expect much in the way of innovation." *Celebrating Bird*, a short biography updated for recordings and literature in 2013, took Sartre on Tintoretto as a model, making Parker a high-culture seeder of sound and avid listener. Biographical digging turned out to be another Giddins gift, as *Satchmo* research revealed Armstrong's birth certificate. Critically, the study lauded how the "Artist as Entertainer" triumphed: "He took jazz away from purists." But that begged certain questions. Giddins appeared more comfortable, as in *Faces in the Crowd*, esteeming the relative antiracism of comedian Jack Benny or Clint Eastwood's LP stash than tackling Spike Lee's musical worldview.

Visions of Jazz, jazz love in the time of twenty-one-CD Dinah Washington and eighteen-CD Nat Cole sets, gave Giddins his own sort of box set. It ranged from jazz precursors like **Bert Williams** and the genre's vaudeville groundings to Don Byron neo-vaudeville, 650 pages and seventy-nine new and revised entries later. A third short biography, of **Duke Ellington**, split into several entries, took seriously the still not-quite-classical composer's notion, "You can't

write music right unless you know how the man who'll play it plays poker."
Giddins honored Benny Goodman without denying swing's "colonial iniqui-
ties," worked out Oedipal issues with **Frank Sinatra**, came back at Davis via his
1970s Duke tribute "He Loved Him Madly" (new out of old), and surprisingly
claimed "No artist has given me more pleasure" of Cecil Taylor (eleven-CD
Berlin box). *Visions* ended with jazz struggling: Dee Dee Bridgewater one of
only a half-dozen great jazz singers under sixty, Joe Henderson and Joe Lovano
as apprentice types aging into mastery. In this context, Black Power debates
having long since shifted to hip-hop and academic jazz studies, Giddins's ecumenicalism inspired Burns and Burns's detractors alike.

The market for long-form music writing dwindling, Giddins concluded
his *Voice* column (see *Weather Bird*), did more with classic film and literature
(*Natural Selection* and *Warning Shadows*), and made a pragmatic peace with
academia: in conjunction with bebop scholar Scott DeVeaux, he created the
trade book, textbook, and listening guides *Jazz*. But his key work was the study
in depth of Crosby, the most popular musical performer of the mid-twentieth
century, abandoned in the twenty-first. Here, Giddins's unflagging gift for
moving through a body of work extended even to studio publicity reports and
the accounts of a radio program's musical director. Spending hundreds of pages
on only six years of Crosby's career in the 1940s earned some complaints, but
Giddins understood that this period in the crooner's career provided an imperial demonstration of what could be recorded, how a performer's reach might
be extended. Both men, the artist and his biographer, had proven the limitless-
ness of repertoire, not to mention those who wrote and performed it.

JAZZ STUDIES CONQUERS THE ACADEMY

Robert G. O'Meally, ed., The Jazz Cadence of American Culture, *1998*

———

This large volume and its sequel, *Uptown Conversation: The New Jazz Studies*, came of importantly cushy origins: a study group on jazz meeting at the
Institute for Research in African-American Studies, then the Center for Jazz
Studies, at Columbia University, funded by the Ford Foundation. Jazz had
been institutionalized in the Cold War and LP era via State Department
tours, **Marshall Stearns**'s Institute of Jazz Studies, and Martin Williams at

the Smithsonian. But this era of jazz studies operated outside the earlier nexus of Black players and white critics: the African American O'Meally was **Zora Neale Hurston** Professor of American Literature at Columbia, stamped officially with the lineage of the Harlem Renaissance, **Ralph Ellison** and **Albert Murray**'s dialogues, **Amiri Baraka** and Black Arts, **Stuart Hall** cultural studies.

Jazz Cadence offered a syllabus, collecting published work and suggestive epigrams. Instead of *Jazzmen*'s Bunk Johnson standing for a lost New Orleans, this revived Sterling Brown on blues as folk poetry and Hurston herself on "Characteristics of Negro Expression"; John Kouwenhoven connecting jazz to skyscrapers and bubble gum as Americana in 1956; and **Barry Ulanov**, the only traditional jazz critic, on Ellington's programmatic mix. Black voices dominated, including musicians, literary greats, artists, scholars, and critics, in answer to Baraka's "Jazz and the White Critic" and **Nathaniel Mackey**'s "Other: From Noun to Verb." Minimizing scenes and canons, O'Meally focused on what made American culture "jazz-shaped": links to dance, literature, visual art and popular memory.

The Ellison-Murray vision of jazz and blues as omni-American equipment for living, gumbo equilibrium, turned into a neotraditional orthodoxy by critic Stanley Crouch and musician/Lincoln Center boss Wynton Marsalis, weighed on the book, which deepened that approach, as with an **August Wilson** preface to a play, more than critiqued it, as in Mackey's two theory-driven essays. Yet Brent Hayes Edwards used **James Weldon Johnson** writing to "theorize a black poetics of transcription"; **Eric Lott** worked bebop's aesthetic of displacement to expand modernism. Language and form were complicated as much as clarified: saxophonist Benny Golson deemed Monk songs "fragments that are developed." James Snead brought Hegel and **Ishmael Reed** together to explain jazz uses of repetition and "the cut." Gerald Early explored "high" jazz at Aeolian and Carnegie Hall from James Reese Europe and Paul Whiteman to Goodman and **Holiday**. Hazel Carby reclaimed urban women's blues as race record and tent show, not folk, triumphs. Scott DeVeaux picked apart a construct, the jazz tradition of critics, as Gunther Schuller might have a jazz solo.

Uptown Conversation, mainly newer writing, embraced post-1970 jazz and theory. **George Lipsitz** attacked neotraditional jazz views, now staged by Ken Burns for PBS. George Lewis detailed the flawed racial encounter between the avant-garde Association for the Advancement of Creative Musicians and New York's downtown music community. Farah Jasmine Griffin's "When Malindy Sings" used a Dunbar poem to consider "black woman's voice as the origin of black male literary and musical productivity." **Louis Armstrong** appeared, but through his photo collages and Betty Boop cartoons: "I shall try to read a great man's telltale smile," O'Meally wrote. Vijay Iyer, combining a UC Berkeley PhD with piano work that later earned him a MacArthur, treated improvisation as embodied cognition. If Mackey writing on Victor Zuckerkandl's *Sound and Symbol* in *Jazz Cadence* was not challenging enough, now Herman Beavers looked at how N., a character in Mackey's novel *Bedouin Hornbook*, came at Zuckerkandl, too.

Jazz studies as aesthetically omnivorous cultural history had been coalescing before *Jazz Cadence* added clout. Krin Gabbard represented a path less tied to African American studies and theory, yet pursued jazz connections to other art forms and jazz narratives as "fabulation." His edited collections *Jazz Among the Discourses* and *Representing Jazz* shared such work as Bernard Gendron on debates between "moldy fig" traditionalists and modernists. Gabbard's *Jamming at the Margins* intersected jazz and movies from Jolson, *Young Man with a Horn*, and Kay Kiser to *Mo' Better Blues*; *Hotter Than That* considered trumpet players as public figures with a magician's concision. John Gennari's *Blowin' Hot and Cool* gave a deeply researched, textured overview of generations of jazz criticism whose influence on this book can be seen across multiple entries. DeVeaux's landmark *The Birth of Bebop* was subtitled *A Social and Musical History*. "To construe the bop revolution as 'anticommercial' is naive," De-Veaux wrote, unconcerned to fit the music in a jazz evolution narrative or leftist revolutionary one. He focused on Coleman Hawkins, Dizzy Gillespie, and even Woody Herman as professional musicians exploring "progressive" identities within Minton's or 52nd Street, comfortable explaining half-diminished chords or beboppers as "brash New Yorkers with an attitude." He would coauthor *Jazz* with critic **Gary Giddins**, the textbook and trade editions furthering a new incarnation of the constructed tradition he had once critiqued.

There were many ways in now. Robin D. G. Kelley, a fan of new jazz who in *Uptown Conversation* celebrated **Greg Tate** for Burnt Sugar as much as his writing, was a historian fitting music with his explorations of Black radicals. *Thelonious Monk*, a massive biography, was undertaken in part as inaugural Louis Armstrong Professor of Jazz Studies at Columbia. Theorizing was sublimated into exhumed links between Monk and fellow New York performer Julius Monk, whose great-grandfather owned Monk's in North Carolina; between Monk's Big Apple sensibility and a West 63rd Street housing complex community center. In detailing the original myth of Monk as idiot savant and "High Priest of Bebop," Kelley used jazz studies strategically. A follow-up, *Africa Speaks, America Answers*, applied similar particularity to "transnational encounters," such as Guy Warren's commercially failed deployment of Ghanaian highlife and Randy Weston's happier journey from Brooklyn to Lagos. "African American musicians were seeking new spiritual and ideological alternatives," Kelley wrote, more sympathetic to such beliefs than most white jazz critics would have been. His advisee, Eric Porter, made that contrast the basis of *What Is This Thing Called Jazz? African American Musicians as Artists, Critics, and Activists.* Sequential chapters developed a countertradition, showing how Ellington, **Mingus,** Baraka, Abbey Lincoln, and Marsalis, among others, redefined the music at different conjunctures. Porter reversed decades of jazz assumptions one case study at a time.

Another Columbia regular, Ingrid Monson, sought "a more cultural music theory and a more musical cultural theory," giving weight to topics prone to airiness. Her "The Problem with White Hipness" viewed the hipster as troubling stereotype for professional Black musicians. *Saying Something*, an ethnography of improvisation more conceptually oriented than Paul Berliner's earlier *Thinking in Jazz*, drew on such informants as clarinetist Don Byron to capture musicians' spoken language as jazzlike figuration and an "intermusicality" of references extended for cosmopolitan purposes. Detailing the conversation performed in a Freddie Hubbard recording, Monson could then decry "the poststructuralist deprecation of the 'speaking subject,' vernacular knowledge, and the phenomenal world." At Harvard, her academic title became Quincy Jones Professor of African American Music, supported by the Time Warner Endowment. *Freedom Sounds* focused on jazz's radicalization, recast to pull out the genre's embeddedness in Jim Crow; hard bop as "a blackening of modernist aesthetics"; Cold War trips to Africa (echoing Kelley and Penny Von Eschen's *Satchmo Blows Up the World*); jazz fundraising for CORE and SNCC, and debates in *Down Beat* about "Crow Jim." Monson cogently explained why many of her students remained in a pre–Black Power permanent 1962.

Along with prioritizing African American perspectives, jazz studies attacked gendered assumptions about musicianship. Both O'Meally and Griffin wrote books about Billie Holiday, and "jazz-shaped" framings took matters off the bandstand. Angela Davis's work on *Blues Legacies*, too, made Holiday's work a centerpiece. In *Swing Shift*, Sherrie Tucker, a student of Davis's, focused on "All-Girl Bands" of the 1940s. Tucker used Soundies in place of recordings and prioritized the complicated ethnicity of Willie Mae Wong of the International Sweethearts of Rhythm, billed as from San Francisco's Chinatown but actually from Mississippi; Phil Spitalny, auditioning white women in his underwear to join his saccharine House of Charm orchestra; collegiate Black Prairie View Co-Eds, born in Texas, booked by Harlem's Savoy Ballroom; the Sharon Rogers All-Girl Band, still holding reunions forty-six years later. Welcomed to the Columbia fold as another Armstrong visiting professor, Tucker coedited *Big Ears* to survey jazz studies of gender. Ingrid Monson ruminated on her blonde, blue-eyed self as Quincy Jones Professor, Jayna Brown connected dancers to Baudelaire flaneurs, and Porter reconceived jazz theorist George Russell as an Afrofuturist bound by masculinist codes. Tucker's *Dance Floor Democracy* aimed to "tangle with," not untangle, music at its most socialized, with a *Rashomon*-like telling of the "integrated" Hollywood Canteen in World War II Los Angeles, where servicemen danced with starlets, sometimes across race lines; servicewomen watched from a mezzanine; a gay 4F served drinks; and an FBI agent left notes Tucker read in redaction.

For all that jazz studies accomplished, the impulse to interrogate category worked to dissolve jazz as a useful container. **Guthrie Ramsey Jr.**'s *Race Music* instead considered African American music's "changing same," in Baraka's famous formulation, as Afromodernism—a term Monson too embraced in *Freedom Sounds*—rather than a musical genre. What would doing so mean for a "Center for Jazz Studies"? And while Dale Chapman's *The Jazz Bubble: Neoclassical Jazz in Neoliberal Culture* used the record label Verve and Bay Area club Yoshi's to explore how jazz was tied to urban renewal efforts, more needed to be done on jazz in relationship to popular music, business, and cultural institutions, elements in the genre's move toward an art music of subsidized cosmopolitanism. Yet as a bookshelf of fully formed work, as a network of funded scholarship, jazz studies had no serious rival. Columbia scholars produced the first version of popular music studies fully welcomed by the American academy.

PART VII

TOPICS IN PROGRESS

FIGURE 7.1 Cover of
José Esteban Muñoz,
*Disidentifications:
Queers of Color and
the Performance of
Politics*, 1999. Author's
collection.

———————

FIGURE 7.2 Cover
of Guthrie Ramsey Jr.,
*Race Music: Black
Cultures from Bebop to
Hip-Hop*, 2003. Author's
collection.

BLACK CULTURES FROM BEBOP TO HIP-HOP

RACE
MUSIC

"A masterwork."—*Library Journal* (starred review)

GUTHRIE P. RAMSEY, JR.

FIGURE 7.3 Cover of
Jonathan Sterne, *The
Audible Past: Cultural
Origins of Sound Repro-
duction*, 2003. Author's
collection.

———

FIGURE 7.4 Cover of
Jennifer Egan, *A Visit from
the Goon Squad*, 2010.
Author's collection.

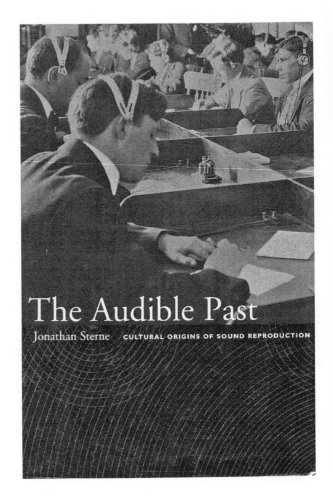

JENNIFER EGAN

A VISIT
FROM THE
GOON
SQUAD

by the author of THE KEEP

PARADIGMS OF CLUB CULTURE, HOUSE
AND TECHNO TO RAVE AND EDM

Simon Reynolds, Energy Flash: A Journey through
Rave Music and Dance Culture, *1998*

———

Suiting remix culture, there were dueling versions of this U.K. take on what became EDM, electronic dance music. *Energy Flash* was published alongside an American edition, *Generation Ecstasy*, that stressed what *Spin* and others, circa the success of groups like Prodigy and Daft Punk, called electronica. An updated *Energy Flash* mostly brought the two editions together in 2012. Reynolds, early a postpunk critic for the British weekly press, called himself a "fundamentally rockist" listener who learned to hear dance as psychedelia. He found "hardcore" dance genres such as gabber more innovative than so-called "intelligent" techno: composerly types like Autechre. Yet intellectualism applied to scenesterism was his modus operandi as he surveyed Chicago house, Detroit techno, London raves and the drug ecstasy, sampling instruments, theorists like Gilles Deleuze and Félix Guattari, and Irvine Welsh's novel *Trainspotters*. His prose reveled in nodal particulars: "The machinic, trance-inducing side of house exemplified by 'Washing Machine' took another turn in 1987, when jack tracks evolved into 'acid tracks': a style defined by a mindwarping bass sound that originated from a specific piece of equipment, the Roland TB 303 Bassline." Subgenre after subgenre agitated the narrative, a barrage the update called "the last blast of full-tilt futurism in mainstream pop culture." No distillation was more influential than this one.

But the literature took disparate forms, since reckoning with EDM, successor to hip-hop in the groove pantheon, meant considering virtual sounds, "glocal" styles, Black cultural traffic, dance via gender and sexuality, a post–physical object music business, neoliberal social networks, and academia-infiltrated undergrounds. Sarah Thornton's *Club Cultures*, published before Reynolds, researched dance culture in England as acid house emerged, participants drawing on Black U.S. sounds and decades of stylized British undergrounds. Observers and participants alike had read Dick Hebdige on subculture. Difference was no longer deviance, or dissidence; for "Thatcher's children," it meant contempt for ordinary people. Media didn't have to incorporate the underground: it now summoned it into existence. Drawing on Pierre Bourdieu's notions of cultural capital, Thornton introduced "subcultural capital"—credibility, style, and hip as fungible assets. In the chapter "Exploring the Meaning of the Mainstream (or why Sharon and Tracy Dance Around their Handbags)," Sharon and Tracy were not going to ever be cool: a function of gendered assumptions that Thornton traced to Andreas Huyssen's modernism divide and bequeathed to **Carl Wilson**'s book on Céline Dion. Hebdige thought of the mainstream as *Top of the Pops* and tabloids; for Thornton, it was no less relevant to understand how a *Time Out* listing built up a key club, how "anticommercial" was now a category of commercial. Sharon and Tracy had more company in the middle than *i-D* realized.

Kodwo Eshun's 1998 *More Brilliant Than the Sun*, attributed to "a concept engineer, an imagineer at the millennium's end," achieved cult status by emphasizing Afrofuturism, drawing on Paul Gilroy's Black Atlantic theories in a more-Reynolds-than-Reynolds language of late jazz "mutantextures" and DJ "skratchadelia." Prone to scoffing at "trad" and "confessional" U.S. cultural tendencies, Eshun's approach wielded "sonic fiction" as a form of science fiction: P-Funk cosmologies of the One linked to Fremen gathering spice in the novel *Dune*. "The unified self is an amputated self," Eshun wrote, rejecting straightforward identity politics: "By now, I've stopped saying 'Black culture.'" If whites could exoticize old bluesmen, Blacks could do the same to Kraftwerk and new wave synners, he thought. Hailing hip-hop as an "analogy engine," he proposed, amazingly: "A Flock of Seagulls are like Blind Lemon Jefferson." Eshun exaggerated tendencies present in the EDM literature from the start. Ulf Poschardt's *DJ Culture* saw a student of media theorist Friedrich Kittler take on everything from Alan Freed and disco to hip-hop, house, and Germany's Love Parade spectacle, in a kind of Hegelian herky-jerk: "critique of ideology comes to an end where political actions prove to be necessary. In the case of DJ culture, this means wherever the ghetto sets about becoming the world, erecting autonomous zones in the sphere of influence of power, or directly approaching power's mechanisms of suppression. The intellectual as Foucault saw him must then—after the most precise examination—always stand on the side of the weak and the oppressed." Poschardt became a media executive, editor of the German *Vanity Fair*. You couldn't make this shit up.

But you could retheorize it, led by Mark Fisher, Eshun's former colleague in borderline cultural studies academia (Cybernetic Culture Research Unit, or CCRU, at University of Warwick) and Reynolds's twenty-first-century blog bro under the name K-punk. Fisher conceived *Capitalist Realism*, the "no alternative" ideology of Thatcher's hard power neoliberalism and any number of cultural soft power forms, to explain why digital millennialism was not going to be an easy utopia. In *Ghosts of My Life*, and after his suicide the memorial collection *K-punk*, he clarified "hauntology": how failures of past futurisms, frozen progress, tormented everything from the vinyl crackle in Tricky and Burial albums to Al Bowlly Depression numbers revived by Dennis Potter and The Caretaker. Reynolds popularized these ideas, adding his flair for examples, in *Retromania*. Hauntology pointed out why postmodern concepts had turned, on the other side of Y2K, into gloomier readings of "ruptures, revolts, and revolutions as ghostly residue." Steve Goodman's *Sonic Warfare* used Eshun and Reynolds as well, putting the sound bombs of global militarism and problematic futurisms against global sound-system cultures and a "politics of frequency," championing electronic musics of the Black Atlantic. Robin James's *Resilience & Melancholy* put a clearer frame on these notions, treating resilience, exemplified by the "soars" of pop EDM choruses, as a "Look I Overcame" ideology of personal rebounding and neoliberal anticollectivism—akin to Naomi Klein's description of disaster capitalism, with melancholy a disruption to this "just do it" ethos. In *Sound of Culture*, Louis Chude-Sokei explored "Black Technopoetics," such as Mad Professor's 1985 dub album *A Caribbean Taste of Technology* and **William Gibson**'s use of dub in *Neuromancer*, a topic extended with a hip-hop emphasis in Roy Christopher's *Dead Precedents*.

Much of the best academic work on post-disco dance and electronic music used Thornton's approach, ethnography mixed with cultural studies mapping. Ben Malbon's *Clubbing*, Jeremy Gilbert and Ewan Pearson's *Discographies*, and Maria Pini's *Club Cultures and Female Subjectivity* all extended topics *Club Cultures* had raised, keeping a British focus. Moving to New York, Kai Fikentscher's *"You Better Work!"* considered underground dance sensibilities as a continuum from disco to house, with "the gay factor" a central element alongside questions of music, mediation, and race. (Tim Lawrence would expand this portion of our awareness with his 1980s study, *Life and Death on the New York Dance Floor*.) Targeting queer world making and performance studies theory, Fiona Buckland's *Impossible Dance* had her informants—"It was always about, let this black girl sing"—convey performative re-embodiment.

Marlon Bailey's *Butch Queens Up in Pumps* navigated Detroit ballroom culture (in the voguing sense), while Micah Salkind's *Do You Remember House? Chicago's Queer of Color Undergrounds* offered an expansive reading of dance in the context of urban gentrification, broadcast "remediation," and generation-later nostalgia. Alejandro Madrid's *Nor-tec Rifa!* told a border story of Tijuana hipsters using beats as "simulacra" to both comment on globalization and revive local elements with "third-degree kitsch." Kiri Miller's *Playing Along* and *Playable Bodies* looked at gaming culture: *Guitar Hero* and *Rock Band* in the first book, *Just Dance* and *Dance Central* in the second, noticing how notions of musicality were transformed, how issues of masculine virtuosity were blown up, how players were surveilled by their own equipment. EDM study writ large transformed ethnomusicological inquiry.

Meanwhile, EDM itself proved a multigenerational, worldwide force, prompting any number of critical-journalistic takes in the more travelogue vein of Reynolds. Dan Sicko's *Techno Rebels* was a key book on that most futuristic genre of electronification, with a particularly post-wall Berlin emphasis given by Tobias Rapp's *Lost & Sound*. Martin James's *State of Bass* centered on jungle, a U.K. style that a generation later fed into grime, covered well as a story of race and neoliberal austerity in Dan Hancox's *Inner City Pressure*. **David Toop**'s *Ocean of Sound* explored ambient chill-outs with room for Debussy. Aram Sinnreich's *Mashed Up* took on the mash-up moment of tracks recombinated across genre lines. More academically, Hillegonda Rietveld's *This Is Our House* offered a cartography of the house genre worldwide, Mark Butler's studies, *Unlocking the Groove* and *Playing with Something that Runs*, gave laptop beats their music theory due, and Oliver Julien and Christopher Levaux's edited collection, *Over and Over*, scrutinized repetition. For a study of rave fiction by the likes of Irvine Welsh and Jeff Noon, see Simon Morrison's *Dancefloor-Driven Literature*. There were memoirs written by DJs. Moby's *Porcelain* recalled the early days as a variant on punk hardcore: "I wasn't succeeding as a musician playing by rules that some old person had created." His sequel, *Then It Fell Apart*, was apparently the opposite: some old person claiming to have dated Natalie Portman. Jace Clayton's *Uproot* set a more worldly and nuanced tone: "I slipped a dancehall riddim underneath Egyptian cabdriver *chaabi*, then used a hip-hop breakbeat to bulwark Rachid Taha's remake of Dahmane El Harrachi's exile classic 'Ya Rayah.' The Lebanese contingent went wild, but a concerned Emirati came up to the booth. 'Could you play less Arabic music?' He pointed to two blond Western girls he was getting down with. Arabic language alienated them, whereas the *niggas* and *bitches* of my rap a cappellas made them want to party."

Had electronic music won, and what might that mean given its post-vernacular routes? Michaelangelo Matos's *The Underground Is Massive* reported on how EDM had finally "conquered America": twenty-five hundred shivering attendees in a horse stable one 1990s moment; "electronica" slotted as newest new wave in another; Coachella making a European festival model work domestically and unveiling Daft Punk in a 2006 pyramid. By 2011, EDM was pure party pop. David Stubbs's *Mars by 1980* savored Daft Punk instead within a lineage of electronic art experiments that sometimes sold: hip-hop producer J Dilla's *Donuts* reworking cartoon music auteur Raymond Scott's "Lightworks" in the spirit of Karlheinz Stockhausen—to Stubbs, the twentieth century's greatest composer. And Matthew Collin, author of the best Ecstasy study, *Altered State*, returned to *Rave On* as EDM generated $7 billion in 2015, $63 million to DJ Calvin Harris alone. Detroit police chief James Craig, cousin to techno legend Carl, urged people to arm themselves as the city's population dipped to twentieth in size, nationally. Berlin's Love Parade suffered a gentrification battle, like seekers/sleaze conflicts in Ibiza, or Vegas, where casinos embraced the celebrity DJ: playing house with house money. There were drug-free rave scenes to cover in China and Dubai, but also idealistic figures like Black Coffee and Spoek Mathambo in South Africa. EDM's triumph was to circulate *everything*, yet the results very much included David Guetta's "Fuck Me I'm Famous Night," homage to Bianca Jagger parading in on a white horse at 1970s disco's Studio 54. Was this the future of music or No Future at all?

PERFORMANCE STUDIES, MINORITARIAN IDENTITY, AND ACADEMIC WILDNESS

José Esteban Muñoz, Disidentifications: Queers of Color and the Performance of Politics, *1999*

———

In his second book, *Cruising Utopia*, this performance theorist recalled growing up Cuban and queer in Florida, listening to punk bands and reading *Creem* magazine. "Tony and I sit in his beige Nissan Sentra and we speculate about this band the Germs and the provocative lyrics to such songs as 'Sex Boy' and 'Ritchie Dagger's Crimes.' What can they possibly mean? we asked ourselves, already almost knowing." Muñoz faced an issue, though, noted in *Disidentifications*. The willfully racist language in "Los Angeles" of X, leading band of his favorite scene, intended as edge trimming, forced him to tactically seek punk on different terms: "we desire it but desire it with a difference." "Minoritarian subjects," queers of color at center, transformed this "failed interpellation"—Louis Althusser's concept of hailing language—to provide a counterpublic sphere. For the cover of *Disidentifications*, Muñoz used a striking image of drag performer and *Fertile LaToyah Jackson* fanzine author Vaginal Creme Davis—punker than the New York Dolls could ever be, it feels easy to write.

But explore that comparison. At about this time, **Simon Frith** was examining *Performing Rites* in conversation with zine provocateur Frank Kogan, culminating a process that took wild rock criticism by figures like **Richard Meltzer** and **Lester Bangs** into a popular music studies summation. Muñoz, meanwhile, with "Famous and Dandy Like B. 'n' Andy: Race, Pop, and Basquiat," prioritized Warhol and his hip-hop-linked artist friend rather than Pop Art and the Velvet Underground yet again. The largely straight, white, and male notion of punk as antibourgeois extremity gave scant priority to punks situated as nonnormative to begin with. In turn, the vision of punk and new wave in Muñoz and collaborators Judith/Jack Halberstam, Karen Tongson, Tavia Nyong'o, Alexandra Vazquez, Christine Bacareza Balance, Shane Vogel, Joshua Chambers-Letson, **Josh Kun**, and Drew Daniel, among others, led to a prominent academic positioning with little time for the earlier literature. When Chambers-Letson conceived *After the Party: A Manifesto for Queer of Color Life*, around "the party" as both revelry and Marx's political inheritors, he echoed unaware a similar Bangs punning on party, back in the acousticity shredding essay "James Taylor Marked for Death."

The generational difference involved language as much as identity. Disidentification authors were grounded in theory (e.g., Jean-Luc Nancy's *Being Singular Plural*). The emphasis on performance over canonization, genre, and scene meant minor figures like Vaginal Creme Davis could be stressed for staging a vibrant cultural "imaginary." Kun's book called this world making *Audiotopia*, reworking Foucault's heterotopia. Halberstam detailed *Female Masculinity* in collaboration with drag kings and the LGBTQ punk band Tribe 8, writing: "the historical bloc can easily describe an alliance between the minority academic and the minority subcultural producer." Halberstam studies of queer temporality and notions of productive failure led to tussles with longtime feminist Susan Faludi over *Gaga Feminism* ("I am not real. I am theater," Gaga had said), a context not unlike Muñoz's powerful writing on MTV *Real World* celebrity and AIDS activist Pedro Zamora in *Disidentifications*. Where a **Greil Marcus** saw punk as vernacular speech applied to millenarian ends, a shattering break, here melancholia mattered as sentiment; performativity routinized a new quotidian. Davis, to Muñoz, was an organic intellectual.

Queer of color critique was fundamentally what one of Muñoz's teachers, Eve Sedgwick, called reparative reading, uniting groups. In work initiated before his death in 2013, issued incomplete in 2020 as part of a "Perverse Modernities" book series that Halberstam coedited, Muñoz described a "brown commons," linked to a "sense of wildness," connecting social gatherings and movement cultures of many kinds. For Vazquez, this meant centering a queer of color analysis around the contours of Cuban music. Balance connected Filipino performances to the punk artistry of **Jessica Hagedorn**. Tongson sketched an Inland Empire of SoCal suburban immigrants dancing to 1980s Top 40 as queer inauguration in *Relocations*, then offered a book for her namesake, *Why Karen Carpenter Matters*. Vogel took up the Harlem cabaret of Lena Horne and the "black fad performance" of 1950s calypso. In *Disidentifications*, Muñoz evoked *choteo*, a Cuban notion of mockery to undermine authority, and *chusmería*, the refusal of bourgeois comportment, to propose as politics "a tactical refusal to keep things 'pristine' and binarized, a willful mismatching of striped and floral print genres, and a loud defiance of a rather fixed order." *Cruising Utopia* sought, instead of punk negation, a "queer futurity": Samuel Delany finding "contact zones" in sexual gatherings, Kiki and Herb tap dancing to PJ Harvey's "Rid of Me" as cabaret, and club icon and outlaw Kevin Aviance singing "Cunty" among the inspirations—Muñoz somehow connected the last to Du Bois on spirituals. He was reading **Fred Moten**, listening to Magnetic Fields sing "Take Ecstasy with Me." In the popular music scholarship of performance studies, a gesture could resonate as much as a recording, given persuasive theorizing: Francesca Royster on "eccentric" soul performers, Drew Daniel on his Germs and Throbbing Gristle punk fanship, or Daphne Brooks putting Aida Overton Walker's vaudeville on top of the bill.

A Muñoz tribute issue of *Social Text* called "Being With," multiracial punk fans crowding the stage on its cover, paid homage by stretching conceptually. Tavia Nyong'o, whose own theories of punk queerness should eventually take book form to go with his work on Frederick Douglass in *The Amalgamation Waltz* or drag legends and Delany fiction in *Afro-Fabulations*, stressed "the prioritizing of methexis over mimesis." This meant, in Muñoz's words, "how the particular participates in a larger form; in Greek tragedy it literally means group sharing, accounting for the way in which an audience takes part in a drama, adding to it, augmenting it." Lauren Berlant, a kindred theorist whose writing on sentimentality, intimate public spheres, and cruel optimism augmented

Muñoz, noted his resistance to easy identity assumptions: "what he called the 'compelled durational performances' of queer temporality involve disidentification, the constant work and play of identifying, détourning, resisting, and enjoying the scene of taking a licking." Jonathan Flatley, extending the study of Warhol farther, as in his book *Like Andy Warhol*, stressed "'liking things,' which I understand as a basic affective openness. . . . Drag practices are for Warhol not only a crucial part of this archive but, in their accumulation of likenesses, also a model for it." Halberstam recalled a book that he, Nyong'o, and Muñoz had hoped to create from their conversations, "Three Paths to the Wild," covering race, anarchy, punk, sexuality, desire. "Queer theory, too," Halberstam wrote, "must come down on the side of chaos, must remain in productive tension with 'the grotesque and the destructive,' and must stay monstrous."

LEFT OF BLACK: NETWORKING A NEW DISCOURSE

Mark Anthony Neal, What the Music Said: Black Popular Music and Black Public Culture, *1999*

———

Neal's books matured in parallel to the field he mentored so determinedly: Black writers taking over the discourse of Black music, attuned to how music came out of the Black public sphere, reflecting a post-soul sensibility conscious of how that counterpublic was constantly riven and transformed, virtual as much as actual. Also, the MAN (his preferred moniker) had great taste in records and an instinct for intersectional analysis—feminism, class, sexuality, bohemianism fomented his politics alongside race, leaving something solid even when the sentences flagged.

What the Music Said gave provisional history to the jook-to-funk and N.W.A story as "communal critique." Mentor figures such as historian Robin D. G. Kelley, critics **Nelson George** and **Greg Tate**, cultural studies theorist **Tricia Rose**, and activist-intellectual Michael Eric Dyson informed the attempted update of **Amiri Baraka**'s *Blues People*. Ahead of musicologist **Guthrie Ramsey Jr.**, eventually a close colleague, Neal stressed the Chitlin Circuit tradition and (via Farah Jasmine Griffin, a central figure in new jazz studies) "South in the city" Black migration. He picked musical elements to emphasize that white historians largely had not, like the Hammond B3 connecting hard bop to proto-soul. (Gospel scholar Ashon Crawley would return to the B3.) Neal was both researching and networking a new synthesis. His aversion to consumerism ("mass consumer culture, which stifles voices of critique and dissent") was rigid, though his take on media was more supple: records reconstructed lost social space, the studio "mimicking the diversity of communal voices." An important aspect of his writing was its pessimism. Born of postindustrial fracturing that sent the Black bourgeois off to Quiet Storm soul nostalgia in the suburbs, hip-hop repeated the sins of swing and disco. The music's critique element had "become the very spectacle that it attempts to counter."

Soul Babies, the writing loosened by columns at PopMatters.com, sought a Black postmodernism. "You Remind Me of Something: Toward a Post-Soul Aesthetic" was keyed to an epigraph from Neal's childhood friend, the pivotal hip-hop feminist Joan Morgan, on the need for literary voices as sampled, layered, and even contradictory as the music. The previous book had stressed class: now, with keyword "queer" added, "meta-identities" were explored, from Cosby and Poitier's *Uptown Saturday Night* trilogy as beginning crossover to Dave Hollister's "Baby Mama Drama" and the Black family. Neal spent two chapters on post-soul intelligentsia, with room for comedian Chris Rock, novelist Paul Beatty, and singer Jill Scott, whose phrasing "metaphorically manipulates accepted urban histories, recovering moments within those histories." *Songs in the Key of Black Life* brought more of this identity-by-identity review, astute on Alicia Keys in the symbolic hood or Laura Nyro and LaBelle as epiphany, on hip-hop "Celebrity Gramscians" and a range of "pomo bohos." Still, it was slighter than the previous volume, the appraisals odd in retrospect: Bilal revered, Beyoncé dismissed: "coyly tries to get us to believe that she is an 'independent' woman."

"What the hell is a black male feminist?" *New Black Man*, part of the rush that gave MAN four books in six years—and a move from SUNY Albany to Duke University—hinted at an answer as he confronted the elephant in the Black cultural studies room: "the performance of black masculinity continues to be the dominant creative force within hip-hop." But the book he called *New Black Man*'s "fraternal twin," *Looking for Leroy*, waited an additional eight years, in which writing such as **Fred Moten**'s *In the Break* raised the intellectual stakes, Neal's grad students circulated, and he started a webcast promoting activist scholarship, *Left of Black*. Chapters focused on Black men whose "legibility" was up for grabs: **Jay-Z**, R. Kelly, and Luther Vandross from music, Avery Brooks and Idris Elba from Hollywood, contextualized around specific performances and queerings of the gangsta/bourgeois dichotomy. A nuanced look at

Shawn Carter's hip-hop cosmopolitanism elevated the monolithic approach to commodification earlier. And the return to Kelly, a frequent Neal subject, used "Trapped in the Closet" for a history of soul singer melodrama that sought to upgrade the category of minstrelsy. Neal worked hard to seemingly riff casually.

AEROBICS AS GENRE, MANAGING EMOTIONS

Tia DeNora, Music in Everyday Life, *2000*

It may seem a modest framing when you go to Spotify and see the option to click on a section devoted to "Genres & Moods." But music sociologist Tia DeNora, writing years before the globals perfected streaming, made the same move intellectually. Yes, there were categories of sound like blues. But there were also categories like "aerobics music." We were all DJs, DeNora argued, reflexively tailoring an everyday soundtrack, using music to work a crowd of exactly one. DeNora saw music as a formal continuum: her first book, *Beethoven and the Construction of Genius*, looked with **Howard Becker** *Art Worlds* eyes at how Vienna society required a particular kind of artistic hero. After *Music in Everyday Life*, she began a multiyear project in collaboration with Gary Ansdell, studying music's use in mental health programs at St. Mary Abbots Rehabilitation and Training (SMART), leading to their *Musical Pathways in Recovery* and her separate study, *Music Asylums*. From this perspective, music was "collective, holistic, *ecological*." There was never good music, only the questions "Good for whom, where, when and how?" The SMART singers, performing "Swing Low Sweet Chariot" at a dying man's request, represented transcendence.

DeNora chose to exclusively interview women, some in the United Kingdom, some in the United States, for her late 1990s *Music in Everyday Life* ethnographies. Her account of music in relationship to aerobics, karaoke, therapy, and retail captured a shift to a view of women as managers—in the workforce, but with similar perspicaciousness as consumers handling emotions. The British arts administrator who used Schubert to regulate her mood, the therapist in upstate New York needing country radio in the morning, became DeNora's rebranding of a Paul Willis, Birmingham cultural studies motorbike boy ethnography. An aerobics mix that gave the body something to "latch" onto in the workout (Eurovision hit "Yodel in the House of Love" had never received such expert defense), retail use of George Michael to make purchasing an outfit appealing—this was music as "prosthetic," used by people conscious of "emotional stances and scenarios associated with particular physical forms—sentimentality, romance, anger, rage, calculation and so forth." DeNora's shuffled categories invited all sorts of follow-ups: we might see *Every Song Ever*, by critic Ben Ratliff, as an example. Mixing standard categories, Ratliff in a "Sadness" chapter worked from Nick Drake to metal, agreeing with Albert Murray's vernacular notion that sadness in blues was overstated but still finding in listening a form of "guarding ourselves" and in sad styles like flamenco a "consensual code."

By foregrounding sentimental rather than vernacular uses of music, DeNora found her way back to that sworn enemy of popular music, **Theodor Adorno**, looking to revitalize his legacy in *After Adorno*. She had no interest in his Schoenbergian modernist allegiances or anti-empiricism, but valued his seeing music as an "affordance structure" creating pathways for certain praxis. To DeNora, "Ted" could be used—as with his categorizing of emotional listeners—as a cartographer of musical cognition, so long as the Frankfurt School superciliousness was burned off. A more general book on sociological method, *Making Sense of Reality*, connected Adorno to the Slow Food movement— equally disgusted by the generic. For DeNora, all culture, popular included, contested and enacted reality. Rarely had the sentimental been so thoughtfully romanticized. "Thus, the 'everyday' is never 'ordinary.' It is the site where the extraordinary achievement of 'dwelling-in-the-world-with-others' is achieved. Making sense of reality is the means for that end and it can thus be seen as a form of devotion."

CONFRONTING GLOBALIZATION

Thomas Turino, Nationalists, Cosmopolitans, and Popular Music in Zimbabwe, *2000*

———

Globalization became a major music topic in the 1980s, with Paul Simon's rock-star employment of South African styles on *Graceland* and Japan's Sony introducing a portable Walkman and buying the biggest U.S. record company, Columbia. Was this story America in the world, the Black Atlantic diaspora, cultural imperialism, postmodern hybridity, or multinational neoliberalism?

As ethnomusicologists, journalists, and industry scholars grappled with the question, its dynamic shifted. By the 2010s, Psy's massive YouTube hit "Gangnam Style" and groups like BTS represented a South Korean K-Pop scene modeled on Motown or Sweden's Cheiron Studios, not authenticity driven like Cuba's revived *Buena Vista Social Club*. To encompass this expanded category, a concept emerged, represented well by Turino's take on the Thomas Mapfumo and *chimurenga* story one worldbeat nation over from South Africa: cosmopolitanism. Tied loosely to heritage, cosmopolitans networked routes instead of roots—singers and players in a planetary pop conundrum.

Fittingly, two Swedish authors—songwriter, radio presenter, and sometime academic Roger Wallis and musicologist Krister Malm—gave world music its first signature study, *Big Sounds from Small Peoples* (1984). With glimpses of such figures as "Sri Lanka's cassette king," Atu Moolchand, the duo identified with a global industry confronting piracy, imminent digitalization, and possible new markets: "Island Records, for instance, created a lot of its wealth by exploiting reggae, notably the work of Bob Marley. Island are now looking very closely to Africa." David Coplan, trained in ethnomusicology by Alan Merriam, published *In Township Tonight!* Soon read by *Graceland* fans, its vernacular emphasis idealized Sophiatown, the integrated Johannesburg neighborhood "giving urban African culture its pulse, rhythm, and style during the 1940s and '50s . . . a slum of dreams, a battleground of the heart." Christopher Waterman's ethnography of *juju*, urban Nigerian pop whose amplification arguably enhanced tribal Yoruba values, and Jocelyne Guilbaut's work on *zouk*, an Antillean style, applied methods reserved for non-pop categories. Peter Manuel surveyed *Popular Musics of the Non-Western World*, then innovated with *Cassette Culture*, using India to capture the democratizing and "folk" blurring effects of technology.

Debates about worldbeat as cultural studies energized upper-echelon ethnomusicology. Mark Slobin's *Subcultural Sounds* contrasted transnational "superculture" with continent-shrinking (soon, internet) "interculture." **Charles Keil** and **Steven Feld**'s *Music Grooves* staged a cross-generational conversation. Veit Erlman's *Music, Modernity, and the Global Imagination* put *Graceland* in the context of music "bracketing new time-space arrangements," culture as constant displacement, and Ladysmith Black Mambazo's collaborations with Paul Simon put in contrast to their work with a Black star, Michael Jackson. Timothy Taylor engaged the question longest, alert to specifics and skeptical of marketing rhetoric. *Global Pop* was a 1990s take: caught up in hybridities, itemizing authenticities. A decade after, *Beyond Exoticism* placed globalization against earlier colonialism and imperialism, corporate against feudal and state, turning his approach on marketing and taste. *Music and Capitalism*, still later, centered on neoliberal globalization strategies—branding, for instance.

Turino's book, the most sustained mix of research and theory to that point, surveyed Zimbabwe from the 1930s to 1990s, asking: "How *do* you get people who did not use money or think of music making as acoustic labor one hundred years ago to shape their aesthetics, music, and dance so as to compete more effectively in mass-national and transnational markets?" He saw an emergent musical professionalism, centered on "cosmopolitan loops" and alliances, as pivotal to the answer. Africans did not set aside nationalism, but postcolonial leadership came from a cosmopolitan class that in different eras valued assimilation, then racial pride; a seemingly folk instrument, the mbira (thumb piano) grew stature in urban performances as an invented tradition not unlike bluegrass. Many moves reacted to the United States. Dorothy Masuka learned from Ella Fitzgerald. Mapfumo, the country's Marley figure, began as a rock and roller. Strongman Robert Mugabe's party, ZANU, used chimurenga first to rework known songs with new messages. Mapfumo's electrified mbira fusion owed to former villagers supporting urban clubs, not unlike Muddy Waters in Chicago. And his postindependence worldbeat status created further fusions. One had to investigate these conjunctures, Turino concluded, not assume outcomes. Still, his own preferences, revealed in the later book *Music as Social Life*, were for participatory music practices more than the record and concert world's "presentational" ones.

Extending Turino, endlessly readable journalist Banning Eyre gave the global pop case study what might be called a compound view: situated in the ramshackle live-work world of performers. *In Griot Time*, recounting a guitar apprenticeship in Mali with Djelimady Tounkara, found inspiration in John Miller Chernoff's *African Rhythms and African Sensibility*: "you must immerse yourself in the social world that produced it, a world that encompasses ideas, beliefs, rituals, and values." But that world now included the Cuba flight Tounkara missed, which meant that Ry Cooder played guitar on the *Buena Vista* sessions. Eyre documented postrevolutionary Africa; worldbeat minutiae; mysterious funders; media programs like *Top Étoiles*; a different cassette pirate king (Kalwani, a Liberia and Sierra Leone–based Pakistani); and charismatic figures such as Oumare Sangaré crisscrossing the sleepy Malian scene. Tounkara made a James Brown guitar part a Wassoulou hit for his Rail Band. Eyre, whose next project, *Lion Songs*, tracked Mapfumo from Harare to Oregon, gave the great bandleader a Tounkara riff that fueled a hit in Zimbabwe. Called to jot down musicking as best a white traveler could, Eyre didn't theorize globalization so much as wince and hold the exchange's loose currency, an invested cosmopolitan.

In the books that followed Turino and Eyre's, cosmopolitans were every-where: freewheeling visionaries and intemperate cogs in a nexus extracting value from difference. Israeli sociologist Motti Regev's *Pop-Rock Music: Aesthetic Cosmopolitanism in Late Modernity* provided an overview text, competing modernities shown through a rock prism; similarly, Simone Varriale's *Globalization, Music and Cultures of Distinction* gave Bourdieu-style taste analysis to Italian pop-rock music criticism, as weekly publications "crafted an economic cosmopolitanism that magnified 'modern' promotional and commercial practices." Michael Denning's *Noise Uprising* used the global pop outburst that followed electric recording in the 1920s to supply globalization's port town and working-class origin story. Michael Bull's *Sound Moves* found the iPod device "sounding out cosmopolitanism"—via shuffle? **Lise Waxer**'s *City of Musical Memory* studied vinyl revivalists in Columbia, echoed later by Richard Shain's *Roots in Reverse* on the "tropical cosmopolitanism" of Cuban music–loving Senegalese: "extensive overlapping networks in Dakar that went well beyond the walls of a music club or recording studio, taking in the realms of academia, the media, politics, commerce, and government." Describing Senegal too, Catherine Appert's *In Hip Hop Time* called rappers there "cosmopolitan subjects who consciously engage, and at times subvert, global narratives." Timothy Taylor was not convinced, wondering in *Beyond Exoticism* why global pop discourse centered on aesthetic elites. Alex Perullo's *Live from Dar es Salaam* answered that in a way, centered on Tanzania with a blurb from that nation's Marley figure, Remmy Ongala. Perullo sketched the full music economy of a nation left outside the record industry, like NGO-sponsored events supplanting neoliberal government withdrawal; he saw the city itself as inherently "cosmopolitan, offering youth a chance to be part of worldly ideas, aesthetics, beliefs, and characteristics."

Global pop had seemed, at the tail end of the era of countercultural vernacular, like rock around the whole world's clock. Now, hip-hop took over, an international youth music dismissive of white appropriators and strategically bordered: "glocal" was one term found in such studies as Tony Mitchell's collection *Global Noise*, Eric Charry's anthology *Hip Hop Africa*, and Ian Condry's study *Hip-Hop Japan*. Michael Fuhr's *Globalization and Popular Music in South Korea* began with three vignettes: lines of fans hoping to attend a K-Pop version of MTV's *Total Request Live*; the screens that suffused Seoul; and German fans like himself, using the internet to learn about these new pop sounds from afar. "These phenomena are, however, neither simple copies of Western originals nor the product of single-sided Western cultural imperialism," Fuhr wrote with noteworthy blandness. "They do not represent any Korean cultural essence (or its loss), but are rather the source and the result of ongoing and entwined processes of homogenization and heterogenization, of transnational and multi-directed flows and their tensions, and of disjunctures in circuits of production and consumption."

To what extent was unexamined cosmopolitanism, including versions writ academic, a new iteration of cultural imperialism? With *Modernity's Ear*, Roshanak Kheshti supplied an ethnography of a Bay Area world music label, using Vampire Weekend's Ezra Koenig among others to represent a process of neoliberalization of sonic cultures that she called an "aural imaginary." Hybridity hype met miscegenation tension—the ghost of **Zora Neale Hurston** keeping score. Meanwhile, Martin Stokes's *Republic of Love* applied U.S. theorist Lauren Berlant's ideas of intimate publics to pop in Turkey, moving through generations to capture a queer nightclub singer, *arabesk* originator, and pop diva showcasing ambivalences of Turkishness. Louise Meintjes's *Sound of Africa!* went into a South African recording studio to see music made Zulu. David Novak's *Japanoise* explored "a global music scene forged in circulation," those exchanges not between cultures but constituting them, as a Merzbow used massive feedback to serve humanistic critique. Global pop had become an inevitability; whether cosmopolitanism could vet the impact seemed far from clear.

EVOCATIONS OF CULTURAL MIGRATION CENTERED ON RACE, RHYTHM, AND EVENTUALLY SEXUALITY

Alejo Carpentier, Music in Cuba, *2001 (1946)*

———

"In 1776, a fleet from Europe that had made a long stopover in Havana took some immigrants of 'broken color' to Veracruz. These foreigners brought a Cuban dance called *El Chucumbé*, which immediately became an extraordinary success. The riffraff of this maritime city began dancing this sweet Antillean novelty with the greatest of joy." The vignette was one of many that radio producer, novelist, Surrealist crony, and music critic Carpentier gleaned from primary source documents while returned to Cuba during World War II. Brand it the literature of Cuban music in microcosm: episodic, hugely evocative, a cultural migration centered on race and rhythm, and a challenge—check that year again—to the pop centrality of a country scant miles away that called itself America. It took over a half-century to publish this template in an English edition; others then fleshed out what it hinted at, with Ned Sublette to index the motions and Alexandra Vazquez to savor the details. But more, like Carpentier's sixteen-volume *Obras*, awaited translation.

The author of *Music in Cuba* critiqued "a provincial desire to downplay the importance of black legacies that have greatly contributed to the character of Cuban music." A thousand Africans were on the island by 1534; a song that century, "Son de Ma' Teodora," troped on chopping wood to link parties and percussive guitars. By 1840, as Haiti's revolt relocated the sugar plantations, Blacks dominated professional music. *Danzon, rumba, son*, and other resulting styles won international acclaim though African influences were disclaimed at home, and young composers like Nicolas Espadero accepted European norms even as the blackface minstrelsy *teatro bufo* perpetuated "slum and lowlife mythology." In Carpentier's day, a movement hailing Afro-Cubanism emerged, chastising a dictator-prone republic that banned carnival practices. **Josh Kun**'s *Audiotopia* devoted a chapter to its parallels with the Harlem Renaissance and especially Langston Hughes. Roberto González Echevarría, in the best literary biography of Carpentier, translated a Hughes collaborator, poet Nicolás Guillén: "Europe's going naked / to tan her flesh in the sun, /and prowls Havana and Harlem / for jazz and *son*." Fernando Ortiz was another central figure, theorizing not acculturation but transculturation, a more thorough hybridity, and Cuba as a place where all had "been torn from their place of origin." Carpentier, a Cuban who spoke with a French accent, understood such hybridity as the height of modernism, beyond anything an André Breton could simulate in a parlor game. He strategically delineated bandleaders, Paul Whiteman lesser to the "rhythmic force" of **Duke Ellington**. With the music's brutal genealogy in his head ("A black woman is sold with a group of musical instruments and furniture"), he wrote his first great novel, *The Kingdom of This World*. Its preface named a "marvelous real," a Black Atlantic "patrimony of all the Americas," that birthed Latin American magic realism.

Kingdom, published without the preface, flopped in its 1950s U.S. translation. Havana casinos, mambos, *I Love Lucy*, and perhaps "Latin jazz" made up Cuba in the postwar American imagination, then Castro triumphed in 1959 and even that figment ended too—embargoed. John Storm Roberts, a British expatriate versed in African sounds, became the U.S. champion of *Black Music of Two Worlds* and *The Latin Tinge*, assuredly linking *habanera* to blues, salsa to bugalú and the Puerto Rican–Cuban continuum. But Ned Sublette, a Texan in the New York experimental scene and, like Roberts, an early world music record label entrepreneur, supplied the weightiest pre-Castro history. *Cuba and Its*

Music arrayed vignettes as did Carpentier, but for six hundred pages and with more fact checking: that song about "Ma' Teodora" was pronounced an invention. If Carpentier one-upped European avant-gardes, Sublette called Cuba the most rock-and-roll country on the planet, epicenter of the Dionysian his friend **Robert Palmer** honored. Shakespearean drums, turn of the seventeenth century Panamanian *zarabanda*, eighteenth-century New Orleans as extension of Havana, nineteenth-century *contradanza*: Sublette tracked it all, finding contemporaneity in every archive. Afro-Cuban religious folklorist Lydia Cabrera, Ortiz's counterpart in anchoring Carpentier, rooted Sublette's drumlore, too. He tracked rumba over to the Congo, located the *trovadora* (song poets) of early recordings, made the case for jazz, blues, samba, tango, and son as a modernism defined by liberating Black creativity. Yet *soneros* still had to hide their drums from the cops, even as Don Apiazu's "El Manisero" (The Peanut Vendor) broke globally in 1930. This story culminated with Arsenio Rodriguez, "the most important single figure of Cuban music in the twentieth century," as the drum broke free and mambos rocked the United States. Sublette's "To be continued" stopped in 1952; we await the sequel.

A burst of work exploring dimensions of "Cuban music" (salsa books have a separate entry below) made even Sublette's scope restrictive, as scholars gave portions full book treatment and used cultural studies methods he shunned. Robin Moore's *Nationalizing Blackness* had already revisited Carpentier, Ortiz, and Cabrera's work on race and nation, noting cross pulls of racist anti-Blackness and nationalist racial exoticism. His *Music and Revolution* moved ahead to a Castro regime that associated pop with the Batista regime; once again, Afro-Cuban folklore met official disapproval. Raul Fernandez's *From Afro-Cuban Rhythms to Latin Jazz* offered a brisk 1990 overview; Leonardo Acosta's *Cubano Be Cubano Bop* a Cuban player-scholar's informed account; and David García's *Arsenio Rodríguez and the Transnational Flows of Latin Popular Music* a detailed musicology. Christina Abreu's *Rhythms of Race* followed Cuban musicians to New York and Miami from 1940 to 1960, giving Desi Arnaz and his bandleader Marco Rizo attention alongside Machito and Mario Bauzá—opposite sides of a Cuban race divide. Marc Perry's *Negro Soy Yo* tracked Cuban hip-hop cohering during the national crisis of the 1990s, as darker-skinned Cubans dealt with the introduction of a dollar economy on one side, a Cuban Rap Agency on the other. Benjamin Lapidus's *Changüí* made the Guantanamo origins of a *son* subgenre akin, in blues terms, to Mississippi purism, proving yet again the dynamism of Cuban music culture. "For about a century before the revolution of 1959, hereinafter called stage one, a changüí was a rural party at which participants consumed large quantities of rum, ate roasted pigs, danced, and engaged in musical duels (controversias) which included treseros (tres players) as well as trovadores (improvising singers)."

The danger was that Cuba's migrating musical legacy could become more catalog than inspiration. If Carpentier augured a literature sounding power at the intersection of Europe and the Black Atlantic, a different variant worked from gender, dance, and the proximate United States. Presiding as a literary figure was Guillermo Cabrera Infante, a novelist and critic a generation younger. Infante's *Three Trapped Tigers* located its narrative in the Batista years and Havana casino culture, punning culturally on American English rather than Carpentier's French: the patriarch, along with folklorist Cabrera and poet Guillén, was parodied in the heavily satiric novel. Infante had been driven out of Cuba for his unwillingness to decouple left politics from sexual experimentation and U.S. pop modernity. Alma Guillermoprieto, in *Dancing with Cuba*, remembered a trip she took to teach Merce Cunningham and Martha Graham dance classes in 1970 as a moment of dueling radicalisms. She found on the island a common line: "The fun is over! The Comandante arrived and ordered it to stop!" The prevailing sentiment was "that in Batista's time, a mafioso, Meyer Lansky, stuck his nose in here and succeeded in transforming Cuba into a Yankee whorehouse . . . the rumba and prostitution were the same thing." Great gay writer Lezama Lima had become little read, while Carpentier was "almost a national hero."

Alexandra Vazquez's *Listening in Detail* gave queered Cuba scholarly shape, beginning with cabaret singer Ignacio Villa, aka Snowball, who performed with a singular intimacy. Vazquez prized that example because: "Totalizing attempts to define what and who Cuba is have long inspired possessive attachments to it." Rather than Carpentier, her ancestor of choice was his book's uncredited researcher, Natalio Galán, whose *Cuba y sus sons* remained untranslated. A dancer and gay man, "Galán has the nonsensical, magical, and illegible accompany the scholarly register." Vazquez put female performers such as Graciela, sister of Machito, at her center, but also such commercial features as the omnipresent grunt of mambo king Perez Prado. Her chapter "Cold War Kids" compared her experiences with those of other Cubans, Koreans, and Vietnamese born in the United States to immigrant parents, locating the book's origins in a DVD she watched of the post-Castro Cuban band Los Van performing in her hometown, Miami. Her key question remained only partly answered: "What do Cuba and the United States have to do with each other?"

DIGGING UP THE PRE-RECORDINGS CREATION OF A BLACK POP PARADIGM

Lynn Abbott and Doug Seroff, Out of Sight: The Rise of African
American Popular Music, 1889–1895, *2002*

———

Independent scholars—Abbott living in New Orleans and soon to work at the
Hogan Jazz Archive, Seroff just outside Nashville—this team was the truest
heir to librarian **Dena Epstein**, turning musty descriptive literature into active
history. Even Epstein had abjured newspaper digging, fearing it would swal-
low her up, but Abbott and Seroff confronted the nineteenth-century Black
press on microfilm to trace the years that saw Jim Crow segregation ratified
exactly as ragtime crossed over. They saw their approach as "document-driven":
rather than assert an interpretive frame, the duo divided the book by individual year, emphasized long quotes from exhumed sources, and put material that
didn't fit loose categories into twelve-month miscellanies. Covering a period
largely missed by records, they made the printed description a form of musical reproduction. Chris Ware, the brilliant cartoonist who brought insights
on the period into his occasional zine *The Ragtime Ephemeralist* and graphic
novel *Jimmy Corrigan,* designed a retronuevo front and back cover. This, along
with the acoustic recordings reissue label Archeophone and David Wondrich's
Stomp and Swerve, generated a curatorial scene: vintage pop restored, even
given a new set of teeth, by hobbyists and outsiders.

Like Epstein, Abbott and Seroff made undertold Black narratives their
focus. Frederick Loudin was a hero of *Out of Sight,* outspoken on civil rights as
he led the Fisk Jubilee Singers through Australia, India, Japan, and China, telling Detroit's *Plaindealer* he had to leave the United States to feel his true manhood. Spiritual singing was a global hit (a protégé of Loudin's in South Africa
set a pathway for Ladysmith Black Mambazo), and operatic performers such as
"Black Patti" (Sisserietta Jones), Flora Batson, and Marie Selika were welcomed
to the White House. But minstrelsy with Black performers proved dominant.
Long before **Duke Ellington** tried it, Pullman cars took Richards and Prin-
gle's Georgia Minstrels, starring Billy Kersands, through the South. William
Foote's Afro-American Specialty Company had a modernism that would lead
to Broadway revues. Sam T. Jack's Creole Burlesque welcomed Black women.
In time, the opera singers and Dvořák student Harry Burleigh joined, too. At
the 1893 Columbian Exposition, Loudin's sponsorship of Ida Wells's anti-fair
pamphlet and the belly dancing and Dahomean Midway pushing high culture
"out of sight" meant ragtime as contested conjuncture was inevitable. Whites

FIGURE 7.5: Cover of Lynn Abbott and Doug Seroff, *Out of Sight: The Rise of African American Popular Music, 1889–1895*. Art and design by Chris Ware, an important comics artist who often wrote about the ragtime era. Author's collection.

insisted on travesty; Blacks sought uplift from the vernacular rendered spectacular. And so, a theme park in Brooklyn called Black America. A "rag" dance out of Kansas, called Possum a Loa or Pas Ma La, popularized by Ernest Hogan before his "All Coons Look Alike to Me." Black Patti Troubadours shaping future blues queens.

In subsequent volumes, Abbott and Seroff continued to link African American musical genres (defined in calcified ways by record collectors and genre specialists) with profoundly disruptive intersections of economic, social, and cultural capital. Their gospel quartets book, *To Do This, You Must Know How*, turned on musical instruction, from Fisk University to Birmingham proletariat. *Ragged but Right*, closer to a sequel to *Out of Sight*, and *The Original Blues*, rounding out a trilogy, gave particular weight to the first Black music critic, Sylvester Russell, and to performer reports from the road. Where a **Lawrence Levine** saw folk transference, this view stressed the musical comedy revues that raised and frustrated expectations in the coon song era of late 1890s through 1910, then the vaudeville theaters across the South that launched blues professionally in the 1910s. The *Smart Set* tours of Ernest Hogan, Salem Tutt Whitney, and Sherman Dudley were in a continuum with tented minstrel shows like *Silas Green from New Orleans* and the eventual Theater Owners Booking Association chitlin circuit. Blind Lemon Jefferson, model of seemingly folk-derived country blues, actually utilized a guitar lick taken from Butler "String Beans" May, aka the Elgin Movements man, diamond inlaid in a gold tooth, whose smash success in Chicago in 1911 brought "the full force of southern vernacular entertainment" to the big city. Whitney complained: "What is the use of creating a sketch that makes an intelligent appeal and have it a 'frost,' while another actor may sing the 'Blues,' 'Ball the Jack,' tell a smutty joke or make a ridiculous reference to racial characteristics and be the hit of the bill?" Russell, who merits his own anthology, had a rejoinder: "This low life phase of music which has electrified the world is better performed by degraded southern Negroes than by the best stage artists in existence."

WHEN FAITH IN POPULAR SOUND WAVERS, HE'S WAITING

Theodor Adorno, Essays on Music, *ed. Richard Leppert, 2002*

———

The Frankfurt School's fiercest writer attacked the "culture industry" ("Dialectic of Enlightenment," with Max Horkheimer), and jazz specifically as "pseudoindividuation" and perennial fashion. His was the thumbs-down position in that undergrad anthology staple, the debate with Walter Benjamin over art in the era of mechanical reproduction. But Adorno provided much of the template for how to apply critical theory to music, how to look for structures that governed the choices available sonically or artistically regardless of what got picked and played. His implacable resistance to claims that commercial culture could be liberatory resonated at the end of the twentieth century—one scholar, Colin Campbell, compared him to the indiest of rock bands, Fugazi. But his travail chimed with popular music intellectuals: caught between categories and funding sources, his favorite form the essay driven by "negative dialectics." Topics included *L.A. Times* astrology columns, NBC radio music appreciation programming, and Beckett's *Endgame. Minima Moralia*, short writing done in

U.S. exile from the Holocaust, "may be," as **Greil Marcus** put it, "the gloomiest book ever written." Novelist Thomas Mann took his musical passages on atonality for *Doctor Faustus* and set him in the text as a devil.

Leppert's anthology of some of the music work (he estimated it at four thousand pages of Adorno's ten thousand overall), gave balance to an aphorist of sorts who declared, "The splinter in your eye is the best magnifying glass," and felt: "A successful work is not one which resolves objective contradictions in a spurious harmony, but one which expresses the idea of harmony negatively by embodying the contradictions, pure and uncompromised in its innermost structures." Taught music by Arnold Schoenberg's student Alban Berg, Adorno (1903–69) brought fatalistic sentimentality to the subject, akin to the mysticism of friends Benjamin and Gershom Scholem but more resigned: "It is demythologized prayer, freed from the magic of making anything happen." New music, in its break with convention, represented one of two choices for all music, accepting commodification or accepting marginalization. "The differences in the reception of official 'classical' music and light music no longer have any real significance." Radio symphonies of Beethoven were "the promotion of musical Babbitry." Toscanini embraced the star system. Fascists used folk rhetoric. The legacy: "Nobody really believes in 'culture' anymore, the backbone of spirit has been broken."

Popular culture was too shackled to provide an alternative, from the Hays Office regulating U.S. movie content to Tin Pan Alley how-to's making musical formulas apparent. Adorno recognized structural shifts: "The Form of the Phonograph Record." But he could not hear vernacular voices on those records, writing in 1932 that there was "no longer any 'folk' whose songs and games could be taken up" and specifying of jazz: "The apparent improvisations of hot music are totally the expression of set norms." By 1936, in "On Jazz," he deliberately set to puncture claims of a pop aligned with Cubism and other modernisms, scorning its adherents ("jazz is 'urbane,' and thanks to it, the white-collar employee can feel superior when he sits with his girlfriend in a beer hall"), its sponsored populism ("The more democratic jazz is, the worse it becomes"), and very much its racial meaning: "that the public clamors for 'black jazz' as a sort of brand-name doesn't say much . . . the skin of the black man functions as much as a coloristic effect as does the silver of the saxophone." **Duke Ellington**, he believed after a poor reading of sources, wanted to be Claude Debussy. Later essays extended the bashing: the young swing jitterbug "mummifies the vulgarized and decaying remnants of romantic individualism," the straight pop "composition hears for the listener."

Many subsequent commentators tried to amend Adorno. Music professor Max Paddison, giving a full book to *Adorno's Aesthetics of Music*, saw him as forerunner of such semipopular performers as Frank Zappa, Carla Bley, and Henry Cow. Richard Middleton, in *Studying Popular Music*, thought he simply missed half the story: "shockingly ebullient, vernacular, everyday *noise*." For **Simon Frith**, writing in *Sound Effects*, Adorno's value was precisely his litmus test: "challenging for anyone claiming even a scrap of value for the products that come churning out of the music industry." Sociologist **Tia DeNora**'s *After Adorno* saw value in his ontology: "how music's *formal properties* evinced modes of praxis that in turn were related to, and could inculcate modes of, consciousness." For critic Joshua Clover in "Good Pop, Bad Pop," Adorno's awareness of different temporalities in music could be turned upside down for Top 40 theorizing.

There may still be a weirder Adorno to formulate, drawing on works released in full English editions only this century. His early U.S. tenure at Paul Lazarsfeld's Radio Research Project, collected as *Current of Music*, produced early media studies with a critical edge that cost him the gig. David Jeneman's *Adorno in America* captured him providing hopeless notes, after relocating to Los Angeles, to director William Dieterle on the movie *Syncopation*, showing more facility with jazz than he otherwise let on and fantasizing a "satanic concert" of sorts in a record shop. *Dream Notes* offered a running diary through decades of his night imagination: "I danced with a giant yellowish-brown Great Dane—as a child such a dog had been of great importance in my life. He walked on his hind legs and wore evening dress. I submitted entirely to the dog and, as a man with no gift for dancing, I had the feeling that I was able to dance for the first time in my life, secure and without inhibition. Occasionally, we kissed, the dog and I. Woke up feeling extremely satisfied." His conclusions about those who read astrology were generous, heavy artillery reserved for middle-class liberals espousing authenticity—as in *Minima* #99, an acute defense of artifice. Adorno could never bring to an **Armstrong** what he could to a Mahler or a Kafka. But he was a mutilated giant, sentimental himself about the "touching but impotent Utopian moment," intent to "estrange the world."

CODIFYING A PRECARIOUS BUT GLOBAL
ACADEMIC FIELD

David Hesmondhalgh and Keith Negus, eds., Popular Music Studies, *2002*

By the twenty-first century, **Simon Frith**, the International Association for the Study of Popular Music (IASPM), and the journal *Popular Music*, all based in England, had spawned an ongoing if ever precarious subfield. Popular music studies—essentially cultural studies of popular music—was interdisciplinary, though sociology and media studies were overrepresented. *The Cambridge Companion to Pop and Rock*, edited by Frith with Will Straw and John Street, and *The Popular Music Studies Reader*, edited by Andy Bennett, Barry Shank, and Jason Toynbee, joined Hesmondhalgh and Negus's volume as summations of a field that turned on articles and anthologies as much as authored volumes. An alertness to power dynamics, favoring of postmodern hybridities, and case studies ranging modernity characterized these writers, equally at home with Rough Trade Records and Pierre Bourdieu.

Popular Music Studies coeditor Negus, also central editorially to *Popular Music*, represented the subfield well. A musician turned sociologist, he asked really good questions. *Producing Pop*, a study of the British record business, disclaimed academic and journalistic "cynicism" to stress conflicts between those trying to profit creatively more than the "romance" of indie oppositions between commerce and aesthetic. It also showcased rockism, not a word he used, in the overemphasis in sexist and racist A&R circles on signing cool bands and cutting them slack. *Popular Music in Theory* centered on processes of mediation. Best of all, *Music Genres and Corporate Cultures* took the project to the United States, where Negus examined hip-hop selling as "streets" met corporate suites and majors deploying "portfolio management" kept indies as pets; where country politics turned out to be industry politics for Nashville in a world of multinationals; where salsa was a failed corporatization. If **Richard Peterson** and his peers had offered the production of culture to sociology, Negus danced that mess around, delineating what he called cultures of production.

Many in popular music studies found a similar vantage: someplace between rock critic ballyhoo and **Theodor Adorno**'s cultural theory despair, as conjuncturally focused as Birmingham Centre writers but more adept at texturing musical spheres. Hesmondhalgh, Negus's coeditor on *Popular Music Studies*, also coedited *Western Music and Its Others* with former Henry Cow member Georgina Born. He used his solo research for shrewd commentary on indie culture, then came to prominence with *The Cultural Industries,* a global survey that took up McDonaldization with the dispatch of the English explainer, Raymond Williams to Terry Eagleton. He'd return to the study of songs, noting fallen belief in the vernacular, with *Why Music Matters.* Will Straw, never publishing his dissertation on the mid-1970s to mid-1980s music industry, made an impact with articles: "Systems of Articulation" conceptualized scenes as supplement to subcultures and dance scenes as challenge to rock. Jason Toynbee's *Making Popular Music* took up cultures of production from performer perspectives, a view of "social authorship" theorizing open-ended commercialism while retaining left beliefs; he'd apply this to a notable study of Bob Marley's shaping by the postcolonial music industry represented by Island Records. Keir Keightley's "Reconsidering Rock" was a highlight of *The Cambridge Guide,* delineating modernist authenticity and romantic authenticity; he went on to hi-fi systems and gender, LPs and song standards as taste formations, and Tin Pan Alley as tinny anti-Victorianism. Barry Shank gave a detailed history of the Austin music scene across generations in *Dissonant Identities.* He then archived a college radio pantheon, from Velvet Underground and Yoko Ono to Moby, to absorb the theories of Jean-Luc Nancy and Jacques Rancière in his probing study, *The Political Force of Musical Beauty.*

Recruiting diverse U.S. authors and subjects remained a challenge for the field, *Journal of Popular Music Studies* and IASPM-US notwithstanding, but the globalism was a leap forward. *Popular Music Studies* included one look at African American music, David Brackett on mainstream crossover ("Billie Jean") versus R&B success only ("Atomic Dog"). Even this, noting majors treating Black music worlds "like a colony," played to the collection's postimperialist address. The book's stated theme was "meaning, power and value." A study of Black South African men, responding to apartheid by marginalizing Black women from music, flowed into "Girl from Ipanema" as Brazilian song model and Australian hip-hop scholarship. Jocelyne Guilbaut, the only author in all three of the framing collections mentioned above, wrote about calypso as low-budget politics. Black music was "exterior to the inner self" in Japan, an undertheorized aspect of Moti Regev's global "pop-rockization," later a book.

In the U.S., popular music studies methods of academic scholarship would soon be rivalled by historical approaches that required monograph length; sound studies theories that questioned the centrality of popular music; and an African American scholarship IASPM never successfully courted, which emerged instead in jazz and hip-hop studies. *Popular Music* moved its center from sociology to musicology; Negus changed departments, too. What did not change was the emphasis on collections of articles, augmented by a British and increasingly European academic system that disfavored books, leading to Handbooks and Companions galore for yearly research accounting to university bean-counters. This made popular music studies seem, at times, more entrenched and established than if you browsed the biographies of its too-often nontenured scholars. Popular music studies endured because it needed to, forever undervalued, an Anglo-originated echo of Americanization writ planetary.

SALSA AND THE MIXINGS OF GLOBAL CULTURE

Lise Waxer, City of Musical Memory: Salsa, Record Grooves, and Popular Culture in Cali, Colombia, *2002*

———

Waxer, an ethnomusicologist self-described as a Canadian of Chinese and Jewish origins, researched salsa—originally a 1970s New York–centered scene of primarily Puerto Ricans reworking Cuban *son*, but in this case salsa in Cali, Columbia, where a cosmopolitan culture had built up around old records. *Situating Salsa*, to take a phrase from the edited collection she published the same year (which saw her die at thirty-seven from sudden illness), required such intertwining of sound, time, and identity. Salsa's heyday preceded academic study and work written in Spanish was sporadically translated. The writing itself became a genre of musical memory, approaches and backgrounds mixed like the performers.

As salsa first emerged, Fania Records showcased the scene it sold with the movie *Nuestra Cosa*, John Storm Roberts made letters of recommendation in his pioneering studies *Black Music of Two Worlds* and *Latin Tinge*, and world music videographers Hannah Charlton and Jeremy Marres used interview material for the documentary *Salsa* and documentary-plus-book *Beats of the Heart*. A more comprehensive exploration, akin to **Charlie Gillett** on rock and roll or **Bill Malone** on country music, was *The Book of Salsa*, by César Miguel Rondón, a Venezuelan radio journalist focused on the best performances and not rigid on authenticity. Sociologist and mambo fan Vernon Boggs collected journalism, scholarship, and interviews into the grab bag *Salsiology*. There, Juan Flores, later to trace Puerto Rican sound in the book *From Bomba to Hip-Hop*, contrasted subcultural *cocolos* (salsa teens) and *rockeros*.

Salsa studies fully arrived in the 1990s, when cultural studies did, Deborah Pacini Hernandez providing a template with her book on *Bachata* and then, most pivotally, Frances Aparicio's *Listening to Salsa*. Aparicio, later to translate Rondón, came to salsa as a different kind of outsider. A middle-class academic and feminist with Puerto Rican roots, she approached the genre as "personal decolonization" and a chance to query "male gaze and authority." Her book actively used literary writing by Rosario Ferré and Luis Rafael Sanchez to vivify Puerto Rican conceptions of music, race, gender, and class: "The guaracha is the vibrating hunt. The bolero is the feast of the hunter and hunted." She brought in ethnographies of listeners, a la Janice Radway on romance readers, and employed the theories of Mikhail Bakhtin on the dialogic to rebuke **Theodor Adorno**'s dismissal of commodified culture, echoing James Snead's "Repetition as a Figure of Black Culture" to argue for musical pop tropes as anticolonialism. Above all, her focus was gender, from performers to women fans in the emotional economies of working-class communities.

Listening to Salsa's text declared, unusually, an eager anticipation of the completion of Waxer's then dissertation project; Aparicio's later multiauthor collection *Musical Migrations* would be dedicated to her memory. But where Aparicio worked from the likes of **Stuart Hall** and Lawrence Grossberg, Waxer's adviser was ethnomusicologist **Thomas Turino**, who in such important books as *Nationalists, Cosmopolitans, and Popular Music in Zimbabwe* and the later *Music as Social Life: The Politics of Participation* pursued a notion of non-elite cosmopolitanism. Waxer explored how a city on the Caribbean coast had branded itself "world capital of salsa," downplaying localized folk sounds for a record-centered dance scene of retro "viejotecas" linked back to "musica antillana" brought by sailors to red-light districts—the perfect imaginary for a community of migrants to urban life. She provided evocative ethnography of "Life in the Vinyl Museum," attentive to collector subcultures and a live scene that produced the internationally recognized Grupo Niche, "company bands" sponsored by drug cartels, and all-women and all-child ensembles reinforcing changes in social norms. She grooved to street festivals where "the dancing throng becomes an electric outpouring of joy and celebration," using the ideas **Stephen Feld and Charles Keil** sketched in *Music Grooves* of participatory uses of records by consumers to fashion a complex urban pop map.

The salsa studies that Aparicio and Waxer crafted from intersecting lineages and combined in *Situating Salsa* scrutinized—like counterparts **Richard Peterson** and **Diane Pecknold** in country music studies—hardcore/soft-shell dichotomies, here termed *salsa dura* (hard) and *salsa romántica* or *monga* (flaccid). The two broke down the gender disruptions of La Lupe early and La India later, coming over from Latin freestyle pop. They contemplated Appadurai-type flows of people and sounds in a quintessential globalization. "In many ways salsa's diverse, multiracial heritage and complex spread through the world reflects my own disjunct sense of personal identity," Waxer wrote, while Aparicio explored "the multiple, contradictory, and conflictive levels of textuality, musicality, and performance." An emphasis on work by performers and journalists aimed at hierarchies of academia. A chapter by Christopher Washburne, a tall, white trombone player who'd moved into ethnomusicology after years spent playing in New York salsa bands, anticipated *Sounding Salsa*, his account of bandstand and offstage. There, Marc Anthony added "I am Latino" after "I am Puerto Rican" got no love from a California audience; gunshots made perilous the locked stage door of a club contemptuous of its hired help, informing a discussion of violence as sonic vibe; pianist Larry Harlow was summoned by a Medellín drug lord; and clave patterns were used and misused in charged authenticity rhetoric.

Recasting identity along with music became the underlying modality of salsa literature. Marisol Berríos-Miranda, in both the Waxer and Aparicio collections, sought to distinguish Puerto Rican nativism from Cuban sound structures, insisting this was different from white borrowings of Black material. Queens kid Will Hermes affirmed the New Yorkness of the salsa story by incorporating Fania and its artists into his equally punk, hip-hop, disco, and minimalism-inclusive chronicle of the city, *Love Goes to Buildings on Fire*. Ruth Glasser, giving historical perspective to Boricuan aural multiplicity in *My Music is My Flag*, felt compelled to begin "What's a nice Jewish girl from Brooklyn doing studying Puerto Rican music?" Sydney Hutchinson, editor of the globe-spanning *Salsa World*, focused on dancers rather than players, led off: "I began dancing salsa as a teenager in Tucson, Arizona. My formal training consisted of a single dance lesson in a nightclub, which was soon shut down (perhaps my age—only sixteen at the time—had something to do with the closure)." Salsa, it was said, juxtaposed two rhythms—and seemingly two of everything else.

MUSICALS AS POP, NATIONALISM, AND CHANGING IDENTITY

Stacy Wolf, A Problem Like Maria: Gender and Sexuality in the American Musical, *2002*

———

Between 2002, when theater professor Wolf brought out the first book in a new paradigm of academic work on musicals, and 2011, when she edited an *Oxford Handbook of the American Musical* with musicologists Raymond Knapp and Mitchell Morris, a literature solidified. Or, as Wolf more tellingly put it in the *Handbook*'s introduction, the study of works like *Oklahoma!* had "grown rapidly into a legitimate field." Legitimate theater, legitimate academia: this codification into handbooks and the like bears considering in tandem with the tenor of the scholarship involved.

Pre-Wolf et al., one found interventions. D. A. Miller's *Place for Us*, like **Wayne Koestenbaum**'s *Queen's Throat*, brought queer visibility and superstar academic theory to gay fanship, a topic echoed less audaciously in John Clum's *Something for the Boys*. Geoffrey Block's *Enchanted Evenings* saw a Harvard musicology PhD tackle Broadway accessibly enough for public library placement, on his way to a second edition and the editing of book series on musicals for Yale and Oxford. Legitimization here meant applying "traditional musicological practices," such as archival scrutiny of compositional histories, with a work-centered focus on "how music and lyrics serve, ignore, or contradict dramatic themes and ideas." This was musicology agreeing to the emphasis on effectivity found in the hands-on study *American Musical Theatre*, by workshop director Lehman Engel. Ethan Mordden, a hyperprolific professional writer—from fictional *I've a Feeling We're Not in Kansas Anymore: Tales from Gay Manhattan* to *Opera Anecdotes*—and a sharp-witted critic, surveyed what worked on Broadway decade by decade, from the 1920s in *Make Believe* to the 1970s in *One More Kiss,* then added *Happiest Corpse I've Ever Seen* for the next twenty-five years and *Anything Goes* as a single book summation. To stick with *Make Believe,* producer Flo Ziegfeld was "the most bewitched heterosexual in the history of the theatre," while every choice in making and remaking *Show Boat* got a tag and appraisal.

But *A Problem Like Maria* was the *Show Boat* of new scholarship, making a coherent synthesis from the intersection of musicals and humanities scholarship on identity and power, situating "from a feminist, lesbian perspective" how shows and star texts could signify, including tomboy Mary Martin, butch Ethel Merman, femme Julie Andrews, gay-identified Barbra Streisand, and lesbian fan accounts of *Sound of Music*. A celebrity marriage or Sinatra TV duet received meaningful scrutiny; how strippers in *Gypsy*'s second act looked back at the spectator resembled parallel popular music studies writing on **Madonna**'s "Open Your Heart." A welcoming read, the book was ideal for graduate students considering future study. Wolf followed with the more undergraduate *Changed for Good: A Feminist History of the Broadway Musical*, covering *Wicked*, for example, as a women's revamping of the kind of duet seen opening Rodgers and Hammerstein works.

The musical was inherently open to the topical understudy becoming the lead: female- and queer-identified; nationally and often colonially or frontier-themed; African American– and classical style–appropriating; Jewish-composed and -produced; a theatrical realm for middlebrow profit. Theater scholar David Savran's *A Queer Sort of Materialism* situated 1950s musical theater in culture critic Dwight Macdonald's assailing of middlebrows and sociologist Pierre Bourdieu's tallying of cultural capital a generation beyond that, finding the status consciousness in *Rent* marketing. Savran's later *Highbrow/Lowdown* expanded this, examining theater a *Vanity Fair* generation earlier as akin to a jazz of cosmopolitanism and cultural illegitimacy more than canonical sound, tapping out the revues of Astaires and Gershwins, the hybrid fantasy of Jewish jazz and "Oriental" form. Andrea Most's *Making Americans* emphasized the Jewish part, the stage as space to self-fashion a mainstream role, from the feminized masculinity of Eddie Cantor to the liberal politics of Rodgers and Hart, then Hammerstein. Most knew this sequence was closed to Black performers, finding as much deflection as progressivism: she wrote of Hammerstein, "His ability to fight against racial prejudice on the one hand and unwittingly indulge in it on the other defines the difficulties and contradictions of the postwar Jewish liberal position on race."

Raymond Knapp's two big books, *The American Musical and the Formation of National Identity* and *The American Musical and the Formation of Personal Identity*, took the compendium approach of earlier works by David Ewen (*Complete Book of the American Musical Theater*) or Gerald Bordman (*American Musical Theatre*), but added cultural and social history, attention to race and sexuality, and musicological grounding, language for readers with needs beyond coffee-table books. Knapp was more skilled at case studies than cultural studies, glossing conjunctures less memorably than Wolf, Savran, and Most: "motivic integration" in *West Side Story*, yes, but **Alex Ross** related that better, in *The Rest Is Noise*, to the musical's gay, left, and Jewish creators. Yet the range of the volumes, stressing national mythology in the first, gendered identities—especially camp—in the second, made a statement about the extent of the field that went beyond efforts to define Knapp's "MERM: Musically Enhanced Reality Mode." (As in Ethel?) His final chapter in his second book began, revealingly: "The American musical has long suffered from a kind of inferiority complex, with many of its critics and practitioners decrying a perceived gap in value between musicals and opera, its 'high-art' counterpart." From a pop perspective, the gap in value was at least as much in the opposite direction.

The *Oxford Handbook* featured contributions by Knapp, Wolf, Savran, and Block, Todd Decker's *Show Boat* scholarship, and newcomers like Jim Lovensheimer, who had issued a study of *South Pacific* and race, gender, colonialism, literary adaptation, etc., to inaugurate Block's Oxford series. (That Oxford University Press came up so often was a tribute to the legacy of longtime editor Sheldon Meyer there, a force for work on jazz, Broadway, and American popular culture and social history in general.) The authors all cited each other, reinforcing a sense of the field as connected across disciplinary lines. From Knapp and Morris, adeptly putting Nora Bayes singing "How Can They Tell That Oi'm Irish?" in a Tin Pan Alley lineage, to material on cast albums, regional theater, and much else, the volume felt usefully comprehensive though a bit bland, as with many such handbooks. It also replicated an issue many in the field commented on, a tendency to represent Black perspectives rather than let Black authors speak for themselves. Where jazz studies, a kindred academic field, looked back to the likes of **Ralph Ellison**, **Zora Neale Hurston**, or **James Weldon Johnson** for inspiration, musical theater studies authors rarely seemed compelled by writing that predated Gerald Mast's great *Can't Help Singin'* in the 1980s. Yet with such work as Lawrence Maslon on cast albums in *From Broadway to Main Street* and Jake Johnson's *Mormons, Musical Theater, and Belonging in America*—taking up a Red State subject the makers of the hit musical *Book of Mormon* hardly knew at all—the tunes they called show remained a ripe area for popular music exploration, one of the few genres in the tapestry to never fully embrace the vernacular or suffer its fall.

In that vein, and as a coda: Not contributing to the handbook, yet often cited there, was Scott McMillin, a Cornell English professor with Elizabethan expertise, who passed away before the publication of *The Musical as Drama*, a small gem and somewhat different path. McMillin respected and applied the newcomers, but wrote with an older era's dash: musicals, he said, were "the major form of drama produced so far in America" and he wondered "if the standards of the university are up to dealing with" them. Calling the book version of musicals "progressive time" and the songs they set up for attendees "repetitive time," he urged the abandonment of any validation of "integrated" musicals or Wagnerian total work, preferring Brechtian stress on alienation and estrangement. McMillin valued things that stuck together without losing their difference, a vantage that included a role for sentiment. He loved musicals to the extent they produced a "spirit of disunification" and "surplus of identity," only worrying that Stephen Sondheim's innovations needed to be politicized and joined to African American and Latino American identities. Indeed, he all but predicted *Hamilton*.

MUSICAL FICTION AND CRITICISM BY THE GREATEST USED BOOKSTORE CLERK OF ALL TIME

Jonathan Lethem, Fortress of Solitude, *2003*

———

With its major characters named **Dylan** and **Mingus**, a middle section framed around fictitious liner notes, and an ending pegged to Brian Eno's *Another Green World*, the novel *Fortress of Solitude* had popular music beatboxing through every page. In addition, the greatest used bookstore clerk of all time published two volumes of arts criticism, *The Disappointment Artist* and *The Ecstasy of Influence*; a rock-band novel, *You Don't Love Me Yet*; a 33⅓ monograph on the Talking Heads album *Fear of Music*; an edited *Da Capo Best Music Writing 2002* collection; and *Shake It Up*, a Library of America collection of rock criticism spanning decades. Lethem didn't cloak his obsessions, or stint on them.

The forms of popular music here, touchstone (Dylan), erudite (Lethem's favorite band was the Go-Betweens), and soulful (*Fortress* and *Disappointment* both theorized Marvin Gaye), connected to Lethem's love of movies (he wrote dazzlingly about *Star Wars* and *The Searchers*), comics, and science fiction. This wasn't just his personal trademark. It branded his literary cohort—Mekons and Wussy fan Jonathan Franzen, *Spin Alternative Record Guide* and *Village Voice* contributor Colson Whitehead, "rap nerd" Zadie Smith, Taylor Swift–basher Rick Moody, San Francisco punk connoisseur **Jennifer Egan**, uber-indie Dave Eggers, etc. But even in this company, Lethem stood out for his insistence that, while the jumble of references might appear to be postmodern eclecticism, everything good in his writing should connect: his personal history, his critical lists, and the way these shaped his staunch preferences and no less fetishized moments of shame, "disgraced, wrenched between concurrent selves." Lethem said his writing should be read outside "the context of academic, scientific, or journalistic discourses," for "impulses to beguile, cajole, evoke sensation, and even to manipulate." To that end, he crafted flirty *Rolling Stone* profiles of the crustiest godfathers: James Brown and Bob Dylan. One could be **Gilbert Seldes** waxing wise for magazines like *Vanity Fair* in the 1920s on the *Lively Arts* now, and still be a version of his terse nemesis Ernest Hemingway, too. Post-vernacular modernism collapsed the difference between critic, novelist, and subject.

Fortress of Solitude appeared after Lethem's path—from selling books at Moe's in Berkeley by his onetime Bennington classmates Donna Tartt and Bret Easton Ellis to emergence as a genre pastiche novelist and Philip K. Dick/ Charles Willeford proponent—yielded to critical success and public recognition as a "New York writer" with the arty mystery novel *Motherless Brooklyn*. Lethem now recollected his childhood on Dean Street in brownstone Brooklyn circa the "souring of utopian optimism in the mid-seventies, a historical cliché." Cobble Hill offered a hotbed of culture: stoopball and Black girls singing new hits on the streets. An artist father and his son took up residence next to a performer father and his. Dylan, one of the only white kids in his public school, was "yoked" for his lunch money, trying—**Ralph Ellison**'s aphorism wasn't mentioned, though invisibility came up—to slip that by changing his role as the butt of the joke. He turned to Mingus, a graffiti tagger, for friendship. Americana seer Leslie Fiedler's schema of interracial friendship in America wasn't evoked explicitly, just Dylan's erotic longing "to merge his identity in this way with the black kid's, to lose his funkymusicwhiteboy geekdom in the illusion."

Culture, especially "the middle space they conjured and dwelled in, a bohemian demimonde, a hippie dream," failed them all. In the 1990s end chapters, Dylan, now a rock-critic type with his racial projections transferred into soul reissues and R&B biopics, visited Mingus, a jailed crackhead, and Mingus's venerated father, equally drug-addled, neither of whom had spiritual room for music. The magic ring that bonded the two boys once, let them fly together, reappeared a last time to cunningly destroy the yoker, the boogeyman from the projects, rapping gangsta style in his final scene. Dylan's dad was honored for hackwork he did for money while feverishly pursuing an avant-garde obsession that others couldn't understand. There was a flashback to the two, culture rather than drug addicts, getting Dylan's stuff out of a college modeled on Bennington. Brian Eno played in their car, from an album with a lyric Lethem didn't quote: "I can't see the lines I used to think I could read between."

POETIC ONTOLOGIES OF BLACK MUSICAL STYLE

Fred Moten, In the Break: The Aesthetics of the Black Radical Tradition, *2003*

———

Was this wordy or pithy? "Blackness is, therefore, a special site and resource for a task of articulation where immanence is structured by an irreducibly improvisatory exteriority that can occasion something very much like sadness and very much like devilish enjoyment." Both? Then come in. A poet and essayist, Moten made the ontology of jazz, blues, funk, and all the rest a space of analytic boom bap. He had his own pet words: appositional rather than the more structuring oppositional. Interinanimation via John Donne. He was profusely indebted to the no less devilish theorist and poet **Nathaniel Mackey**, but really to a couple of key passages—just enough to begin a reworking. He published in Duke's Refiguring American Music series a book of verses, named for his mother, *B Jenkins*, that often took the form of a title at the poem's end as well as beginning, paired figures like "johnny cash/rosetta tharp" but also the academics "ann cvetkovich/kathleen stewart." In 2018, he published three books of articles, the first perfectly titled *Black and Blur*.

In that blur, that break beat, that "broken circle," Moten gave Black vernacular from **Louis Armstrong** to James Brown and rapper Rakim a scrutiny its epic celebrants had rarely slowed down for. The first chapter of *In the Break* was called "The Sentimental Avant-Garde." Moten restored the sentimental because slavery's trauma—and here Saidiya Hartman's work *Scenes of Subjection* was central, on Frederick Douglass recalling the screams of his whipped Aunt Hester—cut through to post-soul suffering, rerouting the confident authenticity claims of countercultural figures like Black Power poet and theorist **Amiri Baraka**. Embodiment, staying Black and proud, was a rigged John Henry fight against the drilling machines. The avant-garde message needed to once again be abolition: of racism, capitalism, macho. How could that be expressed? By finding good company: Samuel Delany, Black queer science fiction elder, for example, on a "writhing mass" of different flesh. Moten elaborated in *Black and Blur*, marking "the unfinished business of abolition and reconstruction that is our most enduring legacy of successful, however attenuated struggle." And note this part: "sentimentalism is too often and too easily dismissed by students and devotees of power, especially in its connection to what they dismiss as identity politics."

With Burning Spear's dub-heavy "do you remember the days of slavery?" filling his head, Moten could connect cultural studies interpellation and vaudeville interpolation, mourn for the way the late **José Esteban Muñoz**, whose position steering the performance department at NYU he took over, had let Cubanidad and Latinidad interrupt each other, and then still bluntly demand of Black British cultural studies scholar Paul Gilroy, antithetical to U.S. Blackness, "Who the fuck you talking to?" *Stolen Life*, the second volume of *consent not to be a single being*, detonated Kant to continue the political project of Moten's work with Stefano Harney, *The Undercommons*: Black study appositional to the university, where "a kind of impossible publicness emerges in and from the radical exclusion from the political." Here, too, sound mattered: "It's the site of a kind of unruly music that moves in disruptive, improvisational excess—as opposed to a kind of absenting negation—of the very idea of the (art)work, and it is also the site of a certain lawless, fugitive theatricality, something on the order of that drama that **Zora Neale Hurston** argues is essential to black life." The concluding volume, *The Universal Machine*, began: "what you have here is a swarm." But what particulars swarmed, how influential this blurry swarm became! Only Moten could link the philosopher Emmanuel Levinas's disdain for a dancing civilization to the rock critic and future Bruce Springsteen manager Jon Landau, hearing indulgence rather than expansiveness in Curtis Mayfield. Vernacular-sentimental? He didn't take sides, he took asides.

RESCUING THE AFROMODERN VERNACULAR

Guthrie Ramsey Jr., Race Music: Black Cultures from
Bebop to Hip-Hop, *2003*

———

This book became as important for what it modeled as for what it achieved. Putting down the Bud Powell dissertation required by the "jazz-centrism" of his University of Michigan graduate music program, Ramsey engaged his full musical training, not some reduction. That had included playing gospel in churches and watching his family interact with music—dad "the resident spoon virtuoso," neighbor dancing a mean James Brown, parties to funk. And yes, time spent singing madrigals in high school. "In one space, P. D. Q. Bach. In the other, 'Jungle Boogie.' Each of these was, of course, a parody of larger musical traditions but ones that were viewed as musically exclusive." Ramsey Sr. passed away, the family mourned in "home-cooked" cultural space to the Gap Band's "Yearning for Your Love," and Ramsey Jr. realized the subject he needed to write about surrounded him.

That personal first chapter set up a second, "Disciplining Black Music," no less agile, as Ramsey conceptualized "an interdisciplinary musicology of postwar black musical style written from 'the bottom up,' or so I would like to think." The disclaimer was not incidental: Ramsey was as wry as he was learned. His family members became central to his scholarship, Rosses on his mom's side arriving in Chicago from the South, where the Ramseys already lived; the flow of regions, races, and rhythms comprising an "Afro-modernity" that spoke to Marshall Berman's musical and vernacular account of modernity in *All That Is Solid Melts into Air* and Tera Hunter's explorations of working-class Black women in Jim Crow Atlanta in *To 'Joy My Freedom*. Ramsey understood how ethnicity was **Stuart Hall**, Birmingham "bricolage," but insisted on Blackness as singular. He granted postmodern individualism but held to "collective sensibility" as actual practice, hailed **Amiri Baraka**'s R&B theorizing while critiquing his future father-in-law (by marriage to Kellie Jones, daughter from the family left during the Black Power moment) for his unease with Christianity and commercialism, his notion of pure Blackness. When Ramsey defended "vernacular" for its "elasticity," he knew the term was under siege.

Revitalizing the vernacular, and its study, became *Race Music*'s focus. A chapter on blues contrasted as Afromodern Dinah Washington's sexy but respectable presentation (like an *Ebony* cover model; Adam Green's *Selling the Race* made a fine subsequent counterpart), R&B jumper Louis Jordan, and Cootie Williams fighting jazz pretense to validate dance. Family members told stories for a chapter on collective memory and "community theater"; jazz itself was how the migrated southerners referred not to music but northern urbanity. Then modernism itself became the subject, as "critiqued, teased and taunted" by Black musical texts that refused to divide into art, pop, and folk. Whether looking back to the first Black music scholar, **James Trotter**, for New Negro rhetoric (or, via postmodern era literary theorist Houston Baker, "renaissancism"), considering the partial liberation of "record men" at indie labels and race-averse progressives like bebop critic Leonard Feather, or taking up **Eileen Southern** in contrast to Baraka, Ramsey made every sequence in the Black music story a study in conflict and tension, not "the cultural 'smoothening' that **Alain Locke** did in *The New Negro*." The narrative lost steam in the final two chapters, on postindustrial hip-hop. You could imagine the younger Black scholars Ramsey worked with at University of Pennsylvania, *Black Music Re-*

search Journal, or the blog *Musiqology*, grinning at that, confident that race music scholarship had room for all.

SOUND STUDIES AND THE SONGS QUESTION

Jonathan Sterne, The Audible Past: Cultural Origins of
Sound Reproduction, *2003*

————

Sound studies, launched into prominence by this book and author, wasn't sure what it thought about music. Overtly, the ambition of fostering language promoting an "ensoniment" in place of an enlightenment, opposing "acoustic modernity" to visually rooted approaches, would have seemed all ears on deck. But Sterne was disinvested in popular culture; he omitted virtually all references to it. His favorite music writer appeared to be **Theodor Adorno,** not for the Schoenberg adoration but a notion that a "prehistory of the gramophone could take on an importance that might eclipse that of many a famous composer." Sterne was an adept scholar, gifted at putting media into cultural studies conjunctures. He touched on subjects in this book: **Alice Fletcher** and Frances Densmore's recordings of Native Americans, for example. Still, his heart was in telephony, tympanic models, audile techniques—not songs and their publics.

A second book, *MP3: The Meaning of a Format*, elegantly applied similar methods, sketching a "general history of compression" for the format—in the sense of CDs or Blu-ray as a format, not sitcoms or country music. A characteristic sentence explained, "Perceptual coding was part of a larger shift in thinking about sound media, from considering audio in terms of transduction and noise suppression to terms of technological decomposition and recomposition." Here, music entered a bit, as engineers and executives set format "standards" around musical ones, notably Suzanne Vega's "Tom's Diner" and a touch of Norman Blake—"I had to slip in some bluegrass," a protocols-aligner offered. Again, Sterne's scholarship was estimable, his demolition of the notion that file sharing could be seen as a gift economy one of many sharp delineations. Yet his lack of interest in the other kind of format meant he missed out on speculating about streaming via Spotify's killer app: the listener- and eventually industry-generated playlist. Sterne saw only "casual use" in MP3s, not how pop exchanges anchored "transectorial innovation."

In the introduction to his *Sound Studies Reader*, Sterne said Du Bois, in *Souls of Black Folk*, "turned to sound as a key modality," an odd distillation of the original sentiment about "a haunting echo of these weird old songs in which the soul of the black slaves spoke to men." Much of the contents could be read through this sound/song divide: older work such as Attali's *Noise* that emphasized music; newer work that spoke about "auditory dimensions" and the like. Soundscapes of modernity, the catacoustics of old Quaker halls, industrial din on the factory floor, telephony redux—these versions of the larger audio repertoire tended to dominate over the note about, say, Pink Floyd in Friedrich Kittler's *Gramophone*. The last two sections of the *Reader* occasionally let the music play: Kodwo Eshun on Afrofuturism, Michael Veal on dub, Alexander Weheliye on R&B uses of vocoders collectively rendering sound studies the party mix of the *Matrix* trilogy. Then back to Mladen Dolar joking about "semiotics of coughing" and Lacan.

That sound studies could coexist with popular music itself was partially, but far from fully demonstrated by another collection of the time, editors Kara Keeling and **Josh Kun**'s *Sound Clash: Listening to American Studies*. Here, Jessica Teague's reading of questions of recording and live performance in the **August Wilson** play *Ma Rainey's Black Bottom*, the blues voice and its stress on a life *lived*, set the tone: aesthetic contemplation and the full range of "sonic blackness" would serve as a primary subject. Both Nina Sun Eidsheim and Gayle Wald considered opera singer Marian Anderson, **Eric Lott** drew on rock critic **Robert Palmer** to think about blues singer Howlin' Wolf, and Barry Shank applied French theory to Moby's use of an **Alan Lomax** field recording of Vera Hall. If Sterne had explored "canned music" as an embalming technique, Jennifer Stoever's chapter introduced the concept of a "sonic color line" to return to the first rock-and-roll movie, *Blackboard Jungle*, using the feckless teacher's tape player rather than the Bill Haley megahit detonating the credits to consider how recordings reproduced the living. The resulting book, *Sonic Color Line*, with subjects from Frederick Douglass to Lena Horne, was highly influential, connected to other work published on her blog *Sounding Out!* Sound studies, Gus Stadler rightly charged in "On Whiteness and Sound Studies," had a race problem. As that started to be addressed, a new question appeared. Did it also have a songs problem?

DYLANOLOGIST CONVENTIONS

Bob Dylan, Chronicles: Volume One, *2004*

———

There would eventually be a multiple-edition *Rough Guide to Bob Dylan*, whose author, Nigel Williamson, claimed nobody in popular music had received more scribbling. Yet beyond the memoir of sorts, *Chronicles*, there was never a great Bob Dylan book—perhaps, as with his Nobel Prize, that was a way he challenged the category of literature. Digesting his great oeuvre and its commentators made one a Dylanologist—by definition a comic figure, like a Trekkie, caring far too much about one thing at the expense of everything. His long-since performative rather than disrupting style, a pastiche of roots, Rimbaud, and random, precluded evaluation. Nobody had the expertise. And as Lee Marshall, his savviest academic reckoner, noted, "cultural studies generally has paid very little attention to Dylan," so he never got revisionist study focused on race, gender, or the emergent category of the singer-songwriter. Far too much writing came out, from a hungry sentiment that there'd been not nearly enough.

Criticism mutated so writers on Dylan would not come off as his clueless character, Mr. Jones. **Nat Hentoff**, linked to Greenwich Village and progressive music across category, conducted early features, offering Dylan as **Charles Mingus**: difficult and worth the trouble. (Articles are compiled in Benjamin Hedin's *Studio A* and Carl Benson's *Bob Dylan Companion*.) A young Paul Williams became the first Dylanologist by 1966, essays collected in *Watching the River Flow* linking *Blonde on Blonde* to Thomas Pynchon and other gnostics. Williams later authored three volumes on Dylan as "Performing Artist," watching *Renaldo and Clara*, the scorned Rolling Thunder tour film, as obsessively as he X-rayed Philip K. Dick. **Ellen Willis**'s 1967 "Dylan," for both countercultural *Cheetah* and then *Commentary*, read Dylan's media personae as his art and became her job application for the new role of rock critic: the *New Yorker* hired her. **Robert Christgau**'s "Rock Lyrics are Poetry (Maybe)," took up the perennial of sung artistry against words on page—he went to *Esquire*. Reviewing *Self Portrait* in *Rolling Stone*, **Greil Marcus**, destined to write multiple Dylan books, announced himself in 1970 with the lede "What is this shit?" Closest to a Dylan peer, Paul Nelson of the Dinkytown folk scene's *Little Sandy Review*, defended the electric move in *Sing Out!* and wrote the first *Rolling Stone Illustrated History* entry on Dylan, reprinted in Kevin Avery's collection of Nelson's work, as a private eye investigation: "In a Dylan song . . . physical objects are no longer merely physical objects but become moral and intellectual properties as well; the whole world is flattened into a plasticity, not physical, and we are free to float with the images in all their kinetic brilliance." To which the dick's client responded: "Elegant romantic hogwash."

By 1971, with the singer-songwriter category established and its progenitor on extended sabbatical, books appeared. Dylan's own *Tarantula*, scheduled for 1966 initially, read as even more formless than his liner notes, but still suggestive: the raw material of songs, including an Abbott and Costello variant up there with "Ballad of a Thin Man" and references to "Louie Louie," Ernest Tubb, Henry Miller, and an Aretha "crystal jukebox queen of hymn & him diffused in drunk transfusion." Michael Gray's *Song & Dance Man* assayed Dylan's many influences: here folk, there John Donne. This became gigantic and blues focused by 2000's *Song & Dance Man III*. Toby Thompson's *Positively Main Street*, starting as a *Village Voice* series, built its Dylan-in-Minnesota theme around the artist's first muse, Echo Holstrom, and a new journalism "gush" prose.

Anthony Scaduto provided the first real biography: "In the beginning was Scaduto," Clinton Heylin's later effort proclaimed. Semiauthorized, it presented Dylan as "an outsider even as a child," the music-loving Jew from a Catholic small town in the Eisenhower era turned cultural sponge arguing **Woody Guthrie**'s authenticity in the Village with Dave Van Ronk. Van Ronk said of Dylan, and Scaduto agreed: "He does happen to be a genius who is entitled to a certain amount of nonsense." Dylan's lover and rival Joan Baez gave a droll interview: "I'd slip a Librium into his coffee." The golden years lingered: "When you heard 'Rolling Stone' back then it was like a cataclysm, like being taken to the edge of the abyss." Scaduto's best stuff ended there.

The Dylan who emerged from domesticity in the mid-1970s with an arena tour, comeback album, and revue had two literary bastions: the now-established rock press and downtown New York's eternal underground. Key interviews by the likes of Ron Rosenbaum and Jonathan Cott date to this period, collected in James Ellison's *Younger Than That Now* and Cott's *Essential Interviews*. Off-Broadway playwright Sam Shepard was commissioned to be the Rolling Thunder dramatist and ended up with a compelling *Logbook*. "I mean he still writes some good songs, but it's not like it was back then," a character said. Dazed but not confused, Shepard noted the racial absurdity of a company with no Black performers serenading a Black prisoner (unfairly convicted boxer Rubin "Hurricane" Carter), compared Baez's onstage impersonation of Dylan in whiteface to minstrelsy and medicine shows, and concluded: "Dylan is an invention of his own mind. The point isn't to figure him out but to take him in." More prosaically, *Rolling Stone* correspondent Larry "Ratso" Sloman filed long about the tour's dysfunctional workings, though Joni Mitchell reaming Sloman for his sexist conception of rock artistry was the more memorable takeaway—this moment would get a semifictional reworking in a 2019 Martin Scorsese documentary.

Over the next two decades, as both Dylan and rock criticism were felt to decay, cronies and Dylanologists took over. Robert Shelton, first to review "Do I Call You Bob or Bobby?" in the *New York Times*, belatedly issued *No Direction Home*, respected more for its candid interviews with Dylan than the author's fuzzy conclusions. (Marcus gave readers of his Real Life column relevant pages to skip to.) The best "book" was inside *Biograph*, the box set that reshuffled Dylan's career into a five-album jingle jangle, with a memorable tracks overview, including many unreleased recordings, given to **Cameron Crowe**—Dylan his own cantankerous archivist. Inspired, if more hapless, Dylanology argued the past as guidepost to the present. Key autodidacts like Gray, Heylin, and John Bauldie, operating in fan publications that became books, reconstructed every day, every recording version, ate up every document. As sacramental offering, this fan service helped shape the "Bootleg Series" of unreleased studio and live recordings. Dylan's relationship to Blind Willie McTell *and* the *Infidels* outtake "Blind Willie McTell" received absurd documentation.

What happened next surprised everybody: Dylan's reputation bumped up several notches. Marcus's 1997 *Invisible Republic* centered on the *Basement Tapes*—not the 1975 version of the 1967 recordings, but an at that point unreleased totality, which he connected to Harry Smith's Folkways *Anthology*: Dock Boggs, for example, as exemplar of a weird-ass, cross-racial, vernacular republicanism. One could quibble: "We just sat there and laughed all day and all night," Robertson had told Sloman. But Marcus's portrayal grew persuasive when Dylan's *Time Out of Mind* appeared the same year as *Invisible Republic*, sounding like Smithtown with paved roads. The critic's intense need for dramatization found later form in *Like a Rolling Stone*, which narrated takes of Dylan's greatest song, and *Bob Dylan by Greil Marcus*, in which his account of the 1990s revival matched *Mystery Train* on the **Elvis** Christmas special.

After 2000, Dylan books appeared as regularly as baseball write-ups. The bulk of Gray and Heylin's many doorstops came out. Howard Sounes's unauthorized *Down the Highway* revealed that Dylan had married and parented with one of his gospel singers in his born-again years. Christopher Ricks, knighted and benighted literary scholar, published *Dylan's Visions of Sins*, awkwardly comparing the songwriter's wordings to scads of canon. Mike Marqusee ably contextualized and defended Dylan's protest songs—nobody else was as historically grounded—in *Chimes of Freedom*. David Hajdu's *Positively Fourth Street*, on the mixed doubles of Dylan and Baez, her sister Mimi and Richard Fariña, captured experimental folk expressiveness and emergent pop-biz competitiveness. Greenwich Village girlfriend Suze Rotolo's memoir *A Freewheelin' Time* represented an activist red diaper baby who chafed at the scene's unrecognized conservatism. Marqusee had noted, "Resentment and fear of women, as well as unexamined sexist assumptions, infuse Dylan's music of the mid-sixties," but Rotolo was concisely devastating on what it meant to be Dylan's "chick," a rare moment of revisionism.

Academics were increasingly part of the Bob Dylan library, free to particularize. Lee Marshall's book concentrated on the underpinnings and variations of Dylan's star image, putting Willis in conversation with Bourdieu. **Keith Negus**'s short study attempted musicology, just quick notes but still to more effect than Wilfrid Mellers's earlier *A Darker Shade of Pale*. In *Bob Dylan in America*, Princeton's Sean Wilentz, "historian in residence" at BobDylan.com, recalled his father's Eighth Street Bookshop as a young Bob stomping ground and put some of Marqusee's historical frame and Marcus's secret history style around different nodes, still too wed to baby-boomer orthodoxy to end up with more than a fuller version of a preset story.

Perhaps it came down to the artist. As even Dylan's revival approached its twenty-year mark, the singer on the road to his Nobel, books extended a shrug: what more was there to prove? David Kinney's *Dylanologists* made sympathetic sport of the subculture of obsessive listeners, from those who collected bootlegs and memorabilia to those who wrote all the books and articles. **Elijah Wald**'s *Dylan Goes Electric!* presented the same anti-Marcus spirit as his **Robert Johnson** book, arguing that Seeger had a point in the battle with Dylan. (Marqusee had contrasted Grossman and **Alan Lomax** just as effectively.) There was room for both versions, Wald argued, folk's beloved community and the counterculture's romanticized individuality.

But the Dylan seen in books as far back as *Tarantula* increasingly ruled his own literature: the unrepentant plagiarist who called his 2001 album *"Love and Theft"* after **Eric Lott**'s minstrelsy study; the deadpan protagonist of the post-everything 2003 film he directed, *Masked and Anonymous*; the candid interview subject of the 2005 *No Direction Home* documentary put together from footage filmed by Jeff Rosen, his manager and canny sanctifier. Connecting it all was *Chronicles*, its fabulation admitted: "Whether he really said it or not, it didn't matter. It's what I thought I heard him say that mattered." Internet sleuths revealed how sentences derived from old guidebooks and business manuals. Dylan kept it brief, starting and ending with folk music, minimizing his glory moment, hurting through the wilderness decades, making the quest for songs and voice a saga and trudge. Unless one counted Suze Rotolo (described more than two unnamed wives), Marcus was the only writer Dylan acknowledged: the *Invisible Republic* of song concept resonated and he championed **Robert Johnson** against Dave Van Ronk like Marcus taking on Wald. "You want to write songs that are bigger than life," Dylan reflected, that "go past the vernacular." And if "Some critics would find the album to be lackluster and sentimental, soft in the head"? "Oh well." Dylan had become the Dylanologist in residence.

TWO EDITIONS OF A FIELD EVOLVING FASTER
THAN A COLLECTION COULD CONTAIN

Murray Forman and Mark Anthony Neal, eds., That's the Joint! The Hip-Hop Studies Reader, *2004, 2012*

In the second, dramatically revised (twenty-five new pieces of forty-four total) edition of this collection, Andreana Clay's Lil' Kim–referencing "I Used to Be Scared of the Dick" explored hip-hop masculinity as a tool for queer women of color. Clay wrote in a breezy first person—"my natural is curled tight"— but affixed cultural studies: "Black male masculinity occupies a space both in and outside of heteronormativity through the rejection and absorption of it. Similarly, Black queer women reject heteronormativity in both their identity and desire at the same time that we embrace mainstream cultures like hip-hop." Clay's essay built upon hip-hop feminist Joan Morgan, whose *When Chickenheads Come Home to Roost* was excerpted in both editions. And it first appeared in *Homegirls Make Some Noise*, coedited by Gwendolyn Pough, present in *That's the Joint*'s first edition with an essay that only loosely addressed gender; in 2004, those were still rare. By 2012, one found a plethora and Morgan was pursuing a PhD. A decade after **Tricia Rose**, hip-hop offered more opportunities to academic writers than to journalists.

Hip-hop studies less featured canonical revisionism, a la jazz studies and the pop-rock takes of popular music studies, than a merging of those fields with ethnic studies approaches to identity and social critique. This removed the imperative to codify great performers—Gil Rodman on Eminem in 2012 was *That's the Joint*'s only single-artist case study, focused not on his flow but "public performances of cultural miscegenation." Though critical voices such as Danyel Smith, dream hampton, and Jon Caramanica were shaped by hip-hop or, as with Kelefa Sanneh and Sasha Frere-Jones, the intersection of hip-hop and indie, few wrote books; for marshaling of prominent critics, see Raquel Cepeda's solid 2004 compilation *And It Don't Stop*. The subsections of *That's the Joint* reflected hip-hop studies emphases: historiography, authenticity, space/place, gender, politics, aesthetics, and culture industries.

The first edition was shaped by the 1990s culture wars that saw a once-grassroots, then nationally popular hip-hop become controversial, to some for profanity and sexism, to others for commodification. The authenticity and politics debates turned on the new Black public academics Forman identified with a "liminal zone where the 'hood and the university converge": Michael Eric Dyson preacherly (N.W.A types "must be challenged to expand their moral vocabulary"), Todd Boyd mixed on Ice Cube, Bakiri Kitwana branding a Hip-Hop Generation. By contrast, Paul Gilroy's diasporic theories, Robin Kelley's critique of social science, and coeditor Neal's postindustrial soul exposition deconstructed myths of urban scenes by outsiders *and* insiders. The space and place material reflected an overreliance on postmodernism, for example "glocalization" (global networks of local scenes). Cheryl Keyes, on female rapping, and Kyra Gaunt, on her way to writing an acclaimed book on Black girls' play as a rapping variant, were rare ethnomusicologies. Material on aesthetics and cultural industries was patchy: scholars weak on hip-hop, culturally versed writers weak on theory.

Eight years later, the president now a hip-hop fan, the second edition culled a field no longer hypothetical, and as diverse as any in the history of popular music writing. More chapters derived from full books, such as **Jeff Chang**'s hip-hop history *Can't Stop Won't Stop* and hip-hop aesthetics collection *Total Chaos*, bringing a stronger sense of historiography. Authenticity and spatial debates exchanged the postmodern for multicultural and global: Usama Kahf on the Palestinian perspective, Oliver Wang on Asian American MCs, Alex Perullo in Tanzania, a roundtable on indigenous rappers worldwide. Imani Perry, whose book *Prophets of the Hood* was worth reading in full, imbricated gender and commodification, drawing on **Albert Murray** in key ways. Like the ethnographies of DJ sampling by Joseph Schloss (see his books on crate digging and break dancing), this edition showcased scholars reconciling their listening and conceptual training. Hip-hop studies remained an activism-oriented field, writers discussing confrontations with Nelly over misogynist lyrics rather than Marley Marl productions. Musicology lagged, though less than in earlier eras: books like Loren Kajikawa's *Sounding Race in Rap*, J. Griffith Rollefson's *Flip the Script*, or editor Justin Williams's *Cambridge Companion to Hip-Hop* were being completed. More archivally rooted history studies needed undertaking. Perhaps, given how the field rapidly evolved from fans to tenured scholars, the future would offer a unique distancing twist: hip-hop-studies studies.

REVISIONIST BLUESOLOGY AND TANGLED INTELLECTUAL HISTORY

Elijah Wald, Escaping the Delta: Robert Johnson and the Invention of the Blues, *2004*

———

Even the 1960s blues revival got a revival in the millennial years, record collectors now as romantic as their icons. Or problematic. Robert Johnson, proclaimed *King of the Delta Blues Singers* on a 1961 Columbia Records LP, was Exhibit A. Who coronated this unknown figure with two recording sessions to his name, first member of the 27 club in 1938? Who tagged Delta blues, a genre label nobody used back in the day? How, after that LP moved just a few thousand copies, did a 1990 CD box set sell a purported million? Three novels inspired by Johnson, including ones by well-known authors Walter Mosley and Sherman Alexie, appeared in 1995 alone; 2001 saw *Ghost World*, a film about a record collector and his Skip James masterpiece. A record label called itself Revenant, for figures returned from death. "People go to Mississippi to look at things that aren't there anymore," wrote critic Francis Davis, who had done the same. Wald's no less bemused and self-implicated study represented peak revisionist bluesology: a "Cross Roads" lane expansion. Marybeth Hamilton's *In Search of the Blues* soon dug up more diggers.

A Robert Johnson Reader, should one ever appear, could start with producer John Hammond, whose "Sight and Sound" in 1937 was the first to review Johnson songs, under the pseudonym Henry Johnson, for the leftist *New Masses*. Like critic **Otis Ferguson**, putting Johnson into a *New Republic* records column in 1940, "Voices, When the Wind is Right," collected in his *Reader*, Hammond drew a contrast by dismissing the less pure Lead Belly. Blues writing, in this way, was a reality show competition from the onset: the arrival of a "folkloric authenticity" ethos, to use Karl Hagstrom Miller's concept in *Segregating Sound*. Field recordings collector **Alan Lomax** hunted Johnson stories on a 1941 Mississippi trip and discovered Muddy Waters before he left sharecropping. That tale would be told, belatedly and cornily, in *The Land Where the Blues Began*, then revised to include Black coresearcher John Work in *Lost Delta Found*, coedited by Waters biographer Robert Gordon. **Rudi Blesh's** 1946 jazz history, *Shining Trumpets*, made "Hellhound on My Trail" a kind of musical Rosetta stone: tortured lost greatness. The fusion of jazz rhetoric and moldy blues records drove *Jazzmen* coeditor **Frederic Ramsey Jr.** to idealize the wandering blues singer in a project that became the photobook and somewhat florid travelogue *Been Here and Gone*; "Hellhound" was quoted in a chapter on "men who carried the devil on their backs." Ramsey inspired **Samuel Charters** to switch from jazz, too, and Charters's 1959 *Country Blues* was pivotal, self-aware revivalism: a short Robert Johnson chapter mulled his appeal to bohemians like Charters yet obscure impact in Black blues life. A "blues Mafia" of collectors thought Charters too open to pop blues—Lonnie Johnson, for example—and put out an album in protest: *Really! The Country Blues*. Their guru, a recluse named James McKune, idolized Charley Patton's gnarled gnosticism. It was in his bleak Williamsburg YMCA room, Hamilton wrote, "that the Delta blues was born."

Hamilton, an expert historian with previous work on Mae West and Little Richard, saw in the resulting intellectual chronicle that she presented a set of revered vernacular scholars purpling prose to capture Johnson and Delta blues: "their writing takes on the hues of romance." **Peter Guralnick**, first of the boomer critics connecting rock back to Delta blues, profiled James, Waters, and Johnny Shines in his 1971 collection *Feel Like Going Home*. He then turned a *Living Blues* article into *Searching for Robert Johnson*, which noted he'd been as seduced by Charters as Charters was by Blesh: "Robert Johnson became the personification of the existential blues singer, unencumbered by corporeality or history, a fiercely incandescent spirit who had escaped the bonds of tradition by the sheer thrust of genius." **Greil Marcus** made Johnson the key originator in his rock-and-roll study *Mystery Train*, that song about stones in his passway a challenge no entitled white supplicant could rise to. **Robert Palmer** described as *Deep Blues* the legacy of the plantation Patton worked on in Mississippi, asking, Hamilton noted, "How much history can be transmitted by pressure on a guitar string?" Even historians such as **Lawrence Levine** were inspired to answer the question, not challenge its premises.

For Wald, dedicating *Escaping* to folk musician Dave Van Ronk, "whose ideas formed the foundations of this work," and leading with a quote from adamantly nontraditionalist blues guitarist B. B. King's book with **David Ritz** ("scholars associate the blues strictly with tragedy"), the stakes were at least as much musical. To overvalue Robert Johnson was to collaborate in a process that resulted in Lonnie Johnson, Black crossover artist turned blues nonperson, and Eric Clapton, white blowhard turned rock god. A busker and hitchhiker himself, Wald—author of good books on Josh White as excluded-by-politics blues figure, dancing girls as the part of rock and roll the arty Beatles destroyed, and **Bob Dylan**'s electric set at Newport in 1965 presented with affection for Pete Seeger, among many others—oversold his revisions, shouting for attention. *Escaping* didn't fully credit similar scholarship, from Charters at the time to **Susan McClary**'s feminist reaming of blues genericism in *Conventional Wisdom* and **George Lipsitz**'s use of Johnson in *Possessive Investment in Whiteness: How White People Profit from Identity Politics*. Marcus slammed Wald in *Mystery Train* revisions for gutting Johnson's artistry, citing a portion of *Chronicles* where Dylan argued with Van Ronk about Johnson's singularity. Yet Marcus protégé John Jeremiah Sullivan noticed in his essays collection, *Pulphead*, how Wald lovingly distilled Johnson's pop-savvy recordings sensibility, track by track. The coda of Wald's study denounced the myth that the bluesman had sold his soul at the crossroads. That became the centerpiece of Barry Lee Pearson and Bill McCulloch's *Robert Johnson Lost and Found*, which tracked the story to a 1966 Pete Welding essay and found time to also denounce a more Afrocentric recounting of Johnson, Julio Finn's *The Bluesman*, where the devil became a Legba figure. Patricia Schroeder's study of his *Mythmaking* presented Johnson as a cultural studies text, invoking theorist Jacques Derrida on hauntology.

Johnson's mythical status only expanded—see YouTube for Barack Obama singing his "Sweet Home Chicago" at a White House blues gathering that included B. B. King and Mick Jagger—and the debates around his blues legacy persisted. (In 2020, a relative, Annye Anderson, released the memoir *Brother Robert*. Combined with a 2019 biography, *Up Jumped the Devil*, by two long-time blues researchers, Bruce Conforth and Gayle Dean Wardlow, it had the effect of shifting the focus of Johnson's musical life away from the Delta altogether and toward Memphis, the urban center where he heard and played pop of all kinds in the company of his second family.) Biographies of Johnson peers who'd survived rendered human beings, not hellhounds. Besides the King-Ritz book and Gordon on Waters, British critic Charles Shaar Murray's *Boogie Man*, on John Lee Hooker, presented an illiterate figure of pure vernacular ("I don't believe in no *paper*") but also a professional: when Hook went "country blues" to court revivalists, Murray wrote, "it was the acoustic folk-blues posture which represented the *real* sell-out." David "Honeyboy" Edwards's as-told-to memoir, *The World Don't Owe Me Nothing*, called Johnson "whorish" rather than demonic; "hustling" to earn three dollars a night from bootleggers rather than work with plantation types who "treated us like we was property." Ted Gioia, a well-established jazz critic rarely in this book for his tendency to exterminate rather than develop pop theories, debunked the debunkers. In *The Delta Blues*, he sniffed that professors like Hamilton hadn't helped the revival in the first place, surveyed different artists rather than collectors, and validated the devil mythology as "a modern American echoing of a timeless African story." John Milward's *Crossroads* wrapped blues stories and rock stories together, such that a white sixties player like Michael Bloomfield simply "suggested that there was more than one route to the blues."

But most scholars kept chipping away. Paige McGinley's *Staging the Blues*, like **Lynn Abbott and Doug Seroff**'s *The Original Blues*, stressed that vaudeville, not a premodern South, gave the blues life, not least for the central role of women as performers. Clyde Woods's *Development Arrested* showed that the Delta was hardly premodern, anyhow: "slavery and the plantation are not anathema to capitalism but are pillars of it," with a "blues bloc" forming in response that was far more collective in its modern sensibilities than portraits of existential bluesmen had indicated. Ulrich Adelt's *Blues Music in the Sixties* put back the politics Gioia and Milward neglected, considering how a Clapton could both revere Johnson and support racist politician Enoch Powell—each reflected a conservative notion of racial essentialism. The blues journalism of Carlo Rotella, collected in books such as *Playing in Time*, stressed blues trafficking as its own theater: "Dizz, who had studied economics at Southern Illinois University, enjoyed playing the down-home blues sage as much as we enjoyed playing at being barflies and connoisseurs. Each indulged the other." Stephen King's *I'm Feeling the Blues Right Now* examined blues tourism. Adam Gussow's *Beyond the Crossroads* went farther than Wald had, arguing for "Johnson as fearless young modernist who deliberately constructed his songs to offend uptight religionists and attract feminine attentions, signifying on crossroads mythology with ironic intent." Here, the Mississippi tamale trail tribute "They're Red Hot," ragtime joviality, signified as much as the hellhound trail.

Still—to make the most modest of critical assertions—"They're Red Hot" was no "Hellhound." To proclaim greatness in a single vernacular figure was not only romanticization and not only white foolishness. Why was Houston

Baker's *Blues, Ideology, and Afro-American Literature: A Vernacular Theory*, a pivotal study for Black scholars with its attempt to make blues speak to literary theory in a post–Black Power landscape, centered on a crossroads theme and littered with Johnson lyrics, yet ignored by Johnson revisionists? Why did Stanley Crouch, writing the introduction to an unproduced screenplay about Johnson, Alan Greenberg's *Love in Vain*, stress the importance of "Printing the Legend"? Black playwright Bill Harris's *Robert Johnson: Trick the Devil* gave the line "His are different from all the other ones" to a white collector whose family fortune came from selling slaves but didn't discount the genius of his world. Sherman Alexie, exchanging fry bread for tamales, brought Johnson into a *Reservation Blues* and evoked "a guitar made of a 1965 Malibu and the blood of a child killed at Wounded Knee in 1890." The characters in Walter Mosley's *RL's Dream*, Mavis and Soupspoon, recalled their time with Johnson as life's epitome; others couldn't "get that naked." Cops, rape, and researchers mingled with "dreams about catfish frying and juke joint dancing and women laughing open-mouthed while he played." Perhaps that interconnection was the key to what Kimberly Mack reconceived as the fundamentally narrative rather than autobiographical story of *Fictional Blues*. Johnson's uncanny musical-literary appeal survived the genre inventions around him. The Black resistance audible in his recordings, too consequential to fully revise away, is where we should leave this Talmudic saga of texts around texts. Soupspoon confessed he never really had the full blues. "Satan scared me silly."

TRYING TO TELL THE STORY OF A DOMINANT GENRE

Jeff Chang, Can't Stop Won't Stop: A History of the Hip-Hop Generation, *2005*

———

Every music genre came at its all-purpose history differently. With jazz, that kicked off in latter 1930s swing and never ended: large jazz overview volumes, such as **Gary Giddins**'s *Visions of Jazz* or Alyn Shipton's *New History of Jazz,* continued to encompass the whole tradition. Rock and roll books accelerated with late 1960s rock and stayed coherent through grunge a generation later, with diminishing holistic accounts—the bad final *Rolling Stone Illustrated History* edition, overseen by Anthony DeCurtis, or **Jim Miller**'s *Flowers in the*

Dustbin. With hip-hop, however, there was a paradox: the years of the music's greatest commercial success were received ambivalently by those who most loved the culture of rapping to beats. *Can't Stop Won't Stop*, by far the most revered history of the subject, came out in 2005 but barely took the story beyond Dr. Dre and Snoop's 1992 "Nuthin' but a 'G' Thang," setting up without hugely exploring a "new corporate order" rising in the aftermath of the Rodney King verdict L.A. riots. The selling of hip-hop had a vexed relationship with the telling of hip-hop.

Chang, a Bay Area alt-weekly and hip-hop press writer involved with indie labels, positioned a deeper, political "dub history" around the obligatory icons. **Tricia Rose**'s theorizing of hip-hop as postindustrial in *Black Noise* here received an epic rendering: "The Bronx and the Politics of Abandonment" turned on Robert Moses slicing up the borough where the first hip-hop parties emerged. Kool Herc, who DJ'd those parties and wrote Chang's intro ("The hip-hop generation is not making the best use of the recognition and the position it has"), had his sound system's Jamaican origins fit to the thwarted left struggle model Mike Davis used in his L.A. study, *City of Quartz*. Chang exhumed a 1970s Bronx gang truce to contrast with a 1990s L.A. gang truce—moments when people, and music, could breathe. He followed hip-hop from the Bronx to downtown hipsters: Basquiat, Blondie, etc. He traced the music's post–civil rights message, from Public Enemy era representation battles to the "militant incoherence" of the N.W.A revamp and "gangstacentricity." The coda was Sean Combs, dressed for synergistic, cross-promotional success, but Chang's hope was that the hip-hop generation would return to the street struggles that had defined it for him.

Tellingly, *The Big Payback*, the next major hip-hop opus, focused directly on what Dan Charnas subtitled *The History of the Business of Hip-Hop*. In this, Russell Simmons meeting Rick Rubin in an NYU dorm room to partner on Def Jam Records was as big a bang as what Public Enemy actually put out on the label. As **Keith Negus** did in *Music Genres and Corporate Cultures*, Charnas personalized business figures: "everybody gets to be human." "Hip-hop," as he defined it, "resulted from unfettered young urban Black expression finding its own way to the masses after being denied access." He posited a dialectic: "the cultural squeeze that created gangster rap also caused a precipitous rise in Black entrepreneurship." And his extensive journalism captured radio, late to embrace rapping but decisive when the likes of Power 106 and Hot 97 did, along with record labels and artists as business execs, "idealistic islands" within the corporate realms Chang deplored. A cultural crossroads here was Tommy Quon, toting Robert Van Winkle to a crossover radio station in Jackson, Mississippi, whose young music director, Dave Morales, broke "Ice, Ice Baby." If, in that case, it was EMI's Charles Koppelman who raked it in, eventually Combs, Wu-Tang Clan, and **Jay-Z** profited directly. For Charnas, "the vision of hip-hop as a culture without boundaries" connected the savviest rappers and label figures.

Chang and Charnas's books were weighty tomes on hip-hop; the next widely read take was quite the opposite: Shea Serrano's breezy *Rap Yearbook*, which devoted a two-thousand-word essay built around an individual song to each of thirty-six years (1979–2014). Serrano, a *Grantland* writer whose next book was on basketball, took on the chatty fan obsessiveness of the website's figurehead, celebrity sportswriter Bill Simmons; he also brought in, more than Chang or Charnas had, his own background—working-class Mexican American from Texas. At times that approach produced a counter-idealistic truth, similar to the critic Chuck Klosterman on North Dakota rock fans. A Slick Rick story song, Serrano wrote, "managed to make casual misogyny seem cool," then he told of being on a date, finding a wallet with $124 in it, not telling the owner, trying to spend the money, and discovering the $100 bill was bogus. To put this another way, he wrote of a doomed battle rapper that "DMX wanted your dollar because he wanted you to be poor." There was no cutoff required in Serrano's account, no precommercial golden age, and no African American business victory. Hip-hip was Sister Carrie, Great Gatsby, Scarface: by any means necessary, sure, but not necessarily for goals that Malcolm X would have recognized; as often, for ones that Kid Rock would have. He ended with Atlanta star Young Thug: "He's maybe the first post-text rapper, in that he doesn't even really need words."

None of these three writers was African American and issues of identification played out differently in Black-authored summations. Imani Perry's *Prophets of the Hood*, title a pun on profits, was sage on the genre as mixed message—neither underground nor corrupt mainstream, but at best a localized, African American vernacular expression rather than diasporic hybrid. Bakari Kitwana's *The Hip-Hop Generation* was culture wars advocacy, far less ambivalent than original hip-hop scholar Tricia Rose's 2008 *Hip Hop Wars*, promoted with campus tours that Kitwana, CEO of the project, called Rap Sessions. Michael Eric Dyson's slim *Know What I Mean?* featured an intro by Jay-Z, who said he valued Dyson's "ability to come from tough streets in Detroit" and now "talk about pimping in terms laid out by Hegel," outro by another rapper, Nas, and chapter headings that quoted lyrics where rappers like KRS-One or Black Thought mentioned the media-beloved academic. Andreana Clay's *Hip-Hop Generation Fights Back* added layers of LGBT and feminist intersectionality. James Braxton Peterson's *Hip-Hop Headphones* stressed "playlist pedagogy": unlike Serrano, his chosen tracks had to "find connections to current events and social justice issues." **Nelson George** had pointed out in his *Hip-Hop America* that the key was accepting mutability: knowing the difference between hip-hop business and culture industry "permanent business," accepting that women at Black colleges partied to 2 Live Crew.

"No one has contributed as much to the analysis of hip-hop as Adam Krims; in fact, analytical approaches can productively be divided into 'Krims' and 'other.'" Kyle Adams, writing in *The Cambridge Companion to Hip-Hop* (edited by Justin Williams), perhaps needed to get out more, but Krims's *Rap Music and the Poetics of Identity* did reflect an investment by musicologists and ethnomusicologists working with cultural studies methods. Joseph Schloss's two books, *Making Beats* and *Foundation*, studies of sampling ethics and break dancers, were exemplary, joined by Eithne Quinn's reading of gangsta rap as neoliberalism, *Nuthin' but a "G" Thang*, and Mark Katz's *Groove Music* on DJ approaches. While Krims had written, "Any claim I could make to hip-hop authenticity would be preposterous," by the *Cambridge Companion* that separation had been complicated. Anthony Kwame Harrison, author of an ethnography of the Bay Area underground from which Chang launched, made the dynamics of being a Black scholar a self-conscious topic; "nerdcore" appeared as a topic alongside an impressive set of global studies; and doctoral student Chris Tabron recounted producing Mary J. Blige.

In the midst of hip-hop's first commercial peak, rap criticism flourished at publications such as the *Source*, *Vibe*, and the quirkier zine *Ego Trip*, leading to such overviews as *The Vibe History of Hip-Hop*. Modeled on the *Rolling Stone Illustrated History*, if the tamer last version, it included some fine individual writers—Danyel Smith, dream hampton, Sasha Frere-Jones. More idiosyncratic, but idea-drenched and exhilarating, *Ego Trip's Book of Rap Lists* modeled itself on Dave Marsh's *Book of Rock Lists*, with categories like "How About Some Hardcore Parodies?" Finally, Oliver Wang edited a collection, *Classic Material*, with essays on great albums, notable for introducing the writing of Hua Hsu. Strangely, none of these writers (one might add *New York Times* critic Jon Caramanica, too) attempted a single-author book on hip-hop in the 2000s, which saw the genre flourish but its magazines crumble. That might be starting to change. Regina Bradley's *Chronicling Stankonia*, on OutKast and the hip-hop South, was on the verge of publication as this book was finalized. Chang announced that a *Can't Stop Won't Stop* young adult edition, written with DJ and activist Dave "Davey D" Cook, would take the story into the present, if in a truncated version. One could hope that soon, Nicki Minaj, Drake, the Migos-era Atlanta scene, and Kanye West, among many others, would find chroniclers for our bookshelves.

REFIGURING AMERICAN MUSIC—AND ITS INSTITUTIONALIZATION

Josh Kun, Audiotopia: Music, Race, and America, *2005*

———————

In the remarkable *Heartland Excursions*, ethnomusicologist **Bruno Nettl** applied his discipline's estimation of "other" music to his own habitat, the university school of music. Here, I want to write about books by my series editors on this one, Duke University Press's Refiguring American Music (RAM), to think about institutionalization, song, seriousness. And race. By 2005, universities had modestly embraced popular music as a field, but on differently structured terms that affected what could be studied, how, and by whom. New jazz studies à la **Robert O'Meally** represented elite acceptance but also African American scholars taking a lead role. Performance studies, via **Jose Esteban Muñoz** or **Fred Moten**, used the university to stage minoritarian transgression. Scholars in popular music studies, media studies, history, and ethnomusicology proper struggled for support to focus on pop songs. Resisting the déclassé pop music label was **Jonathan Sterne**–type "sound studies," bracketing music altogether. Post–**Gilbert Chase** and **Richard Crawford** musicology dubbed itself "American music" to join classical and jazz composers with some pop allowed.

Belonging mattered. For example, RAM co-editor Nina Sun Eidsheim, in her recent book *Sensing Sound*, noted the "institutional recognition" that sound studies had achieved and hoped her volume, and a *Handbook* she was coediting, would do the same for voice studies. It wasn't scandalous to admit this desire for academic currency; **Stacy Wolf** offered similar hopes for musical theater studies. Eidsheim, a classically trained vocalist with an interest in "vibrational practices" and music as an anthropological "thick event," was more likely to respond to a performer like the new music visionary Meredith Monk or the opera singer who became a civil rights symbol, Marian Anderson, than to Lady Gaga; more likely to read the French musicologist and philosopher Peter Szendy on listening and hit songs, than consider, the way rock critic **Robert Christgau** did in *Book Reports*, how a book on popular music singing by an earlier critic of classical and pop, Henry Pleasants, held up.

By contrast, RAM co-editor Kun wrote for the *San Francisco Bay Guardian*, *Village Voice*, and *New York Times* while ascending academia, a go-to freelancer for coverage of *rock en español* especially. *Audiotopia* was theory-driven in its title, a play on Foucault's heterotopia that stressed how a set of songs could create "small, momentary, lived utopias." But the book began "It all started with a record store and the Rock Island Line." There was a chapter on Mickey Katz, performer of dubious comedic rewrites like "Yiddish Mule Train." Critic **Greg Tate** was likely to be cited alongside ethnic studies pioneer **George Lipsitz.** Eidsheim shared Kun's belief in music's power "to frustrate fixity, to confuse authority and baffle totality." Making that a professional habit was Kun's academic practice, as he put off a second monograph to work on Jewish album cover photobooks, menu collections and sheet music collaborations with the Los Angeles public library. The University of Southern California might have carped at crediting these publications as "research" until the MacArthur fellowship he got for the outreach said otherwise.

"A spectre lurks in the house of music, and it goes by the name of race." Ronald Radano, the third RAM co-editor, wrote this with noted ethnomusicologist Philip Bohlman as part of the introduction to a collection, *Music and the Racial Imagination*. Notions of studying "the music itself" had kept musicologists from racial topics, they argued, while ethno types were too wed to "mid-century scientism." Tera Hunter, in the volume's distillation of her book *To 'Joy My Freedom*, brought historical perspective to the Black working women dancing on Atlanta's Decatur Street in the 1910s as quintessentially modern figures. But elsewhere, the view of Black vernacular was more skeptical. Chris Waterman looked at the song "Corrine Corinna," valuing its hybridity and circulation: "a blues performed by rural Mississippians, but, strangely enough, not a rural Mississippi blues." Brian Currid argued the importance of not assuming a "naturally expressive vernacular," only mapping the space produced by those imagining it. He cited Radano, whose own work in the collection focused on the association of Blacks and rhythm as a problematic reification of modernism and the marketplace.

Radano, mentored in American musicology by Crawford but cultural studies adept, wrote *New Musical Figurations* about a maverick modernist with complicated Chicago genre and Black power roots, Anthony Braxton, contrasting his arc in and out of the mainstream with the neotraditionalism of Wynton Marsalis. *Lying Up a Nation*, titled from **Zora Neale Hurston**'s blues ethnography, *Mules and Men*, looked to tell a less "pure" version of Black music and U.S. modernity, critiquing many lauded authors for presuming racial essence: historian **Lawrence Levine**; theorists Houston Baker, Henry Louis Gates Jr., and Sterling Stuckey; ethnomusicologist Alan Merriam; music historian **Eileen Southern;** and literary agitator **Amiri Baraka**. Radano called for nuance and deliberate imprecision, "the sonic-textual concept of black resonance," noting that in Hurston's work, or work by **Ralph Ellison** and **Langston Hughes**, "the voice of vernacular authenticity that so appealed to Baker and Gates was always revealed through these ironic twists." Covering a span from **Lucy McKim Gar-**

rison's *Slave Songs* to jazz, he asked: "Can we embrace the claims of vital groove and essence while also challenging the racialism that routinely goes hand in hand with them?"

Audiotopia, too, made race and sweeping claims its focus, beginning with a chapter that too dismissively debunked **Walt Whitman**'s seeming multiplicity as whiteness easy listening. Kun validated Katz as an embarrassment to Jewish assimilators; detailed using the kind of terms Radano had and Emily Lordi's *Black Resonance* would the impact of James Baldwin listening to Bessie Smith; and made the painter Basquiat and sound-seer Rahsaan Roland Kirk exemplars of Afro-diasporic sound. He gave that other Whitman, Langston Hughes, back his connections to Afro-Cubanists like Nicolás Guillén and the Mexican border, and ended with a rock en español chapter: "a post-national network of diasporas, migrations, and flows." Sentimental about "the varied carols I hear," Kun was clear about his reasons for rescuing, to use a term he took from theorist **Theodor Adorno**, "congealed history," insistent that "racial difference is performed against the grain of a suffocating nationalism."

Once again, the contrast with Eidsheim was instructive, though both drew on Muñoz's strategically multifaceted identity claims in *Disidentifications*. Her *The Race of Sound* used the "black acousmatic," how recordings cut off bodies, to make anti-essentialist assertions about music and race, like Radano in *Lying*. Voice needed to be heard as collectively produced, not singular. Its qualities were cultural, not innate. And the interpretive leader was the listener, not the performer. There were many graphics and charts. Resistant to any notion of cultural fidelity, for instance Angela Davis's take on the blues as Black radicalism, Eidsheim wanted readers to train themselves to focus on "style and technique." A young, white Billie Holiday impersonator on *Norway's Got Talent*, the Japanese-produced hologram Hatsune Miku, or misgendered vocalist Jimmy Scott were her kinds of examples, viewed as "radical resistance on a much deeper epistemological level."

Three non-Black authors, taking up Blackness and music across space and time. How much had the field evolved since a century previously, when Henry Krehbiel theorized *Afro-American Folksongs: A Study in Racial and National Music*, too? Anti-essentialist perspectives might be as dismissive as essentialist ones, if they theorized the U.S. Black vernacular out of its popular music centrality. These issues were not particular to the RAM authors. A different survey could look at Georgina Born, a white, British experimental musician connected to the improvisational scene that bordered punk and fostered the writer **David Toop**. She became a prominent U.K. academic with prestige anthologies that gave skillful and interdisciplinary attention to *Western Music* *and Its Others*, then *Music, Sound, and Space*, but found little room for African American authors and subject matter.

There were no easy answers because, as Radano and his coeditor, Tejumola Olaniyan, noted in yet another weighty collection, "elite cosmopolitanism" and "a rich lexicon of subversive hipness" had become currency for a reconstituted global imperialism. *Audible Empire*, they called this. Michael Denning theorized vernacular recording as resistance to colonialism, with historian Penny Von Eschen hailing the Jamaican dub poet Linton Kwesi Johnson as Black vernacular radicalism personified, "lines that sounded like a bass-line." But Chinese popular music scholar Andrew Jones's neat concept of the music genre as a kind of "shipping container" was more typical of how this story was seen to end, "vernacularization" in the form of Grace Chang, "Mambo Girl," a form of "hollowing out." Kun's article in the book proposed a compromise of sorts, the metaphor of a DJ crossfading: moving between channels without silencing either. And jazz studies language scholar Brent Hayes Edwards, a powerful voice in "counterarchival" revisionism, ranged from antipolitical South African ethnomusicology to Kenyan novelist Ngũgĩ wa Thiong'o to assess views of jazz outside the West. The best of this work held imperial scholars as accountable as nations and corporations, listening as skeptically to new languages of expertise as cultural studies did to the latest product of global pop hybridity.

COUNTRY MUSIC SCHOLARS PIONEER GENDER AND INDUSTRY ANALYSIS

Diane Pecknold, The Selling Sound: The Rise of the Country Music Industry, *2007*

———

Nobody had looked through the Country Music Hall of Fame archive for the business papers of the Country Music Association, the most important trade organization in American pop promotion. For Pecknold, getting a PhD in history after working for indie rock concert booking agency Billions and also teaming with another historian, Kristine McCusker, on the collection *A Boy Named Sue: Gender and Country Music*, the double impetus was clear. Business came down to individuals concerned about status and aesthetics alongside profits. And country people weren't a thousand remakes of Hank Williams: to consider gender, class, and race, those supporting the music with those making it, told that history anew. Along the way, she pioneered the history of music formats, radio set-ups structured differently than genres, and with her peers made country the most gender-inclusive genre of popular music scrutiny ever.

Country had already been an important site of revisionist thinking: **Nick Tosches**'s expansionist criticism, **Robert Cantwell** centering minstrelsy within *Bluegrass Breakdown*, **Richard Peterson**'s sociology of culture explorations in *Creating Country Music*, and Joli Jensen's semiotics approach to how *The Nashville Sound* built hominess around an increasingly corporate product. For *A Boy Named Sue*, Jensen explained Patsy Cline's belated posthumous canonization as polysemic crossover: uptown and down home, pop and hardcore country, feminist and yet less radical than the new image suggested. The book's editors made clear their intent to step past the women's reclamation project of Mary Bufwack and Robert Oermann's *Finding Her Voice*. Gender analysis would now be charged with considering how framings of femininity and masculinity had been "used to establish and defend the stylistic and institutional boundaries separating country music from pop, rock 'n' roll, folk, and other genres."

The *Boy Named Sue* authors and their growing network made those boundaries core to a new history. Jocelyn Neal, a musicologist by training, contributed an assured ethnography of country dance halls, finding "diverse communal identities" even in an era of "Achy Breaky" line-dancing and Clear Channel radio chains. Neal's first book, *The Songs of Jimmie Rodgers*, showed how cover versions of the music's first superstar migrant, by the likes of Dolly Parton, salved positional shifts in country as a whole. (Two kindred books by critic Barry Mazor, *Meeting Jimmie Rodgers: How America's Original Roots Music Hero Changed the Pop Sounds of a Century*, and *Ralph Peer and the Making of Popular Roots Music* on Rodgers and his A&R figure, added journalistic digging and savvy evaluation to Neal's study.) Neal institutionalized the new paradigm with a textbook, *Country Music: A Cultural and Stylistic History*. McCusker, who provided a key chapter in *A Boy Named Sue* on Jeanne Mueunich's turn into "Sunbonnet Girl" radio barn-dance singer Linda Parker, commercialized youth version of "the sentimental mother," extended that method to figures like comedian Minnie Pearl in *Lonesome Cowgirls and Honky-Tonk Angels*. Michael Bertrand's chapter on **Elvis Presley**'s sexuality added a gender component to his *Race, Rock, and Elvis*. Barbara Ching, whose *Wrong's What I Do Best* scraped at abjection in male honky-tonkers, deromanticized the "macho nostalgia" of alt-country, leading to *Old Roots, New Routes: The Cultural Politics of Alt.Country Music*, coedited with fellow English professor Pamela Fox. Fox's own study, *Natural Acts: Gender, Race, and Rusticity in Country Music*, was the most theoretically sophisticated on gender questions, superb on country memoirs. *Old*

Roots, New Routes included work by Pecknold and also ethnomusicologist Aaron Fox, influential for his Texas honky-tonk survey in *Real Country,* which made the language of that scene prickly to the touch. Most recently, Stephanie Vander Wel's *Hillbilly Maidens, Okies, and Cowgirls* added musicological analysis to McCusker's work on early country women—singing has rarely been so well contextualized.

Clearly, this was a booming area of study. In 2013, Pecknold published another edited collection, *Hidden in the Mix*, pinned to country and race. It featured two other careful historians. Patrick Huber, who wrote about Black hillbillies, used *Linthead Stomp* to consider Fiddlin' John Carson and other early commercial figures as modern Piedmont area mill workers, not throwbacks; he would go on to coauthor *A&R Pioneers: Architects of American Roots Music on Record* with Brian Ward, about Ralph Peer's peers. Charles Hughes's part of *Hidden* focused on 1970s southern soul and country intersections, the subject too of his *Country Soul*, which refused the easy assumption that an integrated recorded studio was an equitable one. A sequel by Pecknold and McCusker, *Country Boys and Redneck Women*, added to the mix Nadine Hubbs, whose work there on Gretchen Wilson's "Redneck Woman" expanded into her influential and white-working-class focused *Rednecks, Queers, and Country Music*, denouncing country sorts' written-off position in cultural hierarchies. Also making the latter book was musicologist Travis Stimeling, considering Taylor Swift's voice in relationship to adolescent girls and country norms. Stimeling's *Cosmic Cowboys and New Hicks* looked at rock/country mergings in hippie Austin, and his editing of both a *Country Music Reader* and *Oxford Handbook of Country Music* further institutionalized the new approaches. This cohort tended not to be superstar academics; their annual meet-up was the International Country Music Conference at Nashville's Belmont University, where earlier scholars like Malone and journalists like Mazor and Jewly Hight (author of *Right by Her Roots: Americana Women and Their Songs*) joined Pecknold, Neal, Stimeling, et al.—country once again resisting subdivision. For the format's tightening after September 11, 2001, with the Dixie Chicks banned for comments critical of President Bush and all women losing airplay, see Chris Willman's well-reported account, *Rednecks & Bluenecks*.

Even within this ample literature, *The Selling Sound* stood out for its skill at illustrating how commercialism, and anxiety about commercialism, motivated country as much as the music itself. Looking at 1920–47, Pecknold found "Hillbilly music was above all a creature of radio" and documented the disdain aimed at it by Tin Pan Alley and progressive reformers; advertisers were validating by comparison. With Acuff-Rose publishing and country charts, the music earned segment-of-pop status by the 1950s, raising new fears of crossover even as more anxiousness came at the audience. "I think that when they refer to country and western music as trash, they are referring to the American people as trash," Little Jimmy Dickens wrote in testimony to Congress that Pecknold unearthed. The Country Hall was scrutinized, as an industry effort to define and add respectability to the genre. That contrasted with how politicians courted, and films like Robert Altman's *Nashville* depicted, the audiences proliferating when the format boomed. But her key chapter followed the creation of the Country Music Association in the late 1950s and its woman-led work steering radio stations to become all country, using a new rhetoric: "It will be sophisticated, it will not be 'hokeyed' up, it will be a tight Top 40 format, but with country music." And: "We are all going to get rich with this."

WHERE DOES CLASSICAL MUSIC FIT IN?

Alex Ross, The Rest Is Noise: Listening to the Twentieth Century, *2007*

———

Few books were as warmly welcomed as this longtime *New Yorker* music critic's look at classical composers: awards, MacArthur fellowship, no wonder us pop types get tetchy. But that raises a question worth a skim. To what extent could classical in the United States, given its social and at times financial prominence, its role as an ideal for figures in jazz, rock, or musical theater, be viewed as itself a form of popular music?

Other entries in this book touch on answers. Musicologists in the **Oscar Sonneck**, **Gilbert Chase**, **H. Wiley Hitchcock**, and **Richard Crawford** vein emphasized "American music"—hence the Society for American Music and its Grove Dictionaries. This subfield prioritized composers, including Gershwin types; space for the popular grew but the conservatory persisted. Democratic cultural figures celebrated admixtures, from **Walt Whitman** admiring opera as one of many songs to historian **Lawrence Levine** denouncing the "sacralization" of culture in *Highbrow Lowbrow* and **Wayne Koestenbaum** going browless in his writing on opera queens. Whether **Alain Locke** or **Eileen Southern**, Black intellectuals often preferred Black folk styles transformed to classical form; the European composer Dvořák's support for that move reverberated, though **Duke Ellington**—the best candidate—found his longest works controversial and even an honorary Pulitzer denied him. Middlebrow authors, such as **Sigmund Spaeth** and **David Ewen**, sought a genteel reconciliation, bitterly denounced by radical theorist **Theodor Adorno** as the "Radio Symphony" but shown as industry reality by historians such as William Kenney and David Suisman recounting the first star tenor of records, Caruso. **John Cage**, a classical dissident, joined the pop pantheon by charismatic refusal. And the cultural studies–informed musicology of **Susan McClary** or **Christopher Small**, with **Tia DeNora** a fellow traveler in sociology, applied the same tools to both classical and popular—musicking was musicking.

Joseph Horowitz, a *New York Times* critic who became an orchestra director and cultural influencer, explored classical's broader place in a trio of books. *Understanding Toscanini* used the cult around the Italian conductor, as he led not only the New York Philharmonic but the NBC Symphony Orchestra (raising Adorno's ire), to examine middlebrow classical, big on pomp and light on modernism. *Wagner Nights* notated an earlier U.S. craze for the German opera composer: conductor Anton Seidl, critic Henry Krehbiel, Brünnhilde as New Woman. All this, to Horowitz, challenged Levine's notion of high culture shunting aside the rest. His summary, *Classical Music in America*, prioritized U.S. presenters of culture as more innovative than composers, contrasted inbred Boston and outward-facing New York, and again made conductors a key, with market-aware touches like Leopold Stokowski, in matinee idol fashion, lying about his age. Horowitz perceived a schism as American popular music "displaced high culture as a national marker," classical relegated to a Walt Disney *Fantasia* appearance. Krehbiel had prophesied in 1908 that opera in America would remain marginal until "the vernacular becomes the language of the performances and native talent provides both works and interpreters. The day is far distant, but it will come." Had that day come, between Broadway, Leonard Bernstein's "crowning compositional achievement" *West Side Story*, and the "post-classical" experimental triumph, *Einstein on the Beach*? Not for Horowitz.

Ross didn't challenge Horowitz's "rise and fall" narrative so much as build enough history around classical to make its popular appeal irrelevant. He felt that way about rock, too, he confessed in an essays collection, *Listen to This*, having only heard it through the punk DJs on his Harvard college radio station. To Ross, what he preferred to call "the music" rather than classical was "always dying, ever-ending. It is like an ageless diva on a nonstop farewell tour." If anything, jazz and rock's accumulated erudition proved all music became classical in time. The epilogue of *The Rest Is Noise* argued: "the impulse to pit classical music against pop culture no longer makes intellectual or emotional sense." The first third of the book, set before Hitler's rise, positioned Schoenberg's atonalism off not only Adorno, his one-time student and champion, but Thomas Mann's novelization of that modernist moment, *Doctor Faustus*. Ross looked for other correspondences where he could: "the glassy chords of Thelonious Monk have a Schoenbergian tinge." As generous to academic lit as to literature itself, he drew on Carol Oja's *Making Music Modern*, a pivotal study of 1920s New York, where Gershwin debuted "Rhapsody in Blue" as Antheil did the even clankier *Ballet Mecanique*; critic Carl Van Vechten abandoned European sounds for ragtime; and ultramoderns joined composers' leagues with more melodic students of France's Nadia Boulanger such as Copland, Thomson, and Blitzstein. "Yes, we want our musical tastes to be governed by the young sophisticates rather than by Mrs. **Carrie Jacobs Bond**," Nicolas Slonimsky wrote in 1929, another modern at war with (feminized) sentiment.

Ross tracked modernization across continents, comparing ***Show Boat*** to Brecht and Weill's *Threepenny Opera*, but the events of his middle section— fascism, Stalinism, New Deal Americana—centered the United States as inexorably as Schoenberg, Adorno, and Mann's arrival in California. For a time, classical music was the stuff of patriotic totalitarians. Composers in Cold War America, reasonably, renounced this, embracing dissonance and difficulty, though JFK poured money into culture, too. Ultimately, Ross preferred a story in which "the music" exchanged multiplicity for either cultural dominance or uncompromised purity. He acknowledged the "absent center" of Black composers denied a dominant place, celebrated the arrival of gay composers such as Benjamin Britten, considered a musical like *West Side Story,* music by classical conductor (and gay man) Leonard Bernstein, "an uncompromisingly modern work." In *Listen to This*, he wrote about experimental rockers Radiohead, Björk, and **Bob Dylan**, even queer cabaret duo Kiki and Herb. But he most typically celebrated composers such as Steve Reich, John Adams, and James Luther Adams, with loose ties to Black musical sources or rock and punk lineages, but few anxieties about their rarefied, stable positions. A musicologist Ross cited, Robert Fink, made a strong case in *Repeating Ourselves* for minimalism as a realistic engagement with advertising and mediated desire, not to mention a kissing cousin of disco. As with *The Rest Is Noise*, this approach worried less about whether cultivated compositions engaged audiences, instead asking how creatively their makers had themselves been listening, engaging music beyond ornate chambers.

Early in the twentieth century, another magazine modernist destined to enter the literary pantheon, Willa Cather, wrote a novel, *Song of the Lark*, that in a sense re-created Sister Carrie, but as a *bildung* narrative of a heart-land woman's idiosyncratic classical voice training. (Ross would tell Cather's story, at least in relationship to music, in *Wagnerism*, a book that appeared as this one was wrapping up and that explores the afterlife of Wagner's leitmotifs and other influences on the forms and conceptualizing of culture well beyond music alone. Once again, he took a Horowitz premise—this time *Wagner Nights*—and submerged it in a postmodern worldliness of reference that here ranged through Darth Vader.) Early in the twenty-first century, musicologist Mina Yang wrote *Planet Beethoven*, opening with an image of another young conductor in the United States from afar, Gustavo Dudamel, asserting a rock star's aura at the Hollywood Bowl. Later, she told the story of Baby Mozart marketing campaigns and complained that for Alex Ross, "commercialism is a sign of life."

Was the critique valid? Increasingly, it seemed, in books like Philip Gentry's *What Will I Be*, a look at music and identity in Cold War America where John Cage sat comfortably next to Doris Day and doowop vocal groups in a chapters list, that Adorno's worry that in capitalist classical cultures "everything becomes 'theme,'" a brand extension, was accepted. But as the **Greil Marcus** test—or **Stuart Hall**–type cultural studies, for that matter—had long since demonstrated, incorporation by capitalism wasn't the final word on any subject. You had to listen for what came next: exactly Ross's patient life endeavor, not unlike **Gary Giddins**'s vision of jazz. If **Robert Johnson** at the crossroads was one resonant myth, a Marcus myth, Faustian pacts outlined another, the Ross myth. In the United States at least, "the music"—to the extent that, for better or worse, it was understood to never really just be about that—could be coaxed to contain it all.

POPTIMISM, 33⅓ BOOKS, AND THE STRUGGLES OF MUSIC CRITICS

Carl Wilson, Let's Talk about Love: A Journey to the End of Taste, *2007*

———

The 33⅓ series of short monographs on individual albums began in 2003 with *Dusty in Memphis* by the perfectly positioned Warren Zanes, a musician (Del Fuegos), academic (visual and cultural studies PhD), and independent scholar (Rock and Roll Hall of Fame education department, then Tom Petty's biographer). Fifteen years later, with publisher Continuum sold to Bloomsbury, there were 135 titles in the series proper and climbing, with 33⅓ Global spinoffs for Brazil and Japan. Too much material for this squib to encompass, but the books deserve recognition as occupationally syncretic twenty-first-century popular music writing—sentence slinging in the age of the side hustle.

Two titles were said to be the most popular. Kim Cooper straddled pop and "unpopular culture" in her focus on Neutral Milk Hotel's *In the Aeroplane over the Sea*, as indie-defining an album as existed post-Nirvana. She gave a longer account than even the hardcore fan magazine *Uncut* might afford, based on interviews, and stayed out of the way critically. Wilson, later the contrarian website *Slate*'s music columnist, was all critic. His choice of Céline Dion's *Titanic* companion might have seemed the opposite of Cooper's approach. But the subtitle, unique in the series (an expanded edition, with essays by admirers of the first, changed it to *Why Other People Have Such Bad Taste*), gave the game away: this was an indie reckoning, via sociologist Pierre Bourdieu on cultural capital, with taste as elitism.

Wilson opened with a glimpse of Elliott Smith, doomed indie icon, miserable at an unlikely Academy Awards performance, alongside the all-too-present Dion, then questioned his own aversion as "guilty displeasure." He bruited taste biographies and reframed musical subcultures as breeding grounds of snobbery. His repositioning of Dion considered global pop from a working-class French Quebec perspective, sad songs through history (via **Charles Hamm**), Kant and Hume on taste into rock critics and rockism. Bourdieu's *Distinction* got a chapter: "coolness is a social category." Punk got asked, "Why, finally, should subversion be the *sine qua non*?" And by the end, he made clear that part of what he was doing was allowing for the fiercest forms of vernacular wheat-from-chaff record collection curating to dissolve in schmaltz—sentiment and tears: Dion fans in Vegas, Wilson alone at home mourning the end of his marriage.

A 33⅓ title might feature a favorite musician, like Colin Meloy of the Decemberists, on a favorite album: *Let It Be* by the Replacements, not **the Beatles**. Or impassioned musicology: Susan Fast denouncing the valuations that marginalized a Michael Jackson album like *Dangerous*. Writers in the imperiled magazine and newspaper business pursued passion projects: Michaelangelo Matos on *Sign 'O' the Times*, Geeta Dayal on *Another Green World*. Academics, working on a project much faster than a university press volume, showcased other sides of themselves: Daphne Brooks, better known for work on Aida Walker or Aretha Franklin, took up Jeff Buckley's *Grace*. The 33⅓ authors, often recruited through public calls for proposals, came to represent a vital community of form-obsessed contemplators and job collectors who loved nothing more than to play with an album's shape: its origins and impact, ability to register a social shift or provide the perfect text to soundtrack an idea.

A few boomers aside, the authors tended to be from rock and soul's later generations: happy to revisit, like Douglas Wolk, *Live at the Apollo*'s relationship to the Cuban Missile Crisis, or, like Jenn Pelly, postpunk's Raincoats as "women destroying isolation together." Some albums were famous and heralded, others obscure or more symptomatic, but that mattered less. This was writing not to make history but add to it, not to define opinions but live inside them. Unlike some cultural studies and social media writing, the presence of a central work kept aesthetics from becoming subsidiary. Those interviewed were off the promo cycle and friendlier for it. The series collectively reinforced a sense of popular music as an expository endeavor, a process. The money was crap: $3,000 advances in the early days, down to $500 years later. But for thirty thousand words, the floor was yours.

Structural pressures, from the internet to general economic malaise, had made both popular music as an industry and popular music writing precarious to start the new century. Publications like *Spin* and *Vibe* ceased print runs, with the *Village Voice* slowly curbed, too, and then closed altogether. Academics also suffered, with adjunct employment greeting many after long PhD training. The annual Pop Conference my partner **Ann Powers** and I began to organize in 2002, at the museum then called Experience Music Project, now Museum of Pop Culture, was one response, bringing academic and nonacademic writers together to bolster the ranks. (It was where Wilson debuted his Dion writing.) Three books that I edited resulted: *This Is Pop, Listen Again,* and *Pop When the World Falls Apart.* Another source of validation came from Da Capo's *Best Music Writing* roundups, published from 2000 through 2011, with guest editors a mix of critics (Powers, **Greil Marcus**, **Alex Ross**, **Nelson George**, **Robert Christgau**) and fiction writers (Mary Gaitskill, Nick Hornby, **Jonathan Lethem**).

Many of the same authors featured in each of these venues: the Pop Conference regulars in Wilson's expanded version of his book were as likely to come from academia (Jason King, Daphne Brooks, Drew Daniel) as to be writers with well-known bylines like Powers or Jody Rosen. The crew were frequently called poptimists for resisting centering criticism on the subjects or values of earlier rock and rap cohorts. (Promoting the reconsideration was Kelefa Sanneh's "The Rap against Rockism," a pivotal essay by a then–*New York Times* critic featured in the first Pop Conference collection who mostly turned to nonmusic topics at the *New Yorker*.) A poptimism defined by a Dion rethink involved commercial winners, yes, but also figures who, for reasons of background and experience, changed the mainstream when they entered it. If the internet and gig economy subtracted security, social media and streaming archives made self-publication and research easier than ever, the link to a cool performance on YouTube or Twitter thread substituting for the cultural studies era journal footnote. An imperative to bring non-straight-white-male voices forward diversified the ranks of authors.

Trends at the University of Texas Press showed something of what was possible. The Music Matters series, coedited by former *Voice* editor turned journalism professor **Evelyn McDonnell**, might feature academic and podcaster Karen Tongson on *Why Karen Carpenter Matters*, or longtime *Voice* critic and retired union worker Tom Smucker on *Why the Beach Boys Matter*. The same press's American Music series came under the co-editorship of Jessica Hopper, a social media firebrand who'd titled her own book *The First Collection of Criticism by a Living Female Rock Critic* and then used a short gig overseeing MTV.com to create a radical space for decently funded music writing. One of Hopper's regular authors, poet Hanif Abdurraqib, a Midwesterner with ties to emo and hip-hop, found surprising public recognition for his 2017 collection, *They Can't Kill Us until They Kill Us,* then unlikely sales with *Go ahead in the Rain*, a contemplation of rappers Tribe Called Quest that gave UT Press its first *New York Times* best-seller appearance in decades. Music writing wasn't always nice work anymore. But you could get it if you tried.

NOVELISTS COLLEGIAL WITH INDIE MUSIC

Jennifer Egan, A Visit from the Goon Squad, *2010*

———

When this Pulitzer-winning novel appeared, the relationship between fiction writers and at least a rarefied variant of popular music had become implicitly collegial. The models were novelist-critic types like **William Gibson, Jessica Hagedorn**, and **Jonathan Lethem**. Cool writers, like their friends from school in cool bands, craft-brewed the vernacular. Each confronted the postindustrial creative economy and multicultural globalism. And each was then slammed, after 9/11 by the collapse of American empire, within cities by the obscene gentrification they'd helped foster, and after digital everything arrived by format shifts that presented as unthinkable, paranormal—science fiction. If older novelists such as **Theodore Dreiser** and **F. Scott Fitzgerald** succumbed to modernity as a Faustian compact, novelists beyond the American century understood it as pop futurity, a text to deconstruct.

Jonathan Franzen, defender of the novel of society, was also a huge fan of the ultimate obscure rock critic's band, the Mekons, and brought those two tendencies to *Freedom*, his love triangle between Patty and Walter Berglund, classy progressives, and muse Richard Katz, leader of Jeff Tweedy and *Spin*-endorsed groups like the Traumatics. By the time the characters attended a Bright Eyes show at the 9:30 Club, a few things had become obvious. Bands "doing small-venue gigs attended by scruffy, well-educated white guys who were no longer as young as they used to be" were an endnote to "that era when we pretended rock was the scourge of conformity and consumerism, instead of its anointed handmaid." Cultural, social, economic, and political forms of capital were variant enough to make romance and bourgeois solidity, perennials for the novelist, fresh again. And American music could apparently still be treated as an all-white subject.

For Richard Powers and Michael Chabon, cross-race alliance was the only way music could be redemptive, or fail instructively. Powers's *The Time of Our Singing*, an epic that ranged—with a time travel twist—from Black opera singer Marian Anderson defying the Daughters of the American Revolution on the Washington Mall in 1939 to the Million Man March of 1995, focused on the children of German Jewish émigré David Strom and Philly Negro Delia Daley. "What exactly *are* you?" their three kids were asked. Music became an answer, from conservatory "white culture game" ("We're *uplift*") to the arrival of Black identity assertions. In James Weldon Johnson's novel *Autobiography of an Ex-Colored Man*, a German with European high-art methods fortifying him humbled the protagonist, a ragtime pianist. Nearly a century later, Powers's novel had the classically trained pianist son marvel at a gospel-improvising relative, learn vernacular from jazz and blues records, and then teach in post–Black Panthers Oakland, asked to play Wreckin' Cru on piano: "I tried the line again, this time juked up, hammered out, fitted with a good Baroque figured bass." "Call me Ishmael," Chabon wrote as the epigram to *Telegraph Avenue*, then made a not-so-kidding attribution to **Ishmael Reed**, novelist of the viral vernacular. Set in Berkeley, where partners Archy Stallings and Nat Jaffe ran Brokeland Records, specializing in jazz, and their wives had to accept that they would "never understand" vinyl, the novel seemed even more of a white projection of Black groove traditions undergoing "a kind of apocalypse" than Powers's, including a scene of State Senator Barack Obama offering marriage advice.

Novelists of color, increasingly prominent, found ways to foreground the inglorious history of musical whitesplaining. Former *Village Voice* television critic Colson Whitehead's *John Henry Days* imagined responses to *Chicago Defender* ads seeking info on that folk song, tracing them to the condescending early twentieth-century scholarship of Guy Johnson and Howard Odum. It was a panoramic view of lore that imagined the historical Henry alongside Tin Pan Alley song pluggers, down-home recorders, Paul Robeson, and a couplet that went "**Roland Barthes** got hit by a truck / That's a signifier you can't duck." Whitehead was acidic: the white scholar who "glorie[d] over the more vulgar versions of the ballad," the junket-seizing freelancer as unkillable roach, once at *Crawdaddy*, then *Stone*, now an infestation of "unadorned, service-oriented prose." *Slumberland*, former poetry slam champion Paul Beatty's novel about the "charade of blackness," might have been even more sardonic. The narrator in Berlin, as DJ Darky, quoted **Bert Williams**'s anthem of anomie, "Nobody"; remade lineages ("Audio Two's 'Top Billin' as rapped in the whistled language of the Nepalese Chepang"); pursued "The Perfect Beat" and declined an invite to score *Real Recognizes Real*: "I'd never score anything titled with black street vernacular." British-Indian journalist and former *Wallpaper* music editor Hari Kunzru's *White Tears* made the object of a record collector quest, bluesman Charlie Shaw, into an instrument of murderous vengeance: "he was never far, somewhere just around the corner, scuffing and shuffling his patent leather shoes, laughing his great rich hearty laugh. A mouth like a trap." Most dramatically, Marlon James's *A Brief History of Seven Killings* fictionalized an assassination attempt on Bob Marley into a baggy assemblage, staging a confrontation between Jamaican gangsters and a white *Rolling Stone* critic writing about their culture. They forced him to read his words aloud as they tortured him: "Man, people like me just excite you, eh? Put a white journalist beside him own 'Stagger Lee' and your brain go bananas." A door shut.

Prodigy Zadie Smith, who grew up in a later version of the London **Colin MacInnes** had once called *England, Half English*, showcased musical analysis in her writing, the Black diasporic sensibility and gender readings of her novels aligning with the critic's sensibility in her *New York Review of Books* essays and *Vibe* pieces, when they could get her. *White Teeth* introduced Millat and his crew, "a kind of cultural mongrel" of "Nation Brothers, Raggas, and Pakis." *On Beauty*, perhaps her best novel, was set in a university Black studies department, son Levi's hip-hop mix rejected at a faculty party for Al Green, Levi rejected in a different way at his clerk's job in a record store by single mom LaShonda: "all those girls who didn't give a fuck who the hell Gram-ski was."

Carl, a poetry slammer, was hired by the department's librarian to write a "context card" on Tupac. Husband and wife bonded reenacting a university glee club performing a samba version of U2. *Swing Time*, focused on the nexus of dance and pop from Astaire in the title to a **Madonna** stand-in character, had less pull as a novel but much Smith criticism—the narrator often offered *New York Review of Books* sentences: "for Astaire the person in the film was not especially connected with him." Bête noire Tracey's "world seemed childish to me, just a way of playing with the body, whereas I could walk down the hall and attend a lecture called something like 'Thinking the Black Body: A Dialectic.'" No one was more dialectical than Smith, who regularly put bodies and subcultures in conflict with spheres of discourse.

Dana Spiotta, a product of New Jersey suburbs, Los Angeles media, and (like most in this entry) Generation X displacement, also used identity splinters to prick the associations readers brought to music novels; her works included the major *Eat the Document* and intriguing *Stone Arabia*. (Don DeLillo, whose *Great Jones Street* had provided a template for the bohemian rock novel, was an early supporter.) Taking its title from an unreleased **Bob Dylan** film, *Eat* positioned Jason, collector of rarities like the Beach Boys *Smile* sessions and member of the "marginalites," against his mother, who could say "I met Dennis Wilson once," had appeared in cult films, and was still hiding from the government twenty-six years later. Divided by modes of participation, the two also enacted a generational debate over the meaning of the sixties, Spiotta giving X'er detail to "1970s split-level vernacular," suburbia as "a freak's dream world," and the "artificial vibrato of early-to-middle-period predigital synths." The former Caroline Sherman had fallen for a staunch vernacularist once, but now "The feeling she had for her son was sentimental, it was frightening, it was unimpeachable." When he came at her with Walter Benjamin on capitalist contradictions, she was ready: "He was talking about art, not people." *Stone Arabia*, pitting Nik, who invented his own rock-star life, down to fake clippings, against his enabling sister, imagined a "**Greil Marcus** Professor of Underground, Alternative, and Unloved Music"—but Nik was named for **Nik Cohn**, inventor of *Saturday Night Fever* and the *Rock Dreams* text. Spiotta's ontologies of musical worth in rock went deliriously beyond fake.

By centering on gender as an avenue into dream states of musical creation or consumption, novelists could range from gentrification to globalization and posthuman frontiers. Oberlin-to-Brooklyn author Emma Straub's *Modern Lovers*, named for proto-punk Jonathan Richman's band and featuring an epigram from Pavement ("If I could settle down / Then I would settle down") and a band called Kitty's Mustache, made indie-pop page turning out of real estate and omnivore taste. A son got into Brown with this thesis proposal: "My plan is to write a novel that both celebrates the youthful embrace of reckless love and the way that older people struggle with those same feelings some decades down the line. I plan to incorporate ideas from Jacques Derrida and Michel Foucault as well as to draw inspiration from hypertext-based internet platforms." New Nashville author Ann Patchett's *Bel Canto* adapted a real-life hostage crisis to put an opera singer in Latin America with her admiring Japanese CEO acolyte and a cast out of a film like *Traffic*, gaining a wide readership for how it substituted singing, and women's agency, for thriller action. And genre provocateur David Mitchell's magisterial and goofy genre piece *Cloud Atlas* nested stories about the conceits of civilization from slavery to corporatism and a neo-slave future. Music factored most heavily in the second narrative, about Robert Frobisher's indenture to composer Vyvyan Ayrs and the symphony as minaret, but Mitchell's reworking of a Loudon Wainwright lyric hinted at his full musical palette. (His rock novel, *Utopia Avenue*, appeared as this book was being finalized.) The material set in the "Corpocracy" brooded over consumerism and fashion as part of a "weak are meat the strong do eat" parable, and his science fiction and steampunk leanings inscribed variations of his theme across all modernity.

Egan, with ties to San Francisco, Brooklyn, and metafiction, structured her acclaimed book less as a novel than as a set of short stories with common reference points, a vinyl concept album with a designated A Side and B Side. The most talked-about short story, best read on her website, surveyed a futuristic, melted America through a single family's experience, presented via a set of PowerPoint slides and another experiment with blinkered communication: "Great Rock and Roll Pauses." If Egan's musical acumen was ordinary, her literary reach exceeded that of her many peers in the special category of music fiction. She conveyed media industries and the music business within that, the sexism of its executives but their gleeful risk taking and the women who more than took their bait. As with a great singer-songwriter, details registered in the terse prose: "Lou did some lines off Jocelyn's bare butt." The action shuffled, more CD than vinyl in that way, across fifty years, from counterculture to 9/11 to twenty years after, from pop as romance to relics in the desert. "Seventeen, hitchhiking. He was driving a red Mercedes. In 1979, that could be the beginning of an exciting story, a story where anything might happen. Now it's a punch line." Egan knew the tradition and ended with what might have been *Sister Carrie's* story: "It was another girl, young and new to the city, fiddling with her keys."

YOUTUBE, STREAMING, AND THE POPULAR MUSIC PERFORMANCE ARCHIVE

Will Friedwald, A Biographical Guide to the Great Jazz
and Pop Singers, *2010*

———

A prolific critic in the "you must remember this" category, Friedwald delineated the Bing Crosby and Sarah Vaughan continuum of pre-rock vocalists for decades, accumulating the lore of a New York jazz and cabaret scenester talking with managers, performers, and peers at shows, writing liner notes, plowing through promos and collecting rarities. There was much in his wheelhouse: artist anecdotes, connections between different eras and cover versions, and an ability to generalize from specifics: how Fred Astaire flicked rhythm using the extra syllables in *necessarily* in "Nice Work If You Can Get It"; the consequences of singers in the 1950s LP era being gifted a fantasy realm after Peggy Lee's Latinized rearrangement of Rodgers and Hart's "Lover" into a "polyrhythmic, polycultural, polyeverything." His writing could be sniffy, with "the cultural holocaust known as the late sixties" a frequent target. But he was always having a good time: **Ethel Waters** was "the only major vocalist who could sing the blues with rolled Rs."

Though his books ranged from a leading account of **Frank Sinatra**'s artistry to one that devoted a chapter each to how standards like "Stormy Weather" unfolded in recordings, *A Biographical Guide to the Great Jazz and Pop Singers* was his testament. To win this hot-dog-eating contest, Friedwald worked through eight hundred double-columned pages of alphabetized greats plus lesser figures grouped by topics like crooning and nods outside his specialty: **Bob Dylan** got nine affectionate pages, same as Frank, though fewer than Bing's thirteen. Music streaming needed to arrive, for a reader to spot listen (Spotify listen) while reading. But mostly, the media performances of these singers, from radio to movies to television, had to become available. "This is why God invented YouTube," Friedwald wrote, as he steered readers to Jack Teagarden returning to "Rockin' Chair" with Louis Armstrong on a 1957 *Timex All-Star Show*, the facial gestures and dialogue as pivotal as the moaned gutturals and upturned brass. When Friedwald told us the place to capture original piano man Matt Dennis was performing his saloon song "Angel Eyes" in an Ida Lupino film, *Jennifer*, we could find the whole movie online and quickly scroll fifty-five minutes in.

Friedwald was reflecting and critically demarcating a new archive, vital to correcting the paucity of scholarship on show-business figures who dominated mainstream entertainment for decades, on jazz as a spin on mass media more than principled resistance to it. He pulled his punches on racial appropriation, but he was terrific on the ambiguities of ethnicity: how in an ethos of assimilation, for example, the Andrews Sisters "were demonstrably ethnic—and yet they were not." There was a book within this book about the first album era, inspired by Sinatra but seized particularly by women singing outside their raised identity: across race lines, but also those of class, sexuality, region, genre: Lee, June Christy, Anita O'Day, Chris Connor, Jo Stafford, Kay Starr, Jeri Southern, Eartha Kitt, Abbey Lincoln. Fun was Friedwald's most serious subject, followed closely by the joys of listening through, and watching, the collected works. We came to the end of a century and were entrusted with a new toolkit to return us to the beginning.

IDIOSYNCRATIC MUSICIAN MEMOIRS—PERFORMER AS WRITER IN THE ERA OF THE ARTIST AS BRAND

Jay-Z, Decoded, *2010*

————

Musical form-futzer **Bob Dylan**'s *Chronicles* valued a seemingly minor encounter with a 1930s-identified poet over a "Like a Rolling Stone" rehash because that interaction with Archibald MacLeish's class politics and classroom aesthetics interested him more. A strand of idiosyncratic memoirs followed, leaving Wikipedia material alone. Jay-Z, who "saw the circle" of rappers as a preteen in Brooklyn and never left that hip-hop center, collaborated with (an uncredited) dream hampton, an activist critic and filmmaker with ties to the *Village Voice*, on a lyrics primer: the umpteenth iteration of a songbook. The first verse chosen? "Public Service Announcement," created when Elizabeth Méndez Berry, fresh off writing barbed appraisals of the brilliant but seemingly apolitical rapper for Oliver Wang's *Classic Material* collection of essays on hip-hop albums, challenged him for wearing a revolutionary's image on a T-shirt. Jay-Z thought about it and, next beat he could, rapped: "I'm like Che Guevara with bling on, I'm complex / I never claimed to have wings on."

The point, he insisted, was hip-hop's confrontational essence and multiple meanings: "it plants dissonance inside your head." The story of the rapper and the story of the hustler, artist, and agent collided in a way that remade art—two flows, just as the rapper worked off a DJ's straighter beat. But the contrast also remade commerce and the mainstream. "Everything that hip-hop touches is transformed by the encounter," he wrote, in the manner of a cultural studies academic, "especially things like language and brands, which leave themselves open to constant redefinition." He stressed a lyric that compared Reagan to 9/11 mastermind Osama bin Laden, wrote about the war on drugs as "a war on us," noted his pride at eclipsing the rock band Oasis and becoming one of Obama's symbolic cronies. The former Def Jam CEO related to managerial uses of music: "guys in corporate offices who psych themselves up listening to my music, which sounds odd at first, but makes sense." He didn't discount authenticity, but the bigger triumph was reconciling sentimentality and vernacular, like Scarface getting terrible news at the studio and compressing it into his guest verse on the spot. Blues truth? Tin Pan Alley potboiling? He told another story about the hard-knock lies he'd concocted to clear an *Annie* interpolation: a sweet, utterly untrue tale of winning an essay contest and getting to see the show. And returned to his central theme. "Rap is built to handle contradictions."

The same year as *Decoded*, another Manhattan invader, Patti Smith, published *Just Kids*, about how she and transgressive photographer Robert Mapplethorpe came of age in the Andy Warhol Pop Art version of a bohemia as eternal as her beloved Arthur Rimbaud. Smith befriended Harry Smith, creator of the fabled Folkways collection, while living at the Chelsea Hotel, and playwright Sam Shepard when he drummed for the Holy Modal Rounders. Artist or rock critic? She recalled 1966, when she was pregnant with a child she chose not to raise and was dismissed from college, sharing family quarters with fellow rocker Janet Hamill, "spending long evenings discoursing on the **Beatles** versus Rolling Stones." The mix was everything: "I tacked pictures of Rimbaud, Bob Dylan, Lotte Lenya, Piaf, Genet, and John Lennon, over a makeshift desk where I arranged my quills, my inkwell, and my notebooks—my monastic mess." She listened to opera, Coltrane, Stones, Baez, Dylan, Vanilla Fudge, Motown, called herself and Mapplethorpe "a curious mix of *Funny Face* and Faust." Mapplethorpe caught *Midnight Cowboy* and cottoned to one of Jay-Z's favorite words. "Hustler-hustler-hustler. I guess that's what I'm about."

A key moment found Smith changing her hair from Joan Baez– to Keith Richards–influenced and instantly being elevated; put in a Factory star's play, pushed by Dylan crony Bobby Neuwirth to turn poetry into songs. What made art life *vivid*? Kerouac "infused his being onto rolls of Teletype paper." A Metropolitan Museum curator of photos showed her nudes of Georgia O'Keefe shot by Alfred Stieglitz with Mapplethorpe. Shepard bought her a cool guitar and they wrote the play *Cowboy Mouth* together. *Creem* published a suite of her poems, causing more reactions than even her haircut. She took up pot after watching *The Harder They Come*. United with lifelong member of her band guitarist Lenny Kaye, around a doowop article and "Rock and Rimbaud" performances, recorded in Hendrix's Electric Lady studio. For the Mapplethorpe photo on her first album, she threw a jacket over her shoulder, **Frank Sinatra** style. "I was full of references."

Quirky bohemians proliferated, the reader in the bookstore or digger in the crates now virtually indistinguishable from the self-educated musician. Richard Hell's *I Dreamed I Was a Very Clean Tramp* put another Strand Books framework on CBGB punk. Roots drummer Ahmir "Questlove" Thompson's memoir, *Mo' Meta Blues*, told his life through record collecting. Carrie Brownstein's *Hunger Makes Me a Modern Girl* made such choices as riot grrrl Olympia, grad school, and *Portlandia* sketches a kind of gender blurring of art yen. Even the most conventional, Bruce Springsteen's *Born to Run*, which made damn sure it talked about his biggest hits, had "a story to tell" (Jay-Z lingo) about a hustler and "bit of a fraud," journeying from a version of Smith's Jersey seclusion to therapy sessions. This, not the ossified tributes to **Elvis** on *Ed Sullivan*, was the part Springsteen turned into a smash Broadway musical turn, his version of Stephen King's treatise on horror, *Danse Macabre*, in its conviction that one need not be a revolutionary to make personal neuroses nectar for a mass audience. "I recognize terror as the finest emotion and so I will try to terrorize the reader. But if I find that I cannot terrify, I will try to horrify, and if I find that I cannot horrify, I'll go for the gross-out. I'm not proud." Nor Springsteen and the rock-out.

Why had presentations of musicians as artisans of ambiguity replaced the pantheism of *Hammer of the Gods, Brother Ray*, or *Coal Miner's Daughter*, all premised on the performer's elevation away from the ordinary? One explanation was suggested by Anita Elberse's *Blockbusters*, a Harvard Business School professor's canny take on superstardom in a synergistic post-internet media convergence that required each celebrity to treat their brand like a start-up. Here, *Decoded* was presented as a case study: an ad firm with a book budget to market a pop star got a would-be search engine (Bing) to subsidize a campaign built on finding promotional pseudoevent counterparts to the "Easter egg" qualities of the lyrics Jay-Z so vitally annotated, in a precursor to the Genius.com website. If no genre, let alone the record business itself, could supply a star's heat, or a semipopular figure's mortgage, legitimacy swaps became embedded. Did the Dylan Nobel Prize give pop or literature more aura? Both/and.

But these books also came as late chapters in a now-familiar sequence, traced with fond asperity by Kevin Young in *The Grey Album*, named after the full-length Danger Mouse mash-up of Jay-Z's *Black Album*, lyrically, and the

Beatles' so-called White Album, musically. Young, a former Harvard college radio DJ who identified with such other Black Kansan poets as **Langston Hughes**, Gwendolyn Brooks, and Barack Obama, would go on to control the pipes to two faucets of popular music literature: archives (he directed the Schomburg Center for Research in Black Culture, then was named director of the Smithsonian's National Museum of African American History and Culture) and slicks (he edited the *New Yorker*'s poetry). In tribute to hustlers and hype he also studied *Bunk*, a history of phonies and the true-crime tabloid hype that had overlapped "blackness" since minstrel George Washington Dixon— recall Dale Cockrell's history, *Demons of Disorder*. Summon, too, critic Joan Morgan's insistence on a Black feminism "brave enough to fuck with the grays." *Grey Album*, topically expansive as **Fred Moten** but looser stylistically, engaged everything from the difference between dialect and vernacular in Paul Laurence Dunbar's poetry of masks and caged bird song to the "Crazy" blues of Mamie Smith, long before Danger Mouse and CeeLo moved on to Gnarls Barkley. A Black modernity survey, sweepingly pitched but shaggily narrated, it turned increasingly personal as it approached the hip-hop present, finding kinship between post-soul dialectics and the strategic refusals of Young's pre-soul Negro idols. All mashed up. And a particularly American place for my own decoding to end.

ACKNOWLEDGMENTS

It may be hard to distinguish the notes of gratitude in what follows from obligations of full disclosure. This book is about the very different kinds of writers who have tackled the question of pop, case by case, over time. I came into that picture in the 1990s, as a history grad student at UC Berkeley and record reviewer for alternative weeklies like the *San Francisco Bay Guardian*. After I got through qualifying exams, *Spin* hired me, first to edit their *Spin Alternative Record Guide*, then as a staff editor. Then it was on to the *Village Voice*, where I was music editor and a BUF (bargaining unit freelancer, health insurance included) as the decade ended. I next took a job at a new museum in Seattle, Experience Music Project, these days Museum of Pop Culture, where in 2002 I founded an annual gathering, the Pop Conference, bringing academics and nonacademics into conversation with each other. It continues to this day and more than anything else underlies this book's sense of mission. A return to academia came next: dissertating from afar and irritable at an adviser requiring orthodox history, I tossed off a 33⅓ book on a Guns N' Roses album to remind myself what I sounded like winging it.

These days, I'm tenured, coedit the academic *Journal of Popular Music Studies*, and can mostly make my own choices about topics and methods. But I'm mad that there isn't a *Village Voice* music section to read anymore, still root for writing that throws in stuff nobody would have expected or makes you stop to admire a sentence. And I spend a lot of my time with folks of the same ilk, the Pop Conference gang, so I'm friendly with many of those in this book.

Notably, Robert Christgau shaped my basic taste, helped bring me into the *Village Voice*, has avidly supported the Pop Conference since he co-keynoted the first one, and oh yeah, co-officiated at my wedding. Josh Kun, whom I edited at the *Voice*, series-edits me this time and helped brainstorm the book's basic structure, alongside Pop Conference stalwart and Duke editorial director Ken Wissoker; thanks, too, to Refiguring American Music series editors Ronald Radano and Nina Sun Eidsheim. Critic pals mentioned in these pages include Gina Arnold, Jeff Chang, Joshua Clover, Chuck Eddy, Jessica Hopper, Barry Mazor, Evelyn McDonnell, Simon Reynolds, Alex Ross, Jody Rosen, my *Spin Guide* collaborator Rob Sheffield, RJ Smith, and Carl Wilson. Pop Conference cronies who advised me on entries here include Christine Bacareza Balance, Lara Langer Cohen, Daniel Goldmark, Jewly Hight, Charles Hughes, my *Journal of Popular Music Studies* coeditor Robin James, Mark Katz, Keir Keightley, Roshanak Kheshti, Raymond Knapp, Jennifer Lena, Emily Lordi, Eric Lott, Greil Marcus, Michaelangelo Matos, Jeffrey Melnick, Oliver Wang, S. Alexander Reed, Barry Shank, Greg Tate, Steve Waksman, Gayle Wald, and Christi Jay Wells. But honestly, others cited deserve mention for shaping my sense of things in their work and our personal interactions: Daphne Brooks, Jayna Brown, Ashon Crawley, Alice Echols, Robert Fink, Nadine Hubbs, Karl Hagstrom Miller, Tavia Nyong'o, Diane Pecknold, David Ritz, Carlo Rotella, Gus Stadler, Karen Tongson, Elijah Wald.

Talking out and writing early versions of material here made the whole crazy enterprise more plausible: thanks to the Pop Conference, IASPM-US conference, and global IASPM biennial for hosting versions. A talk to a faculty seminar in Denmark became a chapter in *Music Radio* connecting vernacular and sentimental with my radio themes of genre and format: thanks to Morton Michelson, coauthor of *Rock Criticism from the Beginning*, for the invite. A presentation at Estudios de Rock Ecuador gave me the rare opportunity to present a translated overview—thanks to Hugo Burgos and Kembrew McLeod for that. *Journal of Popular Music Studies* let me focus on the question of academics and nonacademics in an article, "Old Books for New Ceremonies: CliffsNotes to the Literature of American Popular Music"—thanks to Oliver Wang for his edits. And the *Oxford Research Encyclopedia of American History* let me summarize rock and roll for an entry, which meant summarizing its books, another good dress rehearsal—thanks to Doug Rossinow for reaching out.

Librarians Cynthia Miller and Sarah Sahn at my work institution, University of Alabama, were a great help, as were the folks at my neighborhood library, Vanderbilt's Anne Potter Wilson Music Library: Holling Smith-Borne, Michael Jones, Robert Rich, Jacob Schaub, and especially Sara Manus. UA made my writing much easier with a research sabbatical and a Leadership Board fellowship. Thanks to former Arts and Sciences dean Robert Olin for that, former American Studies chair Lynne Adrian for the nomination—and to the department overall, especially new chair Edward Tang clearing my schedule when needed and Rich Megraw, ace scanner Stacy Morgan, and Mairin Odle for thoughts on the manuscript. Thanks to Ryan Bañagale, Robert Fink, Daniel Goldmark, and Marissa Moss for art images. To everybody on Facebook, like my friend dating back to Berkeley, Jesse Berrett, who threw out a book suggestion when I asked about yet another topic, thanks for making reading books and writing sentences feel more communal than it otherwise might have. And to cantankerous Bebe Weisbard, who knows what she likes (and might prefer Steve Waksman's books!), thanks for taking some pride in your goofy dad.

Ann Powers has been my companion through each of these stages: Berkeley, alt-weeklies, New York, Seattle and PopCon, Tuscaloosa, and now Nashville, where she's a critic for NPR Music and I commute to Bama midweek. We've always talked books, movies, TV, politics, people, values, as much as we have records. I take for granted a dialogue with a music-writing eminence—first-ballot Hall of Famer, as Jody Rosen would put it. It's impossible to imagine this book existing without her. Can I say with love that she's my greatest conflict of interest of all?

WORKS CITED

Abbott, Lynn, and Doug Seroff. *The Original Blues: The Emergence of the Blues in African American Vaudeville, 1899–1926*. University Press of Mississippi, 2017.

Abbott, Lynn, and Doug Seroff. *Out of Sight: The Rise of American Popular Music, 1889–1895*. University Press of Mississippi, 2002.

Abbott, Lynn, and Doug Seroff. *Ragged but Right: Black Traveling Shows, "Coon Songs," and the Dark Pathway to Blues and Jazz*. University Press of Mississippi, 2007.

Abbott, Lynn, and Doug Seroff. *To Do This, You Must Know How: Music Pedagogy in the Black Gospel Quartet Tradition*. University Press of Mississippi, 2015.

Abdurraqib, Hanif. *Go Ahead in the Rain: Notes to A Tribe Called Quest*. University of Texas Press, 2019.

Abdurraqib, Hanif. *They Can't Kill Us Until They Kill Us*. Two Dollar Radio, 2017.

Abreu, Christina. *Rhythms of Race: Cuban Musicians and the Making of Latino New York City and Miami, 1940–1960*. University of North Carolina Press, 2015.

Acosta, Leonardo. *Cubano Be Cubano Bop: One Hundred Years of Jazz in Cuba*. Smithsonian, 2003.

Adams, Alice. *Listening to Billie*. Knopf, 1978.

Adelt, Ulrich. *Blues Music in the Sixties: A Story in Black and White*. Rutgers University Press, 2010.

Adler, Bill. *Love Letters to the Beatles*. Putnam, 1964.

Adorno, Theodor. *Current of Music: Elements of a Radio Theory*. Edited by Robert Hullot-Kentor. Polity, 2009.

Adorno, Theodor. *Dream Notes*. Translated by Rodney Livingstone. Edited by Christoph Gödde and Henri Lonitz. Polity, 2007.

Adorno, Theodor. *Essays on Music*. Edited by Richard Leppert. University of California Press, 2002.

Adorno, Theodor. *Minima Moralia: Reflections from Damaged Life*. 1951. Translated by E. F. N. Jephcott. Verso, 1985.

Ake, David. *Jazz Cultures*. University of California Press, 2002.

Albertine, Viv. *Clothes, Clothes, Clothes, Music, Music, Music, Boys, Boys, Boys*. Dunne/St. Martin's, 2014.

Aletti, Vince. *The Disco Files 1973–78: New York's Underground, Week by Week*. DJhistory .com, 2009.

Alexie, Sherman. *Reservation Blues*. Grove, 1995.

Allen, William Francis, Charles Pickard Ware, and Lucy McKim Garrison, eds. *Slave Songs of the United States*. Simpson, 1867.

Almond, Marc. *Tainted Life: The Autobiography*. Sidgwick and Jackson, 1999.

Amos, Tori, and Ann Powers. *Tori Amos: Piece by Piece*. Broadway, 2000.

Anderson, Annye C., with Preston Lauterbach. *Brother Robert: Growing Up with Robert Johnson*. Hachette, 2020.

Andersen, Mark, and Mark Jenkins. *Dance of Days: Two Decades of Punk in the Nation's Capital*. 2003. Akashic, 2009.

Ansdell, Gary, and Tia DeNora. *Musical Pathways in Recovery: Community Music Therapy and Mental Wellbeing*. Routledge, 2016.

Aparicio, Frances. *Listening to Salsa: Gender, Latin Popular Music, and Puerto Rican Cultures*. Wesleyan University Press, 1998.

Aparicio, Frances, and Cándida Jáquez, eds. *Musical Migrations: Transnationalism and Cultural Hybridity in Latin/o America*. Palgrave Macmillan, 2003.

Appadurai, Arjun. *Modernity at Large: Cultural Dimensions of Globalization*. University of Minnesota Press, 1996.

Appert, Catherine. *In Hip Hop Time: Music, Memory, and Social Change in Urban Senegal*. Oxford University Press, 2018.

Armstrong, Louis. *Louis Armstrong's 50 Hot Choruses for Cornet*. Transcribed by Elmer Schoebel. Melrose, 1927.

Armstrong, Louis. *Louis Armstrong's 125 Jazz Breaks for Cornet*. Transcribed by Elmer Schoebel. Melrose, 1927.

Armstrong, Louis. *Satchmo: My Life in New Orleans*. Prentice Hall, 1954.

Armstrong, Louis. *Swing That Music*. Longmans, Green, 1936.

Arnold, Gina. *Exile in Guyville*. Bloomsbury, 2014.

Arnold, Gina. *Half a Million Strong: Crowds and Power from Woodstock to Coachella*. University of Iowa Press, 2018.

Arnold, Gina. *Kiss This: Punk in the Present Tense*. St. Martin's, 1997.

Arnold, Gina. *Route 666: On the Road to Nirvana*. St. Martin's, 1993.

Atkins, Ace. *Crossroad Blues*. Dunne/St. Martin's, 1998.

Attali, Jacques. *Noise: The Political Economy of Music*. 1977. Translated by Brian Massumi. University of Minnesota Press, 1985.

Austin, William W. *"Susanna," "Jeannie," and "The Old Folks at Home": The Songs of Stephen C. Foster from His Time to Ours*. Macmillan, 1975.

Avery, Ken. *Everything Is an Afterthought: The Life and Writings of Paul Nelson*. Fantagraphics, 2011.

Azerrad, Michael. *Come as You Are: The Story of Nirvana*. Three Rivers, 1993.

Azerrad, Michael. *Our Band Could Be Your Life: Scenes from the American Rock Underground, 1981–1991*. Little, Brown, 2001.

Badger, Reid. *A Life in Ragtime: A Biography of James Reese Europe*. Oxford University Press, 1995.

Bag, Alice. *Violence Girl: East L.A. Rage to Hollywood Stage, a Chicana Punk Story*. Feral House, 2011.

Bagge, Peter. *Buddy Does Seattle: The Complete Buddy Bradley Stories from "Hate" Comics, Vol. I, 1990–94*. Fantagraphics, 2005.

Bailey, Marlon. *Butch Queens Up in Pumps: Gender, Performance, and Ballroom Culture in Detroit*. University of Michigan Press, 2013.

Baker, Dorothy. *Young Man with a Horn*. Houghton, Mifflin, 1938. Reissue with afterword by Gary Giddins, NYRB Classics, 2012.

Baker, Houston. *Blues, Ideology, and Afro-American Literature: A Vernacular Theory*. University of Chicago Press, 1984.

Balance, Christine Bacareza. *Tropical Renditions: Making Musical Scenes in Filipino America*. Duke University Press, 2016.

Balfour, Victoria. *Rock Wives: The Hard Lives and Good Times of the Wives, Girlfriends, and Groupies of Rock and Roll*. Morrow, 1986.

Ballard, J. G. *The Atrocity Exhibition*. Cape, 1970.

Balliett, Whitney. *Alec Wilder and His Friends*. Houghton Mifflin, 1974.

Balliett, Whitney. *American Musicians II: Seventy-One Portraits in Jazz*. Oxford University Press, 1996.

Balliett, Whitney. *American Singers: Twenty-Seven Portraits in Song*. Oxford University Press, 1988.

Balliett, Whitney. *The Sound of Surprise: 46 Pieces on Jazz*. Dutton, 1959.

Bañagale, Ryan Raul. "Isaac Goldberg: Assessing Agency in American Music Biography." *American Music Review* 39, no. 2 (2010): 8–9, 15.

Bane, Michael. *The Outlaws: Revolutions in Country Music*. Country Music Magazine Press/Doubleday/Dolphin, 1978.

Banes, Sally, and John Szwed. "From 'Messin' Around' to 'Funky Western Civilization': The Rise and Fall of Dance Instruction Songs." In *Dancing Many Drums: Excavations in African American Dance,* edited by Thomas DeFrantz, 169–204. University of Wisconsin Press.

Bangs, Lester. *Blondie*. Delilah, 1980.

Bangs, Lester. *Mainlines, Blood Feasts, and Bad Taste: A Lester Bangs Reader*. Edited by John Morthland. Anchor, 2003.

Bangs, Lester. *Psychotic Reactions and Carburetor Dung*. Edited by Greil Marcus. Knopf, 1987.

Baraka, Amiri [LeRoi Jones]. "6 Persons." 1974. In *The Fiction of LeRoi Jones/Amiri Baraka*. Hill, 2000.

Baraka, Amiri [LeRoi Jones]. *The Autobiography of LeRoi Jones*. Freundlich, 1984.

Baraka, Amiri [LeRoi Jones]. "Black Art." In *Black Fire: An Anthology of Afro-American Writing*, edited by LeRoi Jones and Larry Neal, 302–3. Morrow, 1968.

Baraka, Amiri [LeRoi Jones]. "Black Dada Nihilismus." In *The Dead Lecturer: Poems*. Grove, 1964.

Baraka, Amiri [LeRoi Jones]. *Black Music*. Morrow, 1967.

Baraka, Amiri [LeRoi Jones]. *Blues People*. Morrow, 1963. Introduction: Quill, 1999.

Baraka, Amiri [LeRoi Jones]. *Digging: The Afro-American Soul of American Classical Music*. University of California Press, 2009.

Baraka, Amiri [LeRoi Jones]. "Dutchman." In *Dutchman and the Slave: Two Plays*. Morrow, 1964.

Baraka, Amiri [LeRoi Jones]. "Jazz and the White Critic: A Provocative Essay on the Situation of Jazz Criticism." *Down Beat*, August 15, 1963.

Baraka, Amiri. *The Music: Reflections on Jazz and Blues*. Morrow, 1987.

Baraka, Amiri [LeRoi Jones]. *Preface to a Twenty Volume Suicide Note*. Totem, 1961.

Baraka, Amiri [LeRoi Jones]. "The Screamers." In *Tales*. Grove, 1967.

Barcella, Laura, ed. *Madonna and Me: Women Writers on the Queen of Pop*. Soft Skull, 2012.

Barrett, Mary Ellin. *Irving Berlin: A Daughter's Memoir*. Simon and Schuster, 1994.

Barthes, Roland. *Image—Music—Text*. Translated by Stephen Heath. Hill and Wang, 1977.

Barthes, Roland. *Mourning Diary: October 26, 1977–September 15, 1979*. Translated by Richard Howard. Hill and Wang, 2010.

Barthes, Roland. *Mythologies*. Translated by Annette Lavers. Macmillan, 1972. *The Complete Edition*, translated by Richard Howard. Hill and Wang, 2012.

Barthes, Roland. *Roland Barthes*. Translated by Richard Howard. Hill and Wang, 1977.

Barthes, Roland. *S/Z: An Essay*. Translated by Richard Miller. Hill and Wang, 1974.

Bartmanski, Dominik, and Ian Woodward. *Vinyl: The Analogue Record in the Digital Age*. Bloomsbury, 2015.

Basie, Count, as told to Albert Murray. *Good Morning Blues: The Autobiography of Count Basie*. Random House, 1985.

Bauldie, John, ed. *Wanted Man: In Search of Bob Dylan*. Penguin, 1992.

Bayton, Mavis. *Frock Rock: Women Performing Popular Music*. Oxford University Press, 1998.

The Beatles. *The Beatles Anthology*. Chronicle, 2000.

Beatty, Paul. *Slumberland*. Harvill Secker, 2008.

Becker, Howard S. *Art Worlds*. University of California Press, 1982.

Becker, Howard S. *Exploring Society Photographically*. Mary and Leigh Block Gallery, Northwestern University, 1981.

Becker, Howard S., ed. *The Other Side: Perspectives in Deviance*. Free Press of Glencoe, 1962.

Becker, Howard S. *Outsiders: Studies in the Sociology of Deviance*. Free Press of Glencoe, 1963.

Becker, Howard S., ed. *Social Problems: A Modern Approach*. Wiley, 1966.

Becker, Howard S. *Sociological Work: Method and Substance*. Aldine, 1970.

Becker, Howard S. *Telling about Society*. University of Chicago Press, 2007.

Becker, Howard S. *Tricks of the Trade: How to Think about Your Research while You're Doing It*. University of Chicago Press, 1998.

Becker, Howard S. *Writing for Social Scientists*. University of Chicago Press, 1986.

Becker, Howard S., Robert R. Faulkner, and Barbara Kirshenblatt-Gimblett, eds. *Art from Start to Finish: Jazz, Painting, Writing, and Other Improvisations*. University of Chicago Press, 2006.

Becker, Howard S., and Robert R. Faulkner. *"Do You Know . . . ?" The Jazz Repertoire in Action*. University of Chicago Press, 2009.

Becker, Howard S., and Robert R. Faulkner. *Thinking Together: An E-Mail Exchange and All That Jazz*. USC Annenberg Press, 2013.

Becker, Jane. *Selling Tradition: Appalachia and the Construction of an American Folk, 1930–1940*. University of North Carolina Press, 1998.

Bederman, Gail. *Manliness and Civilization: A Cultural History of Gender and Race in the United States, 1880–1917*. University of Chicago Press, 1995.

Belgrad, Daniel. *The Culture of Spontaneity: Improvisation and the Arts in Postwar America*. University of Chicago Press, 1998.

Belsito, Peter, and Bob Davis. *Hardcore California: A History of Punk and New Wave*. Last Gasp, 1983.

Belz, Carl. *The Story of Rock*. Oxford University Press, 1969.

Bennett, Andy, Barry Shank, and Jason Toynbee, eds. *The Popular Music Studies Reader*. Routledge, 2006.

Benson, Carl, ed. *The Bob Dylan Companion: Four Decades of Commentary*. Schirmer, 1998.

Bergreen, Laurence. *As Thousands Cheer: The Life of Irving Berlin*. Viking, 1990.

Berlant, Lauren. "On Persistence." *Social Text* 32, no. 4 (2014): 33–37.

Berlant, Lauren. "Pax Americana: The Case of Show Boat." In *The Female Complaint: The Unfinished Business of Sentimentality in American Culture*, 69–106. Duke University Press, 2008.

Berlin, Edward. *King of Ragtime: Scott Joplin and His Era*. New York: Oxford University Press, 1994. Rev. ed., Oxford University Press, 2016.

Berlin, Edward. *Ragtime: A Musical and Cultural History*. University of California Press, 1980.

Berliner, Paul. *Thinking in Jazz: The Infinite Art of Improvisation*. University of Chicago Press, 1994.

Berman, Marshall. *All That Is Solid Melts into Air: The Experience of Modernity*. Simon and Schuster, 1982.

Bernard, Emily. *Carl Van Vechten and the Harlem Renaissance: A Portrait in Black and White*. Yale University Press, 2012.

Berrett, Joshua, ed. *The Louis Armstrong Companion: Eight Decades of Commentary*. Schirmer, 1999.

Berry, Chuck. *Chuck Berry: The Autobiography*. Harmony, 1987.

Berton, Ralph. *Remembering Bix: A Memoir of the Jazz Age*. Harper and Row, 1974.

Bertrand, Michael. *Race, Rock, and Elvis*. University of Illinois Press, 2000.

Beste, Peter. *True Norwegian Death Metal*. Vice, 2008.

Billings, William. *The Complete Works of William Billings*. Edited by Karl Kroeger. 4 vols. American Musicological Society and Colonial Society of Massachusetts, 1977–90.

Billings, William. *The Continental Harmony*. Thomas and Andrews, 1794.

Billings, William. *The New-England Psalm-Singer*. Edes and Gill, 1770.

Billings, William. *The Singing Master's Assistant*. Draper and Folsom, 1778.

Blackburn, Julia. *With Billie: A New Look at the Unforgettable Lady Day*. Vintage, 2006.

Blacking, John. *How Musical Is Man?* University of Washington Press, 1973.

Blesh, Rudi. *Shining Trumpets: A History of Jazz*. Knopf, 1946. 2nd ed., 1958.

Blesh, Rudi, and Harriet Janis. *They All Played Ragtime: The True Story of an American Music*. Knopf, 1950. Rev. ed., Oak, 1966.

Block, Geoffrey Holden. *Enchanted Evenings: The Broadway Musical from "Show Boat" to Sondheim*. Oxford University Press, 1997. 2nd ed., 2009.

Blush, Stephen. *American Hardcore: A Tribal History*. Feral House, 2001. 2nd ed., 2010.

Boggs, Vernon. *Salsiology: Afro-Cuban Music and the Evolution of Salsa in New York City*. Greenwood, 1992.

Bogle, Donald. *Heat Wave: The Life and Career of Ethel Waters*. HarperCollins, 2011.

Bohlman, Philip. *The Study of Folk Music in the Modern World*. Indiana University Press, 1988.

Bolton, Andrew. *Punk: Chaos to Couture*. Metropolitan Museum of Art/Yale University Press, 2013.

Booth, Stanley. *Keith: Standing in the Shadows*. St. Martin's, 1995.

Booth, Stanley. *Rhythm Oil: A Journey through the Music of the American South*. Pantheon Books, 1991.

Booth, Stanley. *The True Adventures of the Rolling Stones*. (Original title: *Dance with the Devil: The Rolling Stones and Their Times*.) Random House, 1984.

Bordman, Gerald. *American Musical Theatre: A Chronicle*. Oxford University Press, 1978. 4th ed., with updates by Richard Norton, Oxford University Press, 2011.

Born, Georgina, ed. *Music, Sound, and Space: Transformations of Public and Private Experience*. Cambridge University Press, 2013.

Born, Georgina, and David Hesmondhalgh, eds. *Western Music and Its Others: Difference, Representation, and Appropriation in Music*. University of California Press, 2000.

Bosse, Joanna. *Becoming Beautiful: Ballroom Dance in the American Heartland*. University of Illinois Press, 2015.

Boulware, Jack, and Silke Tudor. *Gimme Something Better: The Profound, Progressive, and Occasionally Pointless History of Bay Area Punk from Dead Kennedys to Green Day*. Penguin, 2009.

Bourne, Stephen. *Ethel Waters: Stormy Weather*. Scarecrow, 2007.

Bowie, Angie. *Backstage Passes: Life on the Wild Side with David Bowie*. Orion, 1992.

Boyd, Pattie. *Wonderful Tonight: George Harrison, Eric Clapton, and Me*. Crown, 2007.

Boyer, Horace Clarence. *How Sweet the Sound: The Golden Age of Gospel*. Elliott and Clark, 1995.

Boyes, Georgina. *The Imagined Village: Culture, Ideology and the English Folk Revival*. Manchester University Press, 1993.

Brackett, David. *Categorizing Sound: Genre and Twentieth-Century Popular Music*. University of California Press, 2016.

Brackett, David. *Interpreting Popular Music*. Cambridge University Press, 1995. With new preface, University of California Press, 2000.

Brackett, David, ed. *The Pop, Rock, and Soul Reader*. Oxford University Press, 2004. 2nd ed., 2008. 3rd ed., 2013.

Bradley, Adam. *Ralph Ellison in Progress: From "Invisible Man" to "Three Days before the Shooting. . . . "* Yale University Press, 2010.

Bradley, Regina N. *Chronicling Stankonia: OutKast and the Rise of the Hip Hop South*. University of North Carolina Press, 2021.

Brady, Erika. *A Spiral Way: How the Phonograph Changed Ethnography*. University Press of Mississippi, 1999.

Brannigan, Paul, and Ian Winwood. *Birth School Metallica Death, Volume 1: The Biography*. Da Capo, 2013.

Brannigan, Paul, and Ian Winwood. *Into the Black: The Inside Story of Metallica (1991–2014)*. Da Capo, 2014.

Braun, Michael. *"Love Me Do!": The Beatles' Progress*. Penguin, 1964.

Brennan, Matt. *When Genres Collide: Down Beat, Rolling Stone, and the Struggle between Jazz and Rock*. Bloomsbury, 2017.

Bronson, Fred. *The Billboard Book of Number One Hits*. Billboard, 1985.

Bronson, Bertrand. *The Ballad as Song*. University of California Press, 1969.

Bronson, Bertrand. *Traditional Tunes of the Child Ballads*. 3 vols. Princeton University Press, 1959–71.

Brooks, Daphne. *Bodies in Dissent: Spectacular Performances of Race and Freedom, 1850–1910*. Duke University Press, 2006.

Brooks, Daphne. *Grace*. Continuum, 2005.

Brooks, Daphne. *Liner Notes for the Revolution: The Archive, the Critic, and Black Women's Sound Cultures*. Harvard University Press, 2021.

Brooks, Tim. *Lost Sounds: Blacks and the Birth of the Recording Industry, 1890–1919*. University of Illinois Press, 2004.

Brothers, Thomas, ed. *Louis Armstrong in His Own Words*. Oxford University Press, 1999.

Brothers, Thomas. *Louis Armstrong: Master of Modernism*. Norton, 2014.

Brothers, Thomas. *Louis Armstrong's New Orleans*. Norton, 2006.

Broven, John. *Record Makers and Breakers: Voices of the Independent Rock 'n' Roll Pioneers*. University of Illinois Press, 2008.

Brown, Andy, Karl Spracklen, Keith Kahn-Harris, and Niall Scott, eds. *Global Metal Music and Culture: Current Directions in Metal Studies*. Routledge, 2016.

Brown, Jayna. *Babylon Girls: Black Women Performers and the Shaping of the Modern*. Duke University Press, 2008.

Brown, Mary Ellen. *Child's Unfinished Masterpiece: The English and Scottish Popular Ballads*. University of Illinois Press, 2011.

Brown, Wesley. *Darktown Strutters*. Cane Hill, 1994.

Browne, David. *Crosby, Stills, Nash and Young: The Wild, Definitive Saga of Rock's Greatest Supergroup*. Da Capo, 2019.

Browne, David. *Dream Brother: The Lives and Music of Jeff and Tim Buckley*. It Books, 2001.

Browne, David. *Fire and Rain: The Beatles, Simon and Garfunkel, James Taylor, CSNY, and the Lost Story of 1970*. Da Capo, 2011.

Browne, David. *So Many Roads: The Life and Times of the Grateful Dead*. Da Capo, 2015.

Brownstein, Carrie. *Hunger Makes Me a Modern Girl: A Memoir*. Riverhead, 2015.

Broyles, Michael. *Mavericks and Other Traditions in American Music*. Yale University Press, 2004.

Broyles-González, Yolanda. *Lydia Mendoza's Life in Music*. Oxford University Press, 2001.

Bruce, Phyllis Ruth. "From Rags to Roses: The Life and Works of Carrie Jacobs-Bond, an American Composer." Master's thesis, Wesleyan University, 1980.

Bruce, Robert. *So You Want to Write a Song?* Mayfair, 1935.

Buckland, Fiona. *Impossible Dance: Club Culture and Queer World-Making*. Wesleyan University Press, 2002.

Buell, Bebe, with Victor Bockris. *Rebel Heart: An American Rock 'n' Roll Journey*. St. Martin's, 2001.

Bufwack, Mary, and Robert Oermann. *Finding Her Voice: The Saga of Women in Country Music*. Crown, 1993.

Bull, Michael. *Sound Moves: iPod Culture and Urban Experience*. Routledge, 2008.

Burchill, Julie, and Tony Parsons. *The Boy Looked at Johnny: The Obituary of Rock and Roll*. Pluto, 1978.

Burford, Mark. *Mahalia Jackson and the Gospel Field*. Oxford University Press, 2018.

Burlin, Natalie Curtis. "Negro Music at Birth." *Musical Quarterly* 5, no. 1 (1919): 86–89.

Burroughs, William S. *Naked Lunch*. Grove, 1959.

Burt, Stephen. "'O Secret Stars Stay Secret': Rock and Roll in Contemporary Poetry." In *This Is Pop: In Search of the Elusive at Experience Music Project*, edited by Eric Weisbard, 200–211. Harvard University Press, 2004.

Butler, Mark. *Playing with Something That Runs: Technology, Improvisation, and Composition in DJ and Laptop Performance*. Oxford University Press, 2014.

Butler, Mark. *Unlocking the Groove: Rhythm, Meter, and Musical Design in Electronic Dance Music*. Indiana University Press, 2006.

Byrne, David. *How Music Works*. McSweeney's, 2012.

Cabrera, Lydia. *Afro-Cuban Tales*. Translated by Alberto Hernandez-Chiroldes and Lauren Yoder. University of Nebraska Press, 2005.

Cabrera Infante, Guillermo. *Three Trapped Tigers*. Translated by Donald Gardner and Suzanne Jill Levine, with Guillermo Cabrera Infante. Harper and Row, 1971.

Cadigan, Pat. "Rock On." In *Mirrorshades: The Cyberpunk Anthology*, edited by Bruce Sterling, 34–42. Arbor House, 1986.

Cadigan, Pat. *Synners*. Bantam Spectra, 1991.

Cage, John. *Silence*. Wesleyan University Press, 1961.

Cage, John. *A Year from Monday: New Lectures and Writings*. Wesleyan University Press, 1967.

Cage, John, and Alison Knowles, eds. *Notations*. Something Else, 1969.

Campbell, Colin. "'Three-Minute Access': Fugazi's Negative Aesthetic." In *Adorno and the Need in Thinking: New Critical Essays*, edited by Donald Burke, Colin J. Campbell, Kathy Kiloh, Michael Palamarek, and Jonathan Short, 278–95. University of Toronto Press, 2007.

Campbell, Gavin James. "'Old Can Be Used Instead of New': Shape-Note Singing and the Crisis of Modernity in the New South, 1880–1920." *Journal of American Folklore* 110, no. 436 (1997): 169–88.

Campbell, John C. *The Southern Highlander and His Homeland*. Sage, 1921.

Campbell, Olive Dame. *The Life and Work of John Charles Campbell: September 15, 1868– May 2, 1919*. College, 1968.

Campbell, Olive Dame. "Songs and Ballads of the Southern Mountains." *The Survey*, January 2, 1915, 371–74.

Campbell, Olive Dame, and Cecil J. Sharp. *English Folk Songs from the Southern Appalachians: Comprising 122 Songs and Ballads, and 323 Tunes*. Putnam, 1917.

Cantwell, Robert. "A Picture from Life's Other Side: Lee Smith's 'The Devil's Dream.'" *Appalachian Journal* 20, no. 3 (1993): 276–83.

Cantwell, Robert. *Bluegrass Breakdown: The Making of the Old Southern Sound*. University of Illinois Press, 1984.

Cantwell, Robert. *Ethnomimesis: Folklife and the Representation of Culture*. University of North Carolina Press, 1993.

Cantwell, Robert. *If Beale Street Could Talk: Music, Community, Culture*. University of Illinois Press, 2008.

Cantwell, Robert. *When We Were Good: The Folk Revival*. Harvard University Press, 1996.

Carby, Hazel V. "The Politics of Fiction, Anthropology, and the Folk: Zora Neale Hurston." In *New Essays on Their Eyes Were Watching God*, edited by Michael Awkward, 71–94. Cambridge University Press, 1991.

Carducci, Joe. *Rock and the Pop Narcotic: Testament for the Electric Church*. Redoubt, 1990. Rev. ed., 1995; 3rd ed., 2005.

Carlin, Robert. *The Birth of the Banjo: Joel Walker Sweeney and Early Minstrelsy*. McFarland, 2007.

Carmer, Carl. *Stars Fell on Alabama*. Farrar and Rinehart, 1934.

Carner, Gary, ed. *The Miles Davis Companion: Four Decades of Commentary*. Schirmer, 1996.

Carpentier, Alejo. *The Kingdom of This World*. Translated by Harriet de Onís. Knopf, 1957.

Carpentier, Alejo. *Music in Cuba*. 1946. Edited by Timothy Brennan. Translated by Alan West-Durán. Minneapolis: University of Minnesota Press, 2001.

Carr, Ian. *Miles Davis: A Critical Biography*. Quartet Books, 1982. Rev. ed., expanded, Thunder's Mouth, 1998.

Carr, Patrick, ed. *The Illustrated History of Country Music*. Doubleday, 1979.

Carr, Roy and Tony Tyler. *The Beatles: An Illustrated Record*. Harmony, 1975.

Casillas, Dolores Inés. *Sounds of Belonging: U.S. Spanish-Language Radio and Public Advocacy*. New York University Press, 2014.

Castle, Terry. "My Heroin Christmas: Art Pepper and Me." In *The Professor and Other Writings*, 41–80. Harper, 2010.

Cather, Willa. *The Song of the Lark*. Houghton Mifflin, 1915.

Cepeda, Raquel, ed. *And It Don't Stop: The Best American Hip-Hop Journalism of the Last 25 Years*. Farrar, Straus and Giroux, 2004.

Chabon, Michael. *Telegraph Avenue*. HarperCollins, 2012.

Chadwick, Vernon, ed. *In Search of Elvis: Music, Race, Art, Religion*. Westview, 1997.

Chambers, Iain. *Popular Culture: The Metropolitan Experience*. Routledge, 1986.

Chambers, Iain. *Urban Rhythms: Pop Music and Popular Culture*. St. Martin's, 1985.

Chambers, Jack. *Milestones: The Music and Times of Miles Davis*. Beech Tree, 1983. *Milestones 2: The Music and Times of Miles Davis*. University of Toronto Press, 1985. Combined ed., Da Capo, 1998.

Chambers-Letson, Joshua. *After the Party: A Manifesto for Queer of Color Life*. New York University Press, 2018.

Chanan, Michael. *Repeated Takes: A Short History of Recording and Its Effects on Music*. Verso, 1995.

Chang, Jeff. *Can't Stop, Won't Stop: A History of the Hip-Hop Generation*. St. Martin's, 2005.

Chang, Jeff, and Dave "Davey D" Cook. *Can't Stop Won't Stop (Young Adult Edition): A History of the Hip-Hop Generation*. Wednesday, 2021.

Chang, Jeff, ed. *Total Chaos: The Art and Aesthetics of Hip-Hop*. Civitas, 2008.

Chapman, Dale. *The Jazz Bubble: Neoclassical Jazz in Neoliberal Culture*. University of California Press, 2018.

Chapple, Steve, and Reebee Garofalo. *Rock 'n' Roll Is Here to Pay: The History and Politics of the Music Industry*. Nelson-Hall, 1977.

Charles, Ray and David Ritz. *Brother Ray: Ray Charles' Own Story*. Dial, 1978.

Charnas, Dan. *The Big Payback: The History of the Business of Hip-Hop*. NAL, 2010.

Charry, Eric, ed. *Hip Hop Africa: New African Music in a Globalizing World*. Indiana University Press, 2012.

Charters, Ann. *Kerouac: A Biography*. Straight Arrow, 1973.

Charters, Ann. *Nobody: The Story of Bert Williams*. Macmillan, 1970.

Charters, Ann, and Samuel Charters. *Blues Faces: A Portrait of the Blues*. Godine, 2000.

Charters, Ann, and Samuel Charters. *Brother Souls: John Clellon Holmes, Jack Kerouac, and the Beat Generation*. University Press of Mississippi, 2010.

Charters, Samuel. *The Bluesmen: The Story and the Music of the Men Who Made the Blues*. Oak, 1967.

Charters, Samuel. *The Country Blues*. Rinehart, 1959.

Charters, Samuel. *The Day Is So Long and the Wages So Small: Music on a Summer Island*. Marion Boyars, 1999.

Charters, Samuel. *Elvis Presley Calls His Mother after the Ed Sullivan Show: A Novel*. Coffee House, 1992.

Charters, Samuel. *Jelly Roll Morton's Last Night at the Jungle Inn: An Imaginary Memoir.* Marion Boyars, 1984.

Charters, Samuel. *A Language of Song: Journeys in the Musical World of the African Diaspora.* Duke University Press, 2009.

Charters, Samuel. *The Legacy of the Blues: A Glimpse into the Art and the Lives of Twelve Great Bluesmen: An Informal Study.* Calder and Boyars, 1975.

Charters, Samuel. *New Orleans: Playing a Jazz Chorus.* Marion Boyars, 2006.

Charters, Samuel. *The Poetry of the Blues.* Oak, 1963.

Charters, Samuel. *The Roots of the Blues: An African Search.* Putnam, 1981.

Charters, Samuel. *Songs of Sorrow: Lucy McKim Garrison and Slave Songs of the United States.* University Press of Mississippi, 2015.

Charters, Samuel. *Sweet as the Showers of Rain (The Bluesmen, Vol. II).* Oak, 1977.

Charters, Samuel. *A Trumpet around the Corner: The Story of New Orleans Jazz.* University Press of Mississippi, 2008.

Charters, Samuel. *Walking a Blues Road: A Selection of Blues Writing 1956–2004.* Marion Boyars, 2004.

Charters, Samuel, and Leonard Kunstadt. *Jazz: A History of the New York Scene.* Doubleday, 1962.

Chase, Gilbert. *America's Music: From the Pilgrims to the Present.* McGraw-Hill, 1955. 2nd ed., 1966. 3rd ed., University of Illinois Press, 1987.

Chavez, Alex. *Sounds of Crossing: Music, Migration, and the Aural Poetics of Huapango Arribeño.* Duke University Press, 2017.

Chernoff, John Miller. *African Rhythms and African Sensibility: Aesthetics and Social Action in African Musical Idioms.* University of Chicago Press, 1979.

Cherry Vanilla. *Lick Me: How I Became Cherry Vanilla.* Chicago Review Press, 2010.

Child, Francis James, ed. *The English and Scottish Popular Ballads*, I–V. Houghton Mifflin, 1882–98.

Chilton, John. *Billie's Blues: The Billie Holiday Story, 1933–1959.* Stein and Day, 1975.

Ching, Barbara. *Wrong's What I Do Best: Hard Country Music and Contemporary Culture.* Oxford University Press, 2001.

Christe, Ian. *Sound of the Beast: The Complete Headbanging History of Heavy Metal.* It, 2004.

Christgau, Robert. *Any Old Way You Choose It: Rock and Other Pop Music, 1967–1973.* Penguins, 1973. Expanded ed., Cooper Square, 2000.

Christgau, Robert. *Book Reports: A Music Critic on His First Love, Which Was Reading.* Duke University Press, 2019.

Christgau, Robert. *Christgau's Consumer Guide: Albums of the '90s.* Griffin, 2000.

Christgau, Robert. *Christgau's Record Guide: The '80s.* Pantheon, 1990.

Christgau, Robert. *Christgau's Record Guide: Rock Albums of the '70s.* Ticknor and Fields, 1981.

Christgau, Robert. *Going into the City: Portrait of a Critic as a Young Man.* Dey Street 2015.

Christgau, Robert. *Is It Still Good to Ya? Fifty Years of Rock Criticism, 1967–2017.* Duke University Press, 2018.

Christgau, Robert. "Rock Lyrics Are Poetry (Maybe)." In *The Age of Rock: Sounds of the American Cultural Revolution*, edited by Jonathan Eisen, 230–43. Random House, 1969. First published in *Cheetah*, December 1967.

Christopher, Roy. *Dead Precedents: How Hip-Hop Defines the Future*. Repeater, 2019.

Chude-Sokei, Louis. *The Last "Darky": Bert Williams, Black-on-Black Minstrelsy, and the African Diaspora*. Duke University Press, 2006.

Chude-Sokei, Louis. *The Sound of Culture: Diaspora and Black Technopoetics*. Wesleyan University Press, 2015.

Clarke, Donald. *Billie Holiday: Wishing on the Moon*. Viking, 1994.

Clay, Andreana. *The Hip-Hop Generation Fights Back: Youth, Activism and Post–Civil Rights Politics*. New York University Press, 2012.

Clayton, Jace. *Uproot: Travels in 21st-Century Music and Digital Culture*. Farrar, Straus and Giroux, 2016.

Clifford-Napoleon, Amber. *Queerness in Metal Music: Metal Bent*. Routledge, 2015.

Clover, Joshua. *1989: Bob Dylan Didn't Have This to Sing About*. University of California Press, 2009.

Clover, Joshua. "Good Pop, Bad Pop: Massiveness, Materiality, and the Top 40." In *This is Pop: In Search of the Elusive at Experience Music Project*, edited by Eric Weisbard, 245–56. Harvard University Press, 2004.

Clum, John. *Something for the Boys: Musical Theater and Gay Culture*. St. Martin's, 1999.

Cobain, Kurt. *Journals*. Riverhead, 2002.

Cobb, Buell. *Like Cords around My Heart: A Sacred Harp Memoir*. Outskirts, 2014.

Cobb, Buell. *The Sacred Harp: A Tradition and Its Music*. University of Georgia Press, 1978. Updated ed., 1989.

Cockrell, Dale. *Demons of Disorder: Early Blackface Minstrels and Their World*. Cambridge University Press, 1997.

Cockrell, Dale. *Everybody's Doin' It: Sex, Music, and Dance in New York, 1840–1917*. Norton, 2019.

Cohen, Harvey. *Duke Ellington's America*. University of Chicago Press, 2010.

Cohen, Lara Langer. "Solomon Northup's Singing Book." *African American Review* 50, no. 3 (2017): 259–72.

Cohen, Rich. *The Sun and the Moon and the Rolling Stones*. Spiegel and Grau, 2016.

Cohen, Sara. *Rock Culture in Liverpool: Popular Music in the Making*. Oxford University Press, 1991.

Cohn, Nik. *I Am Still the Greatest Says Johnny Angelo*. Secker and Warburg, 1967.

Cohn, Nik. *King Death*. Harcourt Brace Jovanovich, 1975.

Cohn, Nik. *Pop from the Beginning*. Weidenfeld and Nicolson, 1969. As *Rock from the Beginning*: Stein and Day, 1969. As *Awopbopaloobop Alopbamboom: Pop from the Beginning*: Paladin, 1970. As *Awopbopaloobop Alopbamboom: The Golden Age of Rock*: Da Capo, 1996.

Cohn, Nik. *Triksta: Life and Death and New Orleans Rap*. Knopf, 2005.

Cohn, Nik. *Yes We Have No: Adventures in the Other England*. Knopf, 1999.

Collier, James Lincoln. *Louis Armstrong: An American Genius*. Oxford University Press, 1983.

Collin, Matthew. *Altered State: The Story of Ecstasy Culture and Acid House.* Serpent's Tail, 1997. Updated ed., 2010.

Collin, Matthew. *Rave On: Global Adventures in Electronic Dance Music.* Serpent's Tail, 2018.

Comentale, Edward. *Sweet Air: Modernism, Regionalism, and American Popular Song.* University of Illinois Press, 2013.

Condry, Ian. *Hip-Hop Japan: Rap and the Paths of Cultural Globalization.* Duke University Press, 2006.

Conforth, Bruce, and Gayle Dean Wardlow. *Up Jumped the Devil: The Real Life of Robert Johnson.* Chicago Review Press, 2019.

Coon, Caroline. *1988: The New Wave Punk Rock Explosion.* Hawthorn, 1977.

Cooper, Brittney, Susana Morris, and Robin Boylorn. *The Crunk Feminist Collection.* Feminist, 2017.

Cooper, Kim. *In the Aeroplane over the Sea.* Continuum, 2005.

Coplan, David. *In Township Tonight!: South Africa's Black City Music and Theatre.* Longman, 1985. 2nd ed., University of Chicago Press, 2008.

Corona, Ignacio, and Alejandro Madrid, eds. *Postnational Music Identities: Cultural Production, Distribution, and Consumption in a Globalized Scenario.* Lexington, 2008.

Cott, Jonathan, ed. *Bob Dylan: The Essential Interviews.* Wenner, 2006.

County, Jayne, and Rupert Smith. *Man Enough to Be a Woman: The Autobiography of Jayne County.* Serpent's Tail, 1996.

Coupland, Douglas. *Generation X: Tales for an Accelerated Culture.* St. Martin's, 1991.

Crafts, Susan, Daniel Cavicchi, and Charles Keil. *My Music.* Wesleyan University Press, 1993.

Crawford, Marc. "Miles Davis: Evil Genius of Jazz." *Ebony,* January 1961.

Crawford, Richard. *The American Musical Landscape.* University of California Press, 1993. Updated, with subtitle, *The Business of Musicianship from Billings to Gershwin,* 2000.

Crawford, Richard. *America's Musical Life: An Introduction.* Norton, 2001.

Crawley, Ashon. *Blackpentecostal Breath: The Aesthetics of Possibility.* Fordham University Press, 2016.

Cressey, Paul. *The Taxi-Dance Hall: A Sociological Study in Commercialized Recreation and City Life.* University of Chicago Sociological Series, 1932.

Cross, Charles. *Heavier Than Heaven: A Biography of Kurt Cobain.* St. Martin's, 2001.

Crouch, Stanley. *Kansas City Lightning: The Rise and Times of Charlie Parker.* Harper, 2013.

Crow, Thomas. *The Long March of Pop: Art, Music, and Design, 1930–1995.* Yale University Press, 2014.

Crowe, Cameron. *Fast Times at Ridgemont High: A True Story.* Simon and Schuster, 1981.

Crumb, R. *The Complete Crumb Comics.* 17 vols. Fantagraphics, 1987–2005.

Cruz, Jon. *Culture on the Margins. The Black Spiritual and the Rise of American Cultural Interpretation.* Princeton University Press, 1999.

Cunard, Nancy, ed. *Negro: An Anthology.* Wishart, 1934.

Curtis, Deborah. *Touching from a Distance: Ian Curtis and Joy Division.* Faber and Faber, 1995.

Curtis, Natalie. *The Indians' Book: An Offering by the American Indians of Indian Lore, Musical and Narrative, to Form a Record of the Songs and Legends of Their Race.* Harper, 1907.

Dance, Stanley. *The World of Duke Ellington.* Scribner, 1970.

Daniel, Drew. "How to Act Like Darby Crash." In *Listen Again: A Momentary History of Pop Music,* edited by Eric Weisbard, 286–95. Duke University Press, 2007.

Daniel, Drew. *Twenty Jazz Funk Greats.* Continuum, 2008.

Danielson, Virginia. *"The Voice of Egypt": Umm Kulthum, Arabic Song, and Egyptian Society in the Twentieth Century.* University of Chicago Press, 1997.

Dannen, Fredric. *Hitmen: Power Brokers and Fast Money Inside the Music Business.* Times/Random House, 1990.

Darden, Robert. *People Get Ready! A New History of Gospel Music.* Continuum, 2004.

Darnielle, John. *Masters of Reality.* Continuum, 2008.

Darrell, R. D. "Black Beauty." *Phonograph Monthly Review,* June 1932.

Davies, Hunter. *The Beatles: The Authorized Biography.* McGraw-Hill, 1968. Rev ed., 1978, 1985. Rev. eds., Norton, 1996, 2002, 2010.

Davies, Ray. *X-Ray: The Unauthorized Autobiography.* Abrams, 1995.

Davis, Angela. *Blues Legacies and Black Feminism: Gertrude "Ma" Rainey, Bessie Smith, and Billie Holiday.* Pantheon, 1998.

Davis, Clive, with James Willwerth. *Clive: Inside the Record Business.* Morrow, 1975.

Davis, Clive, with Anthony DeCurtis. *The Soundtrack of My Life.* Simon and Schuster, 2013.

Davis, Erik. *Led Zeppelin IV.* Continuum, 2005.

Davis, Mike. *City of Quartz: Excavating the Future in Los Angeles.* Verso, 1990.

Davis, Miles, with Quincy Troupe. *Miles: The Autobiography.* Simon and Schuster, 1989.

Davis, Sammy, Jr., and Jane and Burt Boyar. *Sammy: An Autobiography of Sammy Davis, Jr.* Farrar, Straus and Giroux, 2000.

Davis, Sammy, Jr., and Jane and Burt Boyar. *Why Me?: The Sammy Davis, Jr. Story.* Farrar, Straus and Giroux, 1989.

Davis, Sammy, Jr., and Jane and Burt Boyar. *Yes I Can.* Farrar, Straus and Giroux, 1965.

Davis, Stephen. *Hammer of the Gods: The Led Zeppelin Saga.* Morrow, 1985.

Dawes, Laina. *What Are You Doing Here? A Black Woman's Life and Liberation in Heavy Metal.* Bazillion Points, 2012.

Day, Charles. *Fun in Black; or, Sketches of Minstrel Life.* De Witt, 1874.

Dayal, Geeta. *Another Green World.* Continuum, 2009.

Decker, Todd. *Music Makes Me: Fred Astaire and Jazz.* University of California Press, 2011.

Decker, Todd. *Show Boat: Performing Race in an American Musical.* Oxford University Press, 2012.

Decker, Todd. *Who Should Sing 'Ol' Man River'? The Lives of an American Song.* Oxford University Press, 2014.

DeCurtis, Anthony, James Henke, and Holly George-Warren, eds.; original ed., Jim Miller. *The Rolling Stone Illustrated History of Rock & Roll,* 3rd ed. Random House, 1992.

DeFrantz, Thomas, ed. *Dancing Many Drums: Excavations in African American Dance.* University of Wisconsin Press, 2002.

Delaunay, Charles. *Hot Discography.* Hot Jazz, 1936.

DeLillo, Don. *Great Jones Street.* Houghton Mifflin, 1973.

DeLillo, Don. *White Noise.* Viking, 1985.

Denning, Michael. *The Cultural Front: The Laboring of American Culture in the Twentieth Century.* Verso, 1996.

Denning, Michael. *Noise Uprising: The Audiopolitics of a World Musical Revolution.* Verso, 2015.

DeNora, Tia. *After Adorno: Rethinking Music Sociology.* Cambridge University Press, 2003.

DeNora, Tia. *Beethoven and the Construction of Genius: Musical Politics in Vienna, 1792–1803.* University of California Press, 1995.

DeNora, Tia. *Making Sense of Reality: Culture and Perception in Everyday Life.* Sage, 2014.

DeNora, Tia. *Music Asylums: Wellbeing through Music in Everyday Life.* Routledge, 2013.

DeNora, Tia. *Music in Everyday Life.* Cambridge University Press, 2000.

Densmore, Frances. *The American Indians and Their Music.* Woman's Press, 1926.

Densmore, Frances. *Chippewa Music.* U.S. Government Printing Office, 1910.

Densmore, Frances. *Chippewa Music II.* U.S. Government Printing Office, 1913.

Densmore, Frances. *Music of Acoma, Isleta, Cochiti, and Zuñi Pueblos.* U.S. Government Printing Office, 1957.

DeRogatis, Jim. *Let It Blurt: The Life and Times of Lester Bangs, America's Greatest Rock Critic.* Broadway, 2000.

DeRogatis, Jim. *Soulless: The Case against R. Kelly.* Abrams, 2019.

DeRogatis, Jim. *Staring at Sound: The True Story of Oklahoma's Fabulous Flaming Lips.* Broadway, 2006.

DeRogatis, Jim. *Turn on Your Mind: Four Decades of Great Psychedelic Rock.* Leonard, 2003.

Des Barres, Pamela. *I'm with the Band: Confessions of a Groupie.* Morrow, 1987.

DeVeaux, Scott. *The Birth of Bebop: A Social and Musical History.* University of California Press, 1997.

DeVeaux, Scott, and Gary Giddins. *Jazz.* College ed. Norton, 2009. 2nd ed., 2015.

DeVeaux, Scott, and Gary Giddins. *Jazz: Essential Listening.* Norton, 2010.

Dick, Bruce, and Amritjit Singh Reed, eds. *Conversations with Ishmael Reed.* University Press of Mississippi, 1995.

DiLello, Richard. *The Longest Cocktail Party.* Playboy Press, 1972.

Dinerstein, Joel. *The Origins of Cool in Postwar America.* University of Chicago Press, 2017.

Dinerstein, Joel. *Swinging the Machine: Modernity, Technology, and African American Culture between the World Wars.* University of Massachusetts Press, 2003.

Di Prima, Diane. *Revolutionary Letters.* City Lights, 1971.

Dixon-Gottschild, Brenda. *Digging the Africanist Presence in American Performance: Dance and Other Contexts.* Greenwood, 1996.

Dixon, Robert, and John Godrich, eds. *Blues and Gospel Records, 1902–1942.* Rust, 1964. 4th ed., with Howard Rye, as *Blues and Gospel Records: 1890–1943.* Oxford University Press, 1997.

Doctorow, E.L. *Ragtime.* Random House, 1975.

Dodge, Roger Pryor. *Hot Jazz and Jazz Dance: Roger Pryor Dodge Collected Writings, 1929–1964*. Edited by Pryor Dodge. Oxford University Press, 1995.

Doe, John, with Tom DeSavia. *Under the Big Black Sun: A Personal History of L.A. Punk*. Da Capo, 2016.

Doe, John, with Tom DeSavia and Friends. *More Fun in the New World: The Unmaking and Legacy of L.A. Punk*. Da Capo, 2019.

Doggett, Peter. *You Never Give Me Your Money: The Beatles after the Breakup*. Harper, 2010.

Dore, Florence. *Novel Sounds: Southern Fiction in the Age of Rock and Roll*. Columbia University Press, 2018.

Doss, Erika. *Elvis Culture: Fans, Faith, and Image*. University Press of Kansas, 1999.

Doucet, Julie. *Dirty Plotte: The Complete Julie Doucet*. Drawn and Quarterly, 2018.

Douglass, Frederick. *My Bondage and My Freedom*. Miller, Orton and Mulligan, 1855.

Douglass, Frederick. *Narrative of the Life of Frederick Douglass, an American Slave. Written by Himself*. Anti-Slavery Office, 1845.

Douglas, Susan. *Enlightened Sexism: The Seductive Message that Feminism's Work Is Done*. Times, 2010. Paperback retitled *The Rise of Enlightened Sexism: How Pop Culture Took Us from Girl Power to Girls Gone Wild*. St. Martin's, 2010.

Douglas, Susan. *Inventing American Broadcasting, 1899–1922*. Johns Hopkins University Press, 1989.

Douglas, Susan. *Listening In: Radio and the American Imagination*. Times, 1999.

Douglas, Susan. *Where the Girls Are: Growing Up with the Mass Media*. Times, 1994.

Douglas, Susan, and Andrea McDonnell. *Celebrity: A History of Fame*. New York University Press, 2019.

Doyle, Roddy. *The Commitments*. Vintage, 1987.

Dreiser, Theodore. *Art, Music, and Literature, 1897–1902*. Edited by Yoshinobu Hakutani. University of Illinois Press, 2001.

Dreiser, Theodore. *Sister Carrie*. Doubleday, Page, 1900.

Dreiser, Theodore. *Twelve Men*. Boni and Liveright, 1919.

Du Bois, W. E. B. *The Souls of Black Folk: Essays and Sketches*. McClurg, 1903.

Duffet, Mark. *Elvis: Roots, Image, Comeback, Phenomenon*. Equinox, 2020.

Duncan, Robert. *The Noise: Notes from a Rock 'n' Roll Era*. Ticknor and Fields, 1984.

Duncombe, Stephen, and Maxwell Tremblay, eds. *White Riot: Punk Rock and the Politics of Race*. Verso, 2011.

Dundy, Elaine. *Elvis and Gladys: The Genesis of the King*. Weidenfeld and Nicolson, 1985.

Durham, Aisha, Gwendolyn Pough, Rachel Raimist, and Elaine Richardson, eds. *Homegirls Make Some Noise: Hip-Hop Feminism Anthology*. Sojourns/Parker, 2007.

Dyer, Richard. "In Defence of Disco." *Gay Left* 8, Summer 1979.

Dyer, Richard. "Paul Robeson: Crossing Over." In *Heavenly Bodies: Film Stars and Society*, 64–136. St. Martin's, 1986.

Dylan, Bob. *Chronicles: Volume One*. Simon and Schuster, 2004.

Dylan, Bob. *Tarantula*. Macmillan, 1971.

Dyson, Michael Eric. *Know What I Mean? Reflections on Hip-Hop*. Civitas, 2007.

Early, Gerald, ed. *Miles Davis and American Culture*. Missouri History Museum Press/University of Chicago Press, 2001.

Echols, Alice. *Hot Stuff: Disco and the Remaking of American Culture.* Norton, 2010.

Echols, Alice. *Shaky Ground: The Sixties and Its Aftershocks.* Columbia University Press, 2002.

Edberg, Mark. *El Narcotraficante: Narcocorridos and the Construction of a Cultural Persona on the U.S.–Mexico Border.* University of Texas Press, 2004.

Eddy, Chuck. *The Accidental Evolution of Rock'n'Roll: A Misguided Tour through Popular Music.* Da Capo, 1997.

Eddy, Chuck. *Rock and Roll Always Forgets: A Quarter Century of Music Criticism.* Duke University Press, 2011.

Eddy, Chuck. *Stairway to Hell: The 500 Best Heavy Metal Albums in the Universe.* Three Rivers, 1991. Updated ed., Da Capo, 1998.

Edwards, Brent Hayes. *Epistrophies: Jazz and the Literary Imagination.* Harvard University Press, 2017.

Edwards, Brent Hayes. "The Literary Ellington." In *Uptown Conversation: The New Jazz Studies,* edited by Robert O'Meally, Brent Hayes Edwards, and Farah Jasmine Griffin, 326–56. Columbia University Press, 2004.

Edwards, David "Honeyboy," as told to Janis Martinson and Michael Robert Frank. *The World Don't Owe Me Nothing: The Life and Times of Delta Bluesman Honeyboy Edwards.* Chicago Review Press, 1997.

Egan, Jennifer. *A Visit from the Goon Squad.* Knopf, 2010.

Eggers, Dave. *A Heartbreaking Work of Staggering Genius.* Simon and Schuster, 2000.

Ehrenreich, Barbara. *Hearts of Men: American Dreams and the Flight from Commitment.* Anchor, 1983.

Ehrenreich, Barbara, Elizabeth Hess, and Gloria Jacobs. *Re-Making Love: The Feminization of Sex.* Anchor, 1986.

Eidsheim, Nina Sun. *The Race of Sound: Listening, Timbre, and Vocality in African American Music.* Duke University Press, 2019.

Eidsheim, Nina Sun. *Sensing Sound: Singing and Listening as Vibrational Practice.* Duke University Press, 2015.

Eisen, Jonathan, ed. *The Age of Rock: Sounds of the American Cultural Revolution.* Random House, 1969.

Eisen, Jonathan, ed. *Age of Rock 2: Sights and Sounds of the American Cultural Revolution.* Random House, 1970.

Eisenberg, Evan. *The Recording Angel: Music, Records and Culture from Aristotle to Zappa.* McGraw-Hill, 1987. 2nd rev. ed., Yale University Press, 2005.

Ekeroth, Daniel. *Swedish Death Metal.* Bazillion Points, 2008.

Elberse, Anita. *Blockbusters: Hit-Making, Risk-Taking, and the Big Business of Entertainment.* Holt, 2013.

Elborough, Travis. *The Vinyl Countdown: The Album from LP to iPod and Back Again.* Soft Skull, 2009.

Ellington, Duke. *Music Is My Mistress.* Doubleday, 1973.

Ellington, Mercer, with Stanley Dance. *Duke Ellington in Person: An Intimate Memoir.* Houghton Mifflin, 1978.

Ellison, Harlan, ed. *Again, Dangerous Visions.* Doubleday, 1972.

Ellison, Harlan, ed. *Dangerous Visions*. Doubleday, 1967.

Ellison, Harlan. *Rockabilly* (subsequently *Spider Kiss*). Fawcett Gold Medal, 1961.

Ellison, James, ed. *Younger Than That Now: The Collected Interviews with Bob Dylan*. Thunder's Mouth, 2004.

Ellison, Ralph. *The Collected Essays of Ralph Ellison*. Edited by John F. Callahan. Modern Library-Random House, 1995.

Ellison, Ralph. *Invisible Man*. Random House, 1952.

Ellison, Ralph. *Juneteenth: A Novel*. Edited by John F. Callahan. Random House, 1999.

Ellison, Ralph. *Living with Music: Ralph Ellison's Jazz Writings*. Edited by Robert O'Meally. Modern Library-Random House, 2001.

Ellison, Ralph. *The Selected Letters of Ralph Ellison*. Edited by John F. Callahan and Marc C. Conner. Random House, 2019.

Ellison, Ralph. *Shadow and Act*. Random House, 1964.

Elson, Louis. *The History of American Music*. Macmillan, 1904.

Emerick, Geoff and Howard Massey. *Here, There and Everywhere: My Life Recording the Music of the Beatles*. Gotham, 2006.

Emerson, Ken. *Doo-dah! Stephen Foster and the Rise of American Popular Culture*. Simon and Schuster, 1997.

Emery, Lynne Fauley. *Black Dance: From 1619 to 1970*. National, 1972.

Engel, Lehman. *The American Musical Theatre: A Consideration*. CBS Legacy Collection, Macmillan, 1967.

Enstad, Nan. *Ladies of Labor, Girls of Amusement: Working Women, Popular Culture, and Labor Politics at the Turn of the Twentieth Century*. Columbia University Press, 1999.

Epstein, Brian. *A Cellarful of Noise*. Doubleday, 1964.

Epstein, Dena. *Sinful Tunes and Spirituals: Black Folk Music to the Civil War*. University of Illinois Press, 1977. Reissued with new preface, 2003.

Epstein, Dena. "The Story of the Jubilee Singers: An Introduction to Its Bibliographic History." In *New Perspectives on Music: Essays in Honor of Eileen Southern*, edited by Josephine Wright and Samuel A. Floyd, 151–62. Harmonie Park, 1992.

Erenberg, Lewis. *Steppin' Out: New York Nightlife and the Transformation of American Culture*. University of Chicago Press, 1981.

Erenberg, Lewis. *Swingin' the Dream: Big Band Jazz and the Rebirth of American Culture*. University of Chicago Press, 1998.

Erlman, Veit. *Music, Modernity, and the Global Imagination: South Africa and the West*. Oxford University Press, 1999.

Eshun, Kodwo. *More Brilliant than the Sun: Adventures in Sonic Fiction*. Quartet, 1998.

Esposito, Joe, and Elena Oumano. *Good Rocking Tonight: Twenty Years on the Road and on the Town with Elvis*. Simon and Schuster, 1994.

Everett, Walter. *The Beatles as Musicians: The Quarry Men through Rubber Soul*. Oxford University Press, 2001.

Everett, Walter. *The Beatles as Musicians: Revolver through the Anthology*. Oxford University Press, 1999.

Ewen, David. *All the Years of American Popular Music*. Prentice-Hall, 1977.

Ewen, David. *Complete Book of the American Musical Theater*. Holt, 1960. Rev. ed., *New Complete Book of the American Musical Theater*, Holt, 1970.

Ewen, David. *Composers of Tomorrow's Music: A Non-Technical Introduction to the Musical Avant-Garde Movement*. Dodd, Mead, 1971.

Ewen, David. *Great Men of American Popular Song: The History of the American Popular Song Told through the Lives, Careers, Achievements, and Personalities of Its Foremost Composers and Lyricists—From William Billings of the Revolutionary War through Bob Dylan, Johnny Cash, and Burt Bacharach*. Prentice-Hall, 1970. Rev. ed., 1972.

Ewen, David. *Hebrew Music: A Study and an Interpretation*. Bloch, 1931.

Ewen, David. *History of Popular Music*. Barnes and Noble, 1961.

Ewen, David. *Life and Death of Tin Pan Alley*. Funk and Wagnalls, 1964.

Ewen, David. *Men and Women Who Make Music*. Little Brown, 1939.

Ewen, David. *Men of Popular Music*. Ziff-Davis, 1944.

Ewen, David. *Panorama of American Popular Music: The Story of Our National Ballads and Folk Songs, the Songs of Tin Pan Alley, Broadway and Hollywood, New Orleans Jazz, Swing, and Symphonic Jazz*. Prentice-Hall, 1957.

Ewen, David. *Songs of America; A Cavalcade of Popular Songs, with Commentaries*. Ziff-Davis, 1947.

Ewen, David. *The Story of America's Musical Theater*. Chilton, 1961. Rev. ed., 1968.

Ewen, David. *The Story of Irving Berlin*. Holt, 1950.

Ewen, Hannah. *Fangirls: Scenes from Modern Music Culture*. University of Texas Press, 2020.

Eyre, Banning. *In Griot Time: An American Guitarist in Mali*. Temple University Press, 2000.

Eyre, Banning. *Lion Songs: Thomas Mapfumo and the Music That Made Zimbabwe*. Duke University Press, 2015.

Fabian, Jenny, and Johnny Byrne. *Groupie*. New English Library, 1969.

Fanon, Frantz. *Black Skin, White Masks*. Translated by Charles Lam Markmann. Grove, 1967.

Farwell, Arthur, and W. Dermot Darby, eds. *Music in America*. Vol. 4 of *The Art of Music*. Edited by Daniel Gregory Mason. National Society of Music, 1915.

Fass, Paula. *The Damned and the Beautiful: American Youth in the 1920s*. Oxford University Press, 1977.

Fast, Susan. *Dangerous*. Bloomsbury, 2014.

Fast, Susan. *In the Houses of the Holy: Led Zeppelin and the Power of Rock Music*. Oxford University Press, 2001.

Fauset, Jessie. "The Gift of Laughter." In *The New Negro*, edited by Alain Locke, 161–67. Albert and Charles Boni, 1925.

Feather, Leonard. *Inside Be-Bop*. Robbins, 1949.

Feld, Steven. *Jazz Cosmopolitanism in Accra: Five Musical Years in Ghana*. Duke University Press, 2012.

Feld, Steven. *Sound and Sentiment: Birds, Weeping, Poetics, and Song in Kaluli Expression*. University of Pennsylvania Press, 1982. 30th anniversary ed., Duke University Press, 2012.

Feldman, Christopher. *The Billboard Book of No. 2 Singles*. Billboard, 2000.

Ferber, Edna. *Show Boat*. Doubleday, Page, 1926.

Ferguson, Otis. *In the Spirit of Jazz: The Otis Ferguson Reader*. Edited by Dorothy Chamberlain and Robert Wilson. December Press, 1982.

Fernandez, Raul. *From Afro-Cuban Rhythms to Latin Jazz*. University of California Press, 2006.

Fikentscher, Kai. *"You Better Work!" Underground Dance Music in New York City*. Wesleyan University Press, 2000.

Filene, Benjamin. *Romancing the Folk: Public Memory and American Roots*. University of North Carolina Press, 2000.

Fink, Robert. *Repeating Ourselves: American Minimal Music as Cultural Practice*. University of California Press, 2005.

Finkelstein, Sidney. *Jazz: A People's Music*. Citadel, 1948.

Finn, Julio. *The Bluesman: The Musical Heritage of Black Men and Women in the Americas*. Quartet, 1986.

Fisher, Mark. *Capitalist Realism: Is There No Alternative?* Zero, 2009.

Fisher, Mark. *Ghosts of My Life: Writings on Depression, Hauntology and Lost Futures*. Zero, 2014.

Fisher, Mark. *K-Punk: The Collected and Unpublished Writings of Mark Fisher*. Repeater, 2018.

Fisher, Rudolph. "The Caucasian Storms Harlem." *American Mercury*, August 1927, 393–98.

Fisher, Rudolph. "City of Refuge." In *The New Negro,* edited by Alain Locke, 57–74. Albert and Charles Boni, 1925.

Fitzgerald, F. Scott. *The Beautiful and Damned*. Scribner, 1922.

Fitzgerald, F. Scott. *Flappers and Philosophers*. Scribner, 1920.

Fitzgerald, F. Scott. *The Great Gatsby*. Scribner, 1925.

Flatley, Jonathan. "Just Alike." *Social Text* 32, no. 4 (2014): 87–104.

Flatley, Jonathan. *Like Andy Warhol*. University of Chicago Press, 2017.

Fletcher, Alice C. *A Study of Omaha Indian Music*. Peabody Museum of American Archaeology and Ethnology, 1893.

Fletcher, Alice C. *The Hako: A Pawnee Ceremony*. U.S. Government Printing Office, 1904.

Fletcher, Alice C. *Indian Games and Dances with Native Songs*. Birchard, 1915.

Fletcher, Alice C. *Indian Story and Song from North America*. Nutt/Small, Maynard, 1900.

Fletcher, Alice C., and Francis La Flesche. *The Omaha Tribe*. U.S. Government Printing Office, 1911.

Fletcher, Tom. *100 Years of the Negro in Show Business: The Tom Fletcher Story*. Burdge, 1954.

Flippo, Chet. *Your Cheatin' Heart: A Biography of Hank Williams*. Simon and Schuster, 1981.

Flores, Juan. *From Bomba to Hip-Hop: Puerto Rican Culture and Latino Identity*. Columbia University Press, 2000.

Floyd, Samuel A., Jr. *The Power of Black Music: Interpreting Its History from Africa to the United States*. Oxford University Press, 1996.

Floyd, Samuel A., Jr., with Melanie L. Zeck and Guthrie P. Ramsey Jr. *The Transformation of Black Music: The Rhythms, the Songs, and the Ships of the African Diaspora*. Oxford University Press, 2017.

Fonarow, Wendy. *Empire of Dirt: The Aesthetics and Rituals of British Indie Music*. Wesleyan University Press, 2006.

Forbes, Camille F. *Introducing Bert Williams: Burnt Cork, Broadway, and the Story of America's First Black Star*. Basic Civitas, 2008.

Forman, Murray, and Mark Anthony Neal, eds. *That's the Joint! The Hip-Hop Studies Reader*. Routledge, 2004. 2nd ed., 2012.

Foster, Morrison. *Biography, Songs and Musical Compositions of Stephen C. Foster*. Smith, 1896.

Fouz-Hernández, Santiago, and Freya Jarman-Ivens, eds. *Madonna's Drowned Worlds: New Approaches to Her Cultural Transformations*. Routledge, 2004.

Fox, Aaron. *Real Country: Music and Language in Working-Class Culture*. Duke University Press, 2004.

Fox, Pamela. *Natural Acts: Gender, Race, and Rusticity in Country Music*. University of Michigan Press, 2009.

Fox, Pamela, and Barbara Ching, eds. *Old Roots, New Routes: The Cultural Politics of Alt.Country Music*. University of Michigan Press, 2008.

Frank, Lisa, and Paul Smith, eds. *Madonnarama: Essays on Sex and Popular Culture*. Cleis, 1993.

Frank, Thomas. *The Conquest of Cool: Business Culture, Counterculture, and the Rise of Hip Consumerism*. University of Chicago Press, 1997.

Franklin, Aretha, and David Ritz. *Aretha: From These Roots*. Villard, 1999.

Franzen, Jonathan. *Freedom*. Farrar, Straus and Giroux, 2010.

Freedland, Michael. *Irving Berlin*. Stein and Day, 1974.

Freeman, Phil. *Running the Voodoo Down: The Electric Music of Miles Davis*. Backbeat, 2005.

Friedenberg, Edgar. *Growing Up Absurd: Problems of Youth in the Organized Society*. Random House, 1960.

Friedwald, Will. *A Biographical Guide to the Great Jazz and Pop Singing*. Pantheon, 2010.

Friedwald, Will. *Jazz Singing: America's Great Voices from Bessie Smith to Bebop and Beyond*. Scribner, 1990.

Friedwald, Will. *Sinatra! The Song Is You: A Singer's Art*. Scribner, 1995.

Friedwald, Will. *Stardust Melodies: A Biography of 12 of America's Most Popular Songs*. Pantheon, 2002.

Frith, Simon, ed. *Facing the Music: A Pantheon Guide to Popular Culture*. Pantheon, 1988.

Frith, Simon, ed. *Music and Copyright*. Edinburgh University Press, 1993. 2nd ed., with Lee Marshall, ed., Routledge, 2004.

Frith, Simon. *Music for Pleasure: Essays in the Sociology of Pop*. Routledge, 1988.

Frith, Simon. *Performing Rites: On the Value of Popular Music*. Harvard University Press, 1996.

Frith, Simon. *The Sociology of Rock*. Constable, 1978.

Frith, Simon. *Sound Effects: Youth, Leisure, and the Politics of Rock 'n' Roll*. Pantheon, 1981.

Frith, Simon. *Taking Popular Music Seriously: Selected Essays*. Ashgate, 2007.

Frith, Simon, and Andrew Goodwin, eds. *On Record: Rock, Pop, and the Written Word*. Routledge, 1990.

Frith, Simon, Andrew Goodwin, and Lawrence Grossberg, eds. *Sound and Vision: The Music Video Reader*. Routledge, 1993.

Frith, Simon, and Howard Horne. *Art into Pop*. Methuen, 1987.

Frith, Simon, Will Straw, and John Street, eds. *The Cambridge Companion to Pop and Rock*. Cambridge University Press, 2001.

Fuhr, Michael. *Globalization and Popular Music in South Korea: Sounding Out K-Pop*. Routledge, 2015.

Furia, Philip. *Irving Berlin: A Life in Song*. Schirmer, 1998.

Gaar, Gillian. *She's a Rebel: The History of Women in Rock & Roll*. Seal, 1992. 2nd ed., expanded, 2002.

Gabbard, Krin. *Better Git It in Your Soul: An Interpretive Biography of Charles Mingus*. University of California Press, 2016.

Gabbard, Krin. *Hotter Than That: The Trumpet, Jazz, and American Culture*. Faber and Faber, 2008.

Gabbard, Krin. *Jammin' at the Margins: Jazz and the American Cinema*. University of Chicago Press, 1996.

Gabbard, Krin, ed. *Jazz among the Discourses*. Duke University Press, 1995.

Gabbard, Krin, ed. *Representing Jazz*. Duke University Press, 1995.

Gaines, Donna. *Teenage Wasteland: Suburbia's Dead End Kids*. Pantheon, 1991.

Gaisberg, Frederick. *The Music Goes Round*. Macmillan, 1942.

Gammond, Peter, ed. *Duke Ellington: His Life and Music*. Phoenix House, 1958.

Gamson, Joshua. *The Fabulous Sylvester: The Legend, the Music, the Seventies in San Francisco*. Holt, 2005.

Gamson, Joshua. *Freaks Talk Back: Tabloid Talk Shows and Sexual Nonconformity*. University of Chicago Press, 1998.

Gann, Kyle. *No Such Thing as Silence: John Cage's 4′33″*. Yale University Press, 2010.

García, David. *Arsenio Rodríguez and the Transnational Flows of Latin Popular Music*. Temple University Press, 2006.

García, David. "Embodying Music/Disciplining Dance: The Mambo Body in Havana and New York City." In *Ballroom, Boogie, Shimmy Sham, Shake: A Social and Popular Dance Reader*, edited by Julie Malnig, 165–81. University of Illinois Press, 2009.

García, Enrique. "The Industry and Aesthetics of Latina/o Comic Books." In *The Routledge Companion to Latina/o Popular Culture*, edited by Frederick Luis Aldama, 101–9. Routledge, 2016.

Garland, Phyl. *The Sound of Soul: The Story of Black Music*. Regnery, 1969.

Garman, Bryan K. *A Race of Singers: Whitman's Working-Class Hero from Guthrie to Springsteen*. University of North Carolina Press, 2000.

Garrett, Charles Hiroshi, ed. *The Grove Dictionary of American Music*. 2nd ed. Oxford University Press, 2013.

Garrett, Charles Hiroshi. *Struggling to Define a Nation: American Music and the Twentieth Century*. University of California Press, 2008.

Gates, Henry Louis, Jr., ed. *The African American National Biography*. Oxford University Press, 2008.

Gaunt, Kyra. *The Games Black Girls Play: Learning the Ropes from Double-Dutch to Hip-Hop*. New York University Press, 2006.

Gehman, Richard. *Sinatra and His Rat Pack: The Irreverent, Unbiased, Uninhibited Book about Frank and the Clan*. Belmont, 1961.

Gelatt, Roland. *The Fabulous Phonograph: From Tin Foil to High Fidelity*. Lippincott, 1955. 2nd rev. ed., Macmillan, 1977.

Gendron, Bernard. *Between Montmartre and the Mudd Club: Popular Music and the Avant-Garde*. University of Chicago Press, 2002.

Gennari, John. *Blowin' Hot and Cool: Jazz and Its Critics*. University of Chicago Press, 2006.

Gentry, Linnell. *A History and Encyclopedia of Folk, Country, Western and Gospel Music*. Privately printed, 1961.

Gentry, Philip. *What Will I Be: American Music and Cold War Identity*. Oxford University Press, 2018.

George, Nadine. "Dance and Identity Politics in American Negro Vaudeville: The Whitman Sisters, 1900–1935." In *Dancing Many Drums: Excavations in African American Dance*, edited by Thomas DeFrantz, 59–80. University of Wisconsin Press, 2002.

George, Nelson. *Blackface: Reflections on African Americans in the Movies*. HarperCollins, 1994.

George, Nelson. *Buppies, B-Boys, Baps and Bohos: Notes on Post-Soul Black Culture*. HarperCollins, 1992. 2nd ed., Da Capo, 2001.

George, Nelson. *City Kid: A Writer's Memoir of Ghetto Life and Post-Soul Success*. Viking, 2009.

George, Nelson. *The Death of Rhythm & Blues*. Pantheon, 1988.

George, Nelson. *Elevating the Game: Black Men and Basketball*. HarperCollins, 1992.

George, Nelson. *Hip Hop America*. Viking Penguin, 1998.; Expanded ed., 2005.

George, Nelson. *The Hippest Trip in America: Soul Train and the Evolution of Culture and Style*. HarperCollins, 2014.

George, Nelson. *The Nelson George Mixtape: Volume 1*. Pacific, 2019.

George, Nelson. *The Plot against Hip-Hop*. Akashic, 2011.

George, Nelson. *Post-Soul Nation: The Explosive, Contradictory, Triumphant, and Tragic 1980s as Experienced by African Americans*. Viking Penguin, 2005.

George, Nelson. *Where Did Our Love Go? The Rise and Fall of the Motown Sound*. St. Martin's, 1985.

George, Nelson, and Alan Leeds, eds. *The James Brown Reader: 50 Years of Writing about the Godfather of Soul*. Plume, 2008.

George-Warren, Holly. *Janis: Her Life and Music*. Simon and Schuster, 2019.

George-Warren, Holly. *A Man Called Destruction: The Life and Music of Alex Chilton, from Box Tops to Big Star to Backdoor Man*. Penguin, 2014.

George-Warren, Holly. *Public Cowboy No. 1: The Life and Times of Gene Autry*. Oxford University Press, 2007.

George-Warren, Holly, ed. *The Rolling Stone Book of the Beats: The Beat Generation and the American Culture*. Hyperion, 1999.

George-Warren, Holly, and Michelle Freedman. *How the West Was Worn*. Abrams, 2001.

Gibson, William. *Burning Chrome*. Arbor House, 1986.

Gibson, William. *Idoru*. Putnam, 1996.

Gibson, William. *Neuromancer*. Ace, 1984.

Gibson, William. *Pattern Recognition*. Putnam, 2003.

Giddins, Gary. *Bing Crosby: A Pocketful of Dreams: The Early Years, 1903–1940*. Little, Brown, 2001.

Giddins, Gary. *Bing Crosby: Swinging on a Star: The War Years, 1940–1946*. Little, Brown, 2018.

Giddins, Gary. *Celebrating Bird: The Triumph of Charlie Parker*. Beech Tree/Morrow, 1987. Rev. ed., University of Minnesota Press, 2013.

Giddins, Gary. *Faces in the Crowd: Players and Writers*. Oxford University Press, 1992.

Giddins, Gary. *Natural Selection: Gary Giddins on Comedy, Film, Music, and Books*. Oxford University Press, 2006.

Giddins, Gary. *Rhythm-a-ning: Jazz Tradition and Innovation*. Oxford University Press, 1985.

Giddins, Gary. *Riding on a Blue Note: Jazz and American Pop*. Oxford University Press, 1981.

Giddins, Gary. *Satchmo*. Doubleday, 1988.

Giddins, Gary. *Visions of Jazz: The First Century*. Oxford University Press, 1998.

Giddins, Gary. *Warning Shadows: Home Alone with Classic Cinema*. Norton, 2010.

Giddins, Gary. *Weather Bird: Jazz at the Dawn of Its Second Century*. Oxford University Press, 2004.

Giddins, Gary, and Scott DeVeaux. *Jazz*. Norton, 2009.

Gilbert, David. *The Product of Our Souls: Ragtime, Race, and the Birth of the Manhattan Musical Marketplace*. University of North Carolina Press, 2016.

Gilbert, Jeremy, and Ewan Pearson. *Discographies: Dance Music, Culture and the Politics of Sound*. Routledge, 1999.

Gillespie, Dizzy. *To Be, or Not . . . to Bop: Memoirs of Dizzy Gillespie*. Doubleday, 1979.

Gillett, Charlie. *Making Tracks: Atlantic Records and the Growth of a Multi-Billion-Dollar Industry*. Dutton, 1974.

Gillett, Charlie. *The Sound of the City: The Rise of Rock and Roll*. Outerbridge and Dienstfrey, 1970. Rev. ed, Pantheon, 1984.

Gilroy, Paul. *The Black Atlantic: Modernity and Double Consciousness*. Harvard University Press, 1993.

Gioia, Ted. *Delta Blues: The Life and Times of the Mississippi Masters Who Revolutionized American Music*. Norton, 2008.

Giovanni, Nikki. *Gemini: An Extended Autobiographical Statement on My First Twenty-Five Years of Being a Black Poet*. Bobbs-Merrill, 1971.

Glasser, Ruth. *My Music Is My Flag: Puerto Rican Musicians and Their New York Communities, 1917–1940*. University of California Press, 1995.

Gleason, Holly, ed. *Woman Walk the Line: How the Women in Country Music Changed Our Lives.* University of Texas Press, 2017.

Gleason, Ralph. *Celebrating the Duke, and Louis, Bessie, Billie, Bird, Carmen, Miles, Dizzy, and Other Heroes.* Little, Brown, 1975.

Glenn, Susan. *Female Spectacle: The Theatrical Roots of Modern Feminism.* Harvard University Press, 2000.

Goffin, Robert. *Horn of Plenty: The Story of Louis Armstrong.* Translated by James Bezou. Allen, Towne and Heath, 1947.

Goldberg, Isaac. *George Gershwin: A Study in American Music.* Simon and Schuster, 1931.

Goldberg, Isaac. *Tin Pan Alley: A Chronicle of the American Popular Music Racket.* Day, 1930.

Golden, Eve. *Vernon and Irene Castle's Ragtime Revolution.* University Press of Kentucky, 2007.

Goldman, Albert. *Elvis.* McGraw-Hill, 1981.

Goldman, Vivien. *Revenge of the She-Punks: A Feminist Music History from Poly Styrene to Pussy Riot.* University of Texas Press, 2019.

Goldmark, Daniel. "Making Songs Pay": Tin Pan Alley's Formula for Success." *Musical Quarterly* 98, nos. 1–2 (2015): 3–28.

González Echevarría, Roberto. *Alejo Carpentier: The Pilgrim at Home.* University of Texas Press, 1991.

Goodman, Fred. *Mansion on the Hill: Dylan, Young, Geffen, Springsteen, and the Head-on Collision of Rock and Commerce.* Times/Random House, 1997.

Goodman, Steve. *Sonic Warfare: Sound, Affect, and the Ecology of Fear.* MIT Press, 2010.

Goodwin, Andrew. *Dancing in the Distraction Factory: Music Television and Popular Culture.* University of Minnesota Press, 1992.

Gordon, Kim. *Girl in a Band: A Memoir.* Dey Street, 2015.

Gordon, Robert. *Can't Be Satisfied: The Life and Times of Muddy Waters.* Little, Brown, 2002.

Gordy, Berry. *To Be Loved: The Music, the Magic, the Memories of Motown.* Warner, 1994.

Gould, Jonathan. *Can't Buy Me Love: The Beatles, Britain, and America.* Harmony, 2007.

Gourse, Leslie, ed. *The Billie Holiday Companion: Seven Decades of Commentary.* Schirmer, 1997.

Gracyk, Theodore. *Rhythm and Noise: An Aesthetics of Rock.* Duke University Press, 1996.

Graham, Sandra Jean. *Spirituals and the Birth of a Black Entertainment Industry.* University of Illinois Press, 2018.

Graham, T. Austin. *The Great American Songbooks: Musical Texts, Modernism, and the Value of Popular Culture.* Oxford University Press, 2013.

Granata, Charles. *Sessions with Sinatra: Frank Sinatra and the Art of Recording.* Chicago Review Press, 1999.

Gray, Michael. *Song and Dance Man: The Art of Bob Dylan.* Hart-Davis-MacGibbon, 1972. 2nd ed., as *The Art of Bob Dylan: Song and Dance Man.* Hamlyns, 1981. 3rd ed., as *Song and Dance Man III: The Art of Bob Dylan.* Continuum, 2000.

Gregory, James, ed. *The Elvis Presley Story.* Hillman, 1960.

Green, Abel. *Inside Stuff on How to Write Popular Songs.* Paul Whiteman/Robbins Music, 1927.

Green, Adam. *Selling the Race: Culture, Community, and Black Chicago, 1940–1955.* University of Chicago Press, 2007.

Greenberg, Alan. *Love in Vain: The Life and Legend of Robert Johnson.* Doubleday, 1983.

Greene, Bob. *Billion Dollar Baby.* Atheneum, 1974.

Greenfield, Robert. *Exile on Main Street: A Season in Hell with the Rolling Stones.* Da Capo, 2006.

Greenfield, Robert. *S.T.P.: A Journey through America with the Rolling Stones.* Saturday Review Press, 1974.

Greenlaw, Lavinia. *The Importance of Music to Girls.* Faber and Faber, 2007.

Griffin, Farah Jasmine. *If You Can't Be Free, Be a Mystery: In Search of Billie Holiday.* Free, 2001.

Griffin, Farah Jasmine, and Salim Washington. *Clawing at the Limits of Cool: Miles Davis, John Coltrane, and the Greatest Jazz Collaboration Ever.* Dunne, 2008.

Grossberg, Lawrence. *Bringing It All Back Home: Essays on Cultural Studies.* Duke University Press, 1997.

Grossberg, Lawrence. *Dancing in Spite of Myself: Essays on Popular Culture.* Duke University Press, 1997.

Grubbs, David. *Records Ruin the Landscape: John Cage, the Sixties, and Sound Recording.* Duke University Press, 2014.

Guarino, Lindsay, and Wendy Oliver, eds. *Jazz Dance: A History of the Roots and Branches.* University Press of Florida, 2014.

Guilbaut, Jocelyne. *Zouk: World Music in the West Indies.* University of Chicago Press, 1993.

Guillermoprieto, Alma. *Dancing with Cuba: A Memoir of the Revolution.* Pantheon, 2004.

Guillermoprieto, Alma. *Samba.* Knopf, 1990.

Guralnick, Peter. *Careless Love: The Unmaking of Elvis Presley.* Little, Brown, 1999.

Guralnick, Peter. *Feel Like Going Home: Portraits in Blues, Country, and Rock 'n' Roll.* Outerbridge and Dienstfrey, 1971.

Guralnick, Peter. *Last Train to Memphis: The Rise of Elvis Presley.* Little, Brown, 1994.

Guralnick, Peter. *Lost Highway: Journeys and Arrivals of American Musicians.* Godine, 1979.

Guralnick, Peter. *Sam Phillips: The Man Who Invented Rock 'n' Roll.* Little, Brown, 2015.

Guralnick, Peter. *Searching for Robert Johnson: The Life and Legend of the "King of the Delta Blues Singers."* Dutton, 1989.

Guralnick, Peter. *Sweet Soul Music: Rhythm and Blues and the Southern Dream of Freedom.* Harper and Row, 1986.

Guralnick, Peter, and Ernst Jorgensen. *Elvis Day by Day: The Definitive Record of His Life and Music.* Ballantine, 1999.

Gussow, Adam. *Beyond the Crossroads: The Devil and the Blues Tradition.* University of North Carolina Press, 2017.

Guthrie, Woody. *Born to Win.* Edited by Robert Shelton. Macmillan, 1965.

Guthrie, Woody. *Bound for Glory*. Dutton, 1943.

Guthrie, Woody. *House of Earth: A Novel*. Edited by Douglas Brinkley and Johnny Depp. Harper Perennial, 2013.

Guthrie, Woody. *Pastures of Plenty: A Self-Portrait*. Edited by Dave Marsh and Harold Leventhal. Harper and Row, 1990.

Guthrie, Woody. *Seeds of Man: An Experience Lived and Dreamed*. Dutton, 1976.

Habell-Pallán, Michelle. *Loca Motion: The Travels of Chicana and Latina Popular Culture*. New York University Press, 2005.

Hagedorn, Jessica. *Danger and Beauty*. Penguin, 1993. Expanded ed., City Lights, 2002.

Hagedorn, Jessica. *Dangerous Music*. Momo's, 1975.

Hagedorn, Jessica. *Dogeaters*. Pantheon, 1990.

Hagedorn, Jessica. *The Gangster of Love*. Houghton Mifflin, 1996.

Hajdu, David. *Positively Fourth Street: The Lives and Times of Joan Baez, Bob Dylan, Mimi Baez Fariña, and Richard Fariña*. Farrar, Straus and Giroux, 2001.

Hajeski, Nancy J. *Beatles: Here, There, and Everywhere*. Thunder Bay, 2014.

Halberstam, Jack. [Judith Halberstam.] *Female Masculinity*. Duke University Press, 1998.

Halberstam, Jack. *Gaga Feminism: Sex, Gender, and the End of Normal*. Beacon, 2012.

Halberstam, Jack. [Judith Halberstam.] *In a Queer Time and Place: Transgender Bodies, Subcultural Lives*. New York University Press, 2005.

Halberstam, Jack. [Judith Halberstam.] *The Queer Art of Failure*. Duke University Press, 2011.

Halberstam, Jack. *Trans: A Quick and Quirky Account of Gender Variability*. University of California Press, 2018.

Halberstam, Jack. "Wildness, Loss, Death." *Social Text* 32, no. 4 (2014): 137–48.

Hale, Grace. *A Nation of Outsiders: How the White Middle Class Fell in Love with Rebellion in Postwar America*. Oxford University Press, 2010.

Haley, Alex. "Miles Davis: The Playboy Interview." *Playboy*, September 1962.

Hall, Stuart. "The Great Moving Right Show." *Marxism Today*, January 1979. Reprinted in *Selected Political Writings: The Great Moving Right Show and Other Essays*, edited by Sally Davison, David Featherstone, Michael Rustin, and Bill Schwarz, 172–86. Duke University Press, 2016.

Hall, Stuart. "Notes on Deconstructing 'The Popular.'" In *People's History and Socialist Theory*, edited by Raphael Samuel, 227–40. Routledge/Kegan Paul, 1981.

Hall, Stuart, and Tony Jefferson, eds. *Resistance through Rituals: Youth Subcultures in Post-War Britain*. Hutchinson University Library, 1976.

Hall, Stuart, and Paddy Whannel. *The Popular Arts*. Hutchinson Educational, 1964.

Hamilton, Jack. *Just around Midnight: Rock and Roll and the Racial Imagination*. Harvard University Press, 2016.

Hamilton, Marybeth. *In Search of the Blues*. Basic, 2008.

Hamm, Charles. *Irving Berlin: Songs from the Melting Pot: The Formative Years, 1907–1914*. Oxford University Press, 1997.

Hamm, Charles. *Music in the New World*. Norton, 1983.

Hamm, Charles. *Putting Popular Music in Its Place*. Cambridge University Press, 1995.

Hamm, Charles. *Yesterdays: Popular Song in America*. Norton, 1979.

Hamill, Pete. *Why Sinatra Matters*. Little, Brown, 1998.

Hammond, John [Henry Johnson]. "Sight and Sound." *New Masses*, June 8, 1937.

Hancock, Black Hawk. *American Allegory: Lindy Hop and the Racial Imagination*. University of Chicago Press, 2013.

Hancox, Dan. *Inner City Pressure: The Story of Grime*. HarperCollins, 2018.

Handy, W. C., ed. *Blues: An Anthology*. Albert and Charles Boni, 1926.

Handy, W. C. *Father of the Blues: An Autobiography*. Macmillan, 1941.

Handy, W. C. *A Treasury of the Blues - Complete Words and Music of 67 Great Songs from Memphis Blues to the Present Day*. Charles Boni, 1949.

Hardwick, Elizabeth. *Sleepless Nights*. Random House, 1979.

Harker, Dave. *Fakesong: The Manufacture of British 'Folksong,' 1700 to the Present Day*. Open University Press, 1985.

Harney, Stefano, and Fred Moten. *The Undercommons: Fugitive Planning and Black Study*. Autonomedia, 2013.

Harris, Bill. *Robert Johnson: Trick the Devil (A Play)*. Applause, 2000.

Harris, Charles K. *After the Ball: Forty Years of Melody*. Frank-Maurice, 1926.

Harris, Charles K. *How to Write a Popular Song*. Harris, 1906.

Harris, Michael. *The Rise of Gospel Blues: The Music of Thomas Andrew Dorsey in the Urban Church*. Oxford University Press, 1992.

Harris, Trudier. *The Power of the Porch: The Storyteller's Craft in Zora Neale Hurston, Gloria Naylor, and Randall Kenan*. University of Georgia Press, 1996.

Harrison, Anthony Kwame. *Hip Hop Underground: The Integrity and Ethics of Racial Identification*. Temple University Press, 2009.

Harrison, George. *I, Me, Mine*. Simon and Schuster, 1980.

Hartman, Saidiya. *Scenes of Subjection: Terror, Slavery, and Self-Making in Nineteenth-Century America*. Oxford University Press, 1997.

Hazzard-Gordon, Katrina. *Jookin': The Rise of Social Dance Formations in African-American Culture*. Temple University Press, 1990.

Hasse, John Edward. *Beyond Category: The Life and Genius of Duke Ellington*. Simon and Schuster, 1993.

Hasse, John Edward, ed. *Ragtime: Its History, Composers, and Music*. Schirmer, 1985.

Hebdige, Dick. *Cut 'n' Mix: Culture, Identity and Caribbean Music*. Comedia/Routledge, 1986.

Hebdige, Dick. *Hiding in the Light: On Images and Things*. Comedia/Routledge, 1988.

Hebdige, Dick. *Subculture: The Meaning of Style*. Methuen, 1979.

Hedin, Benjamin, ed. *Studio A: The Bob Dylan Reader*. Norton, 2004.

Heesch, Florian, and Niall Scott, eds. *Heavy Metal, Gender and Sexuality: Interdisciplinary Approaches*. Ashgate, 2016.

Heilbut, Anthony. *The Fan Who Knew Too Much: The Secret Closets of American Culture*. Knopf, 2012.

Heilbut, Tony. *The Gospel Sound: Good News and Bad Times*. Simon and Schuster, 1971. As Anthony Heilbut, 25th anniversary ed., Limelight, 1997.

Hell, Richard. *I Dreamed I Was a Very Clean Tramp: An Autobiography*. Ecco/HarperCollins, 2013.

Helton, David. *King Jude: A Novel*. Simon and Schuster, 1969.

Hemphill, Paul. *The Nashville Sound: Bright Lights and Country Music*. Simon and Schuster, 1970.

Hentoff, Nat. *Jazz Is*. Random House, 1974.

Hentoff, Nat. *The Jazz Life*. Dial, 1961.

Hentoff, Nat, and Albert J. McCarthy, eds. *Jazz: New Perspectives on the History of Jazz*. Rinehart, 1959.

Herder, Johann Gottfried, and Philip Bohlman. *Song Loves the Masses: Herder on Music and Nationalism*. University of California Press, 2017.

Hermes, Will. *Love Goes to Buildings on Fire: Five Years in New York That Changed Music Forever*. Farrar, Straus and Giroux, 2011.

Hernandez, Gilbert. *Bumperhead*. Drawn and Quarterly, 2014.

Hernandez, Gilbert. "Love and Rockets." Collected in *Love and Rockets*, vol. 10, *X*. Fantagraphics, 1993.

Hernandez, Gilbert. *Palomar: The Heartbreak Soup Stories, A Love and Rockets Book*. Fantagraphics, 2003.

Hernandez, Jaime. *Locas: The Maggie and Hopey Stories*. Fantagraphics, 2003.

Hernandez, Jaime. *Locas II: Maggie, Hopey and Ray*. Fantagraphics, 2009.

Hernandez, Los Bros. *Love and Rockets: Music for Mechanics*. Fantagraphics, 1985.

Herrera-Sobek, María. *The Mexican Corrido: A Feminist Analysis*. Indiana University Press, 1990.

Hersch, Charles. *Subversive Sounds: Race and the Birth of Jazz in New Orleans*. University of Chicago Press, 2007.

Herskovits, Melville. *The Myth of the Negro Past*. Harper, 1941.

Hertsgaard, Mark. *A Day in the Life: The Music and Artistry of the Beatles*. Delacorte, 1995.

Hesmondhalgh, David. *The Cultural Industries*. Sage, 2002. 2nd ed., 2007; 3rd ed., 2012.

Hesmondhalgh, David. "Indie: The Institutional Politics and Aesthetics of a Popular Music Genre." *Cultural Studies* 13, no 1 (1999): 34- 60.

Hesmondhalgh, David. *Why Music Matters*. Wiley-Blackwell, 2013.

Hesmondhalgh, David, and Keith Negus, eds. *Popular Music Studies*. Arnold/Oxford University Press, 2002.

Heylin, Clinton. *Bob Dylan: Behind the Shades: A Biography*. Summit, 1991. 2nd ed., *Bob Dylan: Behind the Shades Revisited*. Morrow, 2001.

Heylin, Clinton. *From the Velvets to the Voidoids: A Pre-Punk History for a Post-Punk World*. Penguin, 1993. Updated ed., Chicago Review Press, 2005.

Hickey, Dave. "In Defense of the Telecaster Country Outlaws." *Country Music*, January 1974.

Hickey, Dave. *Air Guitar: Essays on Art and Democracy*. Art Issues Press, 1997.

Hight, Jewly. *Right by Her Roots: Americana Women and Their Songs*. Baylor University Press, 2011.

Hilburn, Robert. *Corn Flakes with John Lennon: And Other Tales from a Rock 'n' Roll Life*. Rodale, 2009.

Hilburn, Robert. *Johnny Cash: The Life*. Little, Brown, 2013.

Hilburn, Robert. *Paul Simon: The Life*. Simon and Schuster, 2018.

Hill, Constance Valis. "Katherine Dunham's *Southland*: Protest in the Face of Repression." In *Dancing Many Drums: Excavations in African American Dance*, edited by Thomas DeFrantz, 289–316. University of Wisconsin Press, 2002.

Hill, Constance Valis. *Tap Dancing America: A Cultural History*. Oxford University Press, 2010.

Hilmes, Michele. *Only Connect: A Cultural History of Broadcasting in the United States*. Wadsworth/Thomson Learning, 2002. 4th ed. Wadsworth/Cengage, 2014.

Hilmes, Michele, and Jason Loviglio, eds. *Radio Reader: Essays in the Cultural History of Radio*. Routledge, 2001.

Hirshey, Gerri. *Nowhere to Run: The Story of Soul Music*. Times, 1984.

Hirshey, Gerri. *We Gotta Get out of This Place: The True, Tough Story of Women in Rock*. Atlantic Monthly Press, 2001.

Hitchcock, H. Wiley. *Music in the United States: A Historical Introduction*. Prentice-Hall, 1969. 2nd ed., 1974; 3rd ed., 1988; 4th ed., 2000.

Hitchcock, H. Wiley, ed. *The Phonograph and Our Musical Life: Proceedings of a Centennial Conference, 7–10 December 1977*. Institute for Studies in American Music, 1980.

Hitchcock, H. Wiley. "William Billings and the Yankee Tunesmiths." *Hi-Fi/Stereo Review* 16, no. 2 (February 1966): 55–65.

Hitchcock, H. Wiley, and Stanley Sadie, eds. *The New Grove Dictionary of American Music*. Macmillan, 1986.

Hoffman, Charles, ed. *Frances Densmore and American Indian Music*. Museum of the American Indian, Heye Foundation, 1968.

Hoggart, Richard. *The Uses of Literacy: Aspects of Working-Class Life*. Chatto and Windus, 1957.

Holiday, Billie. *Billie Holiday: The Last Interview and Other Conversations*. Melville House, 2019.

Holiday, Billie, with William Dufty. *Lady Sings the Blues*. Doubleday, 1956. 50th anniversary ed., introduction by David Ritz, Harlem Moon/Broadway/Random House, 2006.

Holleran, Andrew. *Dancer from the Dance*. Morrow, 1978.

Holmes, John Clellon. *Go*. Scribner, 1952.

Holmes, John Clellon. *The Horn*. Random House, 1958.

Holmstrom, John, and Bridget Hurd, eds. *Punk: The Best of Punk Magazine*. It/HarperCollins, 2011.

Home, Stewart. *Cranked Up Really High: Genre Theory and Punk Rock*. Codex, 1995.

Hood, George. *History of Music in New England*. Wilkins, Carter, 1846.

Hopkins, Jerry. *Elvis: The Biography*. Simon and Schuster, 1971.

Hopkins, Jerry, and Danny Sugerman. *No One Here Gets out Alive: The Biography of Jim Morrison*. Plexus, 1980.

Hopper, Jessica. *The First Collection of Criticism by a Living Female Rock Critic*. Featherproof, 2015.

Horkheimer, Max, and Theodor Adorno. "Dialectic of Enlightenment." 1947. Translated by John Cumming. Herder and Herder, 1972. Translated by Edmund Jephcott. Stanford University Press, 2002.

Hornby, Nick. *High Fidelity*. Riverhead, 1995.

Horowitz, Daniel. *Consuming Pleasures: Intellectuals and Popular Culture in the Postwar World*. University of Pennsylvania Press, 2012.

Horowitz, Joseph. *Classical Music in America: A History of Its Rise and Fall*. Norton, 2005.

Horowitz, Joseph. *Understanding Toscanini: How He Became an American Culture-God and Helped Create a New Audience for Old Music*. Knopf, 1987.

Horowitz, Joseph. *Wagner Nights: An American History*. University of California Press, 1994.

Hoskyns, Barney. *Glam! Bowie, Bolan and the Glitter Rock Revolution*. Gardners, 1998.

Hoskyns, Barney. *Hotel California: The True-Life Adventures of Crosby, Stills, Nash, Young, Mitchell, Taylor, Browne, Ronstadt, Geffen, the Eagles, and Their Many Friends*. Wiley, 2006.

Hoskyns, Barney. *Lowside of the Road: A Life of Tom Waits*. Crown, 2009.

Hoskyns, Barney. *Say It One Time for the Brokenhearted: Country Soul in the American South*. Harper Collins, 1987. Rev. ed., BMG, 2018.

Howard, John Tasker. *Our American Music: Three Hundred Years of It*. Crowell, 1931.

Howard, John Tasker. *Stephen Foster: America's Troubadour*. Crowell, 1934.

Hubbard, W. L., ed. *History of American Music*. Squire, 1908.

Hubbs, Nadine. *Rednecks, Queers, and Country Music*. University of California Press, 2014.

Huber, Patrick. *Linthead Stomp: The Creation of Country Music in the Piedmont South*. University of North Carolina Press, 2008.

Hughes, Charles. *Country Soul: Making Music and Making Race in the American South*. University of North Carolina Press, 2015.

Hughes, Langston. *The Big Sea: An Autobiography*. Knopf, 1940.

Hughes, Langston. *Fine Clothes to the Jew*. Knopf, 1927.

Hughes, Langston. *The Weary Blues*. Knopf, 1926. Foreword by Kevin Young, 2015.

Hughes, Walter. "In the Empire of the Beat: Discipline and Disco." In *Microphone Fiends: Youth Music and Culture*, edited by Andrew Ross and Tricia Rose, 147–57. Routledge, 1994.

Hunter, Tera. *To 'Joy My Freedom: Southern Black Women's Lives and Labors after the Civil War*. Harvard University Press, 1998.

Hurston, Zora Neale. "Characteristics of Negro Expression." In *Negro: An Anthology*, edited by Nancy Cunard, 39–46. Wishart, 1934.

Hurston, Zora Neale. *Every Tongue Got to Confess: Negro Folk-Tales from the Gulf States*. HarperCollins, 2001.

Hurston, Zora Neale. *Folklore, Memoirs, and Other Writings*. Library of America, 1995.

Hurston, Zora Neale. *Mules and Men*. Lippincott, 1935.

Hurston, Zora Neale. *Their Eyes Were Watching God*. Lippincott, 1937.

Hustvedt, Sigurd Bernhard. *Ballad Books and Ballad Men: Raids and Rescues in Britain, America, and the Scandinavian North since 1800*. Harvard University Press, 1930.

Hutchinson, Sydney. *From Quebradita to Duranguense: Dance in Mexican American Youth Culture*. University of Arizona Press, 2007.

Hutchinson, Sydney, ed. *Salsa World: A Global Dance in Local Contexts.* Temple University Press, 2014.

Inglis, Ian. *The Beatles.* Equinox, 2017.

Jablonski, Edward. *Irving Berlin: American Troubadour.* Holt, 1999.

Jackson, George Pullen. *White and Negro Spirituals, Their Life Span and Kinship: Tracing 200 Years of Untrammeled Song Making and Singing among Our Country Folk: With 116 Songs as Sung by Both Races.* Augustin, 1943.

Jackson, George Pullen. *White Spirituals in the Southern Uplands.* University of North Carolina Press, 1933.

Jackson, Jerma. *Singing in My Soul: Black Gospel Music in a Secular Age.* University of North Carolina Press, 2004.

Jacobs, George, and William Stadiem. *Mr. S: My Life with Frank Sinatra.* HarperCollins, 2003.

Jacobs-Bond, Carrie. *Seven Songs as Unpretentious as the Wild Rose.* Jacobs-Bond, 1901.

Jacobs-Bond, Carrie. *The Roads of Melody.* Appleton, 1927.

James, Catherine. *Dandelion: Memoir of a Free Spirit.* St. Martin's, 2007.

James, Etta, and David Ritz. *Rage to Survive: The Etta James Story.* Villard, 1995.

James, Joseph Summerlin. *A Brief History of the Sacred Harp and Its Author, B. F. White, Sr., and Contributors.* New South, 1904.

James, Joseph Summerlin, Benjamin Franklin White, and E. J. King, eds. *Original Sacred Harp.* United Sacred Harp Musical Association, 1911.

James, Marlon. *A Brief History of Seven Killings.* Riverhead, 2014.

James, Martin. *State of Bass: Jungle—The Story So Far.* Transatlantic, 1997.

James, Robin. *Resilience & Melancholy: Pop Music, Feminism, Neoliberalism.* Zero, 2015.

James, Robin. *The Sonic Episteme: Acoustic Resonance, Neoliberalism, and Biopolitics.* Duke University Press, 2019.

Jarman, Freya, ed. *Oh Boy! Masculinities and Popular Music.* Routledge, 2007.

Jasen, David, and Trebor Jay Tichenor. *Rags and Ragtime: A Musical History.* Seabury, 1978.

Jasen, David, and Gene Jones. *Spreadin' Rhythm Around: Black Popular Songwriters, 1880–1930.* Schirmer, 1998.

Jay-Z. *Decoded.* Spiegel and Grau/Random House, 2010.

Jefferson, Margo. *On Michael Jackson.* Pantheon, 2006. With new introduction, Granta, 2018.

Jeneman, David. *Adorno in America.* University of Minnesota Press, 2007.

Jenkins, Sacha, Elliott Wilson, Chairman Mao, Gabriel Alvarez, and Brent Rollins, eds. *Ego Trip's Book of Rap Lists.* St. Martin's, 1999.

Jensen, Joan M., and Michelle Wick Patterson, eds. *Travels with Frances Densmore: Her Life, Work, and Legacy in Native American Studies.* University of Nebraska Press, 2015.

Jensen, Joli. *The Nashville Sound: Authenticity, Commercialization, and Country Music.* Country Music Foundation Press, 1998.

Joe, Radcliffe. *This Business of Disco.* Billboard, 1980.

Johnson, Denis. *Jesus' Son.* Farrar, Straus and Giroux, 1992.

Johnson, Jake. *Mormons, Musical Theater, and Belonging in America.* University of Illinois Press, 2019.

Johnson, James Weldon. *Along This Way: The Autobiography of James Weldon Johnson*. Viking, 1933.

Johnson, James Weldon. *The Autobiography of an Ex-Colored Man*. Sherman, French, 1912.

Johnson, James Weldon. *Black Manhattan*. Knopf, 1930.

Johnson, James Weldon, ed. *The Book of American Negro Poetry*. Harcourt Brace/World, 1922.

Johnson, James Weldon. ed. *The Book of American Negro Spirituals*. Viking, 1925

Johnson, James Weldon. *God's Trombones: Seven Negro Sermons in Verse*. Viking, 1935.

Johnson, James Weldon. ed. *The Second Book of Negro Spirituals*. Viking, 1926.

Johnson, James Weldon. *Writings*, William Andrews, ed. Library of America, 2004.

Johnson, Joyce. *Minor Characters: A Beat Memoir*. Houghton Mifflin,1983.

Johnson, Robert. *Elvis Presley Speaks!* Rave, 1956.

Jones, Alisha Lola. *Flaming? The Peculiar Theopolitics of Fire and Desire in Black Male Gospel Performance*. Oxford University Press, 2020.

Jones, Gayl. *Corregidora*. Random House, 1975.

Jones, Gayl. "Deep Song." *The Iowa Review* 6, no. 2 (1975): 11.

Jones, Hettie. *How I Became Hettie Jones*. Dutton, 1990.

Jones, Papa Joe, as told to Albert Murray. *Rifftides: The Life and Opinions of Papa Jo Jones*. Edited by Paul Devlin. University of Minnesota Press, 2011.

Joplin, Scott. *The Collected Works of Scott Joplin*. Edited by Vera Brodsky Lawrence. 2 vols. New York Public Library, 1971.

Juanico, June. *Elvis in the Twilight of Memory*. Arcade,1997.

Julien, Oliver, and Christopher Levaux, eds. *Over and Over: Exploring Repetition in Popular Music*. Bloomsbury, 2018.

Julien, Olivier, ed. *Sgt. Pepper and the Beatles: It Was Forty Years Ago Today*. Ashgate, 2008.

Juno, Andrea, ed. *Angry Women in Rock, Vol. 1*. Juno, 1996.

Kahn, Ashley. *Kind of Blue: The Making of the Miles Davis Masterpiece*. Da Capo, 2000.

Kahn, E. J., Jr. *The Voice: The Story of an American Phenomenon*. Harper, 1947.

Kahn-Harris, Keith. *Extreme Metal: Music and Culture on the Edge*. Berg, 2006.

Kajikawa, Loren. *Sounding Race in Rap Songs*. University of California Press, 2015.

Kammen, Michael. *The Lively Arts: Gilbert Seldes and the Transformation of Cultural Criticism in the United States*. Oxford University Press, 1996.

Kaplan, James. *Frank: The Voice*. Doubleday, 2010.

Kaplan, James. *Sinatra: The Chairman*. Doubleday, 2015.

Karpeles, Maud. *Cecil Sharp: His Life and Work*. University of Chicago Press, 1967.

Karpeles, Maud. ed. *English Folk Songs from the Southern Appalachians, Collected by Cecil J. Sharp; Comprising Two Hundred and Seventy-Four Songs and Ballads with Nine Hundred and Sixty-Eight Tunes, Including Thirty-Nine Tunes Contributed by Olive Dame Campbell*. Oxford University Press/Milford, 1932.

Katz, Jonathan. "John Cage's Queer Silence; or, How to Avoid Making Matters Worse." In *Writings through John Cage's Music, Poetry, and Art*, edited by David Bernstein and Christopher Hatch, 41–61. University of Chicago Press, 2001.

Katz, Mark. *Capturing Sound: How Technology Has Changed Music*. University of California Press, 2005.

Katz, Mark. *Groove Music: The Art and Culture of the Hip-Hop DJ*. Oxford University Press, 2012.

Kaufman, Will. *Woody Guthrie, American Radical*. University of Illinois Press, 2011.

Kearney, Mary Celeste. *Gender and Rock*. Oxford University Press, 2017.

Kearney, Mary Celeste. *Girls Make Media*. Routledge, 2006.

Keeling, Kara, and Josh Kun, eds. *Sound Clash: Listening to American Studies*. Johns Hopkins University Press, 2011.

Kehew, Brian. *Recording the Beatles: The Studio Equipment and Techniques Used to Create Their Classic Albums*. Curvebender, 2006.

Keightley, Keir. "Frank Sinatra, Hi-Fi, and Formations of Adult Culture: Gender, Technology, and Celebrity, 1948–62." Ph.D. diss., Concordia University, 1996.

Keightley, Keir. "Long Play: Adult-Oriented Popular Music and the Temporal Logics of the Post-War Sound Recording Industry in the USA." *Media, Culture and Society*, May 2004.

Keightley, Keir. "Music for Middlebrows: Defining the Easy Listening Era, 1946–1966." *American Music*, September 2008.

Keightley, Keir "Reconsidering Rock." In *The Cambridge Companion to Pop and Rock*, edited by Simon Frith, Will Straw, and John Street, 109–42. Cambridge University Press, 2001.

Keightley, Keir. "You Keep Coming Back Like a Song: Adult Audiences, Taste Panics, and the Idea of the Standard." *Journal of Popular Music Studies* 13, no. 1 (2001): 7–40.

Keil, Charles. *Tiv Song: The Sociology of Art in a Classless Society*. University of Chicago Press, 1979.

Keil, Charles. *Urban Blues*. University of Chicago Press, 1966.

Keil, Charles, Angeliki Keil, Dick Blau, and Steven Feld. *Bright Balkan Morning: Romani Lives and the Power of Music in Greek Macedonia*. Wesleyan University Press, 2002.

Keil, Charles, and Steven Feld. *Music Grooves: Essays and Dialogues*. University of Chicago Press, 1994.

Keil, Charles, Angeliki Keil, and Dick Blau. *Polka Happiness*. Temple University Press, 1992.

Kelley, Kitty. *His Way: The Unauthorized Biography of Frank Sinatra*. Bantam, 1986.

Kelley, Robin D. G. *Africa Speaks, America Answers: Modern Jazz in Revolutionary Times*. Harvard University Press, 2012.

Kelley, Robin D. G. *Thelonious Monk: The Life and Times of an American Original*. Free, 2009.

Kennealy-Morrison, Patricia. *Strange Days: My Life with and without Jim Morrison*. Dutton, 1992.

Kenney, William Howland. "Jazz: A Bibliographical Essay." *American Studies International* 25, no. 1 (1987): 3–27.

Kenney, William Howland. *Recorded Music in American Life: The Phonograph and Popular Memory, 1890–1945*. Oxford University Press, 1999.

Kent, Nick. *The Dark Stuff: Selected Writings on Rock Music 1972–1993*. Penguin, 1994.

Kerouac, Jack. *Dharma Bums*. Viking, 1958.

Kerouac, Jack. *On the Road*. New York: Viking, 1957. Reissued as *On the Road: The Original Scroll*, Viking, 2007.

Kerouac, Jack. *Visions of Cody*. McGraw-Hill, 1972.

Kheshti, Roshanak. *Modernity's Ear: Listening to Race and Gender in World Music*. New York University Press, 2015.

Kimball, Robert, and William Bolcom. *Reminiscing with Sissle and Blake*. Viking, 1973.

King, B. B., with David Ritz. *Blues All around Me: The Autobiography of B. B. King*. Avon, 1996.

King, Stephen. *Danse Macabre*. Everest House, 1981.

King, Stephen. *I'm Feeling the Blues Right Now: Blues Tourism in the Mississippi Delta*. University Press of Mississippi, 2011.

Kingsbury, Paul, and Alan Axelrod, eds. *Country: The Music and the Musicians*. Country Music Foundation/Abbeville, 1988.

Kinney, David. *The Dylanologists: Adventures in the Land of Bob*. Simon and Schuster, 2014.

Kirchner, Bill, ed. *A Miles Davis Reader*. Smithsonian, 1997.

Kittler, Friedrich. *Gramophone, Film, Typewriter*. Translated by Geoffrey Winthrop-Young and Michael Wutz. Stanford University Press, 1999.

Kitwana, Bakari. *The Hip-Hop Generation: Young Blacks and the Crisis in African-American Culture*. Civitas, 2002.

Klein, Joe. *Woody Guthrie: A Life*. Knopf, 1980.

Klosterman, Chuck. *Fargo Rock City: A Heavy Metal Odyssey in Rural Nörth Daköta*. Scribner, 2001.

Knapp, Raymond. *The American Musical and the Formation of National Identity*. Princeton University Press, 2005.

Knapp, Raymond. *The American Musical and the Formation of Personal Identity*. Princeton University Press, 2006.

Knapp, Raymond, Mitchell Morris, and Stacy Wolf, eds. *The Oxford Handbook of the American Musical*. Oxford University Press, 2011.

Knopper, Steve. *MJ: The Genius of Michael Jackson*. Scribner, 2015.

Koestenbaum, Wayne. *The Queen's Throat: Opera, Homosexuality, and the Mystery of Desire*. Poseidon, 1993.

Kogan, Frank. *Real Punks Don't Wear Black*. University of Georgia Press, 2006.

Kopkind, Andrew. "The Dialectic of Disco: Gay Music Goes Straight." *Village Voice*, February 12, 1979.

Koskoff, Ellen, ed. *Women and Music in Cross-Cultural Perspective*. University of Illinois Press, 1987.

Kostelanetz, Richard. *John Cage, Writer: Previously Uncollected Pieces*. Limelight, 1993.

Kot, Greg. *I'll Take You There: Mavis Staples, the Staple Singers, and the March up Freedom's Highway*. Scribner, 2014.

Kot, Greg. *Ripped: How the Wired Generation Revolutionized Music*. Scribner, 2009.

Kot, Greg. *Wilco: Learning How to Die*. Broadway, 2004.

Kouwenhoven, John. *The Beer Can by the Highway: Essays on What's "American" about America*. Doubleday, 1961.

Kouwenhoven, John. *Made in America: The Arts in Modern Civilization*. Doubleday, 1948.

Krasilovsky, M. William, and Sidney Schemel. *More about This Business of Music.* Billboard, 1967. Five editions through 1994.

Krasilovsky, M. William, and Sidney Schemel. *This Business of Music.* Billboard, 1964. Ten editions through 2007.

Krasner, David. *Resistance, Parody, and Double Consciousness in African American Theatre, 1895–1910.* St. Martin's, 1997.

Krauss, Chris. *I Love Dick.* Semiotext(e), 1997.

Krehbiel, Henry. *Afro-American Folksongs: A Study in Racial and National Music.* Schirmer, 1914.

Kreuger, Miles. *Show Boat: The Story of a Classic American Musical.* Oxford University Press, 1977.

Krims, Adam. *Rap Music and the Poetics of Identity.* Cambridge University Press, 2000.

Kronengold, Charles. "Exchange Theories in Disco, New Wave, and Album-Oriented Rock." *Criticism* 50, no. 1 (2008): 43–82.

Kruse, Holly. *Site and Sound: Understanding Independent Music Scenes.* Lang, 2003.

Kun, Josh. *Audiotopia: Music, Race, and America.* University of California Press, 2005.

Kun, Josh. *Songs in the Key of Los Angeles.* Angel City, 2013.

Kun, Josh. *To Live and Dine in L.A.: Menus and the Making of the Modern City.* Angel City, 2015.

Kunzru, Hari. *White Tears.* Knopf, 2017.

Kureishi, Hanif, and Jon Savage, eds. *The Faber Book of Pop.* Faber and Faber, 1995.

La Chapelle, Peter. *Proud to Be an Okie: Cultural Politics, Country Music, and Migration to Southern California.* University of California Press, 2007.

Lahr, John. *Sinatra: The Artist and the Man.* Random House, 1997.

Laing, Dave. *One Chord Wonders: Power and Meaning in Punk Rock.* Open University Press, 1985.

Landau, Jon. *It's Too Late to Stop Now: A Rock and Roll Journal.* Straight Arrow, 1972.

Lang, Lang, with David Ritz. *Journey of a Thousand Miles: My Story.* Spiegel and Grau, 2008.

Lapidus, Benjamin. *Origins of Cuban Music and Dance: Changüí.* Scarecrow, 2008.

Lawrence, Tim. *Life and Death on the New York Dance Floor, 1980–1983.* Duke University Press, 2016.

Lawrence, Tim. *Love Saves the Day: A History of American Dance Music Culture, 1970–1979.* Duke University Press, 2004.

Leland, John. *Why Kerouac Matters.* Viking, 2007.

Lena, Jennifer. *Banding Together: How Communities Create Genres in Popular Music.* Princeton University Press, 2012.

Lennon, Cynthia. *A Twist of Lennon.* Avon, 1980.

Lennon, John. *In His Own Write.* Simon and Schuster, 1964.

Leonard, Candy. *Beatleness: How the Beatles and Their Fans Remade the World.* Arcade, 2014.

Leonard, Marion. *Gender in the Music Industry: Rock, Discourse and Girl Power.* Routledge, 2007.

Lethem, Jonathan, ed. *Da Capo Best Music Writing 2002: The Year's Finest Writing on Rock, Pop, Jazz, and More.* Da Capo, 2002.

Lethem, Jonathan. *The Disappointment Artist: Essays.* Doubleday, 2005.

Lethem, Jonathan. *The Ecstasy of Influence: Nonfictions, Etc.* Doubleday, 2011.

Lethem, Jonathan. *Fear of Music.* Continuum, 2012.

Lethem, Jonathan. *Fortress of Solitude.* Doubleday, 2003.

Lethem, Jonathan. *Motherless Brooklyn.* Doubleday, 1999.

Lethem, Jonathan. *You Don't Love Me Yet.* Doubleday, 2007.

Lethem, Jonathan, and Kevin Dettmar, eds. *Shake It Up: Great American Writing on Rock and Pop from Elvis to Jay Z.* Library of America, 2017.

Levine, Lawrence. *Black Culture and Black Consciousness: Afro-American Folk Thought from Slavery to Freedom.* Oxford University Press, 1977.

Levine, Lawrence. *Highbrow/Lowbrow: The Emergence of Cultural Hierarchy in America.* Harvard University Press, 1988.

Levine, Lawrence. *The Unpredictable Past: Explorations in American Cultural History.* Oxford University Press, 1993.

Lewisohn, Mark. *The Beatles Day by Day.* Three Rivers, 1990.

Lewisohn, Mark. *The Beatles Live!: The Ultimate Reference Book.* Holt, 1986.

Lewisohn, Mark. *The Complete Beatles Chronicle.* Harmony, 1992.

Lewisohn, Mark. *The Complete Beatles Recording Sessions: The Official Story of the Abbey Road Years, 1962–1970.* Hamlyn, 1988.

Lewisohn, Mark. *Tune In: The Beatles All These Years, Volume 1.* Crown Archetype, 2013. Extended special ed., Little, Brown, 2013.

Lhamon, W. T., Jr. *Deliberate Speed: The Origins of a Cultural Style in the American 1950s.* Smithsonian, 1990.

Lhamon, W. T., Jr. *Jump Jim Crow: Lost Plays, Lyrics, and Street Prose of the First Atlantic Popular Culture.* Harvard University Press, 2003.

Lhamon, W. T., Jr. *Raising Cain: Blackface Performance from Jim Crow to Hip Hop.* Harvard University Press, 1998.

Lhamon, W. T., Jr. "Whittling on Dynamite: The Difference Bert Williams Makes." In *Listen Again: A Momentary History of Pop Music*, edited by Eric Weisbard, 7–25. Duke University Press, 2007.

Light, Alan, ed. *The Vibe History of Hip Hop.* Three Rivers, 1999.

Limón, José. *Américo Paredes: Culture and Critique.* University of Texas Press, 2012.

Lion, Jean Pierre. *Bix: The Definitive Biography of a Jazz Legend.* Continuum, 2005.

Lipsitz, George. *Dangerous Crossroads: Popular Music, Postmodernism, and the Poetics of Place.* Verso, 1994.

Lipsitz, George. *Footsteps in the Dark: The Hidden Histories of Popular Music.* University of Minnesota Press, 2007.

Lipsitz, George. *Midnight at the Barrelhouse: The Johnny Otis Story.* University of Minnesota Press, 2010.

Lipsitz, George. *The Possessive Investment in Whiteness: How White People Profit from Identity Politics.* Temple University Press, 1998.

Lipsitz, George. *Time Passages: Collective Memory and American Popular Culture.* University of Minnesota Press, 1990.

Lipsitz, George. *Upside Your Head! Rhythm and Blues on Central Avenue.* Wesleyan University Press, 1993.

Lloyd, Richard. *Neo-Bohemia: Art and Commerce in the Postindustrial City.* University of Chicago Press, 2005.

Lock, Graham. *Blutopia: Visions of the Future and Revisions of the Past in the Work of Sun Ra, Duke Ellington, and Anthony Braxton.* Duke University Press, 2000.

Locke, Alain, ed. *The New Negro.* Albert and Charles Boni, 1925.

Lomax, Alan. *Folk Songs of North America.* Doubleday, 1960.

Lomax, Alan. ed. *Hard Hitting Songs for Hard-Hit People.* Oak, 1967.

Lomax, Alan. *The Land Where the Blues Began.* Pantheon, 1993.

Lomax, Alan. *Mister Jelly Roll: The Fortunes of Jelly Roll Morton, New Orleans Creole and "Inventor of Jazz."* Duell, Sloan and Pearce, 1950. 2nd ed., University of California Press, 1973. Rev. ed., including preface to 1993 ed., 2002.

Lomax, John A. *Adventures of a Ballad Hunter.* Macmillan, 1947.

Lomax, John A. *Cowboy Songs and Other Frontier Ballads.* Sturgis and Walton, 1910. New ed., revised and enlarged by John A. Lomax and Alan Lomax, Macmillan, 1937.

Lomax, John A., *Folk Song: U.S.A.* Duell, Sloan and Pierce, 1947.

Lomax, John A., *Our Singing Country: A Second Volume of American Ballads and Folk Songs.* Macmillan, 1941.

Lomax, John A., and Alan Lomax. *American Ballads and Folk Songs.* Macmillan, 1934.

Lord, Tom. *The Jazz Discography.* 34 vols. Lord Music Reference, 1992–2004.

Lordi, Emily J. *Black Resonance: Iconic Women Singers and African American Literature.* Rutgers University Press, 2013.

Lordi, Emily J. *The Meaning of Soul: Black Music and Resilience since the 1960s.* Duke University Press, 2020.

Lornell, Kip. *Happy in the Service of the Lord: African-American Sacred Vocal Harmony Quartets in Memphis.* University of Illinois Press, 1988.

Lott, Eric. *Love and Theft: Blackface Minstrelsy and the American Working Class.* Oxford University Press, 1993. 20th anniversary ed., foreword by Greil Marcus, 2013.

Loza, Steven. *Barrio Rhythms: Mexican American Music in Los Angeles.* University of Illinois Press, 1993.

Lummis, Charles. *Spanish Songs of Old California.* Lummis, 1923.

Lydon, John. *Anger Is an Energy: My Life Uncensored.* Dey Street, 2014.

Lydon, John, with Keith Zimmerman and Kent Zimmerman. *Rotten: No Irish, No Blacks, No Dogs.* Picador, 1994.

Lynn, Loretta, with George Vecsey. *Coal Miner's Daughter.* Regnery, 1976.

MacDonald, Ian. *Revolution in the Head: The Beatles' Records and the Sixties.* Holt, 1994.

MacInnes, Colin. *Absolute Beginners.* MacGibbon and Kee, 1959.

MacInnes, Colin. *Absolute MacInnes: The Best of Colin MacInnes.* Edited by Tony Gould. Allison and Busby, 1985.

MacInnes, Colin. *City of Spades.* MacGibbon and Kee, 1957.

MacInnes, Colin. *England, Half English.* MacGibbon and Kee, 1961.

MacInnes, Colin. *Sweet Saturday Night: Pop Song 1840–1920.* MacGibbon and Kee, 1967.

Macías, Anthony. *Mexican American Mojo: Popular Music, Dance, and Urban Culture in Los Angeles, 1935–1968.* Duke University Press, 2008.

Mack, Kimberly. *Fictional Blues: Narrative Self-Invention from Bessie Smith to Jack White.* University of Massachusetts Press, 2020.

Mackey, Nathaniel. *Bedouin Hornbook.* University of Kentucky Press, 1986.

Mackey, Nathaniel. *Discrepant Engagement: Dissonance, Cross-Culturality and Experimental Writing.* Cambridge University Press, 1993.

Mackey, Nathaniel. *Paracritical Hinge: Essays, Talks, Notes, Interviews.* University of Wisconsin Press, 2005.

Madonna. *Sex.* Warner, 1992.

Madrid, Alejandro. *Nor-tec Rifa! Electronic Dance Music from Tijuana to the World.* Oxford University Press, 2008.

Madrid, Alejandro, ed. *Transnational Encounters: Music and Performance at the U.S.-Mexico Border.* Oxford University Press, 2011.

Magee, Jeffrey. *Irving Berlin's American Musical Theater.* Oxford University Press, 2012.

Mahar, William. *Behind the Burnt Cork Mask: Early Blackface Minstrelsy and Antebellum American Popular Culture.* University of Illinois Press, 1999.

Malbon, Ben. *Clubbing: Dancing, Ecstasy and Vitality.* Routledge, 1999.

Malnig, Julie. "Apaches, Tangos, and Other Indecencies: Women, Dance, and New York Nightlife of the 1910s." In *Ballroom, Boogie, Shimmy Sham, Shake: A Social and Popular Dance Reader,* edited by Julie Malnig, 72–92. University of Illinois Press, 2009.

Malnig, Julie, ed. *Ballroom, Boogie, Shimmy Sham, Shake: A Social and Popular Dance Reader.* University of Illinois Press, 2009.

Malone, Jacqui. *Steppin' on the Blues: The Visible Rhythms of African American Dance.* University of Illinois Press, 1996.

Malone, Bill C. *Country Music, U.S.A.: A Fifty-Year History.* University of Texas Press, 1968. Rev. eds., 1985, 2002, 2010 (with Jocelyn Neal); 2018 (with Tracey E. W. Laird).

Malone, Bill C. *Don't Get above Your Raisin': Country Music and the Southern Working Class.* University of Illinois Press, 2002.

Malone, Bill C. *Singing Cowboys and Musical Mountaineers: Southern Culture and the Roots of Country Music.* University of Georgia Press, 1993.

Mann, Thomas. *Doctor Faustus: The Life of the German Composer Adrian Leverkühn, as Told by a Friend.* 1947. Translated by John Woods. Knopf, 1997.

Manning, Frankie, and Cynthia Millman. *Frankie Manning: Ambassador of Lindy Hop.* Temple University Press, 2007.

Manuel, Peter. *Cassette Culture: Popular Music and Technology in North India.* University of Chicago Press, 1993.

Manuel, Peter. *Popular Musics of the Non-Western World.* Oxford University Press, 1988.

Marcoux, Jean-Philippe, ed. *Some Other Blues: New Perspectives on Amiri Baraka.* Ohio State University Press, 2021.

Marcus, Greil. *Bob Dylan by Greil Marcus: Writings, 1968–2010.* Public Affairs, 2011.

Marcus, Greil. *Dead Elvis: A Chronicle of a Cultural Obsession.* Harvard University Press, 1991.

Marcus, Greil. *Double Trouble: Bill Clinton and Elvis Presley in a Land of No Alternatives.* Holt, 2001.

Marcus, Greil. *The History of Rock 'n' Roll in Ten Songs.* Yale University Press, 2014.

Marcus, Greil. *Invisible Republic: Bob Dylan's Basement Tapes.* Holt, 1997. As *The Old, Weird America: The World of Bob Dylan's Basement Tapes.* Picador, 2000. Rev. ed., 2010.

Marcus, Greil. *Lipstick Traces: A Secret History of the 20th Century.* Harvard University Press, 1989.

Marcus, Greil. *Like a Rolling Stone: Bob Dylan at the Crossroads.* Public Affairs, 2005.

Marcus, Greil. *Mystery Train: Images of America in Rock 'n' Roll Music.* Dutton, 1975. 2nd rev. ed., 1982; 3rd rev. ed., 1990. 4th rev. ed., Plume, 1997; 5th rev. ed., 2008; 6th rev. ed., 2015.

Marcus, Greil. *Ranters and Crowd Pleasers: Punk in Pop Music, 1977–1992.* Doubleday, 1993. As *In the Fascist Bathroom: Writings on Punk, 1977–1992.* Harvard University Press, 1999.

Marcus, Greil. *Real Life Rock: The Complete Top Ten Columns, 1986–2014.* Yale University Press, 2015.

Marcus, Greil, ed. *Rock and Roll Will Stand.* Beacon, 1969.

Marcus, Greil, ed. *Stranded: Rock and Roll for a Desert Island.* Knopf, 1979.

Marcus, Greil. *Three Songs, Three Singers, Three Nations.* Harvard University Press, 2015.

Marcus, Greil, and Werner Sollors, eds. *A New Literary History of America.* Harvard University Press, 2009.

Marcus, Greil, and Sean Wilentz, eds. *The Rose and the Briar: Death, Love and Liberty in the American Ballad.* Norton, 2004.

Marcus, Sara. *Girls to the Front: The True Story of the Riot Grrrl Revolution.* Harper Perennial, 2010.

Mark, Joan. *A Stranger in Her Native Land: Alice Fletcher and the American Indians.* University of Nebraska Press, 1989.

Markey, Dave, and Jordan Schwartz. *We Got Power! Hardcore Punk Scenes from 1980s Southern California.* Bazillion Points, 2012.

Marling, Karal Ann. *Graceland: Going Home with Elvis.* Harvard University Press, 1996.

Marovich, Robert. *A City Called Heaven: Chicago and the Birth of Gospel Music.* University of Illinois Press, 2015.

Marqusee, Mike. *Chimes of Freedom: The Politics of Bob Dylan's Art.* New Press, 2003. As *Wicked Messenger: Bob Dylan and the 1960s,* rev. and expanded ed., Seven Stories, 2005.

Marre, Jeremy, and Hannah Charlton. *Beats of the Heart: Popular Music of the World.* Pantheon, 1985.

Marsh, Dave. *Born to Run: The Bruce Springsteen Story.* Doubleday, 1979.

Marsh, Dave. *Fortunate Son: The Best of Dave Marsh.* Random House, 1985.

Marsh, Dave. *The Heart of Rock & Soul: The 1001 Greatest Singles Ever Made.* Plume, 1989.

Marsh, Dave. *Louie: The History and Mythology of the World's Most Famous Rock 'n Roll Song.* Hyperion, 1993.

Marsh, Dave, and John Swenson, eds. *The Rolling Stone Record Guide.* Rolling Stone Press, 1979. Updated ed., 1983.

Marsh, J. B. T. *The Story of the Jubilee Singers: With Their Songs.* 2nd ed. Holder and Stoughton, 1875.

Marshall, Lee. *Bob Dylan: The Never Ending Star.* Polity, 2007.

Martin, George, with Jeremy Hornsby. *All You Need Is Ears: The Inside, Personal Story of the Genius Who Created the Beatles.* St. Martin's, 1979.

Martin, George. *Making Music: The Guide to Writing, Performing and Recording*. Morrow, 1983.

Martin, George. *Playback: An Illustrated Memoir*. Genesis, 2002.

Martin, George, with William Pearson. *With a Little Help from My Friends: The Making of Sgt. Pepper*. Little, Brown, 1994.

Martin, George R. R. *The Armageddon Rag*. Poseidon, 1983.

Maslon, Laurence, ed. *American Musicals, 1927–1949: The Complete Books and Lyrics of Eight Broadway Classics*. Library of America, 2014.

Maslon, Laurence. *Broadway to Main Street: How Show Tunes Enchanted America*. Oxford University Press, 2018.

Mason, Bobbie Ann. *Elvis Presley: A Life*. Viking, 2002.

Mast, Gerald. *Can't Help Singin': The American Musical on Stage and Screen*. Overlook, 1987.

Matos, Michaelangelo. *Can't Slow Down: How 1984 Became Pop's Blockbuster Year*. Hachette, 2020.

Matos, Michaelangelo. *Sign 'O' the Times*. Continuum, 2004.

Matos, Michaelangelo. *The Underground Is Massive: How Electronic Dance Music Conquered America*. Dey Street, 2015.

Matza, David. *Delinquency and Drift*. John Wiley, 1964.

Mazor, Barry. *Meeting Jimmie Rodgers: How America's Original Roots Music Hero Changed the Pop Sounds of a Century*. Oxford University Press, 2009.

Mazor, Barry. *Ralph Peer and the Making of Popular Roots Music*. Chicago Review Press, 2014.

McClary, Susan. *Conventional Wisdom: The Content of Musical Form*. University of California Press, 2000.

McClary, Susan. *Feminine Endings: Music, Gender, and Sexuality*. University of Minnesota Press, 1991.

McClary, Susan. "Introduction: The Life and Times of a Renegade Musicologist." In *Reading Music: Selected Essays*, ix–xv. Ashgate, 2007.

McClary, Susan. *Reading Music: Selected Essays*. Ashgate, 2007.

McClary, Susan, and Robert Walser. "Start Making Sense: Musicology Wrestles with Rock." In *On Record: Rock, Pop, and the Written Word*, edited by Simon Frith and Andrew Goodwin, 277–92. Pantheon, 1990.

McCracken, Allison. *Real Men Don't Sing: Crooning in American Culture*. Duke University Press, 2015.

McCrumb, Sharyn. *The Ballad of Frankie Silver*. Dutton, 1998.

McCrumb, Sharyn. *The Hangman's Beautiful Daughter*. Scribner, 1992.

McCrumb, Sharyn. *If Ever I Return, Pretty Peggy-O*. Scribner, 1990.

McCrumb, Sharyn. *She Walks These Hills*. Scribner, 1994.

McCusker, Kristine M. *Lonesome Cowgirls and Honky-Tonk Angels: The Women of Barn Dance Radio*. University of Illinois Press, 2008.

McCusker, Kristine M., and Diane Pecknold, eds. *A Boy Named Sue: Gender and Country Music*. University Press of Mississippi, 2004.

McDonnell, Evelyn. *Queens of Noise: The Real Story of the Runaways*. Da Capo, 2013.

McDonnell, Evelyn, ed. *Women Who Rock: Bessie to Beyonce. Girl Groups to Riot Grrrl.* Black Dog/Leventhal, 2018.

McDonnell, Evelyn, and Ann Powers, eds. *Rock She Wrote: Women Write about Rock, Pop and Rap.* Delta, 1995.

McGinley, Paige. *Staging the Blues: From Tent Shows to Tourism.* Duke University Press, 2014.

McGraw, Hugh, ed. *The Sacred Harp, 1991 Revision.* Sacred Harp, 1991.

McKay, David P., and Richard Crawford. *William Billings of Boston: Eighteenth-Century Composer.* Princeton University Press, 1975.

McKay, George. *Senseless Acts of Beauty: Cultures of Resistance since the Sixties.* Verso, 1996.

McKinney, Devin. *Magic Circles: The Beatles in Dream and History.* Harvard University Press, 2003.

McLeod, Kembrew. *The Downtown Pop Underground: New York City and the Literary Punks, Renegade Artists, DIY Filmmakers, Mad Playwrights, and Rock 'n' Roll Glitter Queens Who Revolutionized Culture.* Abrams, 2018.

McMillin, Scott. *The Musical as Drama.* Princeton University Press, 2006.

McNally, Karen. *When Frankie Went to Hollywood: Frank Sinatra and American Male Identity.* University of Illinois Press, 2008.

McNeil, Legs, and Gillian McCain. *Please Kill Me: The Uncensored Oral History of Punk.* Grove, 1996.

McPheeters, Sam. *Mutations: The Many Strange Faces of Hardcore Punk.* Rare Bird, 2020.

McRobbie, Angela. *The Aftermath of Feminism: Gender, Culture and Social Change.* Sage, 2009.

McRobbie, Angela. *Feminism and Youth Culture: From "Jackie" to "Just Seventeen."* Macmillan, 1990. 2nd ed., Routledge, 2000.

McRobbie, Angela. *In the Culture Society: Art, Fashion and Popular Music.* Routledge, 1999.

McRobbie, Angela. *Postmodernism and Popular Culture.* Routledge, 1994.

McRobbie, Angela. "Settling Accounts with Subculture: A Feminist Critique." *Screen Education* 34 (1980), 37–49.

McRobbie, Angela. *Zoot Suits and Second-Hand Dresses: An Anthology of Fashion and Music.* Unwin Hyman, 1988.

Medovoi, Leerom. *Rebels: Youth and the Cold War Origins of Identity.* Duke University Press, 2006.

Mehr, Bob. *Trouble Boys: The True Story of the Replacements.* Da Capo, 2016.

Meintjes, Louise. *Sound of Africa! Making Music Zulu in a South African Studio.* Duke University Press, 2003.

Melnick, Jeffrey. *A Right to Sing the Blues: African Americans, Jews, and American Popular Song.* Harvard University Press, 1999.

Mellers, Wilfrid. *Music in a New Found Land: Themes and Developments in the History of American Music.* Barrie and Rockcliff, 1964; Knopf, 1965.

Mellers, Wilfrid. *Twilight of the Gods: The Music of the Beatles.* Viking, 1973.

Mellers, Wilfrid. *A Darker Shade of Pale: A Backdrop to Bob Dylan.* Oxford University Press, 1985.

Melly, George. *Revolt into Style: The Pop Arts in Britain*. Lane, 1970.

Meloy, Colin. *Let It Be*. Continuum, 2004.

Meltzer, Richard. *The Aesthetics of Rock*. Something Else, 1970.

Meltzer, Richard. *Gulcher: Post-Rock Cultural Pluralism in America (1649–1980)*. Straight Arrow, 1972.

Meltzer, Richard. *A Whore Just Like the Rest: The Music Writings of Richard Meltzer*. Da Capo, 2000.

Merriam, Alan. *The Anthropology of Music*. Northwestern University Press, 1964.

Metz, Allan, and Carol Benson, eds. *The Madonna Companion: Two Decades of Commentary*. Schirmer, 1999.

Mezzrow, Mezz, and Bernard Wolfe. *Really the Blues*. Random House, 1946. Reissue, with introduction by Ben Ratliff, New York Review Books, 2016.

Middleton, Richard. *Studying Popular Music*. Open University Press, 1990.

Miles, Barry. *Paul McCartney: Many Years from Now*. Holt, 1997.

Miles, Emma Bell. *The Common Lot and Other Stories: The Published Short Fiction, 1908–1921*. Edited by Grace Toney Edwards. Ohio State University Press, 2016.

Miles, Emma Bell. *Once I Too Had Wings: The Journals of Emma Bell Miles, 1908–1918*. Edited by Steven Cox. Ohio State University Press, 2014.

Miles, Emma Bell. *The Spirit of the Mountains*. James Pott, 1905.

Miles, Emma Bell. *Strains from a Dulcimore*. Edited by Abby Crawford Milton. Hartsock, 1930.

Millard, Andre. *America on Record: A History of Recorded Sound*. Cambridge University Press, 1995. Rev. ed, 2005.

Miller, D. A. *Place for Us: Essay on the Broadway Musical*. Harvard University Press, 1998.

Miller, James. *Flowers in the Dustbin: The Rise of Rock and Roll*. Simon and Schuster, 1999.

Miller, James [Jim Miller], ed. *The Rolling Stone Illustrated History of Rock & Roll*. Rolling Stone Press/Random House, 1976. Rev. ed., 1980.

Miller, Karl Hagstrom. "Revisiting Minstrelsy: *Love & Theft* at Twenty." *American Music* 33, no. 2 (2015): 274–80.

Miller, Karl Hagstrom. *Segregating Sound: Inventing Folk and Pop Music in the Age of Jim Crow*. Duke University Press, 2010.

Miller, Kiri. *Playable Bodies: Dance Games and Intimate Media*. Oxford University Press, 2017.

Miller, Kiri. *Playing Along: Digital Games, YouTube, and Virtual Performance*. Oxford University Press, 2012.

Miller, Kiri. *Traveling Home: Sacred Harp Singing and American Pluralism*. University of Illinois Press, 2008.

Miller, Norma, with Evette Jensen. *Swingin' at the Savoy: The Memoir of a Jazz Dancer*. Temple University Press, 1996.

Milligan, Harold Vincent. *Stephen Collins Foster: A Biography of America's Folk-Song Composer*. Schirmer, 1920.

Milliken, Robert. *Lillian Roxon: Mother of Rock*. Thunder's Mouth, 2005.

Milner, Greg. *Perfecting Sound Forever: An Aural History of Recorded Music*. Faber and Faber, 2009.

Milward, John. *Crossroads: How the Blues Shaped Rock 'n' Roll (and Rock Saved the Blues)*. Northeastern University Press, 2013.

Mingus, Charles. *Beneath the Underdog*. Knopf, 1971.

Mitchell, David. *Cloud Atlas*. Random House, 2004.

Mitchell, David. *Utopia Avenue: A Novel*. Random House, 2020.

Mitchell, Tony, ed. *Global Noise: Rap and Hip Hop Outside the USA*. Wesleyan University Press, 2002.

Moby. *Porcelain: A Memoir*. Penguin, 2016.

Moby. *Then It Fell Apart*. Faber and Faber Social, 2019.

Monson, Ingrid. *Freedom Sounds: Civil Rights Call Out to Jazz and Africa*. Oxford University Press, 2007.

Monson, Ingrid. "The Problem with White Hipness: Race, Gender, and Cultural Conceptions in Jazz Historical Discourse." *Journal of the American Musicological Society* 48, no. 3 (1995): 396–422.

Monson, Ingrid. *Saying Something: Jazz Improvisation and Interaction*. University of Chicago Press, 1996.

Moody, Rick. *Garden State*. Pushcart, 1992.

Moody, Rick. *On Celestial Music: And Other Adventures in Listening*. Back Bay Books/Little, Brown, 2012.

Moorcock, Michael. *The Final Programme*. Avon, 1968.

Moore, Allan. *The Beatles: Sgt. Pepper's Lonely Hearts Club Band*. Cambridge University Press, 1998.

Moore, Robin. *Music and Revolution: Cultural Change in Socialist Cuba*. University of California Press, 2006.

Moore, Robin. *Nationalizing Blackness: Afrocubanismo and Artistic Revolution in Havana, 1920–1940*. University of Pittsburgh Press, 1997.

Moore, Ryan. *Sells Like Teen Spirit: Music, Youth Culture, and Social Crisis*. New York University Press, 2010.

Moore, Scotty, as told to James Dickerson. *That's Alright, Elvis: The Untold Story of Elvis's First Guitarist and Manager, Scotty Moore*. Schirmer, 1997.

Morath, Max. *I Love You Truly: A Biographical Novel Based on the Life of Carrie Jacobs-Bond*. iUniverse, 2008.

Morath, Max. *Three Songs: A Study of Carrie Jacobs-Bond and Her Music*. University of Colorado Boulder, College of Music, American Music Research Center, 2017.

Mordden, Ethan. *Anything Goes: A History of American Musical Theatre*. Oxford University Press, 2013.

Mordden, Ethan. *Happiest Corpse I've Ever Seen: The Last Twenty-Five Years of the Broadway Musical*. St. Martin's, 2004.

Mordden, Ethan. *I've a Feeling We're Not in Kansas Anymore: Tales from Gay Manhattan*. St. Martin's, 1985.

Mordden, Ethan. *Make Believe: The Broadway Musical in the 1920s*. Oxford University Press, 1997.

Mordden, Ethan. *One More Kiss: The Broadway Musical in the 1970s*. Palgrave Macmillan, 2004.

Mordden, Ethan. *Opera Anecdotes*. Oxford University Press, 1985.

Morgan, Joan. *She Begat This: 20 Years of the Miseducation of Lauryn Hill*. Simon and Schuster, 2018.

Morgan, Joan. *When Chickenheads Come Home to Roost: A Hip-Hop Feminist Breaks It Down*. Simon and Schuster, 1999.

Morneweck, Evelyn Foster. *Chronicles of Stephen Foster's Family*. 2 vols. University of Pittsburgh Press, 1944.

Morris, Keith, with Jim Ruland. *My Damage: The Story of a Punk Rock Survivor*. Da Capo, 2016.

Morris, Mitchell. *The Persistence of Sentiment: Display and Feeling in Popular Music of the 1970s*. University of California Press, 2013.

Morrison, Simon. *Dancefloor-Driven Literature: The Rave Scene in Fiction*. Bloomsbury, 2020.

Morrison, Toni. *Jazz*. Knopf, 1992.

Morrison, Toni. *Playing in the Dark: Whiteness and the Literary Imagination*. Harvard University Press, 1992.

Morrissette, Noelle. *James Weldon Johnson's Modern Soundscapes*. University of Iowa Press, 2013.

Morthland, John. *The Best of Country Music*. Doubleday/Dolphin, 1984.

Mosley, Walter. *RL's Dream*. Norton, 1995.

Most, Andrea. *Making Americans: Jews and the Broadway Musical*. Harvard University Press, 2004.

Moten, Fred. *B Jenkins*. Duke University Press, 2009.

Moten, Fred. *Black and Blur*. Duke University Press, 2018.

Moten, Fred. *In the Break: The Aesthetics of the Black Radical Tradition*. University of Minnesota Press, 2003.

Moten, Fred. *Stolen Life*. Duke University Press, 2018.

Moten, Fred. *The Universal Machine*. Duke University Press, 2018.

Mötley Crüe, with Neil Strauss. *The Dirt: Confessions of the World's Most Notorious Rock Band*. Regan, 2001.

Mould, Bob, with Michael Azerrad. *See a Little Light: The Trail of Rage and Melody*. Little, Brown, 2011.

Mudrian, Albert. *Choosing Death: The Improbable History of Death Metal and Grindcore*. Feral House, 2004.

Mudrian, Albert, ed. *Precious Metal: Decibel Presents the Stories behind 25 Extreme Metal Masterpieces*. Da Capo, 2009.

Mullen, Brendan, and Marc Spitz. *We Got the Neutron Bomb: The Untold Story of L.A. Punk*. Three Rivers, 2001.

Mumford, Kevin. *Interzones: Black/White Sex Districts in Chicago and New York in the Early Twentieth Century*. Columbia University Press, 1997.

Muñoz, José Esteban. *Cruising Utopia: The Then and There of Queer Futurity*. New York University Press, 2009.

Muñoz, José Esteban. *Disidentifications: Queers of Color and the Performance of Politics.* University of Minnesota Press, 1999.

Muñoz, José Esteban. "Preface: Fragment from the Sense of Brown Manuscript." *GLQ: A Journal of Lesbian and Gay Studies* 24, no. 4 (2018): 395–97.

Muñoz, José Esteban. *The Sense of Brown.* Edited by Joshua Chambers-Letson and Tavia Nyong'o. Duke University Press, 2020.

Murakami, Haruki. *Norwegian Wood.* Translated by Jay Rubin. Vintage International, 2000.

Murray, Albert. *The Blue Devils of Nada: A Contemporary American Approach to Aesthetic Statement.* Pantheon, 1996.

Murray, Albert. *Collected Essays and Memoirs.* Edited by Henry Louis Gates Jr. and Paul Devlin. Library of America, 2016.

Murray, Albert. *The Hero and the Blues.* University of Missouri Press, 1973.

Murray, Albert. *Murray Talks Music: Albert Murray on Jazz and Blues.* Edited by Paul Devlin. University of Minnesota Press, 2016.

Murray, Albert. *The Omni-Americans: Black Experience and American Culture.* Outerbridge and Dienstfrey, 1970.

Murray, Albert. *South to a Very Old Place.* McGraw-Hill, 1971.

Murray, Albert. *Stomping the Blues.* McGraw-Hill, 1976.

Murray, Albert, and John F. Callahan, eds. *Trading Twelves: The Selected Letters of Ralph Ellison and Albert Murray.* Modern Library, 2000.

Murray, Charles Shaar. *Boogie Man: The Adventures of John Lee Hooker in the American Twentieth Century.* St. Martin's, 2000.

Nancy, Jean-Luc. *Being Singular Plural.* Translated by Robert Richardson and Anne O'Byrne. Stanford University Press, 2000.

Nash, Alanna. *Baby Let's Play House: Elvis Presley and the Women Who Loved Him.* HarperCollins, 2010.

Nash, Alanna. *The Colonel: The Extraordinary Story of Colonel Tom Parker and Elvis Presley.* Simon and Schuster, 2003.

Nash, Alanna. *Elvis Aaron Presley: Revelations from the Memphis Mafia.* HarperCollins, 1995.

Nathan, Hans. *Dan Emmett and the Rise of Early Negro Minstrelsy.* University of Oklahoma Press, 1962.

Neal, Jocelyn. *Country Music: A Cultural and Stylistic History.* Oxford University Press, 2013.

Neal, Jocelyn. *The Songs of Jimmie Rodgers: A Legacy in Country Music.* Indiana University Press, 2009.

Neal, Mark Anthony. *Looking for Leroy: Illegible Black Masculinities.* New York University Press, 2013.

Neal, Mark Anthony. *New Black Man: Rethinking Black Masculinity.* Routledge, 2005.

Neal, Mark Anthony. *Songs in the Key of Black Life: A Rhythm and Blues Nation.* Routledge, 2003.

Neal, Mark Anthony. *Soul Babies: Black Popular Culture and the Post-Soul Aesthetic.* Routledge, 2002.

Neal, Mark Anthony. *What the Music Said: Black Popular Music and Black Public Culture*. Routledge, 1999.

Negus, Keith. *Bob Dylan*. Equinox, 2008.

Negus, Keith. *Music Genres and Corporate Cultures*. Routledge, 1999.

Negus, Keith. *Popular Music in Theory: An Introduction*. Wesleyan University Press, 1996.

Negus, Keith. *Producing Pop: Culture and Conflict in the Popular Music Industry*. Arnold, 1992.

Nehring, Neil. *Flowers in the Dustbin: Culture, Anarchy, and Postwar England*. University of Michigan Press, 1993.

Nelson, Willie, with David Ritz. *It's a Long Story: My Life*. Little, Brown, 2015.

Nettl, Bruno. *Becoming an Ethnomusicologist: A Miscellany of Influences*. Scarecrow, 2013.

Nettl, Bruno, ed. *Eight Urban Musical Cultures*. University of Illinois Press, 1978.

Nettl, Bruno. *Encounters in Ethnomusicology: A Memoir*. Harmonie Park, 2002.

Nettl, Bruno. *Heartland Excursions: Ethnomusicological Reflections on Schools of Music*. University of Illinois Press, 1995.

Nettl, Bruno. *Music in Primitive Culture*. Harvard University Press, 1956.

Nettl, Bruno. *The Study of Ethnomusicology: Twenty-Nine Issues and Concepts*. University of Illinois Press, 1983. 2nd ed., as *Thirty-One Issues and Concepts*, 2005; 3rd ed., as *Thirty-Three Discussions*, 2015.

Nevin, Robert P. "Stephen C. Foster and Minstrelsy." *Atlantic Monthly*, November 1867.

Newton, Francis [Eric Hobsbawm]. *The Jazz Scene*. McGibbon and Kee, 1959.

Nicholson, Stuart. *Billie Holiday*. Northeastern University Press, 1995.

Nisenson, Eric. *'Round about Midnight: A Portrait of Miles Davis*. Dial Press, 1982. Updated ed., Da Capo, 1996.

Norman, Philip. *Shout! The Beatles in Their Generation*. Fireside/Simon and Schuster, 1981.

Northup, Solomon. *Twelve Years a Slave: Narrative of Solomon Northup, a Citizen of New-York, Kidnapped in Washington City in 1841, and Rescued in 1853 from a Cotton Plantation near the Red River in Louisiana*. Derby and Miller; Derby, Orton and Mulligan; Sampson Low, 1853.

Novak, David. *Japanoise: Music at the Edge of Circulation*. Duke University Press, 2013.

Nyong'o, Tavia. *Afro-Fabulations: The Queer Drama of Black Life*. New York University Press, 2018.

Nyong'o, Tavia. *The Amalgamation Waltz: Race, Performance, and the Ruses of Memory*. University of Minnesota Press, 2009.

Nyong'o, Tavia. "In Finitude: Being with José, Being with Pedro." *Social Text* 32, no. 4 (2014): 71–85.

O'Brien, Glenn, ed. *The Cool School: Writing from America's Hip Underground*. Library of America, 2013.

O'Brien, Lucy. *Madonna: Like an Icon*. HarperCollins, 2007.

O'Brien, Lucy. *She Bop: The Definitive History of Women in Rock, Pop and Soul*. Penguin, 1995. 2nd ed., as *She Bop II*, Continuum, 2004. Rev. 3rd ed., as *She Bop: The Definitive History of Women in Popular Music*, Jawbone, 2012.

O'Dair, Barbara, ed. *Trouble Girls: The Rolling Stone Book of Women in Rock*. Rolling Stone Press/Random House, 1997.

Odum, Howard W., and Guy B. Johnson. *The Negro and His Songs: A Study of the Typical Negro Songs of the South*. University of North Carolina Press, 1925.

Odum, Howard W., and Guy B. Johnson. *Negro Workaday Songs*. University of North Carolina Press, 1926.

Oja, Carol. *Making Music Modern: New York in the 1920s*. Oxford University Press, 2000.

Oliver, Paul. *Barrelhouse Blues: Location Recording and the Early Traditions of the Blues*. BasicCivitas, 2009.

Oliver, Paul, and Robert "Mack" McCormick. *The Blues Come to Texas: Paul Oliver and Mack McCormick's Unfinished Book*. Edited by Alan Govenar. Texas A&M University Press, 2019.

Oliver, Paul. *Blues Fell This Morning: The Meaning of the Blues*. Horizon, 1960. 2nd ed., Cambridge University Press, 1990.

Oliver, Paul. *Blues off the Record: Thirty Years of Blues Commentary*. Hippocrene, 1984.

Oliver, Paul. *Conversation with the Blues*. Horizon, 1965. 2nd ed., Cambridge University Press, 1997.

Oliver, Paul. *Savannah Syncopators*. Stein and Day, 1970.

Oliver, Paul. *Screening the Blues: Aspects of the Blues Tradition*. Oak, 1968.

Oliver, Paul. *Songsters and Saints: Vocal Traditions on Race Records*. Cambridge University Press, 1984.

Oliver, Paul. *The Story of the Blues*. Chilton, 1969.

O'Meally, Robert G., ed. *The Jazz Cadence of American Culture*. Columbia University Press, 1998.

O'Meally, Robert G. *Lady Day: The Many Faces of Billie Holiday*. Arcade/Little, Brown, 1991.

O'Meally, Robert G., Brent Hayes Edwards, and Farah Jasmine Griffin, eds. *Uptown Conversation: The New Jazz Studies*. Columbia University Press, 2004.

Ortiz, Fernando. *Fernando Ortiz on Music: Selected Writing on Afro-Cuban Culture*. Edited by Robin Moore. Temple University Press, 2018.

Osborne, Richard. *Vinyl: A History of the Analogue Record*. Ashgate, 2012.

Pacini Hernandez, Deborah. *Bachata: A Social History of a Dominican Popular Music*. Temple University Press, 1995.

Paddison, Max. *Adorno's Aesthetics of Music*. Cambridge University Press, 1993.

Palmer, Robert. *Blues and Chaos: The Music Writing of Robert Palmer*. Edited by Anthony DeCurtis. Scribner, 2009.

Palmer, Robert. *Deep Blues*. Viking, 1981.

Palmer, Robert. *Rock & Roll: An Unruly History*. Harmony, 1995.

Palmer, Robert. *A Tale of Two Cities: Memphis Rock and New Orleans Roll*. Institute for Studies in American Music, 1979.

Pannassié, Hugues. *The Real Jazz*. Translated by Anne Sorelle Williams. Smith and Durrell, 1942.

Paredes, Américo. *Between Two Worlds*. Arte Público, 1991.

Paredes, Américo. *Cantos de Adolescencia: Songs of Youth (1932–1937)*. Edited by V. Olguín and Omar Vásquez Barbosa. Arte Público, 2007.

Paredes, Américo. *Folklore and Culture on the Texas-Mexican Border*. Edited by Richard Bauman. University of Texas Center for Mexican American Studies, 1993.

Paredes, Américo, ed. *Folktales of Mexico*. University of Chicago Press, 1970.

Paredes, Américo. *George Washington Gomez: A Mexicotexan Novel*. Arte Público, 1990.

Paredes, Américo. *The Hammon and the Beans and Other Stories*. Arte Público, 1994.

Paredes, Américo. *The Shadow*. Arte Público, 1998.

Paredes, Américo. *A Texas-Mexican Cancionero: Folksongs of the Lower Border*. University of Illinois Press, 1976.

Paredes, Américo, ed. *Toward New Perspectives in Folklore*. University of Texas Press, 1972.

Paredes, Américo, ed. *The Urban Experience and Folk Tradition*. University of Texas Press, 1971.

Paredes, Américo. *"With His Pistol in His Hands": A Border Ballad and Its Hero*. University of Texas Press, 1958.

Paredez, Deborah. *Selenidad: Selena, Latinos, and the Performance of Memory*. Duke University Press, 2009.

Paskman, Dailey, and Sigmund Spaeth. *"Gentlemen, Be Seated!": A Parade of the Old-Time Minstrels*. Doubleday, Doran, 1928.

Patchett, Ann. *Bel Canto*. Perennial, 2001.

Patterson, Michelle Wick. *Natalie Curtis Burlin: A Life in Native and African American Music*. University of Nebraska Press, 2010.

Pavlić, Ed. *Who Can Afford to Improvise?: James Baldwin and Black Music, the Lyric and the Listeners*. Fordham University Press, 2015.

Paz, Octavio. *The Labyrinth of Solitude: Life and Thought in Mexico*. Grove, 1962.

Pearson, Barry Lee, and Bill McCulloch. *Robert Johnson: Lost and Found*. University of Illinois Press, 2003.

Peck, Abe, ed. *Dancing Madness*. Rolling Stone Press, 1976.

Pecknold, Diane, ed. *Hidden in the Mix: The African American Presence in Country Music*. Duke University Press, 2013.

Pecknold, Diane. *The Selling Sound: The Rise of the Country Music Industry*. Duke University Press, 2007.

Pecknold, Diane, and Kristine McCusker, eds. *Country Boys and Redneck Women: New Essays in Gender and Country Music*. University Press of Mississippi, 2016.

Peiss, Kathy. *Cheap Amusements: Working Women and Leisure in Turn-of-the-Century New York*. Temple University Press, 1986.

Pegg, Bruce. *Brown Eyed Handsome Man: The Life and Hard Times of Chuck Berry*. Routledge, 2002.

Pekar, Harvey. *From Off the Streets of Cleveland Comes . . . American Splendor: The Life and Times of Harvey Pekar*. Doubleday, 1986.

Pelly, Jenn. *The Raincoats*. Bloomsbury, 2017.

Peña, Manuel. *The Mexican American Orquesta. Music, Culture, and the Dialectic of Conflict*. University of Texas Press, 1999.

Peña, Manuel. *Música Tejana: The Cultural Economy of Artistic Transformation*. Texas A&M University Press, 1999.

Peña, Manuel. *The Texas-Mexican Conjunto: History of a Working-Class Music*. University of Texas Press, 1985.

Peña, Manuel. *Where the Ox Does Not Plow: A Mexican American Ballad*. University of New Mexico Press, 2008.

Pepper, Art, and Laurie Pepper. *Straight Life: The Story of Art Pepper*. Schirmer, 1979.

Perry, Imani. *Prophets of the Hood: Politics and Poetics in Hip Hop*. Duke University Press, 2004.

Perry, Marc. *Negro Soy Yo: Hip Hop and Raced Citizenship in Neoliberal Cuba*. Duke University Press, 2015.

Perullo, Alex. *Live from Dar es Salaam: Popular Music and Tanzania's Music Economy*. Indiana University Press, 2011.

Peterson, James Braxton. *Hip-Hop Headphones: A Scholar's Critical Playlist*. Bloomsbury, 2016.

Peterson, Richard. *Creating Country Music: Fabricating Authenticity*. University of Chicago Press, 1997.

Peterson, Richard. "Why 1955? Explaining the Advent of Rock Music." *Popular Music* 9, no. 1 (1990): 97–116.

Peterson, Richard, and Roger M. Kern. "Changing Highbrow Taste: From Snob to Omnivore." *American Sociological Review* 61, no. 5 (1996): 900–907.

Petkov, Steve, and Leonard Mustazza, eds. *The Frank Sinatra Reader*. Oxford University Press, 1995.

Petrusich, Amanda. *Do Not Sell at Any Price: The Wild, Obsessive Hunt for the World's Rarest 78 rpm Records*. Simon and Schuster, 2014.

Phillips, Caryl. *Dancing in the Dark*. Secker and Warburg, 2005.

Pillsbury, Glenn. *Damage Incorporated: Metallica and the Production of Musical Identity*. Routledge, 2006.

Pini, Maria. *Club Cultures and Female Subjectivity: The Move from Home to House*. Palgrave Macmillan, 2001.

Pisani, Michael V. *Imagining Native America in Music*. Yale University Press, 2005.

Pleasants, Henry. *The Great American Popular Singers*. Simon and Schuster, 1974.

Pohl, Frederik. *The Way the Future Was: A Memoir*. Ballantine, 1978.

Pollock, Bruce. *Hipper Than Our Kids: A Rock & Roll Journal of the Baby Boom Generation*. Schirmer, 1993.

Polsky, Ned. *Hustlers, Beats and Others*. Aldine, 1967.

Ponce, Martin Joseph. *Beyond the Nation: Diasporic Filipino Literature and Queer Reading*. New York University Press, 2012.

Popoff, Martin. *The Collector's Guide to Heavy Metal*. Collectors Guide, 1997.

Porter, Eric. *What Is This Thing Called Jazz?: African American Musicians as Artists, Critics, and Activists*. University of California Press, 2002.

Porterfield, Nolan. *Last Cavalier: The Life and Times of John A. Lomax, 1867–1948*. University of Illinois Press, 1996.

Poschardt, Ulf. *DJ Culture*. Quartet, 1998.

Powers, Ann. *Good Booty: Love and Sex, Black and White, Body and Soul in American Music*. Dey Street/Morrow, 2017.

Powers, Ann. *Weird Like Us: My Bohemian America*. Simon and Schuster, 2000.

Powers, Richard. *The Time of Our Singing*. Farrar, Straus and Giroux, 2002.

Pratt, Linda Ray. "Elvis, or the Ironies of a Southern Identity." In *Elvis: Images and Fancies,* edited by Jac Tharpe, 3–10. University Press of Mississippi, 1979.

Presley, Priscilla, with Sandra Harmon. *Elvis and Me*. Putnam, 1985.

Pugh, Megan. *America Dancing: From the Cakewalk to the Moonwalk*. Yale University Press, 2015.

Puzo, Mario. *The Godfather*. Putnam, 1969.

Pynchon, Thomas. *The Crying of Lot 49*. Lippincott, 1966.

Pynchon, Thomas. *V*. Lippincott, 1963.

Quinn, Eithne. *Nuthin' but a "G" Thang: The Culture and Commerce of Gangsta Rap*. Columbia University Press, 2005.

Radano, Ronald. *Lying Up a Nation: Race and Black Music*. University of Chicago Press, 2003.

Radano, Ronald. *New Musical Figurations: Anthony Braxton's Cultural Critique*. University of Chicago Press, 1993.

Radano, Ronald, and Philip Bohlman, eds. *Music and the Racial Imagination*. University of Chicago Press, 2000.

Radano, Ronald, and Tejumola Olaniyan, eds. *Audible Empire: Music, Global Politics, Critique*. Duke University Press, 2016.

Radway, Janice. *Reading the Romance: Women, Patriarchy, and Popular Literature*. University of North Carolina Press, 1984.

Ragland, Cathy. *Música Norteña: Mexican Migrants Creating a Nation between Nations*. Temple University Press, 2009.

Rampersad, Arnold. *The Life of Langston Hughes. Volume 1: 1902–1941; I, Too, Sing America*. Oxford University Press, 1986. *Volume II: 1941–1967, I Dream a World*. Oxford University Press, 1988.

Ramsey, Frederic, Jr. *Been Here and Gone*. Rutgers University Press, 1960.

Ramsey, Frederic, Jr., and Charles Edward Smith, eds. *Jazzmen*. Harcourt, Brace, 1939.

Ramsey, Guthrie, Jr. *The Amazing Bud Powell: Black Genius, Jazz History, and the Challenge of Bebop*. University of California Press, 2013.

Ramsey, Guthrie, Jr. *Race Music: Black Cultures from Bebop to Hip-Hop*, University of California Press and Center for Black Music Research, 2003.

Rapp, Tobias. *Lost and Sound: Berlin, Techno and the Easyjet Set*. Innvervisions, 2010.

Ratliff, Ben. *Every Song Ever: Twenty Ways to Listen in an Age of Musical Plenty*. Farrar, Straus and Giroux, 2016.

Redmond, Shana. *Everything Man: The Form and Function of Paul Robeson*. Duke University Press, 2020.

Reed, Ishmael. *Mumbo Jumbo*. Doubleday, 1972.

Reed, Ishmael. *Shrovetide in Old New Orleans*. Doubleday, 1978.

Reed, S. Alexander. "Punking the Bibliography: RE/Search Publications, the Bookshelf Question, and Ideational Flow." In *Ripped, Torn and Cut: Pop, Politics and Punk*

Fanzines from 1976, edited by the Subcultures Network, 245–63. Manchester University Press, 2018.

Regev, Motti. *Pop-Rock Music: Aesthetic Cosmopolitanism in Late Modernity*. Polity, 2013.

Reid, Jamie, and Jon Savage. *Up They Rise: The Incomplete Works of Jamie Reid*. Faber and Faber, 1987.

Reising, Russell, ed. *Every Sound There Is: The Beatles' Revolver and the Transformation of Rock and Roll*. Ashgate, 2002.

Rettenmund, Matthew. *Encyclopedia Madonnica*. St. Martin's, 1995. Rev. ed., as *Encyclopedia Madonnica 20: Madonna from A to Z*. Boy Culture, 2015.

Reynolds, Christopher. "Documenting the Zenith of Women Song Composers: A Database of Songs Published in the United States and the British Commonwealth, ca. 1890–1930." *Notes* 69, no. 4 (2013): 671–87.

Reynolds, David S. *Beneath the American Renaissance: The Subversive Imagination in the Age of Emerson and Melville*. Knopf, 1988.

Reynolds, David S. *Walt Whitman's America: A Cultural Biography*. Knopf, 1995.

Reynolds, Simon. *Energy Flash: A Journey through Rave Music and Dance Culture*. Picador, 1998; Soft Skull, 2012. U.S. ed., as *Generation Ecstasy: Into the World of Techno and Rave Culture*. Little, Brown, 1998.

Reynolds, Simon. *Retromania: Pop Culture's Addiction to Its Own Past*. Faber and Faber, 2011.

Reynolds, Simon. *Rip It Up and Start Again: Postpunk, 1978–1984*. Faber and Faber, 2005.

Reynolds, Simon, and Joy Press. *The Sex Revolts: Gender, Rebellion and Rock 'n' Roll*. Harvard University Press, 1995.

Rhodes, Lisa. *Electric Ladyland: Women and Rock Culture*. University of Pennsylvania Press, 2005.

Rice, Anne. *The Vampire Lestat*. Knopf, 1985.

Rice, Edward LeRoy. *Monarchs of Minstrelsy, from "Daddy" Rice to Date*. Kenny, 1911.

Rice, T. *Jim Crow*. Riley, c. 1832.

Rice, T. D. *Jim Crow, American: Selected Songs and Plays*. Edited by W. T. Lhamon Jr. Harvard University Press, 2009.

Richards, Keith, with James Fox. *Life*. Little, Brown, 2010.

Ricks, Christopher. *Dylan's Visions of Sins*. Ecco, 2004.

Rietveld, Hillegonda. *This Is Our House: House Music, Cultural Spaces, and Technologies*. Ashgate, 1998.

Riis, Thomas. *Just before Jazz: Black Musical Theater in New York, 1890–1915*. Smithsonian, 1989.

Riley, Tim. *Tell Me Why: The Beatles—Album by Album, Song by Song, The Sixties and After*. Knopf, 1988.

Ritchie, Jean. *Jean Ritchie's Singing Family of the Cumberlands*. Oxford University Press, 1955.

Ritter, Frédéric Louis. *Music in America*. Scribner, 1883.

Ritz, David. "Divided Byline: How a Student of Leslie Fiedler and a Colleague of Charles Keil Became the Ghostwriter for Everybody from Ray Charles to Cornel West." In *Pop When the World Falls Apart: Music in the Shadow of Doubt*, edited by Eric Weisbard, 40–46. Duke University Press, 2012.

Ritz, David. *Divided Soul: The Life of Marvin Gaye*. McGraw-Hill, 1985.

Ritz, David. *Faith in Time: The Life of Jimmy Scott*. Da Capo, 2002.

Ritz, David. *The God Groove: A Blues Journey to Faith*. Howard, 2019.

Ritz, David. *Respect: The Life of Aretha Franklin*. Little, Brown, 2014.

Robbins, Ira, ed. *The Trouser Press Record Guide*. Scribner, 1983.

Roberts, Brian. *Blackface Nation: Race, Reform, and Identity in American Popular Music, 1812–1925*. University of Chicago Press, 2017.

Roberts, John Storm. *Black Music of Two Worlds: African, Caribbean, Latin, and African-American*. Praeger, 1972. 2nd ed., Schirmer, 1998.

Roberts, John Storm. *The Latin Tinge: The Impact of Latin American Music on the United States*. Oxford University Press, 1979. 2nd ed., 1999.

Robertson, David. *W. C. Handy: The Life and Times of the Man Who Made the Blues*. Doubleday, 2009.

Rodman, Gilbert. *Elvis after Elvis: The Posthumous Career of a Living Legend*. Routledge, 1996.

Rogin, Michael. *Blackface, White Noise: Jewish Immigrants in the Hollywood Melting Pot*. University of California Press, 1996.

Rollefson, J. Griffith. *Flip the Script: European Hip Hop and the Politics of Postcoloniality*. University of Chicago Press, 2017.

Rollins, Henry. *Get in the Van: On the Road with Black Flag*. 2.13.61 Publications, 1994.

Rondón, César Miguel. *The Book of Salsa: A Chronicle of Urban Music from the Caribbean to New York City*. 1980. Translated by Frances Aparicio with Jackie White. University of North Carolina Press, 2008.

Root, George. *The Story of a Musical Life: An Autobiography*. Church, 1891.

Rorem, Ned. *Knowing When to Stop: A Memoir*. Simon and Schuster, 1994.

Rose, Al. *Eubie Blake*. Schirmer, 1979.

Rose, Tricia. *Black Noise: Rap Music and Black Culture in Contemporary America*. Wesleyan University Press, 1994.

Rose, Tricia. *The Hip-Hop Wars: What We Talk about When We Talk about Hip Hop—and Why It Matters*. Basic, 2008.

Rosen, Jody. *White Christmas: The Story of an American Song*. Scribner, 2002.

Rosengarten, Theodore. *All God's Dangers: The Life of Nate Shaw*. Knopf, 1974.

Ross, Alex. *Listen to This*. Farrar, Straus and Giroux, 2010.

Ross, Alex. *The Rest Is Noise: Listening to the Twentieth Century*. Farrar, Straus and Giroux, 2007.

Ross, Alex. *Wagnerism: Art and Politics in the Shadow of Music*. Farrar, Straus and Giroux, 2020.

Rossiter, Will, *How to Write a Song and Become Wealthy*. Rossiter, 1899.

Rotella, Carlo. *Playing in Time: Essays, Profiles, and Other True Stories*. University of Chicago Press, 2012.

Rotolo, Suze. *A Freewheelin' Time: A Memoir of Greenwich Village in the Sixties*. Broadway, 2008.

Rourke, Constance. *American Humor: A Study of the National Character*. Harcourt, Brace, 1931.

Rourke, Constance. *Charles Sheeler: Artist in the American Tradition*. Harcourt, Brace, 1938.

Rourke, Constance. *Davy Crockett*. Harcourt, Brace, 1934.

Rourke, Constance. *The Roots of American Culture and Other Essays*. Edited by Van Wyck Brooks. Harcourt, Brace, 1942.

Rourke, Constance. *Trumpets of Jubilee*. Harcourt, Brace, 1927.

Rowland, Mabel, ed. *Bert Williams, Son of Laughter*. English Crafters, 1923.

Rowlands, Penelope. *The Beatles Are Here! 50 Years after the Band Arrived in America, Writers, Musicians and Other Fans Remember*. Algonquin, 2014.

Roxon, Lillian. *Rock Encyclopedia*. Grosset and Dunlap, 1969.

Royster, Francesca. *Sounding Like a No-No: Queer Sounds and Eccentric Acts in the Post-Soul Era*. University of Michigan Press, 2013.

Rubin, Joan Shelley. *Constance Rourke and American Culture*. University of North Carolina Press, 1980.

Russell, George. *Cheer! Boys, Cheer! Memories of Men and Music*. Macqueen, 1895.

Russell, Ross. *Bird Lives! The High Life and Hard Times of Charlie (Yardbird) Parker*. Charterhouse, 1973.

Russell, Ross. *The Sound*. Dutton, 1961.

Rust, Brian. *Jazz Records A–Z, 1897–1931*. Self-published, 1961. As *Jazz and Ragtime Records, 1897–1942: The Classic Jazz Discography*, rev. ed., enlarged, Mainspring, 2002.

Sabin, Roger, ed. *Punk Rock: So What? The Cultural Legacy of Punk*. Routledge, 1999.

Saldívar, Ramón. *The Borderlands of Culture: Américo Paredes and the Transnational Imaginary*. Duke University Press, 2006.

Salkind, Micah. *Do You Remember House? Chicago's Queer of Color Undergrounds*. Oxford University Press, 2018.

Sander, Ellen. *Trips: Rock Life in the Sixties*. Scribner, 1973.

Sanjek, Russell. *American Popular Music and Its Business: The First Four Hundred Years. Volume I: The Beginning to 1790. Volume II: From 1790 to 1909. Volume III: From 1900 to 1984*. Oxford University Press, 1988. Volume III, as *Pennies from Heaven: The American Popular Music Business in the Twentieth Century*, updated by David Sanjek. Da Capo, 1996.

Sandburg, Carl. *American Songbag*. Harcourt Brace, 1927.

Sanneh, Kelefa. "The Rap against Rockism." *New York Times*, October 31, 2004.

Sante, Luc. *Kill All Your Darlings: Pieces, 1990–2005*. Verse Chorus/Yeti, 2007.

Sargent, Helen Child, and George Lyman Kittredge, eds. *English and Scottish Popular Ballads: Student's Cambridge Edition*. Houghton Mifflin, 1932

Savage, Jon. *England's Dreaming: Anarchy, Sex Pistols, Punk Rock, and Beyond*. St. Martin's Griffin, 1991.

Savage, Jon. *1966: The Year the Decade Exploded*. Faber and Faber, 2015.

Savage, Jon. *Teenage: The Creation of Youth, 1875–1945*. Chatto and Windus, 2007.

Savage, Jon, with Hanif Kureishi, eds. *The Faber Book of Pop*. Faber and Faber, 1995.

Savigliano, Marta. *Tango and the Political Economy of Passion*. Westview, 1995.

Savran, David. *Highbrow/Lowdown: Theater, Jazz, and the Making of the New Middle Class*. University of Michigan Press, 2009.

Savran, David. *A Queer Sort of Materialism: Recontextualizing American Theater*. University of Michigan Press, 2003.

Sawyers, June Skinner, ed. *Read the Beatles: Classic and New Writings on the Beatles, Their Legacy, and Why They Still Matter*. Penguin, 2006.

Scaduto, Anthony. *Bob Dylan*. Grosset and Dunlap, 1971.

Scarborough, Dorothy. *On the Trail of Negro Folk-Songs*. Harvard University Press, 1925.

Schaffner, Nicholas. *The Beatles Forever*. McGraw-Hill, 1978.

Schatz, Thomas. *The Genius of the System: Hollywood Filmmaking in the Studio Era*. Pantheon, 1988.

Schaumburg, Ron. *Growing Up with the Beatles: An Illustrated Tribute*. Pyramid, 1976.

Schenbeck, Lawrence. *Racial Uplift and American Music, 1878–1943*. University Press of Mississippi, 2012.

Schloss, Joseph. *Foundation: B-boys, B-girls and Hip-Hop Culture in New York*. Oxford University Press, 2009.

Schloss, Joseph. *Making Beats: The Art of Sample-Based Hip-Hop*. Wesleyan University Press, 2004.

Schreuders, Piet, Mark Lewisohn, and Adam Smith. *The Beatles' London*. Hamlyn, 1994; Updated ed., Portico, 2008.

Schroeder, Patricia. *Robert Johnson: Mythmaking and Contemporary American Culture*. University of Illinois Press, 2004.

Schuller, Gunther. *Early Jazz: Its Roots and Musical Development*. Oxford University Press, 1968.

Schuller, Gunther. *Swing Jazz: The Development of Jazz, 1930–1945*. Oxford University Press, 1989.

Schwichtenberg, Cathy, ed. *The Madonna Connection: Representational Politics, Subcultural Identities and Cultural Theory*. Westview, 1992.

Scott, James. *Domination and the Arts of Resistance: Hidden Transcripts*. Yale University Press, 1990.

Seabrook, John. *NoBrow: The Culture of Marketing, The Marketing of Culture*. Knopf, 2000.

Sears, Benjamin, ed. *The Irving Berlin Reader*. Oxford University Press, 2012.

Seldes, Gilbert. *The Public Arts*. Simon and Schuster, 1956.

Seldes, Gilbert. *The Seven Lively Arts*. Harper, 1924. Rev. ed., Sagamore Press, 1957.

Serrano, Shea. *The Rap Yearbook: The Most Important Rap Song from Every Year since 1979*. Abrams Image, 2015.

Sexton, Adam, ed. *Desperately Seeking Madonna: In Search of the Meaning of the World's Most Famous Woman*. Delta, 1993.

Shain, Richard. *Roots in Reverse: Senegalese Afro-Cuban Music and Tropical Cosmopolitanism*. Wesleyan University Press, 2018.

Shange, Ntozake. *Sassafrass, Cypress & Indigo: A Novel*. St. Martin's, 1982.

Shank, Barry. *Dissonant Identities: The Rock 'n' Roll Scene in Austin, Texas*. Wesleyan University Press, 1994.

Shank, Barry. *The Political Force of Musical Beauty*. Duke University Press, 2014.

Shapiro, Henry. *Appalachia On Our Mind: The Southern Mountains and Mountaineers in the American Consciousness 1870–1920*. University of North Carolina Press, 1978.

Shapiro, Nat, and Nat Hentoff, eds. *Hear Me Talkin' to Ya: The Story of Jazz as Told by the Men Who Made It*. Rinehart, 1955.

Shapiro, Nat, and Nat Hentoff, eds. *The Jazz Makers: Essays on the Greats of Jazz*. Rinehart, 1957.

Shapiro, Peter. *Turn the Beat Around: The Secret History of Disco*. Faber and Faber, 2005.

Shaw, Arnold. *Belafonte: An Unauthorized Biography*. Chilton, 1960.

Shaw, Arnold. *Black Popular Music in America: From the Spirituals, Minstrels and Ragtime to Soul, Disco and Hip-Hop*. Schirmer, 1986.

Shaw, Arnold. *Gene Krupa: First Authentic Life Story of America's Ace Drummer Man*. Pin-Up, 1945.

Shaw, Arnold. *Honkers and Shouters. The Golden Years of Rhythm and Blues*. Macmillan, 1978.

Shaw, Arnold. *The Jazz Age: Popular Music in the 1920s*. Oxford University Press, 1987.

Shaw, Arnold. *Let's Dance: Popular Music in the 1930s*. Edited by Bill Willard. Oxford University Press, 1998.

Shaw, Arnold. *The Money Song*. Random House, 1953.

Shaw, Arnold. *The Rockin' 50s. The Decade that Transformed the Pop Music Scene*. Hawthorn, 1974.

Shaw, Arnold. *The Rock Revolution: What's Happening to Today's Music*. Crowell-Collier, 1969.

Shaw, Arnold. *Sinatra: Twentieth Century Romantic*. Holt, Rinehart and Winston, 1968.

Shaw, Arnold. *The Street That Never Slept*. Coward, McCann and Geoghegan, 1971. As *52nd Street: The Street of Jazz*. Da Capo, 1977.

Shaw, Arnold. *The World of Soul: Black America's Contribution to the Pop Music Scene*. Cowles, 1970.

Shay, Anthony, and Barbara Sellers-Young, eds. *The Oxford Handbook of Dance and Ethnicity*. Oxford University Press, 2019.

Sheed, Wilfrid. *The House That George Built: With a Little Help from Irving, Cole, and a Crew of about Fifty*. Random House, 2007.

Sheffield, Rob. *Dreaming the Beatles: The Love Story of One Band and the Whole World*. Dey Street, 2016.

Sheffield, Rob. *Love Is a Mix Tape: Life and Loss, One Song at a Time*. Crown, 2007.

Shelton, Gilbert. *The Fabulous Furry Freak Brothers Omnibus*. Knockabout Comics, 2008.

Shelton, Robert. *The Country Music Story: A Picture History of Country and Western Music*. Bobbs-Merrill, 1966.

Shelton, Robert. *No Direction Home: The Life and Music of Bob Dylan*. Morrow, 1986.

Shepard, Sam. *The Rolling Thunder Logbook*. Penguin, 1976.

Shiner, Lewis. *Glimpses*. Morrow, 1993.

Shiner, Lewis. *Outside the Gates of Eden*. Subterranean, 2019.

Shiner, Lewis. *Say Goodbye*. St. Martin's, 1999.

Shiner, Lewis. *Slam*. Doubleday, 1990.

Shipton, Alyn. *A New History of Jazz*. Continuum, 2001.

Shirazi, Roxana. *The Last Living Slut: Born in Iran, Bred Backstage*. Igniter, 2010.

Shotton, Pete, and Nicholas Schaffner. *John Lennon: In My Life*. Stein and Day, 1983.

Sicko, Dan. *Techno Rebels: The Renegades of Electronic Funk*. Billboard, 1999. 2nd ed., Painted Turtle, 2015.

Silverman, Kenneth. *Begin Again: A Biography of John Cage*. Northwestern University Press, 2010.

Simond, Ike. *Old Slack's Reminiscence and Pocket History of the Colored Profession from 1865 to 1891*. 1891. Bowling Green State University Press, 1974.

Simonett, Helena. *Banda: Mexican Musical Life across Borders*. Wesleyan University Press, 2001.

Sinatra, Nancy. *Frank Sinatra: An American Legend*. General, 1995.

Sinker, Daniel, ed. *We Owe You Nothing: Punk Planet: The Collected Interviews*. Akashic, 2001. Expanded ed., 2007.

Sinnreich, Aram. *Mashed Up: Music, Technology, and the Rise of Configurable Culture*. University of Massachusetts Press, 2010.

Sklaroff, Lauren. *Red Hot Mama: The Life of Sophie Tucker*. University of Texas Press, 2018.

Slichter, Jacob. *So You Wanna Be a Rock & Roll Star: How I Machine-Gunned a Roomful of Record Executives and Other True Tales from a Drummer's Life*. Broadway, 2004.

Slobin, Mark. *Folk Music: A Very Short Introduction*. Oxford University Press, 2011.

Slobin, Mark. *Subcultural Sounds: Micromusics of the West*. Wesleyan University Press, 1993.

Sloman, Larry "Ratso." *On the Road with Bob Dylan*. Bantam, 1978.

Small, Christopher. *The Christopher Small Reader*. Edited by Robert Walser. Wesleyan University Press, 2016.

Small, Christopher. *Music of the Common Tongue: Survival and Celebration in African American Music*. J. Calder, 1987. Rev. ed., Wesleyan University Press, 1999.

Small, Christopher. *Music, Society, Education*. John Calder, 1977. Reissue, with foreword by Robert Walser, Wesleyan University Press, 1996.

Small, Christopher. *Musicking: The Meanings of Performing and Listening*. Wesleyan University Press, 1998.

Smethurst, James. *Brick City Vanguard: Amiri Baraka, Black Music, Black Modernity*. University of Massachusetts Press, 2020.

Smith, Charles Edward, Frederic Ramsey Jr., Charles Payne Rogers, and Bill Russell. *The Jazz Record Book*. Smith and Durrell, 1942.

Smith, Christopher. *The Creolization of American Culture: William Sidney Mount and the Roots of Blackface Minstrelsy*. University of Illinois Press, 2013.

Smith, Danyel. *Shine Bright: A Personal History of Black Women in Pop*. One World/Random House, 2021.

Smith, Eric Ledell. *Bert Williams: A Biography of the Pioneer Black Comedian*. McFarland, 1992.

Smith, Lee. *The Devil's Dream*. Putnam, 1992.

Smith, Patti. *Just Kids*. Ecco/HarperCollins, 2010.

Smith, RJ. *The Great Black Way: L.A.'s Central Avenue in the 1940s and the Lost Negro Renaissance*. Public Affairs, 2006.

Smith, Willie the Lion. *Music on My Mind*. Doubleday, 1964.

Smith, Zadie. *On Beauty*. Penguin, 2005.

Smith, Zadie. *Swing Time*, Penguin, 2016.

Smith, Zadie. *White Teeth*. Random House, 2000.

Smucker, Tom. *Why the Beach Boys Matter*. University of Texas Press, 2018.

Snead, James. "Repetition as a Figure of Black Culture." In *Black Literature and Literary Theory*, edited by Henry Louis Gates Jr., 59–80. Methuen, 1984.

Søderlind, Didrik, and Michael Moynihan. *Lords of Chaos: The Bloody Rise of the Satanic Metal Underground*. Feral House, 1997.

Sonneck, O. G. "The Bibliography of American Music." *Proceedings and Papers of the Bibliographical Society of America 1* (1906): 50–64.

Sonneck, O. G. *Bibliography of Early Secular American Music*. McQueen, 1905.

Sonneck, O. G. *Early Concert-Life in America (1731–1800)*. Breitkopf and Härtel, 1907.

Sonneck, O. G. *Early Opera in America*. Schirmer/Boston Music, 1915.

Sonneck, O. G. *Francis Hopkinson, the First American Poet-Composer (1731–1791), and James Lyon, Patriot, Preacher, Psalmodist (1735–1794): Two Studies in Early American Music*. McQueen, 1905.

Sonneck, O. G. *Miscellaneous Studies in the History of Music*. Macmillan, 1921.

Sonneck, O. G. *Report on "The Star-Spangled Banner," "Hail Columbia," "America," "Yankee Doodle."* U.S. Government Printing Office, 1909.

Sotiropoulos, Karen. *Staging Race: Black Performers in Turn of the Century America*. Harvard University Press, 2006.

Sounes, Howard. *Down the Highway: The Life of Bob Dylan*. Grove, 2001.

Southern, Eileen. *Biographical Dictionary of Afro-American and African Musicians*. Greenwood, 1982.

Southern, Eileen. *The Music of Black Americans*. Norton, 1971. 2nd ed., 1983; 3rd ed., 1997.

Southern, Eileen, ed. *Readings in Black American Music*. Norton, 1971. 2nd ed., 1983.

Spaeth, Sigmund. *The Art of Enjoying Music*. Whittlesey House, 1933.

Spaeth, Sigmund. *Barber Shop Ballads and How to Sing Them*. Simon and Schuster, 1925.

Spaeth, Sigmund. *Great Symphonies: How to Recognize and Remember Them*. Garden City, 1936.

Spaeth, Sigmund. *History of Popular Music in America*. Random House, 1948.

Spaeth, Sigmund. *Read 'Em and Weep: The Songs You Forgot to Remember*. Doubleday, Page, 1927.

Speck, Samuel H. *The Song Writers' Guide*. Jerome H. Remick, 1910.

Spellman, A. B. *Four Lives in the Bebop Business*. Pantheon, 1966.

Spigel, Lynn. *TV by Design: Modern Art and the Rise of Network Television*. University of Chicago Press, 2008.

Spiotta, Dana. *Eat the Document*. Scribner, 2006.

Spiotta, Dana. *Stone Arabia*. Scribner, 2011.

Spitz, Marc. *Poseur: A Memoir of Downtown New York City in the '90s*. Da Capo, 2013.

Springsteen, Bruce. *Born to Run*. Simon and Schuster, 2016.

Stadler, Gustavus [Gus]. "On Whiteness and Sound Studies." *Sounding Out!*, July 6, 2015.

Stadler, Gustavus. *Woody Guthrie: An Intimate Life*. Beacon, 2020.

Stearns, Marshall. *The Story of Jazz*. Oxford University Press, 1956.

Stearns, Marshall, and Jean Stearns. *Jazz Dance: The Story of American Vernacular Dance*. Macmillan, 1968.

Steffan, Karinne. *Confessions of a Video Vixen*. Amistad, 2005.

Stein, Daniel. *Music Is My Life: Louis Armstrong, Autobiography, and American Jazz.* University of Michigan Press, 2012.

Steinem, Gloria. "John Lennon: Beatle with a Future." *Cosmopolitan*, December 1964.

Steinke, Darcey. *Suicide Blonde.* Atlantic Monthly Press, 1992.

Sterling, Bruce. "Dori Bangs." *Isaac Asimov's Science Fiction Magazine*, September 1989. Reprinted in *Globalhead: Stories.* Random House, 1994.

Sterling, Bruce, ed. *Mirrorshades: The Cyberpunk Anthology.* Arbor House, 1986.

Sterling, Bruce. "We See Things Differently." *Semiotext(e) SF* 5, no. 2 (1989): 27–42.

Sterling, Bruce. *Zeitgeist.* Spectra, 2001.

Sterne, Jonathan. *The Audible Past: Cultural Origins of Sound Reproduction.* Duke University Press, 2002.

Sterne, Jonathan. *MP3: The Meaning of a Format.* Duke University Press, 2012.

Sterne, Jonathan, ed. *The Sound Studies Reader.* Routledge, 2012.

Stevenson, Robert. "America's First Black Music Historian." *Journal of the American Musicologist* 26 (1973): 383–404.

Stimeling, Travis. *Cosmic Cowboys and New Hicks: The Countercultural Sounds of Austin's Progressive Country Music Scene.* Oxford University Press, 2011.

Stimeling, Travis, ed. *The Country Music Reader.* Oxford University Press, 2014.

Stimeling, Travis, ed. *The Oxford Handbook of Country Music.* Oxford University Press, 2017.

Stokes, Geoffrey. *The Beatles.* Rolling Stone Press/Times Books, 1980.

Stokes, Geoffrey. *Star-Making Machinery: Inside the Business of Rock and Roll.* Vintage, 1977.

Stokes, Martin. *Republic of Love: Cultural Intimacy in Turkish Popular Music.* University of Chicago Press, 2010.

Stoever, Jennifer. *The Sonic Color Line: Race and the Cultural Practices of Listening.* New York University Press, 2016.

Stowe, David. *Swing Changes: Big-Band Jazz in New Deal America.* Harvard University Press, 1994.

Strangways, A. H. Fox, in collaboration with Maud Karpeles. *Cecil Sharp.* Oxford University Press/Humphrey Milford, 1933. 2nd ed., 1955.

Straub, Emma. *Modern Lovers.* Riverhead, 2016.

Straw, Will. "Sizing Up Record Collections: Gender and Connoisseurship in Rock Music Culture." In *Sexing the Groove: Popular Music and Gender*, edited by Sheila Whiteley, 3–16. Routledge, 1997.

Straw, Will. "Systems of Articulation, Logics of Change: Scenes and Communities in Popular Music." *Cultural Studies* 5, no. 3 (1991): 361–75.

Straw, Will. "Value and Velocity: The 12-Inch Single as Medium and Artefact." In *Popular Music Studies*, edited by Keith Negus and David Hesmondhalgh, 79–92. Arnold/Oxford University Press, 2002.

Stubbs, David. *Mars by 1980: The Story of Electronic Music.* Faber and Faber Social, 2018.

Sublette, Ned. *Cuba and Its Music: From the First Drums to the Mambo.* Chicago Review Press, 2004.

Suisman, David. *Selling Sounds: The Commercial Revolution in American Music.* Harvard University Press, 2009.

Sullivan, John Jeremiah. *Pulphead: Essays*. Farrar, Straus and Giroux, 2011.

Szendy, Peter. *Hits: Philosophy in the Jukebox*. Translated by Will Bishop. Fordham University Press, 2012.

Szendy, Peter. *Listen: A History of Our Ears*. Translated by Charlotte Mandell. Fordham University Press, 2008.

Szwed, John. *Alan Lomax: The Man Who Recorded the World*. Viking, 2010.

Szwed, John. *Billie Holiday: The Musician and the Myth*. Viking, 2015.

Szwed, John. *So What: The Life of Miles Davis*. Simon and Schuster, 2002.

Talese, Gay. "Frank Sinatra Has a Cold." *Esquire*, April 1966.

Tate, Greg. "The Electric Miles, Parts 1 and 2." *Downbeat*, July–August 1983. Reprinted in *Flyboy in the Buttermilk: Essays on Contemporary America*. Simon and Schuster, 1992.

Tate, Greg, ed. *Everything but the Burden: What White People Are Taking from Black Culture*. Broadway, 2003.

Tate, Greg. *Flyboy in the Buttermilk: Essays on Contemporary America*. Simon and Schuster, 1992.

Tate, Greg. *Flyboy 2: The Greg Tate Reader*. Duke University Press, 2016.

Tate, Greg. "Silence, Exile and Cunning: Miles Davis in Memoriam." *Village Voice*, October 15, 1991. Reprinted in *Flyboy in the Buttermilk: Essays on Contemporary America*. Simon and Schuster, 1992.

Taylor, Derek. *As Time Goes By*. Straight Arrow, 1973.

Taylor, Derek. *It Was 20 Years Ago Today*. Simon and Schuster, 1987.

Taylor, Timothy. *Beyond Exoticism: Western Music and the World*. Duke University Press, 2007.

Taylor, Timothy. *Global Pop: World Music, World Markets*. Routledge, 1997.

Taylor, Timothy. *Music and Capitalism: A History of the Present*. University of Chicago Press, 2016.

Taylor, Yuval, and Jake Austen. *Darkest America: Black Minstrelsy from Slavery to Hip-Hop*. Norton, 2012.

Teachout, Terry. "An American Icon." *New York Times*, November 5, 1995.

Teachout, Terry. *Duke: A Life of Duke Ellington*. Gotham, 2013.

Teachout, Terry. *Pops: A Life of Louis Armstrong*. Houghton Mifflin Harcourt, 2009.

Thompson, Ahmir "Questlove," and Ben Greenman. *Mo' Meta Blues: The World According to Questlove*. Grand Central, 2013.

Thompson, Katrina. *Ring Shout Wheel About: The Racial Politics of Music and Dance in North American Slavery*. University of Illinois Press, 2014.

Thompson, Robert Farris. *African Art in Motion: Icon and Act*. University of California Press, 1974.

Thompson, Robert Farris. *Tango: The Art History of Love*. Pantheon, 2005.

Thompson, Toby. *Positively Main Street: An Unorthodox View of Bob Dylan*. Coward-McCann, 1971.

Thornton, Sarah. *Club Cultures: Music, Media and Subcultural Capital*. Wesleyan University Press, 1996.

Tingen, Paul. *Miles Beyond: Electric Explorations of Miles Davis, 1967–1991*. Billboard, 2001.

Toll, Robert. *Blacking Up: The Minstrel Show in Nineteenth-Century America*. Oxford University Press, 1974.

Tomkins, Calvin. *The Bride and the Bachelors: Five Masters of the Avant-Garde*. Viking, 1965.

Tongson, Karen. *Relocations: Queer Suburban Imaginaries*. New York University Press, 2011.

Tongson, Karen. *Why Karen Carpenter Matters*. University of Texas Press, 2019.

Toop, David. *Exotica: Fabricated Soundscapes in a Real World*. Serpent's Tail, 1999.

Toop, David. *Flutter Echo: Living within Sound*. Ecstatic Peace Library, 2019.

Toop, David. *Haunted Weather: Music, Silence, and Memory*. Serpent's Tail, 2004.

Toop, David. *Into the Maelstrom: Music, Improvisation and the Dream of Freedom, before 1970*. Bloomsbury, 2016.

Toop, David. *Ocean of Sound: Aether Talk, Ambient Sound and Imaginary Worlds*. Serpent's Tail, 1995.

Toop, David. *Rap Attack: African Jive to New York Hip Hop*. South End, 1984.

Toop, David. *Rap Attack 2: African Rap to Global Hip Hop*. Serpent's Tail, 1992

Toop, David. *Rap Attack 3*. Serpent's Tail, 2000.

Toop, David. *Sinister Resonance: The Mediumship of the Listener*. Continuum, 2010.

Tosches, Nick. *Country: The Biggest Music in America*. Stein and Day, 1977. Rev. ed., as *Country: Living Legends and Dying Metaphors in America's Biggest Music*, 1985. 3rd ed., as *Country: The Twisted Roots of Rock 'n' Roll*. Da Capo, 1996.

Tosches, Nick. *Dino: Living High in the Dirty Business of Dreams*. Doubleday, 1992.

Tosches, Nick. *Hellfire: The Jerry Lee Lewis Story*. Dell, 1982

Tosches, Nick. *The Nick Tosches Reader*. Da Capo, 2000.

Tosches, Nick. *Unsung Heroes of Rock 'n' Roll: The Birth of Rock in the Wild Years before Elvis*. Scribner, 1984.

Tosches, Nick. *Where Dead Voices Gather*. Little, Brown, 2001.

Toynbee, Jason. *Bob Marley: Herald of a Postcolonial World?* Polity, 2007

Toynbee, Jason. *Making Popular Music: Musicians, Creativity and Institutions*. Arnold/Oxford University Press, 2000.

Trotter, James. *Music and Some Highly Musical People: The Lives of Remarkable Musicians of the Colored Race*. Lee and Shepard, 1878.

Troupe, Quincy. *Miles and Me*. University of California Press, 2000.

Troutman, John W. *Indian Blues: American Indians and the Politics of Music, 1879–1934*. University of Oklahoma Press, 2009.

Trynin, Jen. *Everything I'm Cracked Up to Be: A Rock & Roll Fairy Tale*. Harcourt, 2006.

Tucker, Mark, ed. *The Duke Ellington Reader*. Oxford University Press, 1993.

Tucker, Mark. *Ellington: The Early Years*. University of Illinois Press, 1991.

Tucker, Sherrie, ed. *Big Ears: Listening for Gender in Jazz Studies*. Duke University Press, 2008.

Tucker, Sherrie. *Dance Floor Democracy: The Social Geography of Memory at the Hollywood Canteen*. Duke University Press, 2014.

Tucker, Sherrie. *Swing Shift: "All-Girl" Bands of the 1940s*. Duke University Press, 2000.

Tucker, Sophie. *Some of These Days: The Autobiography of Sophie Tucker*. Doubleday, Doran, 1945.

Turino, Thomas. *Music as Social Life: The Politics of Participation*. University of Chicago Press, 2008.

Turino, Thomas. *Nationalists, Cosmopolitans, and Popular Music in Zimbabwe*. University of Chicago Press, 2000.

Turner, Fred. *From Counterculture to Cyberculture: Stewart Brand, the Whole Earth Network, and the Rise of Digital Utopianism*. University of Chicago Press, 2006.

Turner, Kay. *I Dream of Madonna: Women's Dreams of the Goddess of Pop*. Collins, 1993.

Tyler, Anne. *A Slipping-Down Life*. Knopf, 1970.

Ulanov, Barry. *Duke Ellington*. Creative Age, 1946.

Ulanov, Barry. *A History of Jazz in America*. Viking, 1952.

Vale, V., ed. *Search and Destroy 1–6, the Complete Reprint: The Authoritative Guide to Punk Culture*. V/Search, 1996.

Vale, V., and Andrea Juno, eds. *RE/Search #4/5: William S. Burroughs/Brion Gysin/Throbbing Gristle*. RE/Search, 1982.

Vale, V., and Andrea Juno, eds. *RE/Search #6/7: Industrial Culture Handbook*. RE/Search, 1983.

Vale, V., and Andrea Juno, eds. *RE/Search #8/9: J. G. Ballard*. RE/Search, 1984.

Vale, V., and Andrea Juno, eds. *RE/Search #10: Incredibly Strange Films*. RE/Search, 1986.

Vale, V., and Andrea Juno, eds. *RE/Search #11: Pranks!* RE/Search, 1986.

Vale, V., and Andrea Juno, eds. *RE/Search #12: Modern Primitives*. RE/Search, 1989.

Vale, V., and Andrea Juno, eds. *RE/Search #13: Angry Women*. RE/Search, 1992.

Vale, V., and Andrea Juno, eds. *RE/Search #14: Incredibly Strange Music Vol. I*. RE/Search, 1993.

Vale, V., and Andrea Juno, eds. *RE/Search #15: Incredibly Strange Music Vol. II*. RE/Search, 1994.

Vander Wel, Stephanie. *Hillbilly Maidens, Okies, and Cowgirls: Women's Country Music, 1930–1960*. University of Illinois Press, 2020.

Van Vechten, Carl. *Nigger Heaven*. Knopf, 1926.

Van Vechten, Carl. *Parties*. Knopf, 1930.

Vargas, Deborah. *Dissonant Divas in Chicana Music: The Limits of La Onda*. University of Minnesota Press, 2012.

Varriale, Simone. *Globalization, Music and Cultures of Distinction: The Rise of Pop Music Criticism in Italy*. Palgrave, 2016.

Vazquez, Alexandra. *Listening in Detail: Performances of Cuban Music*. Duke University Press, 2013.

Vermorel, Fred. *Starlust: The Secret Fantasies of Fans*. Comet, 1985.

Vermorel, Fred. *Vivienne Westwood: Fashion, Perversity, and the Sixties Laid Bare*. Overlook, 1996.

Vermorel, Fred, and Judy Vermorel. *The Sex Pistols: The Inside Story*. Tandem, 1978. Rev. ed., Allen/Starr, 1981.

Vogel, Shane. *The Scene of Harlem Cabaret: Race, Sexuality, Performance*. University of Chicago Press, 2009.

Vogel, Shane. *Stolen Time: Black Fad Performance and the Calypso Craze*. University of Chicago Press, 2018.

Von Eschen, Penny. *Satchmo Blows Up the World: Jazz Ambassadors Play the Cold War*. Harvard University Press, 2004.

Vowell, Sarah. *Radio On: A Listener's Diary*. St. Martin's, 1997.

Wagnleitner, Reinhold. *Coca-Colonization and the Cold War: The Cultural Mission of the United States in Austria after the Cold War*. University of North Carolina Press, 1994.

Waksman, Steve. *Instruments of Desire: The Electric Guitar and the Shaping of Musical Experience*. Harvard University Press, 1999.

Waksman, Steve. *This Ain't the Summer of Love: Conflict and Crossover in Heavy Metal and Punk*. University of California Press, 2009.

Wald, Elijah. *Dylan Goes Electric! Newport, Seeger, Dylan, and the Night That Split the Sixties*. Dey Street, 2015.

Wald, Elijah. *Escaping the Delta: Robert Johnson and the Invention of the Blues*. Amistad, 2004.

Wald, Elijah. *How the Beatles Destroyed Rock 'n' Roll. An Alternative History of American Popular Music*. Oxford University Press, 2011.

Wald, Elijah. *Josh White: Society Blues*. University of Massachusetts Press, 2000.

Wald, Elijah. *Narcocorrido. A Journey into the Music of Drugs, Guns, and Guerrillas*. HarperCollins, 2001.

Wald, Gayle. *Crossing the Line: Racial Passing in Twentieth-Century U.S. Literature and Culture*. Duke University Press, 2000.

Wald, Gayle. *Shout, Sister, Shout! The Untold Story of Rock-and-Roll Trailblazer Sister Rosetta Tharpe*. Beacon, 2007.

Wald, Gayle. *It's Been Beautiful: Soul! and Black Power Television*. Duke University Press, 2015.

Waldo, Terry. *This Is Ragtime*. Hawthorn, 1976.

Walker, William. *The Southern Harmony and Musical Companion*. Facsimile of 1854 revision. Edited by Glenn C. Wilcox. University Press of Kentucky, 1993.

Walkowitz, Daniel. *City Folk: English Country Dance and the Politics of the Folk in Modern America*. New York University Press, 2010.

Wallach, Jeremy, Harris M. Berger, and Paul D. Greene, eds. *Metal Rules the Globe: Heavy Metal Music around the World*. Duke University Press, 2011.

Wallis, Roger, and Krister Malm. *Big Sounds from Small Peoples: The Music Industry in Small Countries*. Pendragon, 1984.

Walrond, Eric. "Bert Williams Foundation Organized to Perpetuate Ideals of Celebrated Actor." *Negro World*, April 21, 1923. Reprinted in *"Winds Can Wake Up the Dead": An Eric Walrond Reader*, edited by Louis Parascandola, 64–65. Wayne State University Press, 1998.

Wang, Oliver, ed. *Classic Material: The Hip-Hop Album Guide*. ECW Press, 2003.

Walser, Robert. *Running with the Devil: Power, Gender, and Madness in Heavy Metal Music*. Wesleyan University Press, 1993.

Ward, Brian, and Patrick Huber. *A&R Pioneers: Architects of American Roots Music on Record*. Vanderbilt University Press, 2018.

Ware, Chris. *Jimmy Corrigan: The Smartest Kid on Earth*. Pantheon, 2000.

Warwick, Jacqueline. *Girl Groups, Girl Culture: Popular Music and Identity in the 1960s*. Cambridge University Press, 2007.

Washburne, Christopher. *Sounding Salsa: Performing Latin Music in New York City*. Temple University Press, 2008.

Waterman, Christopher. *Juju: A Social History and Ethnography of an African Popular Music*. University of Chicago Press, 1990.

Waters, Ethel, with Charles Samuels. *His Eye Is On the Sparrow*. Doubleday, 1951.

Waxer, Lise. *City of Musical Memory: Salsa, Record Grooves and Popular Culture in Cali, Colombia*. Wesleyan University Press, 2002.

Waxer, Lise, ed. *Situating Salsa: Global Markets and Local Meanings in Latin Popular Music*. Routledge, 2002.

Weheliye, Alexander. *Phonographies: Grooves in Sonic Afro-Modernity*. Duke University Press, 2005.

Weinstein, Deena. *Heavy Metal: A Cultural Sociology*. Lexington, 1991.

Weisbard, Eric. *Top 40 Democracy: The Rival Mainstreams of American Music*. University of Chicago Press, 2014.

Weisbard, Eric, with Craig Marks, eds. *Spin Alternative Record Guide*. Vintage, 1995.

Wells, Christi Jay. *Between Beats: The Jazz Tradition and Black Vernacular*. Oxford University Press, 2021.

Wenders, Wim. *Emotion Pictures: Reflections on the Cinema*. Faber and Faber, 1986.

Wenner, Jann, ed. *Groupies and Other Girls: A Rolling Stone Special Report*. Bantam, 1970.

Wenner, Jann. *Lennon Remembers: The Rolling Stone Interviews*. Straight Arrow, 1971. New ed., Rolling Stone Press/Verso, 2001.

Werner, Craig. *A Change Is Gonna Come: Music, Race & the Soul of America*. Plume, 1998. Rev. ed., University of Michigan Press, 2006.

West, Red, Sonny West, and Dave Hebler, as told to Steve Dunleavy. *Elvis: What Happened?* Ballantine, 1977.

Westheimer, Alfred. *Elvis '56: In the Beginning*. Collier, 1979.

Wexler, Jerry, and David Ritz. *Rhythm and the Blues: A Life in American Music*. Knopf, 1993.

Whisnant, David. *All That Is Native and Fine: The Politics of Culture in an American Region*. University of North Carolina Press, 1983.

Whitburn, Joel, comp. *Billboard Book of Top 40 Hits*, 7th ed. Billboard, 2000.

Whitburn, Joel. *Pop Memories 1890–1954: The History of American Popular Music*. Record Research, 1986.

Whitburn, Joel. *Record Research: Compiled from "Billboard" Magazine's "Hot Hundred" Charts, 1955–1969*. Record Research, 1970.

Whitburn, Joel. *Top Pop Records 1955–1972*. Record Research, 1973.

Whitcomb, Ian. *Irving Berlin and Ragtime America*. Limelight, 1988.

White, B. F., and E. J. King. *The Sacred Harp*. Collins, 1844.

White, Charles. *The Life and Times of Little Richard: The Quasar of Rock*. Harmony, 1984.

White, Newman Ivey. *American Negro Folk Songs*. Harvard University Press, 1928.

White, Timothy. *Catch a Fire: The Life of Bob Marley*. Holt, Rinehart, and Winston, 1983. Rev. ed., Holt, 2006.

White, Timothy. *James Taylor Long Ago and Far Away*. Omnibus, 2001.

White, Timothy. *Music to My Ears: The Billboard Essays*. Holt, 1996.

White, Timothy. *The Nearest Faraway Place: Brian Wilson, the Beach Boys, and the Southern California Experience*. Holt, 1994.

White, Timothy. *Rock Lives: Profiles and Interviews*. Holt, 1990.

Whitehead, Colson. *John Henry Days*. Doubleday, 2001.

Whiteley, Sheila, ed. *Sexing the Groove: Popular Music and Gender*. Routledge, 1997.

Whiteley, Sheila. *Women and Popular Music: Sexuality, Identity and Subjectivity*. Routledge, 2000.

Whiteley, Sheila, and Jennifer Rycenga, eds. *Queering the Popular Pitch*. Routledge, 2006.

Whitman, Walt. "Art-Singing and Heart-Singing." *Broadway Journal* 2, no. 21 (November 29, 1845): 318

Whitman, Walt. *Leaves of Grass*. Fowler and Wells, 1855. Expanded 9th ed., David McKay, 1891–92.

Whitmer, Peter. *The Inner Elvis: A Psychological Biography of Elvis Aaron Presley*. Hyperion, 1996.

Whittlesey, Walter Rose, and Oscar George Theodore Sonneck. *Catalogue of First Editions of Stephen C. Foster (1826–1864)*. U.S. Government Printing Office, 1915.

Wickes, E. M. *Writing the Popular Song*. Home Correspondence School, 1916.

Widgery, David. *Beating Time: Riot 'n' Race 'n' Rock 'n' Roll*. Chatto and Windus, 1987.

Wiederhorn, Jon, and Katherine Turman. *Louder Than Hell: The Definitive Oral History of Metal*. It, 2013.

Wilder, Alec. *American Popular Song: The Great Innovators, 1900–1950*. Oxford University Press, 1972.

Wilder, Alec. *Letters I Never Mailed: Clues to a Life*. Little, Brown, 1975. Annotated ed., University of Rochester Press, 2005.

Wilentz, Sean. *Bob Dylan in America*. Doubleday, 2010.

Wilgus, D. K. *Anglo-American Folksong Scholarship since 1898*. Rutgers University Press, 1959.

Williams, Allan, and William Marshall. *The Man Who Gave the Beatles Away*. Macmillan, 1975.

Williams, John A., and Charles F. Harris, eds. *Amistad: Writings on Black History and Culture*. Random House, 1970.

Williams, Justin, ed. *The Cambridge Companion to Hip-Hop*. Cambridge University Press, 2015.

Williams, Linda. *Playing the Race Card: Melodramas of Black and White from Uncle Tom to O. J. Simpson*. Princeton University Press, 2001.

Williams, Martin. *The Jazz Tradition*. Oxford University Press, 1970. New and rev. ed., 1983; 2nd rev. ed., 1993.

Williams, Paul. *Bob Dylan: Performing Artist, 1960–1973: The Early Years*. Underwood-Miller, 1990.

Williams, Paul. *Bob Dylan: Performing Artist, The Middle Years, 1974–1986*. Underwood-Miller, 1992.

Williams, Paul. *Bob Dylan: Performing Artist, 1986–1990 and Beyond: Mind Out of Time*. Omnibus, 2004.

Williams, Paul. *Bob Dylan: Watching the River Flow: Observations on His Art-in-Progress, 1966–1995*. Omnibus, 1996.

Williams, Richard. *The Blue Moment: Miles Davis's Kind of Blue and the Remaking of Modern Music*. Norton, 2009.

Williamson, Nigel. *The Rough Guide to Bob Dylan*. Rough Guides, 2004. 2nd ed., 2006.

Willis, Ellen. *Beginning to See the Light: Pieces of a Decade*. Knopf, 1981.

Willis, Ellen. *Out of the Vinyl Deeps: Ellen Willis on Rock Music*. University of Minnesota Press, 2011.

Willis, Paul. *Learning to Labour: How Working Class Kids Get Working Class Jobs*. Saxon House, 1977.

Willman, Chris. *Rednecks & Bluenecks: The Politics of Country Music*. New Press, 2005.

Wilson, August. "American Histories: Chasing Dreams and Nightmares; Sailing the Stream of Black Culture." *New York Times*, April 23, 2000.

Wilson, August. *Fences*. Plume, 1986.

Wilson, August. *Joe Turner's Come and Gone*. Plume, 1988.

Wilson, August. *King Hedley II*. Theatre Communications, 2005.

Wilson, August. *Ma Rainey's Black Bottom*. Plume, 1985.

Wilson, August. *The Piano Lesson*. Plume, 1990.

Wilson, August. *Radio Golf*. Theatre Communications, 2008.

Wilson, August. *Seven Guitars*. Plume, 1997.

Wilson, August. *Three Plays*. University of Pittsburgh Press, 1991.

Wilson, Carl. *Let's Talk about Love: A Journey to the End of Taste*. Continuum, 2007. Expanded ed., *Let's Talk about Love: Why Other People Have Such Bad Taste*. Bloomsbury, 2014.

Wilson, Earl. *Sinatra: An Unauthorized Biography*. Macmillan, 1976.

Wilson, James F. *Bulldaggers, Pansies, and Chocolate Babies: Performance, Race, and Sexuality in the Harlem Renaissance*. University of Michigan Press, 2010.

Winters, Paul. *Vinyl Records and Analog Culture in the Digital Age: Pressing Matters*. Lexington, 2016.

Witmark, Isidore, and Isaac Goldberg. *The Story of the House of Witmark: From Ragtime to Swingtime*. Furman, 1939.

Wittke, Carl. *Tambo and Bones: A History of the American Minstrel Stage*. Duke University Press, 1930.

Wolf, Stacy. *A Problem Like Maria: Gender and Sexuality in the American Musical*. University of Michigan Press, 2002.

Wolf, Stacy. *Changed for Good: A Feminist History of the Broadway Musical*. Oxford University Press, 2011.

Wolfe, Bernard. "Ecstatic in Blackface: The Negro as a Song-and-Dance Man." In *The Scene before You: A New Approach to American Culture*, edited by Chandler Brossard, 51–70. Rinehart, 1955.

Wolfe, Tom. *Bonfire of the Vanities*. Farrar, Straus and Giroux, 1987.

Wolfe, Tom. *The Electric Kool-Aid Acid Test*. Farrar, Straus and Giroux, 1968.

Wolfe, Tom. *The Kandy-Kolored Tangerine-Flake Streamline Baby*. Farrar, Straus and Giroux, 1965.

Wolfe, Tom. *The Pumphouse Gang*. Farrar, Strauss and Giroux, 1968.

Wolfe, Tom. *Radical Chic & Mau-Mauing the Flak Catchers*. Farrar, Strauss and Giroux, 1970.

Wolfe, Tom. *The Right Stuff*. Farrar, Strauss and Giroux, 1979.

Wolk, Dougas. *Live at the Apollo*. Continuum, 2004.

Wondrich, David. *Stomp and Swerve: American Music Gets Hot, 1843–1924*. Chicago Review Press, 2003.

Wong, Deborah. *Speak It Louder: Asian Americans Making Music*. Routledge, 2004.

Woods, Clyde. *Development Arrested: The Blues and Plantation Power in the Mississippi Delta*. Verso, 1998.

Woollcott, Alexander. *The Story of Irving Berlin*. Putnam, 1925.

Work, John, Lewis Wade Jones, and Samuel Adams Jr. *Lost Delta Found: Rediscovering the Fisk University-Library of Congress Coahoma County Study, 1941–1942*. Edited by Robert Gordon and Bruce Nemerov. Vanderbilt University Press, 2005.

Wright, Josephine, with Samuel Floyd, eds. *New Perspectives on Music. Essays in Honor of Eileen Southern*. Harmonie Park, 1992.

X, Malcolm, as told to Alex Haley. *The Autobiography of Malcolm X*. Grove, 1965.

Yang, Mina. *Planet Beethoven: Classical Music at the Turn of the Millennium*. Wesleyan University Press, 2014.

Yetnikoff, Walter, with David Ritz. *Howling at the Moon: The Odyssey of a Monstrous Music Mogul in an Age of Excess*. Broadway, 2001.

Young, Kevin. *Bunk: The Rise of Hoaxes, Humbug, Plagiarists, Phonies, Post-Facts, and Fake News*. Graywolf, 2017.

Young, Kevin. *The Grey Album: On the Blackness of Blackness*. Graywolf, 2012.

Young, Kevin, ed. *Jazz Poems*. Knopf, 2006.

Zak, Albin. *I Don't Sound Like Nobody: Remaking Music in 1950s America*. University of Michigan Press, 2010.

Zanes, Warren. *Dusty in Memphis*. Continuum, 2003.

Zeltsman, Nancy, ed. *Alec Wilder: An Introduction to the Man and His Music*. Margun Music, 1991.

Zolten, Jerry. *Great God A'Mighty: The Dixie Hummingbirds: Celebrating the Rise of Soul Gospel Music*. Oxford University Press, 2003.

Zuckerkandl, Victor. *Sound and Symbol: Music and the External World*. Pantheon, 1956.

INDEX

Abbott, Lynn, 117, 191, 386–88, 415
Abdurraqib, Hanif, 432
abolitionism and sentimentality, 27
The Abolition of Work (Shiner), 271
Abreu, Christina, 384
Absolute Beginners (MacInnes), 151–53
Adams, Kyle, 419
Adelt, Ulrich, 415
Adler, Bill, 162
Adorno, Theodor: and Cage, 154; commercial culture criticisms, 388, 427, 429; influence of, 49, 388, 404, 422; responses to, 394; writings of, 388–90; writings on, 378, 390
The Aesthetics of Rock (Meltzer), 188–90
Afro-American Folksongs (Krehbiel), 88, 422
Afro-American Specialty Company, 386
Afro-Cubanism, 383
Afromodernism, 361
Aiken, Conrad, 69
"Alexander's Ragtime Band" (Berlin), 40
Alexie, Sherman, 412, 416
Allen, William, 30–31
All God's Dangers: The Life of Nate Shaw (Rosengarten), 119–20
All You Need Is Ears (Martin), 166
alternative rock and grunge, 265, 326–30

ambient, 352–54, 371
American Humor: A Study of the National Character (Rourke), 85–87
American Splendor (Pekar), 278
American studies: *American Humor: A Study of the National Character* (Rourke), 85–87; beat-bop, 135; interdisciplinary, 282; *Sound Clash: Listening to American Studies* (Keeling and Kun), 405. *See also* Lipsitz, George
America's Music: From the Pilgrims to the Present (Chase), 25, 39, 122–24
anthological modernism, 7
Aparicio, Frances, 394–95
Appalachia, 34, 54–56
Armendariz, Alicia (Alice Bag), 239–40, 277
Armstrong, Louis: and Handy, 77; in *Jazzmen*, 96; Mezzrow on, 110; scatting, 13; Spaeth, 83; writings of, 90–93, 127; writings on, 92–93, 110, 356
Arnold, Gina, 326–27
As Time Goes By (Taylor), 164
Attali, Jacques, 274–75, 331
The Audible Past: Cultural Origins of Sound Reproduction (Sterne), 366, 404–5
Audiotopia: Music, Race and America (Kun), 373, 383, 420–23
Austin, William, 41

autobiographies. *See individual persons*
The Autobiography of an Ex-Colored Man (Johnson),
 19, 52–53, 115, 433
Awopbopaloobop Alopbamboom (Cohn), 182–83
Azerrad, Michael, 239, 327

Baez, Joan, 407
Bag, Alice (Alicia Armendariz), 239–40, 277
Bagge, Peter, 279, 329
Baker, Dorothy, 94–95, 259–60
Baker, Houston, 415–16, 421
Balance, Christine Bacareza, 309–10, 373
Baldwin, James, 97, 192
Baline, Israel. *See* Berlin, Irving
The Ballad of Frankie Silver (McCrumb), 313
ballads: "Barbara Allen," 54; borderlands, 138–39;
 collections, 33–35, 54; communal origins of,
 34; *Cowboy Songs and Other Frontier Ballads*
 (Lomax), 2, 31, 50–51; *The Disappointment; or,
 The Force of Credulity* (Barton), 46; novels,
 312–13; *The Spirit of the Mountains* (Miles), *17*,
 44–45, 312; writings on, 33–34, 312
Balliett, Whitney, 141–42, 199
Bangs, Lester: on British Invasion bands, 216–17;
 and Crowe, 251; and cyberpunk, 269–70; and
 Davis, 301; Elvis obituary, 341; on heavy metal,
 218, 314; *Psychotic Reactions and Carburetor Dung*, 210, 290–91; on punk and white
 supremacy, 238; *Rolling Stone Illustrated History
 of Rock & Roll* contributions, 216–18; writings
 on, 209, 291
Baraka, Amiri (LeRoi Jones): autobiography, 159,
 161; *Blues People*, 129, 134, *144*, 148, 160–61, 184,
 297; on Brown, 8, 160; criticisms of, 421; and
 Davis, 301; and Ellison, 167; on Holiday, 131;
 influence of, 159, 161, 347; "Jazz and the White
 Critic," 160, 358; jazz as noun versus verb, 227;
 Preface to a Twenty Volume Suicide Note, 134;
 Ramsey on, 403
Barcella, Laura, 324
Barthes, Roland, 8, 221–23
Barton, Andrew, 46
the Beatles: collected letters, 162, 323; Lennon,
 162–64, 256; sophistication of, 183; White
 Album, 441; writings on, 162–67, 186, 188, 267
The Beatles (Carr and Tyler), 164
The Beatles (Davies), 163
The Beatles (Inglis), 166
The Beatles (Stokes), 165
The Beatles as Musicians (Everett), 163
The Beatles Day by Day (Lewisohn), 165–66
Beatles Forever (Schaffner), 164–65
The Beatles Live! (Lewisohn), 165

The Beatles' London (Lewisohn, Schreuders, and
 Smith), 166
beat literature, 133–36
Beatty, Paul, 434
The Beautiful and the Damned (Fitzgerald), 62–63
bebop, 359
Becker, Howard, 129, 157–59
Bederman, Gail, 50
Bedouin Hornbook (Mackey), 288–89, 359
Beginning to See the Light: Pieces of a Decade (Willis),
 257–58
Beiderbecke, Bix, 94–96, 127
Bel Canto (Patchett), 436
Berlant, Lauren, 74, 75–76, 336–37, 374–75
Berlin, Edward, 116, 282
Berlin, Irving: "Alexander's Ragtime Band," 40;
 sentimentality, 10; "Supper Time," 121; writings
 on, 1, 71–74, 84, 198, 248
Berman, Marshall, 403
Berry, Chuck, 218, 249, 292–93
Berton, Ralph, 95
Bertrand, Michael, 342–43, 424
Best Music Writing roundups, 431
A Bibliography of Early Secular American Music
 (Sonneck), *18*, 45–47
The Big Sea memoir (Hughes), 78
Billboard Book of Number One Hits (Bronson), 201
Billboard Book of Top 40 Hits (Whitburn), 202
Billboard charts, 201
Billings, William, 4, 20–22, 25, 331
*Biographical Dictionary of Afro-American and
 African Musicians* (Southern), 196
*A Biographical Guide to the Great Jazz and Pop
 Singers* (Friedwald), 437–38
Black and Blur (Moten), 401
Black Culture and Black Consciousness (Levine),
 225–26
Black diaspora, 213
Blackface (George), 296
blackface minstrelsy: Chase on, 123; dance, 177;
 as first American pop genre, 22; honesty claims,
 41–42; as non–African American, 247–48;
 paradoxes of, 27; sexuality, 11; songbooks, 4;
 working-class connections, 24; writings on, 24,
 27–28, 42, 225, 283, *306*, 334–37. *See also* Foster,
 Stephen; Rice, Thomas Dartmouth
Blacking, John, 261
Black Manhattan (Johnson), 65, 115
Black music: African origins of, 223–24; versus
 classical music, 227–28; pain-pleasure tensions,
 27–28; performer road reports, 387–88; sentimentality and vernacular, 11, 27; whites and,
 88; women and, 5–6; writings on, 4, 28, 32–33,

52, 67, 69–71, 76, 114–17, 185, 194–98, 224, 228, 244, 295–97, 305, 324–26, 386–88. *See also* blues; Ellison, Ralph; hip-hop; jazz; Moten, Fred

Black Noise (Rose), 213, 346–47, 417

Blesh, Rudi, 96–97, 114–17, 119, 123, 340, 413

Block, Geoffrey Holden, 75, 396, 398

Blowin' Hot and Cool (Gennari), 359

bluegrass, 267–69

Bluegrass Breakdown: The Making of the Old Southern Sound (Cantwell), 267–69, 424

blues: anthologies, 76–78; Handy, 76–77, 196, 280; King, 184, 242, 414; revivalists, 148–51; white advocacy for, 148; writings on, *101*, 110–11, 129–33, 134, 142, *144*, 148–51, 160–61, 184, 205–7, 219–21, *234*, 240–42, 245–47, 255, 280–82, 297, 344–45, 412–16. *See also* Baraka, Amiri (LeRoi Jones); Johnson, James Weldon; Johnson, Robert (blues musician)

Blues All around Me (Ritz and King), 242, 414

Blues Music in the Sixties (Adelt), 415

bluesology, revisionist, 412–16

Blues People (Baraka), 129, 134, *144*, 148, 160–61, 184, 297

Bogle, Donald, 120

Bohlman, Philip, 34, 262, 421

Boogie Man (Murray), 414

Booth, Stanley, 265–67, 340–41

borderlands ballads, 138–39

Born, Georgina, 422

Bosse, Joanna, 179

Bound for Glory (Guthrie), *100*, 104–6

Bourdieu, Pierre, 430

Boyar, Burt, and Jane Boyar, 287

Boyd, Valerie, 87

The Boy Looked at Johnny: The Obituary of Rock and Roll (Burchill and Parsons), 236–40

A Boy Named Sue (Pecknold and McCusker), 349, 423–24

Brackett, David, 320, 332, 392

Brady, Erika, 36

Braun, Michael, 162–67

Brennan, Matt, 13

A Brief History of Seven Killings (James), 434

Bronson, Bertrand, 33–34

Bronson, Fred, 201

Brooks, Daphne, 66, 350, 430

Brooks, Tim, 66, 117

Los Bros Hernandez, 3, 277–79

Brother Ray: Ray Charles' Own Story (Ritz and Charles), 240–42

Brown, James, 188, 255, 272

Brown, Mary Ellen, 34

Brown, Sterling, 358

Browne, David, 273

Brownstein, Carrie, 330, 440

Broyles, Michael, 21–22

Bruce, Robert, 49

Bufwack, Mary, 349, 424

Buppies, B-Boys, Baps & Bohos (George), 296–97

Burchill, Julie, 236–40

Burlin, Natalie Curtis, 35–36, 38, 75

Burroughs, William, 133, 263

Burt, Stephanie, 326

The Businesses of Musicianship from Billings to Gershwin (Crawford), 330–31

Butler, Judith, 349

Cadigan, Pat, 271

Cage, John, 125, 153–55, 187, 283, 427

The Cambridge Companion to Pop and Rock (Frith, Straw, and Street), 391–92

Campbell, Gavin James, 25

Campbell, Olive Dame, 34, 54–56

Can't Buy Me Love (Gould), 166

Can't Stop Won't Stop: A History of the Hip-Hop Generation (Chang), 416–19

Cantwell, Robert: *Bluegrass Breakdown: The Making of the Old Southern Sound*, 267–69, 424; and Bohlman, 34; *Ethnomimesis*, 268–69; on Guthrie, 105, 269; review of *The Devil's Dream*, 313; *When We Were Good*, 269; writings of, 283

capitalism, 370, 429

Carby, Hazel, 89, 358

Careless Love (Guralnick), 343–44

Carmer, Carl, 26

Carmichael, Hoagy, 94, 127–28, 199–200

Carpentier, Alejo, 382–85

Carr, Ian, 299

Carr, Roy, 164

Caruso, Enrico, 332, 426

Casillas, Dolores Inés, 140–41

Catalogue of First Editions of Stephen C. Foster (Whittlesey and Sonneck), 40

Cather, Willa, 428–29

Cepeda, Raquel, 411

Chabon, Michael, 433

Chadwick, Vernon, 342

Chambers, Iain, 213

Chambers, Jack, 299

Chambers-Letson, Joshua, 373

Chanan, Michael, 125

Chang, Jeff, 411, 416–19

Charles, Ray, 240–42, 272

Charnas, Dan, 417–18

Charters, Ann, 65, 135–36, 149

Charters, Samuel, 30, 135–36, 148–50, 340, 413

charts, 201–2

Chase, Gilbert: American music emphasis, 426; *America's Music: From the Pilgrims to the Present*, 25, 39, 122–24; on Billings, 4, 20–21; on Ellington, 123; on Foster, 41, 122–23; *The New Grove Dictionary of American Music*, 283; on Shaw, 245; and Small, 227; and Sonneck, 46, 122; on vernacular music, 9

Chavez, Alex, 141

Cheney Family, 29

Child, Francis James, 33–35, 50, 54

Ching, Barbara, 424

Christgau, Robert: on Berry, 218, 249; *Christgau's Record Guide*, 232, 248–50; on Dylan, 406; on Ferguson, 259; influence, 296; on Madonna, 322; and Meltzer, 189; memoir, 250; *The New Grove Dictionary of American Music*, 282–83; and the Rolling Stones, 217, 266; semipopular artist category, 30, 237, 249; on Shaw, 245; on Small, 227

Christgau's Record Guide (Christgau), 232, 248–50

Christine (King), 313

Christy, George, 40–41, 334

Chronicles: Volume I (Dylan), 406–10, 438

Chude-Sokei, Louis, 65–66, 370

City of Musical Memory (Waxer), 381, 393–95

Clapton, Eric, 414, 415

classical music, 226–28, 397, 426–29

Clay, Andreana, 410, 418

Clifford-Napoleon, Amber, 316–17

Cline, Patsy, 424

Clinton, George, 196

Clive: Inside the Record Business (Davis), 203–5

Cloud Atlas (Mitchells), 436

Clover, Joshua, 329, 390

Cobain, Kurt, 327

Cobb, Buell, 26

Cockrell, Dale, 24, 336, 441

Cohen, Lara Langer, 28

Cohen, Phil, 211

Cohn, Nik: *Awopbopaloobop Alopbamboom*, 182–83; on Elvis, 340; literary tributes, 435; *Saturday Night Fever*, 182, 243, 435; writings, 182–83, 187, 218, 340; *Yes We Have No*, 182–83

Coleman, Ornette, 129, 164, 319, 352

Collier, James Lincoln, 92

Come as You Are (Azerrad), 327

Comentale, Edward, 105, 126

comics, 3, 117, 277–79, 329, 386

The Complete Beatles Chronicle (Lewisohn), 166

Complete Beatles Recording Sessions (Lewisohn), 165

Complete Book of the American Musical Theater (Ewen), 397

Conventional Wisdom (McClary), 414

The Cool School (beats), 134

Coon, Caroline, 236

Cooper, Kim, 430

Coplan, David, 379

Corregidora (Jones), 131, 205–7

cosmopolitanism, 379–82

Costello, Elvis, 218

country: cultural situatedness, 425; Davis's support for, 204–5; hardcore, 177; International Country Music Conference, 425; women and, 215, 349, 424; writings on, 123, *146*, 148–49, 175–77, 229–30, 313, 343, 349, 354–55, 413, 423–26

The Country Blues (Charters), 148–49

Country Boys and Redneck Women (McCusker and Pecknold), 425

Country Music, USA (Malone), 123, *146*, 175–77

Country Music Association, 175

Country: The Biggest Music in America (Tosches), 176, 229–30

Country: The Music and the Musicians (Kingsbury), 176–77

County, Jayne, 239

Coupland, Douglas, 326–27

Covarrubias, Miguel, 76

Cowboy Songs and Other Frontier Ballads (John Lomax), 2, 31, 50–51

Crawford, Richard: *America's Music* introduction, 123; on Billings, 4, 21; *The Businesses of Musicianship from Billings to Gershwin*, 330–31; music business writing, 330–31; musicology, 330–32, 426; publication outlets, 282; on *Show Boat*, 75

Crawley, Ashon, 192

Creating Country Music: Fabricating Authenticity (Peterson), 354–55, 424

Creolization of American Culture (Smith), 337

Crosby, Bing, 355, 357, 437

Crossroad Blues (Atkins), 436

Crouch, Stanley, 415

Crowe, Cameron, 10, 251–52, 408

Cruising Utopia (Muñoz), 372, 374

Crumb, R., 345

The Crunk Feminist Collection (Cooper), 350

The Crying Lot 49 (Pynchon), 156–57

Cuba, 382–85

cultural studies: overview, 4; alternative rock, 329; blackface minstrelsy, 24, 42, 283, *306*, 335–37; Cage, 283; conjunctural analysis, 211, 213–14; and cyberpunk, 270; Dylan, 406; Elvis, 342; feminist, 207, 212–13; hip-hop, 375–77, 419; *The Last "Darky"* (Chude-Sokei), 65–66; *Love and Theft* (Lott), 42, 283, *306*, 335–37; Madonna, 321–23; Mexican American music, 140; Moten, 401–2; Neal, 376; punk, 212, 238; purge of the vernacular, 10–11; ragtime, 117; reggae, 213; *Resistance through Rituals: Youth Subcultures in Post-War Britain* (Hall and Jefferson), 211–14, 252; *Subculture: The Meaning of Style* (Hebdige), 212, 236, 238; subcultures, 212; Waters, 120; world music, 379–80. *See also* Denning, Michael; Frith, Simon; Hall, Stuart

Current of Music (Adorno), 390

Currid, Brian, 421

cyberpunk, 269–71

cylinder recordings, 35–38

dance: electronic dance music, 369–72; jook, 179–80; Lindy hop, 177, 179–80; preservation difficulties, 178; and race, 179–80, 182; salsa, 393–95; swing, 180; tango, 180; tap, 178, 180; writings on, 66, 177–82, 192, 295, 351–52

Dance, Stanley, 112

Dancer from the Dance (Holleran), 242–45

dance studies, 180–81

Dancing in the Dark (Phillips), 66

Dancing Madness (Peck), 242–43

Darnielle, John, 317

Davies, Hunter, 163

Davis, Angela, 132, 207, 360

Davis, Clive, 169, 203–5

Davis, Francis, 131

Davis, Gussie, 47

Davis, Miles, 90, 208, 298–301, 356–57

Davis, Sammy, Jr., 171–73, 287

Davis, Stephen, 275–77

Davis, Vaginal Creme, 373–74

Dawes, Laina, 317

Dayal, Geeta, 430

A Day in the Life (Hertsgaard), 165

Dead Elvis (Marcus), 342

The Death of Rhythm & Blues (George), 244, 295–97

Decker, Todd, 73–75, 398

Decoded (Jay-Z), 438–41

DeCurtis, Anthony, 255, 416

Deep Blues (Palmer), 255–56

DeFrantz, Thomas, 180

Delany, Samuel, 156, 374, 401

DeLillo, Don, 157, 342, 435

Denning, Michael: *Cultural Front*, 105, 118, 132, 134, 213, 287; *Noise Uprising*, 214, 381; on recording technologies, 8, 126, 423

DeNora, Tia, 377–78, 390, 427

Densmore, Frances, 35–38, 261

DeRogatis, Jim, 273

Des Barres, Pamela, 235, 294–95

DeVeaux, Scott, 128, 357–59

The Devil's Dream (Smith), 313

DiLello, Richard, 164

Dinerstein, Joel, 134, 180, 287

Dion, Céline, 430, 431–32

The Dirt (Mötley Crüe memoir), 275, 315–16

The Disappointment; or, The Force of Credulity (Barton), 46

disco, 218, 242–45

Disidentifications: Queers of Color and the Performance of Politics (Muñoz), 310, 364, 372–75, 422

Dixon, George Washington, 22, 336

Dodge, Roger Pryor, 96

Dogeaters (Hagedorn), 3, 308–10

Doggett, Peter, 166

Doss, Erika, 342

Double Trouble (Marcus), 342

Douglas, Susan, 213, 319, 338–39

Douglass, Frederick, 26–28

Dowdy, Helen, 184

Dreiser, Theodore, 42–43, 62, 433

Dresser, Paul, 43

Du Bois, W. E. B., 27, 65, 70, 132, 405

Duffet, Mark, 344

Dufty, William, *101*, 129–33, 240

Duke Ellington Reader (Tucker), 112–13

Dunbar, Paul Laurence, 64, 81–82

Duncan, Robert, 237, 289, 314, 317

Dundy, Elaine, 342

Dyer, Richard, 68, 75, 244

Dylan, Bob: and Berry, 292; *Biograph* box set, 408; in *A Biographical Guide to the Great Jazz and Pop Singers*, 437; *Chronicles: Volume I* (memoir), 406–10, 438; films, 409; influence of, 237, 271; influences on, 104, 148, 335; "Love and Theft" album, 335, 409; sales, 204; sophistication of, 183; *Tarantula* (poetry), 407; *Time Out of Mind* (album), 408; and Whitman, 29; writings on, 210, 257–58, 406–9, 428

Dylan Goes Electric! (Wald), 409

Dyson, Michael Eric, 328, 375, 411, 418

Early, Gerald, 300, 358

Early Concert-Life in America (Sonneck), 46

Eat the Document (Spiotta), 435

Echols, Alice, 244–45

Eco, Umberto, 221

Eddy, Chuck, 314–17

EDM, 369–72

Edwards, Brent Hayes, 13, 52–53, 114, 358, 423

Edwards, David "Honeyboy," 415

Egan, Jennifer, *367*, 432, 436

Eggers, Dave, 328

Ehrenreich, Barbara, 134–35, 338

Eidsheim, Nina Sun, 132–33, 405, 419–20, 422

Eisenberg, Evan, 125

Elberse, Anita, 440

Electric Ladyland (Rhodes), 185, 294

electronic dance music, 369–72

Eliot, T. S., 168

Ellington, Duke: Adorno on, 389; Chase on, 123; and critics, 113–14; Fletcher and, 116; influences, 70; Kerouac on, 135; legacy, 427; Spaeth on, 83; writings of, 112, 127; writings on, 111–14, 219, 221, 356

Ellison, Harlan, 155–57

Ellison, Ralph: on American culture, 93; on "Blue Monday," 220; influence of, 398; *Invisible Man*, 52, 167–68; and Rourke, 87; *Shadow and Act*, 167–69

Elson, Louis, 40

Elvis. *See* Presley, Elvis

Elvis (Goldman), 341–42

"Elvis, or the Ironies of a Southern Identity" (Pratt), 340

Elvis after Elvis (Rodman), 342

Elvis and Gladys (Dundy), 342

Elvis and Me (Priscilla Presley), 342

Elvis Culture (Doss), 342

Elvis Day by Day (Guralnick and Jorgensen), 344

Elvis in the Twilight of Memory (Juanico), 342

Elvis Presley Calls His Mother after the Ed Sullivan Show (Charters), 340

Elvis Presley Speaks! (Johnson), 340, 343

Elvis Presley Story (Gregory), 340

Elvis: Roots, Image, Comeback, Phenomenon (Duffet), 344

Elvis: What Happened (West, West, and Hebler), 341

Emerick, Geoff, 166

Emerson, Ken, 41–42

Emery, Lynne, 179

Energy Flash: A Journey through Rave Music and Dance Culture (Reynolds), 368–72

England's Dreaming (Savage), 238–39

English Folk Songs from the Southern Appalachians (Campbell and Sharp), 54–56

Epistrophies (Edwards), 13

Epstein, Brian, 163–65, 186

Epstein, Dena, 4, 31, 223–24, 386

Erenberg, Lewis, 113, 116, 179–80, 226

Erlman, Veit, 379

Escaping the Delta: Robert Johnson and the Invention of the Blues (Wald), 412–16

Eshun, Kodwo, 369, 405

Esposito, Joe, 342

Essays on Music (Adorno), 388–90

Ethnomimesis (Cantwell), 268–69

ethnomusicology: ballad hunting, 34; *City of Musical Memory* (Waxer), 381, 393–95; Coplan, 379; dance, 179; early works, 261; *Every Tongue Got to Confess* (Hurston), 88; folk music emphasis, 261; hip-hop, 411–12, 419; Merriam, 39, 261; messthetics, 35; *Mules and Men* (Hurston), 6, *60*, 76, 87–89; *Nationalists, Cosmopolitans, and Popular Music in Zimbabwe* (Turino), 378–82; origins, 261; Radano, 421–22; shortcomings, 262; *A Study of Omaha Indian Music* (Fletcher), 35–39. *See also* Feld, Steven; Merriam, Alan; Nettl, Bruno

Ethnomusicology of the Flathead Indians (Merriam), 39

Europe, James Reese, 69, 71, 115–17, 358

Everett, Walter, 163

Everything but the Burden (Tate), 326

Every Tongue Got to Confess (Hurston), 88

Ewen, David, 72, 75, 106–8, 397, 427

Eyre, Banning, 380

The Fabulous Phonograph: From Tin Foil to High Fidelity (Gelatt), 124–27

Farwell, Arthur, 37

Fast, Susan, 316, 430

Fast Times at Ridgemont High (Crowe), 251–52

Fauset, Jessie, 64–65, 67, 70, 78

Feel Like Going Home: Portraits (Guralnick), 343, 413

Feld, Steven, 289, *307*, 344–46, 379, 394

Feminine Endings: Music, Gender, and Sexuality (McClary), *304*, 318–20, 322, 349

feminist critiques: cultural studies, 212–13; Douglas, 213, 319, 338–39; Ehrenreich, 134–35, 338; hip-hop, 349–50, 410; literary methods, 132; Madonna, 322–23, 324; ragtime, 117; rock, 350–51; of subculture analyses, 212. *See also* McClary, Susan

Ferber, Edna, 38, 74–76

Ferguson, Otis, 96, 259–60, 412

Fewkes, J. Walter, 39

fiction: alternative rock and grunge, 329; country, 313; Davis and, 300; disco, 243, 245; Ellington and, 113; Elvis and, 340, 342; Holiday and, 131; Johnson and, 412, 415–16; mountain ballads, 312–13; novels, 432–36; science fiction, 155–56; vinyl records and, 125; Williams and, 66; writers, 3. *See also individual titles and writers*

Fikentscher, Kai, 370

Filene, Benjamin, 34, 51

Fillmore, John Comfort, 36

Fink, Robert, 319, 428

Finkelstein, Sidney, 97

The First Collection of Criticism by a Living Female Rock Critic (Hopper), 350–51, 432

Fisher, Mark, 370
Fisher, Rudolph, 70, 121, 169
Fisk University Jubilee Singers, 31–32, 386
Fitzgerald, F. Scott, 62–63, 77, 173, 433
Flappers and Philosophers (Fitzgerald), 62–63
Flatley, Jonathan, 375
Fletcher, Alice, 35–39, 75
Fletcher, Tom, 114–16
Flores, Juan, 312, 393
Flowers in the Dustbin (Miller), 218, 416–17
Floyd, Samuel, 195
Flyboy in the Buttermilk (Tate), *305*, 324–26
folk, 34, 55; writings on, 2, 29, 31, 34, 40, 50, 54–56, 88, 267–69, 422. *See also* Dylan, Bob; Guthrie, Woody
Ford, Henry, 49
Forman, Murray, 410–12
Fortress of Solitude (Lethem), 399–400
Foster, Morrison, 2, 39–42
Foster, Stephen, 2, 27, 39–42, 122–23, 336
Fox, Aaron, 425
Fox, Pamela, 215, 424
Frank, Lisa, 322–23
Frank, Thomas, 328
Franklin, Aretha, 188, 242
Frank Sinatra Reader (Lear), 284, 324
Franzen, Jonathan, 433
Freedland, Michael, 72
Freedom (Franzen), 433
Friedwald, Will, 92, 131, 284, 437–38
Frith, Simon: on Adorno, 390; *The Cambridge Companion to Pop and Rock*, 391; critiques of, 311; cultural studies, 213, 238; influence, 331; *Sound Effects*, 233, 252–54
Fuhr, Michael, 381–82

Gabbard, Krin, 93, 193, 301, 359
Gaines, Donna, 314–15, 351
Gaisberg, Frederick, 124
Galás, Diamanda, 265
Gamson, Joshua, 339
Gans, Herbert, 158, 221
Gardner, Ava, 286
Garland, Phyl, 6, 184–85, 246, 274
Garman, Bryan, 29
Garrett, Charles Hiroshi, 283, 319
Garrison, Lucy McKim, 5, 9–10, *16*, 30–31, 35, 75, 224
Garrison, Wendell, 30–31
Gates, Henry Louis, Jr., 66, 113, 195–96, 292, 325, 421
Gaye, Marvin, 241
Gelatt, Roland, 124–27

gender: alternative rock and grunge, 327; country, 349, 423–26; heavy metal, 316–17; hip-hop, 410; jazz, 349, 360; Latinx pop, 349; and listening practices, 163; masculinity discourses, 50; musicals, 396–98; rock, 349; salsa, 394–95; in *Show Boat*, 75–76; Tongson on, 349, 351, 374, 432; writings on, 185, 294, 338–39, 349, 396–99. *See also* feminist critiques; women
Gendron, Bernard, 163–64
Generation X (Coupland), 326–27
Gennari, John, 96, 97, 160, 260, 359
Gentry, Linnell, 175
George, Nelson, 244, 250, 295–97, 375, 418–19
George-Warren, Holly, 273
George Washington Gomez (Paredes), 136, 138
Georgia Minstrels, 386
Gershwin, George, 84–85, 107–8, 199
Gibson, William, 269–71, 432
Giddins, Gary: on Armstrong, 92; on Berlin, 73; on Holiday, 131; *Visions of Jazz: The First Century*, 355–57, 416; on Williams, 65; on *Young Man with a Horn*, 94–95
Gilbert, David, 117
Gillett, Charlie, 125, 187–88
Gilroy, Paul: anti-anti-essentialism, 310, 320; on Black Atlantic diaspora, 65, 213; on blackface minstrelsy, 27; on hip-hop ghettocentricity, 11; hip-hop studies, 411; and Moten, 402
Ginsberg, Allen, 133, 135–36
Gioia, Ted, 415
Girl Groups, Girl Culture (Warwick), 319, 339
Girls Together Outrageously (G.T.O.s), 294
Gleason, Ralph, 130, 164, 266, 287, 298, 301
globalization, 182, 308–9, 378–79, 381
"God Bless America" (Berlin), 72–73
Goffin, Robert, 91, 93
Goldberg, Isaac, 1, 6, *59*, 84–85
Goldman, Albert, 341–42
Goldman, Vivian, 350
Goldmark, Daniel, 47
González Echevarría, Roberto, 383
Good Booty (Powers), 181, 192, 295, 351–52
Goodman, Steve, 370
Good Rocking Tonight (Esposito), 342
Goodwin, Andrew, 322
Gordon, Kim, 330
gospel, 175, 190–92
Gould, Jonathan, 166
Graceland (Marling), 342
Graham, T. Austin, 63
Grant, Peter, 276
Granz, Norman, 128, 141
Gray, Judith, 38

Gray, Michael, 407

The Great Gatsby (Fitzgerald), 62

Great Jones Street, 157, 435

Green, Abel, 49

Green, Archie, 175

Gregory, James, 340

Gregory, Montgomery, 70

Griffin, Farah Jasmine, 130, 358, 360

Grossberg, Lawrence, 213, 394

groupies, *235*, 294–95

Grove Dictionary of American Music (Garrett), 201, 282–83

Growing Up with the Beatles (Schaumburg), 164

grunge, 265, 326–30

Guilbaut, Jocelyne, 379, 392

Guillermoprieto, Alma, 181, 385

Gummere, Francis, 34

Guralnick, Peter, 291, 339–40, 343–44, 413

Gussow, Adam, 415

Guthrie, Woody, 29, *100*, 104–6, 134

Gysin, Brion, 263

Habermas, Jürgen, 221

Hagedorn, Jessica, 3, 308–10, 432

Halberstam, Jack, 349, 373

Haley, Alex, 298

Hall, Stuart: bricolage, 225; contemporaries, 221; homologies, 110; influence of, 213–14, 335, 403; *Resistance through Rituals: Youth Subcultures in Post-War Britain*, 211–14, 252

Hamanaka, Vale (V. Vale), 263–65

Hamilton, Marybeth, 256

Hamilton, Richard, 221

Hamm, Charles: on African American music, 247–48; on Berlin, 1, 73, 248; on Foster, 41; on Goldberg, 85; *Musician in a New World*, 331; and Nettl, 261; *The New Grove Dictionary of American Music*, 282; "The Phonograph and Our Musical Life" conference, 125; *Putting Popular Music in Its Place*, 247–48; *Yesterdays: Popular Song in America*, 247–48

Hammond, John, 113, 412

Hancock, Herbie, 298

The Hangman's Beautiful Daughter (McCrumb), 312–13

Happy in the Service of the Lord (Lornell), 191

Hardwick, Elizabeth, 206

Harlem Renaissance: Handy, 76–77, 196, 280; *The New Negro*, 67, 69–71, 76; *Slave Songs of the United States*, 31; Van Vechten, 120–21. *See also* Hughes, Langston

Harney, Stefano, 402

Harris, Charles K., 47–48, 197–98

Harris, Michael, 191

Harrison, George, 164

Harron, Mary, 322

Hazzard-Gordon, Katrina, 179–80

Hear Me Talkin' to Ya (Shapiro and Hentoff), 92, 97, 127–29

Heartland Excursions (Nettl), 420

The Heart of Rock & Soul (Marsh), 217–18

heavy metal, 275–76, 314–17

Heavy Metal (Weinstein), 314

heavy metal writings, 218, 275–76, 291, 314–17, 319, 329

Hebdige, Dick, 212–13, 236, 238, 369

Hebler, Dave, 341

Heilbut, Anthony, 190–92

Hell, Richard, 237, 440

Hentoff, Nat: and Davis, 298, 300; on Dylan, 406; *Hear Me Talkin' to Ya*, 92, 97, 127–29; *The Jazz Life*, 129, 261; *Jazz Makers*, 128; *Jazz: New Perspectives*, 128

Herder, Johann Gottfried, 34–35

Here, There and Everywhere (Emerick), 166

Hermes, Will, 237, 245, 328, 395

Hernandez, Los Bros, 3, 277–79

Hersgaard, Mark, 165

Hesmondhalgh, David, 391–93

Hickey, Dave, 177

Hicks, Dylan, 198–99

Hidden in the Mix (Pecknold), 425

Higginson, Thomas, 30–31

Highbrow/Lowbrow (Levine), 226, 282, 332, 426

Hilburn, Robert, 273

hip-hop: Cuban, 384; cultural controversies, 411–12; gender, 410; global, 381–82; post-industrial framings, 347, 417; Public Enemy, 347; writings on, 297, 347, 349–50, 352, 375–77, 410–19. *See also* Rose, Tricia

Hip-Hop America (George), 297, 418–19

Hip Hop Wars (Rose), 418

Hirshey, Gerri, 272–74

His Eye Is on the Sparrow (Waters), 120–21

History and Encyclopedia of Country, Western, and Gospel Music (Gentry), 175

History of Jazz in America (Ulanov), 97

The History of Rock 'n' Roll in Ten Songs (Marcus), 208

Hitchcock, H. Wiley, 21, 125, 255, 282–83, 426

Hoffman, Charles, 38

Hogan, Ernest, 114, 387

Hoggart, Richard, 211, 221

Holiday, Billie: Blesh on, 96–97; and Jones, 131, 205–6; and Waters, 121; writings on, *101*, 127, 129–33, 240, 360

Holland, Justin, 32

Holleran, Andrew, 242–45
Holmes, John Clellon, 135
homologies, 12, 110, 212–13, 270
Honkers and Shouters: The Golden Years of Rhythm and Blues (Shaw), 245–47
honky-tonk, 176
Hooker, John Lee, 414–15
Hopkins, Jerry, 341
Hopper, Jessica, 350–51, 432
Hornby, Nick, 125
Horowitz, Daniel, 221
Horowitz, Joseph, 427
Hoskyns, Barney, 273
Howard, John Tasker, 40–41
How the Beatles Destroyed Rock and Roll (Wald), 267
Hubbard, Elbert, 81
Hubbs, Nadine, 425
Huber, Patrick, 425
Hughes, Charles, 425
Hughes, Langston: and Afro-Cubanism, 383; and Hurston, 88–89; "Jazzonia," 71; and Mason, 38; and music, 79–80, 88; in *The New Negro*, 70; and Whitman, 29; and Williams, 64; writings on, 2, 77–78
Hughes, Walter, 244
Hunger Makes Me a Modern Girl (Brownstein), 330, 440
Hunter, Tera, 116–17, 226, 403, 421
Hurston, Zora Neale: criticisms of, 206; influence of, 358, 398, 421; and Lomax, 118; and Mason, 38; in *The New Negro*, 70; writings of, 6, 60, 76, 87–89, 358
Hutchinson, Sydney, 139, 395

I Am Still the Great Says Johnny Angelo (Cohn), 182–83
If Ever I Return, Pretty Peggy-O (McCrumb), 312–13
Image—Music—Text (Barthes), 221–23
In Dahomey (Williams), 64, 70
In Dahomey revue, 64, 70, 115, 117
Indeterminacy (Cage), 153–54
The Indians' Book (Mason), 38
indie rock, 265, 326–30
Infante, Guillermo Cabrera, 385
Inglis, Ian, 166
In Search of Elvis (Chadwick), 342
Institute for Studies in American Music, 282
Institute of Jazz Studies, 178, 340, 357
In the Break: The Aesthetics of the Black Musical Tradition (Moten), 289, 376, 401–2
In the Houses of the Holy (Fast), 316
In the Spirit of Jazz: The Otis Ferguson Reader (Ferguson), 259–60

Invisible Man (Ellison), 52, 167–68
Iyer, Vijay, 358–59

Jackson, Bruce, 88
Jackson, George Pullen, 25
Jackson, Michael, 321
Jacobs-Bond, Carrie, 5–6, 80–82
Jagger, Mick, 266–67
James, C. L. R., 221
James, Etta, 241–42
James, Joseph Summerlin, 25
James, Marlon, 434
James, Robin, 351, 370
Janis, Harriet, 114–17, 119
Jay-Z, 193, 418, 438–41
jazz: as popular music form, 12; writings on, 13, *61*, 70–71, 92–97, 114, 123, 127–29, 129, 141–42, 151–53, 157–60, 178, 193–94, 201, 259–61, 261, 288–89, 296–97, 300–301, 340, 349, 355–58, 357–61, 398, 413, 416, 420, 433. *See also* Baraka, Amiri; O'Meally, Robert; Stearns, Marshall; *individual performers*
"Jazz and the White Critic" (Baraka), 160, 358
The Jazz Cadence of American Culture (O'Meally), 357–61
Jazz Dance (Stearns), 177–82
The Jazz Life (Hentoff), 129, 261
Jazz Makers (Hentoff), 128
Jazzmen (Ramsey), *61*, 92, 95–97
Jazz: New Perspectives (Hentoff), 128
Jazz Record Book (Smith), 201
Jefferson, Tony, 211–14, 252
Jeneman, David, 390
Jensen, Joli, 424
John Henry Days (Whitehead), 434
John Lennon: In My Life (Schaffner and Shotton), 165
Johnson, Bunk, 96, 127, 358
Johnson, James Weldon: *The Autobiography of an Ex-Colored Man*, *19*, 52–53, 115, 433; *Black Manhattan*, 65, 115; Hurston on, 89; influence of, 398; Jes Grew, 196; "Lift Every Voice," 53; memoirs, 414; in *The New Negro*, 70; "Under the Bamboo Tree," 168
Johnson, Johnnie, 292
Johnson, Robert (blues musician), 148–49, 208, 230, 412–16
Johnson, Robert (columnist), 340
Jones, Alisha Lola, 192
Jones, Andrew, 423
Jones, Gayl, 11, 131, 205–7
Jones, Hettie, 133–34
Jones, LeRoi. *See* Baraka, Amiri
Joplin, Scott, 114–17

Jorgensen, Ernst, 344
Juanico, June, 342
Juno, Andrea, 263–65, 349

Kahn, E. J., Jr., 284, *285*
Kahn-Harris, Keith, 314, 316
Kammen, Michael, 67
The Kandy-Kolored Tangerine-Flake Streamline Baby (Wolfe), *145*, 173–74
Kaplan, James, 286–87
Karpeles, Maud, 55
Kaufman, Will, 106
Kearney, Mary Celeste, 339, 349
Keeling, Kara, 405
Kehew, Brian, 166
Keightley, Keir, 287, 392
Keil, Charles: on groove music, 337; *Music Grooves: Essays and Dialogues*, *307*, 344–46, 379, 394; and Nettl, 261; and Ritz, 240; and Small, 227; *Urban Blues*, 148, 344–45
Keisker, Marion, 340–41
Kelley, Kitty, 284–87
Kelley, Robin D. G., 359–60, 375, 411
Kenney, William, 332, 426
Kenton, Stan, 128, 141
Kerouac, Jack, *102*, 133–36, 300
Kheshti, Roshanak, 382
King, B. B., 184, 242, 414
King, E. J., 25–26
Kingsbury, Paul, 176–77
Kinney, David, 409
Kirchner, Bill, 299
Kittler, Friedrich, 125
Kittredge, George Lyman, 33
Kitwana, Bakiri, 411, 418
Klosterman, Chuck, 315, 328
Knapp, Raymond, 75, 396–98
Koestenbaum, Wayne, 332–34, 426
Kot, Greg, 273
Kouwenhoven, John, 282, 358
Krasilovsky, M. William, 169–71
Krehbiel, Henry, 88, 422, 427
Krims, Adam, 419
Kuehl, Linda, 132–33
Kun, Josh: alternative rock cultural studies, 329; *Audiotopia: Music, Race and America*, 373, 383, 420–23; influence, 140; *Sound Clash: Listening to American Studies*, 405
Kunzru, Hari, 434

Lady Sings the Blues (Holiday), *101*, 129–33, 240
La Flesche, Francis, 35–37
Laird, Tracey, 177

Landau, Jon, 255
Lapidus, Benjamin, 384–85
The Last "Darky" (Chude-Sokei), 65–66
Last Train to Memphis: The Rise of Elvis Presley (Guralnick), 339–40, 343–44
Lawrence, Tim, 244
Lear, Martha Weinman, 284, 324
Leaves of Grass (Whitman), 28–30
Led Zeppelin, 275–76, 316
Leland, John, 134–35
Lennon, John, 162–64, 256
Lennon Remembers (Wenner), 163–64
Leonard, Candy, 166
Lethem, Jonathan, 271, 399–400, 432
Levine, Lawrence: *Black Culture and Black Consciousness*, 225–26; criticisms of, 421; folk transference, 387; *Highbrow/Lowbrow*, 226, 282, 332, 426; influence of, 331; on opera, 332; popular culture in history, 311
Lewis, Jerry Lee, 229–30
Lewisohn, Mark, 165–66
Lhamon, W. T., Jr.: on Berry, 293; on Davis, 300; on Kerouac, 134; lore cycles, 24, 336; *Raising Cain*, 336; on Rice, 24; on Williams, 66; writings of, 4
"Lift Every Voice" (Johnson), 53
Lilly, Joseph Kirby, 40
Lipsitz, George: career, 311, 318; on identity politics, 414; influence of, 347; *Time Passages: Collective Memory and American Popular Culture*, 310–12; *Uptown Conversation*, 358
Lipstick Traces (Marcus), 182, 210, 236, 238, 311, 373
Listening in Detail (Vasquez), 385
Little Richard, 293
Locke, Alain, 67, 69–71, 76, 88, 403, 426
Lomax, Alan: Cantometrics, 262; and Hurston, 118; and Johnson, 413; and Lead Belly, 226; *Mister Jelly Roll*, 115, 118–20, 183; on Monroe, 268; recordings made, 34, 36, 51, 104, 110, 115, 118, 405
Lomax, John: *Cowboy Songs and Other Frontier Ballads*, 2, 31, 50–51; and Lead Belly, 226; recordings made, 34, 36, 51, 118
The Longest Cocktail Party (DiLello), 164
The Long Night of Lady Day (Holiday documentary), 131
Lordi, Emily, 206
Lornell, Kip, 191
Lost Sounds (Brooks), 117
Lott, Eric: on blackface minstrelsy, 24, 28, 42; cultural studies, 213; on Foster, 42; *The Jazz Cadence of American Culture*, 358; *Love and Theft*, 42, 283, *306*, 335–37; sound studies, 405
Loudin, Frederick, 386
Louis Armstrong's 50 Hot Choruses for Cornet, 90–91

Louis Armstrong's 125 Jazz Breaks for Cornet, 90–91
Love and Rockets (Los Bros Hernandez), 3, 277–79
Love and Theft (Lott), 42, 283, *306*, 335–37
Lovensheimer, Jim, 398
Loza, Stephen, 138–39
Lummis, Charles, 138–39
Lunceford, Jimmie, 295–96
Lynn, Loretta, 80, 214–16

MacDonald, Dwight, 221
MacDonald, Ian, 165
MacInnes, Colin, 151–53
Mackey, Nathaniel, 225, 288–89, 358, 359, 401
Madonna, 320–24, 349
Madrid, Alejandro, 139–41, 371
Magee, Jeffrey, 71, 74
Magic Circles (McKinney), 166
Mahar, William, 336
Mailer, Norman, 110, 129, 134, 336
Malm, Krister, 379
Malnig, Julie, 180–81
Malone, Bill C., 123, *146*, 175–77, 282
Mancini, JoAnne, 7
Manning, Frankie, 180
Manuel, Peter, 125, 262, 379
The Man Who Gave the Beatles Away (Williams), 164
Mapplethorpe, Robert, 439–40
Ma Rainey's Black Bottom (Wilson), *234*, 280–81
Marcus, Greil: on Adorno, 389; on the Beatles, 164, 218; career, 209–10; and Christgau, 249; on Creedence Clearwater Revival, 283; on Dylan, 210, 406, 408; eponymous test, 429; on girl groups, 216; *The History of Rock 'n' Roll in Ten Songs*, 208; influence of, 208, 331; *It Will Stand*, 187; interest in new work, 210; on Johnson, 208; on *King Jude*, 157; *Lipstick Traces*, 182, 210, 236, 238, 311, 373; literary tributes, 435; *Love and Theft* foreword, 335; and Meltzer, 189; *Mystery Train*, 207–10, 341, 414; *The New Grove Dictionary of American Music*, 282; *Ranters & Crowd Pleasers*, 208; *The Rose & the Briar*, 312; secret history, 229; *Stranded*, 208, 210, 252; successes of, 290
Marks, Craig, 327–28
Marling, Karal Ann, 342
Marquesee, Mike, 408–9
Marsh, Dave, 217–18, 238, 282, 322
Marsh, J. B. T., 31
Marshall, Lee, 406, 409
Martin, George, 166
Maslon, Laurence, 74, 200, 398
Mason, Charlotte Osgood, 38
Mast, Gerald, 73, 199–200, 398
Matos, Michaelangelo, 372, 430

May, Butler "String Beans," 388
Mazor, Barry, 424
McCain, Gillian, 236–37, 239, 291
McCartney, Paul, 163
McClary, Susan: *Conventional Wisdom*, 414; *Feminine Endings: Music, Gender, and Sexuality*, *304*, 318–20, 322, 349; influence of, 319, 333; and Lipsitz, 311; *Rock She Wrote* contribution, 348; on Small, 227; writings of, 318–19, 427
McCracken, Alison, 287, 338–39
McCrumb, Sharyn, 312–13
McCusker, Kristine, 349, 423–25
McDonnell, Evelyn, 348, 350–51, 432
McGinley, Paige, 51
McGraw, Hugh, 26
McKim, Lucy. *See* Garrison, Lucy McKim
McKinney, Devin, 166
McLaren, Malcolm, 237–38
McLuhan, Marshall, 221
McMillin, Scott, 398–99
McNeil, Legs, 236–37, 239, 291
McRobbie, Angela, 212–13, 239, 253, 339
Mellers, Wilfrid, 163, 227, 409
Melly, George, 151, 164
Melnick, Jeffrey, 73
Meloy, Colin, 430
Meltzer, Richard, 188–90
memoirs. *See* individual genres; *individual persons*
Merriam, Alan, 39, 261, 345, 379, 421
Metallica, 315, 317
Mexican American music, 139–41
Mezzrow, Mezz, 110–11, 127
Miles, Barry, 165
Miles, Emma Bell, *17*, 44–45, 312
Miller, D. A., 221, 244, 333, 396
Miller, Jim, 164, 216–19, 416
Miller, Karl Hagstrom, 11, 226, 355, 413
Miller, Kiri, 25–26, 371
Milligan, Harold, 40
Milner, Greg, 126
Milward, John, 415
Mingus, Charles, 79, 193–94, 289
Mister Jelly Roll (Alan Lomax), 115, 118–20, 183
Mitchell, David, 436
Mitchell, Joni, 408
Modern Lovers (Straub), 435
Monroe, Bill, 268
Monson, Ingrid, 360–61
Moody, Rick, 271, 329, 399
Moore, Robin, 384
Moore, Scotty, 342
Morath, Max, 81
Morgan, Joan, 349–50, 410, 441

Morneweck, Evelyn Foster, 40–41

Morrison, Toni, 198, 207

Morrissette, Noelle, 52

Morthland, John, 176, 291

Morton, Jelly Roll: and Armstrong, 91; and Lomax, 110, 115, 118; memoirs, 127; *Mister Jelly Roll*, 115, 118–20, 183

Mosley, Walter, 313, 412, 416

Moten, Fred: anti-essentialism, 5; *Black and Blur*, 401; *In the Break: The Aesthetics of the Black Musical Tradition*, 289, 376, 401–2; precursors, 225; on sentimentality, 9, 401; *The Undercommons*, 402

Motherless Brooklyn (Lethem), 400

Mötley Crüe, 275, 315–16

Mould, Bob, 327

MP3: The Meaning of a Format (Sterne), 126–27, 404

Mudrian, Albert, 317

Mules and Men (Hurston), 6, *60*, 76, 87–89

Mumbo Jumbo (Reed), 117, 196–98

Muñoz, José Esteban: and Bangs, 291; *Cruising Utopia*, 372, 374; *Disidentifications: Queers of Color and the Performance of Politics*, 310, *364*, 372–75, 422; and Moten, 402

Murray, Albert: on African American dance, 180; on blues, 131, 219–20, 378; and Ellington, 219, 221; and Ellison, 168; and Giddins, 356; and hip-hop studies, 411; *Omni-Americans*, 219; and Rourke, 87; *Stomping the Blues*, 142, 219–21

Murray, Charles Shaar, 414–15

Music, Society, Education (Small), 226–28

musicals, 75, 396–99

Music and Some Highly Musical People (Trotter), 4, 32–33, 52

music business: the internet, 171; record sales statistics, 170; writings on, 6, 42, 48, 161–71, 203–5, 226, 274–75, 330–31, 355, 391, 417, 423–26

Music Genres and Corporate Culture (Negus), 205, 391, 417

Music Grooves: Essays and Dialogues (Keil and Feld), *307*, 344–46, 379, 394

Musician in a New World (Hamm), 331

Music in Primitive Culture (Nettl), 261

Music Matters series, 351, 432

The Music of Black Americans (Southern), 185, 194–96

Music of the Common Tongue (Small), 228

musicology: the Beatles, 163; Billings, 331; blackface minstrelsy, 336–37; Block, 75, 396, 398; Bracket, 320; classical music, 428–29; country, 425; Crawford, 330–32, 426; *Creolization of American Culture* (Smith), 337; Dixon, 336; Dylan, 409; familialism, 184; heavy metal, 316, 319; hip-hop, 411–12; Hitchcock, 21, 125, 255;

282–83, 426; and race, 319, 421; *Race Music: Black Cultures from Bebop to Hip-Hop* (Ramsey), 184, *365*, 402–4; Radano, 421–22; ragtime, 116, 282; *Running with the Devil* (Walser), 316, 319; *Show Boat*, 75; Sonneck, 46–47, 426; Trotter, 32. *See also* Chase, Gilbert; McClary, Susan; Ramsey, Guthrie, Jr.; Southern, Eileen

Mystery Train (Marcus), 207–10, 208–9, 341, 414

Narcocorridos (Wald), 139

Nash, Alanna, 343

Nathan, Hans, 22, 335

Nationalists, Cosmopolitans, and Popular Music in Zimbabwe (Turino), 378–82

Native American music, 35–39, 404

Neal, Jocelyn, 177, 424

Neal, Mark Anthony, 325, 375–77, 410–12

Negus, Keith, 205, 391–93, 409, 417

Nelson, Paul, 406

Nettl, Bruno, 34, 260–62, 282, 420

Neuromancer (Gibson), 269–71

The New-England Psalm Singer (Billings), 4, 20–22

The New Grove Dictionary of American Music (Hitchcock and Sadie), 282–83

Newman, Randy, 209

The New Negro: An Interpretation (Locke), 67, 69–71, 76

Nirvana, 326–27

Nisenson, Eric, 299

Noise: The Political Economy of Music (Attali), 274–75

Northup, Solomon, 26–28

Novak, David, 382

novels, 432–36. *See also* fiction; *individual authors and titles*

Nowhere to Run: The Story of Soul Music (Hirshey), 272–74

Nyong'o, Tavia, 374

O'Brien, Lucy, 323, 348

O'Connor, Flannery, 77

O'Dair, Barbara, 219, 322, 348

Odum, Howard, 88, 434

Oermann, Robert, 349, 424

Oja, Carol, 428

"Old Folks at Home" (Foster), 336

Oliver, Paul, 148–51, 282

O'Meally, Robert: on Armstrong, 93; on Ellison, 169; on Holiday, 130–32, 360; *The Jazz Cadence of American Culture*, 357–61; jazz studies, 114, 420

Omni-Americans (Murray), 219

One Hundred Years of the Negro in Show Business (Fletcher), 114–16

On the Road (Kerouac), *102*, 133–36

opera, 332–34, 427
The Original Blues (Abbott and Seroff), 415
Osborne, Richard, 126–27
Otis, Johnny, 211
Our Band Could Be Your Life (Azerrad), 327
Out of Sight: The Rise of African American Popular Music, 1889–1895 (Abbott and Seroff), 117, 386–88
Outsiders: Studies in the Sociology of Deviance (Becker), 129, 157–59
Outside the Gates of Eden (Shiner), 271

Page, Jimmy, 294–95
Palmer, Robert, 255–56, 282, 293, 352, 413
Paredes, Américo, *103*, 136–41
Paredez, Deborah, 140
Parrish, Avery, 246
Parsons, Gram, 266
Parsons, Tony, 236–40
Parties (Van Vechten), 179
Patchett, Ann, 436
Pattern Recognition (Gibson), 270
Patton, Charley, 76
Pauline, Mark, 264
Paul McCartney: Many Years from Now (Miles), 165
Pecknold, Diane, 349, 355, 423–26
Peiss, Kathy, 116, 179, 311
Pekar, Harvey, 278
Pelly, Jenn, 431
Peña, Manuel, 137–39
performance studies, 374, 420. *See also* Moten, Fred; Muñoz, José Esteban
Performing Rites (Frith), 254, 373
Perry, Imani, 53, 347, 411, 418
Perullo, Alex, 381, 411
Peterson, James Braxton, 418
Peterson, Richard, 158, 169, 354–55, 391, 424
Petrusich, Amanda, 127, 351
the Philippines, 308
Phillips, Caryl, 66
Pisani, Michael, 35–36
Pleasants, Henry, 282, 286, 420
Please Kill Me (McNeil), 236–37, 239, 291
pop charts, 201–2
Pop Conference, 431
poptimists, 13, 431
popular music studies: in the academy, 421; Brackett, 320, 332, 392; *The Cambridge Companion to Pop and Rock* (Frith, Straw, and Street), 391–92; *Music Grooves: Essays and Dialogues* (Keil), *307*, 344–46, 379, 394; *The Popular Music Studies Reader* (Hesmondhalgh and Negus), 391–93
The Popular Music Studies Reader (Hesmondhalgh and Negus), 391–93

P-Orridge, Genesis, 263–65
Porter, Eric, 360
Poschardt, Ulf, 369–70
The Power of Black Music (Floyd), 195
Powers, Ann: alternative rock criticism, 328; career, 351; *Good Booty*, 181, 192, 295, 351–52; Pop Conference, 431; *Rock She Wrote*, 6, 185, 348–49, 352
Powers, Richard, 433
Pratt, Linda Ray, 342
Preface to a Twenty Volume Suicide Note (Baraka), 134
Presley, Elvis: Charters on, 149; cultural significance, 354; influence of, 176; Malone on, 187–88; precursors, 115; Snake Hips dance, 178; writings on, 208–9, 339–44
Prince, 321–22
A Problem Like Maria: Gender and Sexuality in the American Musical (Wolf), 396–99
psalmody, 20
Psychotic Reactions and Carburetor Dung (Bangs), 210, 290–91
Public Enemy, 347
Pugh, Megan, 181
punk: and cyberpunk, 269–70; queer, 372–75; women in, 229, 236, 239–40, 250, 258, 349–40; writings on, 3, 182, 210, 212, 218, 236–40, 277–79, 291, 311, 317, 329, 351, 373, 440
Punk fanzine, 237
Putting Popular Music in Its Place (Hamm), 247–48
Pynchon, Thomas, 134, 156–57

Queering the Popular Pitch (Whiteley), 349
Queerness in Metal Music (Clifford and Napoleon), 316–17
queer theory: fanship, 396; hip-hop, 410; *Listening in Detail* (Vasquez), 385; opera, 332–34; *Queering the Popular Pitch* (Whiteley), 349; *Queerness in Metal Music* (Clifford and Napoleon), 316–17. *See also* Muñoz, José Esteban
Questlove, 440

Race, Rock and Elvis (Bertrand), 342–43, 424
Race Music: Black Cultures from Bebop to Hip-Hop (Ramsey), 184, *365*, 402–4
Race of Singers (Garman), 29
Radano, Ronald, 421–22
radio, 338–39
Rage to Survive (James), 241–42
Ragtime (Doctorow), 116
ragtime: writings on, 114–17, 226, 279, 282, 386, 403, 421
Ragtime Ephemeralist (Ware), 117, 386

Raimist, Rachel, 350

Raising Cain (Lhamon), 336

Ramsey, Frederic, Jr.: *Jazzmen*, *61*, 92, 95–97; on Johnson, 413; *Race Music*, 184

Ramsey, Guthrie, Jr.: Afromodernism, 361, 403; and Neal, 375; on Powell, 135; *Race Music: Black Cultures from Bebop to Hip-Hop*, 184, *365*, 402–4; on Trotter, 32, 403; writings of, 4, 184, 195, *365*, 402–4

Ranters & Crowd Pleasers (Marcus), 208

rap. *See* hip-hop

Rap Attack (Toop), 352

Rap Music and the Poetics of Identity (Krims), 419

Rap Yearbook (Serrano), 418

Ray, Johnnie, 183

Really the Blues (Mezzrow), 110–11

Recording the Beatles (Kehew), 166

Record Research (1955–1969), 201

records: cylinders, 35–38; writings on, 8, 124–27, 349

Reed, Ishmael, 53, 117, 196–98

Refiguring American Music book series, 420

Regev, Motti, 381, 392

Remembering Bix (Berton), 95

RE/Search (Vale and Juno), 263–65

Resistance through Rituals: Youth Subcultures in Post-War Britain (Hall and Jefferson), 211–14, 252

The Rest Is Noise: Listening to the Twentieth Century (Ross), 397, 426–29

Revolt into Style (Melly), 164

Revolution in the Head (MacDonald), 165

Reynolds, David, 29

Reynolds, Simon, 35, 239, 349, 368–72

Rhodes, Lisa, 185, 294

Rhythm Oil (Booth), 340–41

Rice, Edward LeRoy, 334–36

Rice, Thomas Dartmouth, 4, 22–24, 26–27

Richards, Keith, 266, 292

Riesman, David, 221

Riley, Tim, 165

riot grrrl, 327, 330, 349, 440

Rip It Up and Start Again (Reynolds), 239

Ritchie, Jean, 56

Ritter, Frédéric, 40

Ritz, David, 10, 130, 240–42, 414

Roberts, Brian, 337

Roberts, John Storm, 228, 242, 383, 393

rock: alternative and grunge, 265, 326–30; Berry, 218, 249, 292–93; charts, 201–2; films, 405; groupies, *235*, 294–95; heavy metal, 275–76, 314–17; Led Zeppelin, 275–77; riot grrrl, 327, 330, 349, 440; the Rolling Stones, 265–67, 275;

Semisonic, 330; women/feminism and, 348–51; writings on, 6, 13, 125, *145*, 156–57, 163–67, 173–74, 182–83, 185–90, 208–9, 216–19, 238, 257, 267, 273–76, 282–83, 315–16, 322, 338–44, 348–52, 374, 416, 432–33, 435. *See also* Bangs, Lester; Christgau, Robert; Frith, Simon; Marcus, Greil; *specific performers and genres*

rockabilly, 155–57, 229

Rockabilly [Spider Kiss] (Ellison), 155–56

Rock Encyclopedia (Roxon), 6, 185–87, 274, 338

The Rock Revolution (Shaw), 245

Rock She Wrote (McDonnell and Powers), 6, 185, 348–49, 352

Rockwell, John, 218, 282

Rock Wives (Balfour), 295

Rodgers, Jimmie, 105, 110, 175–76

Rodman, Gil, 342, 411

Rogers, J. A., *58*, 70–71

Rolling Stone Illustrated History of Rock & Roll (Miller), 164, 216–19

Rolling Stones, 265–67, 275

Romancing the Folk (Filene), 34

Roots, George, 80–81

Rose, Tricia: *Black Noise*, 213, 346–47, 417; *Hip Hop Wars*, 418; influence of, 375; *Rock She Wrote*, 348

Rosen, Jody, 1

Rosengarten, Theodore, 119–20

The Rose & the Briar (Marcus and Wilentz), 312

Ross, Alex, 397, 426–29

Rossiter, Will, 47

Rotella, Carlo, 415

Rough Guide to Bob Dylan (Williamson), 406

Rourke, Constance, 85–87, 122, 335

Rowland, Mabel, 64–67

Rowles, Jimmy, 132–33

Roxon, Lillian, 6, 185–87, 274, 338

Rubin, Joan Shelley, 86–87

Running with the Devil (Walser), 316, 319

Russell, Henry, 81

Russell, Sylvester, 387–88

Russell, William, 95–96

Sacred Harp tunebooks, 25–26

Sadie, Stanley, 282–83

salsa, 393–95

Sam Phillips (Guralnick), 344

Sander, Ellen, 156

Sanneh, Kelefa, 431

Saturday Night Fever (Cohn), 182, 243, 435

Savage, Jon, 152, 236, 238–39

Savran, David, 397–98

Say Goodbye (Shiner), 271

Scaduto, Anthony, 407

Scarborough, Dorothy, 88

Schaffner, Nicholas, 164–65
Schaumburg, Ron, 164
Schemel, Sidney, 169–71
Schloss, Joseph, 181, 411, 419
Schuller, Gunther, 92, 132, 142, 199, 282, 331, 358
Schwichtenberg, Cathy, 322, 349
science fiction, 155–56
Sedgwick, Eve, 374
See a Little Light (Azerrad and Mould), 327
Seeger, Charles, 8
Seeger, Pete, 104
Seldes, Gilbert, 67–69, 71–72, 277
Selena, 140
Selling Sounds (Suisman), 42, 48, 226
The Selling Sound: The Rise of the Country Music Industry (Pecknold), 355, 423–26
Semisonic, 330
Senegal, 381
sentimentality, 7–12, 28
Seroff, Doug, 117, 191, 280, 386–88, 415
Serrano, Shea, 315, 418
Seven Guitars (Wilson), 281
The Seven Lively Arts (Seldes), 67–69, 71–72
Seven Songs as Unpretentious as the Wild Rose (Jacobs-Bond), 81
Sexing the Groove (Whiteley), 349
sexism, 208, 258, 294. *See also* feminist critiques
Sex Pistols, 237–38
The Sex Revolts (Reynolds and Press), 349
Sexton, Adam, 321–22
Shadow and Act (Ellison), 167–69
Shank, Barry, 391–92, 405
shape-note singing, 25–26
Shapiro, Henry, 55
Shapiro, Nat, 92, 97, 127–29
Shapiro, Peter, 244
Sharp, Cecil J., 34, 54–56
Shaw, Arnold, 245–47, 282, 285
Sheed, Wilfrid, 200
sheet music industry, 42
Sheffield, Rob, 167, 209, 250–51, 328
Shelton, Robert, 105, 175–76, 408
Shepard, Sam, 407, 439
She Walks These Hills (McCrumb), 313
Shiner, Lewis, 271
The Shining (King), 313
Shining Trumpets (Blesh), 123, 413
Shirelles, 319, 338–39
Shotton, Pete, 165
Shout! (Norman), 165–66
Show Boat (Ferber), 74–76, 200, 428
Simmons, Bill, 315, 418
Simone, Nina, 184
Sinatra, Frank, 172, 198, 284–87, 324, 437

Sinatra! The Song Is You (Friedwald), 284
Sinful Tunes and Spirituals (Epstein), 4, 223–24
singing conventions, 25–26
Sister Carrie (Dreiser), 42–43, 62
Situationism, 237–38
Slam (Shiner), 271
slavery, 225
Slave Songs of the United States (Allen, Ware, and Garrison), 5, *16*, 30–31, 224
Slichter, Jacob, 330
Slobin, Mark, 34, 379
Slumberland (Beatty), 434
Small, Christopher, 226–28, 427
Smith, Charles Edward, *61*, 92, 95–97, 201
Smith, Christopher, 337
Smith, Lee, 313
Smith, Patti, 229, 236, 250, 258, 349–40
Smith, Paul, 322–23
Smith, Willie "the Lion," 116
Smith, Zadie, 434–35
Smucker, Tom, 218, 244, 250, 432
Snead, James, 347, 358, 394
Some Highly Musical People (Williams), 32
Songs of Sorrow (Charters), 30
songwriting guides, 47–49
Sonneck, Oscar George Theodore: *A Bibliography of Early Secular American Music*, *18*, 45–47; *Catalogue of First Editions of Stephen C. Foster*, 40; and Chase, 46, 122; *Early Concert-Life in America*, 46; influence of, 45–46, 224, 330–31; musicology, 46–47, 426
Sontag, Susan, 221
soul: Brown, 188, 255, 272; writings on, 6, 184–85, 241–42, 272–74
Sound and Sentiment (Feld), 345
"Sound and Sentiment, Sound and Symbol" (Mackey), 289
Sound Clash: Listening to American Studies (Keeling and Kun), 405
Sound Effects (Frith), 233, 252–54
The Sound of a Surprise (Balliett), 141–42
The Sound of Soul: The Story of Black Music (Garland), 6, 184–85
The Sound of the City (Gillett), 187–88
sound studies, 404–5, 420. *See also* Sterne, Jonathan
Sound Studies Reader (Sterne), 404–5
Southern, Eileen: *Biographical Dictionary of Afro-American and African Musicians*, 196; Black folk preferences, 426; career, 194–95; criticisms of, 421; and Epstein, 31; *The Music of Black Americans*, 185, 194–96; *The New Grove Dictionary of American Music*, 282; Ramsey, on, 403
So You Wanna Be a Rock & Roll Star (Slichter), 330

Spaeth, Sigmund, 82–84, 334, 427

Speck, Samuel, 49

Spector, Ronnie, 310

Spider Kiss [*Rockabilly*] (Ellison), 155–56

Spin Alternative Record Guide (Weisbard and Marks), 327–28

Spiotta, Dana, 435

The Spirit of the Mountains (Miles), *17*, 44–45, 312

spirituals, 74–75, 224

Spitz, Marc, 329

Springsteen, Bruce, 440

Stearns, Jean, 177–82

Stearns, Marshall, 97, 177–82, 340, 357

Stein, Daniel, 92

Steinke, Darcey, 329

Sterling, Bruce, 269–71

Sterne, Jonathan: *The Audible Past: Cultural Origins of Sound Reproduction*, *366*, 404–5; on cylinder recording, 36; *MP3: The Meaning of a Format*, 126–27, 404; *Sound Studies Reader*, 404–5

Stewart, Jeffrey, 88

Stimeling, Travis, 425

Stoever, Jennifer, 405

Stokes, Geoffrey, 165, 204

Stokes, Martin, 382

Stomping the Blues (Murray), 142, 219–21

Stone Arabia (Spiotta), 435

Story of Jazz (Stearns), 97

Stranded (Marcus), 208, 210, 252

Straub, Emma, 435

Strauss, Neil, 275, 315–16, 328

Straw, Will, 349, 391–92

Stubbs, David, 372

The Study of Ethnomusicology (Nettl), 260–62

A Study of Omaha Indian Music (Fletcher), 35–39

Subculture: The Meaning of Style (Hebdige), 212, 236, 238

Sublette, Ned, 383–84

Suisman, David, 42, 48, 226, 332, 427

Sullivan, John Jeremiah, 414

"Supper Time" (Berlin), 121

swing, 96–97, 180

Swing That Music (Armstrong), 90–93

syncretism, 262

Szwed, John, 118, 121, 129–30, 132, 299

Talese, Gay, 284

Tanguay, Eva, 117

Tanzania, 381, 411

tap dancing, 178, 180

Tarantula (Dylan), 407

Tate, Greg: and Baraka, 159; and Christgau, 250; on Davis, 298, 300; *Everything but the Burden*, 326; *Flyboy in the Buttermilk*, *305*, 324–26; influence of, 325, 375; and Moten, 159

Taylor, Derek, 164, 166, 186

Taylor, Herbert, 47

Taylor, Timothy, 379–81

Teachout, Terry, 92–93, 113–14, 284

Teenage Wasteland (Gaines), 314–15

Telegraph Avenue (Chabon), 433

Tell Me Why (Riley), 165

Tharpe, Rosetta, 191–92, 350

That's Alright, Elvis (Moore), 342

That's the Joint! The Hip-Hop Studies Reader (Forman), 410–12

They All Played Ragtime (Blesh and Janis), 114–17

33⅓ series, 429–32

This Ain't the Summer of Love (Waksman), 275, 291, 317, 329

This Business of Music (Krasilovsky and Schemel), 169–71

Thompson, Ahmir "Questlove," 440

Thompson, E. P., 211

Thompson, Katrina, 337

Thompson, Robert Farris, 181, 227, 325

Thompson, Toby, 407

Thornton, Sarah, 213, 369–70

Three Trapped Tigers (Infante), 385

The Time of Our Singing (Powers), 433

Time Out of Mind (Dylan), 408

Time Passages: Collective Memory and American Popular Culture (Lipsitz), 310–12

Tin Pan Alley, 11, 40, 49, *59*, 84–85

Tin Pan Alley (Goldberg), *59*, 84–85

To Do This, You Must Know How (Abbott and Seroff), 191

To 'Joy My Freedom (Hunter), 116–17, 226, 403, 421

Toll, Robert, 225, 335

tone parallels, 12

Tongson, Karen, 349, 351, 374, 432

Toomer, Jean, 70

Toop, David, 352–54, 371

Top Pop Records, 201–3

Tosches, Nick, 176, 229–30, 336

Toynbee, Jason, 391–92

transnational imaginary, 136, 138–40

Trotter, James, 4, 32–33, 52, 403

Trouble Girls (O'Dair), 219, 322, 348

Troupe, Quincy, 298–99

Troutman, John, 37

Tucker, Mark, 112–13
Tucker, Sherrie, 360–61
Tucker, Sophie, 106, 108–9
Tune In (Lewisohn), 166
Turino, Thomas, 378–82, 394
Turner, Fred, 263, 270
Twelve Years a Slave (Northup), 26–28
Twilight of the Gods (Mellers), 163
Tyler, Anne, 157
Tyler, Tony, 164

Udovitch, Mim, 322, 348
Ulanov, Barry, 97, 111–12, 358
The Undercommons (Moten), 402
"Under the Bamboo Tree" (Johnson), 168
Uptown Conversation (Lipsitz), 358
Urban Blues (Keil), 148, 344–45

V (Pynchon), 134, 156
Vale, V. (Vale Hamanaka), 263–65
Van Ronk, Dave, 407, 410, 414
Van Vechten, Carl: Bernard on, 120; on Ewen, 108;
  and Hughes, 78–80; importance of, 67; in *The
  Kandy-Kolored Tangerine-Flake Streamline Baby*
  (Wolfe), 174; *Parties*, 179; ragtime, 428
Vargas, Deborah, 140
vaudeville, 178
Vazquez, Alexandra, 385
Venturi, Michael, 221
Vermorel, Fred and Judy, 237–38, 323
vernacular, 7–12, 206
vinyl records. *See* records
Violence Girl (Bag), 239–40
Visions of Cody (Kerouac), 300
Visions of Jazz: The First Century (Giddins), 355–57,
  416
A Visit from the Goon Squad (Egan), *367*, 432, 436
Vogel, Shane, 79, 114, 120–21, 373–74
The Voice: The Story of an American Phenomenon
  (Kahn), 284, *285*
voice studies, 420, 422
Von Eschen, Penny, 93, 226, 360, 423
Vowell, Sarah, 328

Waksman, Steve, 275, 291, 293, 316, 317, 329
Wald, Elijah: on dance, 181; *Dylan Goes Electric!*,
  409; *Escaping the Delta: Robert Johnson and
  the Invention of the Blues*, 412–16; *How the
  Beatles Destroyed Rock and Roll*, 267; on
  Johnson, 209, 414; *Narcocorridos*, 139
Wald, Gayle, 110, 191–92, 350
Walker, Aida Overton, 64, 116

Walker, George, 64, 70, 115
Walkowitz, Daniel, 56
Wallis, Roger, 379
Walrond, Eric, 66
Walser, Robert, 316, 318–20
Wang, Oliver, 411, 419, 438
Ware, Chris, 117, 279, 386, *387*
Warhol, Andy, 375
Warwick, Jacqueline, 163, 319, 339
Washburne, Christopher, 395
Washington, Booker T., 64–65
Waterman, Christopher, 379, 421
Waters, Ethel, 120–21, 127, 171, 355, 437
Watts, Shirley, 266
Waxer, Lise, 6, 381, 393–95
The Weary Blues (Hughes), 78–80
We Gotta Get Out of This Place (Hirshey), 272
Weheliye, Alexander, 126, 405
Weinstein, Deena, 314
Wenner, Jann, 163–64
West, Red, 341
West, Sonny, 341
When Genres Collide (Brennan), 13
When We Were Good (Cantwell), 269
*Where the Girls Are: Growing Up with the Mass
  Media* (Douglas), 338–39
Whisnant, David, 44, 55
Whitburn, Joel, 201–3, 218
White, Benjamin Franklin, 25–26
White, Timothy, 273
Whitehead, Colson, 434
Whiteley, Sheila, 349
White Noise (DeLillo), 342
White Tears (Kunzru), 434
Whitman, Walt, 28–30, 85, 134, 426
Whittlesey, Walter, 40
Why Karen Carpenter Matters (Tongson), 351, 374,
  432
Wickes, E. M., 49
Wilder, Alec, 73, 198–200
Wilentz, Sean, 312, 409
Wilgus, D. K., 34, 55, 175
Williams, Allan, 164
Williams, Bert, 6–7, 32, 64–67, 70, 120
Williams, Clarence, 96
Williams, Harry F., 49
Williams, John, 197–98
Williams, Linda, 75–76
Williams, Marion, 190
Williams, Paul, 156, 406
Williams, Raymond, 211, 221
Williamson, Nigel, 406

Willis, Ellen: *Beginning to See the Light: Pieces of a Decade*, 257–58; and Christgau, 249; on Dylan, 257–58, 406; feminist critiques, 10, 208, 257–58; on rock criticism, 217; *Rock She Wrote* contribution, 185; and the Rolling Stones, 266; on the Sex Pistols, 238

Wilson, August, *234*, 280–81, 297, 405

Wilson, Carl, 429–32

Wilson, Dan, 330

Wilson, Edmund, 55, 67

With His Pistol in His Hand (Paredes), *103*, 136–41

Wittke, Carl, 334–35

Wolf, Stacy, 396–99

Wolfe, Bernard, 110

Wolfe, Tom: and the Beatles, 162–63; and Christgau, 249; influence of, 182; *The Kandy-Kolored Tangerine-Flake Streamline Baby*, *145*, 173–74

Wolk, Douglas, 431

women: in Appalachia, 55–56; *Girl Groups, Girl Culture* (Warwick), 319, 339; in gospel, 190; groupies, *235*, 294–95; *To 'Joy My Freedom* (Hunter), 116–17, 226, 403, 421; Juno on, 265; and Native American music research, 35–38; *Rock She Wrote: Women Write about Rock, Pop and Rap* (McDonnell and Powers), 185, 348–49, 352; *Rock Wives* (Balfour), 295; and sentimentality, 9; and sheet music, 42; survey of writers, 5–6, 13; *We Gotta Get Out of This Place* (Hirshey), 272

Woods, Clyde, 415

woofing, 89

Woollcott, Alexander, 1, 72–74

worldbeat, 379–80

world music, 379–80

X, Malcolm, 178

Yang, Mina, 429

Yesterdays: Popular Song in America (Hamm), 247–48

Yes We Have No (Cohn), 182–83

Yetnikoff, Walter, 204, 242

You Don't Love Me Yet (Lethem), 271, 399

You Never Give Me Your Money (Doggett), 166

Young, Kevin, 71, 80, 159, 440–41

Young Man with a Horn (Baker), 94–95

Zappa, Frank, 294

Zimbabwe, 80

zines, 263–65